AL AMERICA,
e

DIES

ATLANTIC

40°

60°

BERMUDA ★ Hamilton

Bahama Islands

ANDROS ★ Nassau

TROPIC OF CANCER

Marianao ★ Havana
io ● Matanzas
CUBA ● Santa Clara

Greater

● Camaguey

● Holguín

Santiago
de Cuba ●

Cap Haitien ●

● Santiago

HAITI DOMINICAN
REP. ★ Santo
Domingo

San Juan
★

Lesser

JAMAICA ★ Kingston
Port au
Prince ★

PUERTO RICO

VIRGIN IS.

ST. KITTS   ANTIGUA

Antilles

GUADELOUPE

Leeward Is.

MARTINIQUE

CARIBBEAN SEA

Antilles

Windward Is.

CURACAO
★ Wilhemstad

● Barranquilla
Maracaibo ●

TORTUGA

MARGARITA

n

● Colón
ANAMA ★ Panama City

★ Caracas

Gulf of Panama

Lake Maracaibo

COLOMBIA   VENEZUELA

To RUSSELL H. FITZGIBBON

In gratitude for his teaching

POLITICAL FORCES IN LATIN AMERICA:

Dimensions of the Quest for Stability

BEN G. BURNETT
Whittier College

KENNETH F. JOHNSON
University of Southern California

Contributors

MARVIN ALISKY
DONALD W. BRAY
JACK B. GABBERT
PAUL E. HADLEY
LOUIS K. HARRIS
ROBERT E. HUNTER
ENRIQUE LOW MURTRA
JOHN D. MARTZ

J. C. M. OGELSBY
L. VINCENT PADGETT
ROBERT L. PETERSON
PETER G. SNOW
ROBERT D. TOMASEK
HOWARD J. WIARDA
JORDAN M. YOUNG

Wadsworth Publishing Company, Inc.
Belmont, California

L. C. Cat. Card No.: 68–10533

Printed in the United States of America

Preface

Instability in government and politics has come to be accepted by most scholars as *the* salient characteristic of political life in Latin America today. Rarely does a year pass in Latin America without major examples of this phenomenon of political instability: the overthrowing of governments, the resignations of cabinets, political assassinations, student riots, labor violence, and organized insurgency or guerrilla warfare. By selecting political instability as the phenomenal theme for this collaborative book, we have sought to implant at the outset a sense of direction and system to what might otherwise appear to be an amorphous mass of geographically punctuated material.

Our primary goal in the writing and directing of this text has been improved pedagogy, through a lucid and orderly discussion of the diverse and often chaotic patterns of behavior that we and our colleagues have observed and studied throughout the nations of Latin America. To this end, we have sought to include the most recent findings of other political and social scientists; we have drawn in depth upon relevant vernacular writings by indigenous Latin American scholars; and we have incorporated the fruits of our own on-going research. To the extent that we have succeeded in fulfilling this primary aim, we should like to express our deep appreciation to our contributors, as well as to the staff at Wadsworth (especially Grace Clifford, Robert Gormley, Roberta Howell, and Robert Mann). Moreover, we are very grateful to a number of outside reviewers, many of whose very helpful suggestions have been incorporated into the text. In this category we are indebted to George I. Blanksten of Northwestern University, José Nun of University of California at Berkeley, K. H. Silvert of Dartmouth College, and William S. Stokes of Claremont Men's College. Of course, as in all writing ventures, the authors assume full responsibility for errors of fact or interpretation.

Ben G. Burnett

143562 *Kenneth F. Johnson*

Contents

1 / FOUNDATIONS OF LATIN AMERICAN POLITICS, Ben G. Burnett and Kenneth F. Johnson   1

The Traditional Political Order   2
Challenges to the Traditional Order   8
Symptoms of Political Instability in Latin America   15

2 / MEXICO, Kenneth F. Johnson   19

The Years of Revolution   19
The Environment of Revolution   28
Mexico's PRI: The Institutional Revolutionary Party   36
The Satellite System of Opposition Parties and Out Groups   39
Governmental Processes, Public Policy, and Public Administration   46
Conclusion and Prognosis   52

CENTRAL AMERICA

3 / GUATEMALA, HONDURAS, EL SALVADOR, AND NICA-RAGUA, Robert L. Peterson   57

Political Environment   58
Political Structures and Roles   67
Constitutional and Institutional Forms   73
Processes of Function and Dysfunction   77
Conclusions   90

4 / COSTA RICA, Robert D. Tomasek   91

Political Environment   91
Political Structure and Roles   95
Characteristics of the Party System   102
Processes of Function and Dysfunction   107
Assessment of Stability and Instability   114

5 / PANAMA, Louis K. Harris   115

    Introduction   115
    Political Environment   118
    Political Input Groups   129
    Political Output Groups   137
    Problems of Function and Dysfunction   139
    Prognosis: Stability or Instability   142

THE CARIBBEAN

6 / HAITI AND THE DOMINICAN REPUBLIC, J. C. M. Ogelsby
145

    Haiti   145
    The Dominican Republic   157

7 / CUBA, Howard J. Wiarda   171

    Introduction: The Significance of Cuba   171
    The Political Environment   172
    Political Structures and Roles   178
    Public Policy: Processes of Function and Dysfunction
      189
    Conclusion: Assessment of Stability and Instability   196

NORTHERN SOUTH AMERICA

8 / VENEZUELA, John D. Martz   199

    Political Environment   200
    Political Structures and Roles   207
    Processes of Function and Dysfunction   217
    Dimensions of Systemic Change   227

9 / COLOMBIA, L. Vincent Padgett and Enrique Low Murtra 231

    Introduction   *231*
    Historical Background   *232*
    The Social Environment of the Political System   *242*
    Ideological Trends in the Political Environment   *247*
    Political Structures and Roles   *248*
    Political Parties, Coalitions, and Factions   *255*
    The Three Branches of Government   *259*
    Processes of Function and Dysfunction   *262*
    Conclusion   *264*

INDO-ANDEAN NATIONS

10 / ECUADOR, Jack B. Gabbert   *267*

    Political Environment   *268*
    Political Structures and Roles   *272*
    Political Processes   *282*
    Assessment of Stability and Instability   *285*

11 / PERU, Marvin Alisky   *289*

    The Environment of Politics in Peru   *289*
    The Political System of Peru: A Developmental Sketch   *293*
    The Contemporary Party Spectrum   *297*
    Institutional Forces and Tradition   *300*
    Electoral System   *301*
    Governmental Structure   *302*
    Contemporary Policy Issues   *306*
    Conclusions   *308*

12 / BOLIVIA, Robert E. Hunter   *313*

    The Political Evolution of Bolivia   *313*
    The Bolivian Revolution   *316*
    The Political Process   *331*
    Contemporary Politics   *332*

13 / CHILE, *Ben G. Burnett*   *337*

    Introduction   *337*
    The Political Environment   *337*
    Political Structures and Roles   *345*
    Political Parties   *353*
    Processes of Function and Dysfunction   *360*
    Conclusion: A Prognosis of Stability and Instability   *368*

SOUTHERN SOUTH AMERICA

14 / PARAGUAY, *Paul E. Hadley*   *373*

    Political Environment   *373*
    Political Structures and Roles   *379*
    The Structure of Government   *385*
    Political Development   *389*
    Prospects for Political Change   *391*

15 / ARGENTINA, *Peter G. Snow*   *393*

    The Political Environment   *393*
    Governmental Structures and Functions   *399*
    Interest Groups   *406*
    The Political Party System   *412*
    A Tentative Prognosis   *422*
    Postscript   *424*

16 / URUGUAY, *Donald W. Bray*   *429*

    The Political Environment   *429*
    Political History   *431*
    Political Structures and Roles—Processes of Function and
      Dysfunction   *436*
    Political Structures and Roles   *437*
    Conclusion   *446*

17 / BRAZIL, *Jordan M. Young*   *447*

    Political Environment   *447*
    Political Structures and Roles   *459*
    Conclusion   *474*

**18 / LATIN AMERICAN POLITICAL THOUGHT: SOME LITER-
ARY FOUNDATIONS,** *Kenneth F. Johnson*   477

    Democratic Liberalism   *480*
    Authoritarian Idealism   *483*
    Three Political Dialectics   *485*
    Democratic Utopianism: The Voyage to Ipanda   *488*
    Contemporary Democratic Progressivism   *492*
    Invectives and Vendettas   *495*
    Political Ideas in the French Idiom   *504*
    Brazilian Political Thought   *506*
    Conclusions   *508*

**19 / STABILITY-INSTABILITY IN LATIN AMERICAN POLI-
TICS,** *Kenneth F. Johnson and Ben G. Burnett*   511

    Stability-Instability as an Interaction System   *515*
    The Price of Stability   *519*
    The Probability of Stability in Latin America   *521*

GLOSSARY   *525*

SELECTED BIBLIOGRAPHY   *529*

INDEX   *545*

POLITICAL FORCES
IN LATIN AMERICA

1 / Foundation of Latin American Politics

BEN G. BURNETT AND KENNETH F. JOHNSON

BEN G. BURNETT, Professor of Political Science at Whittier College, has undertaken field investigation in most of the Latin American nations. He received Danforth and Haynes fellowships and spent 1963–64 in Chile on a Social Science Research Council grant. The author of a number of articles stressing labor and politics in Latin America, he also co-authored (with Moisés Poblete Troncoso) The Rise of the Latin American Labor Movement *and is the author of the forthcoming study,* Political Groups in Chile: The Dialogue between Order and Change.

KENNETH F. JOHNSON, Associate Professor of International Relations and Political Science, and Chairman of the Latin American Studies Program at the University of Southern California, was a Ford Foundation fellow and has pursued research in Mexico, Central America, and Colombia. His writings include "Causal Factors of Latin American Political Instability," "Measurement of Latin American Political Change" (with Russell Fitzgibbon), "Ideological Correlates of Right Wing Political Alienation in Mexico," and a forthcoming study of Guatemalan politics. During the spring and summer of 1967, Professor Johnson served as a Fulbright scholar in Argentina.

In the mass media of the few affluent countries of the world, there is sedulous coverage of political turmoil in the have-not countries. Stories frequently appear about plots and counterplots and chronic manifestations of violence. Through these stories and through recurring proclamations of new "revolutions," the press reinforces a scornful attitude among the affluent toward the world's emerging peoples. There seems to be little patience in the

1

mass media for reporting short but significant steps toward progress, and only rarely are efforts made to clarify the causes of the political instability that racks much of the world.

Indeed, the popular press usually obscures the meaning of political events in the have-not countries through the casual use of the term "revolution." Events that are called revolutions generally are not fundamental changes in the makeup of society but rather confrontations among oligarchical elites battling for power.

Actually, as the frustrations of the poor erupt in demands for a greater share of their societies' scarce political rewards, economic resources, and social privileges, contemporary violence does seem to be increasingly setting the stage for genuine revolutions.

All of this bears on our view of political behavior in Latin America. To understand what is happening there, we must look beyond superficial events to the Latin American experience. We must examine the legacy of the colonial era, the impact of the wars of independence, the social forms implanted early in the republican period, and we must consider certain ecological factors. As Professors Wilgus and D'Eça pointedly observe,

> The revolutions, the dictators, and the constitutions are only symptoms of maladjustment. They reveal the struggle of those peoples to overcome the handicaps of adverse physical environment and racial heterogeneity as well as the curses, inherited from their mother countries, of an aristocratic concept of government.
>
> It is with these points in view that the history of Latin American nations since independence must be studied. And whatever progress these peoples have made must be measured, not by the yardstick of other more fortunate peoples' advancement, but by the magnitude of the obstacles overcome.[1]

THE TRADITIONAL POLITICAL ORDER

Legacy of the Colonial Period

The discovery and conquest of America by Spain and Portugal was an incredible feat. In a few years Iberian expansion subjugated millions of indigenous peoples. The ruling system that was established, was, above all, authoritarian. The monarch, absolute and infallible, owned all the lands in his domain and retained the final authority on any aspect of the lives of his subjects. By a blending of the institutions and the personnel of State and Church, loyalty to the crown was instilled and order maintained. A powerful ruler could almost totally dominate political, economic, and religious processes in his realm; no popular body, such as a parliament, existed to thwart his

---

[1] A. Curtis Wilgus and Raul D'Eça, *Outline-History of Latin America* (New York, Barnes & Noble, 1941), p. 133.

wishes or temper his thoughts. Of course, advisory bodies (especially the Council of the Indies) participated in the formulation of policy for the New World, but they were still the king's coterie, and their goals were customarily those of the crown.

In Spanish America, monarchical policy flowed downward through a hierarchy of viceroys, captains-general and presidents, *audiencias, gobernadores, corregidores,* and *alcaldes mayores.* The Portuguese employed a similar, though not identical, chain of command. Fortunately for the colonists, the oppressive nature of this system was mitigated by the great distances between the mother countries and their colonies and the concomitant slowness of communication. Moreover, European-issued edicts, which might be highly repressive or irrelevant to colonial needs could be appealed (requiring endless delays), interpreted differently in the Americas, or handled with a traditional official response for seemingly impossible orders: *Obedezco pero no cumplo* ("I obey but do not enforce").[2]

Economically, Spain and Portugal adhered to mercantilism, which treated the colonies almost solely as sources of wealth for the mother country. This extractive concept reduced the economic role of the colonists to agricultural and mining pursuits and greatly inhibited the growth of manufacturing. During the early colonial era, colonists were prohibited from trading with nationals of other countries (though ubiquitous smuggling could not be halted), and even trade among the Spanish colonies generally was frowned upon. Land tended to be concentrated in the hands of a few great landowners, or *latifundistas,* favored by the king. Although many who were born in Iberia in the most humble circumstances came to the New World and achieved high administrative and economic positions, the mestizo and Indian populations could rarely aspire to property ownership. Indeed, in the Spanish colonies practically all the good land was allocated to a few Spaniards under the *encomienda* system, "whereby the native occupants of the land remained on the soil in a situation bordering on serfdom, moderated in time to the slightly freer status of peonage."[3]

2 Hubert Herring, *A History of Latin America* (New York, Alfred A. Knopf, 1965), p. 155. For additional background on the history of Latin America, see Helen M. Bailey and Abraham P. Nasatir, *Latin America: The Development of its Civilization* (Englewood Cliffs, N.J., Prentice-Hall, 1960); John A. Crow, *The Epic of Latin America* (Garden City, Doubleday & Company, 1952); Bailey W. Diffie, *Latin American Civilization: The Colonial Period* (Harrisburg, Stackpole Sons, 1945); John E. Fagg, *Latin America: A General History* (New York, Macmillan Co., 1963); Charles E. Chapman, *Colonial Hispanic America: A History* (New York, Macmillan Co., 1933) and *Republican Hispanic America: A History* (New York, Macmillan Co., 1938); C. H. Haring, *The Spanish Empire in America* (New York, Oxford University Press, 1947); J. Fred Rippy, *Latin America: A Modern History* (Ann Arbor, University of Michigan Press, 1958); Donald E. Worcester and Wendell G. Schaeffer, *The Growth and Culture of Latin America* (New York, Oxford University Press, 1956).

3 William L. Schurz *Latin America: A Descriptive Survey* (New York, E. P. Dutton & Co., 1942), p. 57.

In colonial times, economic as well as political policy prevented the rise of a middle class and, in fact, sharply divided the population into haves, almost-haves, and have-nots. By far the most favored were the European-born whites, *peninsulares*, who held most of the high administrative and clerical offices and were in the best position to accumulate great fortunes. The creoles, whites born in the New World (known as *criollos* in Spanish America and *masombos* in Brazil), were less privileged but were still permitted to occupy lower offices and procure a small slice of the economic resources. Considered inferior because of birth in barbarian lands, few creoles ascended to a standing commensurate with the *peninsulares*. The creoles therefore regarded the *peninsulares* with a singular hatred, which was to burst forth in the wars of independence. The vast bulk of the population — those of mixed blood, the Indians, and the Negroes — filled out the bottom of the pyramid, where they wallowed hopelessly in a mire of destitution and wretchedness.

The political, economic, and social life of the colonies revolved mostly around the single task of producing largesse for the crown and its chosen agents. Peninsulars came to the Americas to make their fortunes only in order to return to Spain or Portugal and enjoy the fruits of their exile. There was a profound lack of the type of long-range policy that could benefit the colonies. Personalism characterized political behavior; officeholders considered their posts as proprietary holdings, not as public trusts; the emphasis on quick profits resulted in merciless exploitation of the New World's human and physical resources and in the instillation of the habit of *la mordida* (that is, taking a "bite" from revenues) into the administrative process. Working closely with the colonial administration, the Roman Catholic Church spread its mantle over education, the arts, and welfare services and came to possess some of the largest estates in the hemisphere. The military also played a tremendously important role during the colonial period as the vital coercive arm that sustained the dominant status of the privileged few. In effect, then, the colonial period institutionalized modes of behavior and inculcated sets of attitudes that carried over into the republican era as barriers to reform and, consequently, as factors contributing to political instability.

The Wars of Independence

Naturally, some changes did occur during the several centuries of colonial rule. Spain passed through its Golden Age and, except for a brief flourish under the early Bourbon kings, lost the dynamism and the inspired leadership necessary to hold so great an empire together. In a similar fashion, the Portuguese became slack in their grasp on Brazil, which consequently developed a kind of relaxed identity of its own. Some wealthier creoles traveled abroad, embraced new ideas, and returned to the colonies convinced of the unfairness of the creoles' position in society. Revolutions in France and British North America at the end of the eighteenth century sent shock waves into the Spanish and Portuguese colonies that stimulated lines of thought antithetical to the traditional order. Then, in the early 1800s, the many forces working to transfer control of the old order from the peninsulars to the creoles (and theoretically to the lower classes as well) coincided with the royalist unwillingness to give loyalty to a Bonaparte sitting on the Spanish throne. Thus, what began in 1810 as rebellion against the French emperor ended little more than a decade later when most of the Spanish colonies broke away from Spain. By 1823, in an almost bloodless episode, Brazil had also ended its ties with Portugal.

In many ways, the wars for independence had a disastrous impact on the former Spanish colonies. To begin with, the colonial system had failed to create a reserve of qualified leadership, since the creoles, who were to assume the primary role in forming the new States, had enjoyed few opportunities to learn how to govern. Experience in the municipalities (*cabildos*), almost the only level in the administrative process where the creoles had had a voice, did not prepare them well for the monumental task of unifying and stabilizing the deprived and helpless communities. In addition, the long warfare, which decimated the ranks of young men left few potential competent leaders. The military, long prominent in colonial life, achieved an exaggerated importance as a result of the wars. Military units were little more than groups of combatants unified by personal loyalty to a commander, and battles were fought by means of shifting alliances among such leaders. After independence there was no place, except in politics, for the military officers to quench their thirst for power and wealth. Since political resources were extremely scarce, commanders formerly allied in battle now engaged in vicious battles with each other in the struggle to seize and secure dominion over governments.[4] Not surprisingly, the *caudillo* ("man on horseback," or strong man) emerged as a prototypal Latin American political leader. The early constitutions, often modeled after that of the United States, commonly were utopian or at least lacking in operational relevance to domestic situations. Even the best of such basic documents only got in the way of the ambitions of the *caudillo*, who either ignored or altered the laws. Thus no rule of law could evolve to provide viability for a constitutional system.

In a similar manner, systemic defects distinguished the economic and social realm. The fledgling industries that appeared in the late colonial period largely disappeared during the wars; commerce and mining, mostly controlled by the *peninsulares*, deteriorated rapidly when the Spaniards fled America. Even agriculture, the economic mainstay of virtually all Latin Americans, dropped in productivity. Unfortunately, while the economy declined, the old

---

4 Asher N. Christensen, *The Evolution of Latin American Government* (New York, Holt, Rinehart and Winston, 1951), p. 64.

ways remained substantially the same. Thus the semifeudal land relationships between *peón* and *patrón* and the concentration of enormous estates in a few families' hands continued to be the outstanding characteristics of the republican economic system. These problems in turn, accentuated divisions between the social classes; in most places racial antagonism further aggravated such cleavages by pitting Indians or mestizos against Europeans. For these reasons, probably no more than five percent of all Latin Americans in the immediate post-independence era were able to live above a bare subsistence level.[5]

In summary, the new Latin American nations received the following legacies from the colonial period and the wars of independence: authoritarianism, administrative corruption, political ineptness, and oligarchical monopoly of scarce political and economic resources. Such a set of conditions was not conducive to the establishment of pluralistic, liberal democracies.

Politics in the Nineteenth Century

It has been frequently pointed out that very little really changed in Latin America after the winning of independence. Creole names replaced peninsular names in the power structure, and republican wording supplanted monarchical terminology in governmental administration. However, at least in the first decades, the spirit of government remained much as before. Pío Jaramillo Alvarado stated wryly that independence came on "the last day of despotism and the first day of the same thing."[6]

The oligarchy, which now held a hegemony of political resources, was a triarchy of the great landowners, the high clergy, and ranking military officers. Because of the anarchy that marked the independence period and its immediate aftermath, they had quickly filled positions of power and then threw support to the *caudillo*, whether military or civilian, who might bring stability and thus insure their pre-eminent political and economic standing. Nevertheless, the deficiency of resources, even among the oligarchy, caused a seesaw contest as one aristocratic element and then another seized the government. All of this largely passed over the heads of the mass of the population. Moreover, the working classes rarely got to participate in the spoils, though they were often dragged into the power struggles.

John Kautsky's generalizations on social divisions in traditional societies living on subsistence agriculture and outside the money economy have considerable validity for pre-industrial Latin America.[7] He notes that the aristocracy,

---

[5] Herring, p. 294.

[6] Quoted in George Blanksten, "Revolutions," in *Governments and Politics in Latin America*, ed. Harold E. Davis (New York, Ronald Press, 1958), p. 119.

[7] John Kautsky, *Political Change in Underdeveloped Countries: Nationalism and Communism* (New York and London, John Wiley, 1962). See especially Chapter 1.

in order to function in these closed societies, took on certain attributes that markedly distinguished them from the peasantry: considerable physical mobility, ease of communication among themselves, and a level of literacy. Meanwhile, the peasants were kept in ignorance and poverty, and their servile state imbued them with hopelessness and resignation. Because they were dispersed over huge land areas and commanded no means of giving voice to the nature of their dilemma with their counterparts elsewhere, the peasants were unorganizable and could scarcely be defined as a group. Despite the numerical preponderance of the peasants, they never constituted a collective threat of any sort to the oligarchy.

One social element in Latin America which periodically did inconvenience the aristocracy in the nineteenth century was the tiny but incipient middle sector. Composed of lawyers, teachers, physicians, artists, bureaucrats, lower military officers, and some of the secular clergy, it was a restricted and heterogeneous stratum of society. However, aside from the oligarchy, the middle sector was the one social element possessing a functional degree of literacy, mobility, and ability to articulate demands. With such strengths, as well as with aspirations to acquire status and power, the middle sector placed itself squarely in the path of the oligarchy. During the first half of the nineteenth century, segments of the middle sector coalesced into political-action groups, usually calling themselves Liberals, and attacked the political *status quo*. In order to counter such opposition, the traditional triarchy joined together as Conservatives. In both cases, the so-called political parties that evolved tended to be heavily personalist — almost closed corporations — with little orientation to issues and programs. Still, the Liberals voiced, though often vaguely, anticlerical views and usually espoused federalism, while the Conservatives stood for Church rule and order guaranteed by the military. Both parties relied heavily upon coercive force as their mainstay. Revolutionary ideals borrowed earlier from France and the United States dropped to the wayside: "Liberty, equality, and fraternity gave way to infantry, cavalry, and artillery, as the republics bled themselves in constant warfare."[8] In fact, it seldom made much difference to most of the people whether the Conservatives or the Liberals held office, since both camps were spurred primarily by the desire for power and had no intention of sponsoring concrete social changes which might permit the entrance of lower-class representatives into the councils of government.

In a number of countries, the traditional order marched secure and practically unchanged through the nineteenth century and into the twentieth. Here and there the Church experienced setbacks, the oligarchy opened its doors to new-

---

[8] John J. Johnson, *The Military and Society in Latin America* (Stanford, Stanford University Press, 1964), p. 37.

comers, and government assumed a more progressive posture. But the *lati-fundio* system remained firm, and the *gente decente* ruled. And yet, in a few nations, new forces with new ideas stirred near the end of the last century and demanded social transformation and political accommodation.

CHALLENGES TO THE TRADITIONAL ORDER

Catalysts of Change

Although bloody civil wars and revolts would still disrupt Latin America in the last half of the nineteenth century, these beleaguered Republics grew in their ability to govern themselves; distinguished statesmen and educators came forth, educational facilities expanded, and, in general, a somewhat more stable political pattern evolved out of the wreckage of the first decades of the republican experience. Even the military's pervasive penetration of the political process lost some of its heaviness, and the omnipresence of *caudillo* rule abated. (This development began in Chile in the 1830s, then followed in Argentina after 1860, in Uruguay, in 1890, and in Colombia shortly afterwards.)[9] Simultaneously, some significant modifications of the economy began to appear. Until the 1850s, there was little agricultural production for surplus, and millions of Latin Americans lived quite separate from the money economy; hence, almost no capital could be accumulated for the stimulation of new kinds of economic activity.

Then, in the 1850s, two principal currents converged. The first of these currents was the readiness of foreign entrepreneurs — and at this stage especially the British — to invest capital abroad, where they could tap raw materials for their voracious factories and obtain inexpensive food staples for their laborers. Large areas of Latin America proved capable of fulfilling such requirements and consequently gained a sizable transfusion of capital that energized both urban and rural productivity. An added bonus came in the form of European coal for Latin America's trains and factories (coal was a commodity in short supply outside Chile).[10]

The second current was the positivist concepts of Auguste Comte, which found a welcome reception in intellectual circles in Chile, Argentina, Uruguay, Brazil, Mexico, and elsewhere. According to Comte, man must turn to science to verify the nature of his social environment; he must build a science of society, which ultimately would aid humanity by ferreting out "laws" that explain

---

[9] Edwin Lieuwen, *Arms and Politics in Latin America* (New York, Frederick A. Praeger, 1961), Chapter 1.

[10] Wendell C. Gordon, *The Political Economy of Latin America* (New York and London, Columbia University Press, 1965), Chapter 2; George Pendle, *A History of Latin America* (Baltimore, Penguin Books, 1963), pp. 138–140.

the life cycles of societies. With such laws it would be possible to "mark out a normal or standard line of evolution to which every society might be expected in general to conform...."[11]

The Latin American positivists looked at the United States and Europe and "verified" to their satisfaction certain ingredients of those civilizations which they themselves could well emulate for the advancement of their own peoples. These positivists decided that the normal lines of social development could be best served by inviting a flood of foreign investment capital into Latin America and by encouraging a host of immigrants to supplant what many positivists considered to be the inferiority of Indian labor. Comte's "religion of humanity" had simply been merged with the capitalist ethic of John Calvin.

Later generations took umbrage at the positivists' open-door policy to foreign penetration of their economies; but, in the meantime, a half century of European and North American capital stimulated Latin American development. Rapidly proliferating railroads and telegraph lines extended effective control of the nation to wider frontiers, opened up new lands to farming, and spread feelings of national consciousness among larger numbers of the citizenry. Foreign money, technicians, and inventions modernized old economic sectors and launched new projects. Foreign workers, seeking better wages, poured into Argentina, Uruguay, Venezuela, and a few other regions and brought with them advanced skills necessary for manufacturing. In the 1870s, the invention of refrigerated ships that could transport South American meat to the tables of Europe stimulated the cattle-raising and meat-packing industries. Allied and service industries multiplied and fostered urbanization and the accumulation of some native capital. All of this economic activity had broad social ramifications, not the least of which was the catapulting of new groups into prominence. After World War I, some of these groups issued claims on the political system — claims that seriously threatened the old aristocracy's paramount station in society.

New Groups and Ideologies

Once foreign capital stamps its imprint on a traditional society and fosters basic industrial expansion, the resulting economic factors create conditions for the genesis of three new strata in the social order: (1) A breed of native capitalists may come forth, though commonly they will emerge relatively late in the industrialization process; (2) White-collar employees at once arise in response to industry's demands for supervisory and clerical personnel; and,

---

11 George H. Sabine, *A History of Political Theory* (New York, Holt, Rinehart and Winston, 1950), p. 717.

of course, (3) great numbers of industrial workers appear who operate machines and perform menial chores.[12] This developmental pattern has particular applicability to events in Latin America after the turn of the century.

The industrial expansion of Latin America effected some primary political innovations. Both white-collar and blue-collar workers were inclined to enter politics soon after the formation of their groups. Rather than compete just for spoils, these labor groups sought broader policy aims. They interacted with a new brand of political parties, which offered a doctrinal appeal and which interjected issues into what formerly were almost exclusively personalist campaigns.

Generally speaking, Latin America's native capitalists arrived very late on the economic scene. The late appearance of this stratum probably derived from the old aristocracy's familial and class mores, which frowned on such undertakings. Most of the first national capitalists were Italian, German, French, Middle Eastern and other immigrants who settled in the Americas. In changing from an old to a new culture, these immigrants seemed to carry with them a set of attributes which not only distinguished them from the population in their new surroundings but also propelled them into almost any economic pursuits that would establish their financial solvency. Many indeed are the stories in South America of the *turco* (an inaccurate, unflattering term given to Arab immigrants from the Levant) who rented a small apartment containing no more than a bathroom and a bed and sold baths and a place to sleep to other new arrivals until he could add more beds and finally accumulate a sufficient stake to buy a shop. Why the immigrants turned out to be so different from the society they planted themselves in is open to conjecture:

> It has never been solved whether or not foreigners took the entrepreneurial lead mostly because they were better trained, better informed, and lacking other opportunities, or because they carried a different cargo of mental afflictions. Literate native sons are said to have been afflicted with a horror of machine dirt, a compulsion to be genteel, and low "need achievement" conditioned by authoritarian fathers and servile mothers. By contrast, it is said, the immigrants turned their rage at not being aristocratic into marvelous greed.[13]

Whatever the cause, native industrial capitalists were late in making their presence felt, and then they customarily did so in localities with little immigration (that is, around Medellín, Colombia, and Monterrey, Mexico). Another wave of native capitalists entered the economy in the 1930s, when the State intruded in economic life in order to encourage and protect industrial produc-

---

12 Kautsky, especially, Chapter 1.

13 W. Paul Strassmann, "The Industrialist," in *Continuity and Change in Latin America*, ed. by John J. Johnson (Stanford, Stanford University Press, 1964), pp. 164–165.

tion.[14] Lines between the old arstiocracy and the new native industrialists tended to blur with intermarriage — a phenomenon also occurring in some areas between the aristocracy and established immigrant capitalists. Accordingly, the affluent industrial elite assumed a conservative posture not unlike the old oligarchs, though with the major exception that the new elite covered its bets more carefully by financial and personal ties to all the middle-to-right political parties.

Numerically larger than the native capitalists, the incipient middle sector increased markedly in size as industrialization gained a stronger foothold in Latin America. Although most of the job classifications now present existed in the old middle groups, these classifications assumed far greater importance. Factories required managerial personnel; state economic intervention augmented the number of bureaucrats; added emphasis on public education demanded more teachers; and the military expanded as a result of arms races among several of the Republics (for example, Argentina, Brazil, and Chile). Even more than the old middle sector, the new, larger middle sector was an extremely mixed group, which drew members from upper and lower classes, from various ethnic origins, and from the background of many kinds of skill. Despite the obvious heterogeneity of the new middle sector, as John J. Johnson observes, its members held several interests in common for political action: 1. Overwhelmingly, the new middle sector was located in the huge, burgeoning urban centers. 2. Having a higher than average education themselves, they pushed for wider educational facilities and services. 3. Almost unanimously, the middle sector pinned its hopes for the nation on further industrialization — to such a degree, in fact, that it seemed to be a fetish with them. 4. The middle sector believed that education and industrialization, as well as social welfare and other social enrichments, necessitate State intervention and that economically for example, the State should protect domestic enterprises from competition, amass capital, and stabilize the costs of products through price fixing. 5. More and more the middle groups associated with political parties because urbanization commonly broke the back of the family as a political unit. 6. The middle sector propounded an intensely aggressive form of nationalism that finally ended as economic assertiveness and xenophobia.[15]

In large measure, nationalism provided a foundation for the flowering of national culture by expediting the opening and the enlarging of school facilities, by stimulating national industrial growth through State protectionism, and

---

[14] Strassmann, pp. 165–169.

[15] John J. Johnson, *Political Change in Latin America*, (Stanford, Stanford University Press 1958), pp. 5–11. Other studies of nationalism in Latin America include Gerhard Masur *Nationalism in Latin America* (New York, Macmillan Co. 1966); Arthur P. Whitaker, *Nationalism in Latin America* (Gainesville, University of Florida Press, 1962); Arthur P. Whitaker and David C. Jordan, *Nationalism in Contemporary Latin America* (New York, Free Press of Glencoe, 1966).

by infusing political movements with ideological precepts. Earlier nationalist manifestations had sought to define national territory and to promote its welfare through positivistic materialism. In the early 1900s, idealism replaced positivism as the preponderant ideological force. Adherents to idealism condemned for acts of *vendepatria*, or a sell-out to foreigners, those who had originally encouraged the investment of foreign capital. Thus, the new nationalists attacked the United States for its encroachment upon Latin American economies and for the crassness of its materialist proclivities.

In Uruguay, José Enrique Rodó theorized the new nationalism and José Batlle y Ordóñez sought to implement it. The middle sector sold economic nationalism so well that the ideology also became a concomitant of State policy in the Mexican Revolution and in Argentina, Brazil, and Chile during the 1930s. In all of these cases, the middle sectors usually dictated to the Government or shared the control of it. In addition, nationalism percolated into the urban working classes so that most political groups espoused it as their own. Even the Communists of Chile endeavoured to throw off the image of their international allegiances in order to push themselves into the vanguard of economic nationalism. Following World War II, nationalism transcended earlier defensive forms. Positive concepts of national achievement and dignity were accented in nationalist thought while foreign infiltration was eschewed and varieties of international neutralism were pursued.

In time, in those nations where a measurable middle sector came forth, middle groups tended to ally themselves with the upper-middle-class capitalists in the hope of broadening their own economic base; on other occasions middle groups allied themselves with workers in order to enlarge their own political power. This latter alliance worked only rarely to the advantage of the laborers. Actually, middle-sector leadership often seemed to be inconsistent through unleashing economic nationalism and promoting State intervention and industrialism, while trying to preserve their own interests and reconcile moderate, even traditional, values with the forces activated by these values. Regardless of the periodic anomalies in middle-sector programs and the ambivalence in middle-sector associations, the middle sector emerged as an especially powerful political force in the decades following World War I.

The third of the new groups, the urban working class, grew simultaneously with (but not so much because of) industrial expansion. Even then, it was very late for the working class to begin procuring a part in the decision-making process. This difficulty is explicable in terms of the organizational history of the working class, the strength of its opposition, and the problematic aspects of its political involvements.[16]

---

16 Moisés Poblete Troncoso and Ben G. Burnett, *The Rise of the Latin American Labor Movement* (New York, Bookman Associates, 1960), Chapters 1 and 7; Robert J. Alexander *Organized Labor in Latin America* (New York, Free Press of Glencoe, 1965), Chapters 1 and 2.

Certain patterns of structural similarity generally mark labor's organizational history throughout Latin America. The earliest form of organization was usually the mutual benefit society, created by artisans of a given occupation who were seeking to protect themselves from the risks of job and life through a kind of group insurance coverage. Many of these societies branched out into educational and other services, but only in exceptional circumstances did their activities become politically oriented. Another phase in labor's development occurred toward the end of the last century when the agglomeration of large numbers of workers in such industries as nitrate mining in Chile and meat packing in Argentina created a different kind of organizational need. The oppressive working conditions in many of these enterprises inculcated a kind of elementary class consciousness among a number of segments of labor together with a receptivity to doctrines which explained the reasons for their plight and offered direction for the satisfaction of their basic wants. As a consequence, anarcho-syndicalist and socialist ideologies brought by European immigrants gained immediate attention and encouraged workers to form "societies of resistance." The resistance societies proved intensely anti-capital and generally were short-lived as a result of both the superior coercive powers launched against them by the management-government coalition and of the inexperience of the societies' leadership in treating organizational problems. Nevertheless, the societies served importantly as precursors of the trade unions that made their debut particularly after World War I and constituted the most recent organizational stage in the history of Latin America's labor movement.

Almost half a century after the advent of demonstrable trade-unionist activities in given Latin American nations, organized labor, and the working classes generally, remained chiefly in a supine position; they saw but did not touch the opportunities available to more privileged groups. The frustrations that consequently built up within the working classes often spilled over into acts of violence. This presence of widespread political alienation among laborers has served as a principal root cause of much of the instability that has tormented Latin American political life in recent years.

First, although industrialization undoubtedly helped to enlarge the urban working class, industry never provided jobs for many workers. At best, less than fifteen percent of the working force in Latin America today is employed in manufacturing, whereas the figure for agriculture is approximately forty-seven percent and for personal services nearly thirty-five percent.[17] Still, urbanization is advancing at a tremendous pace in many of the countries as a result of the impoverishment and the frequent violence of rural life and as a result of the city's ostensible attractiveness to the farm laborer. However, instead of finding the Promised Land, the newcomer to the city squats in misery approxi-

17 Gordon, p. 143.

mating the worst he knew in his rural environment. Now, he is "poorly schooled, ill-housed, granted a survival wage by government fiat, cozened by politicians, weakly organized when not regimented."[18]

However, residing in the city does put him in contact with channels to literacy, broader consumption, political influence, and organization for economic self-defense.[19] Even though he is only on the fringe of such opportunities, the new arrival to the urban working class is at least introduced to a conception of the better life, a hope of gaining it, and a rapidly increasing interest in the political process by which he might achieve it. Thus, if few workers actually advance to a very superior economic position as a result of migrating to the city, they do contribute to an ever larger percentage of the total population that is not only potentially alienated but also more and more politically activated. As members of trade unions, which the new urban workers would not have normally known in the rural setting, they are manipulated in countless ways in a struggle with the traditional order. Union ranks are greatly augmented for political ends by cajoling and deceiving unorganized workers who are frequently gullible and who can often be easily moved to participate in demonstrations and street violence. Extremists who wish to incite labor violence have learned that several cups of *aguardiente* or *mezcal* can buy the services of many idle bodies for an afternoon protest and riot. The frequency of such incidents increases with the ever-widening base of frustrations that grows because of the urban labor pool's inability to secure adequate employment and material reward.

Unfortunately for Latin America's organized labor sector, however, its ability to inject claims into the political system with any considerable expectation of success is decidedly limited. Illustrative of this inability are efforts to hold down the pernicious inflation that is constantly vexing many of the region's economies. The workers who suffer most grievously from the inflationary spiral are almost always those who find a government putting a ceiling on their salaries in order to combat inflationary tendencies. Thus, while prices soar, the laborers' wages are frozen, and occasional thawing in wage restrictions never seems to quite catch up with leaps in the prices of basic consumer goods.

Allegedly pro-labor regimes have promulgated labor codes (in Uruguay, Mexico, and Chile years before comparable statutes appeared in the United States) which seemed more restrictive than protective in the manner in which they came to be enforced. Time and time again, trade unionists in pursuit of normal bargaining procedures bumped into a coercive wall of management-government reaction. Irresponsible labor actions often begged such a recourse.

---

[18] Frank Bonilla, "The Urban Worker," in *Continuity and Change in Latin America*, p. 187.
[19] Bonilla, pp. 189–196.

Frequently, however, trade unionism's legitimate techniques confronted governmental inaction, or worse, repression. Perhaps it is no wonder, then, that workers have felt themselves betrayed by the existing format for bargaining, and with mounting frustrations, they turn to extremist movements advocating a total reconstitution of society. This turning to extremism endangers the many reform-minded regimes that are anxious to bring their nations out of the Dark Ages. This extremist tendency is conducive to a chronic instability that breeds violence as a spreading mode of political behavior in Latin America.

SYMPTOMS OF POLITICAL INSTABILITY IN LATIN AMERICA

The clash of new groups with the old, of the impoverished with the well-to-do, or simply of the disenchanted with their environment, takes many forms, from insurgency in the Peruvian highlands and in the Venezuelan cities to street demonstrations in Chile and Uruguay. Actually, as unrelated as these incidents may appear, they have a common theme that is at the heart of the "revolution of rising expectations" and that differs profoundly from the "palace revolutions" of historical infamy. Although the age of the *golpe de estado* (a *coup d'état*, or direct blow at the center of power) and the *cuartelazo* (the "barracks revolt," or physical movement of military units toward power loci) is not past, it is likely that the minority's exclusive possession of political resources is drawing to a close; the next few decades will witness popular groups' thrusts into the sources of power with the subsequent mending or breaking of age-old schema. Naturally, no time schedule for the metamorphosis is easily predictable in such cases, and a time lag persists between countries, but the overall trend seems irreversible.

Among the many agents giving impetus to this era of new directions, the inexorable rush of great quantities of people to the mushrooming cities surely rates as a *sine qua non* of the entire process. By being implanted in urban centers, these disaffected multitudes see in their surroundings the ingredients of a better life. As the expectations of these people rise, they also learn techniques and gain knowledge of the instruments for achieving their gradually elevated goals, and, of fundamental significance, the urban workers now reside close to the very nucleus of power that can remove their dissatisfactions and raise them to a higher rung on the socio-economic ladder. Thus, the traditional order faces unsatiated appetites difficult to appease and challenges impossible to ignore. The contending of reformers and revolutionaries with each other feeds upon and contributes to this mood. By the 1960s, "change" had become the overwhelming concept found almost everywhere in Latin America, and revolution has become the final purpose of many.

However, authentic "revolutions," fundamental economic, social, and political alterations, have transpired in only two nations, Mexico and Cuba. Nonetheless, the outcome of a revolution begun in Bolivia in the 1950s is still undecided, and aborted revolutionary efforts in Guatemala—and some would say in Brazil and Argentina as well—continue to echo throughout those Republics. More recently, the Governments in Venezuela, Peru, and Chile promised organic changes within democratic and peaceful confines, the process which Chilean President Eduardo Frei called the "revolution with freedom."

Instability, which is endemic to most of the Americas, has been a subject of great import for students of Latin American politics. Some of the causal factors for such pervasive instability have been summarized in this Introduction, and they lace the following chapters. In addition, several other studies focus upon political instability. For example, William Stokes deduces that one overriding reason for violence originates in the extensive influence of Hispanic culture in all power relationships, whether they involve family, church, army, schools, or economic institutions. Basically, these relationships are "authoritarian in nature, hence, conditioning the individual to more frequent acceptance of processes of dictatorship, including violence, than processes of political democracy."[20] Another Latin American scholar, Merle Kling, emphasizes the concentration of economic power in a controlling elite which, in turn, exercises a dominant sway over political power. But while control of economic resources is comparatively static, governmental hegemony is not, and that hegemony affords a tempting opportunity for the acquisition of extra wealth. Thus, "chronic political instability is a function of the contradiction between the realities of a colonial economy and the political requirements of legal sovereignty . . . ."[21] Finally, Kenneth Johnson sees political instability in Latin America as originating in the "circular interaction" of three factorial categories: "(1) entrepreneurial deficiencies; (2) high degrees of role substitutability among politically relevant performance entities; and (3) accelerated urbanization and overpopulation."[22]

Whatever the analytical approach, all of these treatises suggest the presence of an overabundance of social strains that produce conflict. Indeed, the great tragedy of Latin America today is that while its political life continues to be chronically unstable, there are enormous social pressures that exacerbate and magnify the instability. The publication *Visión* predicted in 1966 that Latin America's population would reach 750 millions by the year 2000, and further,

---

20 William Stokes, "Violence as a Power Factor in Latin-American Politics," *Western Political Quarterly*, V, No. 3 (September 1952), pp. 466–468.

21 Merle Kling, "Towards a Theory of Power and Political Instability in Latin America," *Western Political Quarterly*, IX, No. 1 (March 1956), pp. 33–34. Italics in original removed.

22 Kenneth F. Johnson, "Causal Factors in Latin American Political Instability," *Western Political Quarterly*, XVII, No. 3 (September 1964), p. 436. This triad of influences is developed in the concluding chapter of this work.

that countries such as Brazil, Venezuela, Guatemala, Mexico, and Colombia would be called upon to invest three times as much as they are now investing of their national resources in education and public welfare in order to meet the pressure of this population explosion.[23] The histories of these nations give little reason to hope that they will ever be able to meet this challenge.

In the concluding chapter of this book, we will argue that Latin America lacks the ideological, associational, and structural resources to achieve its quest for political stability within the near future. Barriers to change take many forms in Latin America, but they may be ultimately traced to ideologies and beliefs that inhibit reform. Thus, writing of the Brazilian Amazon, Charles Wagley tells us:

> Throughout Brazil supernaturalism and folk science are the main elements of the world view of the majority of the rural population. Though this world view is beginning to disintegrate under the impact of more modern ideology coming from the large cities, it still poses a barrier to social change.[24]

And in a monumental work on the "culture of poverty" in the slums of Mexico City, Oscar Lewis gives us a similar insight drawn from an urban setting. Tapping the political ideology of Manuel, one of the *Children of Sánchez*, Lewis relates the attitude of an ex-*bracero* laborer toward American life as he observed it in the state of California and as he contrasted this image with his native Mexico:

> They [in California] have a day, an hour, a fixed schedule set up for everything. It must be a good method because they have lots of comforts. But the government charges them a tax for food, for shoes, for absolutely everything. If our government tried that tax business here, I believe it might even cause a revolution. A person doesn't like to have what's his taken from him.[25]

Since the wars of independence, Latin Americans have often sought to achieve modernity. Often their efforts have failed. Lurking in the background of these failures has been an ideological congeries of values that blends features of the anthropological quotations cited above: (1) mysticism and supernaturalism as a barrier to change in a rural setting and (2) an exaggerated individualism among governors, workers, and entrepreneurs of the urban milieu. Thus a truly public spirit or civic culture is characteristically absent throughout the politics of instability within the nations of Latin America: Community values often suffer neglect as priorities are assigned to ritual functions and private greed.

---

[23] *Visión*, June 10, 1966, pp. 22–23.

[24] Charles Wagley, *Amazon Town* (New York, Alfred A. Knopf, 1964), p. 274.

[25] Oscar Lewis, *The Children of Sánchez* (New York, Random House Vintage Books, 1961) p. 338.

When genuine demands for change have been presented by reformers prepared to eschew these restrictive values, the reformers have usually encountered resistance from groups, institutions, and individuals whose composite force was of a stultifying magnitude. The result of such resistance is that a host of truly progressive Latin Americans are discouraged from even attempting reform, as the testimony of Manuel and the catastrophic "brain drain" out of Argentina, Colombia, and Cuba indicate.

If the vast majority of Latin Americans were to demand change, and if many of them were prepared to use violence to attain it, then the United States would be thwarted in its quest for political stability throughout the hemisphere. Such intrusions by the United States as the Dominican invasion of 1965 may merely aggravate the symptoms of political instability. It is possible that such interventions will ultimately convert moderates into revolutionaries by inciting mass tempers into anticipating the moment they can explode into a radical, substantive redefinition of Latin American society even before their political systems are able to accommodate these changes.

The following chapters consider numerous aspects of the problem of stability in Latin American political life. The general theme of the book is not contrived but weaves prominently throughout the treatise as, indeed, this theme does throughout Latin American politics. The importance of the theme is further evidenced by the conclusion drawn by some American commentators that "communism is merely our competition; the *status quo* is our true enemy."[26]

---

[26] Conclusion drawn on insurgency problems in Latin America by NBC Television, "The Undeclared War," June 15, 1966.

2 / Mexico

KENNETH F. JOHNSON

Seldom has the twentieth century witnessed socio-economic and political change so profound as that which began in Mexico between the years 1910 and 1917. In 1917 it was not obvious, of course, to Mexicans themselves nor to foreign observers just how deep the change went or how lasting it would be. When revolution is attended by violence, the euphoria of the victors is often short-lived and sporadic. Onlookers may miss the fact that a basis for fundamental social change is being laid. They will see only a broken mosaic of intergroup and interpersonal conflict. In Mexico, the revolutionary years saw responsibility for social direction fragmented by civil war among nomadic bands of mercenaries, men like the *hombres de Macias* who pillaged the nation wantonly.[1] Mexico is not unique among Latin American nations for the savagery of her violence; her less developed sister nations have partaken generously of violence as well. Mexico is unique, however, in that her contemporary political system boasts a capacity for stability and human reward that makes Mexico a prototype for democratic achievement within the Latin American family of nations. This capacity is indeed a rare, albeit costly, fruit of revolutionary violence, especially when one views the political experience of the Latin American countries across the historical sweep of the nineteenth and twentieth centuries.

THE YEARS OF REVOLUTION

The symbols which unite the Mexico of today into a people capable of revering a common history were born of social desperation. These symbols were nur-

---

[1] The reference is to Mariano Azuela's classic *Los de abajo*.

tured through great human carnage, sacrifice, and rapine. The Querétaro Club of 1810 produced Ignacio Allende and later Miguel Hidalgo, two creole fore-bears of Mexican nationhood, whose disenchantment with colonial New Spain drove them to arms against the *gauchupines*. Coming at the moment when Napoleon's Continental System had exhausted the mental and physical re-sources of the mother country, Spain, Hidalgo's *grito de Dolores* turned loose upon Mexico a savage uprising of Indian and mestizo masses that was beyond the control of its fanatical padre leader. Once defrocked, the sullen Padre Hidalgo repudiated on his deathbed all he had fought for, and thus the charge of revolution passed into the hands of his more moderate disciple, José Maria Morelos. Like Hidalgo, Morelos was condemned and executed by the Inquisition. But, unlike Hidalgo, Morelos would not recant his alleged heresy, and, significantly, he succeeded in proclaiming Mexican independence. By 1820, however, independence had not materialized, and those who had clamored for it in principle now demanded it in fact. Unwisely they turned to Augustín de Iturbide, a Loyalist officer who had been instrumental in the demise of Morelos and who, lusting for self-aggrandizement, deserted to the rebel cause. Iturbide made an ignominious deal with Vicente Guerrero, a dedicated but gullible patriot leader, whereby their forces were joined under the *Plan de Iguala* in a formal declaration of independence from Spain. Hence independence was a reality in 1821, at least for many Mexicans. However, it was not the independence for which Hidalgo and Morelos had died.

Mexico remained under the joint plagues of clerical privilege and aristo-cratic rule. With the demise of Iturbide's short-lived dream of empire in 1823, Mexico entered upon a disastrous age, which bears the name of Antonio López de Santa Anna, the vain general who viewed his nation's political arena as a laboratory for playful experimentation with games of threat, promise, and deceit. This age was a thirty-year period of trauma, plunder, and war that ended only after Santa Anna had sold a piece of his homeland to the United States in 1853 and then spent much of the proceeds on his own caprice.

The greatest setback to Mexican nationhood during this period was the loss of nearly one-half of her domain when the war with the United States ended with the Treaty of Guadalupe Hidalgo in 1848. With the exit from public life of Santa Anna after 1853, came the Wars of Reform, engineered by Benito Juárez, Melchor Ocampo, and Lerdo de Tejada. From this era emerged a new liberalism symbolized by the Constitution of 1857, whose paper principles have generally prevailed in Mexico to the present day. The *Reforma* produced also the important and fiercely anticlerical *Ley Juárez* and *Ley Lerdo*, legal strictures which abolished ecclesiastical courts, restricted clerical participation in public affairs, and severely curtailed the rights of the Church in landholding and in instruction in public schools. Mexico was following true to the tradition of France in 1789 in that the Mexican "third estate" now clamored for an accounting from its "betters." As could be expected, the beleaguered Church drained its coffers in defense of the Conservative cause only to be tricked into believing that the privileged position of the Church would be secure under a French occupation and Maximilian in the 1860s.

In the interest of collecting debts that had been incurred by past Mexican regimes, the Governments of England, France, and Spain had entered into an agreement in 1861 whereby a joint expeditionary force would be sent to Mexico to demand payment from the new Liberal Government of Benito Juárez. Soon, however, it became obvious that the interests of France were really those of Napoleon III, who, deeply involved in the private intrigues of European royalty, sought to conquer Mexico and to place a Hapsburg monarch on the to-be-created Mexican throne. In the early months of 1862, the treason of several Mexican generals aided the French in occupying the port of Veracruz. Although the Imperial French Army was routed on May 5 at Puebla by a small troop of guerrilla fighters under General Zaragoza, the French succeeded in taking Mexico City by July; President Júarez fled north to maintain a provisional government in Chihuahua near the United States border. Maximilian and his wife, Carlotta, assumed the Mexican throne in the great Castle of Chapultepec in 1864 and believed all the while that they had been invited to do so by the Mexican people. In this, Maximilian and Carlotta were mistaken. Furthermore, the Hapsburg monarchs did not fully understand what had been expected of them by the Conservative Mexican elements who had collaborated with the French in driving Juárez into exile. Maximilian did not return to the Church the property which had been confiscated from it during the *Reforma*, nor did he succeed in endearing the local aristocracy to his Hapsburg tradition. That the common people did not love the European monarchs became clear from the popular protests and disorders in Mexico City. Disorder ultimately broke into a full-scale insurgency and forced Maximilian to flee to Querétaro. There he was tried and executed by the advancing forces of Juárez in 1867 while all European governments stood aghast.

President Juárez unfolded a liberal reform program until his sudden death in 1872. He was succeeded by a provisional government under Sebastián Lerdo de Tejada, which sought to carry on the liberal programs of Juárez. In 1877, General Porfirio Díaz, who then held power by force of arms, was recognized by the Congress as Mexico's constitutional President. Thus began an epoch of more than three decades which has come to be known variously as the *porfiriato* or the *Pax Porfiriana*, during which Porfirio Díaz sustained the longest dictatorship in Latin American political history. Intellectually, the *Pax Porfiriana* was bolstered by a group of socio-economic planners, led by José Y. Limantour, who were enamored with the philosophy of the French positivist Auguste Comte. Known as the *científicos*, their brilliance was more ascriptive than real. They claimed to possess insight into natural laws or observable regularities of human order and conduct and thus felt entitled to the privileged role of making organizational and policy prescriptions for the whole of porfirian Mexico. The assumption of this role meant in actual practice a carte blanche to run the country as the *científicos* saw fit and a wholesale invitation to foreign commercial interests to exploit Mexico's natural resources. Few guarantees were ever reserved for the homeland to participate in the benefits of the new wealth, except, that is, for Díaz and the *científicos*. The Church and the aristocrats regained most of the old privileges that Juárez had taken away.

Díaz, who maintained only the most narrow facade of democracy, on one occasion even held a plebiscite that elected a nominal successor to the executive power. The threat of peasant uprisings in the countryside was held in check by the use of mercenary police forces known as *rurales*, who in truth were little more than commissioned rogues and highwaymen charged with maintaining an ostensible level of order. Justice was largely replaced by the *ley fuga*, which gave an arresting officer the license to shoot any person who "seemed" to be in flight from "justice."

Although the *porfiriato* was Latin America's most enduring dictatorship, its foundations gave way suddenly and collapsed in a manner envisioned by no one at the time. In 1908 two events occurred which foreshadowed the demise of Porfirio Díaz. The first, and the most significant, was the publication of Francisco I. Madero's *The Presidential Succession of 1910*, which cautiously suggested that Díaz might remain in power while allowing opposition groups to elect a Vice-President as a gesture toward a more democratic political system. The second event was that Díaz himself had indeed suggested that he believed in a competitive party system. He had told an American reporter, James Creelman of *Pearson's Magazine*, of these democratic beliefs. However, by the time Creelman's story had been published in the United States, embellished by Latin American correspondents, and returned to Mexico, the story stated that Don Porfirio had promised to resign in 1910. Quickly and brutally, Díaz made it known that such were not his intentions. But the combined impact of these two events, coupled with the antigovernment activities of Pascual Orozco and Pancho Villa, had now brought Mexico to the brink of anarchy. In the face of this threat, the aging dictator resigned on May 25, 1911. One century after Padre Hidalgo's call to arms from the tiny village of Dolores, the cry of revolution was again broadcast throughout the land. This time the cry was "effective suffrage, no re-election, land and liberty."

When Madero successfully proclaimed himself President of the Republic, he accomplished much on the basis of very little strength. He had no program, and the business community which had depended upon Díaz to guarantee its privileged status now looked in vain to Madero for support. Pure democracy as Madero envisioned it was no opiate for a severely backward socio-economic system. The peasants, who were early defectors from his revolutionary cause, charged that Madero had betrayed their charismatic leader, Emiliano Zapata, with promises of land and opportunity. To the Right, the nephew of the exiled Porfirio, Felix Díaz, instituted his own uprising in the hope of resurrecting anew the *científico* cult. Supported by a sizable body of recalcitrant troops, Díaz undertook to battle Madero's forces in February 1913 in what came to be known as the "Tragic Ten Days." Unwisely, Madero had placed his hopes on General Victoriano Huerta who for ten days did fight Díaz' forces in the capital city. It is now suspected, however, that much of the fighting was deliberately staged in order to decimate the ranks of Madero's Loyalists and to enable Huerta and Díaz to make a deal for the assumption of power in Mexico.

Immediately thereafter came one of the blackest moments in the history of Mexico's relations with the United States. The American ambassador, Henry Lane Wilson, took it upon himself to negotiate a plan between Huerta and Díaz whereby the former would become provisional President and the latter the preferred Government candidate at the following election. The United States Embassy was the stage from which this pact was openly proclaimed, to the chagrin and astonishment of the assembled foreign diplomatic corps. Almost immediately afterward, Huerta's forces seized President Madero and Vice-President Pino Suarez and had them summarily executed under the *ley fuga*, now revived from porfirian times.

Huerta was the most inept of dictators. He alienated such regional chieftains as Venustiano Carranza, Pancho Villa, and Emiliano Zapata, who now rose in arms against the Mexico City Government. To make matters worse, Huerta began an exchange of insults with President Wilson, after which American Marines were ordered to seize Veracruz in April 1914. War between the two countries was barely averted through the good offices of the foreign ministers of Argentina, Brazil, and Chile. In 1914 Huerta resigned and fled to Europe with a generous array of loot taken from the Mexican Treasury. In August of that year, he was succeeded by General Carranza, who became a *de facto* President and was later recognized as such by President Wilson. Carranza was forced to flee the capital by an invasion of forces under Pancho Villa and Eulalio Gutiérrez, but Carranza returned safely after a major triumph by his trusted general, one of Mexico's truly great military figures, Alvaro Obregón. Carranza sought to repair the injured relations between his nation and the United States, a task made difficult by the border raids of the Mexican "Robin Hood," Pancho Villa, during 1916.

This period is probably the most critical point in the growth of Mexican nationhood. Her political and military leaders now grew aware that the social fabric of the country was at the point of hopeless cleavage. The chronicle of the events which led to the month of December 1916 tells little or nothing of the euphoria, the pathos, the naked despair of the people of Mexico during this horrendous six-year period. The novel *Los de abajo* referred to earlier does tell this story in the poignant words of a disillusioned revolutionary who was caught up in the anarchy which swept across the countryside like a plague in the aftermath of the revolution. Perhaps it was the pitiful blindness of those who fought onward to their destruction which ultimately produced a vision of lasting order and the conviction to make that vision real. Order was the determination of Venustiano Carranza when he called a Constitutional Assembly into session at Querétaro at the end of 1916. The following February the Assembly promulgated a document which has been the governing format of Mexico to this day.

The Consitution of 1917 embraced most of the Liberal principles of the Juarez-Ocampo-Lerdo Constitution of 1857. The four key features of the new Constitution were the following: (1) Article 3 prohibited clerics from participating ni public educational instruction and severely limited the political rights of religious groups. Specifically, the article proscribed the useof religious titles in the names of political parties and endorsements by religious groups of political parties. (2) Article 27 deprived the Church of landholding and subsoil rights throughout the Republic. (3) Article 33 opened the door for the Mexican President to expel foreign companies and personnel from the land. (4) Article 123 endorsed the principle of collective bargaining, recognized the right of workers to organize into unions, and enumerated principles for land distribution and reform. It is an enormous understatement to say that Mexicans of 1917 were ready for such hopes as these.

Carranza recognized the need for the reforms defined in the Constitution of 1917, but he was not eager to enforce them. His own cronies and followers participated generously in the booty that issued from the Presidency, but little filtered down to the masses. Thus the populace again came to wonder whether the revolution had been for nought, since it resulted in merely a paper document of reform. Pancho Villa's forces in Chihuahua and those of Zapata in Morelos and Guerrero still opposed Carranza's rule. Ignominiously and, it is suspected, with the blessing of Carranza, the legendary Zapata was assassinated in 1919, and thus a revolutionary of wide popular following became a martyr. But Zapata, posthumously, may have had his own requital. The following year Carranza himself was assassinated while attempting to flee the country by way of Tampico. Carranza had refused to honor his 1917 pledge of "no re-election" and in April 1920 had used federal troops to interfere with a Sonora strike involving Luis Morones' newly formed CROM, the Regional Confederation of Mexican Workers. With organized labor and the followers of Zapata still against him, Carranza recognized the precariousness of his situation and abdicated only to lose his life in attempted flight.

General Obregón was proclaimed President for a four-year term in 1920. He tried to implement the land-reform promises of the Constitution, as his predecessor had failed to do, and carried out an ambitious program of public education under the brilliant guidance of the philosopher, José Vasconcelos. Despite an attempted coup by Adolfo de la Huerta, Obregón turned the Presidency over to Plutarco Elías Calles, the constitutional President-elect, in 1924. Whereas Obregón had begun educational and land reforms pursuant to the Constitution of 1917, Calles considered as his special province the implementation of the anticlerical provisions of the Constitution. To this end he confiscated Church lands, abolished religious instruction in public schools, deported priests, forbade the wearing of religious habits in public, and in general waged a Kulturkampf against religious privilege in all its protean forms. A counterrevolution of Rightists and clerical fanatics, under the banner of the *cristeros*, or defenders of Christ, erupted in defiance of Calles. Despite the shock felt by many foreigners over Calles' treatment of the Church, Mexico's relations improved with the United States, largely because of the adept qualities of Ambassador Dwight Morrow, who sympathetically understood the Mexican dilemma and sought constructive channels to aid it.

Once again, in 1928, the question of the presidential succession threatened to visit another bloodbath upon Mexico while rival factions of the military sought to impose their favored candidates. In open contempt of the constitutional prohibition of re-election, Obregón's supporters successfully imposed his candidacy upon the electorate in an election of questionable honesty, as were many of the following elections. Defiantly and before he could take office, the President-elect was assassinated by a religious fanatic who, anachronistically, was allegedly a *cristero* working in the employ of Calles. So vigorously did Calles denounce the affair however and so determined was his appeal for government by law rather than by passion that violence of major proportions was avoided. Calles like other contemporary leaders was not above enriching himself at the public trough but he exhibited moments of progressive conviction, as had Carranza and Obregón which impelled the revolution's "paper gains" to inch forward toward realization.

Congress named Emilio Portes Gil, an intimate and supporter of Obregón, to be provisional President for fourteen months. During this time Calles and his group, which now included Luis Morones, formed Mexico's first revolutionary political party, the PNR, or National Revolutionary Party, which held its first convention in 1929 and nominated Pascual Ortiz Rubio to succeed Portes Gil. The latter, in his *Quince años de política mexicana*, described Ortiz Rubio's defeat of José Vasconcelos in a bitter electoral struggle which pitted the reformist thrust of the revolution squarely against the Conservative forces of clerical reaction. Not only was Ortiz Rubio an *incondicional*, or puppet, for Calles, but he was also a poor one. The Congress challenged the President's budget, and out of the ensuing controversy, Ortiz Rubio saw fit to fire several pro-Calles members of his own Cabinet. With this gesture of contempt at Calles, the great cacique dictated Ortiz Rubio's resignation and replaced him with a wealthy militarist and landowner from Baja California. Abelardo Rodríguez finished the term faithfully in service to his *jefe máximo*. The elections of 1934 saw the Left Wing of the PNR erupt in disgust at a situation in which the Mexican Presidency was obviously being run by Calles from his villa near Cuernavaca. The new revolutionaries were able to impose upon Calles their own favored candidate for the Presidency, General Lázaro Cárdenas, who was promptly elected and assumed office. That Calles had underestimated the General as a potential *incondicional* became painfully obvious. Soon Calles was in exile in the United States marveling at the socio-economic reforms which began to sweep the Republic.

The Cárdenas era (1934-1940) is one of the great steps of the Mexican Revolution during the post-violence period. Casting aside all remnants of bondage to the Calles machine, Lázaro Cárdenas distributed agrarian lands to peasants more generously than had any other previous Chief Executive. He did so via the usufructory device of *ejidos,* or collective farms regulated by the State. Cárdenas inspired strong Conservative opposition by his more strict enforcement of the anticlerical provisions of the Constitution of 1917. He frightened foreign investors by expropriating the foreign-owned oil industries in 1938, and sought political change internally by scrapping Calles' old PRN in favor of a new name, PRM, the Mexican Revolutionary Party. At the same time the old CROM of Luis Morones was replaced with the CTM, the Mexican Confederation of Workers, which came under the new and vigorous leadership of Vicente Lombardo Toledano. With both Calles and Morones exiled to the United States, Cárdenas governed without serious opposition. His support rested squarely on a broadly based configuration of peasantry, urban labor, and the armed forces. The most spectacular of Cárdenas' reforms was clearly the nationalization of the oil industry. The new State oil company, PEMEX, after floundering for over a decade under the pressure of foreign boycotts, eventually infused the Mexican Treasury with a small profit and gave to her people a prominent measure of national pride.

In 1940 Cárdenas gracefully stepped aside and was succeeded by General Manuel Avila Camacho, who carried on, though with less urgency, many of the Cárdenas reform programs. Avila Camacho was matched against the candidacy of General Juan Andreu Almazán whose support came from a number of splinter parties including PAN, the Party of.National Action, which foreshadowed the growth of a permanent political opposition in contemporary Mexico.

The elections of 1946 and 1952 were tranquil compared to the rest of Mexican experience in the twentieth century. The official party, PRM, became the PRI, the Revolutionary Institutional party, during the regime of President

Avila Camacho; and this party supported the successive regimes of Miguel Alemán Valdés and Adolfo Ruíz Cortines. Alemán's rise to fame set a pattern which was soon to be repeated in Mexican political life. He rose from governor of a major state, Veracruz, to campaign manager for Avila Camacho in 1940, and from that position to Secretario de Gobernación in the President's Cabinet. With the end of World War II, it was felt that Mexico needed a President somewhat to the political Right of the Cárdenas tradition who would promote commercial and industrial development.[2] Miguel Alemán Valdés became one of Mexico's most entrepreneurial Presidents. During his regime the nation's industrial economy surged forward toward maturity.

The selection of Adolfo Ruíz Cortines as the PRI standard-bearer in 1952 represented only a mild reaction to the conservatism of the Alemán administration. This selection is somewhat paradoxical inasmuch as Ruíz Cortines was one of the more trusted *Alemanistas* who had followed exactly the same route of ascent as had his predecessor and mentor. Ruíz had always been distinguished, even within Alemán's orbit, as being impeccably honest, and Alemán is known to have assigned to Ruíz certain financial custodial tasks which Alemán did not even trust to himself. Under Ruíz Cortines, Mexico's public administration was purged of many of its former objectionable practices, and definite strides were taken to expand the *ejido* program, public welfare, and other needed social reforms.

In 1958, Adolfo López Mateos brought to the Presidency a distinguished background as a labor mediator and organizer. His service as Secretario de Trabajo in the Ruíz Cortines Cabinet and earlier as a troubleshooter for the Mexican Treasury had attracted the admiration of ex-President Cárdenas which, coupled with López Mateos' long-standing friendship with Miguel Alemán, served ideally in fitting López for the PRI candidacy. He was unusual in that he enjoyed the unanimous support of not only the three principal emeritus figures in Mexican politics at the time, but also the unqualified support of most businessmen, of organized labor, and of the military establishment.

The election of Adolfo López Mateos in 1958 was significant in several respects. It was the first time in Mexican history that the franchise had been extended to women. Moreover, part of the PRI's campaign pledge was the institution of a sweeping program of socialized medicine, medical and dental clinics, and maternity care centers intended particularly for rural and depressed urban neighborhoods. López Mateos generally made good this pledge and

---

2 In his *Breve historia de México*, an embittered José Vasconcelos even goes so far as to argue that the selection of Alemán as Avila Camacho's successor was dictated directly from the State Department in Washington. Undoubtedly apocryphal, this is the image many Mexicans hold today of the voracity of U.S. business interests in Mexico and their governmental ties. The prevalence of this myth in high places is an impediment to the use of U.S. funds in plans for Mexican development.

thereby endeared himself to many Mexicans who otherwise might have remained apathetically on the edge of their national political life. The 1958 presidential campaign was one of the most determined, indeed violent, campaigns since the *cristero* riots of the 1920s. The opposition candidate endorsed by PAN, the National Action Party, was Luis H. Alvarez, an elite-born firebrand who saw Mexico slipping into an abyss of Marxian socialism and ultimately Communist dictatorship. Alvarez was openly the spokesman for clerical interests and for some members of the financial aristocracy.

Political stability was the hallmark of López Mateos' regime. This stability did exist despite several naval and border skirmishes with Guatemala, international friction over relations with Castro's Cuba, and the problem of the salinity in the Colorado River water coming from the United States. Even though Mexico remained a country in which misery and injustice were still widespread, her booming economy, her aggressive trade unionism, the broad range of her social welfare services, her public education system, and her generally enlightened leadership all combined to make Mexico an example of success in terms of the usual consequences of revolutionary violence, for the rest of Latin America. When Gustavo Díaz Ordaz became President in 1964, he inherited the charge of a promising land well guarded by a viable political system.

THE ENVIRONMENT OF REVOLUTION

Beginning with Mexico's "boot," her southern border with Guatemala and British Honduras, the Republic can be divided conveniently into five distinct regions. The first is the rain-forest peninsula of Yucatán, Mexico's least developed region. In Yucatán rudimentary communications, a general scarcity of entrepreneurial skills and poor land combine to retard the growth of new markets and of an industrialized economy. The peninsula is a frontier wilderness and is the home of much of Mexico's surviving Indian culture. Mérida is Yucatán's only urban center of important size. The remainder of what may be called Indian Mexico lies in the second region, the wet and rugged south Pacific which is one of Mexico's principal agricultural "bread baskets." This region in turn feeds the third region, central Mexico, which extends from Guadalajara on the west to Veracruz on the southeast and contains approximately sixty-five percent of the Republic's total population. Central Mexico is integrated around the Federal District and the capital city, whose sprawling mass draws people from all corners of Mexico into a crowded urban complex, which has a population now estimated at around seven million. Many of those who migrated to the capital came from Mexico's fourth basic region, the northern desert. It is not totally a desert since it is split at the center by a prominent range of mountains having moderate rainfall and holding a great potential for mining and lumbering as well as for limited agricultural development.

This northern region serves as a cultural buffer, or transition zone, between the United States and the more traditional southern Mexico. Finally, the Baja California peninsula might logically be included as a part of the north. However, Baja California can be viewed as a distinct regional entity because of its unusually varied geography, its potential for economic development in agriculture, mining, and fishing, and its unique socio-economic ties with the United States and particularly with the state of California.

A vast literature on Mexico's demography and patterns of social change exists, but there is much disagreement among experts on whose figures should be considered "official." It is probably safe to say, as a generalization, that population increase and accelerated urbanization are the two most critical internal problems that Mexico must face in the coming years. Mexico's population in 1966 was roughly 40,000,000. Her annual population growth in recent years has been in excess of 1,000,000. Mexico City itself is thought to have quadrupled its population since 1940. Guadalajara, the nation's second city in size and importance, now has a population of well over 1,000,000, and Monterrey, in third place, is not far behind. It is certain that Mexico's economic growth, and more precisely her indices for wealth distribution, are not keeping step with this expanding population.

Urbanization has been one of the striking facts of social change in twentieth-century Mexico. According to a recent sophisticated analysis by a Mexican scholar, who designated communities having less than 2,500 inhabitants as rural, 68.8 percent of the population in 1921 lived in rural communities.[3] By 1930 the figure had been lowered to 66.5 percent, in 1940 to 62.5 percent, and in 1950 only 57 percent of Mexico's population could be considered rural according to the 2,500 standard. The Mexican population living only in communities of over 50,000 inhabitants more than doubled (2.6 times) between 1930 and 1950. Today it is estimated, unofficially, that at least half of Mexico's population lives in urban areas, defined as agglomerations of 15,000 or more people. The realities, and often the myths, of medical care, education, protection against violence, and employment opportunity have accelerated this displacement of people from the country into the city. Mexico's experience with urbanization has nevertheless been more favorable than that of many of her Latin American neighbors largely because of the welfare measures that successive revolutionary governments have taken to relieve human misery. However, a major section of the populace must live in wretched slums.

Natural population increase is, of course, a major factor in urban growth. It is estimated that even if the current birthrate were reduced by 50 percent Mexico's total population will reach 61,000,000 by 1980. By that time, probably, 75 percent of the population will be classified as urban. Raúl Benítez Zenteño

---

3 Raul Benítez Zenteño, *Análisis demográfico de México* (Mexico, UNAM, 1961), p. 30.

has predicted that Mexico's birth rate (3.45 percent for 1960) will decline sharply as urbanization is accelerated.[4] However, his further prediction that the average life expectancy in 1980 for Mexican women will be 72, and for men 68, offers the promise of additional social complications. Future Mexican generations will not only need to grapple with the same enormous slum problem existing today but will also inherit the North American dilemma of what to do with and for the idle aged. The ability of future generations to solve this problem will depend heavily upon their nation's economic growth and upon its creation and equitable redistribution of new wealth.

During the Mexican Revolution and the years since then, agrarian reform has figured prominently in the nation's economic development. The cry "land and liberty" was a hallmark of the Mexican Revolution, although under the tyranny of Díaz, Mexican peasants were forced into a system of perpetual debt peonage which was handed down from father to son. After 1917, successive revolutionary regimes were firmly pledged to redistribute land and to wipe out the remaining *latifundia*. Under General Obregón, some initial, albeit mild, gestures were made toward reform, but the impetus for land redistribution became acute only during the administration of Lázaro Cárdenas in the late 1930s. President López Mateos (1958-1964) redistributed sizable portions of land through the usufructory device of *ejidos*. After fifty years of revolutionary tradition in Mexico, it could be said with certainty that at least one-third of the nation's land mass had been taken from the *latifundistas* and in one way or another placed in the hands of individuals or groups of peasants. Nonetheless, as late as 1950, less than one percent of the farms in Mexico occupied almost fifty percent of her land,[5] and large tracts of land owned by one person persist today despite revolutionary ideology. This fact and the fact that *ejido* lands are usufructory, serve as focal points for political attacks upon the *status quo* by opponents of Left and Right.

Mining has traditionally been an important bulwark of the Mexican economy. Both silver and gold are produced in amounts that are significant in terms of the world market. During the twentieth century, Mexico proved her ability to produce a range of industrial metals for internal consumption. Industrialization is facilitated by the presence of large deposits of coal and iron ore, which give Mexico a decided economic advantage over her immediate neighbors to the south in Central America. Before Lázaro Cárdenas expropriated the foreign oil holdings, Mexico had been one of the world's major exporters of crude oil. The immediate effect of his nationalizations was a protracted slump in oil production, but since the end of World War II, and especially

---

4 Zenteño, pp. 96–97.

5 According to figures quoted by John P. Powelson, *Latin America*: *Today's Economic and Social Revolution* (New York, McGraw-Hill Book Co., 1964), p. 37.

during the Government of Miguel Alemán, the Mexican national oil monopoly PEMEX (Petroleos Mexicanos) has shown active recovery. During the 1960s Mexico was second only to Venezuela in Latin American oil production.

Manufacturing in Mexico accounted for approximately forty percent of the gross national income in 1960. Leading manufacturing sectors are in steel (Altos Hornos de México, founded in 1942), automotive and electronics (nearly 400,000 radios were manufactured in 1959), chemicals, and pesticides. Such figures indicate that Mexico is becoming an industrial nation and has begun its drive toward economic maturity. Yet in spite of this economic growth, serious inequalities exist in the distribution of her national wealth. Comparing only total available working force with gross national product, a superficial measure to be sure, one still finds strong evidence of material inequity. In 1961, for instance, Mexico's total available working force was estimated at 12,000,000. This figure represents a 2.8 percent increase over the 1959-1960 period as compared with an increase in the gross national product of 2.9 percent for the same economic time period.[6] The 2.8 percent increase would not appear to be sufficient to justify optimism over socio-economic mobility opportunities or over improved material rewards for many of the laboring force.

While Mexico's socio-economic picture is clearly one of the brightest in Latin America, it is important to recognize that in, comparison with the United States, wealth distribution in Mexico is seriously inadequate in terms of the standards most Mexicans themselves would prescribe. Census figures from 1950 were analyzed for 4.5 million families, which were classified by their source of income. Of these families, 89 percent received less than $70.00 per month at the 1950 rate of exchange. Moreover, 71 percent received less than $35.00 per month.[7] A more recent analysis of income distribution in Mexico indicates that in 1957, 46 percent of the population subsisted on a monthly income of less than $45.00 and received 14 percent of the country's total income. That study further shows that 5 percent of the total population received 37 percent of the national income.[8] These finding are refined by a study of inhabitants in the city of Oaxaca. According to this study, 69 percent of the respondents in a given sector subsisted on less than the minimum prescribed level, and many of these same respondents lived on less than 10 pesos ($0.80 U.S.) daily. Twenty-eight percent lived on more than 10 pesos daily but on less than 30 pesos ($2.40 U.S.). Only 3 percent had a daily income of more than 30 pesos.[9]

---

[6] Nacional Financiera S.A., *Informe anual* (México, 1961), pp. 27–30.

[7] As quoted by Oscar Lewis in "Mexico Since Cárdenas," in *Social Change in Latin America Today* (New York, Harper & Row, Publishers, 1960), p. 324.

[8] Ifigenia M. de Navarreta, *La distribución del ingreso y el desarrollo económico de México* as quoted by Oscar Lewis, p. 325.

[9] Pedro Yescas Peralta, "Estructura social de la ciudad de Oaxaca," *Revista Mexicana de Sociología*, XX, No. 3 (1958), pp. 767–780.

Distribution of Mexican income on a rural and urban basis is difficult to determine. Based upon recent information, the 1958-1959 average minimum income in Mexican urban areas was 8.29 pesos daily and 6.86 pesos in rural areas. [10] Such gross figures, of course, tell nothing about the shape of the distribution. Table 1 represents the average minimum daily salary spread for key states throughout the Republic.

TABLE 1

Minimum salaries in key Mexican areas[11]

1958-1959

	Pesos per Day	
	Urban	Rural
Baja Calif. Norte	23.00	20.00
Sonora	14.01	14.08
Quintana Roo	14.00	14.00
Distrito Federal	12.00	10.00
Coahuila	11.20	9.31
Chihuahua	10.77	9.62
Morelos	10.50	8.50
San Luis Potosí	7.73	5.87
Zacatecas	6.92	5.68
Querétaro	6.41	4.72
Hidalgo	6.32	4.77
Oaxaca	6.02	4.80
Guerrero	5.88	5.77
Chiapas	5.40	4.28

The high figure for Baja California Norte is consonant with its elevated cost of living, the result of its proximity to the United States. The significant fact about the salary spread depicted above, however, is that incomes in the more favored group of states tend to be more than double those in the less favored group.

As in most Latin American countries, operative systems in Mexico for the distribution of wealth impose wretchedness upon the great majority of the population. Income and consumption statistics for any of the depressed neighborhoods of a major Mexican city tell their own story. Oscar Lewis convincingly unfolds one such tale. In Panaderos, a depressed neighborhood in Mexico

---

[10] Paul Lamartine Yates, *El desarrollo regional de México* (Mexico, Banco de Mexico, 1962), p. 93.

[11] Yates, p. 93.

City, he found that more than 85 percent of the households had an average
monthly income of less than $16.00. "Many families consisting 'of husband,
wife and four children managed to live on 8–10 pesos a day ($0.60 – 0.80 U.S.)
for food. Their diet consisted of black coffee, tortillas, beans and chile."[12]
Not unexpectedly, persons with such a niggardly share in the material
rewards of their society are frequently and prominently among the politically
alienated.

Ultimately, the charge of continuing the revolution and of caring for
Mexico's growing population must fall upon the Government itself. This
charge will require both social reform and economic growth. Rather than
relegating this responsibility to private institutions as many Latin American
nations have done, and with unhappy consequences, the Mexican Government
has placed responsiblity for sustaining economic growth in the hands of one
principal organ. This agency, Nacional Financiera, was created in 1934 and
is officially designated as a development bank. Development banks may be
classified in three ways: those which have only private capital, those which are
exclusive agencies of governments, and those which involve participation by
both government and private capital, Nacional Financiera belongs to the
last group even though the privately held share of its stock, belonging to
banks and insurance companies, constitutes only 9 percent of the total capitaliza-
tion. Recent changes in Nacional Financiera's Organic Law provide, however,
that the private share of the bank's capital may increase to 49 percent.

Nacional Financiera's Board of Directors consists of seven members,
three of whom represent the Government and four of whom are appointed by
private stockholders. The Board of Directors functions as a co-ordinator of credit
policy for public and private banks and is one of the country's most important sources of investment capital. The bank exerts direct fiscal management
over Government corporations such as those involving steel and petroleum
production, the railroads, Aeronaves de México, electricity, major highways,
and numerous related functions. Financing of both public and private enterprises is largely by guaranteed credit, but securities and stock subscriptions
are also accepted.[13] Nacional Financiera makes credit available both to banks
and individual operated privately or as adjuncts of the Government. Direct
loans to individual persons are left to banks and other lending institutions.
Mexico's increasingly vigorous economy testifies to the success of Nacional
Financiera.

Nevertheless, Mexico's economic growth, no matter how promising,
has not cured her social ills; social change is a companion requisite of economic

---

[12] Oscar Lewis, *The Children of Sánchez* (New York, Random House, 1961), p. xvii.

[13] *Informe anual*, pp. 1–15.

development. Robert E. Scott, in a thoughtful and excellent treatise on the Mexican political system, has generalized Mexican society into the following broad groupings: (1) the unintegrated Indians; (2) the peasants, *ejidatarios* (tenants of *ejido* lands) and miscellaneous small farmers; (3) small town and urban middle class; and (4) the urban upper class.[14] Although the overwhelming majority of Mexicans are of Indian descent, only a very small percentage of them, probably not more than ten percent, could be classed ethnically (speaking no Spanish and living in traditional circumstances) as Indians in 1965. Largely apart from the thrust of Mexican political life, the Indian is in many respects a drain on the national economy and a wasted human resource. The Indian prefers isolated village living, often shuns identification with the nation, and resists efforts at economic integration. He is in this respect markedly in contrast to the second grouping listed by Scott. Peasants, *ejidatarios* and small farmers tend to identify actively with the national political life through such functional organizations as the National Peasants Confederation, the League of Agrarian Communities, and the officially sponsored party, PRI. While generally content with a menial socio-economic role, this second social grouping has frequently voiced outrage over its small share in Mexico's material prosperity. During the decade of the 1960s peasants flocked in sizable numbers to support an organization known as UGOCM, the General Union of Mexican Workers and Peasants. Under the fiery leadership of Jacinto López, UGOCM has harrassed rural officials and has committed a number of invasions, or *paracaidismo*, of privately held land. The effect of such actions has been to dramatize the deficiencies of rural life in Mexico rather than to cure them.

Mexico's middle class, the third of Scott's general groupings, is a critical factor in assessing the nation's continuing prospects for political stability. However, his fourth group, the urban upper class, can be dispensed with briefly as the small peak, constituting less than one-half of one percent of the population, of Mexico's socio-economic pyramid. A hereditary and self-perpetuating elite before the Revolution of 1910, the upper class has now been invaded by *nouveaux riches*, who have reached their position via the Revolutionary party and its ever-extending governmental controls over the economy.

Scott estimated Mexico's middle class to be 12.57 percent of the national total.[15] Using different criteria for inclusion, Oscar Lewis has estimated that the middle class is closer to 20 percent of the national total.[16] Because of the time lapse since Scott's and Lewis's works appeared, we can safely assume

---

[14] Robert E. Scott, *Mexican Government in Transition*, (Urbana, University of Illinois Press, revised 1964), pp. 56–95.

[15] Scott, pp. 56–95.

[16] Lewis, "Mexico Since Cárdenas," p. 324.

that the upper figure is now correct and that 25 percent would be a reasonable estimate for the year 1970. Social scientists specializing in Latin American studies are far from agreed on what criteria ought to be used in distinguishing middle-class growth. Most social scientists, however, would accept at least these features as being characteristically middle-class: a tendency to disdain manual labor and a tendency to define one's social and occupational role in terms of acquired intellectual skills. Combined, these characteristics give a measure of socio-economic mobility *potential* which, by Mexican standards, can generally be said to distinguish the middle class from the lower classes.

Regardless of actual socio-economic mobility, the Mexican middle class has influenced governmental social and economic policy. Since World War II, middle-class influences in Mexico, and indeed throughout Latin America, have motivated governmental intervention in commerce and industry for three primary purposes: to protect local industry from outside competition, to assist in the process of capital formation in order to promote industrial growth, and to control prices of consumer necessities on behalf of labor groups. [17] Middle-class influence has exhibited a collaborative spirit in combining State and private capitalism and has successfully substituted organized political parties for the family as a basic political unit. A recent general study contends that large businesses and governments have usurped the position of the family as job finder and that the cadres of white-collar workers, so intimately associated with middle-class development, have found little difficulty in transferring political allegiances.[18]

Even more significant for Mexican political change is the moderating effect of middle-class influence. Businessmen, professionals, government workers, bureaucracy, and social pluralism are all hallmarks of the Mexican urban middle class. Social pluralism, a multiplicity of overlapping group memberships, has a decidedly moderating effect upon overt behavior. An individual's actions as follower or leader in one membership context imply consequences for other memberships he may have. Multiplicity of group memberships broadens one's social base of responsibility for his own behavior, and this broadening tends to discourage extreme actions or unusually radical points of view. In the words of John J. Johnson, the middle sectors have become harmonizers. "They have learned the danger of dealing in absolute postulates, and their political experiences have given them a positive psychology, as opposed to the negative one so often exhibited by opposition groups."[16]

Johnson's statement undoubtedly holds true for the Latin American middle

---

[17] See John J. Johnson, "The Political Role of the Latin American Middle Sectors," *The Annals* (March 1961), p. 24.

[18] Johnson, p. 24.

[19] Johnson, p. 25.

classes in general. In Mexico, however, there is evidence that along with a stabilizing or harmonizing function has gone an increased political awareness and a tendency toward criticism of the *status quo* on the part of urban middle-class elements. That not all such criticism has been directed through politically stable channels will be seen presently in the discussion of political groups. It must be said, however, that Mexico has one of the largest and most stable middle-class aggregates in all of Latin America, and this stability is in itself a tribute to Mexico's dynamic revolution.

MEXICO'S PRI: THE INSTITUTIONAL REVOLUTIONARY PARTY

The assassination of President Obregón in 1928 provided an impetus for Mexico's political leaders to band together in some enduring institutional arrangement whereby the nation might be spared a reoccurrence of the anarchy and the carnage which had marked the revolution. Plutarco Elías Calles, the *jefe máximo*, was at once enlightened and threatened in this respect when he oversaw in 1929 the creation of the National Revolutionary party, PNR. Under President Cárdenas the name was changed in 1937 to PRM, the Mexican Revolutionary party, partly in an effort to obscure any lingering stigma of attachment to the old Calles political machine. In 1945, President Avila Camacho was instrumental in once again changing the party's name to the present one, the Institutional Revolutionary party, PRI.

Until the election of Lázaro Cárdenas in 1934, Calles had been able to dominate Mexican political life through the PNR and through a series of strategically located *incondicionales*, or puppets, whom he successfully manipulated. He made a mistake, however, in his choice of a candidate for the election of 1934. His candidate, Lázaro Cárdenas, had no fear of losing the election. There was virtually no opposition, and had there been, Calles would have seen to it that the votes were counted "properly." Despite this certainty, Cárdenas stumped the country thoroughly into many remote villages, and thus let it be known that the future President of Mexico cared enough about the common folk to carry his appeal to their doorstep. There is no doubt that Cárdenas endeared himself to the masses and captured a popular mandate that no other President has ever enjoyed. If Cárdenas seemed to represent a continuation of any revolutionary tradition, it was that of Zapata's "land and liberty." Cárdenas was entirely too charismatic in his own right to fall quietly into line as another Calles *incondicional*. Thus, when the opposing forces were joined in issue, it was Calles who left the country for permanent exile.

Whereas Calles had organized his official party on a regional basis, somewhat reminiscent of Díaz' *rurales* but without the violence, Cárdenas preferred a functional, or sectorial, organization. The PRM was reorganized into four sectors: agrarian, labor, popular, and military. The agrarian sector contained a number of subsidiary organizations designed to integrate peasants and small landholders into the party. Prominent among these two groups was the CNC, the National Confederation of Peasants. The labor sector was integrated around the CTM, the Mexican Workers Confederation, under the leadership of the Socialist intellectual Vicente Lombardo Toledano. The popular sector appealed primarily to urban small businessmen, professionals, students, and public employees, while the military sector obviously was meant to represent the armed forces.

Cárdenas' sectorial system featured informal reciprocity agreements whereby congressional seats were apportioned among the four sectors. Although one state might be represented by senators and deputies who came from only one or two sectors, the remaining sectorial organizations were pledged to support these candidates in exchange for having their own candidates supported reciprocally in other states. The intention was to give each sector nearly equal representation at the national level. The Presidency, of course, was considered nonsectorial, or party-wide. So comprehensive and far-reaching was the development of this system that it seemed to presuppose the impossibility of any serious threat from politically relevant opposition parties. Indeed, the official party controlled the ballot boxes in such a manner as to make it difficult, often hazardous, for opposition groups to register whatever popular mandate they might have.

Under President Avila Camacho in 1945, the military sector of the PRI was dropped as a gesture of demilitarization in Mexico's growing commitment to a civilian stewardship of the revolution and as a revulsion against the specter of cacique rule then plaguing many other of the Latin American nations. The official party, PRI, thus emerged as the semimonolithic structure which it is today. At its top is the President of the Republic. and immediately beneath him is a Central Executive Committee, CEC, whose president and members are elected by the party's National Assembly, which meets every three years. The CEC is the official presidium of the PRI and as such is the highest and most important agency within the party. Next in order of prestige is the Grand Commission, which is elected by the National Assembly and functions as a permanent interim committee while the Assembly is out of session. Its function, generally, is to represent not only the Assembly itself but also the grass-roots sectors of the party and to watch over the activities of the party's Central Executive Committee. The National Assembly itself follows the Grand Commission in the chain of command. The membership of the National Assembly is fed by the general party membership, including the popular, agrarian, and labor sector organizations, all of which have a prominent voice in the regional committees organized in each of the twenty-nine states, and including a series of municipal committees beneath the regional committees. The Federal District and Mexico City are further subdivided into district committees.

The interested scholar who wishes to pursue in greater detail the complex and fascinating organization of the PRI is referred to any of several excellent recent studies that are cited at the conclusion of this discussion. The PRI is a unique phenomenon in Latin American politics. Since 1929 PRI and its forebears have maintained a virtual monopoly of elective and appointive offices in Mexico. Significantly, this monopoly has been accomplished without a single major outbreak of violence or insurgency, and the State has not been seriously threatened with coups from either the Left or the Right. The PRI must be given credit for advancing Mexico across an economic period of beginning growth and into her present drive toward maturity. Her people enjoy more social welfare benefits than do the citizens of most Latin American nations, and employment opportunities, while leaving much to be desired, are not in the hopeless state of affairs that one finds in such countries as Honduras, Colombia, and Bolivia. The PRI can rightfully claim the credit for most of these accomplishments, because no other group from its earliest beginnings onward has been able to control the machinery of government during most of the present century.

Describing the implications of Adolfo López Mateos' electoral victory in 1958, Philip Taylor observed that Mexico seems to be a "smoothly running authoritarian regime."[20] Taylor's statement holds much of the secret of the PRI's role as chief stabilizer in the Mexican political system. PRI has benefited from the lessons of political authoritarianism which have been felt so poignantly in other Latin American nations. Authoritarianism, when its fruits are reserved for the enjoyment of an elite minority, generates severely alienated out groups, who in turn threaten the *status quo*. Ideologically, these groups may have little or nothing in common except a singularity of purpose in deposing an exploitative elite. It makes no difference whether the elite in question is defined in social, economic, racial, spiritual, or functional terms. The practice of authoritarianism by Latin American elites has always generated widespread alienation and has ultimately led to violence. The *porfiriato* was Latin America's longest dictatorship, and it ended in one of the most horrendous bloodbaths the modern world has ever seen. The lesson of the *porfiriato* was that the people must be made to feel, or be deceived into believing, that the Government is theirs and that it really seeks to improve their way of life. Since the revolutionary mechanism was institutionalized into a party in 1929, successive regimes have sought to extend this feeling of belonging into the grass roots of Mexican society.

Yet surely the Mexican political system is not an idyllic picture of pure and unfettered democracy. We know that Mexican bureaucrats have been among the world's most voracious in their greed. Dishonesty has been and

---

20 Philip B. Taylor, Jr., "The Mexican Elections of 1958: Affirmation of Authoritarianism," *Western Political Quarterly* (September 1960), p. 729.

still is rampant throughout the country's public administration. There is much electoral fraud although it is decreasing.

Clearly the PRI has its elements of corruption, but to say that a regime can be improved upon is not to argue that its continued existence is unjustified. The author has found among a limited group of severely alienated leftist intellectuals in Mexico the feeling that the PRI is only a cadaver, a shabby lingering reminder of the great *fracaso* that once was the revolution. Such a view is also shared among a few leftists in the academic circles of the United States. But, before passing judgment upon Mexico, perhaps we should first look at ourselves. In the matter of spoils, we North Americans can lay no claim to an orderly house, as the Jacksonians, the Grant regime, Cleveland, and Harding all testify.

In Mexico, where spoils have occurred, the benefits of these spoils have filtered farther down the socio-economic pyramid than has been the case in most other Latin American countries. Perhaps this observation is a pejorative way of praising. Nevertheless, PRI has come to symbolize Mexico; ideologically PRI has tried to make itself available to the Mexican people at the most humble level of society. The PRI commands allegiance to the system even though those who give allegiance may often be hungry. Mexico therefore enjoys political stability as it is known in few of her sister Republics. The classic and most definitive statement of PRI's role has been rendered by L. Vincent Padgett: "... From the standpoint of stability within the Mexican political system and citizen participation in the molding of policy, the emerging function of the party as an instrument of mediation between government and people has been most important .... An 'official' party need not necessarily be an instrument of imposition. It may be a device for bridging the gap between authoritarianism and representative democracy."[21]

THE SATELLITE SYSTEM OF OPPOSITION PARTIES AND OUT GROUPS

PRI occupies the center of the Mexican party spectrum, although when placed within the context of a world-wide political continuum, PRI would certainly be located to the left of center. To the left of PRI in Mexico is a loose configuration of Marxist-oriented groups whose principal ideological bond is a common dissatisfaction that the Revolutionary party has not been sufficiently Communist or sufficiently anti-North American. In August of 1961, a convention of prominent leftists, featuring representatives of the Mexican

---

[21] L. Vincent Padgett, "Mexico's One-Party System: A Re-Evaluation," *The American Political Science Review*, (December 1957), p. 1008.

Communist party, the Popular Socialist party, and a number of other splinter groups, was held in Mexico City. Ex-President Lázaro Cárdenas served as the ideological mentor. These meetings displayed a broad consensus in favor of nationalization of all natural resources, expulsion of most foreign capital investments, closer ties with Castro's Cuba, and a broad "go-it-alone" policy that was highlighted by a vitriolic anti-Yankeeism. The convention also decided that a new leftist entity was needed to cement and coordinate the efforts of the various groups into a unified front. Thus a new movement, the MLN, or National Liberation Movement, was proclaimed. It was intended to be an organ of the far Left. As David Garza said, "What is perhaps most revealing about the political orientation of the Movement of National Liberation is the inclusion of Communists in the ranks of its National Committee."[22]

MLN immediately called itself a grass-roots organization which ultimately would rival PRI. This image was short-lived, however; during the first year of MLN's existence, Vicente Lombardo Toledano took his Popular Socialist party, PPS, out of the MLN. His action resulted partly from reluctance to embrace Maoist Communism, which seemed to be gaining currency within the MLN, and partly from rivalry between himself and Lázaro Cárdenas. This withdrawal caused discontent within PPS itself. The UGOCM, the General Union of Mexican Workers and Peasants, under Jacinto López, agreed to pull out of MLN only under severe duress from Lombardo. MLN die-hards countered this blow to their prestige by trying to capitalize on the prestige of Lázaro Cárdenas and proclaimed a radical campaign to renew his vigorous agrarian reform measures of the 1930s. Braulio Maldonado Sández, an ex-governor of Baja California and a PRI renegade, called for armed peasant uprisings and insurgent *paracaidismo* in the countryside against the incumbent "traitors" of the revolution. An MLN organizer and labor leader from Morelos, Rubén Jaramillo, was murdered under mysterious circumstances which pointed to government complicity, although this charge has never been proved. An agrarian reform subsidiary known as CCI, the Independent Peasant Front, was formed, with Lázaro Cárdenas again serving as godfather, but supported by a directorate consisting of known members of the Mexican Communist party.

The central dilemma of the Mexican Left is that it is divided principally between supporters of two aging giants who do not seem prepared to compromise in favor of a united front. Vicente Lombardo Toledano is famous throughout the hemisphere as the founder of CTAL, the Latin American Workers Confederation. His PPS has predominated in Mexico's leftist out group camp because of PPS willingness to come to terms with the PRI on matters of poten-

---

22 David T. Garza, "Factionalism in the Mexican Left: The Frustration of the MLN," *The Western Political Quarterly*, (September 1964), p. 451.

tial ideological cleavage. In the presidential campaign of 1964, PPS was virtually conscripted by PRI as its "official" opposition of the Left and was inscribed as a legal political party by the Secretaría de Gobernación. In return, PPS, that is, Lombardo, promised to support the presidential candidacy of the PRI's standard-bearer in return for assured seats in Congress. This *rapprochement* further widened the breach between PPS and the Cárdenas-oriented MLN, which formed its own campaign front, the FEP, the Popular Electoral Front, and ran Professor Ramón Danzós Palomino for the Presidency. Danzós Palomino, who was also an official of the Mexican Communist party, was denied inscription as a legal candidate. Also wearing the illegal colors of FEP in 1964 was the honored painter, David Alfaro Siquieros, who, from his jail cell in Mexico City, campaigned as a protest gesture for a seat in the Senate.

Seen from the vantage point of the 1960s, the Marxist Left does not appear to constitute a serious threat to the stability of the Mexican political system. This threat is absent essentially because the official PRI has traditionally taken a sufficiently Marxist bent of its own to embrace within its ranks most of Mexico's leftist ideological sentiment. Probably for this reason also, Christian Democracy of the Chilean, Peruvian, or Venezuelan variety, which is Socialist-oriented, has never become a major leftist opposition force in Mexico. The only leftists who cannot find an ideological home within the PRI are for the most part intransigent Communists who are satisfied with nothing short of a Maoist hard line. An example of such intransigence is a group known as SMACP, the Mexican Society of Friends for Peoples China. Should the warring factions of the Left, PPS and MLN, ever resolve their differences, and especially if this resolution were to occur within the lifetimes of their charismatic chiefs, Lombardo and Cárdenas, then the relevance of the Mexican Left could be vastly enhanced. This relevance could also be strengthened by any visible major shift of PRI to the right of center, a possibility to which we shall return later.

Although it is doubtful that the Mexican Left constitutes a force of major political relevance as the decade of the 1960s draws to a close, there is less reason to doubt the growing relevance of organized out groups on Mexico's political Right. Rightist out-group sentiment in Mexico has two principal organizational forms, Unión Nacional Sinarquista and Partido de Acción Nacional. The term *"sinarquista"* is a corruption of two words, *"sin"* and *"anarquia,"* meaning "without anarchy" or in better English, "with order." Order, *orden*, as the name of its official journal implies, is the hallmark of UNS. It is intended to be an order of Christian democracy, first under God, then under a God-fearing state. All *Sinarquistas* are said to be ardent Roman Catholics. Sinarquistas are disciplined soldiers of a militant theocratic faith and frequently use the word "soldier" in self-description. The ideology *sinarquismo* embraces a strong economic conservatism.

Unión Nacional Sinarquista was proclaimed from León, Guanajuato, in

1937 by a committee consisting of José Antonio Urquiza, José Trueba Olivares, Manuel Zermeño, Juan Ignacio Padilla, and Rubén and Guillermo Mendoza Heredia. So intense was popular frenzy against their declarations that the governor of Guanajuato drove these early *Sinarquistas* from his state. They then established offices in Mexico City and began publication of the mimeographed *El Boletín* in an effort to develop a national organization.

Although José Antonio Urquiza is most often referred to as the founder of UNS, its first national chief to hold working office was José Trueba Olivares, who still lives in his native León as a retired attorney. The assassination of Urquiza in 1938 was the first of many crises for UNS. An ambiguous period ensued throughout the war years of the 1940s of rioting and disorder, which the *Sinarquista* and the Communists blamed on each other. It is fair to say that the *Sinarquistas* caused considerable difficulty for the Governments of Lázaro Cárdenas (1934–40), Manuel Avila Camacho (1940–46), and Miguel Alemán (1946–52). Since the labor riots of 1958, however, *sinarquismo* has tended to function as a pacific, although not a passive, civic opposition.[23] As an ideology that is essentially reactionary, *sinarquismo* found little congruency between its own image of the ideal state and the realities of contemporary Mexico. Thus, as a new presidential succession approached in 1964, the fighting song of UNS, *Fe Sangre Victoria*, was heard anew as were rumors of another *Sinarquista* intrusion into the political arena.

The campaign year 1964 opened with the promise of a strong rightist opposition alliance. An agreement had been concluded in December 1963, whereby UNS would support candidates of a new political formation known as Partido Nacionalista de México (PNM). This formation was a Christian Democratic party, (allegedly financed by the Catholic laymen's organization, Acción Católica Mexicana). The new party was created during 1963 and was officially registered as a political party with the Secretaría de Gobernación. UNS was not registered and did not wish to consider itself a political party; however, by supporting PNM candidates, UNS could exert itself politically, and PNM could acquire needed popular support.

In March 1964, the registration of PNM was suddenly cancelled on the ground that the party no longer had the legally required membership of seventy-five thousand for official registration. A different view of that event was expressed by spokesmen for several of the related groups. Their version of the loss of register was that a union of PNM (which had official register) and UNS (which claimed popular voting membership in excess of two million) posed a serious threat to PRI, especially in the light of PRI's pledge to support the new electoral

---

23 A more full discussion of *sinarquismo* is found in Kenneth F. Johnson, "Ideological Correlates of Right-Wing Political Alienation in Mexico," *The American Political Science Review* (September 1965); and by the same author (with Duane W. Hill), "A Cross-Cultural Approach to Political Alienation" *The Rocky Mountain Social Science Journal*, (May 1965).

law giving opposition parties greater representation in Congress. The thought of twenty *Sinarquistas* seated in the Cámara de Diputados was, understandably, no source of comfort to the incumbent regime. Because of the cancelled registration and the forced dissolution of the PNM-UNS alliance, PNM slipped quietly into the shadows of Conservative reaction, and UNS retired, not without cries for radical action, to its pacific role as critic. In June, 1964, an announcement came from José Trinidad Cervantes, National Chief of Unión Nacional Sinarquista, that his followers were to vote for the candidate of their conscience in order to fulfill their constitutionally required duties as citizens.

Since 1940 the only formal opposition to PRI has been offered by PAN, the Party of National Action. PAN emerged as part of the Conservative reaction to the socialistic reforms of the Lázaro Cárdenas regime during the 1930s. Principal targets of reactionary attack were the sweeping nationalizations of industry, the stricter enforcement of the anticlerical provisions of the Constitution of 1917, and the hastened distribution of agricultural lands through the use of *ejidos*. PAN was formed at a Mexico City convention in 1939. The founder of PAN, Manuel Gómez Morín, is still active in the party's national organization. Since its founding, PAN has always offered presidential and congressional candidates, except in 1946 when it eschewed the Presidency. PAN carefully avoids attacks on important symbols of Mexican nationhood; thus the Constitution of 1917 is upheld except for the anticlerical provisions, as a great instrument of human equality. Continuing in the role of critic, PAN charges that the controlling PRI has bastardized this great work through administrative abuses of liberty.

Today's *Panistas*, or members of PAN, include the *abolengo*, old families of distinguished ancestry whose wealth and position have been reduced or threatened by the Revolutionary party; certain of the *nouveaux riches* who aspire to greater place; many of the upwardly mobile middle class who "never quite made it" and blame officialdom; and an uncertain base of peasants and artisans whose susceptibility to Church influence has placed them within PAN ranks. Never having been able to claim more than twelve percent of the officially reported vote in a presidential election, PAN holds the image of a weak and ineffectual opposition to PRI.

PAN played a significant role in the 1964 presidential election. The PAN candidate, José González Torres, attacked the *status quo* on points of issue that were, in some ways, similar to the campaign pronouncements of Barry Goldwater in the concurrent American electoral period. Goldwater called for administrative decentralization, branded as unconstitutional the concentration of power in the hands of the President, and decried the corruption and the weakness of state and local governments. In González Torres' native Michoacán, he condemned socialism as a spreading leftist disease. PAN demanded an end to the *ejido* program of state-supported collective farms and condemned the Banco Ejidal for dishonest lending and foreclosure practices. A major point of the PAN attack was the program of free and compulsory textbooks for the public schools. This program had been initiated during the López Mateos regime and was promised continued support by all PRI candidates in this campaign. PAN's principal objection to the program was that the compulsory books made no mention of God or of religion. *Panistas* viewed this omission as a deliberate campaign to "de-Christianize" Mexico and to forever relegate the Church to the status of lower-class citizenship in the national political life.

The presidential succession of 1964 represented a major advance for political maturity in Mexico, although no one seriously doubted that Díaz Ordaz would win. In round figures, González Torres got approximately twelve percent of the eleven million votes that were cast on July 5, 1964.[24] PAN won two *diputados* in districts and eighteen others by means of proportional representation. The election was conducted calmly, with little or no reported violence, and only a few charges of voting irregularities were made. It appears certain that the pledge of clean elections was honored. The election of Díaz Ordaz marked an important "first" in recent Mexican history. It was the only time in PAN's history that one of its candidates publicly acknowledged defeat without charging fraud or disparaging the outcome. On July 11, 1964, President-elect Díaz Ordaz openly thanked PAN for its attitude and lauded the concession of defeat as an example of Mexico's maturing democracy. A cartoon in a Mexico City daily had earlier commented wryly on PAN's plight, "*Hay algo peor que no ganar . . . perder, sin fraude.*"[25] ("The hardest way to lose is honestly.")

That Mexico had gained a measure of political maturity can easily be seen in the contrast between the campaign of 1964 and that of 1958. The earlier presidential campaign period saw the triumph of Adolfo López Mateos marked by severely critical pronouncements by PAN's leadership. Luis H. Alvarez blamed all the ills of Mexico and of the world on the PRI. He cursed his defeat as an enormous fraud, leaving strained relations between the two parties. There was certainly a great amount of fraud in the 1958 election but not enough by itself to have taken the Presidency away from Alvarez. However, the election was conducted in a tense atmosphere that involved the murder of one PAN campaign worker and several attacks on Alvarez himself. The violence of the opposition to his presidential candidacy undoubtedly accounted for much of PAN's extreme alienation in 1958. That none of these misfortunes was visited upon José González Torres in 1964 made this campaign appear much less antagonistic. Significantly, the only reported violence of serious propor-

---

[24] According to *Visión*, (24 julio 1964), p. 10.

[25] *Novedades*, (15 junio 1964). (Caricatura de GUASP.)

tions in the campaign was directed against the PRI. An attack by stone-throwers on Diáz Ordaz in Chihuahua City and a frustrated dynamite attempt in Nuevo Casas Grandes were officially blamed by the regime on the leftist Frente Electoral del Pueblo. One of its leaders, Braulio Maldonado Sández, a former governor of Baja California Norte, was deported as a result of the incident. Similar happenings during the 1958 campaign were blamed exclusively, and in many cases unfairly, on Acción Nacional and on the *Sinarquistas*.

The presidential succession of 1964 not only demonstrated Mexico's capacity for stable politics — for relatively honest vote counting, little or no violence, few reports of intimidation, and a frank concession by the losers — but also revealed certain clues to the possibility that the political party system might be gravitating toward a competitive two-party, or even three-party, system. Traditionally, and notwithstanding the activities of opposition groups, Mexico had been considered by most scholars to be a single-party system. However, when several months prior to the voting in July, Unión Nacional Sinarquista entered into its previously mentioned coalition agreement with the Partido Nacionalista de México, the Secretaría de Gobernación cancelled the PNM registration, ostensibly on the ground that the party lacked the legally required membership. Later it was discovered that the cancellation was a reaction to the threat of a large *Sinarquista* vote for PNM candidates for the Cámara de Diputados.[26] UNS spokesmen claimed that the party could muster a popular vote in excess of one million. Under Mexico's new electoral law, this number of votes could place up to twenty *Sinarquistas*, or their sympathizers, in the Congress. Moreover, it was learned that the original demand for cancellation of the PAN registration came from the national committee of Acción Nacional itself, which feared loss of its own status as Mexico's principal opposition party. In acceding to the PAN demand, PRI not only acknowledged the political relevance of the satellite Right but also co-opted PAN as an "official opposition" of the Right. Similarly, as noted earlier, PRI had co-opted PPS from the Left as another favored, or "official opposition," party.

It is too soon to tell, of course, whether these groups might become totally assimilated into the Revolutionary party and thus leave the single-party system intact. It is clear, however, that in 1964 a precedent, although perhaps not a firm one, was established for the growth of multi-party democracy in Mexico, a possibility explored more thoroughly in the concluding prognosis. Suffice it to conclude here that Mexico's most severely alienated political groups are the hard-line Marxist followers of FEP and the semi-fascist devotees

---

[26] According to confidential informal testimony received by the author during the electoral period.

of UNS on the right.[27] With the leftist PPS and the rightist PAN now being drawn closer to the centerist PRI, it is doubtful whether either of the extremist out groups of alienates will be able to upset the stability of Mexico's current political system.

GOVERNMENTAL PROCESSES, PUBLIC POLICY, AND PUBLIC ADMINISTRATION

The Mexican party system, the PRI and the cooperating satellite groups, tends to circumscribe all major aspects of administrative decision-making and public-policy formation throughout Mexico and at all levels of government. Thus, any consideration of governmental structures and functions must presuppose that programs, offices, and the personnel to run them must first enjoy the sanction of the official party.

In the structure of the Mexican Government, probably the most powerful man beneath the President is the Minister of *Gobernación*, an office roughly equivalent to a combination of the Departments of Justice and of the Interior in the United States. President Díaz Ordaz held this post until his selection as the PRI candidate for the 1964 election. *Gobernación* has been a major prize for competition within the Mexican power structure. Beneath *Gobernación* and the other Cabinet posts is the Congress, which in Mexico is bicameral and consists of a a 60-member Senate and a 180-member Chamber of Deputies. PRI has always controlled the Senate in its entirety. PRI's control over the Chamber has been challenged only mildly, and then it is likely that when opposition forces were admitted, the admittance was done deliberately as a way of erecting a facade of democracy. In 1958 PAN elected 4 deputies, and PPS elected 1. The introduction of proportional representation in 1964 raised PAN's total of deputies to 20 and that of PPS to 10. Opposition parties have never been able to win Senate seats away from PRI, a circumstance which many foreign observers view as more than curious. No heuristic purpose would be served here by detailing the facts of parliamentary procedure in the Mexican Congress, because it is virtually a "rubber stamp" for the National Executive, his Cabinet, and the dominant party, PRI.

Mexico's present electoral system went into effect in 1964 and was a major feature of the Díaz Ordaz campaign. The law provides for what is termed a "mixed" system of proportional representation. This law applies only to the Chamber of Deputies; senatorial seats, 2 from each of the 29 states, are won by popular plurality vote. A registered party can win seats either on a plurality basis in an individual electoral district, or on the basis of deputies at large, known as *diputados de partido*. For deputies at large, the party would have to win at least 2.5 percent of the total national vote for

---

27 A statistical comparison of PAN and UNS alienated attitudes is contained in Kenneth F. Johnson, "Ideological Correlates...."

deputies. This rule is a means of eliminating parties which contest in only a few states. Winning this percentage means an automatic receipt of 5 deputy seats, and 1 additional seat is awarded for each one-half percent of the national total, up to a limit of 20 seats. In the 1964 election, two PAN candidates for the Chamber were declared winners in electoral districts in León and Chihuahua. In addition, the party received 18 deputies at large as a result of its percentage of the total national vote. PPS won 10 deputies by means of proportional representation, and the PARM* won 5. So long as Mexican elections continue the precedent of honesty set in 1964, it is likely that the new electoral system may help to reshape the traditional structure of decision-making at all levels of Mexican government.

Mexico is one of the few Latin American States which claims federalism as the organizing principle of its political and governmental subdivisions. Scholars have generally agreed, however, that Mexican federalism is more of a paper myth than a political reality. The twenty-nine states, the two territories, and the Federal District are severely limited in the amount of indebtedness, bonded or otherwise, which they may incur and are intimately tied financially to the national Government. Both politically and administratively, the President of the Republic has the legal power to remove the governor of a state, and governors have the corresponding power, in fact if not legally, to remove mayors and other local officials. The threat of removal has been widely used, normally in cases that involve local corruption so severe as to become an embarrassment to the President or to members of his Cabinet.

It is convenient to think of Mexico's internal public policy spectrum in terms of three broad areas: agrarian reform, economic development, and accommodation of social change. In the area of agrarian reform, the Mexican Revolution was instrumental in developing present policy; among the principal goals of the revolution was the destruction of the *latifundia*, the great landholdings. During the Cárdenas era and later under López Mateos, land distribution through the device of *ejidos* took on proportions of major public policy. Although the majority of Mexican peasants still have little hope of acquiring their own land, the *ejidos* have absorbed much of the rural unemployment, and with continued opening of new lands, the *ejidos* offer a realistic future for many who choose the rural life. Unfortunately, the *ejido* program has not aided enough rural families to check the drain of people out of rural Mexico and into the city slums. In all likelihood, the *ejido* program will continue to be a major policy commitment of future Mexican Governments, but the success of that program will be intimately tied to the overall growth of Mexico's economy.

William P. Glade has summarized the broad outlines of the Mexican

---

* Partido Auténtico de la Revolución Mexicana, a right of center and Catholic-oriented party.

Government's economic policy in terms of four interrelated developments having their origins in the revolution and in subsequent programs: "(1) the deliberate and progressive Mexicanization of the economic system; (2) the adoption and elaboration of a policy of aggressive State interventionism; (3) the evolution of political instruments for building a viable consensus on national policy; and (4) the formulation and implementation of economic and social policies productive of 'industrial goodwill.'"[28] Creation of the Banco de México in 1925 to be the sole bank to issue money and to centralize banking functions was an important first step in the direction of Mexicanizing the economic system. State interventionism was stimulated by the creation of Nacional Financiera in 1934 and subsequently by the creation of subsidiary mortgage and development banks to aid the growth of autonomous local industries. Political instruments for building a national consensus on public policy emanated largely from the PRI in the form of its sectorial organizations. In addition, such governmental organs as the Mexican Social Security System and CONASUPO, a food and clothing distribution program in depressed neighborhoods, have done much to mold favorable public opinion on behalf of the revolutionary regime. In terms of industrial good will, important investments have been made in major items of social overhead capital such as highways, bridges, and irrigation. These projects are administered largely under SCOP, the national Secretariat of Communications and Public Works.

Foreign capital is welcome in Mexico although it may not always be sought out so ostentatiously as would be the case in other Latin American countries. A major source of foreign exchange that is highly favorable to Mexico's balance of payments situation is tourism, especially tourists from the United States. Constantly improving air, rail, and highway travel have brought annual increases in American dollars spent in Mexico. Tourism has become especially important to the Mexican economy since the termination of the migratory worker, or *bracero*, agreement with the United States in in 1965.

The final broad area of Mexican public policy, accommodation of social change, is clearly the most critical for the decade of the sixties and will undoubtedly continue as such into the near future. As noted earlier, urbanization as a result of natural population increase plus displacement from the countryside is contemporary Mexico's most acute form of social change. Approaches to the solution of her urban problem raise important questions for both policy and public administration at all levels of Mexican government.

Provision of public services to urban areas in Mexico is largely a function of state governments, which levy taxes, receive federal subsidies, and, in turn, make subventions to municipalities. The basic taxes which support state regimes

---

28 William P. Glade Jr. and Charles W. Anderson, *The Political Economy of Mexico* (Madison, University of Wisconsin Press; 1963), p. 52.

are levied upon property, sales and commerce, gasoline, alcohol, "usurious income" (interest), inheritance, income tax on salaries, and special assessments for public works. Evaluation of the effectiveness of Mexican fiscal mobilization on an input-output basis is stymied by a consideration applicable to most Latin American countries. Because of the absence of detailed expenditure and revenue reporting requirements, it is usually impossible to determine receipts and outlays accurately.

Aside from the absence of strict accountability in Mexican fiscal management, there are a number of built-in factors of instability in the tax structure itself which impede the ability of government to solve the increasingly complex problems of an accelerated urbanization. In certain states, the *ley de hacienda* gives the state treasury broad discretion in granting property tax exemptions.[29] This provision has obvious value as a political patronage device. An ex-governor of Baja California Norte writes that, upon taking office, he found more than fifty percent of the eligible real estate in the entire jurisdiction unlisted on the tax rolls.[30] Another tax loophole exempts bookstores and like establishments from the sales tax on the grounds that they are cultural enterprises.[31] This provision is commonly interpreted to mean that an enterprise which handles any sort of printed matter may be totally exempt from the sales tax. All Mexican states exempt the salaries of federal employees from payment of the local income tax. Employers are authorized to deduct income tax from the salaries they pay but, again, as a result of primitive accounting techniques, there is little certainty or stability in actual receipts. The *ley de hacienda* in Sonora even includes the curious-sounding exemption of "end-of-year gifts" which do not exceed one month's salary to public employees.[32] This provision is thoroughly fraught with suspicious overtones.

Mexican *municipios*, or municipalities, have relatively little power to tax or to mobilize fiscal resources through bonded indebtedness. With respect to taxation alone, the sales taxes belong to the state and federal governments. Property tax is normally a state prerogative, so the only remaining tax base for the *municipio* is the issuing of business licenses and various permits for street vendors and other miscellaneous small-scale activities. A lesser-known and seldom-admitted source of municipal revenues is the tolerance, through indirect licensing, of prostitution and related vice activities.

In the area of public services which help to accommodate social change, several major services are provided on a shared basis between federal, state,

29 *Ley de hacienda del estado de Sonora*, No. 81, Arts. 182–187.

30 Braulio Maldonado Sández, *Baja California: comentarios políticos* (México, Costa-Amic, 1960), p. 31.

31 *Ley de hacienda* Art. 264.

32 *Ley de hacienda*, Arts. 531–537.

and local levels of government. Major highways and state roads are constructed and maintained by the federal Secretaría de Comunicaciones y Obras Públicas (SCOP), the state governments, and local private initiative on an equal basis of thirty-three percent each. Private initiative, in this case, may be a local government or a local civic group. The latter is frequently the case. A similar financial arrangement prevails in the area of domestic water service. In view of the unwillingness of local groups to invest in public services, this arrangement often means that roads maintained in the countryside by the state and federal governments are in relatively good condition while urban streets go unimproved. The American driver is often shocked to find that the pavement of a major Mexican highway ends at the city limits of a given *población* and simply resumes on the other side of the urban area.

The Mexican Government undertakes public assistance and welfare activity on a large scale through a nationally coordinated Social Security Institute and by means of the national lottery, which raises part of the financial resources for the program. Minimal unemployment compensation, medical service, and basic consumer goods are available through the Government's various welfare services. Welfare is almost entirely a federal program designed to benefit both urban and rural areas. One of the most striking of Mexico's welfare services is CONASUPO, Compañía Nacional de Subsistencias Populares which operates with an annual budget of nearly four million pesos (320,000 dollars), an operating budget surpassed in Mexico only by those of PEMEX, the National Railroads, and the Social Security system.[33] CONASUPO operates mobile stores in trucks which distribute staple consumer goods for minimal prices and under a rationing system to both urban and rural poor communities. This service has alleviated much human misery in Mexico, especially in rural areas. The system has been skillfully advertised by the PRI as a grass-roots identification symbol for group allegiance and has done much to endear the official regime to thousands of Mexicans who might otherwise provide recruiting ground for alienated and belligerent groups.

In Mexico's effort to accommodate the demands of acute social change that are generated by the growth of urban areas, the country faces a cultural dilemma which is characteristic of most Latin American nations. Cultural tradition and social values permit corruption in public office; corruption results in a dearth of public welfare services and in the reluctance of the private sector to contribute to these goals. Resulting losses in public revenues make service cutbacks and exploitive taxation increasingly necessary. The dishonesty which characterizes much of Mexican public administration depends upon a tightly controlled information system within a narrow conspiracy of key individuals. The absence in the past of an effective two-party system strengthened these

[33] *Vision*, (18 febrero 1966), p. 28c.

controls. Largesse is trickled downward and upward by means of *mordidas*, or payoffs, made to numerous officials. The actual public allocation of fiscal resources then becomes a function of personal relationships within the bureaucracy. Informal working relationships are reinforced by the built-in factors of instability contained in the treasury laws cited above, which provide ample opportunity for self-enrichment by individuals.

Much of the effectiveness of Mexican governmental adaptation to urbanization depends upon state governors, who set general norms for the administration and allocation of fiscal resources. The governor attains his position largely because he promotes the national program of the PRI in his state. Intense citizen pressure upon Mexico City for relief from excessive corruption in any state regime may lead to presidential intervention. Padgett notes the downfall pattern of state governors who have become offensive to Mexico City and are removed from office by the President:

> The penalty for incapacity has become quite clearly defined. Disturbances occur in the *municipios*. Repetition of such happenings brings editorial comment in state and national newspapers. Continuing tensions, conflicts and press criticisms finally drive the beleaguered state administration to abuse of the police power. Petitions of grievances then pile upon the desks of policy makers at the national level.. . . Such is the pattern of the downfall of state governors . . .[34]

Recognizing the threat of alienation and instability in urban areas, the Mexican Government has taken steps, through policies of long-range planning, to avoid the potentially damaging consequences of uncontrolled urbanization. In 1960 the Mexican Government adopted a realistic scheme to relieve some of the socio-economic pressure upon Mexico City. The Government created a satellite city, Ciudad Bernardino de Sahagún, based on planned industrialization with both state and private capital participating. The Italian firm Fiat and the Japanese Toyota Co. have been attracted to the site. The experiment shows that planned industrial cities on a regional basis can retrain displaced peasants for technical vocations and can relieve population pressure on central cities.[35]

As urbanization continues in Mexico, demands for job sources and social welfare services multiply. Frustrated demands for both public and private socio-economic accommodation contribute to political alienation at all levels of Mexican government. Continued clustering of people in cities is creating a greater opportunity for the articulation of political demands by opposition parties and is increasing popular pressure for modifications in the present one-party political structure of the country.

---

[34] Padgett, p. 1005.

[35] Cf. Jorge Hernández M. y Solomón Nahmad, "La política del estado como factor del desarrollo social regional," *Revista Mexicana de sociología* (enero-abril), 1961.

CONCLUSION AND PROGNOSIS

As Mexico entered the last half of the 1960s there were robust signs of her continuing revolutionary strength. Víctor Urquidi wrote that Mexico's industrial work force increased from 9 percent of the total in 1940 to almost 14 percent in 1960 and that during the same 20 years the industrial worker's share in the economy increased by an average of 2 percent annually.[36] In 1965 the Mexican automotive industry produced, though certain components were imported, and sold over 96,000 automobiles and trucks. This number represents an increase of nearly 6 percent over the previous year. Regional centers like Saltillo, Monterrey, and Guadalajara are becoming major industrial complexes in their own right. It would seem that Mexico has entered the age of mass production and may be approaching that of mass consumption. Urquidi further asserted, "fortunately for present-day generations of Mexicans, the Mexican Revolution produced a new economic concept, that of the '*estado propulsor*,' the state as motivator of the economy, and with it a social structure in which private initiative would be limited only by technology, education, market conditions, and the legislative determinations of the nation."[37]

There is no doubt that the benefits of Mexico's industrial achievement have filtered farther down the socio-economic pyramid than has been the case in most other Latin American nations. Nevertheless, the distribution of wealth is still seriously lopsided, and the poverty of rural villages and urban slums is an unpardonable disgrace, especially to a country with Mexico's wealth-producing potential. Against the squalid picture of slum life contained in Oscar Lewis's, *The Children of Sánchez*, Víctor Urquidi's pronouncement augurs poorly for the overall impact of the revolution. On the other hand, we must defend the revolution for its obvious achievement of political stability, without which socio-economic progress would have no chance at all. The earlier suggested interpretation of the Mexican political system as co-optative rather than as exclusive and authoritarian is surely a hopeful signpost for the future, but only if major politically relevant out groups are continually welcomed into the PRI's family of officialdom. At the time of this writing, there is reason to ponder this interpretation with care.

During 1965 relations between the PRI and Lombardo Toledano's PPS grew strained over charges by the latter that PRI had no intention of allowing a true opposition bloc to grow in Congress and that the ten PPS deputies were no more than a showcase opposition. On the other hand, PRI's co-opted right-wing opposition, PAN, showed signs of moving closer toward the official family. PAN's national leaders frequently spoke of their party as being in the

---

36 Víctor Urquidi, "El sector público en México," in *Progreso 64/65 Visión*, 1965, p. 73.

37 Urquidi, p. 73.

process of changing from a dogmatic opposition to one that would be democratic and loyal. One highly bizarre event actually teamed PAN with reformist PRI elements who were seeking to make the official party more responsible to its own grass-roots organizations. This event occurred on December 4, 1965, when Senator Alfonso Ruiseco Avellaneda, the head of PRI's regional organization in Baja California Sur, challenged PAN President Adolfo Christlieb Ibarrola to a duel to the death in the stadium of Mexico's National University. The proceeds of the duel were to be used to establish a specialized voting register throughout the nation that would guarantee honest elections. Christlieb accepted the challenge, but, of course, the duel never came about; the purpose of the challenge had been more the dramatization of recent scandals in municipal elections than a proposal for serious action.

Interestingly enough, PAN continued to retain control of the municipal government of Garza García in Nuevo León, certainly a precedent-setting achievement for an opposition group in Mexico. Again cynics claimed that Garza García was no more than another special enclave showcase for the PRI, despite the fact that PAN's mayor took vigorous action to purge the municipal government of graft and undertook to professionalize the police force through higher wages and civil service requirements. According to some reports, the reforms carried out by PAN in Garza García were so extensive as to be of little "showcase" value to the official regime.

Within PRI itself there were signs of strain that hinged upon the esoteric dialogue over intra-party democracy versus imposition from above. Shortly after taking office as president of PRI's Central Executive Committee, Carlos Madrazo had promised to work toward greater internal democracy within PRI. Specifically, he had promised honesty in the municipal elections of 1965 and had pledged the PRI to honor whatever popular choice that might be made. The widely publicized example of Garza García had made a lasting impression. However, Madrazo went beyond that example and advocated that local committees of PRI ought to choose their own municipal candidates in conjunction with the rank-and-file membership as opposed to the standard practice in most states of having such candidacies imposed by the state political bosses. Madrazo's recommendation proved too bitter a pill for PRI stalwarts to accept. Madrazo, as president of the PRI, was perhaps the third most powerful man in Mexico, but even he could not wipe out overnight PRI's graft-ridden patronage base, an important timber in the framework of PRI. On December 4, 1965, scarcely one year after assuming office, Madrazo resigned. Wild speculation on the possibility of total disintegration within the PRI, of a rightist coup by followers of Miguel Alemán, and of a rumored threat of open insurgency by the National Liberation Movement, MLN, then followed. That none of these fears has yet materialized is testimony to the endurance of PRI and to the overall stability of the Mexican political system.

Certainly Madrazo's resignation precipitated a crisis for the PRI, yet in taking this nearly unprecedented action, he may have promoted the very goals which he had championed and which had led to the open controversy during his initial term in office. For the first time in many years, PRI had been forced to air its dirty linen in public, and its leaders scrambled furiously to remold a public image of party unity. Many observers feel that PRI will now be forced by its own membership into a self-democratization process. If that observation is true, Madrazo's sacrifice will not have been wasted. Undoubtedly, the realization of this possibility will mean that the co-optation of loyal out groups will also continue and that Mexico will continue to enjoy political stability.[38] As we postulated earlier, political stability through some form, whether democratic or otherwise, of satisfying the demands of competing power groups is a requisite for socio-economic development, and only through such growth can Mexico expect to solve her chronic social problems. Failure to solve them means a continuing potential for political alienation and insta-bility. This potential will be especially acute in urban areas whose poorer districts are becoming havens for social renegades.

As a result of intimate ties with PRI and its sectorial organizations, labor groups in Mexico offer only a slight alienation potential that could command political relevance. Organized laborers who are unemployed enjoy social welfare benefits which are generous by most Latin American standards. The Mexican Armed Forces are fully pledged to a non-political role, and their rewards are sufficiently high to discourage severe political alienation. Extremists of the political Left, the MLN and the FEP, are a definite minority and show little chance of offering a strong united front. The *Sinarquistas*, rightly or wrongly, are disgraced with the taint of neo-fascism, racism, and clericalism and hold only a limited potential for upsetting the *status quo* by violent means. Finally, as in all Latin American countries, we must ultimately consider the students who, at the various university campuses, do hold a potential for articulating alienated sentiment and for violent upheaval. This potential was dramatized in April of 1966, when some three thousand law students paralyzed Mexico's National University for several days and forced the rector to resign under threat of death.

The key to Mexico's future stability lies in the solution of the social and economic problems of her burgeoning urban areas, where the potential for alienation, political instability, and outright insurgency is most acute. Increased

---

[38] In a later writing Robert E. Scott has suggested a thesis which is roughly complementary to the present argument. He asserts that in the early revolutionary years, and indeed until the present day, political authoritarianism was necessary for national progress, but that once achieved, "material development has allowed. . . democratic seeds to sprout and grow into demands for abandonment of the less formal authoritarian political structures." (In Pye and Verba, *Political Culture and Political Development* (Princeton, Princeton University Press, 1965), p. 394.)

flexibility in what has been until now a semi-authoritarian, single-party system will surely contribute toward the solution of these problems by incorporating more competing points of view into the national political life. To say that a regime may be improved upon is not to argue its continued existence is unjustified. Governmental history shows that the more enduring schemes are those which are most amenable to self-perpetuated reform from within. This observation explains much of the fragility of dictatorships which become totalitarian. The rotten timbers of the *Pax Porfiriana* crumbled, as no one thought they would, before the cry of a timid little man who believed in effective suffrage and no re-election. At the same moment, a bigger and more audacious man was screaming for land and liberty. Neither man survived the revolution, but the schemes of the former, Madero, were better suited to change from within and have endured as symbols of loyalty which bind the Mexican people together both culturally and politically. Zapata wanted all or nothing; although ultimately he too became a revolutionary symbol, his movement achieved much less than Madero's did.

Perhaps today, as the decade of the 1960s draws to a close, the successors to Madero and Zapata have come to realize and accept the imperative for institutional and ideological change in Mexico is to take her place among the major powers of the world. Such slogans as *"sufragio efectivo — no reelección"* may simply have to be changed to read "more suffrage for more people and re-election for those with demonstrated competence." The cry *"tierra y libertad"* may have to be converted into "housing and job opportunities in urban areas with equitable interest rates and better wages". The ethics and aesthetics of revolutionary symbolism will live on in Mexico, as indeed they should. Future stability will demand, however, that they be subject to interpretation as guides for appropriate worldly action aimed toward a better life for Mexican generations to come.

3 / Guatemala, Honduras, El Salvador, and Nicaragua

ROBERT L. PETERSON

ROBERT L. PETERSON, Associate Professor of Political Science at the University of Texas at El Paso, has concentrated his field research in Mexico and in Central America. His writings include "Social Structure and the Political Process in Latin America."

The Central American Republics of Guatemala, Honduras, El Salvador, and Nicaragua reflect the often observed contradiction between political theory and political practice in Latin America. Invariably, the many constitutions of these four states have proclaimed responsible, representative rule and have established formal institutions for the protection of individual rights and liberties within a democratic governmental framework. Almost equally constant, however, has been the utilization of the political process for authoritarian ends, for personal advantage, for advancement and protection of special interests, and for denial of the very rights granted by organic law. In brief, constitutional powers have often been arbitrarily enlarged while corresponding legal obligations have been ignored and negated in practice.

At the same time, none of these countries has been immune to modernizing forces currently sweeping the developing lands of the world. Economic development, social reform, political democratization and integration, education, respect for human dignity, and individual well-being are all fundamental issues in the political systems of the four states; the manner in which these problems are resolved will determine the future course of social, economic, and political relationships in the Central American region.

In this chapter we will examine the political systems of Guatemala, Honduras, El Salvador, and Nicaragua and the corresponding role played by the political process in the changing social structures of the Republics. First, the political environment will be described in terms of the relevant geographical, social, and historical bases of politics in the area. Secondly, the character and nature of political structures and roles will be analyzed and interpreted in the context of the actual workings of the political process. Finally, a comparative assessment will be made of instability and stability in the states under discussion in an attempt to clarify the direction of political change in each political system.

POLITICAL ENVIRONMENT

Population, Geography, and Human Ecology

Together, Guatemala, Honduras, El Salvador, and Nicaragua make up a combined area of some 146,000 square miles with an estimated population of approximately 11 million persons.[1] As a result of the nature of the physical terrain, settlement patterns are closely related to geographical factors.

Forming the major part of the Central American isthmus, which connects North and South America, the four Republics are characterized by coastal lowlands, rugged mountains, and high plateaus. Within this general threefold pattern of geographical diversity, the great majority of people, with the exception of those in Nicaragua, are concentrated on the plateaus, while the lowlands remain relatively uninhabited. In Guatemala, most of the people live in the highlands, which comprise a little more than one-third of the total land area, while the tropical lowlands, constituting another third of Guatemala's territory, contain few inhabitants. The final one-third of the country, the El Petén region of the northern plain, is also sparsely populated. El Salvador, with a relatively large population, has a more even settlement pattern, though the more elevated parts of the country are more densely populated than the lowlands. Honduras' population is found mainly in the central and western parts of the nation; the north-eastern section is largely uninhabited. In contrast to this general pattern of highland settlement, Nicaragua's population is clustered in the lowlands of the Pacific and along the western mountain slopes.

An examination of the relation between land and people reveals a number of significant facts. Population density is relatively low. Except for El Salvador, which has an estimated 275 persons per square mile, there are fewer than 100

---

[1] The combined figures for population and land area can be broken down as follows:

	Population	Area in Square Miles
Guatemala	4,378,341	42,042
Honduras	1,068,000	44,880
El Salvador	2,854,000	8,186
Nicaragua	1,536,240	50,780

The reader should be warned that even the most basic data for the Central American states can be unreliable. Consequently, the above figures are at best approximations and estimates, though the population figures for Guatemala and Nicaragua are taken from the most recent census in each of the two states (1964 and 1963, respectively).

inhabitants per square mile in the region, and in Nicaragua, the figure falls to a mere 22 inhabitants per square mile. However, higher population densities are obtained by comparing population and arable land. Estimates place approximately 2,100 inhabitants per square mile of arable land in El Salvador, 573 in Guatemala, 521 in Honduras, and 378 in Nicaragua. Since the greater percentage of the populations in all four states is rural, density figures have important political significance, especially for the overriding question of land reform.

Social Structure

Much of the character of present-day life in Guatemala, Honduras, El Salvador, and Nicaragua is a product of the social systems of these states. In large measure these social structures are an outgrowth of the Spanish colonial period and still reflect the system of social privileges and class values established at that time.

Geographically isolated, lacking easily accessible precious metals, and except for Guatemala, lacking large Indian populations for agricultural work, the area occupied today by Guatemala, Honduras, El Salvador, and Nicaragua was given little notice by the Spaniards. A small number of *peninsulares* and creoles, however, received large land grants from the Spanish crown and came to form the original nucleus of a wealthy upper class. Similarly, by the beginning of the nineteenth century, the region's commercial life was effectively monopolized by a small group of European Guatemalans who were able to combine the natural advantages of geography with the contrived advantage of commercial ties with the merchants of Cádiz, Spain.

Thus the colonial class structure came to be marked by the domination of native-born Spaniards, the *peninsulares*, over both the native-born white elements, the creoles, and the mestizos, Indians, and Negroes. The non-white groups were far below the *peninsulares* and the creoles in the social scale. To a large extent then, class structure tended to reflect an additional racial distinction. However, it would be inaccurate to classify the colonial class structure as simply a dual one. Also present in colonial society was a small number of embryonic bourgeoisie, or artisans, traders, scribes, and the like, who tended to identify themselves with the upper class or, at least, saw their own interests as being clearly distinct from those of the lower class. At the lower end of the social scale, in those regions where large Indian settlements were established, such as in Guatemala, the early appearance of mestizos soon brought about a distinction between these elements and the Indians, who occupied an inferior social position. Even among the Indians, however, an indigenous social structure paralleled the dominant Spanish structure in that a distinction was made between the Indian masses and the native Indian aristocracies.

The first instance of the system of large landholdings, which provided an important basis for the colonial social structure, was the *repartimiento,* under which the Spanish crown granted land to individual Spaniards. Labor for this system was obtained by seizing large numbers of Indians as *de facto* slaves and forcing them to work the land and the mines or to build churches and roads. The brutalities of the *repartimiento,* indistinguishable from a system of slave labor, led to the establishment of the *encomienda,* under which the Spanish crown allotted Indian groups to individual *encomenderos.* Legally, the *encomienda* was a feudal institution; a set of mutual obligations was established whereby the *encomendero* was to provide for the spiritual and physical welfare of the Indians, who, in turn, were required to labor on the *encomienda.* In reality, however, the *encomienda,* like the *repartimiento,* meant virtual enslavement for the Indian. Despite repeated attempts by the Spanish crown during the colonial period to outlaw the *encomienda,* it persisted until its final demise in the eighteenth century, when new but similar labor practices began to replace the old system. In Guatemala, for example, a refined version of the *mandamiento* system, whereby "reciprocal" agreements were made between Indian and landlord, the former agreeing to work out an advance payment from the latter, persisted until 1894.

In effect, then, the Indian often occupied a socio-economic position hardly distinguishable from that of the Negro slave, despite legal provisions to the contrary. Nor did the dissolution of colonial ties, as exemplified in the case of the Guatemalan *mandamiento* system, improve conditions among the lower social groups. In a number of instances, in fact, the lower social groups, especially the Indian, experienced a deterioration in their objective social position. The only significant alteration in the class structure was the replacement of the *peninsulares* by the creoles at the top of the social system.

In contemporary Central America, this class structure, with a few alterations, has retained much of its basic colonial character. The survival of the *latifundio,* the dominance of large *latifundio* owners, the historical position of the Church, and the conservative orientation of the army have produced a hostility to socio-economic change and the enlargement of opportunities for the lower classes. In this sense differences in the class structures of the individual states are a matter of degree rather than of kind.

In general terms, the present-day class structure is characterized by the usual threefold social division; within this tripartite structure, however, six important social groups stand out: the upper class, the intelligentsia, the middle sectors, the urban proletariat, the rural proletariat and the peasantry.

The upper class. The still dominant element within the upper class is the large landowner. In union with upper-class Church and army officials, landowning interests have been able to maintain both their social and economic power and the traditional society upon which that power depends. Because of that dominant position, this group has also been able to control the political process in the promotion of its own interests.

The intelligentsia. The intelligentsia contains both an upper-class and a middle-class segment, though the latter is now much more important than the former. According to John Friedmann, the term "intellectual" in an underdeveloped society

> ... refers quite generally to the educated minority, including principally those who are undergoing or have completed a higher education.
> The intellectual elite in this sense is a small and highly conscious social group, cohesive in relations to the rest of society though often divided among itself.[2]

More sharply, the intelligentsia can be considered to consist mainly of bureaucratic, administrative elements and of professional people, including some indigenous merchants. Of substantial importance within this group are academicians, lawyers, doctors, leaders of student organizations, scientists, and engineers. It is important to note that consciousness of socio-economic inequalities is undoubtedly greatest within this group. This fact is reflected in this group's being not only the most active in the area of reform but also the most revolutionary of the social groups.

The middle sectors. The middle sectors in Guatemala, Honduras, El Salvador, and Nicaragua are still relatively small. As has often been pointed out, the middle sectors are anything but homogeneous. Nevertheless, certain traits appear to be fairly common to what might be termed the modern middle sector of the middle class. The modern middle sector is a product of the modern industrial and commercial forces which have increasingly been felt within the Central American region during the twentieth century. Among these traits are the essential urban character of the sector, the confidence in industrialization as the basic means by which to resolve national problems, the support of public education and of improvement within professional and cultural education, the nationalist sentiments, often protectionist and anti-North American, the support of social legislation and agrarian reform, the belief in state economic intervention, and the basic democratic views. To be sure, there are individuals in the modern middle sector who would disavow one or more of these traits — the industrialist might look askance at a government nationalization program — but, in general, these traits are prevalent within the urban middle sector.

The urban proletariat. Situated below the middle class, but in many ways related to it, is the urban proletariat. The special and growing importance of this group lies in its formation of labor movements, through which the urban proletariat is beginning to assert itself. There are a number of common

---

2 John Friedmann, "Intellectuals in Developing Societies," *KYKLOS*, XIII (1960), p. 520.

interests between the urban proletariat and the modern middle sectors which tend to draw the two groups together, not the least of which are the feelings of both groups that they have been denied social opportunity and status within the existing social structure.

The rural proletariat and peasantry.   Also related by a number of bonds of affinity to the urban proletariat and to the modern middle sectors is the rural proletariat. Along with the peasantry, however, this group, situated at the bottom of the social structure and having little opportunity to articulate its interests in the political process, has experienced the worst social situation of any social grouping. That the rural proletariat is now beginning to assert itself is of importance for the future of the area.

Foreign interests.   Peripheral to the domestic social structure, but exerting an important influence upon it, are the various foreign interests within the region. Because of the mainly agricultural and nonindustrial economic interests of these concerns the practical effect of foreign corporations has been helping to maintain traditional class lines rather than to undermine social stratification.

The class basis of political groups.   This brief and general view of the class structures reveals why class forms one of the primary bases for the classification of political groups within the region and why these groups tend to form along class lines. In the first place, the high degree of social stratification tends to create class resentments. The consequence of these resentments is that interest groups must often claim to act in the interest of a particular class as a whole if they are to obtain their own objectives. Thus political figures often appeal on the basis of class though they couch their language in universal, moralistic terms. This phenomenon can be seen from any number of different viewpoints. Viewed negatively, political appeals may take the form of appeals against the dominant social class, as can be seen in the almost constant middle-class appeals for professionalization or even abolition of the army, a traditional power prop of the upper class. Viewed positively, such class appeals can be accompanied by programs designed to increase the power of labor unions as an alternate instrument of political power, even of violence. Secondly, social class is a reflection of profound economic differences. It is not surprising, therefore, that economic interests and class interests often tend to converge, as the present-day hostility of the middle sectors toward the upper class indicates. Thirdly, to the extent that the class structure represents a racial distinction there is an element of racism within the groups which claims to act in the name of a particular social group. Finally, representing in many respects a class or subclass relation, the rural-urban relation in all four states has an important bearing upon the groups acting within the class structure. For example, middle-class and lower-class leaders in urban areas are finding that their interests are increasingly bound up with the interests of similar groups in the rural areas and, consequently, are attempting to assert themselves as the natural leaders of the hitherto depressed rural classes. A rural-urban interaction, then, is developing along essentially class lines, and it should have, and to some extent already has had, an important impact upon political life.

Historical Perspective: Independence to 1930

Independence from Spain. Independence came to Central America more by default of Spanish authority than by any contrived and concentrated effort to throw off the colonial yoke. The success of the independence movements in other parts of Latin America, particularly in Mexico, offered the small number of wealthy Central American creoles an opportunity to break the domination of the *peninsulares.* The facts of geography and the pattern of settlement, however, prevented any outright transfer of political power. Moreover, the success of the Mexican Revolution and the establishment of Mexican independence brought about a significant moderation in royalist sympathies within Central America. On September 15, 1821, upper-class leaders, both civil and religious, met in Guatemala City and declared the independence of the region. The mere declaration of independence, however, brought about little consensus on the form and direction of the new Government. Peninsular domination of important political offices during the colonial regime meant that the creoles were ill-prepared to carry out the affairs of an independent government. Furthermore, factionalism was reflected in Guatemalan domination of the area, and the local predominance of provincial capitals presented important political problems. Consequently, the Spanish captain general, Gabino Gainza, who had opportunely become reconciled to separation from the mother country, was able to control the executive power and allowed local governors in Honduras, El Salvador, Nicaragua, and Costa Rica to do the same. In addition, a *junta consultiva* was formed for the purpose of aiding executive authorities until a permanent government could be constituted.

Creation of the United Provinces of Central America. Conservative elements within the region looked to union with Mexico, now ruled by Agustín de Iturbide, who had been proclaimed emperor. Iturbide, not without ambition, dispatched letters promoting Mexican amalgamation to the local governmental units in Central America, and, in 1822, the creole *junta consultiva*, sensing majority support for annexation, brought Central America under Mexican control. Not unexpectedly, opposition to annexation resulted in violence in El Salvador, in Costa Rica, and in Nicaragua. The conflict was temporarily resolved in 1823, when Iturbide was deposed in Mexico, and the Central American provinces, meeting in a constituent assembly in the summer, were able to agree upon the formation of the United Provinces of Central America. The Constitution of the newly formed political entity was based in good part upon the United States Constitution; executive power was vested in a federal President, though the Constitution also provided for five provincial presidents. As would be expected, political participation was limited strictly to the propertied classes.

Disintegration of the federation. The constitutional creation of a Central American federation did little, if anything, to bring about effective political federation. From 1823 to the dissolution of the federation in 1838, the United Provinces were caught in a web of violent factionalism and localism, most prominently seen in the conflict between Liberals and Conservatives. Supporting clericalism, the Conservative party accepted the exclusive position which had been given to the Catholic Church within the federation but demanded a unitary, rather than a federal, state. The Liberals, in contrast, were anticlerical and supported the federation. Both groups, however, were elitist organizations, and tensions arising out of concrete political issues were greatly exacerbated by the rivalry of personal leaders on both a national and a local level. In the words of Mary P. Holleran,

> it became apparent that a common resort of both parties . . . when reduced to extremities was prolific of evil consequences. It was, namely, the practice of allying themselves by bribery or otherwise with the most successful military commanders who were willing to become their tools. The power thus acquired was often turned by the military despot against both parties.[3]

Continued Guatemalan domination. The disintegration of the United Provinces in 1838 produced five independendent states. Guatemala, however, continued to dominate the area down to Costa Rica, which was able to remain somewhat outside the political conflicts of the area. Between 1838 and 1865, Guatemala was under the political control of Rafael Carrera, a Ladino peasant who had come to power on the basis of the fortuitous circumstances of a cholera epidemic. Using the epidemic as an excuse for discrediting the Liberals on the one hand and championing the Church on the other, Carrera was able to amass a group of Indian and Ladino peasants to destroy the federation and establish Conservative-clerical control of Guatemala. The Conservatives, in turn, were controlled by an elite of large landowners and high Catholic clergy, and the pseudo-popular base of the revolution was soon forgotten in the interests of the Conservative clique.

Factionalism, internal dissensions within the ruling class, and the ever-present threat of the Liberal party brought about Guatemalan intervention in the states of Honduras, El Salvador, and Nicaragua throughout this period. However, as Dana Munro has found,

---

[3] Mary P. Holleran, *Church and State in Guatemala* (New York, Columbia University Press, 1949), p. 73.

these Conservative governments, although usually controlled by the wealthiest and most respectable classes in the community, did little to improve the desperate political and economic situation into which the continual civil war had plunged the new republics, partly because of frequent changes in the personnel of the governments and frequent dissensions within the ruling class, and partly because of the inherent weakness of administrations established and upheld by the force of a foreign government.[4]

British and U.S. intervention.   It was also during this period that foreign interventions from outside the Central American region first became important in the internal affairs of the Central American states. Following the war between the United States and Mexico, rivalry between Great Britain and the United States became open in Central America. Great Britain had previously been able to maintain and enlarge its economic and strategic interest in Central America by encouraging factionalism and internal dissension within the area. With the California gold strike in 1848, United States' interests in the region became more direct, especially with the establishment of a Nicaraguan transit line by Cornelius Vanderbilt and with the British occupation of San Juan del Norte, which formed the port of entrance into the Vanderbilt line. The situation became embroiled by the internal rivalry between the Conservatives and the Liberals, locally based in Granada and León, respectively, and by the attempt by the Liberals to regain power by the use of foreign mercenaries under the command of William Walker, a United States soldier of fortune. The outcome of the whole situation was the defeat of the Conservatives and the accession of Walker to the Nicaraguan Presidency. Walker, however, was soon challenged by the Conservative Governments of the other Central American states with a great deal of instigation and assistance from Vanderbilt and the British. In 1857, Walker was defeated, though he was to make two more abortive attempts to invade the region.

Liberal seizure of political power.   Carrera's death in 1865 gave the Liberal factions in Central America an opportunity to seize political power. In 1871 Justo Rufino Barrios, a member of a well-to-do Ladino family, succeeded in establishing Liberal control over Guatemala. Previously, Liberal cliques had swept into power in El Salvador and Costa Rica. A year after the Liberals captured power in Guatemala, the Liberal party in Honduras gained the Presidency. Now established in four of the five Central American states, the Liberals proceeded to carry out certain "reforms." In Guatemala, a ruthless attack was launched upon the Catholic Church, the Conservative party, and the old landed elite while a number of moderate economic reforms were initiated. In spite of all these "progressive" aspects of the Barrios regime,

---

[4] Dana G. Munro, *The Five Republics of Central America* (New York, Oxford University Press, 1918), p. 32.

democracy was hardly established, the position of the masses in general, and of the Indian in particular, remained much the same as before, and while a not insignificant number of large landholders were deprived of their socio-economic status, they were replaced by new landowners from the elite in power, including generals, middle-class managers, and immigrants.

In the meantime, Barrios, like his Conservative predecessor, continued to intervene in neighboring states. Although Liberal Presidents had been installed in Honduras and El Salvador, Barrios soon became dissatisfied with them and, in 1876, undertook their replacement. Barrios again intervened in Honduras in 1883.

Conservative control in Nicaragua.   During this same period Nicaragua was under Conservative control as a result of the Walker fiasco. The Conservatives were able to maintain this control without the dominance of a single individual because of the ability of the various Conservative cliques to check each other, an ability which prevented the ascendancy of any one single clique. In this way Presidents were limited to the exact terms of their office, the Conservatives were able to mitigate internal jealousies, and upper-class interests as a whole were supported.

Beginnings of foreign enterprise.   This period also saw the entrance of large-scale foreign enterprise into Central America in the form of railways and the banana industry. In addition, the coffee industry was actively promoted by the Liberal Central American Governments. By the end of the nineteenth century, however, another round of long-term dictatorships had been established in Guatemala under Manuel Estrada Cabrera, who was to rule despotically until his overthrow in 1920. Honduras was under the control of Policarpo Bonilla, an army officer, while El Salvador was dominated by another army officer, Tomás Regaldo. In Nicaragua, the Liberal José Santos Zelaya, having taken advantage of factionalism within the Conservative party to overthrow the Government in 1893, had consolidated his power. In all states the power and influence of the upper class stood firmly behind the established Governments.

The twentieth century.   The same patterns of factionalism, violence, intervention, and the like were carried over, en masse into the twentieth century. After the overthrow of Estrada Cabrera in Guatemala, the usual period of factional conflict ensued, which ended in 1931 with the dictatorship of Jorge Ubico. Until 1933 Honduras was engulfed in a continuing factional struggle, in which the balance of power was held by the army. In El Salvador continuous conflict between upper-class families was temporarily resolved by the accession of the Meléndez family to political power in 1913. Their accession inaugurated seventeen years of political domination, which ended in 1930 through the revolutionary capture of power by Maximiliano Hernández Martínez. Zelaya's rule in Nicaragua was abruptly ended in 1909 with the approval of the Taft administration in the United States. Following the canons of the United States "dollar diplomacy," foreign investments in Nicaragua increased, and the United States undertook the supervision of the Nicaraguan Treasury. From 1912 to 1925 and from 1927 to 1933, Nicaragua was under the occupation of United States Marines.

Consolidation of foreign enterprise. The early twentieth century also witnessed the consolidation of large-scale foreign enterprise in Central America. Monopolistic in organization, such enterprises accommodated themselves to the traditional neo-feudal economic structure. Moreover, these foreign interests took an active role in the local politics of the region in order to promote and maintain their own already advantageous positions.

United States intervention. Unlike the situation in the nineteenth century, intervention from outside the Central American region became more important during the early part of the twentieth century than intervention from within the region. Thanks to President Theodore Roosevelt's desire to construct a canal across the Isthmus, Panama became independent in 1903 with the aid of United States intervention. Dependent on the canal ever since, Panama quickly fell into the regional pattern of upper-class political domination. Nicaragua, as previously noted, was under direct United States economic and political supervision for the greater part of the period from 1912 to 1933, and the United States also intervened in a politically chaotic Honduras in the early 1920's. None of these interventions significantly altered the traditional patterns of politics in Central America although Panama has been dependent upon the Canal ever since it was built.

POLITICAL STRUCTURES AND ROLES

Contemporary political structures and roles in Guatemala, Honduras, El Salvador, and Nicaragua are a product of historical, social, and political factors and a consequence of modern forces beginning to have an effect on the region. Consequently, political parties, interest groups, constitutional institutions, and formal governing apparatus tend to be a somewhat paradoxical combination of the old and the new, of the past and the future. The basic feature of the present-day situation, however, is social, economic, and political tension of a magnitude never before felt in the region.

Political Parties

A significant indicator of the dual nature of the political structures of Guatemala, Honduras, El Salvador, and Nicaragua can be seen in the realm of political parties. The traditional pattern of Liberal and Conservative parties has been quantitatively altered, for the most part by the emergence of new political parties and by the development of a middle-class outlook in a number of political parties in the region. A classification of political parties in these states — a somewhat hazardous undertaking in view of the transitional nature of contemporary politics — must, therefore, take into account this twofold pattern of traditional and contemporary parties.

Russell H. Fitzgibbon has attempted to formulate a typology of Latin American political parties generally in terms of whether or not the party's ideology is primary or secondary with respect to party organization and operation. Such a distinction can be applied to Guatemala, Honduras, El Salvador, and Nicaragua in terms of ideologically-based parties and traditional political parties.[5] This distinction, however, must be supplemented with a further political party type, which may be either traditional or reformist. This type is the personalist party, which, unlike personalist parties in the past, can align itself with modern elites. Thus, depending on the place of the personalist party within the socio-economic spectrum, a personalist party may, on the one hand, be indistinguishable in outlook from the traditional parties or, on the other hand, be associated with ideologically based parties.

Traditional parties. Within the contemporary political process, the rubrics "Conservative" and "Liberal" have fallen into disuse in Guatemala and El Salvador. Traditional *status quo* parties, however, are still prevalent, especially in Nicaragua, and play an important role in the frustration of socio-economic change. However, some of the traditional groupings, particularly the descendants of the old Liberal parties, have been forced to broaden their membership and advocate more progressive political programs or be replaced by new political groups. The Liberal party of Honduras is an example of a traditional party forced to become more progressive. Between 1949 and 1953, the Liberal party changed in leadership and in party program through the influence of new middle-class elements within its ranks. In 1954 the party supported the agricultural workers' strike against the United Fruit Company and consequently obtained the support of most of the banana workers and of a good number of workers and peasants in the rest of the country.

Catholic parties. The Social Catholics are another group which must be included among the newer parties of the region which are of increasing consequence as political parties. A Catholic action organization, the Christian Democratic party, has arisen in Guatemala and in El Salvador. The Party in El Salvador is now the second largest party in the country. Catholic social action centers around papal encyclicals dealing with social and economic

---

[5] Russell H. Fitzgibbon, "The Party Potpourri in Latin America," *Western Political Quarterly*, X (March 1957), p. 11.

justice, and, in the newer forms of the movement, attempts to overcome socio-economic and political problems through the application of Christian precepts.

Communist parties. Communist parties have also developed in response to contemporary transformation in the region and, in the case of Guatemala, one reached considerable size in the 1950s. In Guatemala however, the gains of the Communist party were short-lived. The relative weakness of the Communist parties cannot be considered as a sign of social and political stability for one of the changes which could result from current ideological and social transformation could considerably strengthen the appeal of communism.

Other ideological parties. Other ideological parties range from the currently unimportant to the impotent. Socialist organizations have sprung up from time to time but have generally withered away. A similar fate has befallen agrarian parties. Labor parties have also been organized, but their parochial and somewhat personalist nature has prevented them from obtaining even a modicum of success. By and large, labor tends to be assimilated within a party of wider ideological or personalist appeal.

Personalist parties. Personalist parties, as already indicated, run the gamut of socio-political outlook. Of significance have been the more socially-minded personalist organizations such as the outlawed *Partido Revolucionario de Unificación Democrática* (PRUD), which flourished from 1950 to 1960 under Colonel Oscar Osorio in El Salvador.

Contemporary party complexion. The nature of political parties in the four countries being considered bears out what has been previously stated. The following summary is currently accurate, but political parties can be extremely short-lived, and rapid shifts in nomenclature and programs can occur in the party spectrum.

In Guatemala, political parties were reconstituted after the 1954 counter-revolution. In the presidential and congressional elections in March 1966, the three major contesting parties were the Partido Revolucionario (PR), the Movimiento de Liberación Nacional (MLN), and the Partido Institucional Democrático (PID). Although often termed a "leftist" party, the PR is politically moderate and the only one of the three parties not closely identified with the military. The MLN is headed by army officers, most of whom were associated with the leader of the 1954 counterrevolution, Colonel Carlos Castillo Armas. The PID was the vehicle of the controlling military regime in the March elections and is a rather loosely organized group of conservative and military elites. In addition to these three parties, the Christian Democratic party (DCG) claims an important following but was not allowed to participate in the last presidential elections. There are also a number of smaller organizations and associations, or political party organizations lacking sufficient voter signatures to qualify as officially recognized parties, as well as the illegal Communist party (PGT).

The two major political parties in Honduras are the Liberal and Nationalist parties, which reflect the traditional Conservative-Liberal cleavage in that state. As previously noted, the Liberal party has attempted to function as a moderate, reform-minded party since at least 1954. It obtained power in December 1957, with the delayed assumption of the Presidency by Ramón Villeda Morales. The Nationalist party, on the other hand, continues to be the bastion of traditional conservatism in Honduras. This party advocates retention of the socio-economic *status quo*, though not without certain innovations.

As in the case of Guatemala and Honduras, El Salvador also requires a certain number of voter signatures before a political organization can legally qualify as a political party. At present, the three largest parties are the Partido de Conciliación Nacional (PCN), headed by the former President of El Salvador, Lieutenant Colonel Julio Adalberto Rivera, the liberal Partido Demócrata Cristiano (PDC), and the Partido Acción Renovadora (PAR). In addition there are numerous small political associations representing various positions on the political spectrum.

The major political parties of Nicaragua are all conservative with little except personalities to distinguish them. The governing party is the Nationalist Liberal party, while the Nicaraguan Conservative party (PCN) is the only other party to hold seats in the National Congress. The Traditional Conservative party (PCT) has refused to participate in recent elections and, like the smaller Independent Liberal party, is not officially recognized as a political party.

Interest Groups

The traditional pillars of political rule in this Central American region have been the army and the Church: the higher officers and officials of these institutions have been recruited from the upper class or absorbed into it. In more recent times, nonetheless, new or previously impotent interest groups have emerged to challenge the historical primacy of upper-class elites. Most prominent of these interest groups have been middle-class groups which have attempted to extend their power to lower classes through the assumption of leadership and intellectual guidance. It is important to note that, as in the case of the traditional political process, these new groups are lacking in explicit political function. In part, this lack is the result of the continued existence of traditional political elements and of the consequent dearth of new political roles developing inside the political process. In part, these groups' lack of function is also the result of the transformation process itself and of the political instability brought about by the transition from one ideological and social structure to another. Moreover, the propensity of interest groups to be organized along class or subclass lines has tended to broaden further the interests and the outlook of both past and present regional groups.

A quantitative indicator of the essentially class nature of Central American interest groups can be seen in the decreasing number of such groups as one moves down the social scale. Consequently, the emergence of middle-class interest groups and of middle-class leadership of lower-class groups can be expected to become more pronounced as basic transformations take place within the social systems of the individual states.

Upper-class interest groups. The traditional upper-class landowning and agricultural associations within the upper class remain prominent. Also important are certain industrial associations, which include members of the *nouveau riche.* Some of these associations have formal or informal bonds with prosperous foreign elements. In Guatemala, for example, upper-class interest groups include national and regional landholding associations, a number of guilds, manufacturers and merchants groups, agricultural producers associations, various civic organizations, and a number of other miscellaneous groups and associations.[6] Similar types of associations, with the same general emphasis upon occupational groupings, are found in Honduras, El Salvador, and Nicaragua. A special type of interest group which is found with some frequency in local Central American areas centers around a predominant local individual, who is variously called *gamional, caudillo, guayacán,* or *cacique.*

Middle-class interest groups. Not unexpectedly, modern middle-sector interest groups are found primarily in urban areas. It is important to remember, however, that a significant aspect of the current transformation in the region lies not only in the formation of distinctive middle-class interest groups but also in the penetration of middle-class values and aspirations into other classes as well. As already mentioned, this penetration is obvious within lower-class interest groups. But perhaps of equal importance is middle-class penetration of certain upper-class interest groups, particularly of neo-capitalist groups and of those groups which have no fundamental stake in the traditional ideological and social order. Through the promotion of economic change beneficial

---

[6] In Guatemala the following would have to be considered upper-class interest groups: the Asociación Guatemalteca de Agricultores; the Cámara de Industriales; the Cámara de Comercio; the Asociación Guatemalteca de Productores de Algodón; the Asociación General de Industriales de Guatemala; the Sindicato Patronal de Industriales; the Asociación General de Salineros de Guatemala; the Asociación Guatemalteca de Productores de Aceites Esenciales; the Asociación General de Agricultores de Occidente; the Cooperativa de Ganaderos de Guatemala; the Asociación de Agricultores de Pamaxán; the Asociación de Caficultores de Oriente; the Cooperativa de Ganaderos de Occidente; the Asociación General de Comerciantes Guatemaltecos; the Cámaras Unidas de Comercio é Industria; the Asociación Guatemalteca de Instituiones de Seguros; the Banco Agrícola Mercantil; the Rotary Clubs; the Club Guatemala; the Country Club; and several religious and civil brotherhoods and groups. The newspaper *El Imparcial,* the electoral unions, and the Conservative parties also act substantially as upper-class interest groups. Mario Monteforte, Toledo, *Guatemala: Monografía Sociologica* (México, D.F., Universidad Nacional Autonoma de México, 1959), pp. 268–269.

to upper-class industrial and commercial elements and through more fluid social arrangements, the middle class has been able to produce a degree of group schism and the beginnings of group transformation and has thus strained the relation between the agricultural, landowning sector of the upper class and the nonagricultural sectors. Thus in the Guatemalan upper-class-oriented interest groups mentioned above, the nonagricultural groups have experienced a high degree of instability and of intragroup conflict. Though these groups are not yet alienated from the upper class, it may be expected that, as the middle class in Guatemala is able to challenge upper-class domination, these nonagricultural upper-class sectors will increasingly come to adopt a middle-class outlook.

Like upper-class interest groups, middle-class groups are organized along occupational lines and particularly on the basis of profession. As such, occupational groups in the middle class are but another reflection of the transitional nature of Central American life, which includes traditional, modern, as well as revolutionary elements. The modern middle sectors have come to exercise, depending on the degree of transformation of the individual states of the region, a determining voice in these organizations to an increasing extent. Predominantly middle-class manufacturing and commercial groups have been less hampered by traditional elements and are becoming more and more vocal as their numbers grow under the impact of economic development. Also active in the assertion of middle-class interests are the varous university student and faculty organizations which have become prominent in the region.

Lower-class interest groups.   Within the lower classes, explicit interest groups, with the important exception of labor unions, are almost nonexistent. Labor unions, focusing on the urban proletariat, however, have become more and more powerful. There have been both explicit and tacit relations between labor unions and middle-class elements; labor leaders, for instance, have often come directly from the ranks of modern middle sectors. Nonetheless, with the proliferation of labor movements has come the domination of individual labor leaders, the so-called labor *caudillos.* Even in this respect, though, the injection of personalism into the labor movement is indicative of the need for disciplined behavior; the labor *caudillo,* by and large, is a *caudillo* of the Left, who challenges the traditional social system.

Inter-class interest groups.   Cutting across class boundaries are a number of interest groups, the most important of which are the army and the Church. These traditional allies of the landowning class have, in recent times, been subjected to much the same type of pressures as the nonagricultural upper-class interest groups have. The process of change has gone much further in the Church, especially with the appearance of middle-class Catholic social action organizations, than in the army. In fact, the contemporary Church in Guatemala, Honduras, El Salvador, and Nicaragua exhibits a rather schizophrenic personallity; one sector of the Church upholds traditional ideological and social standards, and the other advocates fundamental change. Less noticeable are similar cleavages within the army, or "public" forces, though social and economic discontent has been manifested at times by the political activities of middle-class junior officers. In general, the army has remained the most powerful instrument for maintaining the *status quo* and has, in truth, been strengthened in this role by United States programs of military assistance. Whether or not the middle classes will be able to establish a more powerful and a more secure base within the army will undoubtedly depend upon the course of developments within other areas of social and political life. The continued existence of the army as the protector of the *status quo*, nevertheless, not only hinders social change but ensures violent upheaval in the process of transformation. Moreover, it should be emphasized that the enlisted ranks of the army, conceivably an important potential social revolutionary force, are still largely dependent upon upper-class higher officers, or upon one particular officer, for social prestige and economic rewards. In these circumstances, middle-class junior officers find it extremely difficult to establish a widespread basis of power among the rank and file since they can offer no immediate gains to rank-and-file interests, at least in the absence of more general social and political transformation within society as a whole.

CONSTITUTIONAL AND INSTITUTIONAL FORMS

Although constitutional and institutional forms in the four states under discussion can be highly deceiving, these forms are important both as partial reflections of the current transformations in the political process and as indicators of future aspirations and desires. Moreover, as transformation within the political process becomes more complete and more stabilized, such forms may be expected to converge more closely with actual political practice than they did in the past. Before looking at political transformation in terms of actual class and group activities, therefore, it is necessary to describe the constitutional bases of government and the organization of executive, legislative, and judicial power.

As noted earlier, breaks in constitutional and institutional continuity have often been more apparent than real. For example, since the breakup of the United Provinces the Central American states have been unitary in form and have retained a separation of powers system at the national governmental level. Similarly, within the individual states provisions of previous constitutional and institutional structures have been inserted verbatim into new constitutional frameworks. In Guatemala, for instance, the present Constitution, though modified in 1945 and 1956, rests upon the Constitution of 1879. This continuity and longevity often reflects the lack of issues in the traditional political process and the predominance of personalities and cliques.

The present Constitution of Guatemala was adopted in 1956; that of Honduras in 1965; that of El Salvador in 1962; and that of Nicaragua in 1950. According to the basic laws of each Constitution, the individual states are sovereign, democratic, republican, and representative. Sovereignty resides in the people, who exercise political power directly through their elected representatives in accordance with individual guarantees of freedom of speech, of press, and of assembly. The national Governments are unitary, and governmental power is divided between legislative, executive, and judicial bodies. All citizens, subject only to qualifications of age and to constitutionally prescribed rules of eligibility, are granted the right to vote.

Legislative Power

Legislative power is vested in a unicameral legislature called the National Congress in Guatemala, the Chamber of Deputies in Honduras, and the Legislative Assembly in El Salvador. The Nicaraguan Congress is bicameral, consisting of a Chamber of Deputies and a Senate. Actual legislative powers are enumerated in detail in Central American Constitutions and include the power to enact laws, to amend the Constitution, to approve the national budget, to exercise supervision over the executive branch (including the power of impeachment), to declare war, and to approve international treaties and conventions. A somewhat unusual power is exercised by the Nicaraguan Congress, which may declare a "General State of Economic Emergency," in which case "guarantees" of freedom of trade, of contract, and of industry and freedom from *ex post facto* laws are suspended. The Constitutions of Guatemala, Honduras, and El Salvador also provide for a Permanent Legislative Committee to function during adjournment of the full legislative organ.

Executive Power

In the constitutional organization of executive power, the Central American states exhibit what has been termed "attenuated presidentialism." In Guatemala, Honduras, El Salvador, and Nicaragua, the President must exercise power in conjunction with a Council of Ministers, who share separate and joint responsibility with the President. Ministers may be interpellated by the legislature and must countersign "decrees, decisions, orders and rulings of the President of the Republic."

Because of the historical prominence of *caudillismo* and *continuismo*, the Constitutions are an attempt to elaborate a detailed system of presidential checks in addition to the requirements of ministerial countersignature and responsibility. Immediate re-election is forbidden in all siates, and the President in Guatemala is not allowed to be re-elected to office for at least two terms.

Relatives, as well as vice-presidents and ministers of state, of incumbent Presidents are not eligible for immediate election to the Presidency though these restrictions vary in length of time in the different Constitutions. The Guatemalan Constitution of 1956 provides that "no leader or chief of a *coup d'état*, armed rebellion or similar movement which alters the constitutional order" may be elected in the period in which the Constitution "was interrupted or the following period," a provision which "legalizes" *coups d'état* by inference. Finally, ministers of state cannot be relatives of the incumbent President.

As in the case of legislative powers, the duties and power of the President are given detailed constitutional enumeration. The President may appoint and remove ministers; is the supreme commander of the armed, or "public", forces; must observe and enforce the Constitution; participates in the drafting, promulgation, and publication of laws, regulations, decrees, and decisions in accordance with provisions for ministerial approval; receives and appoints diplomatic personnel; and is charged with the conduct of foreign relations as well as the performance of the general duties of a Chief Executive. In addition, all Constitutions contain provisions for the exercise of emergency powers by the Executive, though here, as elsewhere, fairly detailed provisions are laid down for the assumption of these powers.

Judicial Power

Judicial power is constitutionally vested in Supreme Courts of Justice, which vary in composition, and in various appellate and inferior courts. In general, the judicial power includes the authority to hear cases of *amparo*, related to writs of injunction and habeas corpus in Anglo-American law, and to hear civil, penal, commercial, and labor disputes. The Courts also exercise the power of judicial review to a greater or lesser extent. One of the most explicit grants of judicial review is found in the 1950 Salvadorian Constitution, which states in Article 95:

> Included within the power of administering justice, the courts have the power to declare, in cases on which they must pronounce judgments, the inapplicability of any law or order of the other Powers which is contrary to the provisions of the Constitution.

Similarly, the Guatemalan Constitution provides that "in every action and appeal, the interested parties may petition for a declaration of the unconstitutionality of the law involved therein." In Honduras, judicial review is restricted to the Supreme Court of Justice. The Nicaraguan Constitution, on the other hand, appears to limit judicial review to the exercise of contentious administrative jurisdiction and to decisions on the constitutionality of laws vetoed by the President on grounds of unconstitutionality.

Local Government

Municipal governments are subordinate to the national administration in the Central American states, though "autonomy" is encouraged on the local level. Throughout the region the general pattern of territorial and administrative hierarchy has been found by Richard N. Adams to be one in which

> local autonomy is at a minimum and in most cases not encouraged. The peculiar situation exists in the *municipio*-district where a *municipio* that may develop economically to the point where it is financially productive is threatened with total loss of what autonomy exists.[7]

Special mention should be made of the municipal organizations of the Guatemalan Indian communities. Manning Nash has observed that

> technically the Indian *municipios* are governed by organizations similar to those which govern the *municipio;* in practice, the municipal organization is a compromise between the internal organization of local Indian society and the wider political network in which they find themselves embedded. Seen from the point of view of the national Government, municipal governments in the Indian communities tie the local society to the nation. For the Indian, that is only part of its task; from his point of view the municipal organization is seen as a different kind of structure.[8]

Although disrupted to some extent during the important social revolution of 1944–1954, the basic institutional structure of local Guatemalan Indian societies rests upon a fairly elaborate civil-religious hierarchy. Within this hierarchy there is a dual series of graded offices or positions which are functionally separate, one dealing with religion, the other with civil matters. Common symbols and the fact that individuals alternate between civil and religious offices form a structural bond in communal organization. Nash has found that

> the difference between the two ladders is conceptual. Indians tend to think of them as one system. And the term civil-religious hierarchy recognizes this fact of interrelation. From the point of view of the Indian in local society, the hierarchy represents fixed tasks of communal service to which he must devote a number of years from his adult life. Each man who serves in an office is really above the very lowest rungs, a representative of a family. And it is family units, rather than individuals, which pass through the cycle of public service.[9]

---

[7] Richards N. Adams, *Cultural Surveys of Panama-Nicaragua-Guatemala-El Salvador-Honduras* (Washington, D. C., Pan American Sanitary Bureau, 1957), p. 584.

[8] Manning Nash, "Political Relations in Guatemala," *Social and Economic Studies*, VII (March 1958), p. 67.

[9] Nash, p. 67.

Political and Social Rights

Outside national and local governmental structure, Central American constitutions evidence a great concern with political and social rights. In the case of the former, individual rights include the usual guarantees found in democratic constitutions. Social and economic rights, unlike political rights, are a relatively recent constitutional phenomenon though some of these rights, such as the inviolability of the family, have been asserted traditionally. Labor, employer-employee relations, social security, hours, and the protection of women and minors in their work are all illustrative of this new constitutional concern in the region. The degree of realization of the constitutions here, however, has depended more on the particular regimes in actual power than on constitutional provisions. In any event, these provisions at least indicate an awareness of the increasing importance of new groups, parties, and forces within the Central American region.

PROCESSES OF FUNCTION AND DYSFUNCTION

The development of a remarkable diversity of interests and the accompanying tension exhibited in the institutional structures of Guatemala, Honduras, El Salvador, and Nicaragua have given the political process in each state an ambivalent and unstable character apparent, as seen in the previous section, in the groups and forces which are struggling for power and ascendancy today. Ambivalence and instability are, of course, concomitants of social and ideological change. Thus an important aspect of present-day change in each individual Republic lies in both the importance of political power as a means to realize modern social and economic goals and the transformation of the political process itself into an arena where formerly excluded interests and groups now vie for political ascendancy.

In this section the relation between social issues and political change will be examined in the context of recent political developments in each state in order to delineate more clearly and concisely the transitional nature of contemporary politics in the region. At stake in these developments are the very nature of society itself and the future course of socio-political relationships.

Guatemala

The 1944 Revolution. At the beginning of the 1930s, Guatemala was hardly distinguishable from its Central American neighbors in terms of either its socio-economic structure or its political process. Dominated by upper-class landholding cliques in association with the army, high-ranking ecclesiastical officials, and foreign corporations, Guatemala appeared to be an unlikely setting for fundamental social upheaval. This appearance was greatly reinforced in 1931 when General Jorge Ubico captured the Presidency. Ubico's rule was reactionary, even for Guatemala. Daniel James, no particular friend of the revolution which overthrew Ubico, has aptly summarized his regime in the following words:

> ... Ubico's passion for order and efficiency became pure and simple tyranny when applied to civil liberties and to progressive ideas in general. It was more than a peasant's life was worth to be caught evading a forced-labor contract, much less trying to organize or join a labor union. Students found reading a banned book, politicians discovered voicing opinions critical of Ubico, and anyone apprehended in an attempt to form or encourage a political opposition could be, and usually were, jailed, exiled or executed. Some of Guatemala's finest men spent their best years in exile. Those who desired a modicum of democracy were usually charged with "sedition" or "communism," which helps explain why after 1944 the charge of Communist was greeted by most Guatemalan leaders with mistrust and suspicion.[10]

Despite upper-class control of the political process and the heavy-handedness of the Ubico dictatorship, a modern middle sector had been developing in Guatemala since the 1870's. Although small in number compared to other sectors of the population, these middle-class elements increasingly bore the brunt of the Ubico dictatorship. Release came in the revolution of October 20, 1944. In both inception and purpose, the October revolution was middle-class in nature, a product of the leadership of young intellectuals, junior army officers, students, and professional men. Their objectives were to be found in the desire to establish a middle-class social and ideological order in place of the traditional social order which had been supreme in Guatemala since colonial days. Thus the 1944 revolution, unlike the political upheaval and violence of the past, was to be fundamental in nature, dedicated to the liquidation of feudalism, the organization of a modern (revolutionary propaganda used the word "capitalist") economic system, and the rearrangement and revitalization of the social structure. To these ends the revolutionary middle class found the political process indispensable and were quick to increase the scope of governmental activity and regulation; the middle class introduced norms of economic planning and direction, agrarian reform, the protection and integration of Indian communities, the defense of workers, and the limitation of individual rights, particularly upper-class property rights.

Once in political power, however, the middle sectors found that the task of implementing these goals had just begun. Even the political position of the

---

10 Daniel James, *Red Design for the Americas: Guatemalan Prelude* (New York, John Day and Co., 1954), pp. 36–37.

revolutionary elements was shaky — there were some thirty-one plots against Juan José Arévalo in the six years of his Presidency. The middle sectors possessed no material economic foundations to give themselves permanence. Thus it became readily apparent that the middle class must adjust the socio-economic structure to its own advantage if it was to survive. However, the difficulties in establishing a new social order and the small and unstable nature of the middle class itself increasingly produced a trend in favor of more radical political control, ultimately communism, so that the ruling elite might perpetuate itself in power. This trend created a number of internal contradictions within the middle sectors and finally led to the overthrow of the revolutionary regime, headed by Jacobo Arbenz Guzmán, in 1954. The political character of this ambivalence can be best understood within the context of the evolution that took place in national and local political structures in Guatemala in the period from 1944 to 1954.

National goverment.   One of the outstanding achievements of revolutionary government in Guatemala was the high degree of integration between democratic political forms and political practice, at least until near the end of the revolutionary period. In 1946, for instance, suffrage was extended to women, and the December 1944 elections were probably the freest held in Guatemala to that date. Slowly, but perceptibly, however, democratic political reform became secondary to other matters.

The Presidency.   The historical predominance of the office of the Presidency was carried over into the revolutionary period and under Arbenz regained much of its traditional flavor. In most respects, in fact, the ideological ambiguities and contradictions which arose during the course of the revolution can be seen in the nature of the two men who occupied the Presidency from 1945 to 1954.

Juan José Arévalo was of middle-class origin and was an educator. His particular political philosophy centered around what he termed "spiritual socialism." For Arévalo, spiritual socialism meant the alleviation of feudalism in Guatemala through the utilization of "discreet measures and programs" which would socially integrate and economically improve the greater mass of the Guatemalan people. As has often been pointed out, Arévalo's political and social theory did not go beyond the highly general principles which represented the ideal of a middle-class ideological and social order. *Arevalismo* became the practical standard of government. The instability of the middle class and the difficulty of implementing "discrete measures and programs," combined with the strong and intransigent opposition of upper-class and foreign interest groups, began to undermine the type of middle-class ideological and social order which had been generally endorsed in the revolution. Schneider has argued that, had Arévalo been able to transform the favorable attitude of the masses into effective support for a well-planned and realistic program, these obstacles would have been formidable but not insurmountable. As it turned out, the enthusiasm of the young revolutionaries could not off-set their total lack of experience, and the first years of the new government were characterized by improvisation. The unrealistic masses who had hoped for miracles from the schoolteacher president were disappointed by the slowness of progress during these difficult years of adjustment. Even the young idealists upon whom the revolution depended for motive power became disillusioned by the disparity between promise and fulfillment.

In this atmosphere of frustrated hopes, opportunism began to creep into the revolution while the opponents of social and economic reform became increasingly intransigent.[11]

Parenthetically, it might be added that United States support for middle-class revolution in Guatemala at this time might well have provided a basis of stabilization through the alleviation of frustrated hopes. In any event, the abdication of a middle-class *status quo*, communization, and the pursuance of the revolution in more radical directions became clear under the Presidency of Jacobo Arbenz Guzmán, whose social origins, interestingly enough, were in the upper class. This change can be seen not only in the growth of Communist activities and power between 1951 and 1954 but also in the following developments: the expansion of bribery and corruption on the part of leading politicians; the aggressiveness of the official political parties, which more and more took on the character of their opposition among conservative landowning groups; the application of illegal methods in order to enforce conformity; the utilization of agrarian reform as a governmental political instrument affecting both middle-class and small proprietors as well as feudal elements while mainly benefiting peasants who belonged to official political parties; the growth of rural and urban opposition among middle and lower classes; the imposition of economic austerity, which particularly hurt the middle class; and the continued narrowing of the political liberties which had been established in 1945.

The legislature and judiciary.   Not unlike the traditional political process, the legislative and the judicial branches of the Government were subordinated to the President during the period, though this subordination was much less pronounced under Arévalo than under Arbenz. Nonetheless, revolutionary middle-class elements came to dominate both branches of government. In 1953, for example, the Guatemalan Congress included sixteen teachers, eight lawyers, two farm union leaders, two railroad workers, and at least twelve other

---

11 Ronald M. Schneider, *Communism in Guatemala, 1944–1954* (New York, Frederick A. Praeger, 1959), pp. 20–21.

deputies who could be considered of middle-class status — a total of at least forty out of fifty-six deputies.[12]

Local Government. Some of the more profound effects of the revolution were felt in the political structures of Guatemalan rural *municipios.* In Indian villages the traditional civil-religious hierarchy underwent severe strain. According to Nash,

> the sentimental and personal attachment of Indians to national goals and organizations was actively fostered. The civil wing of the hierarchy was to function as part of a political party or to be ignored in favor of persons pertaining to a political party. Officials were elected to civil offices despite their previous service or age. This reformulation of the role of hierarchy engendered conflicts within the community, centering about the strains associated with elective mechanisms, voluntary participation in public office, and the separation of religious from civil offices. The Indian population, now seen as a mass basis for the government, was asked to act as individuals, to be recruited to government organization, to appear in rallies, vote in elections, join unions, and to sanction leadership oriented away from local society.[13]

The intrusion of Indians into the political process on both a national and a local level brought about conflict, primarily in the rural areas, with Ladinos. The attitude of Ladinos in San Miguel Acatán is probably typical of this Indian-Ladino tension. Here the attitude among older Ladinos was one of puzzlement and confusion — and antagonism to Indian acculturation and progress. Among younger Ladinos, however, there was an admission that progress depended upon some sort of racial amalgamation.[14]

The 1954 Counterrevolution. By 1954, revolutionary forces and groups had become debilitated to the extent that the opposition, with the aid of the United States Government, which was concerned over the degree of Communist infiltration in the Guatemalan Government and over the expropriation of United States commercial interests, was able to launch a successful counterrevolution under the leadership of Colonel Carlos Castillo Armas.

---

[12] K. H. Silvert, *A Study in Government: Guatemala* (New Orleans, Tulane University Press, 1954), p. 43.

[13] Nash, p. 72.

[14] Morris Siegel, "Culture Change in San Miguel Acatán," *Phylon,* XV (June 1954), p. 175. In an opinion survey taken at the University of San Carlos during the summer of 1956, Solomon Lipp found that about one-half of the student group surveyed favored racial mixture with the Indian while an almost equal number desired to avoid racial amalgamation though expressing some flexibility on the subject. Only 4.5 percent were unalterably opposed to racial mixture. At the same time 83.2 percent of the group felt that Indians should be allowed the same privileges and rights as Ladinos while 13.2 percent expressed the opinion that Indians should not be discriminated against but that Ladinos should retain their dominant societal position. The percentage of students favoring outright Indian discrimination was 3.6. Solomon Lipp, "Attitudes and Opinions of Guatemalan University Students," *Sociology and Social Research,* XLIV (May–June 1960), pp. 337–338.

The 1954 counterrevolution re-oriented Guatemala back to the more traditional course of its history. Although Castillo Armas himself and a number of his supporters were reform-minded, the power of the landowners, of the high army officials, and of the important ecclesiastical officers in the counter-revolutionary movement was sufficient to swing the new Government to an approximation of the traditional social order; the Government re-established and redefined the traditional socio-economic foundations of power. Former officials of the Ubico regime were brought back into the Government; the agrarian law was cancelled and expropriated property turned back to the original owners; political opposition was suppressed; and civil liberties were curtailed. The traditional pattern of Indian-Ladino relations was resumed, and labor legislation, was, for practical purposes, voided. In 1956, a new Constitution was drawn up in a Constituent Assembly composed mainly of conservative Catholic elements.

Castillo Armas' assassination in July 1957 ushered in a period of political unrest. In a patently fraudulent election, General Miguel Ydígoras Fuentes assumed office on March 2, 1958. Like his predecessor, Ydígoras Fuentes faced the problems and contradictions inherent in the return to traditional politics. Although the Government advocated social and economic reform, the upper class remained in political control of the country. In these circumstances, Ydígoras' attempts to institute basic reform were half-hearted at best. In the area of agrarian reform, for example, a comparison between land distribution in the period from 1952 to 1954 and in the period from 1955 to 1958 shows the timid, perhaps indifferent, approach which had been taken to this most basic problem following the revolution. Under Ydígoras, agrarian reform was further de-emphasized by transferring the Office of Agrarian Affairs from direct presidential control to an agency within the Ministry of Agriculture. The small number of lands distributed were mostly taken from idle, nationally owned farms.[15] In addition, a drastic decline in coffee prices on the international market began at almost the same time that Ydígoras assumed office, and the President was faced with the unpleasant task of imposing austere controls over the economy.

Political reaction to Ydígoras took the form of attempts to overthrow his government. Student protests, strikes, and general unrest forced the President to suspend political liberties on a number of occasions. Such measures, however, only made the opposition more determined in its efforts. When Juan José Arévalo, by now an outspoken leftist and admirer of the Cuban Fidel Castro, returned to Guatemala City in March 1963 and announced his intention to run for the Presidency in the scheduled December elections, the military, under the leadership of Ydígoras' War Minister, Colonel Enrique

---

15 Nathan L. Whetten, *Guatemala: The Land and the People* (New Haven, Conn., Yale University Press, 1961), pp. 166–167.

Peralta Azurdia, forced Ydígoras out of political office and into exile. Fearing a return to the revolutionary programs of the period from 1944 to 1954, Peralta assumed extraordinary powers, suspended the Constitution and political rights, and dissolved the National Congress. At the same time, Peralta announced his intention to return government to civilian rule.

On March 6, 1966, elections were held. Three political parties ran candidates: the moderate Revolutionary party (PR), the Democratic Institutional party (PID), and the National Liberation Movement (MLN). The Revolutionary party candidate, Julio Méndez Montenegro, was the victor in an ostensibly honest election. Each side charged the other with fraud and with attempting to "destroy the democratic process". Notwithstanding, Julio Méndez took office on July 1, 1966.

Despite all the political maneuvering, what might best be termed the legacy of the 1944–1954 revolution remains in Guatemala. Perhaps most important in this respect is the realization among the middle and lower classes that change can occur and that a traditional society need not be accepted as inevitable and transcendent. If this observation is true, and there is every indication that it is, then the temporary reversal of the modern sectors in Guatemalan politics and the discrediting of their activities and programs is not permanent. Whether needed social and economic reform can take place within a democratic framework, or whether desires for fundamental change will be directed into more radical and totalitarian channels is a question unanswered at present. The recent appearance of guerrilla movements in the countryside indicates that the longer necessary reforms are stifled, the greater is the possibility of violent upheaval in the near future.

Honduras

The Carías and Gálvez regimes. Of the four states under discussion, Honduras and Nicaragua have experienced the least social tension and erosion of the traditional social order. From 1932 to 1949, Honduras was under the control of General Tiburcio Carías Andino, a traditional *caudillo*. In fact, though, the outstanding feature of Carías' political career was that he bowed to electoral defeat in 1928 with hardly a backward glance and actually released his hold on the Government in 1949. During these years Carías invoked *continuismo* and ruled in accordance with the dictates of the traditional ideological and social system. According to Lewis Hanke's summary,

> His [Carías'] conservatism led him to oppose suffrage for women and labor organization, and under his regime democratic institutions withered. Although generally lenient with opponents, he felt that serious lawbreakers should be discouraged, and some three hundred prisoners, including some political transgressors, were kept at public work in the capital while chained to heavy balls.

With complete power in his hands for many years, he failed to accomplish any resounding material progress.[16]

In 1949 Juan Manuel Gálvez succeeded to the Presidency. Although a personal friend of Carías, Gálvez was able to assert a suprising degree of independent power and even attempted to institute some mild economic reforms. Given the socio-economic structure in Honduras and the nearly complete monopolization of land by upper-class elites, such reforms were only superficially aimed at basic improvement and in 1954 were challenged by the more revolutionary forces of social change. As John D. Martz has remarked,

> it was only a matter of time ⋯ before the combined forces of poverty, illiteracy, disorganization, and exploitation would unite, demanding better working and living conditions, formal organization, and adequate land reforms.[17]

The 1954 *Banana Strike.* The specific challenge came in the form of a general labor strike centered on the United Fruit Company, which had long enjoyed the favor of the upper classes and the Government in Honduras. Although there is little doubt that the strike was first led by Communist and pro-Communist elements, many of whom came from outside Honduras, especially from Guatemala, within a month these elements were purged out of the General Strike Committee, which had been set up to supervise the strike, and were replaced by anti-Communist middle-class elements. At the same time the Government, which supported the strike, refused to break it but agreed with officials of the United Fruit Company that the strike was Communist-inspired. In the meantime the United States ambassador in Tegucigalpa, Whiting Willauer, expressed the hope that the strike could be settled amicably and that the settlement "would be facilitated if both the United Fruit Company and the workers realize that their common interests are greater than their differences."[18] In reality, however, the differences were greater than common interests, for as far as UFCO was concerned, the symbiotic relation between the company and the traditional political order was in jeopardy. The strike lasted from early April to mid-July, 1952, and the strikers finally won wage boosts, paid vacations, hospital facilities for their families, and a housing construction program, though these considerations were forthcoming only after the fruit company had lost some fifteen million dollars in unpicked ba-

---

[16] Lewis Hanke, *Mexico and the Caribbean* (Princeton, N. J., D. Van Nostrand Co., 1959), p. 21.

[17] John D. Martz, *Central America: The Crisis and the Challenge* (Chapel Hill, N. C., University of North Carolina Press, 1959), p. 131.

[18] Robert S. Alexander, *Communism in Latin America* (New Brunswick, N. J., Rutgers University Press, 1957), p. 375.

nanas.[19] Undoubtedly, the greatest importance of the strike lay in the fact that labor had finally won the right to organize in Honduras and that socio-economic reform could no longer be totally prevented by blind obstructionism. Moreover, the 1954 strike gained the support of the Liberal party, which abandoned its traditional, conservative orientation, and thereby gained the support of the modern middle sectors in Honduras.

The banana strike, as subsequent events were to prove, was but a skirmish in which labor won legal recognition but in which the supporters of the traditional social system remained supreme. After a turbulent election, the Liberal Ramón Villeda Morales appeared to have won the Presidency in 1955. He was denied office, however, and Juan Lozano Díaz, Gálvez's vice-president, proceeded to rule by decree until removed by a military junta in 1956. In December 1957, the office of the Presidency was finally turned over to Villeda Morales. Although reform-minded, Villeda Morales had to be constantly on guard against the possibility of a Conservative-military *golpe del estado*. As a consequence, his social and economic program was adjusted to the limitations of the political system. Perhaps most notable were Villeda Morales' efforts in the areas of education and agrarian reform. In the latter area was a controversial nationalist provision prohibiting foreigners from owning property within thirty miles of the coast. However, despite Villeda Morales' caution the military intervened and deposed the President ten days before the scheduled October 1963 elections and thus prevented what appeared to be an easy electoral victory for the Liberal party. Executive control was assumed by Colonel Osvaldo López Arellano, a staunch Conservative, and a series of political manipulations began to insure the ascendency of the Honduras Right Wing in the political process. In elections marked by fraud, a legislative assembly was chosen in February 1965, with the Nationalist party gaining a majority of seats. A new Constitution was drawn up, and in March of the same year, López was elected President for a six-year term.

El Salvador

The Hernández and Osorio regimes. Social instability has become pronounced in El Salvador since 1950. Between 1931 and 1941, El Salvador was under the control of Maximiliano Hernández Martínez and the army. Hernández, a fantastic and ruthless individual, was able to form an important power base in the peasantry but actually did nothing to destroy the traditional privileges of the upper class. In fact, the social *status quo* received vigorous enforcement from his regime. In 1932, for example, peasants agitating for a program of land reform were summarily shot down by landlords. This situ-

---

[19] Martz, pp. 139–140.

ation developed into a more general conflagration in which the Government intervened on the grounds of stamping out a "Communist plot fomented by Mexican agents." Forced to resign in the wake of a nationwide strike in 1944, Hernández Martínez was replaced by a rapid succession of Presidents, including a Chief Justice of the Supreme Court, a police officer, and a Falangist. In 1948, however, army support was gained for a four-man junta. Two years later, Lieutenant Colonel Oscar Osorio, aided by army officers and the Partido Revolucionario de Unificación Democrática (PRUD), was able to seize control of the Government. Unlike his predecessors, Osorio actually attempted to institute his reforms under a general Program of Economic Development and Social Well-Being which included economic diversification; industrialization, particularly in the area of light industry; improved living conditions; the development of electrical power; and a housing program. Nonetheless, by the end of his presidential term, in the face of the powerful opposition of El Salvador's landowners, Osorio had not touched upon the most fundamental problems of the country or on the problem of agrarian reforms specifically. It should be emphasized that

> perhaps the most complete monopoly of economic, social, and political power by the agriculturalists is found in the Republic of El Salvador. Virtually all the arable land of the country is owned by a limited number of great families whose principal wealth is in coffee plantations. These same families, however, also control the nation's cattle industry and the expanding sugar and rice cultivation. They also control most of the banking system and a large part of the nation's commerce, including most of its foreign trade.
>
> This same small band of coffee planters constitutes the nation's aristocracy and dominates its social life. They also have the last word in the country's politics. Though the government which has ruled El Salvador since December, 1948, has ostensibly been controlled by the Army and has been a reform regime, even the military has not dared to touch the interests of the landholding aristocracy.[20]

The overthrow of Lemus and the continuation of military rule. José María Lemus, yet another army officer, won the election of 1956 with the support of Osorio. The election, itself a fiasco, was mainly "notable because of the refusal of the people to revolt despite a most Gilbert and Sullivan atmosphere."[21] Once in power, Lemus attempted to continue the reforms started by Osorio, though the sharp decline in coffee prices placed severe strains on the economy. Fundamental land reform, however, remained outside the province of government action.

Middle-class discontent with the Lemus regime began in September 1960 with the holding of antigovernment demonstrations by the General Association

---

[20] Robert J. Alexander, "Political Parties and Pressure Groups in the Caribbean," in A. Curtis Wilgus, ed., *The Caribbean: Its Political Problems* (Gainesville, University of Florida Press, 1956), p. 82.
[21] Hanke, p. 19.

of University Students. In the wake of these demonstrations and the spread of dissatisfaction, Lemus attempted to impose a state of siege by charging that Communists were threatening to overthrow the legitimate Salvadorian Government. On October 20, however, the intervention of a group of army officers forced Lemus out of office, and a military-civilian directorate was established. The new junta, consisting mainly of middle-class army officers and civilians, appeared to be pledged to a more basic program of socio-economic reform than had the previous Governments. The fact that the new Government legalized a previously outlawed political party, which supported revolution *á la* Fidel Castro, however, gave the more traditional elements in El Salvador, who were already uneasy over the directorate's announced program of socio-economic reform, an opportunity to harass the new regime with accusations of "communism" or "pro-communism." On January 25, 1961, a number of high-ranking army officers were successful in overthrowing the junta and establishing their own civil-military directorate. The new junta immediately pledged itself to a program, not of socio-economic reform, but of "anti-communism" and, interestingly enough, "anti-Osorioism." In fact, it was evident that "anti-Osorioism" was much more important to the traditional military elements than anti-communism. In accordance with this new policy, Osorio was forced into exile, and the activities of PRUD were greatly curtailed.

The junta was able to obtain the agreement of five right-of-center political parties to support the junta's exercise of power until elections could be called. In addition, a program of socio-economic reform was finally outlined on paper, but little was done to implement the program. Actual elections were set for December 17, 1961, to choose a constituent-legislative assembly to revise the 1950 Constitution. The five political parties which had reached agreement with the junta when it came into power split into a Government party, called the National Conciliation party (PCN), and into the United Democratic Opposition. The opposing group based its campaign on the charge that the governing junta represented a small power-grabbing military clique; the pro-Government forces lashed back with the charge that the opposition represented a small wealthy minority. Not unexpectedly, the pro-Government party won the election by a 3 to 1 majority. The most interesting aspect of the election, however, was the joining of middle-class elements, a number of which had been associated with PRUD, with a number of wealthy landowners and the few Communists left in El Salvador. The modern middle sectors opposed the junta because of its conservative, *status quo* outlook; the landowners because of the distrust in which they have held the military since the "betrayal" of 1950; and the Communists because of both the anti-Communist orientation of the junta and the possibilities of championing the side of social reform.

The presidential election of April 29, 1962, was uncontested. The PCN candidate, Lieutenant Colonel Julio Adalberto Rivera, a member of the directorate, was elected President. Significantly, less than twenty percent of the eligible voters bothered to cast ballots. In the March 1964 legislative elections, however, the opposition was able to gain some governmental representation. This pattern was repeated in the March 1966 legislative elections when the Christian Democrats, who enjoyed a rapid growth in popular support especially in the urban centers, obtained fifteen seats. The ruling PCN aquired thirty-one seats, and lesser parties picked up the remaining six.

Rivera's administration has been relatively progressive. Reform of election, banking, and income tax laws and the establishment of minimum wage laws, tenement rent reductions, and other social reforms have given El Salvador a modicum of social and economic development. In the March 1967 Presidential elections, the Government was able to win a significant victory when the officially endorsed candidate of the PCN, Colonel Fidel Sánchez Fernández, prevailed over strong leftist opposition from the Christian Democrats and a coalition alleged to be Communist-dominated. At the same time, however, the political system is anything but stable. Rivera's reforms earned him the animosity of the Conservative sectors and liberal opinion tends to support civilian rule. The resolution of these problems will severely test the ability of the new Administration to govern effectively.

Nicaragua

Perhaps the most outstanding, and certainly the most dubious, result of the long United States occupation of Nicaragua was the establishment of a well-trained National Guard under Anastasio Somoza, who quickly built up an unchallengeable power position in Nicaragua and, after the end of occupation, assumed the Presidency in 1937. From that time until 1956, Nicaragua was dominated by Somoza, who fully upheld the traditional social order. Not without his own reform program, Somoza, like other contemporary Central American *caudillos*, instituted his own program of economic development, of which an important part was the attraction of foreign capital and enterprises. Economic development, however, was not to alter the traditional neo-feudal economic structure. To this end,

a chaotic and backward country was given a measure of economic progress. Yet the new roads he [Somoza] built seem ordinarily to lead to or go near one of his many ranches. His private commercial interests included distilleries, sugar mills, cotton gins, lumber, cattle, cement, soap, textiles, ice-making, a steamship line, and even a barber shop. Through these numerous enterprises he was able to build up one of the greatest personal fortunes in the Western Hemisphere, estimated at $ 60 million, a tremendous amount to have been accumulated in a poor country with about one and a quarter million people.[22]

22 Hanke, p. 24.

Indeed, sixty million dollars in 1950 represented more than the total Nicaraguan income from agriculture, forestry, and fishing and only 30 percent less than the total national income in the same year. Similarly, large landholdings were protected. Of all farms in Nicaragua, 1.7 percent accounted for some 42.1 percent of all agricultural land, whereas 50.4 percent of the farms covered a mere 5.4 percent of the land area.

Opposition was not tolerated, and middle-class and lower-class groups were required to pledge their allegiance to the President. The principal Nicaraguan trade union, Obrerismo Organizado de Nicaragua, became personally tied to Somoza but failed to gain the support of many working-class elements who were opposed to the President. For a while, Somoza was able to form a working arrangement with Nicaragua's Communists. This arrangement was highlighted by a visit in 1943 from Lombardo Toledano, leader of the Communist-controlled Confederación de Trabajadores de América Latina and a year later by the founding of the Confederación de Trabajadores de Nicaragua, which quickly was to become Nicaragua's leading labor union.[23] But after 1948, recognizing the Communists' growing strength and appeal and the rivalry between the United States and the Soviet Union on the international scene, Somoza turned on the Nicaraguan Communists and Communist-based organizations and reduced them to impotence.

Like so many other Central American *caudillos* and Presidents, Somoza became embroiled in the affairs of neighboring states, particularly Costa Rica. In 1948 and again in 1955, tensions between Nicaragua and Costa Rica reached the point of open hostility. Relations between Somoza and José Figueres, President of Costa Rica from 1953 to 1958, were especially uncongenial; the former claimed that the Costa Rican President was implicated in "Communist plots" to assassinate him.

The stifling effects of Somoza's rule offered Nicaragua's middle classes little opportunity to develop, much less to adopt a revolutionary outlook. Even Somoza's assassination in 1956—the work of a discontented Nicaraguan rather than the result of an outside plot—failed to introduce any basic changes in this situation as Somoza's two sons, Anastasio, Jr., and Luis, quickly seized the reins of power. Luis served in the Presidency from 1957 to 1963. In the 1963 presidential elections, René Schick Guitiérrez, the officially sanctioned candidate, was elected President. Upon his death in early August 1966, the National Congress elected Schick's Minister of Interior, Lorenzo Guerrero, to serve as provisional President. Meanwhile, the Nationalist Liberal party nominated General Anastasio Somoza to be its standard-bearer in 1967.

A growing resentment of the long dynasty of the Somoza family erupted in January, 1967, when opposition elements engaged in a brief but bloody

---

23 Moisés Poblete Troncoso and Ben G. Burnett, *The Rise of The Latin American Labor Movement* (New York, Bookman Associates, 1960), p. 120. Alexander, p. 38.

clash with government forces. Claiming that the violence was initiated by "Communists and Communist sympathizers," the Government instituted a number of repressive measures aimed at immobilizing the opposition.

To no one's surprise, in February 1967 General Anastasio Somoza easily won the presidential election. Thus, despite some rumblings of discontent and the subsequent death of Luis Somoza, Nicaragua continued to remain firmly committed to the *status quo.*

CONCLUSIONS

Political instability has been chronic in Guatemala, Honduras, El Salvador, and Nicaragua since the first days of independence. Nevertheless, the instability felt in the region today is quite different from that of the past. Although Honduras, El Salvador, and Nicaragua have yet to experience actual social revolution, these states cannot be expected to remain immune to modern ideological, social, economic, and political forces which are being felt in other parts of the hemisphere and of the world. In Guatemala, where the beginnings of fundamental revolution were felt after 1944, ideological ambivalence and the increasing subversion of the political system brought about a return to traditional rule in 1954. Consequently, Guatemala differs little today from its neighbors, with the important exception of the problem of Ladino-Indian relations.

The future course of political relations in the four states is subject to the interaction of a number of dependent and independent variables and to the nature of outside forces. Nevertheless, the quest in each state for a more just social and economic order now appears irresistible. Within this quest, and in fact an integral part of it, the political process and the uses to which it is put, may well be the single most important factor in the future of the region. In this respect, it may be that the most significant development in the last decade and a half has been the creation of the Central American Common Market (ODECA). Composed of Guatemala, Honduras, El Salvador, Nicaragua, and Costa Rica, ODECA looks forward to the eventual economic amalgamation of the Central American region. Beyond this eventuality the common market looks forward to a long-standing Central American aspiration, political reunification. Although the problem of Central American economic and political amalgamation will undoubtedly have to await the outcome of the contemporary social struggle within the region, there is no reason to view that struggle with pessimism, for it may well be that social change will ultimately produce renewed regional vitality, which would allow a better life for all sectors of the area's population. At present, however, the greatest problem besetting each state seems to be the unwillingness or the inability on the part of governing elites to meet political and social challenges in a concrete manner. As a result, political tension and instability will probably increase in the foreseeable future.

4 / Costa Rica

ROBERT D. TOMASEK

ROBERT D. TOMASEK, Associate Professor of Political Science at the University of Kansas, acted as Director of the University of Kansas Junior Year in Costa Rica and has been the recipient of Watkins and Doherty grants for research in Latin America. Among his published works are "Defense of the Western Hemisphere: A Need for Re-examination of United States Policy," "British Guiana: A Case Study of British Colonial Policy," "El Problema de los Latifundios en Latinoamérica," and Latin American Politics: 24 Studies of the Contemporary Scene.

The Costa Rican commitment to democracy as both a social and a political way of life has distinguished the country not only from Central America but also from most of South America as well. For this reason Costa Rica is often singled out for special study. Her democracy has evolved over a long period of time and has been caused by a number of accumulative factors. Many of these factors have been geographic, social, and economic in nature; they are basic to an understanding of the country's political process.[1]

POLITICAL ENVIRONMENT

Factors of Homogeneity and Integration

The geography of Costa Rica has been instrumental in furthering the integration process. The heart of the country is the central plateau, the *meseta central*, consisting of approximately 770 square miles of fairly level terrain at an elevation of 3,000 to 4,000 feet. About three-fourths of the nation's approximately 1,400,000 people are found on the *meseta central;* the capital city of

---

[1] For an interesting comparative study of factors conducive to democracy in Costa Rica and to dictatorship in Nicaragua, see James L. Busey, "Foundations of Political Contrast: Costa Rica and Nicaragua," *Western Political Quarterly*, XI (September 1958), pp. 627–659.

San José, which has a population of about 150,000, the three smaller cities of Alajuela, Cartago, and Heredia, and a large number of smaller towns are all situated on the central plateau. A good network of roads throughout the *meseta* ties the cities and towns together. This facility of movement, along with an abundance of schools and mass media, has been conducive to political alertness among the people. The *meseta* is also the economic center of the country; it contains the bulk of medium and light industry and most of the national market. The altitude of the *meseta* has enabled Costa Rica to raise a high grade of coffee and has also resulted in an invigorating, spring-like climate for the people living there. Costa Rica is often identified simply with the *meseta central*.

The other areas of the country are less well integrated. The coastal regions on the Caribbean and Pacific sides are predominately hot, rainy, jungle and forest areas that support mainly a United Fruit banana-plantation industry and the raising of some cacao. The two coastal towns of Puerto Limón and Puntarenas are connected to San José by railways, but the Limón and Golfito coastlands are still isolated in many ways from the activity of the *meseta central*. The peninsula of Guanacaste in the northwest, although traversed by the Pan American highway, is also quite separate and different from the *meseta central* in its terrain, which resembles west Texas, in the production of cattle and grain predominantly on large landholdings, and in the mestizo people who originally migrated from Nicaragua. Political parties have penetrated these areas, but political participation by the inhabitants has been lower than in the area of the *meseta*.

Ethnically the Costa Rican people are fairly homogeneous. The inhabitants of the *meseta central* are almost exclusively Spanish in origin. Not more than three thousand Indians remain, and they live mainly on isolated reservations in the remote parts of the country. That the Indian population is small and isolated has meant that Costa Rica has not had the great Indian assimilation problems which countries such as Guatemala, Ecuador, and Peru have had. Also living in Costa Rica are about twenty thousand Negroes who are descendants of migrants from the West Indies, principally Jamaica. Most of these Negroes live in the province of Limón and on the Pacific coast and work on the banana plantations or raise cacao.

The special nature of the Costa Rican class system has also been an important integrating factor. One cannot say the country has a classless society. There is a wealthy class consisting of large-coffee-plantation owners, cattle ranchers, exporters, and industrialists; a middle class, which includes most professionals; a lower middle class of teachers, shopkeepers, and white-collar workers; and a lower class, which includes factory workers and small, independent-coffee-plantation owners. However, the class system is different from many others in Latin America. The wealthy class is not offensively ostentatious, in most cases has been productive instead of parasitic, and has harbored little class contempt. On the other end of the social scale, there is not a distinct, impoverished lower class made up of workers living in slums or of *peones* working for large landowners. Many of the lower-class people have their own small homes or apartments and tend to identify with the middle classes. The large number of schools has provided at least a minimal education for most of the people and has facilitated social mobility. The Costa Ricans think of their society as being egalitarian; in politics, one does not find class-oriented parties based on such ideologies as conservatism, socialism, and communism.

The uniqueness of the land ownership pattern is especially pertinent in explaining Costa Rica's homogeneous society. The country is not an ideal rural paradise of small, independent holdings as some have pictured it.[2] There are large coffee *fincas* on the *meseta central*, particularly near Cartago, and in Guanacaste one-half of the cultivated land is occupied by fifty-three large estates. However, about eighty percent of the farmers own some land and account for most of the agricultural sales in the country. The basic rural unit is not the large *latifundio* characterized by absentee ownership, *peón* shacks, and arduous working conditions; instead, the basic rural unit is a small or medium-sized plot given to the raising of coffee or food crops, where the owner often lives in a brightly painted house and has running water and access to schools. The Costa Rican farmer's stake in society has made him a political participant and has precluded a Communist or Castroite movement from feeding on agrarian discontent. The tenure system has also meant that there is no solid bloc of large landholders defending their interests through a Conservative party or through special elitist influence.

Historical Conditioning Factors

The roots of Costa Rican democracy can be traced to the colonial period and the uniqueness of the colonization pattern in Costa Rica. The country lacked gold and silver, and this meant that the earliest conquistadores were not interested in the country. Furthermore, when the first settlers filtered in from Nicaragua, they discovered that they could not work the thirty thousand Indians on large estates. The Indians were either too ferocious, or fled to the mountains, or were shipped to Panama or to the mines of Peru. The settlers had to cultivate their own small plots, and since little intermarriage between the settlers and Indians occurred, no large mestizo group which was distinct from the whites emerged.

---

2 For the best objective discussion of the land tenure system, see James L. Busey, *Notes on Costa Rican Democracy* (Boulder, University of Colorado Press, 1962), pp. 60–72.

During the colonial period the settlers lived in isolation, poverty, and intellectual darkness. The location of the *meseta central* resulted in a lack of communications with the outside world. Transportation to the coasts was so difficult that the settlers found no advantage in raising cash crops. There were no colonial universities comparable to the ones in Guatemala and Nicaragua. Most of the settlers were illiterate and lacked any vestige of a cultural life.

Cut off from the sentiments felt elsewhere in the hemisphere, the settlers did not participate in the wars of independence against Spain. The settlers discovered that they had to do their work themselves or perish, and Costa Rican historians point out that from this poverty was born a sort of rough egalitarianism.

The introduction of coffee in the 1880s to the *meseta central* was largely instrumental in removing much of the poverty and isolation from the country. The exportation of the high grade coffee necessitated the building of railroads to the coast. Coffee exportation also led to a sizeable increase in export taxes for the Government, and the growers made profits that could be used to import a variety of articles. Some large coffee *fincas* were established as a result of the coffee boom, but most of the public lands on the *meseta* went to poorer cultivators, who added to the number of small proprietors that already lived there. Later in the century the introduction of banana plantations in the coastal areas added to the sources of governmental revenue.

The stress on education was an important development of the late 1800s. In 1860 the literacy rate was eleven percent, but after that date a number of Presidents who had been teachers emphasized the building of schools, and in 1866 compulsory free education was instituted. Today the literacy rate in Costa Rica is a high seventy-eight percent.

Costa Rican politics of the 1800s, especially before 1889, was by no means completely democratic and orderly. Not only were there a number of dictators, but also, before 1889, seven of twenty-five governments came into power through violence. Moreover, the elections for the Presidency that did take place were not genuinely competitive. Even under these conditions, however, the politics of this period was somewhat unique compared to the chaos found elsewhere in Latin America. The dictators, for example, were not crude, illiterate despots who ruled for periods of from ten to twenty-five years; they were usually civilians who governed in a restrained manner for short periods of time and who occasionally contributed to economic development. Furthermore, the non-competitive presidential elections usually reflected the people's consensus, and Costa Rica was fortunate in having a number of Presidents of a high intellectual and moral caliber.[3]

---

[3] A more detailed analysis of the politics of this long period is found in James L. Busey, "The Presidents of Costa Rica," *The Americas*, XVIII (July 1961), pp. 55–70.

Since 1889 the democratic pattern has prevailed except for two important occasions. The first was the Tinoco dictatorship from 1917 to 1919. The second was focused around the events of the 1940s leading to the 1948 civil war. In the 1940s the Republicano Nacional party, under the leadership of Calderón Guardia, monopolized politics and became increasingly oppressive in national elections. Political tension erupted in the 1948 presidential election when the holdover legislature canceled the narrow victory of Otilio Ulate over Calderón Guardia. Under the leadership of José Figueres, a volunteer army composed of such people as farmers and professionals was formed to fight the Picado Government, the two-thousand-man army, the followers of Calderón Guardia, and the Communists raising havoc in San José. Spasmodic fighting lasted six weeks, and before a truce was called, the Figueres forces had lost 56 men and the Government forces 1,500 men out of a population of 870,000. Calderón Guardia and Teodoro Picado fled abroad, and José Figueres headed an interim government from May 8, 1948 to November 8, 1949, until the Presidency was restored to Otilio Ulate. A tragic episode for Costa Rica, the 1948 civil war has had lasting political repercussions.

POLITICAL STRUCTURE AND ROLES

In many Latin American countries the military, the Catholic Church, students, and political parties are all instrumental in exerting influence on the political system. In Costa Rica, however, it is the parties that predominate in political importance while the other groups have little or no influence. The Legislative Assembly and the President also play significant roles.

The Lack of a Military Establishment

Costa Rica is unique in Latin America in that it does not have a military establishment. A well-trained and inconspicuous police force of about 1,250 men provides internal order and is completely non-political. Therefore, military participation in decision-making in either a direct or an indirect way does not exist, and the chance of a *coup d'état* is minimal. Moreover, the country does not budget money for jets, tanks, artillery, and other expensive weapons. The lack of a military force also has implications for foreign policy in that Costa Rica has been strongly against military dictatorships. The country has also been a proponent of disarmament in Latin America; Costa Rica particularly took the initiative in advocating disarmament during President Echandi's administration. This civilian spirit, immediately noticeable to foreigners, pervades the entire country.

A number of historical forces has been responsible for the failure of militarism to make much headway in the country. In the colonial period the scarcity of valuable resources and the poverty and isolation of the people resulted in few inducements for military adventurers. The movement for independence in most of Latin America involved a great deal of fighting and violence, but in Costa Rica independence was declared in 1821 without effort or bloodshed. The settlers had felt none of the stirrings of revolution and had actually declared their solidarity with Spain on a few previous occasions. Thus no conflict situation arose from which military heroes could emerge to use their popularity and their troops to plague politics in later decades.

Some militarism was prevalent after 1821 but was generally moderate in comparison to that of other Latin American countries during the same period. Of Costa Rica's strong Presidents and dictators, only three were from the military profession, and they ruled for not more than sixteen years altogether. Even when the military intervened to overthrow governments, it tended to withdraw and to allow civilians to determine the question of presidential succession.

Only one invasion of Costa Rica helped the military to entrench itself for a short period. This invasion was the filibuster invasion under William Walker in 1856 and in 1857, but was eventually defeated. The country did not later experience United States Marine intervention, with the consequent training of national guards by the United States to provide internal order, as Nicaragua and the Dominican Republic did.

In the 1900s the Costa Rican stress on education led to spending much of the money that could have been used by the military; the people have often boasted that they have more teachers than soldiers. By 1948 even the small existing military force was permanently disbanded by the Figueres forces after they won the civil war. Since that date the country has relied principally on volunteers and on the Organization of American States for protection. When the exile invasions from Nicaragua took place in late 1948 and in 1955, volunteers were armed and rushed to Guanacaste, where they were able to defeat the aggressors while OAS observation teams put a halt to any further outbreaks of fighting.

The country has not experienced any Castroite-influenced guerrilla activity in the mountains or in the coastal areas since 1959, as have some of the other Central American countries. Any guerrilla activity would probably receive little popular support.

The Catholic Church

In such countries such as Colombia, Ecuador, and Argentina, the Catholic Church has been a major or a minor political power. In Costa Rica, however, the influence of the Church has been negligible, even in the 1800s when the greatest Church involvement in politics occurred elsewhere. The Church in

Costa Rica is official, but the continued lack of financial support has meant that only a small number of churches and priests are to be found in the country.

The Church has not been completely quiescent. In the 1940s it was pleased with President Calderón Guardia's Christian social philosophy based on the Papal encyclicals, although it by no means gave him direct backing. During that period the Church showed a tolerance to the Communist party that was somewhat unusual in Latin America. In recent years Church activity has been slight although the Church has reminded Costa Ricans that they have a civic obligation to vote and has seemed to be behind some of the anti-Castro movements within the country.

In Costa Rica there has been no Conservative party to back the interests of the Church; and no Radical party has won support by being zealously anti-clerical. The three main parties in Costa Rica have differed on other kinds of issues; questions such as public aid to Church Schools have not arisen during the country's political campaigns. Although a Christian Democratic party has been founded, its strength so far has been minute.

The Students

The university students of some Latin American countries are minor power groups. In Costa Rica, however, the party organization within the University of Costa Rica is not as structured and efficient as it is, for example, in Venezuela or in Peru. The students rarely riot in the streets or join labor unions in strikes as is often done elsewhere. There are no guerrilla groups for the students to join, no dictators to be overthrown, and no military with which to skirmish; the usual reasons for vigorous student action are largely lacking in Costa Rica. The students have at most staged peaceful demonstrations in the streets of San José. Even being vigorously anti-United States has not been popular in the university, a phenomenon that emphasizes the unique nature of Costa Rican students. Nevertheless, many of the professors at the University of Costa Rica have been actively involved in the political parties; some have even filled secondary leadership positions. The Liberación Nacional party seems to have the dominant strength at the university. The candidate of the Republicano Nacional and Unión Nacional parties for the 1966 presidential election was a former dean of economics, however, and that fact alone could perhaps equalize the advantages the parties have had in recruiting from the University of Costa Rica.

Political Parties

Before the 1940s, political parties in Costa Rica were fluid groups that lacked ideology, organization, and a strong base of support. They were opportunistic, often attaching themselves to the most popular presidential candidates. Surprisingly, perhaps, Costa Rican democracy was able to develop without a strong party system. In the last twenty-five years, however, a viable party system has emerged that has had important repercussions on all aspects of politics.

Partido Republicano Nacional. The oldest and most personalist of the present Costa Rican parties is the Partido Republicano Nacional, founded by Dr. Rafael Calderón Guardia. The party's origin during the bleak years of the depression and the subsequent efforts of the party to meet the problems of unemployment and of low export prices explain much of its popularity today; the voters' perception of the party seems to be centered around Dr. Calderón as a popular colorful leader who carried out needed social reforms during a period of economic troubles.

Dr. Calderón Guardia has long dominated the party. He is a doctor who became well known through his treatment of the poor. In his youth he was influenced by Christian social philosophy and by the hardships of the depression in Costa Rica. After organizing the party and being elected President for the 1940–1944 period, he was instrumental in passing a number of social-security laws and a new labor code.[4] These laws were passed with the support of the Communist party, and in return some Communists were appointed to important governmental positions. Dr. Calderón Guardia has never been a Marxist but has used Communist support for his own ends.[5]

In 1944 Teodoro Picado, a lawyer and a friend of Calderón, was elected President. The Government became increasingly oppressive. It was able to retain the support of many of the workers who had been aided by Calderón's New Deal and of some of the old politicians, but an alliance of businessmen, professionals, professors, and students began actively to oppose the Government. In the 1948 presidential election, these latter groups backed Otilio Ulate, a respected publisher and the head of the new Unión Nacional party. He won in a close election. When the Republicano-dominated holdover legislature canceled the election and arrested Ulate, the civil war broke out in Costa Rica which ultimately led to the installation of Ulate as President and the flight of Calderón and other Republicano leaders abroad.

The disrespect for the election results and the subsequent involvement of some of the Republicano leaders in unsuccessful exile invasions from Nica-

---

[4] For an expression of Calderón's social ideas and their origin and a description of legislative measures to carry them out, see Dr. Rafael Calderón Guardia, *El gobernante y el hombre frente al problema social costarricense* (San José, author, 1944).

[5] See Robert J. Alexander, *Communism in Latin America* (New Brunswick, Rutgers University Press, 1957), pp. 383–391, for a description of the origin of the Communist party, the extent of its alliance with Calderón, and the tactics, amount of support, and role of the party in the 1948 civil war.

ragua in late 1948 and in 1955 led many to predict the rapid demise of the party. Instead, however, the party has been able to make a surprising comeback. In Costa Rica's unicameral Congress, the party has increased its number of deputies from 3 of 45 (7 percent) in 1953, to 11 of 45 (24.5 percent) in 1958, and finally to 19 of 57 (33 percent) in 1962. In the 1962 presidential election, the first in which the party ran its own candidate since 1948, Calderón came in second with 35 percent of the national vote.[6]

The election results indicate that the party has a certain appeal among some of the rural peasants and among a good many of the city workers. The party lacks support from most of the upper classes and from most of the middle sectors, although some young professionals are vigorous in the secondary leadership positions and would like to make the party more programmatic. The organization of the party has improved in recent years but is still very weak, which indicates that factors other than organizational effort explain most of the vote. The party has been lax in formulating a modern development program of specific issues. The mass support of the party thus seems to be explained by a personal attachment to Calderón alone, or to him in conjunction with his old New Deal. Some support also seems to be the result of Calderón's extreme dislike of José Figueres, the leader of the Liberación Nacional party.

Partido Unión Nacional. The Partido Unión Nacional is a modern Conservative party understandable only in terms of the Costa Rican political environment. Since 1946, when the party was started by the newspaper publisher Otilio Ulate, its fortunes have varied considerably. In 1948 Ulate won the presidential election with the support of all those who were against Calderón. Although at first thwarted from taking office, Ulate was finally able to serve his term from 1949 to 1953. During this period he attempted to heal the political wounds of the civil war and provided an honest, disinterested government adhering to Conservative fiscal policies.[7]

In the 1953 presidential election, the party's candidate was badly defeated by José Figueres of the Liberación Nacional, but in 1958 was able to elect Mario Echandi as a result of support from the Republicano party at a time when the Liberación party was split. In 1962 Ulate, collecting only 14 percent of the national vote, ran a poor third. In Congress, the party support has dwindled from 33 (73 percent) of the 45 deputies in 1949 to 8 (14 percent) of the 57 deputies in 1962.

---

6 The election data of Table I were taken from the official election records examined in the office of the Supreme Tribunal of Elections. This office does not have a detailed breakdown of elections previous to 1949. The voting, broken down by provinces, for the 1953, 1958, and 1962 presidential and congressional elections can also be found in Joaquín Zalazar Solorzano, *De una derrota a la victoria del P.L.N.* (San José, Vargas, 1962), pp. 34–40.

7 See John D. Martz, *Central America: The Crisis and the Challenge* (Chapel Hill, University of North Carolina Press, 1959), pp. 229–263, for a detailed account of the policies of this and the following administrations.

The party has a strong economic program that stresses the role of private enterprise and the market economy. Though the party is not extreme to the extent that it could be called a laissez-faire party, it nevertheless is deeply suspicious of governmental involvement in the economy. The party also has a traditionalist appeal in that it often appears to be more attuned to the old ways of doing things in Costa Rica than the other parties seem to be. The party also contrasts itself to what it calls the highly personalistic Republicano party and the highly organized, left-of-center Liberación party.

The Partido Unión Nacional is supported by much of the upper class of Costa Rica, especially by large-coffee-plantation owners, bankers, traders, and industrialists. However, the party cannot be categorized as simply a Rightist upper-class party; it has a certain amount of support among the middle sectors and, with its stress on property rights, appeals to some of the thousands of independent landowning farmers. The tradition-oriented are generally attracted to the party. The leadership of Otilio Ulate also explains much of the support of the party. Ulate's vigorous editorial stands in *Diario de Costa Rica* and his concern for all classes have made him respected and popular in the past. The party's main weakness seems to be its lack of support by the urban working class.

Financially the party is quite well off as a result of sizable contributions from some of its more wealthy supporters. In its organization, however, it is even weaker than the Republicano Nacional party and only organizes itself prior to each election although recent efforts have been made to correct this deficiency.

Partido Liberación Nacional. The Liberación Nacional party has been designated by its own leaders and by observers abroad as a party of the *Aprista* type.[8] A brief examination of the leaders, the program, the organization, and the base of support of the Partido Liberación Nacional would seem to bear out this claim.

Parties of the *Aprista* type in Latin America have been led by men like Haya de la Torre of Peru, Rómulo Betancourt of Venezuela, and Juan Bosch of the Dominican Republic—men who could be called intellectuals and professionals belonging to the middle sectors. Of the three main Liberación Nacional leaders, José Figueres and Daniel Oduber seem to belong to this type. José Figueres especially is the embodiment of the *Aprista* leader, and much of the party growth has been built around his actions. He helped found the party, became famous in the civil war of 1948 by forming a volunteer army to fight against the Republicano Government, and was elected President in an overwhelming victory in 1953. He is a personal friend of other *Aprista* leaders,

---

[8] For the characteristics of these parties, see Robert J. Alexander, "The Latin American Aprista Parties," *The Political Quarterly*, XX (July–September 1949), pp. 236–247.

reads widely, travels, takes an interest in world problems, and as a result of his 1948 role and his personal crusade against Central American dictators, is of heroic stature to many of the lower classes in Costa Rica.[9]

Daniel Oduber, who ran unsuccessfully for the Presidency in 1966, is a young, well-educated professional who has worked hard for the party. He has long been a dynamic leader of the party's left wing, which desires to accelerate the Government's role in the economy. He has traveled widely, has studied abroad, and has been Foreign Minister. Francisco Orlich, President from 1962 to 1966, is a lifelong friend of Figueres and has played an important role in party organization. His ownership of coffee and sugar plantations, shoe factories, a grocery chain, and other enterprises puts him in the upper class and not only makes him somewhat atypical of an *Aprista* leader but also helps to explain his leadership of the right wing of the party.

The Liberación party, as are other parties of the *Aprista* type, is strongly programmatic in respect to economic development and social reform. The party adheres to a belief in a mixed economy in which the Government plays a large role whenever it is necessary to facilitate economic growth. The party has established autonomous public corporations in housing, banking, and electric power but has not, however, carried out any important governmental nationalization. With respect to social reform, the party finds itself in a rather unusual position for an *Aprista* party since there is no great Indian problem or large landholding problem in Costa Rica. The party, however, has worked on taxation measures and has made them more equitable and productive.

The party has built up its organization continuously since 1948 and today is by far the best organized party in Costa Rica. Having an active body of militants who can deliver the vote and a vigorous youth and women's section, the party's objective is to develop a permanently structured party that will be constantly active between elections.

A breakdown of the composition of the Liberación party indicates again that it is *Aprista* in nature since it attracts many of the middle sectors, the workers in the cities, and the farmers in the rural areas. The party is especially popular among the professionals and the professors. In the cities the party has not lost worker support as has happened to some extent to the *Aprista* party in Peru and to the Acción Democrática party in Venezuela. In the rural areas the Partido Liberación Nacional not only attracts many of the small farmers but also some of the large coffee landholders. The latter belong to the upper class, as do some of the industrialists and bankers who belong to the party. The personalism of Figueres and the developing organization account for much of the party's strength, but of even more importance is the fact that the

---

[9] See Robert J. Alexander, *Prophets of the Revolution* (New York, Macmillan, 1962), pp. 144–173, for a description of the personality, the rise to power, and the beliefs of Figueres.

Liberación stands for modern economic development, which furthers many disparate interests and is conducive to a widespread appeal.[10]

CHARACTERISTICS OF THE PARTY SYSTEM

The characteristics of a party system as a whole are much harder to point out than the attributes of individual parties. The importance of a party system for Costa Rican life, however, necessitates an elaboration of the more important characteristics.

A Three-Party System with Uncertain Future Trends

One of the most noticeable traits of the Costa Rican parties is that party strength has shifted considerably since the 1930s. This shift not only makes it difficult to predict future trends but also generates some reservations in the assessment of whether the party system has been a one-, two-, or three-party system. The dominance of the Republicano Nacional party from 1940 to 1948 and that of the Liberación Nacional party from 1953 to 1958 indicate one-party traits of the system. Since 1949, however, it seems more accurate to call it a three-party system, provided that further clarification is made of this concept. The three parties, if one uses Duverger's categories, consists of a majority-bent party, a major party, and a medium party.[11]

The Liberación Nacional party is large, but it does not have the dominant strength of, for example, the PRI of Mexico. The former can best be categorized as a majority-bent party, meaning that from 1953 to 1966 it has or has come close to a majority in the three Congresses, has held the Presidency two out of three times, and has been much stronger than Duverger's category of a major party. The Republicano Nacional party seems to fit the major-party classification since it received 24 percent and 33 percent of the deputies in the 1958 and 1962 congressional elections and 35 percent of the popular vote in the 1962 presidential election. Finally, the Unión Nacional has dropped since 1949 to the status of a medium party because it received only 14 percent of the deputies and 14 percent of the popular vote in the 1962 congressional and presidential elections.

One of the most difficult predictions to make is whether the Liberación Nacional party will reach the strength of the PRI in Mexico and transform

---

10 For an excellent presentation of this latter thesis, see Charles W. Anderson, "Politics and Development Policy in Central America," *Midwest Journal of Political Science*, V (November 1961), pp. 333–338.

11 For Duverger a majority-bent party has above 40 percent, a major party 20–40 percent, a medium party 9–20 percent, and a minor party 0–9 percent of the congressional strength. See Maurice Duverger, *Political Parties* (London, Methuen, 1954), pp. 283–299.

Costa Rica into a one-party State. To do this the Partido Liberación Nacional would have to substantially outgrow its majority-bent status by greatly increasing its number of deputies, by winning all of the future Presidencies, and by relegating the other two parties to a minor-party category. There is no assurance that this growth will occur. The party actually dropped from its 66 percent average high in the 1953 elections to a leveling off at about 50 percent in the 1958 and 1962 elections and a shade below 50 percent in the 1966 elections. From 1962 to 1966, the party was faced with innumerable economic difficulties caused mostly by the eruption of the volcano Irazú. The party entered the 1966 presidential campaign with a popular candidate, Daniel Oduber, and without leadership splits but still failed to garner a majority vote. Future presidential elections will probably find José Figueres running at least once again, but other popular leaders will have to arise, and any splits like the one in 1958 will have to be avoided. Finally, the organization of the party is good and is continually being improved but must be improved to a much greater extent before the party achieves the effectiveness of the Mexican PRI.

Much of this prediction, of course, depends on the future prospects of the other two parties. The Republicano Nacional party, with its electoral comeback since 1958, would again seem to be on the ascendancy. This strength, however, may be deceiving. Calderón Gardia is old and was discouraged after his 1962 presidential defeat. Since the party is oriented around his personality and past accomplishments, his future retirement and the failure to build up other leaders could lead to the demise of the party. The Unión Nacional party, with its noticeable electoral decline since 1949, is in somewhat the same predicament. Otilio Ulate, still the party leader, has aged considerably and has lost a great deal of popularity. Mario Echandi, who has formed his own branch of the party, cannot run until 1970 and does not seem to be a potential winner of the Presidency because of his somewhat inactive past term of office and because of his feuding with Ulate. The chances of both parties are also reduced as a result of their weakness in organization and in the types of programs that would sustain them in the long run.

On the presidential level the two parties would seem to have a chance only when they combine their efforts behind a joint candidate. Even this tactic has not always given them over 50 percent of the popular vote, as the 35 percent and the 46 percent in the 1953 and the 1958 presidential elections, respectively, indicate. However, this tactic has given the two parties more strength than they had in the 1962 presidential election, when separate candidates ran. For the 1966 presidential election, the three feuding leaders, Calderón Guardia, Otilio Ulate, and Mario Echandi shrewdly signed a coalition pact to choose José Joaquín Trejos, a former dean of economics at the University of Costa Rica who had remained aloof from politics, as their presidential candidate. He was considered the ideal candidate to rally the diverse opposition parties. Moreover, he was billed as a man with "clean hands" and as an economist who could solve the Government's chronic budgetary and trade deficits mainly by placing a greater stress on private enterprise.

On the congressional level it is hard to predict what will happen to opposition parties. Costa Rica's electoral system of proportional representation in each of the seven provinces should retard any possible trend toward a one-party system. (See Table 1.) With only seven provinces as electoral districts, the number of deputies elected from each is generally large, enabling the second-place and third-place parties to utilize their vote almost to its fullest extent. However, if the Republicano Nacional and Unión Nacional parties should lose heavily in future popularity, proportional representation can at best only delay their decline and not prevent it, especially since the parties have no regional base to fall back upon. In 1966, the combined Partido Unificación Nacional, made up of *Calderonistas*, *Ulatistas*, and *Echandistas*, obtained twenty-seven congressional seats, or one less than the Partido Liberación Nacional.

Non-Regional Parties

The distinctiveness of the central plateau, the northern province of Guanacaste, and the coastal areas has meant that a cerain amount of regionalism is prevalent in Costa Rica. Conceivably each of the three parties could have the nucleus of its strength in certain regions, or other regionally oriented parties could exist. However, such regionalism has not occurred. The three parties are national in scope; their strength is distributed through all of the seven provinces. The scope of these three has minimized the chances of regionally-based parties. The few that have been formed to take up the specific concerns of Guanacaste or Limón, for example, have been unable to elect deputies even by means of proportional representation.

Minimal Splintering within the Parties

The parties in Costa Rica have held together fairly well compared with the splintering so common in many of the other party systems of Latin America. There have been leadership differences within each party, however, that are worth noting. In the Liberación Nacional party there has been a right-center-left-wing division over the amount and the rate of governmental involvement in the economy, with Oduber on the left, Figueres in the center, and Orlich on the right. The party has also had struggles over who should receive the presidential nomination. These struggles resulted in Rossi's independent candidacy in 1958 and the dissatisfaction when Oduber lost to Orlich in 1962. It may be more important to note, though, that the Rossi followers were readmitted

TABLE 1

Recent Party Strength in Congress by Provinces*

SAN JOSÉ
1958 — 16 Deps. — Lib. 6, Ind. 2, Rep. 4, Unión 4 (Vote 84,578 —
E.Q. 5,286)
1962 — 20 Deps. — Lib. 9, Rep. 7, Unión 3, Ac. Dem. 1 (Vote 155,202 —
E.Q. 7,760)

ALAJUELA
1958 — 8 Deps. — Lib. 4, Rep. 2, Unión 2 (Vote 39,298 — E.Q. 4,912)
1962 — 11 Deps. — Lib. 6, Rep. 3, Unión 2 (Vote 69,418 — E.Q. 6,310)

CARTAGO
1958 — 6 Deps. — Lib. 3, Ind. 1, Rep. 1, Unión 1 (Vote 24,238 —
E.Q. 4,039)
1962 — 7 Deps. — Lib. 4, Rep. 2, Unión 1 (Vote 46,476 — E.Q. 6,639)

PUNTARENAS
1958 — 5 Deps. — Lib. 2, Rep. 2, Unión 1 (Vote 16,306 — E.Q. 3,216)
1962 — 6 Deps. — Lib. 3, Rep. 2, Unión 1 (Vote 30,814 — E.Q. 5,135)

GUANACASTE
1958 — 5 Deps. — Lib. 3, Rep. 1, Unión 1 (Vote 18,794 — E.Q. 3,758)
1962 — 6 Deps. — Lib. 3, Rep. 2, Unión 1 (Vote 32, 218 — E.Q. 5,369)

HEREDIA
1958 — 3 Deps. — Lib. 1, Rep. 1, Unión 1 (Vote 15,143 — E.Q. 5,047)
1962 — 4 Deps. — Lib. 2, Rep. 1, Unión 1 (Vote 27,843 — E.Q. 6,960)

LIMÓN
1958 — 2 Deps. — Lib. 1, Unión 1 (Vote 8,159 — E.Q. 4,079)
1962 — 3 Deps. — Lib. 2, Rep. 1 (Vote 14,966 — E.Q. 4,988)

* The parties abbreviated are Liberación Nacional, Independiente, Republicano Nacional, Unión Nacional, and Acción Democrática Popular. The vote denotes the valid votes cast in the province, and E.Q. is the electoral quotient necessary to elect one deputy.

to the party and that Figueres' overwhelming popularity has strengthened the large center position and has placated most of the left-wing leaders, so that splits. which have plagued, for example, the Acción Democrática party in Venezuela, have been prevented.

In the Republicano Nacional party the differences have occurred between the older leaders, who believe that Calderón is still the mainstay of the party, and some of the younger members, who would like to revamp the leadership, develop a specific program, and work more on organization. Although these differences are sharp, the party has still held together. In the Unión Nacional party a personal feud between Ulate and Echandi developed in the early 1960s as a result of Ulate's criticism of Echandi's somewhat inactive governmental policy. Mario Echandi has since formed his own small party, while Ulate has retained control of most of the Unión Nacional party members.

Recent Origin and the High Degree of Personalism within the Parties

The Costa Rican party system, which developed in the 1940s, is new compared with other party systems in Latin America. The only other party systems of more recent origin are those of Brazil and the Dominican Republic; these two systems developed after 1945 and after 1960, respectively. The effects of the newness of the party system are several. A traditional party identification such as that of the southern Democrats in the United States or that of the Conservatives and the Liberals in Colombia is minimal as a result of the short lifespan of Costa Rican parties. The newness also partially explains the weak organization of the Republicano and Unión Nacional parties. Finally, personalism is enhanced, since most of the organization of each party is centered around an original party leader.

The personalism of the party leaders is indicated by many supporters calling themselves *Figueristas, Calderonistas, Ulatistas,* and *Echandistas.* The parties, and especially the Liberación Nacional, are based on many factors other than the personal magnetism of the leaders, as mentioned previously. However, the element of personalism is prevalent and accentuated because of the personal animosity of the party leaders. José Figueres has hated Calderón as a result of the 1948 civil war and has had a personal feud with Ulate during the past several years. Otilio Ulate has disliked Calderón for attempting to prevent him from taking office in 1948, has sniped away at Figueres through the Ulate newspaper, and has had a falling out with Echandi. During elections such as the 1962 presidential race, the personal wounds are aggravated in campaigning, and much of this emotional feeling is carried over to the voters.

Generally Heterogeneous and Moderate Parties

The Costa Rican parties are not class parties in the sense that one thinks of the Conservative, Socialist, and Communist parties of Latin America.[12] Generally each party incorporates a mixture of different classes, occupational groups, and urban and rural supporters. There are differences in the support of each party, as described previously, but the parties are generally heterogeneous in nature. The egalitarianism of the Costa Rican people minimizes the class factor in politics. The strong charismatic personalism of the party leaders is also important; personalism is a phenomenon that in many ways transcends or modifies interest politics.

The three Costa Rican parties are not polarized at the extremities of the right-to-left spectrum. The Liberación and Republicano parties are both non-

---

[12] The *Acción Democrática Popular* party, which is left-wing and pro-Castro, does exist. However, in 1962 its candidate for President received only one percent of the vote, and the party elected only one congressional deputy from San José province.

Marxist and vie especially for lower-class support. In order to gain this support, the former stresses economic development, and the latter uses memories of its "New Deal of the 1940s." The Unión Nacional is right-of-center but is by no means a large landholder party of the Conservative type. All of the parties are strongly anti-Castro and pro-United States with varying degrees of enthusiasm and are generally agreed on other foreign policy issues as well.

Nevertheless, the seriousness of the party struggle for political power, illustrated by the 1948 clash and the 1948 and 1955 exile invasions (largely backed by the Republicano Nacional party) should not be minimized. After 1955, though, that party decided to continue its political struggle through peaceful electoral procedures, and the party system has become stabilized to the extent that all parties are considered legitimate within the context of Costa Rican democracy.

PROCESSES OF FUNCTION AND DYSFUNCTION

The Electoral Process

The elections for the Presidency, for the Legislative Assembly, and for the offices of municipal officials in Costa Rica take place at the same time every four years on the first Sunday of February. A candidate for the Presidency needs over forty percent of the popular vote in order to be declared the winner. If no candidate receives this percentage, a second run-off election between the top two contenders is held on the first Sunday in April. In the 1948 and 1953 presidential elections, there were only two candidates, so the forty-percent figure was not relevant. In the 1958 and 1962 presidential elections, however, the leading candidate was afraid that the nonattainment of the forty-percent vote would lead to the united support of the second-place candidate by the other parties in the run-off election; this unification, would, of course, enable the latter candidate to emerge victorious. As it turned out, the fears were unwarranted.

For elections to the unicameral Legislative Assembly, proportional representation under a modified Hare system is used. The Legislative Assembly was changed from 45 to 57 deputies during the 1962 elections in accordance with the new census figures. At present the deputies are apportioned among the 7 provinces in the following way: San José 20, Alajuela 11, Cartago 7, Puntarenas 6, Guanacaste 6, Heredia 4, and Limón 3. The ballots in the various provinces list the names of candidates for deputy by party lists. In the 1966 election the formal pact of the Republicano Nacional and Unión Nacional parties allowed them to present a joint list of candidates in each province in order to receive the fullest advantage from proportional representation.[13]

---

[13] For the complete pact between the two parties, see *La Prensa Libre*, (October 11, 1965), p. 11.

Elections since 1949 in Costa Rica have been genuinely competitive and free from violence and fraud. It took a long time, however, for the electoral procedure to be perfected. Prior to 1913, Presidents and deputies were chosen by indirect vote. It was not until 1926 that the secret ballot and a regular system of voter registration were introduced. The elections through most of the 1940s were notorious for their irregularities and intimidation. In 1948 the presidential election results were suspended by highly questionable legal procedures, and this suspension resulted in the chaotic civil war of that year.

The reasons for the changes which began with the 1949 congressional election are several. The Supreme Tribunal of Elections established that year has perhaps been the most instrumental factor. The tribunal is autonomous and has under its supervision the important duties of registering voters, of issuing identification booklets to citizens, of appointing the members of electoral boards, of interpreting legislation about electoral matters, of counting the votes, and of hearing formal complaints about election violations. The tribunal, like many other electoral courts in Latin America, has been prestigious and effective. Another important reason for the changes has been the strong growth of the Liberación Nacional party since 1949. It stands to benefit the most from free elections and, more important, firmly believes in political democracy. This belief was illustrated in the 1958 elections, when President Figueres invited observers from the United Nations to view the electoral process. Finally, the strong belief of the Costa Ricans in civil liberties would seem to assure a continuation of electoral propriety.

Political Participation and Mobilization

In Costa Rica there are many reasons for expecting a high degree of popular participation in the electoral process, especially since the 1953 elections. The literacy rate of seventy-eight percent is extremely high for Latin America; only Argentina, Uruguay, and Chile have a higher rate. In the schools civic duties are stressed. Illiterates have the right to vote, a right denied in so many other Latin American countries. Voting is mandatory although the enforcement of the law is not generally observed. Women have had voting privileges since the 1953 elections. There has been no violence, terrorism, or threat of military intervention in the elections since 1949. Since there is proportional representation in the election of deputies, and since several of the presidential elections since 1948 have been unpredictable, no voters should have felt that their vote would be wasted. Finally, the compactness of the central plateau in Costa Rica facilitates good voting turnouts.

The nature of the election campaigns should also lead to a great amount of political participation.[14] The campaigning is long, often lasting a year and

---

[14] A case study of an election campaign is found in Harry Kantor, *The Costa Rican Election of 1953: A Case Study* (Gainesville, University of Florida Press, 1958).

a half. The previously dormant organizations of the Republicano Nacional and Unión Nacional parties suddenly become active and strive to compete with the Liberación Nacional party in organizational effectiveness. This competition involves an outpouring of party flags and posters, continual radio broadcasts, numerous statements printed in the newspapers of support for particular candidates by prominent people, and the provision for all types of transportation by the party militants to make it easier to vote. Most of the four or five Costa Rican newspapers are highly partisan and probably reinforce their readers' political predispositions through the one-sided coverage of campaign news. Oral discussion about the candidates and their beliefs is substantial and vigorous, especially in San José.

In every election the parties recall the events of the 1948 civil war and try to apportion the responsibility for it to their opponents. The civil war has become a point of reference for much of Costa Rica's political life and seems to have led to an emotional campaign involvement of the voters who experienced the 1948 events. With the passing of years, one would expect the fervor of the debate to diminish, but whenever persons such as José Figueres, Calderón Guardia, and Otilio Ulate, who were involved in the 1948 events, run as presidential candidates, one is amazed by the ferocity of the campaign and the way in which many of the people seem to immerse themselves in the political struggle all over again.

The amount of political participation of the people can be determined to a certain extent by an analysis of the actual electoral figures for the 1953, 1958, and 1962 elections. Before 1953 electoral participation was not particularly impressive. Although 80 percent of those who were registered voted, those registered averaged only 20 percent of the Costa Rican population. Thus the amount of the population which voted was an average 17 percent.[15]

In the 1953 election the addition of the women's vote and the importance of the election increased registration from a previous average 20 percent to a high 33 percent. Surprisingly, however, the voting turnout decreased from approximately 80 percent to 67 percent, which, although higher than United States presidential election rates, is not particularly high in comparison with many other countries. In the 1958 election the registration advanced only from 33 percent to 34 percent, and the voting actually declined from 67 percent to 65 percent. The 1962 election saw an impressive heightening of electoral participation. Registration increased from 34 percent to a very high 40 percent, and the voting turnout increased from 65 percent to 81 percent, which is comparable to percentage rates in Britain, Israel, and the Scandinavian countries. Altogether 33 percent, an increase of 11 percent from the 1953 and 1958 elections, of the Costa Rican population voted in the election. The heightened electoral in-

---

15 For specific figures from 1889 to 1953, see Kantor, p. 29.

volvement in 1962 may have been the result of a larger percentage of women making use of their voting rights, of the controversial nature of the three presidential candidates, and of more effective party organization. The voting turnout of 81 percent was not constant throughout the country but varied from 86 percent in Heredia, to 85 percent in Cartago, to 84 percent in Alajuela, to 82 percent in San José, to 78 percent in Guanacaste, to 75 percent in Limón, and to 66 percent in Puntarenas. These figures indicate that the three most isolated provinces had the poorest electoral participation.

The elections since 1953 indicate that many new voters are entering the political scene. In the 1958 election there were 32,054 more voters than in 1953, and in the 1962 election there were 161,563 more voters than in 1958, an expansion of the voting electorate by 70 percent. This pattern of expansion gives a certain fluidity to Costa Rican politics since the parties cannot rely solely on their past followers but must continually assess what effect campaign issues and strategies will have on the new voters.

Politically Relevant Decision-Making

In Costa Rica the bulk of the important decision-making is done by the Legislative Assembly and by the President. The political parties' instrumental role in politics has already been pointed out, and it is worth emphasizing again that the military, the Catholic Church, and the students have negligible or no influence on the decision-making process. This fact enhances the importance of the legislature, of the Presidency, and of the parties, and contrary to practices in many other Latin American countries, allows for decisions to be made by the constitutionally designated authorities.

Before the 1940s these conditions were different in that the locus of power was primarily in the presidential office. Many factors accounted for this location of power. The political parties were shifting cliques that lacked organization and ideology and were either dominated by the President or provided only ineffective opposition to him. The President determined who would run for Congress on his ticket, often manipulated the election returns to get his men in Congress, and then expected it to be subservient to his demands. He was usually able to control the budget without close legislative scrutiny, often decreed legislation himself, and used patronage and the spoils of office to the utmost effectiveness. Fortunately, Costa Rica has had a number of competent Presidents who used their powers more to develop the country than to enhance their own personal position. This was not always the case, however, and, since the 1948 civil war, there has been a determined effort to limit the powers of the President.

The unicameral Legislative Assembly has provided the most checks on the President and has developed a vigorous legislative spirit which is highly responsive to national concerns. The factors responsible for this development are not easy to assess, but some can be mentioned. The deputies cannot be immediately re-elected to a four-year term and thus feel less compulsion to follow the President, especially since the President cannot be re-elected until two four-year terms have passed. Building a future legislative career is not geared to backing a particular president. The small size of the Legislative Assembly, which consists of only fifty-seven members, gives the deputies a feeling of importance and enables all of those who desire to do so the chance to participate in debate. The Legislative Assembly, supposed to meet in regular sessions during six months of each year, actually meets almost continuously throughout the entire year. This practice permits passage of more legislation and provides for an uninterrupted surveillance of the President.

The Legislative Assembly has the constitutional authority to keep a close watch on the executive branch. The Assembly can conduct interpellations of the ministers and censure them by a two-thirds vote of the deputies present. The Constitution holds the President and his ministers responsible for impeding or obstructing popular elections, for refusing to publish or execute the laws, and for violating a specific law by action or omission. The Legislative Assembly is not hesitant to formulate charges and condemnations of the executive branch, and these are given wide publicity in the newspapers and through the broadcasting of the sessions. When the party opposition is strong in the Legislative Assembly, the President finds it even more difficult to enact his program. No bills are assured of automatic legislative approval, as usually happens in the Mexican Congress. In the workings of the legislative branch, obstruction does not become an end in itself but rather the right of the deputies to examine carefully all facets of legislation.

The deputies are not overly concerned with local interests as are their counterparts in the United States, and although provincial interests are by no means ignored, the focus in the Assembly is generally on legislation that will benefit the nation as a whole. Various factors account for this emphasis: The Government is unitary and not federal; the electoral districts are large provinces; residency within a province is not a requirement for candidacy; and ineligibility for an immediate second term makes the deputy less concerned about cultivating the special interests of his province.

Presidents in Costa Rica are by no means debilitated, but, certainly since 1949, a President would find it almost impossible to become despotic. The obstacles confronting a President with such designs are innumerable. The Constitution of 1949 stipulates that a President cannot become a candidate again until two intervening four-year terms have passed. This law prevents situations such as the one when President Calderón Guardia (1940–1944) again ran as a candidate in 1948. President Otilio Ulate (1949–1953) had to wait until 1962 before he could again enter the presidential race. The Costa Ricans do not believe that any one man is indispensable as President; ninety-four percent of those who voted in a 1953 plebiscite voted against reducing the two-term intervening period to one term. Presidents in certain other Latin American countries have tried to circumvent the ban on immediate re-election by controlling their successor's actions from behind the scenes. In Costa Rica, however, any President with such aims would find that he would have to control the actions of the next two Presidents before he could run again—an extremely difficult task. This task is made even harder by the fact that Presidents cannot interfere in or participate in election campaigns. Presidents of Costa Rica seem to have accepted these restrictions and the public's perception of the role of the President. For example, José Figueres, the most popular politician and potentially the most powerful man in Costa Rica, did not attempt to control the actions of President Orlich, as some thought he would, and did not even press for the presidential nomination by the Liberación Nacional party in 1966, eight years after his 1953–1958 presidential term.

Any President with designs for becoming autocratic would find himself hindered in many other ways. There is no military force that could be used by a President to suppress his enemies. The state of siege, or restriction of civil liberties, that is sometimes misused by Presidents elsewhere in Latin America to thwart the political opposition is in Costa Rica taken almost completely out of the hands of Presidents. The Legislative Assembly by a two-thirds vote has the authority to proscribe civil liberties up to thirty days, and since it meets continuously, the presidential emergency powers are extremely limited in the use of the state of siege. Conditions under which a state of siege could be imposed are hardly ever prevalent anyway since Costa Rica is not plagued with abortive coups, riots, terrorism, and guerrilla activity.

Presidents in Costa Rica do not issue decree legislation as is done so often elsewhere in Latin America. Decree legislation can be an important presidential power since it involves not only the interpretation of congressional acts but also many matters Congress never even considers. The extensive use of the device of decree legislation by some Latin American Presidents, especially when Congress is not in session, makes them the principal lawmakers.

The Presidents of Costa Rica also find it virtually impossible to spend money in excess of the amount allotted in the budget by Congress, an eventuality that is constitutionally accepted for customary practice in many other Latin American countries. The office of Comptroller General, somewhat comparable to the U.S. General Accounting Office, provides a check on public expenditures before their release. The comptroller is independent of executive influence since he is appointed by the Legislative Assembly for eight years, the term beginning two years after that of the President.

A number of autonomous institutions such as the Supreme Electoral Tribunal, the state banking system, the state insurance monopoly, and various economic enterprises, including the railroad to Puntarenas, a housing corporation, an electricity company, and the tourist promotion corporation constitute in effect a fourth branch of government. The directors of these autonomous agencies are normally appointed with the participation of the Legislative Assembly; thus a number of functions are kept free of excessive Executive control.

The judicial branch is also independent of presidential manipulation. The seventeen Supreme Court judges are appointed by the Legislative Assembly for eight years, thus bridging two presidential terms. Furthermore, the judges are re-elected for subsequent eight-year terms unless specifically determined otherwise by a two-thirds vote of the Legislative Assembly. In some of the other Latin American countries, the judges are appointed by the President for a period equal to his term, a practice which leads to judges who are often highly subservient to presidential desires.

The attitude of the Costa Rican people toward their Presidents and the Presidents' conception of their own role are other factors pointing to the distinctiveness of the executive office. Some of the past Costa Rican Presidents, such as Calderón Guardia and José Figueres, have had a great amount of popularity, and the personalistic tendencies in the parties have already been pointed out. However, all of the Presidents have been criticized unmercifully soon after attaining office, and it has long been a practice of Costa Rican Presidents to defend their policies through explanatory letters to the editors of newspapers. The people look upon the President as merely another human being afflicted with all of the frailties common to the species.

The President is definitely not the Mexican presidential or Vargas *patrón* type who takes care of the people's every need, dispenses favors, and provides a strong sense of security. The Costa Rican President is rather the leader of his party followers fending off the attacks of the opposition. The literacy of the Costa Rican people and their sense of independence help to preclude overly protective types. Moreover, the country does not have masses of landless peasants moving to the outskirts of cities and substituting for their landlord *patrón* a national *patrón* such as the late Vargas in Brazil. The Presidents, although commanding respect, are still thought of as equals, especially when they are seen driving their own cars or walking unescorted by Secret Service police.

Costa Rican Presidents are neither excessively strong nor excessively weak. They have been able to utilize facets of the country's political system to their own advantage. Most foreign policy is in their hands, which indicates why Costa Rica's relations with Nicaragua could shift so considerably from the Figueres administration to the Echandi administration. In pressing presidential domestic legislation, the Presidents do not have to worry about obstruction from a second chamber of Congress. Furthermore, the country has not had a six-party system of the Chilean sort, which would have forced the Presidents to construct shifting legislative coalitions and party Cabinets in order to pass measures successfully. Presidents Ulate and Figueres actually had a sizable legislative majority during their administrations, and the latter especially was able to enact most of his program.

Much of a President's strength depends on what he wants to make of his office. President Ulate was a compromiser with the main objective of healing the wounds of the 1948 civil war. President Figueres was a strong President because he was able to combine his energetic qualities with a large popular mandate and a legislative majority toward the goal of involving the Government in economic activities and social reforms. President Echandi represented forces that believed in the effectiveness of the free enterprise system and was thus deliberately inactive. Finally, President Orlich lacked national stature, had continual trouble holding a legislative majority, and was swamped by economic problems—all of which made him a weak President regardless of the intentions he may have had.

ASSESSMENT OF STABILITY AND INSTABILITY

Costa Rica is not completely free of political and economic problems. The political party system has been strengthened with the growth of the Liberación Nacional party, but the future of the other two parties is in doubt unless they can improve their organization and groom the best of their younger men for leadership positions. The country will need a viable party system to meet the present and future economic challenges. The country has been set back by volcano damage. The population is continually increasing, and by the year 2000 Costa Rica will have five million people. Colonization in the south and elsewhere will have to absorb much of the rural population growth, as land on the *meseta central* has long been utilized. Furthermore, the country needs to diversify its crops and depend less on coffee. In the cities new industrial growth will have to flourish, possibly under the Central American free market, or Costa Rica will be faced with a growing problem of discontented, unemployed workers.

The stabilizing factors in Costa Rican society and politics should enable the country to meet future problems. It is integrated ethnically and does not have the land tenure and class problems of most other Latin American countries. The people are literate and patriotic, no large group feels alienated from society, and they are interested in politics. Fortunately for political stability, memories of the 1948 civil war are slowly disappearing. There is no military to intervene in politics, and Costa Rican Presidents do not ride roughshod over the Legislative Assembly. All of the parties have accepted the electoral process as the proper arena to carry out their political struggles. Costa Rica's commitment to the democratic process was demonstrated once again on February 6, 1966, when José Joaquín Trejos, candidate of the Partido de Unificación Nacional, a coalition group, defeated Daniel Oduber, the favored nominee of ex-President José Figueres and his Partido de Liberación Nacional. As a general prediction, Costa Rica will probably continue to be politically stable and will be regarded as a model democratic society in Latin America.

5 / Panama

LOUIS K. HARRIS

LOUIS K. HARRIS, Professor and Chairman of the Department of Political Science at Kent State University, has taught at the Universidad Nacional Autónoma de México under a Fulbright fellowship and at the Universidad de Panamá in a program sponsored by the Agency for International Development. His scholarly contributions include several studies, published in Spanish, on the scope and methods of political science, as well as a forthcoming book on Panama.

INTRODUCTION

Panama, the youngest member of the American family of nations, has had a unique union of interests with the United States. Though the relations of these two David and Goliath nations have been very close, there have been serious misunderstandings at times, as witness the destructive riots of 1964. "Panama and the United States are like two brothers who are united in fraternity but with separate interests which have not harmonized."[1] "Gringos" are perhaps better known in Panama than in any other Latin American country—certainly the actions of North Americans in the isthmian republic have been closely scrutinized and criticized. The major project that binds these two nations together has been conducive to both conflict and cooperation.

Panamanian internal and external politics are inseparable. Since Panama was first founded in 1501 as a stepchild of Spain, gold and canal diggers have plundered the Isthmus. As an *audiencia,* as a province, and as a Republic, this

---

[1] Ricardo Alfaro, *Medio siglo de relaciones entre Panamá y los Estados Unidos* (Panamá, Talleres de la Imprenta Nacional de Panamá, 1959), p. 38.

"key of the oceans" has been sought and fought for as "the crossroads of the world and the heart of the universe," first by Spain and later by Colombia, Britain, France, and the United States. Relations with the United States since 1901 have altered and complicated Panamanian economics, social problems, and political behavior. Politics are still molded in significant degree by what transpires in the Canal Zone, though in recent years Panamanian leaders have resolved to rid themselves of the "canal mentality" that distracts and debilitates development of the interior.

The unique features of Panama are manifold and determine its political character. The international influence of the Republic is far out of proportion to its 29,000 square miles and 1,300,000 population; its S-shaped territory has been geologically gutted by the United States, which preaches hemispheric solidarity; and, having leased part of its territory to the complete control of a foreign power, Panama is the only country with a "state" within a state. The cosmopolitan country is "a bizarre and unique little nation" and perhaps the most unpredictable in Central America.[2]

Panama has always had special commercial and military significance for the United States. A canal across the Isthmus had been a long-standing objective of United States foreign policy, and though Uncle Sam's contribution to Panama's independence has probably been overstated, there is no doubt of United States influence over Panamanian politics and government organization. Resentment at that influence has created Socialists and super-patriots and set the stage for political maneuverings. Comprehension of political forces in Panama must start with the recognition of the importance of the Canal in the economics and politics of the country. Panamanians are torn between pride in and shame for North Americans; "they are our critical friends, our trustworthy but uneasy allies."[3] The more resentful Panamanians dub *Norte Americanos* "dollar diplomats" and "big stick" imperialists. Resentment leads to violence over events which in themselves may seem relatively unimportant, such as flying a flag and naming a bridge.[4] Such issues, however, are symptomatic of deep-seated feelings.

Panamanians tend to believe that *Tío Sam* owes much to their country. They remind *el Gringo* that Panamanian labor and land are responsible for the Canal that shortens by 7,873 miles the distance between New York and San Francisco; that 82 percent of the commercial cargo transiting the Canal originates in or is destined for the United States; and that the Canal, Panama's major asset, is particularly important to the United States during wartime,

---

[2] John D. Martz, *Central America, the Crisis and the Challenge* (Chapel Hill, The University of North Carolina Press, 1959), pp. 318–19.

[3] John and Mavis Biesanz, *The People of Panama* (New York, Columbia University Press, 1955), p. 380.

[4] The riots of 1964 were provoked by American students in the Zone flying only the United States flag. Presidents Eisenhower and Kennedy had authorized flying Panama's flag alongside that of the United States. Previously, emotions flared, and a minor riot occurred in 1963 over naming the new bridge across the Canal.

since, for example, 5,300 combat vessels and 8,500 craft carrying troops and cargo crossed the Canal during World War II. The importance of the Canal can also be statistically seen by noting that 240,000 ships of all types and more than 930,000,000 tons of cargo have gone through the Canal since it opened.[5] Panamanians view the Canal as their most important God-given resource.

On the other hand, North Americans, particularly those who live in the ten-mile strip and who efficiently run the Canal, are likely to feel that the Canal is one of the seven wonders of the world and that, without their own mastery of the physical tropical world, Panama would still be a mosquito-ridden, unsanitary, backward nation rather than one of the most literate, healthy, developing countries in Latin America. Panamanians, though more often insisting that their vexation be resolved in principle than in pragmatic terms, will concede the value of the approximately $100 million channeled from the Canal into the neighboring economy each year. Such assistance, however, only seems to whet their appetite for what they deem rightfully theirs.

With a background of cultural conflicts, Panamanian politics become inflammatory. The United States is a ready-made scapegoat for Panama's own failures, and the by-product of this tendency to blame the United States is that attention is distracted, even that of revolutionary students, from Panamanian political mistakes. In such a social context, political oratory may degenerate nationalism and liberty into xenophobia and license. In several ways Panama represents a failure in human relations. Two perceptive sociologists note that Americans "have spent little effort and less money in bringing the human picture up to date, making the zone a more accurate showcase of what we like to think is the American way of life." Though speculating that this failure may prove more damaging than "a Communist saboteur dropping a bomb in a locks chamber,"[6] the two sociologists recognize that it is easier to build canals than construct social and economic organization.

Panama can be described as two cultural communities separated by a boulevard. Political passions run so high that piecemeal concessions by the United States, such as a two-million-dollar bridge designed to "reunite" North and South Americans, fail to close the gap of misunderstanding. Prodded by the riots of 1964, which took twenty-three lives, the administrations of both countries seem to sense the inadequacy of piecemeal concession. Presidents Lyndon B. Johnson and Marco Robles announced concurrently that a new treaty, replacing the outmoded one of 1903, will recognize Panama's sovereignty over the area of the present Canal Zone. The riots of 1964 seem to have been diagnosed correctly as something more than Caribbean tempests, Communist plots, or campaign devices. Whatever the cause of these riots, they

---

[5] Ruben D. Carles, *Panamá* (Panamá, Los Talleres de la Estrella de Panamá, 1962), p. 54.

[6] Biesanz, p. 62.

testify to the need to study Panamanian politics within the context of problems related to the Canal.

POLITICAL ENVIRONMENT

Geopolitical Factors

The same geological accident that produced Panama and gave it a commercial advantage also explains numerous political paradoxes. Political behavior results in part from the geographic quirk that makes Panama a logical commercial crossroads. Because of the narrowness of the Isthmus, and because the mountains at this point dip to only 312 feet above sea level, the idea of a canal route in this region dates back to 1500. These same geographic features led to the construction by the United States of the Panamanian railroad (completed in 1855) and led to the bankrupt French canal project in the 1880s and the successful United States engineering feat of 1904–1914.

Geography has geared the economy to international commerce and has thus helped create a psychological reliance on solutions from outside the nation. Other geographic effects can be observed: (1) Tropical location, with a humidity count that even in the dry season remains above 83 percent, adversely affects health and vitality. (2) The constant heat and other general characteristics of the tropics fortify the Spanish cultural legacy of aversion to work. (3) The tropical jungles and heavy rains combine with mountainous terrain to make the development of adequate highways and railroads nearly impossible. Farmers having no access to markets and being removed from the money economy, leads to a self-sufficiency of the rural economy and a lack of balanced economic growth. (4) Heavy rainfalls and physical barriers isolate communities and create regionalism. As in most Latin American countries, the population is maldistributed: eighty-five percent of the population lives on the Pacific slopes and practically none in the Darien jungles. (5) Climate, soil, and location produce a monocultural economy. (6) The dearth of mineral deposits makes industrialization problematic even if economically and politically desirable.

There are advantages, however, to Panama's geographic location. Tourism is a major source of income, and the Republic, which is about half the size of Florida, serves as the nexus for numerous aviation lines. Because of its central position in the Americas, Panama not only hosts numerous private and public conferences but still harbors Bolivarian dreams of one day being the capital of an inter-American confederation. Nevertheless, Panamanians believe there has been an inefficient or exploitative utilization of their geographic position and that they have not gained the benefits that nature designed. They readily search for someone to blame for the failure to gain those benefits.

Economic Determinants

Panama provides a clear example of a developing country. The country lacks investment in productive sectors while possessing a general low rate of economic growth. Location is the key to the Panamanian specialized type of economy, which emphasizes the merchandising sectors. The metropolitan region (defined as the area close to the Canal), where nearly fifty percent of the population is concentrated, is urban and commercial. The rest of the country's economy, though changing, is still basically rural, self-sufficient, and severed from urban and world markets, though investments by the United Fruit Company, especially in Chiriquí and Bocas del Toro, involve the economy in world markets. Economically the country is tied closely to the United States.

The Zone may be both an asset and a liability to Panama. Zonians, partially in the interest of "good neighbor" relations, are increasingly buying Panamanian goods when quality and prices compare favorably with those of the world markets. However, the local economy is subject to intense internal and external pressures; economic expansions and contractions resulting from world crises affect employment in the Zone. Fluctuations in the Zone's demands for goods and services produce prosperity and depression. In postwar years, when demands are more normal, Panamanians allege that the United States uses their country as a dumping ground for surplus labor. Regardless of the truth of such allegations, the importance of the United States and of the Zone to the economy is unquestionable. In 1963 the unemployment rate in the metropolitan area was 19 percent. Shortly after the January 9, 1964 riots and the rupturing of diplomatic relations with the United States, that figure climbed to twenty-four percent. Recently the number of Panamanians employed in the Zone has decreased, but total wages paid by the Panama Canal Company have increased. This type of unemployment situation is one which demagogic leaders and alienated groups exploit and one which benefits supporters of Communism.

One of the many economic and political paradoxes in Panama results from the interior-metropolitan dichotomy. On one hand, much is made of the argument that greater advantages should be gained from the Canal, but on the other hand, leaders suggest greater economic balance and more emphasis on the isolated interior. Perhaps these dual objectives are complementary. Certainly the industrial, the commercial, and indirectly the agricultural economic potentials, are in the metropolis. Here, too, are the markets, manpower, transportation, and water. In addition, since fifty-three percent of the working force is engaged in agriculture, there can be no doubt that the agricultural workers are not producing adequately for the urban population. The interior serves only as a partial granary for the metropolitan area. Cattle production has improved, but even this improvement has not meant much of an increased consumption of beef by the lower class. While most Panamanians are without an adequate diet of animal protein, the producers of beef attempt to develop foreign markets.

Militating against improvement in agricultural production are such factors as the country's rank of nineteenth in railroad mileage and of fifteenth in highway mileage in Latin America. The most serious deterrent, however, is that only 3 percent of the land is in agricultural production. Large land tracts have long been in the hands of rich politicians. Concentration of ownership is seen in the fact that 1.5 percent of the proprietors own 50 percent of the arable land, most of which is undercultivated.[7] A majority of the *campesinos,* or farmers, are squatters, and only 8 percent of the farmers own the land they work.

Another characteristic of the economy is its apparently unfavorable balance of trade. Unable to be self-sufficient in food and to export in quantities, Panama must rely upon one "product," the Canal. The unfavorable balance is compensated for by the Zone's direct purchases ($23 million in 1962) and by workers' wages ($33 million that same year).[8]

To escape economic difficulties, Panama, like most Latin American countries, has resorted to economic nationalism. Industrialization, as a means of achieving independence from the United States, and government, as the vehicle for realizing this end, are the twin gods of salvation. In the attempt to produce all basic needs, parasitic industries are perpetuated through tariffs. Two reservations about the protectionist policies of the Government are possible: these policies are retrogressive, and the country's resources do not justify the diversification promised. Emphasis on industry may be merely a means of creating a new, or perpetuating the old governing class. Though certain industries (cement, brewery, and an oil refinery) are important, it is questionable whether Panamanian wealth is sufficiently distributed to develop the domestic markets essential to industrialization. Panamanian businessmen lack a sense of consumer service and are governed by the belief in low volume and high prices. On the other hand, because of Panama's favorable location for commercial relations, the prognosis might indeed be bright if agricultural production could be stepped up and if practices like those of the "Free Port of Colón" were extended.

Endeavors to develop economically are difficult. Though Panama has a per capita income of $487, which places the country fifth among Latin American states, development is stymied by many factors. Concentration of land; insufficient and/or inactive capital; poor health; inadequate transportation; lack of education in the use of vaccinations, fertilizers, insecticides, and improved seeds; and the prevalence of corruption, graft, and nepotism all help to retard economic development. Furthermore, because an unusually high percentage of the population is under sixteen years of age, much of the national income is spent for education and medical care. Socio-psychological factors also probably explain difficulties in development.

Demographic and Social Considerations

The social makeup of the Panamanian nation nearly defies description. It is indeed a melting pot. The cultural impact upon the original Indians by

---

[7] House of Representatives, *Special Study Mission to Latin America: Venezuela, Brazil, Argentina, Chile, Bolivia, Panama,* Report No. 70, 87th Cong., 1st. Sess. (Washington, D.C., U.S. Printing Office, 1961).

[8] J. C. Metford, "The Background to Panama," *International Affairs,* XL, No. 2 (April 1964), 279.

various strains from Mediterranean Europe, Africa, Asia, and North America is obvious. The Spanish legacy is superimposed upon Indian, Negroid, and Caucasian ethnic elements. In a study of four important social groups, urban Panamanians, rural Panamanians, West Indian Negroes, and North American Zonians, the problem of gaining national unity in a country characterized by "contrasts between the sophisticated and the primitive, the cosmopolitan and the provincial, the old and the new"[9] is highlighted. In the construction of the Canal, Americans imported the best and cheapest labor possible and left behind a rich but complicated social milieu.

The problem of defining the social composite is seen in the demographers' confusion over whether to classify the country as predominately mestizo or mulatto. The safest classification is "mixed blood." The mulatto-mestizo segment ranges between 50 and 65 percent of the total population. Pure Indians constitute about 10 percent, whereas their Negro and Caucasian counterparts approximate 10 to 15 percent each. There is, however, no difficulty in classifying individuals on the social ladder: whites rank first, mestizos and mulattoes are next, and Negroes rank last. Aggravated by the political, economic and geographic situations described above, the social conditions implied by this class structure lead to deep social chasms, which may be unbridgeable. Such conditions combine with pronounced poverty and traditional patterns of oligarchical rule to create an "underdeveloped country."

Attitudes toward race are equally perplexing. Panamanians are less likely than North Americans to classify themselves as Negro. In fact, according to the 1940 census, official figures show only one in seven as Negro and seven in ten as mestizos. Since that date there has been no official attempt to classify Negroes. The question of race per se has only occasionally become a political issue, and candidates of all races have held public office, including two Negro vice-presidents. Nevertheless, racial discrimination of the informal, extralegal type exists. Panamanians, though, are unwilling to admit it, particularly to gringos. The Panamanians may distinguish West Indian and Panamanian Negroes by insisting, for example, that one's color is an accident but that hair texture is a reliable indicator of race. If racial discrimination is admitted, it may be blamed on Zonian influence.

Many West Indians, who are largely Jamaicans and are frequently called *chombos,* have Hispanized their names, joined the Catholic Church, taken advantage of Article 9 of the Constitution, which makes it easy for those born on Panamanian soil to become citizens, and have marched as super-patriots in demonstrations against Uncle Sam. Such efforts may garner greater social acceptance. Yet the *chombos* are nearly voiceless in politics. Toward West Indians, Panamanians are antagonistic, an attitude that former President Arnulfo Arias sensed when he suggested their expatriation or removal to isolated areas of the country. The West Indians, who, like many others, came to the Isthmus to make money, have been reduced to being the "hewers of wood and

---

[9] Biesanz, p. 5.

drawers of water." With their British background, they are frequently alienated from Americans and Panamanians and feel insecure and resentful.[10] No longer British subjects, but not quite Americanized or Panamanianized, the West Indians are without country and deep roots.

The Panamanian social structure is composed of several important national and racial components. Though perhaps not as polarized into the "somebodies" and the "nobodies" as the structure of most Latin American societies is, nevertheless, classes in Panama are clearly distinguished. They are determined by "family and racial background, money, occupation, education, social *savoir faire,* and political power. . . ."[11] At the top of the social ladder stand a few families, totaling (depending upon the source) from five to fifty. They are invariably active in politics and through land and other types of ownership exert great influence. These families manipulate political behavior and anti-United States sentiment. The presence of American forces nearby enables the elite to shift responsibility from their own shoulders. Such distraction seems to strengthen past and present power patterns.

The middle class, though not large, is evident and growing. It can be characterized as competitive and ambitious, and though likely to be predominantly mulatto-mestizo, it may include Negroes, whites, a few workers, and members of the professional class. The two requisites for membership in the middle sector are attractive clothing and secondary or college education.[12] Opportunities for gaining middle-class status are good, but the inclination of individuals in this group to emulate the upper class hinders the middle class from becoming in the near future an influential, independent force. The possibility of a genuine middle-class or lower-class takeover of the Government may be reduced as the elite or their representatives recognize the need for reform in order to maintain control.

The social advantages of the twentieth century have not been conferred upon the majority of Panamanians. For example, there is an estimated urban housing shortage of 42,000 units.[13] Of the 211,009 houses in 1960, 61 percent were substandard, and one-half of them lacked potable water and covered floors. Of the total population, at least 300,000 live in 1 room with 4 or more persons. Though co-operative efforts by Panama and the United States have improved housing conditions in recent years, the situation is made worse by high birth rates and mass exodus to cities. In urban housing, hygienic conditions are bad; 36 percent of the population lacks potable water, and 41

[10] Biesanz, p. 84.

[11] Biesanz, pp. 202, 207.

[12] Biesanz, p. 211.

[13] For basic data on demographic, social, and economic characteristics, see the following: Inter-American Development Bank, *Social Progress Trust Fund, Fourth Annual Report,* 1964, pp. 407–21; Departamento de Planificación, *Programa de desarrollo económico y social* (Panamá, 1963), pp. 25–124; and Roy Tasco Wesley, *Hechos sobre Panamá* (Panamá, n.d.), pp. 1–36.

percent is without sewage services. The housing condition is symptomatic of other social problems. It should be mentioned, however, that Panama is superior to most Latin American countries in the categories of infant and general mortality rates and in the numbers of doctors, nurses, and hospital beds.

Basic demographic data are also essential to comprehending Panamanian politics. The Republic has an estimated population of 1,300,000, populating 29,200 square miles. Generally 3 out of 4 persons are classified in the *gente baja,* or have-not, category. The natural birth rate increase is 3.2 percent. As noted above, most of the population is located on the Pacific slopes and along the Canal. There are 14 persons per square mile, but they are maldistributed; density varies from 33 in the Province of Panama to 0.3 in the Chagres area.

Other aspects of population distribution also have significance. According to the 1960 census, 4 of every 10 inhabitants are urban. Panama City, with a population at that time of 273,000, had 61 percent of the total urban population, or more than 4 times that of the next largest city, Colón. Panama City serves as the political, administrative, social, commercial, and industrial center of the country. This "big-headedness" is characteristic of other Latin American capital cities. Though Panama's working force is still rural, the trend toward urbanization is seen in the fact that the urban population during the 1950s increased by 45 percent, while the population of the whole country increased by 33 percent. In that same period the population of the capital increased by 51 percent. These statistics signalize problems in health, employment, and housing. The slums, referred to as *casas brujas,* are extensive in and around the capital.

Another statistic relating to population distribution in Panama that is significant to a country seeking social improvement and economic development is that 43 percent of the population is under 15 years of age. Furthermore, this trend is becoming more pronounced. Though the total population is increasing at a 3 percent rate, the younger group is growing at a 3.4 percent rate. These figures emphasize the problems of educational facilities and of future employment opportunities.

Other basic data affect political behavior. The low marriage rate of 3.5 per 1,000 (compared to 3.3 divorces per 10,000) results from the practice of *uniones de facto.* These consensual unions, which in 1950 were more numerous than the formalized marriages in all but two provinces, result from poverty and a value system that stresses freedom (interpreted to mean that one may have as many *queridas* as he can afford) and masculinity. It should be stressed that the above divorce rate in no way indicates the number of broken homes. Panamanian fathers have notorious tendencies to desert wives and children. Perhaps only one school child out of three lives with his parents. The Constitution handles the problem, as much as the written word can, by conferring equality on all children before the law and by requiring from fathers the same responsibilities toward illegitimate as toward legitimate children. It is understandable why attempts to institute "Mother's Day" have been a notable success and attempts to institute "Father's Day" a marked failure.

Selected data lead to brighter prognoses. Perhaps most encouraging is the literacy rate of 72 percent. Moreover, as noted above, Panama compares favorably with other Latin American countries in health and medical facilities. On these counts, objective analysis would give credit to the United States for its help.

One other set of statistics sheds light on the nature of political problems. Exports have increased in recent years from $39 million in 1960 to $72.6 million in 1963, an increase of 86 percent. Bananas, while declining from 45 to 35 percent of total exports in that period, were still the leading export product. As a result of the construction of a petroleum refinery in 1962, oil exports accounted for 32.5 percent of the exports in 1963 and were the second most important export. Shrimp exports, 8.5 percent of the total, were third in importance. Cacao, meat, and sugar were of lesser significance.

The value of Panamanian imports, however, invariably exceeds that of exports. The former increased from $109.4 million in 1960 to $163 million in 1963. Figures indicate a persistent trade deficit, which is financed primarily by surpluses in trade with the Zone. At a cursory glance, there appear to be deficits of $97 million and $90 million in 1962 and 1963 respectively; however, in those two years there were surpluses of trade with the Zone of $68 million and $63 million. These figures do not include income from tourists, which would probably run about $14 million in a non-riot year. Thus this apparent unfavorable balance of trade is unreal; it is another complex dimension in social and international relationships.

Educational Conditions

Panamanians have long been committed to mass education. *Norte Americanos* like to believe that this commitment stems from the United States' influence. Article 78 of the Constitution states that primary education is obligatory and that, through the secondary level, public schools are gratuitous. Article 61 obligates the State to educate those minors whose parents are unable to do so. In giving emphasis to this constitutional prescription, the Government is inclined to devote about 25 percent of its expenditures (21 percent and 28 percent in 1958 and 1962 respectively) to education. Of the 1965 budget of $86.5 million (excluding expenditures of autonomous agencies), $21 million went to the Ministry of Education.

Primary education is free and compulsory for children from 7 to 16 years old. Six grades of education are required for admittance to secondary, normal, or vocational schools. Generally, upper-class and middle-class people are strongly inclined to enroll children in private schools and thereby leave public schools to the lower classes. In 1961 there were 1,372 primary schools with 171,159 children studying under 5,550 teachers. In the same year there were 136 secondary schools accommodating 42,171 students under 1,852 teachers.[14] In 1963 a Catholic university was created; up to that time there had been only one institution of higher learning, La Universidad Nacional de Panamá, whose enrollment increased from 3,320 in 1958 to 5,434 in 1962, while the number of professors jumped from 138 to 193. The colleges, called schools, in the university are as follows: Public Administration and Commerce; Law and Political Science; Natural Sciences and Pharmacy; Philosophy, Arts, and Education; Engineering; Architecture; and Medicine. Two new schools, Agronomy and Dentistry, have recently opened.

The reputation of the university has improved in the opinion of the middle class, but the institution still operates primarily for those of lower strata. Because many of the students have jobs, nearly all classes are scheduled after five o'clock. The traditional autonomy of the university, the political motivation of its student body, and the absence of extracurricular activities—all help to create revolutionary sentiment on campus. Well-to-do Panamanians tend to send their children, particularly their sons, to United States and European universities. In 1958–59, 557 Panamanians were studying in North American universities.

In spite of healthy traits, there are signs that the educational system is deficient. Twenty-eight percent of the population ten years old or over is still illiterate, and a mere one percent has graduated from a university. About half the children leave school before completing sixth grade. Teaching methods are generally formal, verbal, and stilted, leaving little room for independent thought by students. The official *Program of Economic and Social Development* admits that the educational level remained about the same in 1961 as it was in 1945; in other words, the State in the immediate post World War II period handled educational resources inefficiently. However, such criticisms should not detract from the fact that educational opportunities in Panama are superior to those in most Latin American countries.

Constitutional Context and Governmental Forms

Containing 22,000 words, the Constitution of 1946 is one of the longest in Latin America. Like its counterparts the document attempts, and fails, to alter realities. As a modern document, it is filled with political and socioeconomic rights dealing with health, education, labor, culture, and family. The right of private property is guaranteed, but so is its expropriation when in the social interest.[15] The basic document creates a unitary, democratic Republic with a separation of powers in the Government. The earlier Constitutions of 1904 and 1940, as well as that of 1946, show that the United States has exercised strong influence over the organization of the State.

The country is divided into nine provinces, headed by governors, who are named by the President and accountable directly to him. Each province is

---

[14] Wesley, *op. cit.,* p. 13.

[15] For reference to constitutional content, see Russell H. Fitzgibbon, *The Constitutions of the Americas* (Chicago, The University of Chicago Press, 1948), pp. 604–50.

divided into municipal districts; the latter are divided into *corregimientos,* and they, in turn, are subdivided into *regimientos.* The most important of the subdivisions are the municipalities, which are described by the Constitution as autonomous and which are scheduled to become more important under present plans for economic development. The municipalities elect *alcaldes* and municipal councils. The former are the chief executive functionaries and, along with the council, enjoy autonomy in the establishment of special taxes, preparation of budgets, and the expenditure of revenues. It is doubtful whether other Latin American countries with unitary forms of government have governmental functions more decentralized than Panama does. Within the limits of legal prescription, municipal governments have wide administrative functions. Initiative and referendum exist at this level.

Regarding suffrage, the privilege of voting is extended in national and municipal elections to anyone who is twenty-one years old; no distinction is made on the basis of race, civil state, sex, religion, or political affiliation. Although revolutionary Panamanians are frequently cynical about the utility and efficacy of the ballot box as a reliable means for basic change, they nevertheless prize and exercise the constitutional right to vote.

Historic Perspective

Panamanian politics, though sometimes volatile and unpredictable, are determined in part by historic patterns. For over three centuries the Isthmus has played a vital role in international relations and world commerce and has had special strategic significance for the United States. As a result of being visited over the centuries by conquerors, exploiters, and tourists, Panamanians are cosmopolitan and tolerant of dissent. As an independent Republic born in 1903, the country has had a short but troubled history. Even earlier, Panama's relations with its mother country, Spain, and later with Colombia, were not happy. Neither have relations always been cordial with other sister Republics, including the United States and Costa Rica.

Panamanians resent the "Black Legend" which states that Teddy Roosevelt fathered independence. The wielder of the big stick, through the use of naval vessels, assured the success of the movement for independence, but he did not instigate and wage the revolution. Manifesting Panamanian unhappiness with Colombian rule (1821–1903), 53 local rebellions and revolts occurred within the 57-year period between 1846 and 1903. The tendency to downgrade Panamanian participation and overstate the United States' contribution stems from the belief that Roosevelt "took the Canal."

The Spanish discovered Panama in 1501 and made it, in 1533, the capital of an *audiencia.* The conquistadores enslaved but failed to extinguish local natives. Negro slaves, brought to Panama as early as 1517, were not emancipated legally until 1821. Throughout the long colonial period, Spaniards were willing to take Indian and Negro mistresses and thus produced a complex social characteristic which, in conjunction with foreign domination, has worked against a sense of national unity.

As in other areas of Latin America, missionaries were used as carriers of Spanish culture. For a short while colonial Panama had a measure of administrative discretion but was later placed under the viceroyalty of Nueva Granada. After the defeat of Spanish forces, the province voluntarily placed itself, in 1821, under the Republic of Colombia, which cavalierly misgoverned the area until Panama gained its independence in 1903. By treaty in 1846, Colombia gave the United States the right to intervene in Panama when necessary to protect the forty-seven miles of railroad, which took five years to build at a cost of $150,000 a mile.[16] The completion of the railroad ended the pack-mule era, which had lasted for three centuries. Probably the most important political pattern to emerge from the colonial period was oligarchical power. Three centuries of colonial history established a state paternalism that does not rub away readily.

Another important pattern sanctioned by time is economic cycles of prosperity and depression. The major events determining Panama's history have occurred outside the Isthmus. In the colonial period conditions were prosperous, particularly after the discovery of Peru when Spanish fairs were held at Portobello. Fortune also smiled briefly when Panama was designated as the capital of Colombia. Still later, the California gold rush and the consequent construction of the railroad had healthy economic effects, as did the heavy investments in the 1880s by the French in their attempts to construct a canal. United States' efforts, first during the construction days and later in building up the Canal as a military bastion, had the same results. Economic dislocation followed each prosperous period. The important conclusion from this cyclical condition is that Panamanians tend, with historic justification, to look to external forces and events for solutions to internal problems. The Panamanians are inclined to believe that good fortune will come from either the heavens, foreign powers, or the lottery tickets sold on nearly every street corner. Understanding this dependence on external forces is basic to comprehending present political currents.

The key date in recent history is 1903, the year in which the new nation became independent but legally bound to respect United States' "use, occupation, and control" of a ten-mile strip of Panamanian soil. The 1903 convention, known as the Hay-Bunau-Varilla Treaty, gave to the United States the right to intervene in Panamanian domestic affairs when necessary to maintain order or to protect the Canal. The agreement uses phrases such as "Panama grants," "Panama cedes," "Panama renounces." The United States is given the authority to act, in perpetuity, as though sovereign over the Zone. There is no provision for joint administration. The United States was obligated to pay $10 million for the Zone (in addition to the $40 million for the French assets), and an annuity of $250,000. The latter figure was increased to $430,000 in the liberal 1936 amendments to the treaty and was again increased to $1,930,000 in 1955.

---

[16] Biesanz, p. 37.

The 1936 and 1955 amendments represent concessions, but Panamanians continue to agitate for a new treaty rather than for piecemeal change. It is doubtful that they will settle for less than a recognition of Panama as the landlord and of the United States as the tenant. To students at the University of Panama, regardless of their political leanings, the question of sovereignty over the Canal is a burning issue. The 1903 document and its amendments color United States-Panamanian relations and have a disruptive and determinative effect upon internal politics. Understanding the treaty and its effects is essential to historical perspective.

Present Patterns of Political Philosophy

Since 1946 there has been a clear constitutional basis for a welfare state. Acceptance of the idea, however, is of more recent vintage. The Constitution says that:

> "The State will intervene in any kind of private enterprise . . . in order to cause compliance with the ends of social justice . . ."; that "There may be no private monopolies"; that "The individual has the right to the protection, preservation, and restitution of his health . . ."; that "Every individual has the right to the security of his economic means of subsistence in case of incapacity for working. . . . Services of social insurance will be given . . . and will cover cases of illness, maternity, family subsidies, old age, widowhood, orphanage, forced suspension of work, labor accidents, occupational illnesses, and all other contingencies that may affect the capacity to work and consume . . ."; and that "The State will give special protection to peasant and indigenous communities. . . ."[17]

Careful students of Panamanian phenomena realize, however, that constitution-making may be a favorite indoor sport and that the written word is not representative of reality.

Nevertheless, since 1952 and particularly since 1960, there have been signs that the Government, if for no reason but self-preservation, is making limited philosophic adjustments to the basic needs of the dispossessed. There is increased awareness that an unjust distribution of wealth implies an unjust distribution of liberty and that it is impossible to divorce democratic politics from a democratic economy. The etiology of this change is interesting but difficult. It seems reasonable to hypothesize that the haves believe that malnutrition and discontent threaten present institutions. The changes may be traced to the revolutionary ferment of Castro. President José A. Remón, who was assassinated in 1955 by an unknown assailant, expounded a philosophy of social welfare measures; his successor, Ernesto de la Guardia (1956–60), though hardly a reformer nevertheless recognized in his inaugural that "we are at the end of a way and a manner of life which are inadequate to meet the most pressing needs of the country. . . ."[18]

Since 1960, state intervention has been more extensively articulated. The

---

[17] Fitzgibbon, pp. 604–50.
[18] John D. Martz, p. 316.

principal objective of Roberto Chiari's administration (1960–64), as stated by his chief public planner, David Samudio, was " 'to achieve maximum opportunities for all Panamanians for their general well-being.' "[19] Chiari insisted that Panama is at the hour of change and stated that democratic government must be concerned with the misery of its people. In this regard and in compliance with the provision of the *Alianza para el Progreso,* the public sector is more active, particularly in increased investments in housing, hospitals, health centers, sewage systems, road construction, credit, and agricultural reform. In the interests of social improvement, four kinds of reforms are being advocated: (1) governmental, (2) tax, (3) metropolitan (to the end that the urban area close to the Canal is developed), and (4) agrarian.[20] More specifically, the program has nine objectives, including a sustained economic per capita increase of 2.5 percent, more equitable distribution of income and opportunities, greater efficiency in the productive process, agrarian reform, expansion of educational opportunities, improved health facilities, more and better housing, development of a Latin American common market, and strengthening of democratic institutions. Furthermore, the Government is legally obligated to protect the indigent against hazards of illness, old age, injury, death, and motherhood.

Though these reforms would intensify the role of the public sector, a strong commitment to invigorate the private sector also exists. The former is deemed complementary to the latter; the influence of Keynesian economics is felt. In official publications and in campaign oratory, private entrepreneurs are assured that the exercise of economic activities belongs primarily to private individuals. The assumption is that massive public investments can generate an environment favorable to private capital and that such investments can produce a vigorous private production. About three-fourths of the efforts under the official program for economic development rest with private efforts. Corporate, income, and real estate taxes have been increased recently, but present public plans warn against leveling taxes that may scare off private investments; such burdens are dangerous to development. The public position seems to be to increase the efficiency of tax collection rather than to graduate taxes. Such a political philosophy represented not only the Chiari Government but also that of his hand-picked successor, President Marco Robles, elected in 1964.

POLITICAL INPUT GROUPS

Politics, Politicians, and Parties

Politics in Panama is so pervasive and important that it is described as the favorite national sport. Yet political interest does not imply strong political

---

[19] Address given in June 1963 to the Panamanian Association of Business Executives. Taken from a brochure entitled *El programa de desarrollo económico y social* (Panamá, 1963), p. 11.

[20] Departamento de Planificación, pp. 2–8.

parties. Panamanians prefer charismatic leaders to cold, inanimate party machinery and platforms.

Though skeptical about politics, Panamanians invariably turn to it for the redress of grievances. Riches, power, and prestige are the prizes of politics, and the accepted political maxim is "to the victor belong the spoils." Politics "is a blend of cynicism and tolerance, self-interest and patriotism."[21] Politics is a process of moral accommodation as well as a contest for power. "Political decisions in Panama have been made by a few powerful families, by shifting political combinations, by the national police, at times by the clamor of an aroused populace, and often by American authorities."[22] Though Panamanians may confess little faith in democracy, politics is a predominant interest for either social reasons or the reason that politics represents social stepping-stones, *botellas,* or soft jobs, and patronage. Politics is a means of improving one's social status. In one first-year class at the university, about half of the students were working for the Government. Others expressed strong interest in public service.[23]

Two principal issues provoke political behavior: United States occupancy of the Canal and the maldistribution of wealth. Other issues, such as corruption and communism, are of lesser importance. As is the case in Mexico, it is politically advantageous to be anti-gringo. Because of the importance of the Canal, politics is invariably envisioned in terms of the Zone. For example, the influence of the United States upon Panamanian politics was observable in 1956, when Secretary of State John Foster Dulles remarked that the United States has sovereign rights over the Canal to the entire exclusion of the Republic of Panama. Once again the issue of sovereignty over the Zone flared. Time and time again, Panamanian politicians of all colors, to whom nationalism is the key political theme, have alleged that the United States has discriminated unjustly against their Republic and its workers.

The second important general issue concerns the wide disparity in wealth among Panamanians. The traditional and newly formed oligarchies, whose power is largely based on land and selected types of wealth, are calloused toward, if not fearful of, the dispossessed. In the pursuit of basic changes in class and racial relations, words like "sovereignty," "revolution," "economic development," "reform," "independence," and "liberty" make up popular political parlance. The struggle of Panama to obtain equitable distribution of wealth is typical of that of Latin America. The struggle involves the question of what type of change will transpire and who will lead it.

Historically, Panamanian politics has been generally stable, indicating in part that party competition and political stability are compatible. Infrequent resort to arms shows that defeat at the ballot box is bearable. Stability has

---

[21] Biesanz, pp. 138, 154.

[22] Lewis Hanke, *Mexico and the Caribbean* (Princeton, D. Van Nostrand Co., Inc., 1959), p. 28.

[23] This determination was arrived at through limited sampling by the author. The students queried were enrolled in the School of Public Administration and Commerce.

probably resulted from five factors: (1) moderate reforms; (2) promises of additional changes; (3) the integrating effect of nationalism; (4) the power and attitude of the National Guard; and (5) the proximity of the power of the United States, which intervened to supervise elections in 1908, in 1912, and in 1918. The United States has been inclined to favor the party in power, and on occasion to use troops to maintain order, to advance sanitation, and to achieve honest elections. Interestingly, and perhaps because of the proximity of the Zone as a haven for political refugees, only one President has been assassinated.

Nevertheless, change in constitutional order has developed. Social agitation in the 1930s and nationalism in the 1940s led to unstable governments, and the unpredictable currents in the Canal Zone aggravated this instability. Before the De la Guardia administration (1956–60), not one of the previous six Presidents served his full term. Within one decade (1948–58) there were ten Presidents. Since 1956, however, if one disregards the riots between Zonians and Panamanians, a troubled tranquillity has settled over the political horizon. The kind of allegation advanced by the defeated presidential candidate of 1964, Arnulfo Arias, who claimed that the election of Marco Robles was fraudulent, is not as typical of Panamanian politics as of the politics of other Latin American countries. In Panama the threat of violence stems from economic disparities, social imbalance, and political immaturity. *Continuismo* does not seem to be a serious malady; only two Presidents have served more than two terms.

Panama, like other Latin American countries, has two types of political parties, one personalistic and the other ideological. Generally, the parties are devoid of principles and programs and operate in order to dispense favors and patronage. Perhaps the only party having a program, as North Americans use that term, is the reformist Christian Democratic party; "the party system continues to consist of a set of personalist parties among which alliances are constantly changing."[24] Panamanians readily take advantage of not only the constitutional right to vote under Article 102 but also the provision for free party life. Article 103 states that political parties may be regulated by law and prohibits undemocratic parties which are based on sex, race, or religion. Recognizing the divisiveness and irresponsibility of the multi-party system, President Remón (1952–55) utilized the constitutional provision for legal regulation of political parties and pushed through a law which required a party to have forty thousand registered voters in order to qualify for participation in elections. Furthermore, this law required a party to poll forty percent of the vote in order for that party to continue in existence. The law is obviously not now operative and, in the face of Panamanian temperament, would be difficult to administer.

Secondary-school and university students, taking advantage of the lack of

---

[24] Daniel Goldrich, "Requisites for Political Legitimacy in Panama," *Public Opinion Quarterly*, XXVI (Winter 1962), 665.

party leadership, play a leading role in national politics. They lead or generate most of the demands for reforms. Using the tools of rallies, strikes, and parades, and taking advantage of university autonomy, the students offer a moral conscience to the nation. Politics permeates the entire life of the university, but it is commonly contended that most secondary-school and university graduates cease or modify their reformist tendencies soon after graduation.

Prior to 1952, politics was clearly the patrimony of the few: it was a hotly contested game for those who could afford to play. As a result of the fears of crisis and the chaos of political immaturity, Panama turned on two occasions (1940–41 and 1949–50) to the despotic leadership of Arnulfo Arias, who along with his older brother, Harmodio, had risen from obscurity to prominence during the 1930s. During Arnulfo Arias' first brief stint in politics, when he appeared pseudo-fascist and sympathetic to the Axis powers, Panama's relations with the United States were at low ebb. When Arias was ousted, aroused Panamanians blamed the United States.

Confusion resulted from the election of 1948, in which there were five Presidential candidates including Arias. After considerable delay the Government announced that its candidate, Díaz Arosemena, was elected but changed its decision still later to say that there had been a mistake in the vote count and that Arnulfo Arias was the voters' choice. A political paradox of Arnulfo's program was that while strengthening patriotism through such means as requiring the use of Spanish, the program alienated West Indians and Chinese through plans to repatriate or relocate these "un-Panamanian minorities." One may speculate that Arias' considerable popularity, which existed in spite of such programs, can be traced either to his magnetic personality, to his anti-United States attitude, which he denied in his 1964 campaign, or to the lack of alternative political leaders and programs. Arias' term in office was again brief. Frequent changes in leadership between 1948 and 1952 are attributed to the head of the Guardia Nacional, Colonel Remón, whose affection for Arias waned fast, with the result that the charismatic Arnulfo's second term, with a program of "Panama for the Panamanians," lasted only until 1950. Again, of course, the United States was adjudged the culprit in his removal.

After having dominated the political stage from behind the curtains of the Guardia from 1948 to 1952, Colonel Remón decided that he wanted the Presidency for himself. He thereupon seized the Government and offered, to the surprise of many, a constructive leadership to the little Republic until his assassination in 1955. Most sources will overlook Remón's role as head of the Guardia and credit him with being genuinely interested in the resolution of basic problems and in the reduction of graft. Yet many Panamanians, particularly students, who tend to dislike anyone associated with the Guardia, say that Remón's promises were politically motivated and that he did not really reduce corruption or change the country's power configuration. Though there is evidence to validate these indictments, several observations are to Remón's credit: (1) His New Deal type of program served to awaken the interest of the masses—something essential to durable progress; (2) he was unique among Panamanian politicians, having been very pro-Panamanian without appearing to be opposed to the United States; and (3) he secured better treaty arrangements with the United States than did his predecessors. These arrangements included an increase in annuity to $1.9 million and the promise of equal pay for equal work in the Zone. His assassination may have seriously retarded political development in Panama.

Ernesto de la Guardia, the Government candidate and a member of one of the ruling families, won election in 1956. His general promise of *Pan y Libertad* and his specific commitments to tax reform, improved social security coverage, minimum wages, and the development of a petroleum refinery all made De la Guardia seem aware of the need for reforms. The election, in which there were 380,000 eligible voters, was calm, and the verdict was convincing if judged by official results. Nevertheless, the 1956–60 administration was unspectacular and relatively unproductive. Probably this lack of productivity stems from De la Guardia's not being a strong dynamic leader and not being interested in change. His attempts to produce change may also have suffered from his being considered a friend of the United States.

In the 1960 election there were three candidates, all of whom were wealthy. Leading the Liberal party and backed by five other parties was Roberto Chiari, a businessman who had made his money in sugar and milk. Ricardo Arias, who was the Government candidate and a moderate like his predecessor, headed the National Patriotic Coalition. He also came from an influential family. The intellectual, Víctor E. Goytía, backed by a coalition of Liberal parties called the Popular Alliance, was the third candidate.

Chiari's victory was interpreted by some as a return to power by the Harmodio Arias family, which has been a powerful President-maker for about thirty years. It includes Arnulfo, but perhaps of greater import, the sons of his late brother, Harmodio. The family's newspapers, which are frequently anti-United States, can spell political life or death for men and issues. In 1960 these newspapers supported Chiari, whose candidates gained twenty-eight of the fifty-three legislative seats. The National Patriotic Coalition, the Government's party and the main opposition, won eighteen seats. The Alliance, supporting Víctor F. Goytía, obtained seven seats.

Though a member of the Panamanian oligarchy, Chiari, judged by his four years in office, should be classified as one of the most progressive Presidents of Panama. Until the 1964 riots, when it was believed that he failed to use the National Guard soon enough to maintain order, he was in good standing with Washington. He repeatedly warned against rule by the extreme Right and Left. If the President's monopoly of milk in the metropolis and his near monopoly of sugar are disregarded, he represented the kinds of reforms that the Alliance for Progress envisages. Formulated by the able David Samudio under the Chiari administration, the ambitious and systematic seven-year program for social and economic development presages a better

future. The program provides groundwork for improvement in public administration and, in order to do so, attempts to counter corruption and provide for
public planning. Other achievements, such as the construction, with United
States' help, of public schools and housing, may have alleviated symptoms
without reaching the basic cause of the problems of education and housing.
Regardless of these achievements, Chiari's behavior during the 1964 riots is
open to question. Whether he permitted or encouraged the riots, which proved
so destructive of life and property, in order to make himself popular and
enhance the prospects of electing his hand-picked successor is an interesting
but unanswerable question.

Marco Robles, who served in Chiari's Cabinet as Minister of Government, became the 1964 candidate of the Liberal party and of seven other
smaller groups. His candidacy, after lengthy backstage maneuverings, was
blessed by Chiari. Again the main opposition centered around the stormy
petrel of Panamanian politics, Arnulfo Arias, the nationalistic leader of the
Panameñista party, probably the most popular single party in the country. The
third candidate was Juan de Arco Galindo, a former assemblyman and Public
Works Minister. He was supported by a combination of seven political
parties.

As a middle-class compromise candidate of the Liberal party, and as an
individual who lacks charismatic appeal, Robles has had difficulty in uniting
the nation. Securing a sense of unity in a society as polarized as it is in
Panama is always difficult. This difficulty was aggravated by the consequences
of the 1964 riots, which, in addition to leading to a serious loss of private
capital, had the effect of increasing unemployment in the metropolitan area
from nineteen to twenty-five percent. Such conditions breed super-patriots and
demagogues and combine with a lack of social conscience to keep the political
pot boiling. Robles, like his predecessor, seems friendly to Washington and
appears co-operative with the spirit of *La Alianza*. This appearance of friendliness and co-operation may be the important factor which led to the new
Washington policy that has conceded Panama's sovereignty over the Canal. It
is interesting to ask whether this concession was born of principle, of politics
in general—including the prospect for a favorable relocation of the Canal in
Panama—or simply of an interest in strengthening Robles' political position.
If this last possibility is the case, the success of the maneuver is questionable.

Panamanian opinion on the treaty is divided. The Panameñista party still
claims that the 1964 election was fraudulent and that the present Government
is unpopular and therefore cannot represent the country's treaty aspirations.
Furthermore, Arnulfo, claiming to represent 125,000 voters out of an electorate of 290,000, has joined forces with other groups to oppose the proposed
new treaty. The Christian Democratic party, which has proved increasingly
attractive to members of the middle class and which is one of the few parties
with some semblance of ideological roots, objects to the new treaty because it
retains the Zone as a military base, which contradicts the party's policy on

denuclearization. Finally, the newspapers of the Arias brothers have apparently taken issue with the treaty.

On the other hand, there are forces working in support of Robles. Investors of foreign capital in Panama have given him a vote of confidence by returning to the country after the riots, and loans from the United States and international agencies have been readily available. Some of his reform measures enhance his standing in certain quarters. A reform which enhances the lower class's opinion of Robles may be the agrarian reform law, which provided for the distribution in 1964 of 50,000 acres of land, the relocation of 15,000 families, and land titles for squatters.[25] The President has said that the two biggest needs for Panama are a new treaty, which he may be in the process of gaining, and social and economic development of the interior. The latter involves shaking the country from its siesta and opening up the interior so that the rural population can feed the growing urban population. Finally, in assessment of Robles' leadership, it should be noted that thus far Colonel Bolívar Vallarino and his National Guard seem to have backed presidential reforms. The colonel, like some of his fellow members of the elite, apparently recognizes that reforms are the only hope of preventing revolution.

Significant progress has been made since 1960. Final judgment, however, on Chiari and Robles, and indeed on Latin American leaders of their type, who represent evolutionary approaches to basic problems, will have to await more data and history. Needless to say, much is at stake, perhaps including the outcome of the cold war in Latin America.

Political alignments, in preparation for the presidential contest of 1968, are already under way and appear to involve seven major political parties, with the two most important ones being the *Liberal* and the *Panameñista*. David Samudio seems to be one of the most prominent candidates of the Liberal, or government, party. The *Partido Cristiano* has failed to develop, as predicted by numerous sources, into a major political force.

In the consideration of other political groups, organized labor, as an independent force, is nearly excluded from political power. The labor group has not been, and is not, well organized. Historically, there were no unions in Panama until 1920, though there was a strike as early as 1917 by the Canal workers, who were at first organized by the AFL and later organized effectively by the CIO. The divisions characteristic of the labor movement prior to 1955 have now been somewhat overcome with the merger of twenty unions into the Confederación de Trabajadores de Panamá (CTP).[26] The confederation has taken a strong position on equal pay for equal work in the Zone and has tried to organize the banana workers.

The explanation for the backwardness of labor organization is best found

---

[25] Edwin A. Roberts, Jr., "A Report in Depth on Latin America," *The National Observer,* 1964, p. 126.

[26] Víctor Alba, *Historia del movimiento obrero en América Latina* (México, Libreros Mexicanos Unidos, 1964), pp. 409–410.

in the heterogeneous social composite of the Panamanian people. A heavy immigration from the Antillean area and the difference in salary in the Zone have militated against union development. Business elements are in a favorable bargaining position because of the surplus of workers and their poverty. Furthermore, traditional societies are likely to be skeptical of innovation and of organization. It is also possible that the political impotence of labor results from a fairly elaborate network of welfare provisions. If such a correlation does in fact exist, it would be difficult to prove that it results from purposeful strategy.

The weakness of labor is surprising in view of liberal constitutional prescription. Article 63 states that labor is a right and a duty and obligates the State to provide employment when essential to decent existence. Other legal provisions which may have contributed to the political impotence of labor are the minimum wage (established in 1959 at forty cents in the metropolitan areas), the right to organize and strike, compensation for accidents, equal pay for equal work, protection of minors, indemnifications in case of unjust dismissals, the right to vacations, maternity rights, overtime pay, an eight-hour day, and a six-day week. Probably the most realized of these provisions is the social security system, which obligates employers to contribute 5.5 percent, employees 5 percent, and the independently employed 10.5 percent of their salaries. The Panamanian case study, however, serves to remind one of the world of difference between legal prescription and social realities. The prognosis for Panama may depend upon stabilizing demands for labor in the Zone, minimizing labor factions, making labor more productive, and organizing unions as effective defenders of worker rights. Recent governments have admitted that free bargaining between unions and employers will strengthen Panamanian democracy.

As the Constitution's commitment to private property implies, business has played a major role in the determination and administration of public policy. Success in business can depend more on political contacts than on free competition, prices, and quality of merchandise. Successful businessmen are frequently categorized by radical Panamanians as oligarchs. Although this epithet does not seem to have damaged the political power of business, the dynamic, if not powder-keg, character of the political situation leads one to speculate that business would do itself credit by following the counsel of *La Alianza,* that is, to improve the business image and to become more efficient. One of the ways to follow this counsel would be to turn from small-volume business and protectionism to mass production with more reasonable per capita profits. Two characteristics of United States' capitalism, spontaneity and taking risks, show limited signs of taking root in Panamanian business practice.

An example of foreign capital in Panama is the United Fruit Company. Though it is not directly involved in politics, what this company does reverberates in both the political and the economic arenas. The company has 2 divisions in Panama, controls 2 percent of all agricultural land, and employs about 4 percent of the country's labor force. The activities of the company constitute about 5 percent of the total economic activity of the nation, and the company has paid nearly 12 percent of the central Government's tax revenues. Between 1951 and 1955, the company contributed on an average of $21.5 million to the economy and in 1955 paid $4.6 million in income taxes.[27] Excluding direct and indirect income from the Canal, exports of bananas still remain the major source of foreign exchange.

Another area of business that has an incalculable effect on political behavior is the publication of newspapers. Panamanians are avid newspaper readers, as the combined circulation of 75,600 for 8 dailies indicates. There are also 5 weeklies, several journals, about 100 radio stations, 2 television stations (excluding the one in the Zone), and 7,358 television sets.[28] It is generally conceded that about six individuals have almost complete control over what the people read, hear, and see. In large measure these are the same individuals who dominate the country's politics and who are not adverse to arousing political passions in their own interest. These people may deliberately foment anti-gringo attitudes in order to avoid a dialogue on internal political conditions. The defense used by these individuals is that they give the man on the street what he wants to read. Nevertheless, these few individuals obviously are molders of public opinion. It will be interesting to see their effects on treaty negotiations in the next few years.

Political parties, politicians, labor unions, businessmen, and the owners of mass media, the input groups, are all contenders on the battlefield of Panamanian politics. The political and economic structure within which these groups operate is determined by the political output groups of Panama.

POLITICAL OUTPUT GROUPS

Legislative, Executive, and Judicial Structures and Roles

The separation of powers doctrine nominally operates in Panama. Like other Latin American countries, but to a lesser degree, the Executive Will usually prevails over legislative prerogatives.

Panama's legislature is called the National Assembly and is one of the five unicameral legislative branches in Latin America. The Assembly is made up of 53 deputies, who are elected for four-year terms by direct vote and apportioned on the basis of 1 for every 15,000 provincial inhabitants. Each province is guaranteed 1 deputy regardless of its population. Representatives must be at least 25 years old. The Assembly meets for 90 days each year and toward the end of the session selects a Permanent Legislative Commission of five assemblymen to protect, theoretically, legislative powers against executive encroachment. In reality, however, it is doubtful that this "watchdog commit-

---

[27] Stacy May and Galo Plaza, *The United Fruit Company in Latin America* (Washington, National Planning Association, 1958), p. 161.

[28] Wesley, p. 17.

tee" turns out to be more than an advisory body to the President. Nevertheless, the common characterization of the Assembly as a rubber stamp of executive suggestion is open to qualification. The President may eventually get what he wishes, but not without dissent. Two other observations are interesting: (1) Members of the Assembly are obligated to represent their conscience and their country rather than the provinces from which the members are elected; and (2) The state of siege, so much in vogue in Latin America, must be declared by the Assembly when in session. Otherwise, the state of siege can be decreed by the President and countersigned by Cabinet ministers and members of the Legislative Commission.

With slight variation, the executive branch is constitutionally similar to that of the United States. The President is elected for four years, hires and fires almost at will members of his Cabinet, gives as the doctor of the body politic a State of the Union Message, possesses the veto, and must be at least thirty-five years of age and Panamanian by birth. However, there are contrasts with the executive branch as it is known in the United States. The President is elected directly without a cumbersome electoral college; Cabinet ministers have a voice in legislative debate; these same ministers must resign if, by a two-thirds vote, the Assembly expresses a lack of confidence in their competence; the President has the item veto (which can be overridden by a two-thirds vote); and the Chief Executive cannot be re-elected unless there have been at least two intervening terms.

The President's powers are extensive. He has wide appointive and removal power as well as responsibility for preserving order, defending the country, directing foreign relations, collecting revenues, formulating the budget, and promulgating laws. To assist him in these duties, he has seven ministries: Interior; Foreign Relations; Treasury; Public Works; Education; Agriculture, Commerce, and Industry; and Labor, Social Welfare, and Public Health. The Office of the Presidency is headed by a Secretary General, who advises the President on matters of planning, budget, administrative organization, and personnel. Only the President's nominations of judges and diplomats are subject to confirmation by the Assembly. Non-policy-determining positions are legally a part of civil service.

Most sources characterize the executive branch as strong. This generalization is at least half true. However, extralegal political forces, particularly in a highly politicized country like Panama, are certainly restraining. In addition, it should be noted that under the 1946 Constitution, sixteen autonomous and semiautonomous agencies were created, establishing the equivalent of a "headless fourth branch." These agencies have limited presidential power. For example, under the 1961 budget of $155,900,000, the President had control over the expenditure of only $63,000,000.[29] The 1963 plan for economic and social development, in attempting to prevent proliferation of agencies and duplication of effort, recommends more administrative integration, particularly of financial matters. The plan decries restraints on the President.

---

[29] Departamento de Planificación, p. 10.

Theoretically the judicial branch is independent. The Supreme Court consists of nine judges appointed by the President with the advice of the Assembly. The functions of the Supreme Court are divided into civil, criminal, and administrative matters. It has the power of judicial review and is designated as guardian of the legal integrity of the country. The Constitution describes the Court's decisions as final, definitive, and obligatory.

Other Constitutional Guardians

In addition to pressure groups, political parties, legislatures, executives, and judiciaries, there are other contestants in the power struggle. Chief among these, about which little is known, are the religious groups and the military forces. Although Panama is one of the eleven Latin American countries separating Church and State, the Constitution recognizes the Catholic religion to be that of the majority. Freedom of all religions is guaranteed, but Catholicism is taught in public schools, though it is not obligatory if parents dissent. In spite of this constitutional favoritism, a tradition of anticlericalism exists in public schools, and many religions are tolerated. There are numbers of Methodists, Anglicans, Lutherans, Presbyterians, Adventists, and Jews. More research is needed in order to make creditable conclusions on the interaction of political and religious authorities. It would seem difficult, in view of political realities and the high percentage of nominal Catholics, to make a convincing case that organized religion is a major political determinant.

Another guardian of the Panamanian way of life is the military establishment. Here too, more research is needed. Though Panama has no military forces per se, the country does have a National Guard of about 3400 men, who serve not only as defenders of the nation's territorial integrity but also as maintainers of law and order. For example, the Guard was called out twice in 1949 to put down riots and has been deeply involved in Canal riots of 1959, 1964, and 1965. It must also be credited with defeating the Castro-sponsored invasion of 1959 and with maintaining close surveillance over groups that wish to overthrow the Government. Since 1952 the Guard seems to have admitted its subordination to civil authorities. Presently its support appears assured, and indispensable, for President Robles. Since the Guard is headed by a member of the elite, Colonel Bolívar Vallarino, it remains to be seen whether that support will continue in the face of the President's reform measures.

PROBLEMS OF FUNCTION AND DYSFUNCTION

It is obvious from the volatility of Panamanian politics that the electoral and political systems are not representing broad, or at least vociferous, segments of the society. As observed above, sources of power are embedded in the possession of wealth. In penetrating the periphery of the legal facade, one finds that decisions are made not so much by official legislatures, political parties, or vote of the majority as by the possessors of property and the monopolizers of media. This situation results, in part, from the divisive nature of Panamanian politics, which in turn stems from foreign occupancy of the Zone, geographic influence, the Spanish cultural legacy, economic dislocation and imbalance, and social polarization. Implicit in this kind of politics is that the President, usually described as the source of decision-making, actually plays such a role not because he is President, or the leader of a political party, but because he represents the powerful property people and because he comprehends and complies with the political requisites of public office. It may also be true that the presence of United States' forces in the Zone has helped to underwrite the *status quo*. The United States may be unjustly blamed for many failures because Panamanians fail to focus attention sufficiently on their own leaders and political processes.

While going through the motions of democracy on election day, the governing class, recognizing the danger of monopolizing power, has begrudgingly conceded certain reforms. The growth of a more extensive and vocal middle class has also forced the elite to give ground. Examples of this middle-class impact upon the traditional power structure can be found in the recruitment of leaders and administrators. Within the Assembly all shades of the political spectrum are represented, including pro-Castro politicians and vitriolic anti-gringo *políticos*. President Robles, though selected, or sanctioned, by the ruling families, comes from the middle class, which is gaining recognition in the recruitment of civil servants at the managerial level. In noting these exceptions to the general power pattern, it is necessary to remember that the middle class, once it escapes the fear of falling into the have-not category, tends to emulate the top social level.

If by political socialization we mean that the Government attempts to identify with social interests, once again we find a generalization complicated by reservations. Since 1952, Presidents, or at least their ghost writers, have made promises in order to identify themselves with the general welfare. The best concrete example of socialization is the Government's seven-year program for economic and social development. Nevertheless, it is obvious from existing revolutionary sentiments that certain significant groups are disenchanted and aware of inefficiency in their political system. This political strain results largely from lack of social and economic mobility. The extent of the strain is difficult to assess because of the lack of quantification of public opinion and the lack of description of values.

Undoubtedly, many secondary and university students, as well as urban and rural workers, feel politically alienated. To a lesser extent, the middle class shares such feelings. Students, by default, "tend to monopolize the function of expressing demands for reform."[30] Educational systems, foreign as well as domestic, may be training individuals faster than economic and social systems can absorb them and thus may be adding to group alienation. In particular, unemployed university students returning from abroad are likely to feel a sense of frustration, and consequently they turn to the political arena for

---

[30] Daniel Goldrich, p. 666.

redress of grievances. Already bothered with an excess of *botellas,* or soft jobs, and hamstrung by limited revenues, the Government cannot find enough jobs for all those wishing to work for the Government.

The possible alienation of the educated may be more acute in Panama than in many other countries because of its educational record: Panama is third among Latin American countries in the number of teachers per one thousand students, second in secondary school enrollment, and fourth in enrollment in higher education. Overproduction of people trained for professional and technical positions may generate frustrations that will find an outlet in revolutionary political activity, particularly since many of the frustrated are also politically alienated.[31] In an age of nationalism and with an economy that produces little, disenchanted groups are inclined to support revolutionary leaders. A political bandwagon also affords opportunities to move rapidly from a "nobody" to a "somebody" status.

In an interesting study of secondary students at two Panamanian schools, Professors Goldrich and Scott found profound ambivalence among students. Strong majorities opposed violence as a means of deciding political issues and believed that democracy is appropriate for developing nations. Closer votes were recorded in support of the idea that political liberty is more important than material well-being and the idea that governments doing bad jobs should be changed. Goldrich and Scott discovered that the secondary students are highly politicized (although only about forty percent identified with a political party); dissatisfied with the country's present system of values; disdainful of political leaders; inclined to demonstrate discontent; prone to believe that the middle class or the labor unions could govern better than landowners; and convinced that the Government should do more to cope with major problems.[32]

In two first-year classes at the University of Panama, certain student beliefs stand out: primary loyalty is to the State; strong attachments to the family, but not to organized religion, exist; Panama is, and should be, sovereign over the Zone; and the Government should demand, and the United States concede, revision of the 1903 treaty. Though insisting, in answering one question, that nationalism should have priority in the world of values, the students nevertheless backpedaled, in answering another question, which required a choice between nation and family, by favoring the latter by nearly 2 to 1. Additional light is thrown on the value system of fourth-year students:

(1) The most important problems are economic in nature (with frequent reference to unemployment, agriculture, and concentration of wealth). (2) Other leading general categories of problems (in the order of frequency of response) are social, educational, and political in nature. (3) A minority feels that occupancy of the Zone by the United States is a major problem.

---

[31] Daniel Goldrich and Edward Scott, "Developing Political Orientations of Panamanian Students," *Journal of Politics,* XXIII, No. 1 (February 1961), 84–107.

[32] Goldrich and Scott, pp. 84–107.

(4) The chief criticism against the United States is that its attitude toward others, particularly in the Canal Zone, tends to be domineering. (5) Foreign aid represents the best feature of United States' foreign policy. (6) The most important institutions are the family and the State, though several students expressed values frequently associated with religion. (7) The Alliance for Progress is good because it will help Latin America develop.[33]

The crucial question is whether students are permanently alienated from the social and political system. The answer to this question depends on the growth and the distribution of the national income and on such considerations as social mobility and absorption of newly trained individuals, the consequence of present United States-Panamanian negotiations, and the results of Castro's experiments. However, working in behalf of stability or evolutionary change is the tendency of students to modify or cease reformist or radical behavior once a diploma is granted.

PROGNOSIS: STABILITY OR INSTABILITY

The prognosis for Panama is cloudy. The isthmus Republic, like other Latin American states, is in a twilight zone, with impatient groups seeking to change traditional power patterns. Generally, future policy alternatives are threefold: (1) a retreat from recent liberal gestures and a reassertion of the power that stems from property ownership and from the control of mass media and of the military forces; (2) the installation in power, probably by revolution, of groups presently alienated; and (3) the evolution of change similar to, but at a more rapid rate than, what has taken place since 1960. If stability is the objective, some type of change is necessary; external as well as internal forces conjoin against the *status quo*.

Certain questions are crucial to predicting Panamanian politics. Have United States' aid grants and Canal concessions come too late to quiet passions and undercut leftward leanings? Do these concessions manifest an understanding of Panamanians or simply an attempt to secure political alignment? Can the ruling families really be prodded into more progressive policies? If so, would the change be the result of internal politics, of United States' pressure, or of lessons learned from failures in pre-Castro Cuba? Answers to these and other questions hinge on the events in the Canal Zone, the degree of reasonableness and understanding shown by North Americans and Panamanians, the absorption of educated Panamanians into the political and social systems, the attitude of the National Guard toward politics, and the degree of alleviation of poverty.

Certain predictions and prescriptions, though dangerous, are in order. First, the United States is aware of its past errors and complacency and will probably concede major changes in present policy. The agreement to rewrite the 1903 treaty and recognize Panama's sovereignty over the Canal illustrates

---

[33] These findings are the result of questionnaires circulated by the author to students enrolled in the School of Public Administration in 1962–63.

this awareness. This kind of understanding, particularly if accompanied by some type of joint administration of the Zone, should help stabilize local politics and would enhance the United States' prestige and security. Though Panama will probably be inclined toward greater neutrality in world politics, most Panamanians seem to want the United States to concede Panamanian sovereignty but remain to help administer the Canal. Second, the ruling families show signs of confessing past sins or of admitting that self-interest requires commitment to general interests. Public planning, which in itself is an encouraging innovation, is being geared to the general welfare. This attention to the general welfare will probably continue and should encourage stability. Third, optimism for stability can be gleaned from the development of an energetic and enterprising middle class, which will be likely to anchor political vicissitudes or at least to modify their effects. It appears that the elite cannot retain dominant power and that the proletariat lacks the unity and political resources to govern. The middle sector will probably exercise greater control.

On a more pessimistic level, several considerations can be noted. First, the vast reservoir of social need sets the stage for continual acrimonious political conflict during the remainder of the twentieth century. There is little likelihood of immediate moral accommodation of social groups which are severely polarized. The pervasiveness of politics will aggravate conflict unless the state of social mobility is considerably improved. Second, the role of the National Guard is not clearly defined. Though it has appeared to be subordinate to civil authorities since 1952, its power has been indirectly felt and on past occasions directly applied. It remains to be seen whether the Guard will continue to be neutral in the face of social reforms, or whether it would support an elected President in times of widespread unrest. Third, in relating the state of political parties to the question of stability, it is essential to remember that parties are multiple and personalized and fail to offer definitive programs and reliable outlets for pent-up grievances.

Politics in Panama must be characterized as volatile but probably less so than in most Latin American countries. Conditions have improved slowly and will probably continue to do so within a limited democratic context. Predictions must be cautious, however, since Panama is at an important crossroads where various paths to progress intersect.

6 / Haiti and the Dominican Republic

J. C. M. OGELSBY

J. C. M. OGELSBY, Assistant Professor of History at University College of the University of Western Ontario, has carried out research in Spanish, French, and British as well as Haitian, Dominican, Puerto Rican, and Jamaican archives in line with his special interest in imperialism and the Caribbean. Besides "The Crisis in Latin America" (Canadian Broadcasting Corporation University Extension Lectures of 1965), his writing credits include "The Prospects for Democracy in the Dominican Republic" and "Graham Greene's Haiti."

HAITI

The Republic of Haiti shares Hispaniola, the second largest island in the Caribbean, with the Dominican Republic. Haiti's 10,714 of Hispaniola's 29,535 square miles make the country slightly larger than the state of Maryland. The estimated 4,500,000 people of Haiti are crowded into the mountainous western portion of the island.[1] Haiti, the Arawak Indian term for "land of mountains," is aptly named, for the country is dominated by three great ranges of mountains, and all Haitians know that "behind the mountains there are mountains."

---

[1] Statistics for this chapter are drawn from the *Statistical Abstract of Latin America: 1964* (Los Angeles, Latin American Center, University of California, 1965). At this time the author would like to thank the University of Victoria for a grant in aid of research in order to complete this study.

The Political Environment

In the north of Haiti, the peaks of the Massif du Nord tower over the coastal plain. This chain of mountains is an extension of the Central Range, which rises over nine thousand feet on the Dominican Republic side of the border, but which falls to three thousand feet in Haiti. On one of the lower peaks is the famous Citadel of the Haitian king, Henri Christophe. While the northern slopes of the Massif have a heavy amount of rain, the southern side of the mountains is drier. Much of the area bordering along the Gulf of Gonaives is covered with desert growth.

Part of the Massif du Nord, the Montagnes Noires, is divided from the central Chaîne de Mateaux by the Artibonite River Valley, a wide and potentially rich agricultural area. Beyond the Chaîne is the Cul de Sac Plain, which stretches from Port au Prince, the capital city, east into the Dominican Republic; much of this plain is below sea level. South of the Cul de Sac Plain rises another range of mountains, some of which are over eight thousand feet high. These mountains stretch from the Dominican Republic westward for almost two hundred miles along the southern peninsula, whose peculiar shape helps give Haiti's contour the appearance of the head of a dying salmon. On either side of this range are very narrow coastal strips.

The geographical structure of Haiti has militated against the development of a good communications system. In colonial times the sea was the easiest means of communication between cities along the coast; today the airplane takes the place of sailing ships. However, few Haitians ever enjoy the luxury of an airplane flight but must use old trucks and buses that groan and bounce over the few rutted roads that are supposed to link the various provincial towns of the five *départements* with the capital. There is no guarantee, however, that a trip along these roads will ever be completed by vehicle, and most Haitians only travel as far as they are able to walk.

The Republic has a total of 6,857,000 acres, of which roughly thirteen percent is utilized for agriculture and another eighteen percent for pasture; the remaining land is in forest or in bush. Even these estimates can be questioned, for the Haitian peasant has had to struggle so hard to survive that he has proved energetic in his pursuit of arable ground, even to the extent of hanging by rope on the mountainside in order to plant on some outcropping in the heavily eroded mountains.

Haitians farm to survive. Very little of their crops is for export. Coffee is the country's major export and comprises about seventy percent of the total exports. Sisal and sugar are also important products.

Population and Social Structure   Haiti is unique among the Republics in the Americas. It is a Negro Republic, and it is the only Latin American Republic to have gained its freedom from France. Haiti is also unique in that the majority of its people own the land they till; this heavy emphasis on the farming of individual plots accounts for the fact that almost ninety percent of the country's population is rural. The population density is roughly 350 people per square mile, but when this density is equated with the amount of arable land, there are more than 2,200 people per square mile. Such a heavy concentration of people in a land ill-suited for intensive farming has produced a situation in which the majority of the people barely fend off starvation.

So many Haitians live out of touch of the statisticians and the paraphernalia of demographic surveys that it is difficult to find accurate statistics more recent than the United Nations 1950 survey. It is estimated, however, that the population increases at a rate of about 2.2 percent per annum. There are undoubtedly many more births, but the primitive conditions of the people and the prevalence of diseases such as yaws, tuberculosis, malaria, and hookworm produce high infant mortality. Nevertheless, enough survive to increase the population annually and swell the ranks of the over ninety percent of the population that is illiterate. These survivors can on the average expect to live less than thirty-five years. The peasants regard these children as their wealth: *"Pittit ci richesse malhere"* ("children are the riches of the unfortunate").

The majority of Haiti's population is of African descent. Only about 200,000 are Afro-Europeans, but this small group of *gens de couleur,* or *mulâtres,* who are descendants of the French colonists have by tradition comprised the majority of Haiti's elite. The elite consists of approximately two percent of the population, and the members of the elite have been educated in a European cultural tradition. They speak French in preference to the Creole tongue of the masses and are Roman Catholic. In a country where almost everyone has to work with his hands, the elite have prided themselves on not doing so, and by virtue of their prestige and position, they managed to control the conduct of the nation's affairs until very recently.

This small group of Haitians remained virtually unchallenged by the masses until 1946, when a nationalist movement, led by Negro intellectuals from the small but emerging middle class, seized power. The leaders of this movement were determined to make their country more African in outlook by weakening the elite and by increasing Haitian awareness of African culture and traditions. As a result of this so-called "Revolution of 1946," more Negroes have risen above the masses and become members of the elite. Others joined the small number of bureaucrats, teachers, shopkeepers, and office workers in the middle class. Yet this "revolution" has had little impact on Haiti's social structure, for the new recruits to the elite and the middle class, which still only comprises six percent of the population, have preferred to become identified with the older European traditions. This desire for identification with elite values is recognized by the masses, who live outside the money economy. They know that to enter the middle and upper classes is to have money, and money makes color (*neg rich mulate, mulate pauvre neg*). Color means elite values.

The elite and the urban middle class govern the country and are oriented toward national and international affairs. The mass of society exists in the hinterland away from the coastal cities and the capital, and the horizon of the masses is very limited. Its members are primarily concerned with the land and the immediate group that inhabits it, for land is a Haitian's most prized possession. The leading figures in any community are those who have larger holdings; the Haitians call these people the *gros nègre*. They have usually been active in politics or commerce and might well have traveled several times to the capital. Below the *gros nègre* is the largest percentage of the rural population, the peasant freeholder, who works his small plot. The lowest class in rural areas is the landless peasant, whether a sharecropper or an agricultural worker. Paul Moral estimated that in the Département du Nord five percent of the people was *gros nègre,* eighty-five percent possessed small and middle-sized holdings, and ten percent was landless.[2] This estimate for one department could be reasonably assumed to approximate the existing situation in Haiti.

Historical Political Perspective   Haiti became a land of peasant farmers as a result of policies formulated in the early years of the Republic. When the slaves rose against their French masters in 1791, the French colony of Saint Domingue suffered fifteen years of intermittent bloodshed before the slaves achieved their independence. Since 1664 France had claimed the western portion of the island settled only sparsely by cattlemen and buccaneers. French settlers had slowly cleared the plains and planted sugar, which they harvested by importing thousands of West Africans to do the work. The planters lived luxuriously on the profits of the slave-harvested sugar, and by 1780 Saint Domingue was the wealthiest colony in the New World.

The planters dallied with slave girls and servants, and the children resulting from these affairs often received their father's blessing, in which case he educated them to be Frenchmen in spirit if not in race. Yet because of the Afro-European heritage, these people suffered discrimination at the hands of the Europeans, and the *mulâtres* fanned the revolution and benefited by its success. As the only educated people in the new Republic, they replaced the French as the social and intellectual elite. However, the *mulâtres* could not have won the revolution, and it was Negro leadership and the Negro masses who achieved the victory.

On January 1, 1804, the former French colony became Haiti and began a tradition by having as its Chief of State a general of its armies. Jean Jacques Dessalines, a brutal hero of the revolution, became emperor. He ruled for only two years before he was assassinated, but his rule inspired others, and at his death two men divided the tiny nation between them. In the north Henri Christophe became king and ruled his people with an iron hand. In the south, however, the Republic of Haiti took the direction which it would ultimately follow. The colored General Alexandre Pétion exposed the people to constitutional rule, and he permitted them to parcel the land amongst themselves. By this act Haitians broke away from the plantation system and set the stamp on the future social and economic development of the country.

Jean Boyer, who united the country after the deaths of Pétion and

---

[2] Paul Moral, *L'Économie Haitienne* (Port au Prince, Imp. de l'Etat, 1959), pp. 55–56.

Christophe, ruled until 1843. The legacies of the first forty years of the country were a strong Executive, a constitutional form of government, and a Negro peasant society led by a small group of *mulâtres*. The majority of Haitians lived divorced from the urban society that taxed them and ruled them. As they had had no formal education, the world that was meaningful to them was their immediate surroundings and a spiritual world composed of *Le Bon Dieu,* or the good God, and a number of lesser gods. "After God," so the saying goes, "is the State" (*"Aprè Bô-Dié, se héta"*).

The caste structure, the religious life, and the concept of the State are very important to Haitian society. The Haitian peasant has grown up in a tradition of an ordered society. He learns from birth to obey his father and mother; he learns to accept the hierarchical structure of the society in which he lives; he is aware that the State is to be obeyed; and he accepts the religious leadership of the Christian priest or of the *vodun* (voodoo) *houngan,* or priest. The peasant, therefore, is susceptible to the influence of these values, whether they be religious, social, or political in nature. But because his real world and his spiritual world are so limited, it is hard to involve the Haitian in anything that might break down his concept of his world. Thus, as Presidents came and went, often with great rapidity during the period after Boyer's death, they had virtually no impact on the peasants.

The American Government sent in Marines in 1915 to prevent any European power from taking advantage of the breakdown in the political system. The Americans intended to alter the system, but the twenty years of American occupation hardly disturbed the society. Americans directed the building of roads, sewers, schools, and hospitals, established peace in the land, and straightened out Haiti's finances, but the Americans did not change the attitudes of the people. After the Americans left in 1934, political and financial instability returned, the roads rapidly deteriorated, and there were not enough doctors to serve the hospitals. The Haitians remained almost as they had been found, except that the Americans had left them with a Marine-trained Garde d'Haiti and an intellectual reaction against the occupation.

Political Structures and Roles

The historical evolution of Haiti as a peasant society in which distance and poor communication militated against a broadly based political conscious-ness has meant that any party affiliation a Haitian might have is based on his immediate acquaintance with a personality. Politics in Haiti is very personal, and it is rare for political parties to have an ideological framework. In fact, it would almost be fair to say that, once a man reaches the Presidency, opposi-tion political parties collapse or their leaders go into exile. Any sign of weakness in the President, however, spurs the opposition to action; from the time the Negro Charles Herard marched with his men out of the north to remove Boyer, a succession of Presidents has suffered a similar fate.

Doctor François Duvalier, President of Haiti since 1957, has suppressed opposition in the Republic for the time being, but there are a number of his opponents in exile, and a multiplicity of parties opposed to his regime exist outside the country. Duvalier, who has his own personalist party (in September 1963, he called it the Parti Unique de l'Action Révolutionaire et Gouvernementale), has faced invasions from the Comité des Forces Democratique Haitiennes and the Forces Armées Révolutionaires Haitiennes and has beaten them. These were units representing a variety of exile groups which had been formed around leading opponents of Duvalier, but there is every likelihood that these groups would forget their association once they achieved victory and would begin to agitate for their own particular leader.

Only two Haitian parties based in the country or outside it have existed longer than fifteen years. One is the Communist Parti Socialiste Popular (PSP), founded in the early 1930s by one of Haiti's leading writers, Jacques Romain, and the other is the Mouvement Ouvrier Paysan (MOP), which Daniel Fignole established in 1946 as his personal vehicle to the Presidency. Both parties have set social revolution as their goal.

Fignole's Mouvement Ouvrier Paysan was born at the same time as the labor movement in Haiti. The country's rural orientation militated against an early establishment of such a movement, but the increasing emigration from the country into the cities has resulted in the emergence of an urban proletariat anxious to improve their very squalid conditions. Fignole, an inspiring leader, was conscious of their desires and became spokesman for the newly founded Fédération Haitienne des Travaillers (FHT). The Communists founded and controlled the Fédération des Travaillers Haitiens (FTH) as a rival to the FHT, but the FTH did not manage to survive through the regime of Paul Magloire (1950–1956). The FHT did survive and joined in a general strike with some of the thirty-odd unaffiliated unions to prevent Magloire from extending his term of office beyond the constitutional six years. That general strike was instrumental in forcing Magloire to leave the country.

During the chaotic period following Magloire's departure, the individual unions formed into either the Union National des Travaillers (UNT) or the Union National Ouvriers d'Haiti (UNOH). Together the two unions opposed the Duvalier regime, but their leadership was either in exile or in prison, and neither major union has been an effective opponent of the regime. Fignole and his MOP are also in exile. The general strike which was such an effective instrument against Magloire has not yet been a successful weapon against Duvalier.

The Haitian student, representing as he does only a tiny minority of the population, has been effective in his own strike actions. Most Haitian secondary-school and university students have come from the families of the educated elite. These students have usually gone into law or into medicine and then have actively engaged in politics after their graduation. But while students, they have had an opportunity to protest for their own ends or to happily join a general strike in support of political ends. In 1929 students struck when President Borno failed to hold an election. Their strike was instrumental in getting him to resign. More recently the university students were not even cowed by the increasingly authoritarian regime of Dr. Duvalier and struck in November 1960 because one of their officers in the Union National Étudiants Haitiens was in prison. When Duvalier decreed martial law and ordered them to desist, they quickly complied.

The radio and the press have had little impact on the country. The radio is government controlled and informs those who can afford a radio and their friends what it wants them to hear. Newspapers in Haiti have occasionally had that independence of editorial opinion which is treasured in democracies, but with a small literate readership, the Haitian newspapers have not stimulated much activism, whatever their content. When Doctor Duvalier came to power, he insisted that the press praise his administration. If the press did not do so, then it would soon be suppressed. Thus the Roman Catholic daily, *La Phalange,* received a presidential order to cease publication, and the *Haiti Sun,* an English language daily, stopped publication when its editor was asked to leave the country. What are left are uninteresting little sheets like Port au Prince's *Le Matin,* which has a few lines of praise for the administration, some advertisements, and a gossip column.

Haiti has had thirty-five Chiefs of State since its foundation. Twenty-four were forced to resign; seven have been killed in office. Sir Spenser St. John, one-time British Minister to Haiti, wrote an unflattering book about the country in which he aptly described Haitian government as "a despotism tempered by revolution and exile, and occasionally by death."[3]

The Legislature in this atmosphere has little opportunity to be anything more than a rubber stamp for the Executive. The Haitian Constitution prescribes a Legislature consisting of a Senate and a Chamber of Deputies. These bodies sat at least once a year to give some legitimacy to the Executive's decisions; if there was any trouble, the Executive dismissed them. In April 1961, President Duvalier abolished the bicameral Legislature and replaced it with a single chamber whose members, supporters of the regime, were elected by the people in the fascinating election of May 1961. Duvalier still had several years in office at the time, but his name appeared at the top of the election ballot, and when the election results were announced, the over 1,300,000 voters found that they had elected Duvalier to another six-year term in office!

Duvalier's procedure may have been a little unusual, but he knew the Haitian people. Few Haitian Heads of State have been able to extend their period of office beyond the limits established in the Constitution. Those who have tried have usually waited until the last minute to attempt it and have run into heavy opposition. Duvalier never mentioned an extension of his term; he just arranged it and capitalized on the Haitians' amazement and admiration at his daring.

Duvalier, one of the men of the Haitian nationalist movement and a

---

[3] Sir Spenser St. John, *Hayti, or the Black Republic* (London, Smith, Elder & Co., 1889), p. 272.

student of the psychology of his people who admire and venerate a brilliant leader (as long as nothing goes wrong), was not satisfied with just an extension of his term to 1967. He decided to become President for life, a feat which had not been attempted since 1869; he accepted this permanent Presidency in April 1964. The last man to do so was executed, but Duvalier ordered the Legislature to throw out the 1957 Constitution and draw up a new one granting him a life term. The Legislature approved the new Constitution on May 25, 1964, and it is still in force.

Duvalier heads a regime dominated by the Negro middle class and supported by the peasants. He has become what he once condemned in the elite—a Head of State who not only considers himself head of the nation "but first and above all the first of his class."[4] His administration serves the interests of Duvalier and his most loyal supporters. The President, however, trusts no one, and so there have been numerous changes in the Cabinet, in the military force, and in the civil service during the years that he has been in power.

Duvalier has taken advantage of his knowledge of the Haitian society and employs its religious beliefs for his own ends. Like most of the Negro middle class, he had been a Roman Catholic, a status symbol for those who have risen above the masses. The elite has been Roman Catholic since the days of the French Empire. Catholicism is part of the heritage of the elite and has differentiated it from the masses, who have been nominally Roman Catholic but have been spiritually followers of Catholicism and *vodun,* or voodoo.

Vodun has received much unfavorable publicity from sensationalists who have not attempted to understand it, and the Roman Catholic Church has opposed it since the Concordat of 1860 between Haiti and the Vatican permitted the return of the Church to the Republic. Yet the Haitian peasant sees no wrong in adhering to the two religions, and *vodun* has over the years incorporated many Catholic beliefs. *Vodun* is, in fact, an exceedingly sophisticated religion, and knowledgeable students of comparative religion contend that *vodun* is structurally comparable to Christianity, Islam, or Buddhism. *Vodun* certainly has meaning for the Haitian peasant, who sees the universe and his surroundings in *vodun* terms. It also makes his life bearable, which Catholicism or the Protestant sects, which have been active in the country since 1945, have not done.

The Roman Catholic Church has been and is regarded as an enemy of the State by the nationalists who emerged after the American occupation. President Éstime, who led the social revolution of 1946 and brought the middle class Negroes to power, did not trust the Church and banished those priests who criticized his Government. Doctor Duvalier has also done his best to break with the Catholic Church, for ever since the Church made every effort to influence the Government's attitude against *vodun,* the Church has been regarded unfavorably by the nationalist intellectuals. Duvalier recognized

---

[4] Lorimer Denis and François Duvalier, *Problème des classes à travers l'histoire d'Haiti; sociologie politique* (Port au Prince, Au service de la Jeunesse, 1948), p. 3.

that the Church could rally urban discontent, and he proceeded to exile the bishops and French priests who opposed him. His subsequent excommunication did not apparently bother him, and he appointed clerical supporters to the vacant positions. A loyal Haitian priest also joined his Cabinet.

Vodun, the people's religion, gained a new prominence under Duvalier. In the past it has not been acknowledged by the elite regimes as worthy of sophisticated support. However, *vodun* has always had some influence on Haitian politics because not even the most sophisticated is absolutely certain that he can avoid the mysteries of the religion. This aura surrounding *vodun* has proven useful to President Duvalier, who is recognized by the people as having a great interest in the religion, and he has gained a reputation among the masses as being a *houngan*. Several *houngans* also serve on his staff as spiritual advisors.

Haiti's judicial system has never been independent of the Executive, and judges, who owe their appointment to the Executive, have been noted for corrupt practices and subservience to Presidents. The Court of Cassation, which is a court of appeals, is the highest judicial body in the country. Before it can make a judgment, the court must seek Executive opinion and thus foil the very concept of judicial independence and precedence. Any case the court might hear may have been years going through the lower courts in the five *départements,* and justice for those who can afford the courts is a slow process, if not a fruitless one. For the majority of Haitians, however, the formal judicial structure means nothing. Most Haitians are not aware of the forms of justice, and most issues that arise in rural areas are settled by a *juge de paix* appointed by the President. The *juge de paix* is usually a *grand don* (a wealthy peasant) or a *gros nègre* who knows little law but knows the customs of his community, and he bases his decisions on custom.

The courts are, however, useful weapons in the hands of the Executive, who permits the courts to pay lip service to the divisions of power. The courts can also be useful in interpreting the Constitution in favor of Executive action. In May 1957, during the chaotic days that followed the overthrow of Magloire, the high court's judges even ruled that an executive council should be the governing body. When Duvalier and another presidential aspirant declared that the court had no jurisdiction in the matter, the judges admitted it, but they thought somebody ought to rule something. The court now functions as a Duvalier agency.

The most important instrument of power in Haiti has been the army. The birth of the Republic came about because of the Negro army that followed the founders of the Republic, Toussaint L'Ouverture and Jean Jacques Dessalines. The army was the country's first institution. While a few elite and Negro Haitians have taken great pride in serving as officers in the army, the men in the lower ranks have not been as enthusiastic about military service. The Haitian peasant has long preferred his woman to go to town instead of himself for fear he will be conscripted into service.

Every Haitian general was a potential President. Commanders of units in *départements* often tried to use their own troops to achieve the Presidency. These officers did not always succeed, but one Haitian writer points out that it was traditional for army leaders to have "one common thought—to make war on constitutional authority."[5] This atmosphere did not contribute to political stability in the country. Thus, when the Americans occupied the country in 1915, they defeated the old army and created a new *gendarmerie,* which was to be divorced from politics. The Garde d'Haiti, as the *gendarmerie* came to be called, recruited men from the rural areas, educated them, and raised many of these former peasants to command of the Garde by the time of the American withdrawal in 1934.

The Garde, which had considerable pride in itself and its leading officers, did very well under Presidents Vincent (1934–1941) and Lescot (1941–1946), but when Lescot decided to remain President, the apolitical Garde became quite political, and a military junta took control of the country after the Garde had permitted the people to rise against Lescot. The junta then backed Dumarsais Éstime, the candidate of the nationalists, for the Presidency. When he too wished to prolong his term in office, the junta returned to power in 1950. The junta's leader, Colonel Paul Magloire, who could have persuaded the National Assembly to name him President, decided to allow the people to vote directly for the President for the first time. He received their overwhelming approval.

Magloire was a Negro President who eased the tension created between the *mulâtre* and Negro leadership by the "Revolution of 1946." He was also a very popular figure with the masses, but when he appeared to want to remain in power beyond the limit of six years imposed by the Constitution of 1950, the people rebelled in December 1956, and his rivals in the army did not support him. He went into exile with the profits from his monopoly of the Republic's cement and sisal production.

The leading officers watched while several interim Presidents failed to restore order after Magloire's overthrow. The officers finally took control in May 1957. The army leaders then established the rules for the election which they called for September. They ruled that a number of aspirants were ineligible to run and thereby narrowed the field to two candidates, Senator Dejoie and Doctor Duvalier. The army leaders apparently preferred Duvalier because they thought he would be more manageable, and in the election, the first one in which Haitian women had ever voted, Doctor Duvalier won.

Once in power, Duvalier began to subvert the army by dismissing his former supporters in the General Staff and by elevating younger men to important posts. In order to ensure that his power extended into every hamlet and village in the country, he deprived the army of its customary right to appoint the *chefs de section,* or officers of rural police, and selected his own men for these significant positions. The *chef de section,* representing military and governmental authority, can control the lives of the people in his area.

---

[5] Beauge Bercy, *Les péripéties d'une democratie* (Paris, Librairie L. Rodstein, 1941), p. 109.

President Duvalier also decided to weaken the army by creating his own instruments for the internal policing of the nation. He took fervent supporters from the urban and rural masses, gave them guns, and authorized them to serve as his special police. These men, known as the *Tonton Macoute,* Uncle Bogeyman, have gained an international reputation for brutality. Wearing their open-neck shirts, dark glasses, and side-arms, these men can be seen in the streets of Port au Prince swaggering about on their missions of extortion and death.[6] Duvalier has also made the militia an important arm of the Government; these rural peasants man roadblocks, garrison villages, and are readily available to protect Duvalier from attacks on his sanctuary, the white National Palace in Port au Prince. The army has had to accept its role as defender of the territorial sovereignty of the Republic and conforms to the principles of the 1957 Constitution, which declares the army to be apolitical and obedient. Doctor Duvalier has made it so.

Processes of Function and Dysfunction

Every Haitian over twenty-one has the right to vote. In the past the voter had not had an opportunity to elect a President, as the choice of President had been a privilege of the Legislature, but since 1950, when the Haitians were told they could vote for Paul Magloire, the populace has elected the President. This system has not really altered the pattern of political reality; the man who has the power will still get elected. In one way or another, the election will be a foregone conclusion, for it has been a Haitian tradition to channel the votes in the desired direction. The average Haitian has no concept of the rights accorded him by his franchise, and his illiteracy has not helped him improve his knowledge of the electoral procedures. Votes do not even have to be bought, for when the voter cannot read, it is very easy to tell him where to mark his ballot.

The Legislature has until recently consisted of a Senate and a Chamber of Deputies. The twenty-one senators used to be elected to their six-year terms by an assembly composed of leading figures in each *département,* though the senators were really chosen by the Executive. The thirty-seven deputies had been elected by popular vote. In 1961 President Duvalier abolished the Senate and the Chamber and unified the two houses into a popularly elected sixty-seven-member Legislative Chamber. The members of the Chamber serve six years.

The executive branch of the Government makes the decisions which affect the Haitian people. These decisions are usually designed to benefit the President and his allies, and those Presidents who have survived a period of years in office have managed to retire into exile as very rich men. Former President Paul Magloire is reported to have had several millions of dollars overseas when he left the country in 1956. Control of the Presidency permit-

---

[6] Graham Greene's recent novel *The Comedians* (New York, The Viking Press, 1966), convincingly evokes the atmosphere surrounding the role of the *Tonton Macoute* in what Greene calls "the nightmare republic."

ted him to direct the economic and commercial affairs of the country in his interest, and he did so. President Duvalier has also launched into a program which will increase his personal fortune and the fortunes of his few trusted allies. Duvalier's Mouvement Renovation Nationale, a collection agency for funds to carry out personal projects of the President, is but one means to increase the flow of funds into the executive coffers. The success of the program is guaranteed by the fact that Duvalier uses his personal police as collectors, and payment into the fund is really only a supplement to the other taxes that the President has imposed on the people.

Conclusion: A Prognosis of Stability and Instability

Haiti's political life reflects the country's heritage. The great mass of the people at the time of the revolution was illiterate and oppressed. Their leaders cared little about the development of the people and preferred to improve their own material position at the people's expense. The Heads of State, with rare exception, did little to improve the economic or social position of the rural peasants, who comprised over ninety percent of the nation. What politics that existed has been on a personal level, and political ideologies have not had the opportunity to take root among the illiterate masses.

The fact that throughout her history Haiti has remained two nations has also retarded her political development. Government has been for the urban nation, while the rural nation has carried on in its simple, but not unhappy, way. Politics has not been of rural concern unless some peasants have cared to answer the call of adventure and join the forces of some presidential aspirant in his march on Port au Prince. In the city, however, politics has been of greater interest because the urban elite has had access to governmental posts and has had to be constantly aware of possible changes of the Executive.

Haiti has faced two major attempts to change its character. The first was the American occupation, which the American Government hoped would produce stable conditions through the improvement of Haitian political life, communications, education, health, and finances. The twenty-year occupation achieved little. The second attempt was the apparent social revolution of 1946, which raised the Negro middle class to prominence in a political society dominated by the predominantly colored elite. Besides attempts at economic reforms, introduction of an income tax, and an agrarian program, the Negro middle class aimed at ridding Haiti of its elitist overtones. The revolution, however, has yet to occur, and Haiti continues in its original mold.

The Haitians are a fascinating and likeable people. They have survived disease, bad government, revolts, foreign occupation, and near starvation. Throughout, the peasant can only shrug his shoulders at what has gone on in the capital, for his way of life has not been disturbed, and governments mean very little to him. His life is exceedingly stable. But in the capital and the provincial towns is another atmosphere. There the people have grown used to strong presidential control of the country, and each man who has had the opportunity has sought to reap some benefit from the Government, if not to gain something, to at least preserve what he has already acquired. Graft and corruption have become a part of the political system, just as revolts rather than elections have been the usual method of changing governments. Given Haiti's political instability in the past, it is hard to see how there will be an improvement in the future.

THE DOMINICAN REPUBLIC

The Dominican Republic comprises the remaining two-thirds of the island of Hispaniola and exists in an uneasy peace with its island neighbor. The Dominicans, who are Spanish-speaking and who have a greater cultural affinity with Europe, have suffered invasion and occupation at the hands of the Haitians and so have long distrusted them. Certainly, in comparison with the Haitians, the Dominicans possess a more economically favorable natural environment in their land which, they recall, "Columbus loved best."[7]

The Political Environment

Four ranges of mountains, three of them stretching into Haiti, dominate the land, and in the Cordillera Central are the highest mountains in the Caribbean; several of them rise over nine thousand feet. In the north the Cordillera Septentrional rises some three thousand feet above the Atlantic coastal plain. The southern slopes of this range overlook the rich Cibao Valley and the Rio Yaque del Norte, which is 240 miles long. The southeast tip of the range also touches on another fertile plain, La Vega Real, which lies between the coast and the eastern end of the central range.

The massive Cordillera Central divides the Republic. The pine-covered forests of the mountains are cool and wet, but on the southern side the rainfall slackens, and irrigation becomes important in the San Juan Valley, which lies between the central range and the Sierra Neiba, which are five thousand feet high. Below the Sierra Neiba lies a rift valley, the Enriquillo Plain, and this plain and the slopes of the mountains are dry and covered with desert growth. Lake Enriquillo, the dominant feature in the plain, is well below sea level and is separated from the south coast by the lower Baoruco Mountains.

The Republic has 18,816 square miles; it is smaller than Nova Scotia and is about the size of New Hampshire and Vermont combined. Bush, trees, and scrub growth cover over fifty percent of the land, while some twenty-five percent is in meadow and pasture, and twenty percent is used for agricultural purposes. It is the agricultural land which has meant so much to the Dominican economy; sugar has been the major export of the country, and in the last

---

[7] The author would like to thank Professor Howard J. Wiarda of the Department of Government, University of Massachusetts, for his incisive comments on the first draft of this study. Professor Wiarda's unpublished dissertation "The Aftermath of the Trujillo Dictatorship: The Emergence of a Pluralist Political System in the Dominican Republic" (Gainesville, University of Florida, 1965), is a valuable contribution to our knowledge of that country.

five years sugar has supplied between fifty and sixty percent of the country's foreign exchange. Coffee and cacao are the other two major exports, and they account for about eleven percent of the foreign exchange. Other commodities sold abroad include tobacco, chocolate, hides, and a limited amount of minerals, such as bauxite and nickel.

Population and Social Structure

The land which comprises the Republic was first settled by Christopher Columbus' men, who established the first permanent European community on the banks of the Ozama River in 1496. Named in honor of Santo Domingo de Guzmán, Santo Domingo became an administrative center and was the first vice regal capital of Spain's empire in America. For twenty years Santo Domingo was the most important Spanish settlement in the New World. After that time the importance of Santo Domingo diminished as newer and more important conquests on the mainland overshadowed it. Santo Domingo, however, continued to be the administrative capital of the island, whose inhabitants engaged in mining, planting, and cattle raising. The Indians who had inhabited the island before the arrival of the Spaniards did not survive the conquest, and Africans had to be imported to work the mines and the fields. By 1570, when the settlement consisted of only thirty to thirty-five thousand people, the racial composition of the island had assumed an Afro-European complexion. Today, though figures vary, Negroes and whites each comprise about fifteen percent of the Dominican people. The remaining seventy percent is of mixed blood.

The estimated 3,500,000 people in the Republic are heavily concentrated in two areas: the southeast plain surrounding Santo Domingo and the rich agricultural areas of the Cibao and La Vega Real.[8] Santo Domingo has a population of over 300,000, while Santiago de los Caballeros in the Cibao has about 100,000 inhabitants. Other cities with over 25,000 are San Francisco de Macoris in La Vega Real and San Pedro de Macoris to the east of the capital. The estimated 700,000 inhabitants who live in the other municipal centers which dot the island, together with those living in the major cities, make up the urbanized thirty percent of the country; many of these people live in densely populated slums where housing is substandard and conditions are exceedingly primitive.

The heavy concentration of people in primitive conditions within urban areas and the low subsistence level of the rural population undoubtedly contribute to the high infant mortality of 108.3 per thousand in a country which annually averages about 39.8 births per thousand people. Even with this high death rate, the population continues to increase at a rate of about 3.5 percent and thus adds to the difficulties of the country.

---

[8] Statistics quoted throughout are contained in either *República Dominicana en Cifras* (Santo Domingo, Sección de Publicaciones, 1964), or *The Statistical Abstract of Latin America: 1964* (Los Angeles, Latin American Center, University of California, 1965).

Historical Political Perspective

The Dominican Republic has been, like many of its Latin American neighbors, unable to divest itself of its past, when the majority of the land was in the hands of a few families, and members of these families and a small number of businessmen controlled the commercial and financial sectors of the economy. The established landowners, a few businessmen, and the Church dominated the society during the colonial period and continued to do so during the twenty-two years of Haitian rule, which ended in 1844. In that year the Dominicans proclaimed their independence.

The two most important figures to dominate the first thirty years of the Republic came from this landed and business segment of the society. Pedro Santana left his small ranch in the eastern part of the southern plain to become a leader in the struggle against Haiti, as did Buenaventura Báez, a businessman from Azua in the southwest. Santana was the better military leader, but Báez was an ardent intriguer, and between them they managed to stave off Haitian aggressions. Neither of them, however, cared about the independence of the Republic. Santana returned the Republic to Spanish control in 1861, but many Dominicans were unhappy with this foreign domination and forced Spain to withdraw in 1865. Báez, who was very interested in money, tried in his turn to persuade the United States to acquire the country, and only the United States Senate prevented President U. S. Grant from doing so. This unhappy beginning did not contribute to the establishment of a secure society.

The dominant psychological characteristic of the Dominican people is a result of the long conditioning process which began with the first settlement of the area. From the very beginning, there evolved a caste structure attributable to the *hidalgo* mentality of the Spanish conqueror, who did not want to work with his hands. This caste structure has placed the leading families at the top and has relegated the vast majority to a position of inferiority. The great landowners, the big businessmen, and the military leaders have played on this inferiority, even though many of them have also suffered the frustration of being unacceptable to those who comprise the top echelon of the society.[9]

The ambitious but socially inferior Dominican has had to struggle for recognition and has sought to achieve it through political or financial power. This assertion of personality has resulted in the domination of Dominican politics by four men after Báez surrendered his power in 1878. The political confusion that followed Báez's departure was finally resolved by the fifteen-year (1884–1899) dictatorship of the Negro soldier "Lilis" Heureaux. After his assassination parties formed behind Horacio Vásquez and Juan Isidro Jiménez. Vásquez finally emerged as champion only after a twenty-four-year period of chaos, which included the eight-year (1916–1924) occupation of the country by the United States. When Vásquez tried to remain in power

---

[9] Juan Bosch, *Trujillo, Causas de una tiranía sin ejemplo* (Caracas, Editado "Las Novedades," 1959), pp. 26–47.

longer than his six-year term of office, General Rafael Leonidas Trujillo deposed him in 1930. Trujillo ruled his country with an iron hand for thirty-one years until he was assassinated in 1961 by some of his own followers. At this moment in Dominican history, another period of political instability engulfed the people and found the United States once again embroiled in Dominican affairs.

Political Structure and Roles

Since the death of Trujillo, under whom political parties, labor unions, student groups, and other organizations that might influence political decisions came and went at the whim of the dictator, the Dominicans have responded to the vacuum existing after his death and have created a number of organizations centered around special interest groups within the society. That no institutional political framework has existed has meant that personalities and ideological positions have been the main factors in the formation of specific parties.

Political Parties   When Trujillo seized power in 1930, there were seven political parties in existence. The dictator reduced them to one, the Partido Dominicano, and every eligible voter belonged to it. As a student of the dictatorship described the party, it had no doctrine or particular characteristic but was "a fundamental part" of Dominican life and was "Trujillo's major instrument of action."[10] In 1942 Trujillo decided to have an opposition and permitted the Partido Trujillista to form. When this party was not enough to illustrate the democratic intention of his regime, he invited the Communist Partido Socialista Popular (PSP) to come back into the country. For almost two years (1945–1947) the PSP functioned. Then Trujillo drove its adherents underground, and he became an acknowledged anti-Communist. After 1947 he kept a tight control over internal political matters and did so until his death permitted a change in the political life of the country. Then numerous parties and politicians sought to take advantage of the new freedom.

Two parties that had been formed in exile became active in the Republic after Trujillo's death. The most important of the two has been the Partido Revolucionario Dominicano (PRD), founded in 1939 and led by Juan Bosch, a Dominican intellectual and novelist. It has had a democratic-Socialist orientation, and as soon as its leaders had returned to the Dominican Republic, they set about creating an organization which would seek the party's main support from among the urban and rural masses. Bosch proposed to keep the PRD based upon its ideological position rather than upon allegiance to him. In contrast, the other party formed in exile, the Vanguardia Revolucionaria Dominicana (VRD), while a reformist party, was the personal vehicle of Horacio Ornes, a member of a distinguished Dominican family.

The PRD was very successful in its appeal to the voting public, while the

---

[10] Jesús de Galíndez, *La era de Trujillo* (Santiago de Chile, Editorial del Pacifico, 1956), p. 292.

VRD faded into the background as stronger parties developing in the Republic after the assassination came to the fore. The major challenge to the left-of-center PRD was the rightist Unión Cívica Nacional (UCN), whose base was the landowning and business community that lived under the Trujillo regime. The UCN preferred the *status quo* and opposed the reformist and revolutionary tendencies of the leftist parties. In the December 1962 elections, the contest centered around the struggle for the Presidency between Juan Bosch, of the PRD, and Viriato Fiallo, the candidate of the UCN. In a dramatic last-minute upsurge by partisans of the PRD, Bosch, receiving sixty-two percent of the popular vote, won.

To the left of the PRD was the party of the educated and activist youth of the country. This party is the Agrupación Política 14 de Junio (1J4 or *Catorcistas*), founded by a group of young professional men in honor of some exiles who had tried to emulate Fidel Castro's invasion of Cuba by landing on the Dominican coast and who had died on June 14, 1959, at the hands of Trujillo's soldiers. This party has stood for social revolution and has been ardently nationalistic.

These four parties prepared to contest the proposed September 1965 election called by the provisional Government established by the military leaders who had overthrown the Bosch administration in September 1963. These parties were joined by a number of other parties reflecting personal aspirations and ideological positions.

On the far right was the Acción Revolucionaria (AR) of Angel Severo Cabral, who had left the UCN because it was too moderate. The Partido Liberal Evolucionista (PLE), headed by Luis Amiama Tío, one of the two surviving assassins of Trujillo, supported the idea of an authoritarian state in emulation of Trujillo. A more moderate Right-wing party was the Partido Reformista (PR) of Joaquín Balaguer, a former Trujillo advisor and President of the Republic at the time of Trujillo's death; Balaguer had been in exile, and his party had no other leader capable of winning any popular support.

The PRD and the Partido Revolucionario Social Cristiano (PRSC) were the parties of the democratic Left, and the PRSC, because of its religious and social revolutionary character, had a number of supporters. The PRSC candidate finished third in the presidential election of 1962.

The activist Left besides the 1J4 included two Communist groups. The PSP, which in August 1965 became the Partido Communista Dominicana (PCD), was Moscow-oriented and had a hard core of veterans from the Trujillo days. The Movimiento Popular Dominicano (MPD) was also Communist, but in its adherence to Peking, the party reflected the split within the world Communist movement. This party too was small in numbers.

Several other minor parties wished to contest the election, but no party ever had a chance to do so. On April 24, 1965, supporters of a return to constitutional government began a rebellion against the provisional Government. The uprising subsequently led to armed intervention by the United

States and the postponement of any elections until order was restored in the country. In September 1965, the contending forces agreed to hold elections in June 1966, by which time Dominican political aspirants would have an opportunity to develop a new political form-sheet for the election race.

Interest Groups   The labor movement in the Republic had its origins in the period after the death of Heureaux in 1899, but it was not until the United States occupation that unions began to organize in specific industries with the intention of improving working conditions. A national body, the Federación Dominicana de Trabajo (FDT), incorporated most of the unions after 1920. The first political movement was organized in 1926. These activities collapsed under Trujillo, but in 1944 he revived the union movement by ordering the formation of a central organization, the Confederación Dominicana de Trabajadores (CDT). The number of guilds and syndicates then increased to more than one hundred and fifty. Two years later the organized sugar workers struck and won a pay increase. Following this strike, Trujillo ordered tighter government control in order to prevent further strikes, and this government-controlled union survived the death of Trujillo by only six months.

Labor, seeking to purge the Trujillo family control over unions, created a new central organization, the Frente Obrero Unido Pro Sindicatos Autónomos (FOUPSA) in September 1961. FOUPSA's leaders soon let their partisan political affiliations influence their own outlook on the labor movement, and in December 1961 FOUPSA began to lose members. By June 1962, new labor organizations replaced FOUPSA as a major force in the labor movement. As divergent groups struggled for paramount influence over labor, politics clearly had a role in this struggle. By the end of 1962, the Frente Obrero Unido Pro Sindicatos Autónomos-Central Sindical de Trabajadores Dominicanos (FOUPSA-CESITRADO), emerged as pro-PRD, while the Confederación Autónoma de Sindicatos Cristianos (CASC) represented those sympathetic to the social Christian movement.

Another FOUPSA offshoot, FOUPSA Libre, a U.S.-supported group, represented about two hundred unions. Representatives of these unions met in November 1962 to establish a set of principles and to join the International Confederation of Free Trade Unions and the Inter-American Regional Organization of Workers. The delegates chose a new name, the Confederación Nacional Trabajadores Libre (CONATRAL), and pledged to work for democracy while rejecting tyranny from either Left or Right. The leaders of this group, however, were not anxious to work with FOUPSA-CESITRADO or with CASC in presenting a democratic front against potential tyranny, and CONATRAL's efforts to remain apolitical in a politically charged atmosphere found its leaders becoming strongly anti-Communist and fearful of President Bosch's activities. CONATRAL publicly endorsed his overthrow, and its members watched while the new Government harassed CASC and FOUPSA-CESITRADO. CONATRAL ensured by its actions a continual split in labor's ranks. This split would be widened by employers anxious to use it to their own advantage. Given this atmosphere, it is not surprising to find labor . . . among the principal forces fighting on the "Constitutionalist" side in the bloody and destructive civil war which broke out in 1965. Both FOUPSA-CESITRADO and CASC joined the downtown Caamano forces and, though CONATRAL did not look with favor on the Constitutionalists, it could not prevent many of its individual members from joining the struggle.[11]

The divisions within the labor movement have hindered its development as a strong voice in the political life of the country. While the more powerful unions like the dockers, the chauffeurs, the sugar-mill workers, and the electrical workers can usually disrupt the economy of the country to their advantage, smaller unions and the unaffiliated worker have been at the mercy of their employers and of the governments, which have usually supported the employers. Until the laborers speak with a more unified voice, the worker in the Dominican Republic will have to take his chances on obtaining economic and social improvements.

The university students in many Latin American countries have traditionally been very active in politics. Dominican students are no exception, but during the thirty years of suppression under Trujillo, they were not permitted much freedom of expression, and the few moments when they forgot themselves and questioned the regime led to reprisals. As a result, the death of Trujillo released pent-up energies, and students have become participants in the political life of the country. The university student organizations reflect student enthusiasms for causes and political positions. The three major groups are all left of center. Fragua represents the far Left, the Frente Universitario Radical Revolucionario (FURR), is pro-PRD, and the Bloque Revolucionario Universitario Cristiano (BRUC), is sympathetic to the Social Christian movement.

The student elections of January 1964 at the University of Santo Domingo clearly illustrate the student position. At that time 54 percent of the student body voted. Fragua won 2 seats on the University Council and 26 seats in the student assembly with 1452 votes, BRUC with 1157 votes won 1 seat on the Council and 21 assembly seats, and FURR received 66 votes and 3 assembly seats.

A larger body representing student opinion throughout the Republic is the Federación de Estudiantes Dominicanos (FED), whose executive is elected by the various student organizations. In 1964 Fragua replaced the BRUC majority in the Federación.

The active students are for social revolution and tend to be very nationalistic. They are vociferous anti-Americans. In April 1965 they joined enthusiastically in the Constitutionalist struggle against the Dominican military and the American intervention, and it is to be expected that the students will continue to act with vigor against any government which they oppose.

The political parties, the labor unions, and the student groups have been

---

[11] Howard J. Wiarda, "The Development of the Labor Movement in the Dominican Republic," *Inter-American Economic Affairs*, XX (Fall 1966), 60–61.

vociferous and active exponents of their own particular points of view. There are other organizations, particularly from the Conservative business community, that have been influential in supporting governments that protect the interests of these organizations. Thus, the business and professional organizations, the local chambers of commerce, and the landowners, comprising as they do the economic and professional elite of the country, have preferred the *status quo* and have opposed any radical alterations of the political, economic, and social structure of the society. Of the seven governments between the death of Trujillo and the April 1965 uprising, these groups were unhappy with only one, that of Juan Bosch, and were pleased with its demise.

In contrast to the upper echelons of the economic society, the Dominican middle-class professional men and civil servants are too busy trying to achieve material security to have developed a political and social consciousness. They have no defined goals except to avoid falling back among the vast majority of their countrymen, some seventy-five to eighty percent of the Dominican people, who are the small entrepreneurs, the urban laborers, the rural peasants, and the unemployed in both rural and urban areas.[12] The Dominican masses, unfamiliar with the opportunities that their votes afford and conditioned to respond as they have been told to elections, have not yet been able to appreciate their potential as a political force.

One of the great influences on the masses has been the Roman Catholic Church, whose position in the Republic has traditionally been a Conservative one. Church and State are separated, but Roman Catholicism is the official religion of the people, and hardly a national event or holiday occurs that does not have a Catholic ceremony as part of the festivities.

The hierarchy of the Church has usually been allied with the vested interests, and high officials of the Church have at times been asked to lead the country out of political chaos. Thus the people elected Archbishop Fernando Meriño to serve as President of the Republic between 1880 and 1882, and Archbishop Adolfo Nouel was provisional President for less than six months during the hectic years just prior to the American occupation. He had been asked to serve in order to avoid an occupation, but he was unable to restore order.

During Trujillo's period of control, Church leaders remained relatively quiet but at times became effusive in their praise of his rule. Not until 1960 did any members of the hierarchy involve themselves in any condemnation of the dictatorship, and then Trujillo responded with aggressive attacks on the offending bishops. One of the bishops was an American, who three years later was involved in protecting the Church's interest from the reforms proposed by the Bosch Government. At that time the hierarchy of the Church opposed the 1963 Constitution, which among other things sanctioned divorce, authorized State inspection of religious schools, and recognized civil and common-law marriage.

---

[12] Juan Bosch, *The Unfinished Experiment, Democracy in the Dominican Republic* (New York, Praeger, 1965), pp. 66–76.

With the death of the dictator, the Church responded favorably to the reform movement urged by Pope John XXIII in his encyclical *Mater et Magistra* and espoused social reforms and a democratic society in which the Church could play a significant role. Church leaders, therefore, remained neutral in the election campaign of 1962, even though many of them did not favor Bosch's candidacy because he appeared to be too liberal in his religious life. Several clerics openly attacked Bosch as being a Communist, but the bishops, who officially spoke for the Church, refused to associate themselves with these individual priests. However, even the hierarchy could not stand by and allow Bosch's Government to promulgate a Constitution which, the bishops believed, would destroy the Church's traditional position in the country. However, they were unwilling to lead openly an attack on the Government, although an increasing number of the bishops' subordinates became active and vociferous opponents of the Bosch administration. Very few members of the Church were sorry when the armed forces seized control of the country in September 1963. Since that time, however, the Church leadership has continued to call for social justice in the land. But the leaders want these reforms from a government which will recognize that the Church has a significant role to play in the future of the country.

The Church has been an important moral influence in the Republic, but the role of the Church has never been as powerful as that of the country's armed forces in the shaping of the political life of the country. Theoretically responsible for the defense of their country against external attack or internal disorder, the Dominican armed forces and police have involved themselves in an untold number of uprisings against the Executive. Prior to the American occupation, no central control over the army or the police existed. Each provincial governor was in charge of the units within his province, and if he was ambitious for national power, he had at hand the means to achieve it. The history of the period between 1844 and 1916 is filled with examples of local *caudillos* marching at the head of their men to Santo Domingo in order to seize political control of the country.

During the American occupation a complete change in the character of the military occurred. The American officials believed that only through the establishment of a well-trained, politically independent military force could peace and tranquillity be brought to Dominican political life. Therefore the Americans disbanded the old armed forces and prepared to train a new one which would be responsible only to the Executive. In April 1917 the Americans began to recruit men for the Dominican constabulary. U.S. Marines trained the volunteers. The constabulary failed to attract officers from the society's upper echelons, who had opposed the intervention, and became an important steppingstone up the economic ladder for ambitious lower-class men, who might otherwise never have had an opportunity to improve their social or economic position. The armed forces have continued to afford that opportunity.

The constabulary became the National Police once it was apparent that the United States was preparing to leave the control of the country in the hands of the Dominicans themselves. The Americans had hoped that the Dominicans would leave the police force independent of political leaders, but in the end the people merely left it to be controlled by an ambitious young officer, Rafael Trujillo, who within four years of the American departure had become commander of what was now called the National Army and who within six years had used his position to propel himself into the Presidency.

Trujillo used the army as the backbone of his power. But he also developed a navy, an air force, a police force and a secret service to help discourage the opposition. Towards the end of his regime, he organized a special unit of tanks and infantry as part of the Air Force, placed it under the command of his son, and kept it at San Isidro Air Base for use in an emergency. While Trujillo never had an opportunity to employ that special Air Force unit, it was that unit that was to be the arbiter of political affairs in the period after his death. General Elías Wessin y Wessin used it as a counter-revolutionary force in April 1965, and President Balaguer, recognizing it as a potential danger to his administration, ordered the unit incorporated into the Army shortly after his inauguration in July 1966.

The Dominican armed forces under Trujillo were an especially pampered group, for he did not stint on the defense budget. The officers received high pay and other privileges which improved their economic position, yet it was several senior officers in the armed forces who joined with a few civilians in plotting Trujillo's assassination. Since his death the armed forces and the national police have been active in Dominican politics and are still the most powerful institution in the country.

The senior officers in the armed forces, who had received land and commercial rewards from Trujillo, have allied with the landowning and business interests in an attempt to preserve the *status quo*. However, a number of younger officers and men who had not been corrupted by the dictator's largesse joined in the April 1965 uprising because they wished to see a return to constitutional government. They were more in sympathy with professional than with political activity in the armed forces. This recent division in the leadership of the armed forces has only clouded the political situation; the direction that the military will take in the future will depend upon which of the factions is victorious.

Trujillo's former police force is also still a powerful organization. In the 1950s it consisted of about three thousand men and served as another security arm of the dictatorship. In the period after Trujillo's assassination, the police force grew to twelve thousand because the United States Government had urged the creation of a strong apolitical force, and this urging had conformed to the wishes of the ambitious Minister of the Interior, Antonio Imbert Barreras, one of the two surviving assassins of Trujillo. Imbert could see the police as a useful instrument in his own plans for achieving power.

The officers of the police are politically involved. They have been accustomed to using their position to improve their economic and social status within the country, and they are anxious to protect this position. Their men have a reputation for being ruthless in the pursuit of police ends, and they are feared by the majority of the people.

The Three Branches of Government   The executive branch of the Dominican Government has traditionally run the affairs of the country; the Legislature, consisting of a Senate and a Chamber of Deputies, has had little opportunity during the twentieth century to be more than a rubber stamp for the Executive. During Trujillo's regime the dictator, conforming to the Constitution's provision that Presidents should not succeed themselves, did not always fill the Presidency and selected someone to do so while he continued to make the decisions. Since December 1961 there has been only one constitutional President and an elected Legislature. That was the Government elected in December 1962 and overthrown in September 1963. Otherwise, the country has been run by either a Council of State, a triumvirate, or a provisional President.

The judicial system of the country was designed to exist separate from the executive and legislative branches of the Government, but in the Republic the judges have rarely functioned independent of the executive branch. In the early days of the Republic, the law, which is based upon French law as a result of the Haitian occupation, was usually administered by local political bosses and Church officials. However, the Constitutions authorized the establishment of courts to protect individual rights, and the judges, who theoretically have had political immunity, came to be expected to bow to the wishes of the President in the pursuit of justice. Any failure to carry out these wishes resulted in dismissal from this socially respectable position.

Since the death of Trujillo, there has apparently been little change in the traditional opinion that judges respect the will of the President. The triumvirate that ran the Government after the overthrow of Bosch removed three Supreme Court justices, including the President of the Court, in order to have the Court composed of men willing to accede to the Government's wishes.

The Processes of Function and Dysfunction

Constitutional governments have come and gone, and of the country's twenty-three Constitutions, none has lasted more than ten years. The military leaders abrogated the most recent one, promulgated in May 1963, after their overthrow of the Bosch Government.

The Dominican Republic has also had more than fifty Presidents and provisional Presidents, of whom only five have managed to remain in control for any length of time. *Caudillismo,* the exercise of power by a strong personality, has been the rule rather than the exception, and as long as the leader has been able to control the capitol and has had a sufficient number of supporters, he has been able to remain in power. Trujillo lasted longer than any of his predecessors, and as a result, he was able to guide the country in directions that were beneficial to him. He also saw that the senators and deputies, representing the party which he had established to give an air of legitimacy to his rule, did as he ordered. Thirty-one years of this control meant that a whole generation of Dominicans grew up in a political atmosphere that on the surface appeared to be a constitutional democracy, with all the apparatus of parties, elections, and a Constitution, but which was really a dictatorship. The elected representatives, the Government, and the appointed officials all conformed to the dictator's wishes.

Elections have been held in the Republic when the Government has functioned under a Constitution. During Trujillo's period of power, he adhered to the letter of the Constitution and authorized elections for the Presidency and the Legislature at regularly stated intervals. Everyone over eighteen years of age, including women, who received the franchise in 1942, has been eligible to vote in these elections. The Senate has one representative from each of the twenty-six provinces and the Federal District of Santo Domingo, while the Chamber of Deputies has had representation based upon population.

Trujillo's essentially one-party State ensured that his nominees for the Legislature would be elected, but even then every Dominican eligible to vote was expected to belong to the party organization and to exercise his franchise. If he did not, there would be unpleasant questions. Such a system was, of course, anything but democratic, and the Dominicans did not have an opportunity to participate in partisan political elections until December 1962, when they went to vote in an election supervised by the Organization of American States.

The people vote, but the Presidents make the decisions. These decisions have usually been designed to enable the President and his friends to benefit by his control of the country. The President has been able to distribute government positions and civil service posts at will, and he has been able to decide economic and fiscal matters as he sees fit. This kind of power has traditionally been inimical to the best interests of the majority of people who have gone to the polls.

Dominican Presidents are not supposed to seek re-election, but this regulation has not been followed if the President has been able to manipulate matters in his favor. In 1929 Trujillo's predecessor, President Horacio Vásquez, having one year of his term left, began to make motions to extend it. His activity led to opposition and opened the way for Trujillo to seize power. Trujillo served two four-year terms before giving way to two puppets. He became President again in 1942 and remained in office for ten years. Then his brother became the Chief Executive, and it is said that Trujillo's brother always read the daily newspapers in order to find out what he had ordered done.

The political decisions made in the Dominican Republic have been in the hands of the Executive, and policies have conformed to his desires. How the executive branch has arrived at these decisions, what groups have influenced it, and what goals it wishes to achieve have, of course, been predicated on the President's own views and in his interests. Most of the Presidents of the Republic have guided the political affairs of the country in this way. They have tried to reap as much economic advantage for themselves and for their supporters as was humanly possible. In Trujillo's case, he managed to gain personal control over most of the truly productive land in the nation and monopolized economically profitable businesses.

Of the ten Governments that have run the country since Trujillo's death, seven of them have represented the vested interests in the country, and the Executive has attempted to function in such a way as to protect their position. The only elected Governments, representing the will of the majority of the Dominican people, were the Governments of Juan Bosch and, more recently, of Joaquín Balaguer. The Government of provisional President Héctor García-Godoy was formed as a result of the "Act of Dominican Reconciliation" of September 3, 1965, in order to ease the tensions between defenders of the old order and those who sought a return to constitutional government and social revolution. President García-Godoy retired as soon as the Dominican people elected a new administration in the June 1, 1966, election. This election was the third reasonably honest election in the Republic's history.

The OAS-supervised election of December 20, 1962, was only the second election (the U.S.-supervised election in 1924 was the first) run relatively free of coercion, bribery, and rigged ballot boxes. The PRD won the election with 58.7 percent of the popular vote, controlled the Presidency, and had majorities in both the Senate and the Chamber of Deputies. The PRD achieved its success as a result of an intense campaign to win the urban lower class and the rural peasants to the party. It had campaigned for major reforms in the country which would improve the conditions of all the people and not just those of special individuals. The major opponent of the PRD was the UCN, created in 1961 as an "apolitical" group dedicated to the removal of Trujillo elements within the country. The UCN numbered Communists and Conservatives from the middle and upper classes among its early supporters but did not officially become a political party until early in 1962. Other political parties existed and were active during the campaign, but these two parties, which would attract almost one million votes between them, dominated the election campaign. The party that had gained the support of the masses won the election but lost its Government seven months later when the armed forces overthrew it. An armed forces-supported triumvirate ruled until the crisis of April 1965.

The June 1, 1966, elections joined those of 1924 and 1962 in being a genuine expression of the will of the voting public. After an often violent and vitriolic campaign, the voters went to the polls to choose between the two leading candidates, Juan Bosch of the PRD, the candidate supported by the Left, and the PRD's Joaquín Balaguer, the candidate of the Right, who had been former advisor to Trujillo and a past President of the Republic (1960–1961). More than 1,200,000 Dominicans voted, and when the election was over, Balaguer had defeated Bosch by a 3 to 2 margin. The majority of voters had apparently chosen Balaguer because he appeared to offer the best chance for stability in their country. He was a staunch Roman Catholic who had not been identified with the worst excesses of the Trujillo period. In his last days as President, he had begun to distribute Trujillo properties to the masses, and they had not forgotten this action. As the only real alternative to Bosch, Balaguer would have received support from the middle-class and upper-middle-class voters and from the vested interests. Many voters would also have recognised that the military leaders would not see him as dangerous , to their interests.

The United States' presence was also felt in this election. Most Dominicans wanted the O.A.S. units, which were largely components of the U.S. forces sent to the country in April and May 1965, to leave the country. The U.S. Government, while ostensibly neutral, nevertheless showed a preference for the Conservative Balaguer. And because Balaguer had won the election with the support of the masses and obviously has no leftist inclinations beyond introducing certain social reforms that will appease the mass vote, the United States and O.A.S. forces could leave the Republic hoping that the Dominican military forces can quell any civil strife organised by dissident elements on the Left or Right.

Conclusion: Prognosis of Stability and Instability

The Dominican Republic has had three periods of political stability. The longest periods of stability were the dictatorships of "Lilis" Heureaux and of Rafael Trujillo. The former lasted fifteen years and the latter thirty-one. The other major period of stability in the country was the American occupation between 1916 and 1924. Otherwise, the country has faced constant turmoil and change in its political life.

This checkered political history of the country shows that the Dominican people have had little opportunity to become involved in the political process. The overwhelming control of the country by the executive branch and the personal or military factions that have surrounded it and competed for it have kept the Presidency from becoming open to respected constitutional procedures.

The Dominican people are now once again in a period of political instability. The thirty-one years of stability under Trujillo gave way to conflict between those who wish to emulate the dictator by using their power to improve their personal position and those who wish to see greater social justice. Those seeking to improve the social and economic conditions of the country for the benefit of the majority of the people are themselves divided between those who wish to pursue democratic ends and those who would prefer to bring about social justice under a totalitarian regime. This conflict in aims between the various political ideologies and groups ensures that the Dominican people will have little political stability in the future unless they have a strong executive branch supported by an armed force.

The Caribbean

7 / Cuba

HOWARD J. WIARDA

HOWARD J. WIARDA, Assistant Professor of Government at the University of Massachusetts, has been the holder of Rockefeller, National Defense Education Association, Fulbright-Hays, and University of Massachusetts grants for Latin American research. Among his publications are more than a dozen articles dealing with the Caribbean; an edited study, Dominican Republic: Election Factbook; *and a forthcoming book on Dominican politics.*

INTRODUCTION: THE SIGNIFICANCE OF CUBA

The significance of Cuba in the present-day world is far greater than the size or the population of the country would indicate. What occurred in this Caribbean nation with the coming to power of the revolutionary regime of Fidel Castro attracted world-wide attention; the success or failure of the Cuban Revolution became one of the most important—and controversial— themes of the 1960s.

Cuba became important because, as the first openly Communist State in the Americas and as the first Latin American ally of the Soviet Union, it was a center of contention between the two "superpowers." Cuba became a pawn in the cold war rivalry between the United States and the Soviet Union, most notably during the 1962 missile crisis, when these two countries "stood eyeball to eyeball" over the issue of Soviet missiles in the island while the world tensely waited to see who would blink first or whether the confrontation would result in a nuclear war. As a pawn, bartered and manipulated by these superpowers, the interests of Cuba herself were often forgotten.

Cuba also became important as a possible model for rapid social, economic, and political development and modernization. In an era when the aspirations and demands of the peoples of the underdeveloped world, undergoing the "revolution of rising expectation," reached new, higher, and more intense proportions, the Cuban experiment was closely watched not only in Latin America but in other developing areas as well. Whether the nations of these areas will be able to achieve rapid change through more or less democratic systems or whether these nations will resort to some kind of dictatorship is a crucial, but by no means fully decided, issue. Cuba embarked on the latter course, and this course is being either copied or closely scrutinized by many other revolutionary elements in the hemisphere and elsewhere.

Furthermore, the Cuban Revolution and the Castro regime increased the complexity of social and political change in Latin America and dimmed the prospects for the growth of democracy in the area. Instead of the two-part conflict between the defenders of the traditional order and the supporters of social and political democracy, a third force, one which favored totalitarian methods and close alliances with the Communist nations, was interjected into the struggle. Democratic development was made more difficult because the extreme-Left *Fidelistas* and Communists frequently worked in concert with the traditional Conservative forces to frustrate the moderate middle way of the Social Democrats. This kind of alliance was most clearly exemplified in Venezuela during the Presidency of Rómulo Betancourt.

The major reasons for Cuba's significance as a key point of contention in the cold war, as a closely-watched attempt to achieve rapid modernization through dictatorial means, and as a force making democratic development in Latin America more difficult are interrelated. The particular kind of dictatorship which emerged in Cuba is, of course, a Communist one, though with a peculiarly Cuban and *Fidelista* orientation. While the government of the Soviet Union thus has a large stake in seeing that the Cuban experiment succeeds, the United States government, with an avowed interest in promoting democratic processes of government, wishes to see that other alternatives are found. What happens in Cuba, therefore, has enormous implications not only for that country, but for the U.S. and the U.S.S.R., for Latin America, and for much of the underdeveloped world.

THE POLITICAL ENVIRONMENT[1]

With 44,000 square miles of territory, about the size of Pennyslvania, Cuba is the largest island in the Caribbean and contains over half of the total land area of the Antillean chain. Cuba is a lush, tropical country which has proved attractive to successive waves of settlers. A wide variety of crops could

---

[1] A good introduction to the political environment or political culture is Wyatt Mac-Gaffey and Clifford R. Barnett, *Cuba: Its People, Its Society, Its Culture* (New Haven, Human Relations Area Files Press, 1962), republished in paperback as *Twentieth Century Cuba: The Background of the Castro Revolution* (Garden City, New York, Anchor Books, 1965).

be grown in the rich soils, though the raising of sugar cane has predominated, and the gentle slopes make much of the land suitable for mechanized agriculture. The country is wealthy in minerals as well as in land since it contains largely untapped deposits of nickel, iron, chromite, manganese, copper, gold, and petroleum. Though tropical, Cuba's climate is generally temperate, and the island has sufficient and well-distributed rainfall and no frost. The Sierra Maestra, which rises to almost eight thousand feet and is in the eastern end of the island, the much lower Trinidad Mountains in the geographic center, and the Sierra de los Organos in the west are exceptions to the generally moderate relief. The island has not without reason been called the "Pearl of the Antilles."

The importance of Cuba's alluring internal geography is matched by its significant geographical location close to mainland North America and at a strategic point overlooking the sea routes to Central America, the Panama Canal, and the entire Caribbean area. This location has meant that Cuba traditionally has been coveted by major powers, and her domestic politics have often been dominated or determined by the interplay of these powers. Cuba's present status as a pawn watched over by the cold war powers is not unique; historically, the island has long been subject to similar kinds of pressures.

Cuba's population of seven million makes the country densely populated when compared to most of the mainland countries but not so densely populated as some of its Antillean neighbors. The early Spanish *conquistadores* found a small number of Indians on the island, and most of these were soon decimated not so much by force of arms as by the diseases the Spaniards carried. Early in the colonial history of the island, the indigenous population had all but disappeared, with the result that the colonialists were forced to import slaves from Africa to do the manual work.

Despite a large influx of Africans, Cuba's population, in contrast to those of its neighbors, has been predominantly white. The census of 1953 classified 73 percent as of European descent, 12 percent as Negro, 14 percent as mestizo, and 1 percent as Oriental. Though the number of those of "pure" European descent is highly exaggerated and though the darker elements have usually been found at lower levels in the social scale, Cuba has not had the same degree of rigid class-caste stratification found in most of the Antillean and Central American countries.

While color has undoubtedly affected the Cuban's place in society, prejudice has traditionally been more social and economic than racial. The Cuban who has wealth and status is accepted in most social circles regardless of his race.

Prior to Castro, Cuba was also, by most indices of modernization, a comparatively highly developed country. It was approximately sixty percent urban, had a literacy rate of seventy-five percent, and had the best transportation system in Latin America. In 1958, Cuba ranked fifth among the Latin American nations in manufacturing, and its industry was also highly developed. Cuba's per capita income during the 1950s placed the country fourth highest of the twenty Latin American Republics. The island was becoming so prosperous, indeed, that Cuban tourists were spending more in the United States than U.S. tourists were spending in Cuba. The picture of Cuba sketched by many early apologists of the Castro regime as a backward, poverty-ridden land is not completely accurate, particularly in the Latin American context.

There were, of course, enormous gaps between rich and poor, but again, this statement must be tempered by looking at Cuba in comparative perspective. While land ownership was concentrated—thirty-six percent of the farmland was contained in the eight hundred largest *fincas*—the degree of concentration was lower than in much of Latin America. A strong labor movement coupled with prosperity meant that urban workers lived better than did their counterparts in most of Latin America. While conditions in the countryside were wretched by U.S. standards, the majority of Cuba's *campesinos* were considerably more prosperous than the subsistence rural peasants of the Dominican Republic, Haiti, and most countries of Central America. A large and strong middle class, though confined almost exclusively to urban areas and with little self-identification, was beginning to develop. In a perspective of comparison, conditions before the revolution in Cuba were not so bad as *Fidelista* sympathizers assert.

To be sure, Cuba had its share of socio-economic problems. The economy had been sluggish for some time. Reliance on sugar resulted in a one-crop economy, which meant that the island's income was dependent on fluctuations in the world market or on the sugar quotas set by large importers. Sugar, by value, made up seventy-five to eighty percent of Cuba's exports, and efforts to diversify agriculture or to increase industrialization were not proceeding fast enough. The island's overwhelming concentration on the production of sugar tied Cuba to a market over which the country had no control, and fluctuations in the price of sugar made and unmade Cuban Governments during the entire period of independence.

Foreign ownership of basic industries also posed a long-standing dilemma for Cuba, but here again care must be taken in the use of statistics. Cuba has been pictured by many observers sympathetic to Castro as an economic colony of the U.S. It is true that the U.S. owned or controlled large portions of the economy, including some thirty-six percent of the all-important sugar industry and many public utilities. About sixty percent of Cuban exports went to the U.S. in the post World War II period (seventy percent before the war), and Cuba's economy was closely tied to that of the U.S. Earlier in the twentieth century this tie took the form of "dollar diplomacy" when American money could and did help determine the rise or fall of Cuban Governments. U.S. interests in Cuba, which in 1958 totaled only six percent of the total Cuban productive activity, was not so much "imperialism," however, as it was the inevitable effect of a wealthy, expanding U.S. economy. Because of the U.S. investments, Cuba could not achieve complete economic independence; but these investments also meant a quickening of economic activity and a rising prosperity which the island would otherwise not have had. In any case, U.S. economic influence and the nationalist resentment which this influence engendered was not, as some have argued, the only reason, or even among the primary reasons, that the Cuban Revolution came under Communist control.[2]

Perhaps the key problem was that Cuba was not a very highly integrated nation. There was little national consensus on the ends and means of political activity. Large gaps separated rich and poor, and deep and irreconcilable divisions existed between the several sectors that made up Cuba's amorphous middle class. These divisions prevented the growth of a unified national consciousness and of a viable political system.

The Cuban Revolution may best be understood by looking at the country in historical perspective. The colonial institutions which Spain brought to Cuba did not differ markedly from these established in other areas of Latin America. The political system was one of absolutism, of a hierarchy of despotisms, from king to captain general to largely autonomous *hacendado,* or landowner. This system provided no training for self-government or democracy. Church and State were closely united, and the Church established its own absolutism, which buttressed and at times rivaled the State's. The economy was one of exploitation and of agrarian feudalism, and the considerable wealth of the island was siphoned off rather than used for the development of Cuba. Intellectual life was devoted primarily to theology; knowledge was believed to be revealed; and the method of thought was the dialectic and syllogistic scholasticism. In all of these aspects the institutions established by the Spaniards differed markedly from those of the North American colonies.

The early *conquistadores* used Cuba as a jumping-off place for expeditions to other areas bordering on the Gulf of Mexico and the Carribbean. With the more lucrative conquests of Mexico and Peru and the corresponding lack of gold and of a large indigenous population in Cuba, the value of the island was not recognized, and it was largely neglected from 1540 to the eighteenth century. The capture of Cuba by the British in 1762 re-emphasized its strategic importance, however, and the decline of other colonies as sugar producers turned the island into a rich possession based on a slave-plantation economy.

The country was the last of Spain's colonies to achieve independence, and the long struggle shaped what C. A. M. Hennessey called Cuba's "politics of frustrated nationalism."[3] The revolution for independence began in 1868, lasted thirty years, and was finally completed by another foreign power, the United States, which promptly established control over the island. Had José Martí, Cuba's great national independence leader and hero, not died in 1895,

---

[2] On the issue of foreign economic interests, see especially the writings of Alberto Arredondo, "Reformismo agrario y colonialismo mental," *Política* [Caracas], No. 35 (June–August 1964), pp. 41–57; and "Cuba era de los Cubanos," *El Caribe* [Santo Domingo], December 4, 1965, p. 15-A.

[3] C. A. M. Hennessey, "Cuba: The Politics of Frustrated Nationalism" in Martin C. Needler (ed.), *Political Systems of Latin America* (Princeton, N.J., D. Van Nostrand, 1964), pp. 183–205.

three years before independence was fully achieved, twentieth-century Cuban politics might have proceeded differently.

The thirty-year struggle for independence; the succeeding era of severe conflict, revolution, and civil war; plus the introduction of highly organized, international gangsterism into Havana made Cuban politics more violent than that of other Latin American countries. This assertion is difficult to document, but it seems clear that the tradition of revolutionary violence, of butchering one's political rivals—the *paredón,* or what some have called the habit of *pistolismo*—developed in Cuba to an extent unknown elsewhere in the Americas. Extreme violence became an important power factor in Cuban politics.[4]

For the first thirty-six years after the ouster of Spain, Cuban Governments were frequently determined by the U.S. The Platt Amendment, appended to the 1901 Constitution as a condition of independence, provided the basis for the U.S. to intervene "for the preservation of Cuban independence, the maintenance of government adequate for the protection of life, prosperity and individual liberty. . . ." This and other clauses were so broad that the U.S. intervened or threatened to intervene on a number of occasions and thereby manipulated and controlled Cuban Governments. Cuban politicians, in turn, used the threat of U.S. intervention as a device for securing votes and gaining political support. The island was not only a political protectorate of the U.S. during the first third of this century but, as investments increased, an area for economic colonization as well. Cuba did not become a sovereign nation until the Platt Amendment, which provided a degree of political stability but which prevented the development of indigenous governmental institutions, was abrogated in 1934 as an important part of the Good Neighbor Policy of President Roosevelt. At about the same time, the portion of the economy controlled by U.S. business interests began to decline.

Important changes were also occurring in internal Cuban politics during this period. Governments had become increasingly more corrupt, and violence more prevalent. Stimulated by World War I and the boom of the 1920s, however, Cuba began to prosper, and with prosperity came new socio-economic and political groups. A middle class began to develop, and the power of the students, of the army, and of organized labor increased. These groups coalesced to overthrow the hated dictatorship of Gerardo Machado in 1933. The resultant Government of the Liberal Ramón Grau San Martín, not recognized by the U.S. government, and beset by other problems, was also forced out by the army, under Fulgencio Batista.

From 1934 to 1940, Batista ruled through a succession of puppet Presidents. The first three years of his regime were harsh and oppressive, but after 1937 his Government was somewhat liberalized; economic and social reforms were promoted; and the liberal and democratic Constitution of 1940 was promulgated. Under the new Constitution Batista himself ran for President in

---

[4] See William S. Stokes, "National and Local Violence in Cuban Politics," *Southwestern Social Science Quarterly,* XXXIV (September 1953), 57–63.

1940 and was overwhelmingly elected. His candidate was defeated by Grau in the 1944 elections, and to everyone's surprise, Batista acquiesced and stepped down from power.

The administrations of Grau, 1944–1948, and of Carlos Prío Socarras, 1948–1952, were the most democratic in Cuban history. As was true of all pre-Castro Governments, corruption was widespread, but during this eight-year period, democratic processes and freedoms were encouraged and upheld. Grau's and Prío's *Aprista*-like Party of the Cuban Revolution (Auténticos) achieved a preponderant position; civil liberties were generally respected; the Communists, who had dominated the labor movement, were placed on the defensive; and social and economic reforms were promoted. Constitutional government came to an end, however, when Batista staged a coup in 1952 and assumed power.

The second Batista regime interrupted and set back the processes of political development and modernization which had been emerging in Cuba. As his Government became more and more dictatorial, the fledging democratic parties and interest associations were either snuffed out or subjected to government control. As opposition to his dictatorship mounted, Batista relied increasingly on more oppressive tactics, which still further alienated his Government from almost all sectors of the population. After it had become clear that even his army was not fully behind him, Batista flew into exile on New Year's Day, 1959.

Until 1959, the behavioral norms of Cuban politics had thus generally centered around personalistic leadership, structures of patronage, and a social system in which class and status were still important. Personalism had frequently led to dictatorship or to strong executives unfettered by constitutional limitations. The upper class had historically played the role of *patrón* to lower-class elements, disdained manual labor, and lived ostentatiously; the growing middle sectors tended to imitate upper-class ways and values; and the Government often was looked upon as the *patrón* of all. A system of values centered on belief in individual destiny, on extreme nationalism, on personal potential for greatness, and on the integrity of the soul helped shape the revolutionary tradition and tended to lead to an emphasis on conspicuous power, charismatic leadership, and sudden change rather than on gradual but steady advancement. This value system, which further hindered the establishment of a viable and stable political system, carried over into the post-1959 period.

Cuba had never really had an opportunity to evolve into a constitutional, democratic system. Plagued by a one-crop economy and subject to the vagaries of the world market; unintegrated, despite its comparatively high ranking on a number of indices of modernization; harassed by foreign powers, of which the U.S. and the Soviet Union were only the most recent; divided by a violent tradition which made deadly enemies out of political foes; and frustrated by unsuccessful attempts to become fully sovereign and politically independent, the environment of Cuban politics was not conducive to liberal, representative democracy. The first democratic institutions and democratic groups in Cuba were only in their infancy when Batista destroyed them. Into this vacuum and this environment stepped Fidel Castro and the Communists.

POLITICAL STRUCTURES AND ROLES

The Cuban Revolution is one of the most misunderstood events in recent Latin American history. The revolution is shrouded in inaccuracies and myths. Among the most prominent of the myths are (1) that Castro was a Communist all along, (2) that prior to the revolution Cuba was a poor, underdeveloped country, (3) that U.S. imperialism caused the revolution, and (4) that the revolution succeeded because of peasants' and workers' support.[5]

Fidel Castro was born of a good family of moderate wealth in Oriente Province in 1926. He attended the University of Havana, studied law, and became active in politics. He was involved in the Cayo Confites plot to overthrow the dictator Rafael Trujillo of the Dominican Republic and was present in Bogotá, Colombia, at the time of the 1948 uprising. Young Castro joined Eduardo Chibás' Cuban People's party (Ortodoxos), a radical and nationalist but non-Communist splinter from the Auténticos.

Castro's promising career in politics was cut short by the re-establishment of the Batista dictatorship in 1952. The following year, in an abortive attempt to overthrow Batista, Castro led a group of inexperienced university students and recent graduates in an attack on the Moncada military barracks at Santiago and was captured. At his trial Castro delivered his now famous but then unpublicized "History Will Absolve Me" speech, which followed the Ortodoxo program of a restoration of the 1940 Constitution and the advocacy of various social and economic reforms. He was soon released from jail and later went to Mexico, where the preparations for the invasion of Cuba were made.

In December 1956, the Castro invasion force landed on Cuba's south

---

[5] Because the Cuban Revolution is so often misunderstood, students should be very skeptical of the books and articles they read concerning this event. The Cuban Revolution spawned numerous Latin American "experts" overnight, many of whom wrote highly emotional books based on the inadequate knowledge picked up during short visits to the country. Among the better books on the revolution are the following: Daniel James, *Cuba: The First Soviet Satellite in The Americas* (New York, Avon Book Division of the Hearst Corp., 1961); and Theodore Draper, *Castro's Revolution: Myths and Realities* (New York, Praeger, 1962). Other volumes, ranging in point of view from Marxist to ultra-conservative, include Leo Huberman and Paul M. Sweezy, *Cuba: Anatomy of a Revolution* (New York, Monthly Review Press, 1961); Jean Paul Sartre, *Sartre on Cuba* (New York, Ballantine Books, 1961); C. Wright Mills, *Listen Yankee* (New York, Ballantine Books, 1960); Warren Miller, *Ninety Miles From Home* (New York, Crest Books, 1961); Maurice Zeitlin and Robert Scheer, *Cuba: Tragedy in Our Hemisphere* (New York, Grove Press, 1963); Victor Franco, *The Morning After* (New York, Praeger, 1963); William Appleman Williams, *The U.S., Cuba, and Castro* (New York, Monthly Review Press, 1962); Herbert L. Matthews, *The Cuban Story* (New York, G. Braziller, 1961); Ruby Hart Phillips, *The Cuban Dilemma* (New York, I. Obolensky, 1961); Boris Goldensberg, *The Cuban Revolution and Latin America* (New York, Praeger, 1965); Earl E. T. Smith, *The Fourth Floor: An Account of the Castro Communist Revolution* (New York, Random House, 1962); and Fulgencio Batista, *Cuba Betrayed* (New York, Vantage Press, 1962).

coast. Of the eighty-six original invaders, only twelve managed to reach the Sierra Maestra of Oriente Province, where they began a guerrilla campaign. Batista was forced to launch a full-scale assault against the guerrillas and claimed to have wiped them out, but when it was revealed that Castro and his group had survived, the magnetic leader captured the imagination of much of the world and became an international hero. Other resistance groups emerged in the Escambray Mountains and among the students in Havana. Using increased terror, Batista only succeeded in arousing the hostility of ever wider sectors of the population and left the country on January 1, 1959. Batista was not forced out; he simply abdicated. Handed this unexpectedly easy victory, Castro and his followers triumphantly moved on Havana and took control. At this time he had the sympathy of almost all sectors of the population—not just the peasants and workers.

Whether Castro was a Communist from his student days cannot be ascertained with finality. It is most likely that he was not, despite his own statement that he had always been a Marxist-Leninist. Castro was more a *Fidelista* than anything else—an extremely ambitious *caudillo* who sought personal power no matter what the ideology, who at all costs wanted to be the *"líder máximo,"* and whose ambition the Communists were able to exploit. Indeed, the regular, long-time Communist leaders in Cuba had co-operated with Batista and condemned Castro and his followers as *petit-bourgeois* reformers, only working out a mutually beneficial arrangement when it became clear that the Batista regime would not last much longer.

Castro emerges as one who betrayed the democratic and reformist aims of many of those who fought for the revolution. Fidel provided charismatic leadership; the members of the old Communist apparatus, one of the strongest in the hemisphere, provided the needed ideology and organization. The two combined into a revolutionary dictatorship—with Castro at least nominal head—which became aligned with the Communist nations. This alliance took place independently of U.S. activities in and policies toward Cuba.

The type of regime which Castro and the Communists established increasingly came to resemble the model of the totalitarian state. The controls which the regime exercised over all aspects of education, communications, society, the economy, and religion, as well as over the Government and politics, were absolute. Yet totalitarianism under Castro and the Communists was of a distinctively Cuban type; the Cuban variant of the totalitarian state was conditioned by the environment in which it was formed and exhibited many continuities with the nation's past.

Political Norms and Institutions

Cuban politics had traditionally been based more on personalities than on abstract issues or on impersonal groups. Followers were known as *Zayistas,* *Machadistas,* or *Batistianos,* rather than as Liberals, Conservatives, or Autén-ticos. The leader was usually looked upon as a great national *patrón,* and the authority of the *caudillo* most often rested upon a combination of personal power and charisma. Personalism rather than programs, principles, or ideology was the dominant style of Cuban political leadership.

Castro fit this pattern. A large and forceful man with a number of charismatic qualities, he became the *caudillo* of the revolution. Early rivals in his movement, such as Camilo Cienfuegos, Hubert Matos, Manuel Urrutia, and Pedro Díaz Lanz, were either killed, purged, or forced out by the Castro regime with the result that for a time Fidel himself became the only law in the country. Castro is especially adept at exploiting his personal appeal, and his abilities as a leader help explain the longevity of his rule.

Ever since 1959, however, an uneasy relationship has existed between the dominant *Fidelistas* and the Communist leadership of the revolution. The remnants of Castro's 26th of July Movement (named for the anniversary of the 1953 assault on the Moncada barracks) and the more orthodox, old-time Communists, headed by Blas Roca, Lázaro Peña, Carlos Rafael Rodríguez, and Aníbal Escalante, differ in age, ideology, and revolutionary fervor. The alliance between the *Fidelista* and the Communist leaders has not always been peaceful, as illustrated by Escalante's fall from favor; though by sharing some of the spoils of power, the *Fidelistas* and the Communists have prevented their breach from becoming an open divorce. Castro has apparently been able to maintain his own personal authority above these conflicts.

The ideology of the revolution is in many ways more uncertain than its leadership. Ideologies, like party platforms, have traditionally been subordinated to personalities in Cuban politics. This subordination is perhaps best expressed by the Cuban who, when asked to explain Castro's ideology, replied simply, *"Fidelismo es Fidel y Fidel es Fidelista."*

The traditional linking of ideology and personality and the continuation of this linkage in the present Cuban context should not lead one to ignore what is new in this relationship. Castro is not merely a traditional *caudillo* but a "modern" *caudillo* who must justify his actions and programs with an ideology. His ideology has not been constant over a long period of time but has evolved from radicalism, nationalism, and reformism in the Ortodoxo tradition to "humanism" to self-proclaimed Marxism-Leninism. All of these ideas, however, carry a special *Fidelista* flavor. As Theodore Draper concludes, "Castroism represents a particular case of cross-fertilization, as yet difficult to assess with finality, of a Latin American revolutionary tradition and the European Communist tradition."[6]

Similar patterns emerged in the political-party realm. The demise of Castro's 26th of July Movement and the suppression of other political groups soon after the revolution meant that the Communist Partido Socialista Popular was the only political party functioning in the country. The PSP later changed its name to the Cuban Communist party, but the same balance which existed between the orthodox Marxists and the neo-Marxist *Fidelistas* in other

---

[6] *Castroism: Theory and Practice* (New York, Frederick A. Praeger, 1965), p. 55.

areas was also maintained in the PCC. The ideology, leadership, and programs of the party also reflected this blend.

With the exception of the period of Auténtico rule, 1944–1952, political parties had not previously played a significant role in Cuban politics. At the turn of the century, four groups, the Nationalists, the Republicans, the Democratic Union and the Autonomists, plus a large number of smaller factions, competed for power. The Moderates soon replaced the Nationalists, and the Republican became the Liberals, while the Moderates again regrouped, this time as the Conservatives. None of these parties was well organized or had clear-cut ideologies but represented shifting coalitions of diverse, usually personalistic, interests.

The first party with a mass base and a more than temporary program was the Auténticos. The Auténticos were organized by Grau San Martín in the interim between his first short-lived rule during 1933–1934 and his election to the Presidency in 1944. Grau built up a party apparatus, and the Auténticos' organization coupled with its Liberal reform program was sufficient to carry Prío Socarras to the Presidency in 1948. Chibás' Ortodoxos also emerged as a strong party during this period. During Batista's rule most opposition leaders were forced into exile, and the emerging party system ceased to function.

After the assumption of power by Castro and his followers, the several political organizations which backed his regime were welded together into a single official party. The Cuban Communist party, which replaced the PSP, took on increased importance as a means by which the regime extended its control into all aspects of Cuban life. Though the membership of the party was roughly only forty thousand, efforts were made to build up a larger organization so that every unit, whether factory, farm, school, army, or government agency, would have its own cell.

The party organized a large number of branch associations, which further added to its control. These included the Rebel Pioneers, the Federation of Cuban Women, and the Union of Communist Youth. These associations represented an attempt to indoctrinate and mobilize sectors of the population which were not already organized under the regime's surveillance. Party control was also extended to include the administration and supervision of provincial and local authorities.

Though the party appeared to be a monolithic organization, it was made up of diverse interests within the state apparatus. Castro himself headed the Political Bureau and the Secretariat and appointed the members of the Central Committee. Though in all three governing bodies an attempt was made to balance the Communist old guard with the *Fidelista* new guard, the party was overwhelmingly dominated by those personally loyal to Castro himself. Many of those occupying important party posts could not be identified as belonging to either the old or the new guard but were rather bureaucrats who rose to prominence by faithfully serving the regime.

In terms of governmental institutions, the Cuban Revolution did represent a fairly sharp break with the past. Unlike many of the Latin American countries, Cuba has not had a plethora of Constitutions. The Constitution of 1901, modeled after that of the U.S., provided for three branches of government, but the nature of personalistic authority made the Presidency preponderant, and in this as well as in other ways, the Constitution did not reflect the realities of Cuban politics.

Nor did the Constitution of 1940 accurately mirror actual Cuban political processes. In a country where strong, personalistic, and patriarchal rule was a social norm, this Constitution attempted to limit presidential power by providing for a semi-parliamentary system. But parliamentary checks did not effectively control Batista, Grau, or Prío. Like many modern Constitutions, the Cuban basic law also contained a large number of articles dealing with social welfare and the rights of labor, but many of those articles were not fully implemented; the Constitution remained one of the world's most advanced—on paper but not in practice. It is significant that one of the most important items in Castro's program, prior to taking power, was a promise to return to the Constitution of 1940.

The Castro regime did not restore the 1940 Constitution, which the preceding Batista dictatorship had also largely ignored, but relied instead on fitting institutional arrangements to existing circumstances. Under the Fundamental Law of February 7, 1959, the Council of Ministers took over the legislative and executive functions, and members of the Rebel Army assumed governmental posts at the national, provincial, and local levels. Decision-making authority by 1960 came to be vested in the Central Planning Council, in which Castro, his brother Raúl, and the Argentine revolutionary Ernesto "Che" Guevara were the most important members.

The revolution's leaders instigated major changes in other institutions as well. Much of the judicial system was taken over by the revolutionaries, who were more concerned with establishing political control than in preserving legality. In trials in which the verdicts were often determined by popular clamor, revolutionary tribunals purged the administration and the armed forces of Batista supporters. The police were given many of the legal powers formerly reserved for the courts, while the entire judicial system was subordinated to political direction. The office of the President was retained, but neither Manuel Urrutia, who was forced to resign because of his attacks on Communist infiltration, nor Oswaldo Dorticós, who proved more compliant, was permitted to exercise much more than ceremonial powers as "Chiefs of State." José Miró Cardona, the first Prime Minister and a non-Communist Batista foe, also fell out with the regime early in 1959; the office of Prime Minister was then filled by Castro himself.

New institutions were set up to help administer the expanding state functions. The Ministries of Social Welfare, Study of Revolutionary Laws, Economy, and Recovery of Misappropriated Properties were added. The National Institute of Agrarian Reform, which controlled over half of all land and whose functions were much broader than its name would indicate, became one of the most powerful organizations in the new Government, but the power of the Institute was later curtailed. The Department of Industrialization, the Institute for Friendship among Peoples, and the Institute of Savings and Housing were among the important administrative agencies created by the regime. All these institutions further contributed to increased centralization, to a more directed and planned economy, and to tighter political control.

Political Groups

During the 1930s, 1940s, and early 1950s, Cuba had begun to develop into a plural society, a society in which a multiplicity of groups vied for political power. New social aggregates—primarily labor and the middle sectors—and increasingly more important associations of interest, spawned by economic development and industrialization and nurtured by the climate of freedom which existed under Grau and Prío, began to convert Cuba into a competitive system. The development toward a more democratic society, however, which had been interrupted by the Batista dictatorship, was crushed by Castro and the Communists. No group or institution was permitted to remain independent of the regime; all were subordinated to central control and direction.

The Roman Catholic Church was never as strong a force in Cuban politics as in most other Latin American countries. The Church had been discredited in the nineteenth century for opposing Cuba's independence from Spain, and in the 1901 Constitution, Church and State were separated. The Church was predominantly urban, made little effort to work in rural areas, and had little direct influence over the popular classes. Before the revolution, Cuba was officially 85 percent Catholic, but only about 10 percent of the population was considered to be actively practicing their religion. Protestantism was also stronger in Cuba than in other Latin American countries, and African cults, free masonry, secularism, and indifference were common. Only 700 priests (1 for each 10,000 inhabitants—among the lowest ratios in the hemisphere) served some 200 parishes. The Cuban Church was further alienated from the population by the fact that Spanish-born clergy outnumbered the native-born clergy in proportions of about four or five to one; few Cubans went into the priesthood, with the result that the clergy was considered to be anti-nationalistic.

Following the revolution, Castro used the foreign domination of the Church as a rationalization for expelling many priests. A large number of priests had been initially sympathetic to the revolution's aims, but these clerics were also militantly anti-Communist and soon began to speak out against the direction the revolution was taking. When some priests were discovered participating in the April 1961 Bay of Pigs invasion, a mass expulsion of clerics took place, so that in 1965 only a hundred priests were left to man the two hundred parishes. A succession of laws further restricted the Church's power in such areas as education, social work, public utterances, and lay groups. Though no official sanctions were enacted to limit church-going and though the churches remained open and worship was freely allowed, attendance marked one as "different" and raised the question of one's revolutionary loyalties. These unofficial sanctions served to reduce the influence of the Church still more.[7]

The armed forces were not a decisive factor in Cuban politics until the 1930s. The senior ranks especially were discredited by graft and lack of professionalism. The low regard in which the military was held paved the way for the 1933 revolt of the ambitious and more professionalized younger officers, of whom Batista, a sergeant, was the most prominent. Thereafter, the armed forces became increasingly more significant in politics, and it was by military might that Batista again took over power in 1952. The armed forces, further strengthened by U.S. military assistance, served the Batista dictatorship as an instrument of terror and oppression and became steadily more discredited in the eyes of major sections of the population. U.S. aid to Batista was eventually cut off, but the military remained alienated from most of the Cuban people. Unable to wipe out the Castro guerrillas in the early stages of the revolution and unwilling to precipitate a major civil war as the opposition to the dictatorship grew, the armed forces stood by while Batista fled the country and the revolutionaries took over.

One of the first acts of the Castro regime was to purge the armed forces of pro-Batista elements. In the Cuban tradition of the *paredón,* many officers were executed. (It is interesting that among military officers in other Latin American countries, communism is most frequently opposed not as an inimical ideological or economic system but, with the Cuban example clearly in mind, as a system in which the armed forces will be destroyed and its officers killed.) Taking over many governmental posts in the new regime, officers of the Rebel Army supervised political indoctrination and manned the mushrooming administration which economic centralization and planning necessitated.

The regular armed forces were replaced by a militia formed later in 1959. In the face of hostility from abroad, particularly the threat of a United States-backed invasion by Cuban exiles (which was precisely what took place in the Bay of Pigs episode), the militia increased in numbers until it was an estimated 250,000 strong and was given the most modern arms. The Revolutionary Armed Forces (F.A.R.) was created in 1963 to replace the militia, and Cuba's military might contined to grow until it was, with the exception of the U.S. forces, the largest, best equipped, and most powerful in the Caribbean-Central American area.

The armed forces were subjected to the same kind of political indoctrination as other sectors of the population. Cells were organized as a means of educating the predominantly lower-class F.A.R. members in the revolution

---

[7] A good short summary of the role of the Church before and after the revolution is the study prepared by Helen L. Clagett for the Committee on the Judiciary, United States Senate, *The Church and State under Communism: Cuba* (Washington, Government Printing Office, 1965).

and of giving them a stake in politics. The principle of democratic centralism meant that officers were responsible to superiors not only in military matters but for their political views as well. It is likely that, despite the elaborate indoctrination and controls, the relations between the Communist party and the armed forces, as in other Communist countries, will remain an uneasy alliance with continuing problems and tension.

Though not strictly military, the Committee for Revolutionary Defense (C.D.R.) should be mentioned in this context because the committee fulfilled some para-military functions. The C.D.R. supervised some 100,000 "vigilante committees," organized block by block, whose purpose was to report dissenters and fifth columnists and maintain the purity of the revolution. The committees reportedly had over 2,000,000 members, or about 30 percent of the population, and worked closely with armed forces units, especially with the Department of Investigations of the Rebel Army, in order to maintain the regime's tight grip. Created during the period prior to the Bay of Pigs episode, when the underground was active and the threat of invasion imminent, the C.D.R. was a mass organization which reached into nearly every home to maintain vigilance and to denounce counterrevolutionaries.

The bureaucracy has traditionally been a significant force in Cuban politics because of the number and nature of those employed. Next to sugar, the Government was the biggest "industry" and the biggest employer, particularly of educated persons, in the country. Cuba was the first Latin American nation to introduce a merit system in the civil service, but the system was frequently evaded; patronage was the accepted way of filling the many Government posts. Government employment was looked upon as a form of social assistance and as a means of rewarding friends and relatives, with the result that the bureaucracy was deeply involved in the political struggle. Only the first stirrings of a more "modern" and more "rational" government service were beginning to be felt in the 1940s and early 1950s.

The vast switchover from a capitalist to a socialist system called for basic changes in the structure and function of the government service. New agencies and departments were created to administer the planned and centralized economy and the social services, primarily education and health. The reorganization led to disorder and to a large number of major and minor errors, chiefly the result of some disastrous experimentation. The country's resources were often managed in unsuccessful and incoherent ways; as Castro himself admitted, incompetence, excessive paper-shuffling, feather-bedding—traits associated with previous Governments—were carried into the revolutionary era. In the Cuban tradition, many public servants continued to be chosen for their personal loyalty and their political orientation and not necessarily for their administrative skills and competence. Many of the same behavioral norms and practices characterized administration at the provincial and local levels, a fact which caused the party to centralize bureaucratic decision-making still further.

A large number of employer and professional associations had also been organized prior to Castro's assumption of power. Among the more important interest organizations of the business and landowning elite were the National Association of Cuban Sugar Mill Owners, the Association of Cuban Sugar Cane Planters, the Association of Cuban Bankers, and the Employer's Confederation of Cuba. The professionals, whose entry into their respective professions required their compulsory registration in an official association, were organized in the National Bar Association, the Association of Architects, the Association of Civil Engineers, the National Association of Pharmacists, and so forth. These associations served as effective means by which the growing middle sectors, as well as elite groups, could make their interests felt in decision-making.

These same groups were among the first to be destroyed after Castro took power. Employer associations had practically disappeared by the middle of 1960, and the old professional organizations were obliterated shortly thereafter. The professional associations were transformed into voluntary organizations, and later a campaign was begun to place the professionals on a par with unskilled labor. The professionals were treated as salaried workers and had to affiliate with the union section of their occupation; thus, doctors, for example, had to belong to the National Union for Workers of Medicine. The independent political strength of both the business and landholding upper-middle-class and upper-class elements as well as the middle-sector professionals was destroyed at the same time that their property was expropriated. It is not surprising that these elements, many of whom had not been *Batistianos*—as they are often portrayed—but who were initially sympathetic to the revolution, were among the first to be disillusioned, to go into exile, and to become bitterly outspoken Castro foes.

Like the business, landowning, and professional sectors, the Cuban labor movement, one of the oldest and best organized in Latin America, was also a comparatively strong political force, second in importance only to the army. The major federations were the sugar and tobacco workers, who made up the majority of the powerful Confederation of Cuban Workers (C.T.C.). Economic development and industrialization spurred the growth of the unions, which tended to concentrate more on political action than on collective bargaining. The power of labor as a political force was first clearly demonstrated in 1933, when a general strike helped overthrow the Machado dictatorship; by the 1940s most Cuban workers were organized, and their leaders played an important role in politics. Much of the early labor movement, including the dominant C.T.C., was under the direction of the well organized Communists, but during the administrations of Grau and Prío, control was wrested from the Communists, and the labor movement came under the leadership of the more democratic forces. Batista's overthrow of the Auténtico Government in 1952 provided the Communists with a new opportunity to gain control. In return for a free hand in the labor movement, they supported Batista.

Prior to 1959, Cuban labor legislation was among the most advanced of all the Latin American nations. Though some of the social and economic welfare provisions existed only on paper, the strength of the Cuban labor movement meant that much of the legislation was applied in practice since after 1933 Governments generally found it politically expedient to side with the workers in disputes with employers. Most of labor's legal rights and privileges, however, were taken away after Castro and the Communists had consolidated their hold, and the unions' independent political strength was destroyed as well. The Government became the arbiter of salaries, hours, prices, and so on, and left little room for bargaining. Austerity measures were enacted, wages were frozen and in some cases reduced, strikes were prohibited, and salary deductions increased. With eighty percent of the labor force working for the State, it became, for all practical purposes, the only employer. Further, it imposed a system of "voluntary" labor which by 1961 had regimented 2 million of the 2.4 million workers into the Government-controlled C.T.C. Revolucionaria. Labor was politically and economically subservient to the party, and the trade union movement was converted into an appendage of the regime.[8]

The Cuban students were another important sector in the emerging pluralist society which had begun to develop in the 1930s and 1940s. The hemispheric university reform movement led the students to demand and receive increased power in university decisions and autonomy for the university itself. The student federation was in the forefront of the struggle against dictatorship, contributed significantly to the downfall of Machado, and constituted much of the urban resistance to Batista. The majority of the student activists were not Communists but intensely nationalistic and desirous of reform.

After Castro and his followers had completed their triumphal march from Oriente to Havana, one of their first moves was to demand that the students surrender their arms. After that time, the student associations were either crushed or converted into branch organizations of the State. Successive purges of faculty and students rid the schools of those who showed a lack of enthusiasm for the revolution. While the children of peasants and workers received more opportunities for higher education, these were not exempt from the purges either; and the students, who before were one of the most important groups in Cuban politics, became unable to strongly voice their discontent.

The rural peasantry had never been fully integrated into Cuba's social, political, and economic life; economic development, which brought benefits to urban labor and increased the size and strength of the middle class, largely passed the *campesinos* by. They were promised benefits by the Castro regime in the areas of housing, social welfare, working conditions, and, most importantly, national decision-making. While new schools, agricultural projects, housing and social centers, more diversified crops, and fuller employment

---

[8] See Cuban Economic Research Project, University of Miami, *Labor Conditions in Communist Cuba* (Miami, University of Miami Press, 1963).

increased, at least through 1961, the living standards of the rural peasants, the promise of increased political importance was not honored. The *campesinos* were slightly better off economically and socially, but they remained largely unintegrated as a national political force, and their opinions and interests were not often consulted in governmental policies that affected them most closely.

The well-developed communications system was long of major importance in Cuban politics. Most of the media was concentrated in Havana, where major decisions were made, but other areas of the country were comparatively well-blanketed also. The literacy rate was relatively high, and in 1956 Cuba ranked third among the twenty Latin American countries in per capita newspaper circulation. The number of radio stations and receivers was the highest per capita in all of Latin America, and Cuba was eighth highest in the world in terms of per capita television sets. Every major party and the larger interest associations printed their own newspapers and had their own radio programs. As Hennessey states, "It is hard to imagine the Ortodoxos without Chibás' weekly radio talk, or Castro without his mammoth television appearances."

Following the revolution, the tradition of free and independent—and often vituperative—criticism through the widespread communications media was curtailed. *Granma* (named after the boat which carried Castro and his men to Cuba in 1956) replaced *Hoy* and *Revolución* as the official organ of the Communist party and became Cuba's principal newspaper. The entire Cuban press was forced to follow the official party line while news broadcasts consisted of handouts from the Government's news agency, Prensa Latina. Newspapers, radio, and television all came under the strict supervision of the Government and no longer played an independent crusading role in the nation's politics.

In the period prior to the revolution then, a pluralist political system had been developing in the country. Cuba was no longer a traditional, two-class, semifeudal society but a complex nation in which the increasingly differentiated sectors and groups became more conscious of their diverse interests and organized themselves to promote their positions. A wide variety of interest organizations—middle-sector professional and business associations, labor, the students, the communications media, as well as the Church, the business and land owning elite, and the armed forces—competed for political power. Some groups, such as the rural peasantry, were not well represented, while others, such as the political parties, had only enjoyed a short-lived existence. Though the various groups and sectors were not at all well integrated, the beginnings of a modern and developed political system were present.

This development was arrested by the Castro-Communist Government. While the traditionally forgotten sector, the peasantry, received some social and economic benefits, it did not gain much political strength, and the other political groups were either destroyed or brought under the control of the regime. Though some tensions remained between different groups and factions in the Revolutionary Government, Cuba progressively took on the nature of a monolithic totalitarian dictatorship.

PUBLIC POLICY: PROCESSES OF FUNCTION
AND DYSFUNCTION

Castro policies

The policies and decisions undertaken by the Castro regime are unique among the Latin American nations in the two areas of international affairs and domestic socio-economic policy. In international affairs Cuba became the first country in the hemisphere to establish strong and binding political and economic ties with the Soviet Union, China, and other Communist countries. In domestic affairs Cuba, more than any other Latin American country, employed totalitarian techniques to effect fundamental changes in her socio-economic structure. In all the speculation concerning Cuba's role in global politics, the internal revolution has been neglected. Both these aspects of policy deserve attention.

Foreign Policy

Following the abrogation of the Platt Amendment in 1934, overt U.S. intervention in Cuban affairs did not occur as it had in the past. Nevertheless, the U.S. continued to play a major role in the economic and political affairs of Cuba. Because of the U.S. influence, Cuba was equally as affected by non-intervention as by intervention—a fact underscored by Ambassador Earl E. T. Smith's remark that "The United States, until the advent of Castro, was so overwhelmingly influential in Cuba that . . . the American ambassador was the second most important man in Cuba; sometimes even more important than the President."[9] U.S. ascendancy contributed to Cuba's long tradition of frustrated nationalism.

U.S. policy toward Cuba was motivated by two major concerns: the preservation of internal stability and the prevention of political or military dominance of the country by another power. During World War II, the U.S. therefore sought to curb German activities in Cuba. After the war, the U.S. became more concerned with averting the spread of Communist influence to the island. Post-war relations between the two countries were further complicated by the decreasing yet still extensive influence which U.S. concerns exerted over the Cuban economy.

Because the U.S. eventually stopped supporting Batista, he accused the U.S. of undermining his Government. At the same time the Castro forces berated the U.S. for its long support of the dictatorship. Grounds thus existed for future differences, but initially it appeared that cordial relations could be maintained between the U.S. and the new revolutionary regime. The summary trial of *Batistianos,* Castro's unhappy trip to the U.S., the nationalization of U.S. properties, the harboring of anti-Castro exiles in the U.S., the heightened anti-Americanism on the island, the U.S. cancellation of the Cuban sugar quota, and the increasing Communist influence in the Cuban Government—all contributed to the cooling and, eventually, the breaking of relations

---

[9] Quoted in MacGaffey and Barnett, p. 375 (paperback).

between the two countries. The hostility reached its high point in 1961 when an attempt supported by the U.S. to overthrow Castro failed on the beaches at the Bay of Pigs.

After 1961, relations between Washington and Havana changed slightly. The U.S. Government's policy was to treat Cuba as an outlaw in the hemispheric system, to isolate her, and to maintain a strict economic embargo in the hope of strangling the Cuban economy. Cuba continued to look on the U.S. as an imperialist power dedicated to overthrowing the Castro regime. Neither country publicly expressed much interest in working for a relaxation of the tensions between them.

The estrangement between the U.S. and Cuba coincided with the closer alignment between Cuba and the Communist nations. Trade missions and cultural exchanges took place in an ever-increasing number. Technicians and machinery now came from the Communist nations, while trade between Cuba and the Eastern European countries, the Soviet Union, and China replaced the business which had formerly been transacted with the U.S. Cuba's relations with the American nations were severed, and her contracts with the Communist States were correspondingly strengthened.

Rather than being closely bound to the U.S., as had been the case in the past, Cuba under Castro became a satellite of the Soviet Union and was dependent on Moscow for her day-to-day existence. Soviet technicians, money, machinery, arms, trade, and moral support buttressed the Castro regime against collapse. The Soviet Union, the largest producer of sugar in the world, took the place of the U.S. as the subsidizer of the Cuban sugar economy. Cuba's status as a satellite of the Soviet Union was best demonstrated in the missile crisis of 1962, when decisions were made in Washington and Moscow, and Havana's voice was completely ignored. Though Cuba wished to remain politically independent, her economic dependence on the Soviet Union meant that many decisions, both political and economic, were made by the Russians.

Cuba was not only a bone of contention in the cold war conflict between the U.S. and Soviet Union; the country was also caught in the middle of the Sino-Soviet conflict. Because the Cuban leadership saw some rough parallels between China's and Cuba's rural-based revolutions and because the Chinese insistence on fomenting armed uprisings throughout Latin America matched the *Fidelista* vision of leading revolutions in the entire hemisphere, Peking gained a moral edge in the conflict. On the other hand, Cuba's economic and defense needs tied her closely to the Soviet Union. The conflict gave rise to the aphorism that Castro's heart was in China but his pocketbook was in Moscow and produced a series of sharp strains between the three countries. The Soviet Union, however, managed to maintain more influence in Cuban affairs than did China.

The Sino-Soviet differences were also reflected in Cuba's dealings with other Latin American countries. Following China's lead, Cuba attempted to serve as the center for hemispheric revolution and provided arms, propaganda materials, and other equipment to similarly-oriented guerrilla movements. Beards and green fatigues were imitated, and the success of the Cuban Revolution served as an inspiration to those who wanted a violent overthrow of the *status quo* in other countries. As Cuba became more closely tied to the Soviet Union economically, however, the island also tended to follow a less aggressive foreign policy. Further, as the revolution matured and as the nature of the dictatorship and its economic failures were exposed, Cuba became less of an inspiration for other Latin American revolutionaries.

As *Fidelismo* lost much of its attractiveness in Latin America, Cuba's dealings with the developing countries of Asia and Africa increased. Cuba attempted to become the leader of those nations opposed to imperialism and colonialism and to serve as an example of successful revolutionary overthrow of corrupt and oppressive dictatorship. To that end, Cuba began a limited, small-scale program aimed at training and equipping guerrilla leaders from other continents, primarily from Africa. The Afro-Asian-Latin American solidarity conference of 1966, at which eighty-two countries were represented, indicated that Cuba had achieved some success as a leader of revolutionary struggles. Less successful, however, was Cuba's attempt to serve as a model for socio-economic development.

Domestic Policy

The Cuban Revolution attracted world-wide attention not only because it provided an example of a revolution against a prior dictatorship or because of the revolutionary changes in Cuba's international policies but also because of its revolutionary domestic policy. The Cuban Revolution signified an attempt to completely restructure the social and economic nature of the entire society. The Castro Government set out to achieve an ambitious educational program aimed at not only preparing the future labor force but also retraining the present one. Moreover, the regime was determined to instigate a more rapid rate of economic and industrial development and a more equalitarian society by employing the techniques of state direction of the economy, a stress on communal rather than private incentives, detailed planning covering every sector, and strict centralized control. It is upon the success of Cuba's socio-economic revolution that her attractiveness to the underdeveloped nations will rest.[10]

Agrarian reform was the key program for the improvement of the rural sector. The Agrarian Reform Law's basic purpose was to transform agriculture as a means of accelerating the economic development of Cuba and the well-being of her rural workers. Private lands were expropriated, and while some of these lands were distributed to peasants, most of it remained in the

---

[10] The best book on this topic is Dudley Seers and others, *Cuba: The Economic and Social Revolution* (Chapel Hill, University of North Carolina Press, 1964). The usefulness of this volume is limited, however, by the fact that the research and writing were completed in 1962, when Cuba's economic and social reforms were still largely in the planning stage and before the mistakes in these plans became fully apparent.

hands of the State, which reorganized the rural economy along Communist lines. The National Institute of Agrarian Reform (I.N.R.A.) established co-operatives, ran the state farms, mobilized the peasantry into government-run associations, attempted to raise farm productivity, and generally supervised all aspects of agriculture. Along with increased productivity, the regime also sought to diversify agriculture and thus break the hold which sugar had traditionally held over the economy. Massive efforts were made to cultivate new crops, such as cotton and soybeans, as well as to increase the output of the more traditional crops like rice, tobacco, henequen, and potatoes.

The full impact of the enormous changes made by the Castro regime in the agricultural realm will probably require more time before a reasonable and comprehensive assessment can be made. However, it does seem clear that social mobility, standards of living, and opportunities for betterment were somewhat higher for the Cuban peasant than they had been before the revolution. On the other hand, the *campesinos* were not fully represented in national decision-making on questions dealing with their daily existence. Total farm output fell initially below the pre-Castro level, and agricultural productivity sharply declined. Though some of the decline can be attributed to natural causes, such as the lack of rainfall in 1961, the inadequacy of agricultural planning, the neglect of a part of the private sector, and the inefficient operation of the state farms were primarily responsible. The Government also underestimated the difficulties of a rapid change from a one-crop economy to more diversified production, and the numerous problems which arose forced a return to an emphasis on extensive cultivation of sugar cane. The I.N.R.A. did succeed in expanding cultivated areas and in promoting a more stable level of rural employment, but the Institute's efforts to stimulate the production of crops which Cuba had previously had to import were unsuccessful. Cuba's attempts to reform agriculture thus brought decidedly mixed results.

Cuba also chose to try to accelerate industrialization through the device of a planned, centrally-directed economy. The first stage of the plan called for an increase in the output of light industries producing consumer goods, while the second stage would have emphasized heavy industries. The Government decreed the nationalization of public services, foreign companies, and later, the principal Cuban concerns. The Banco Nacional took control of foreign exchange. With the help of technicians and financial aid from the Communist countries, mines were to be developed to exploit Cuba's largely untapped resources and provide raw materials for the proposed new industries. Industrial plants for the processing of the by-products of sugar and for the manufacture of other items were also to be established.

The tensions and dysfunctions brought on by the attempt to industrialize were greater than those resulting from changes in the agricultural sphere. Shortages of technicians, managers, resources, and skilled labor; disastrous planning mistakes; and mechanical breakdowns led to a self-confessed decline in production. The change from a capitalist to a socialist system and the reorientation of trade from West to East resulted in dislocations and near chaos; in shortages which led to the rationing of food, clothing, and other articles; in the shelving of ambitious road-building and housing plans; in the deterioration of capital equipment such as trucks, generators, and pumps; and in the postponing of the promises of improved social welfare and living conditions. The failures were so great that in 1963 Cuba abandoned its ambitious plans to not only diversify agriculture but also rapidly industrialize the economy. The Soviet Union agreed to buy the island's sugar until 1970, and Cuba reverted again to a concentration on sugar production.

The most successful of the socio-economic reforms of the Castro regime was in the field of education. The revolutionary Government treated education as the cornerstone for a complete reconstruction of society and attempted to expand the human resources available for development. The education program was aimed at not only erasing Cuba's illiteracy rate of twenty percent but also raising the technical skills of workers, technicians, and administrators and creating an entirely new system of goals, values, and ideology. Adult education was widely promoted; in 1961, the "year of education," students fanned out into the countryside to teach the illiterates, and all educational facilities were expanded.

Even the relatively successful education programs encountered difficulties, however. The drive to wipe out illiteracy in 1961 was not adequately followed up, which made the regime's claim to have cut the illiteracy rate to four percent appear exaggerated. The exile of upper-class and middle-class elements led to a shortage of teachers, and in general educational quantity at all levels was achieved at the price of quality. Constant political indoctrination provided some previously unaware and politically uninvolved elements a stake in the revolution, but the Marxist-Leninist-*Fidelista* ideology, to which teaching, intellectual life, and all education had to conform, resulted in a stifling dogmatism.

Patterns of Allegiance and Alienation

The Cuban Revolution was clearly not equally popular with all sectors of the population; the increasing drift toward communism domestically and toward ever-stronger ties with the Communist nations internationally brought to the regime the allegiance of certain groups and the alienation of others.

The first to flee the island were those who had been most intimately associated with "The Tyranny," as the Batista dictatorship came to be called. These included the fallen dictator's aides, some high-ranking government officials, military cohorts, Batista family members, and close friends. Compared to the later large-scale exodus of those who had initially thought they would be able to make their peace with the incoming Castro Government, this first group of exiles was numerically of relative insignificance.

Cuban organizations and movements had traditionally been subject to deep divisions and severe splintering, and the revolution was no exception to this tradition. Tensions among the revolutionaries developed almost immediately after Castro's taking power early in 1959. The initial opposition to his now-established Government came from those who had before given him their strongest support. Many of the moderates in the 26th of July Movement and in other groups sympathetic to the revolution became alarmed at the summary trial of the remaining *Batistianos,* at the failure to restore civil liberties and the Constitution of 1940, at the unwillingness of the regime to call elections, and at the increasing influence of the Communists. Castro's more radical proposals and his demagogic appeals further alienated these early supporters, most of whom subsequently resigned or were dismissed from their government posts and went into exile.

The enactment of more radical measures and the increase of Communist dominance in the Government during 1959 and 1960 alienated still others. The expropriation and nationalization of private properties resulted in the exile of the wealthier business and landowning elements. Merchants and small businessmen were soon hurt by the economic measures of the regime, while the professionals became disenchanted for both political and economic reasons. As it became clearer that the new social order would be incompatible with middle-class interests and values, much of the middle class, which had once been sympathetic, turned against the revolution and sought refuge abroad. By the end of 1960 there were 100,000 exiles in the U.S. alone, sixty-nine percent of them were from the upper and middle classes of white-collar workers and professionals. Even more exiles had gone to other Latin American countries.

During 1960 some opposition was still found within Cuba. Dissent became increasingly dangerous, however and, as the communications media were brought under government control, increasingly more difficult. The Church, Havana University, and the business and professional associations continued to express opposition early in 1960, but these organizations too were soon purged or made subservient to the regime. Small guerrilla groups operated in the mountains, especially in the Escambray, until they were decimated, and sporadic urban terrorism and sabotage became less frequent after the second anniversary of the Castro regime. The increasingly totalitarian nature of the dictatorship made open opposition nearly impossible, and by 1961 most of those who had resisted longer also left the country. The total number of exiles climbed to over 300,000, about five percent of the population.

In 1961 there were some two hundred exile organizations operating in the U.S., though most of them fell into two major groups: (1) the conservative *Batistianos* and (2) the center-leftist Auténticos and Ortodoxos. The former were concentrated in Miami, Guatemala, and Nicaragua and were averse to any reforms. The latter were those who had been opposed to Batista, who had, in many cases, been initially sympathetic to Castro and had participated in the revolution, and who desired a government dedicated to liberal social and economic reform.

This latter group coalesced in 1960 into the Democratic Revolutionary Front (D.R.F.), under Manuel Antonio de Varona. The D.R.F. urged a

return to the 1940 Constitution, respect for civil liberties, and the re
of national sovereignty. This group soon became the dominant exile (
tion. It excluded *Batistianos* but appealed for the support of all other
The Movement for Revolutionary Recovery (M.R.R.), headed by Manuel
Artime, professed a similar ideology and claimed to be the only exile organization with an effective arm within Cuba. The Revolutionary Movement of the
People (M.R.P.), under Manuel Ray, had a slightly more leftist and revolutionary program.

Under pressure from the U.S., these groups came together in March
1961 to form the Cuban Revolutionary Council, which was to present a united
opposition to Castro and to organize a provisional government once he was
overthrown. José Miró Cardona was named coordinator-general, though the
council was more an imposed, loose coalition than a tightly unified and
coordinated front. Differences in programs had not been completely worked
out when the council issued a call for a new revolution against Castro.

The "perfect failure," as Theodore Draper expressed it, of the U.S.-
supported April 1961 invasion of Cuba, for which the Council had been
hastily set up, meant the end of the exile unity. Manuel Ray withdrew the
M.R.P. from the council, and the facade of harmony soon collapsed. Subsequent attempts to unite the exiles met with little success.

As the artificial front of exile unity dissolved, the revolutionary hopes of
the exiles faded as well. Many were settled in areas of the U.S. other than
Miami, and the number of applications for U.S. citizenship grew. As increasing numbers became reconciled to a long exile, they adjusted more to life in
their new lands. Many of the exile organizations which had formerly been
military and political became social and fraternal groups. The active anti-
Castro organizations passed into virtual obscurity and only occasionally engaged in propaganda or small-scale military activities against the Castro
regime. Those exiles who continued to leave the island after 1961 did so for a
far greater variety of reasons than did those who had left previously; intense
economic or political feelings were no longer the only criteria. The picture
which emerges of the exiles is that of a group which is completely alienated
from its homeland but which is beginning to adjust to and accept that
alienation.

The Bay of Pigs was also a turning point for opposition within Cuba.
During 1960 some active opposition had persisted, but after the invasion had
been repelled, few expressions of discontent were allowed. Potential opposition groups were broken up or brought under the strict supervision of the
Government, while individual disloyalty was checked by the creation of the
vigilante committees and by the close surveillance of revolutionary loyalties.

Accurate information on the degrees of alienation and allegiance on the
island itself is lacking. Constant indoctrination and propaganda in favor of the
regime tended to be offset by the limited success of its ambitious goals for
social and economic improvement. Estimates were that some thirty-five to
forty percent of the population, primarily among the lower classes, was solidly

in favor of the Government; that a slightly higher percentage was indifferent; and that relatively few were manifestly opposed. Neither those opposed nor those indifferent, however, posed an effective threat to the continuance of the regime.

CONCLUSION: ASSESSMENT OF STABILITY AND INSTABILITY

The Castro Revolution permanently changed Cuba. This revolution was not just a change of the palace guard but a political, social, and economic revolution which altered the entire structure of the nation. The behavioral and institutional transformations that the revolution ushered in are so broad and so deep that the society and the economy can never be restored to their previous state; even if the regime should disappear, Cuba cannot go back to the pre-1959 system.

The nature of the regime itself also changed over time. The revolution settled down and became more ordered and less frenetic. Many soldiers, for example, were ordered to shave their beards in 1960 as a reflection of the transition from revolution to administration, while Castro himself eventually shed the ideal of "direct democracy" in favor of a daily desk job. The hope for a swift transformation from an agricultural to an industrial country gave way to a more realistic assessment of Cuba's potential and led to a re-emphasis on sugar production. With the abandonment of the attempt at totally changing the economy and the abandonment of promoting rapid development, the vision of Cuba's leading a vast hemispheric popular revolution also faded; Castro's techniques and goals held far less appeal than they did in the first visionary and hopeful years of the revolution. The regime became more "rational," predictable, and bureaucratized; the heady days and grandiose dreams of its leaders were ended.

No one can predict with any certainty what the prospects are for the endurance of the Castro Government. Despite widespread indifference and some expressions of open discontent, totalitarian control has made any organized resistance within Cuba very difficult. Many norms and behavioral patterns, such as *personalismo,* the subordination of ideology to charismatic leadership, and the revolutionary tradition, were carried over from the pre-1959 period into the era of the revolution and have helped to diminish the effect of radical changes in other areas and helped to preserve a feeling of continuity. The regime's claim to be within the tradition of such national heroes as Martí also gives the Government a sense of legitimacy. Tensions, most prominently those between the old-guard orthodox Communists and the new-guard *Fidelistas* and between the Revolutionary Armed Forces and the Communist party, continue beneath the surface and could become open clashes. Yet after nine years in power, the regime has so entrenched itself that it could possibly survive even without its charismatic leader.

Tensions also have existed at the international level, though these too have become less pronounced. While the exiles have tended to abandon many of their futile anti-Castro raids and to become accustomed to their newer surroundings, Cuba remains a bone of contention not only in the cold war between the U.S. and the Soviet Union but also the "little cold war" among the Communist nations. U.S. policy changed from active opposition to a more moderate policy of isolation and containment, while the Soviet Union also encouraged the revolution to become less chaotic and more pacific. Cuba's promotion of guerrilla movements in other Latin American countries lessened at the same time that Castroism began to lose its political and socio-economic appeal abroad. The Soviet Union had enough interest in maintaining Cuba as its ally in the Western Hemisphere to justify the continuance of massive annual aid, and the U.S. had enough interest in seeing the Cuban Revolution collapse to continue the U.S. economic embargo, but neither of the superpowers seem eager for a major confrontation over Cuba. In mid-1967, despite some rumblings of internal dissension and of a possible crisis ahead, both Castro's position as the leader and communism seemed secure on the island; the Cuban regime appeared to have become more institutionalized at both the domestic and the international levels.

8 / Venezuela

JOHN D. MARTZ

*JOHN D. MARTZ, Associate Professor of Political Science
and Assistant Director of the Institute of Latin American
Studies at the University of North Carolina, has held Buenos
Aires Convention, National Defense Education, Foreign Areas
Study, Social Science Research Council, and Guggenheim fellowships for research in Latin America. Besides numerous
articles and monographs, his books include* Central America:
The Crisis and the Challenge; Colombia: A Contemporary
Study; *and* Acción Democrática: Evolution of a Modern Political Party in Venezuela. *He also edited* Dynamics of Change
in Latin American Politics: Readings.

The drive for basic socio-economic as well as political change is common
to the emerging areas, and in this Venezuela is no exception. The modernizing
process has taken root in a relatively short period of time, and national life has
already experienced many fundamental transformations in the three decades
since the death of the archetypal *caudillo* Juan Vicente Gómez. The Venezuelan evolution, especially in the form it has been taking since 1958, is perhaps
unique in Latin America for the richness of the basic resources available to
the country. The storied wealth of subsoil deposits of both petroleum and iron
ore has made possible far more ambitious and sweeping programs than can be
undertaken elsewhere. Just one of many illustrations is the fact that in all of
Latin America, only Venezuela has the economic strength to provide significant and truly equitable compensation for the agrarian reform program. Given
the overwhelming regional commitment to modernization, Venezuela has
stood out to many as a leader and an innovator in this respect. For if progress
is impossible in so richly endowed a nation, the poorer countries will see little

realistic prospect for their own development. And in a country that seems to have also developed significant human resources and that has a generation of national leaders combining both the political understanding and the vision that are prerequisites for enlightened approaches to socio-economic weaknesses, there is even greater importance attached to the accomplishments that have been or can be achieved. The broader implications of Venezuelan development, placed in juxtaposition to the diametrically-opposed rationale of the Cuban Revolution, are impressing leaders elsewhere in the hemisphere. Further, the long-range results of the competition between Venezuelan and Cuban attacks on long-standing endemic problems will not be lost on the rest of Latin America.

POLITICAL ENVIRONMENT

Geographic and Economic Features

Geographic diversity is scarcely uncommon in Latin America as a whole, and Venezuela itself is consistent with this pattern. From the snow-capped peaks of the Andes to the uncharted vastness of the Guayanas, the Republic embraces a kaleidoscopic range of climatic and topographical features. With a 1750-mile coastline on the Caribbean, the country is situated astride major transportation routes linking the hemisphere. Claiming an area of 352,000 square miles, which is larger than Great Britain, France, and the Benelux countries combined, the country is roughly the average size for South American countries. Venezuela is customarily divided into four distinct regions: the Andean mountains, the coastal lowlands, the *llanos,* or plains, and the Guayana Highlands.

Venezuela's highest mountains are located in the northeastern finger of the Andean chain known as the Sierra Nevada de Mérida, the highest pinnacles of which exceed 15,000 feet. Running some 300 miles in all, the Sierra Nevada dominates the life and economy of residents, who have largely settled in cities where the elevation is about 5,000 feet, such as San Cristóbal, Mérida, and Trujillo. The center of Conservative political attitudes and strong Church authority throughout national history, this southwestern portion of the nation stands out even today as the sharpest example of Venezuelan regionalism. Succinct characterization of the coastal area to the northeast is less simple. Its central core is the region surrounding the capital city of Caracas. With a metropolitan population that is reaching toward the two million mark, Caracas is the economic and business center of the nation. Fertile soil is found in the valleys about the agricultural city of Valencia and the cattle center of Maracay, both of which are within a short distance of Caracas. This coastal zone extends across the northern tier of the country, while the only other significant subregion is that of Lake Maracaibo to the west, where some two-thirds of Venezuelan petroleum deposits are found. At the eastern edge of the country, sparsely inhabited land merges into the Orinoco River delta, and little significant activity occurs there.

The two remaining geographic regions are more imposing climatically, less developed economically, and stand somewhat beyond the main currents of national life. The *llanos* constitute the flat, low-lying plains drained by the Orinoco River. Situated between the Andes and the coastal range on the north and the Orinoco on the South, the *llanos* are some 600 miles long and 250 miles wide and are largely covered with savanna grasses and scrub bush. During the rainy season, which runs from April to November, much of the *llanos* is flooded, for stream beds are shallow and cannot accommodate the rushing waters. In contrast, the January to April dry season is arid and unproductive, as streams dry up and grasses slowly die. The major industry is livestock-grazing, which was first introduced by the Spanish, but it has always suffered from the seasonal extremes. Fewer than a million Venezuelans live in this area, which constitutes more than one-third of the national territory. To the immediate south of the Orinoco, the Guayana Highlands are the most remote and undeveloped geographic section of Venezuela. Comprising nearly half the national territory, the highlands range from 1500 to 3000 feet in elevation, although the latter figure is more than doubled in a few locations. Mineral deposits are believed to be great, but problems of exploitation and transportation are extreme. While the potential for development is large, the future remains fairly dim. Most of the highlands are unpopulated except for a few small groups of primitive Indians, and the entire region is little known and largely unmapped.

The basic economic pattern of Venezuela has been transformed within the last half-century. For more than four hundred years, the economy was agricultural, relying on the export of coffee, cacao, and a little gold. Foodstuffs were produced for subsistence purposes. As recently as the early 1920s, growing doubt arose over the rate of productivity required simply to feed a population that was less than 3 million. The sudden outburst of a remarkably productive oil well in 1922, however, ushered in the boom in petroleum that has continued to this day. The extraordinary wealth of Venezuelan subsoil deposits has brought the average per capita income to a higher level than that of any other Latin American country although the distribution is anything but equitable. This imbalance has led to a situation which is described in a recent study by the International Bank for Reconstruction and Development, which characterized the nation paradoxically as "one of the world's most prosperous 'less developed' countries." Presently second only to the United States as a producer of petroleum, Venezuela now earns a good ninety percent of its foreign exchange with this product, and around two-thirds of government revenue comes from the output of petroleum.

The enormous sums of government revenue gradually led to an expanded economy in which large foreign and domestic investment came into being. Governmental attention began to center on such matters as public health and education, although concerted, well-planned efforts did not reach into all areas of social and economic policy until the late 1950s. Rapid industrial development has spread in Venezuela, yet at the same time the agricultural sector continues to be underdeveloped, only recently deriving any substantive benefit from the income of petroleum. Less than four percent of Venezuelan land is used for agricultural crops, which are primarily coffee, sugar, cotton, cacao, rice, and corn. With nearly one-third of the labor force engaged in agriculture and nearly forty percent living in rural areas, Venezuela is by no means fully self-sufficient in foodstuffs and must import a number of basic products which are not yet produced in adequate proportions. The 1960 agrarian reform law provided renewed impetus to the effort toward diversification and agricultural self-sufficiency, but the imbalances of the economy, notwithstanding heightened industrialization and agricultural progress, have by no means been erased.

Political History

Something of a colonial stepchild under Spanish rule, Venezuela was never more than peripheral in interest to the mother country. Far removed from the viceregal capitals and consequently even more neglected than would otherwise have been the case, Venezuela became one of the centers for anti-Spanish agitation. Even without the presence and leadership of Simón Bolívar, himself a *caraqueño,* the Venezuelans would have been prominent in the fight for independence. A full decade was necessary before the Spanish were conclusively defeated. Several more years of turbulence came as a result of the uneasy and ill-fated merger with Ecuador and Colombia to form Gran Colombia. The shattering of this union in 1830, ironically the year of Bolívar's death, led to a period of rule and consolidation under the first of several great historical figures, General José Antonio Páez. A *llanero* of humble origins whose troops had been of great service during the independence wars, the rough-and-ready Páez contributed toward the development of Venezuelan nationality for the next eighteen years. Not until 1848, with the advent of a Liberal faction opposed to the long Conservative domination, did Páez and lesser heroes of the wars lose their prominence in national politics.

The early stability and progress were interrupted in 1848 by what was to initiate, with only brief interludes, nearly a quarter-century of internecine fighting, civil war, and largely unprincipled political conflict. Until 1858 the country was ruled by José Tadeo Monagas or, on one occasion, by his brother Gregorio. Allegedly chosen as a Conservative, José Tadeo Monagas soon found it more opportune to become aligned with the Liberals, and his rule became more authoritarian until the outbreak in 1858 of the five-year Federal War. At one point the aging Páez was even recalled from exile in an effort to bring an end to anarchy, but the situation was not firmly resolved until the consolidation of power by the Liberal *caudillo* Antonio Guzmán Blanco in 1870. For eighteen years the self-styled *Americano Ilustre* pursued Liberal policies which included sharp anticlericalism and created a solidly entrenched regime in which his vanity was widely evidenced. Ignoring traditional Liberal demands for decentralized government in his effort to build an impregnable political position, Guzmán Blanco, for all his opportunism and egoism, nonetheless encouraged a sense of Venezuelan nationality and of national culture. His well-organized Government paid off the foreign debt, restored peace to a badly ravaged land, and propelled it forward in such fields as communications and education. His eventual downfall gave way to another period of renewed civil war, personal rivalry, and unprincipled as well as largely incompetent national administration.

The emergence of General Joaquín Crespo in 1892 brought to power a corrupt and inept ruler, who was succeeded seven years later by the remarkably dissolute, extravagant, and venal Cipriano Castro. Capitalizing upon the battlefield death of Crespo and the astute military leadership of his lieutenant, Juan Vicente Gómez, Castro became the first in a succession of military rulers to come out of the Andean state of Táchira and assume national control. Foreign intervention was only narrowly avoided following his imprudent handling of debts outstanding to British, Italian, and French creditors. Eventually forced to seek medical treatment abroad, Castro left the country in the hands of Gómez. Venezuela was to become the personal fief of Gómez, the storied "tyrant of the Andes," until his death of old age in 1935. Although personally unprincipled and unfeelingly ruthless in his methods, the semiliterate *tachirense* wrote an unparalleled tale of one-man authoritarian rule in Venezuela. Shrewdly solidifying the allegiance of regional *caudillos,* he created an aura of personal omnipotence which became legendary. Capitalizing on the sea of oil which began to flow in the early 1920s, he operated a financially responsible administration, avoided the worst of the 1929 depression, and attracted foreign investment. The death of this cruel if enigmatic man opened the floodgates of emotion, and national rejoicing was too widespread for his preappointed successor to restrict.

Although the death of Gómez marked the end of an era, the beginning of the modern period was still at least a decade away. A transitional phase saw the successive military administrations of two more officers from Táchira, Eleazar López Contreras and Isaías Medina Angarita. The former, a *Gomecista* who became known for his political acumen, modified repressive controls while retaining a tight rein over opposition activities. Political opponents were harassed, and freedom of speech was frequently interrupted, while economic policies were not fundamentally dissimilar from those of Gómez. Under Medina, after 1941 a further liberalization of the Government set in, as the rather easy-going President followed the counsel of civilian advisers in enacting overdue reforms. Contractual renegotiation following a revised petroleum law brought the country a greater share of oil companies' profits, and larger sums were provided for health, housing, education, and public works. Additional measures included concessions to women's suffrage and the direct election of members of the lower house. Medina also permitted increasing activity from the opposition, notably the Acción Democrática (AD), a party which was legally created in 1941. The approach of elections in 1946 presented a leadership crisis, which Medina was unable to resolve, and on October 18, 1945, discontented junior military officers and Acción Democrática collaborated to overthrow the Government.

The accession to power of the AD heralded the beginning of the Venezuelan Revolution, but the three-year period known as the *trienio* was abruptly halted by military counterrevolution in November of 1948. With AD leaders such as Rómulo Betancourt, Raúl Leoni, Gonzalo Barrios, and Luis B. Prieto sitting in the seven-man provisional junta, the party had undertaken an immediate and total transformation of national life and society. Political alteration included granting universal suffrage, enacting a popular-election law with direct voting for the Presidency, and adopting of a modern, socially oriented national Constitution. Social and economic reforms followed in short order; educational revisions, health and sanitation measures, low-cost housing, industrial diversification, an increase in the share of petroleum income, the drafting of agrarian reform legislation, and the organization of a national development corporation were all a part of the revolutionary program. After the AD ruled by decree for over two years, the renowned novelist and essayist Rómulo Gallegos was chosen as its presidential candidate and won an overwhelming victory. Less than a year later, a dissatisfied and suspicious military turned on the Government and forced it from power.

Zealously dedicated to a radical and sweeping reform program, the AD had imprudently run roughshod over those who questioned it. Rival political factions, the Church, large landholders, and major business interests had been alienated in large part and thus acquiesced in the military seizure of power. A three-man junta eventually evolved into the unchallenged rule of Lieutenant Colonel Marcos Pérez Jiménez, and the wealthy if avaricious rule he instituted was to survive for a decade. Election returns were falsified in 1952 to permit his retention of office; from that time until 1958, not only the AD but other opposition forces were systematically hunted down, imprisoned or tortured, exiled or killed in the streets. Relying both upon keen instincts and the backing of well-financed military leaders, he presided over a period of booming prosperity in Venezuela but did little to improve the grossly inequitable distribution of national wealth. Pérez Jiménez profited enormously from his Presidency, and in his penchant for grandiose construction schemes squandered huge sums while social and economic difficulties mounted. The inevitable popular uprising, inspired by party and student leaders and encouraged by increasingly disgruntled military men, led to the flight of the dictator and a year's provisional rule under Rear Admiral Wolfgang Larrazábal. National elections in December 1958 led to the establishment of popular and representative government under the AD's Rómulo Betancourt.

Organizing a coalition government including both the Christian Democratic COPEI and the Unión Republicana Democrática (URD), Betancourt attempted by more gradual and evolutionary means to institute reforms resembling those envisaged during the *trienio*. Confronted by economic difficulties which had accumulated under Pérez Jiménez, Betancourt gradually succeeded in surmounting that crisis, and by the conclusion of his term, Venezuela was more prosperous than ever before. The pattern of wealth distribution also improved. Politically he was plagued by a factious Congress, in which his party lost its majority, while the URD withdrew from government and became bitterly antagonistic. Even more serious was the campaign of terror and violence mounted by Venezuelan Communists and fellow-traveling members of the Movimiento de Izquierda Revolucionaria (MIR). The self-styled Fuerzas Armadas de Liberación Nacional (FALN) initiated a campaign of urban terrorism intended to force military intervention in politics, after which the extreme Left might lead a "popular" revolution against the military dictatorship that would presumably ensue. Despite widespread bombing, machine-gunning, bank robbery, and measures designed to produce international publicity, the FALN was unable to destroy military support of Betancourt or to bring about his overthrow. The extremists were overwhelmingly repudiated by Venezuelan public opinion when over ninety-one percent of the electorate defied their threats by voting for presidential and congressional candidates. The winner was the AD's Raúl Leoni. Inaugurated in early 1964, he proceeded with the basic policies of the preceding administration, constituted another coalition Cabinet, which broadened the popular base of the Government and, aided by the reduction in extremist violence, presided over an increasingly pacific and prospering Republic.

Society and Political Attitudes

Venezuelan social structure, under direct and indirect influences of the petroleum enterprise in particular and the process of modernization in general, has undergone drastic changes. As the economy has changed from an agrarian base to reliance on subsoil deposits with a concomitant drive toward industrialization, society as well has been transformed. At a basic level is the change from an overwhelmingly rural population thirty years ago to the present situation, in which nearly two-thirds of the people are urban. Population mobility also increased strikingly, as census figures reveal that in the 1930s eleven percent of the Venezuelans lived outside their native state, while today the figure is almost exactly double. More important than such statistics, however, is the disappearance of a traditional society largely characterized by a classic colonial mentality, where virtually no middle class existed to fill the chasm between the miniscule social elite and the mass of *campesinos* and agricultural workers. Similarly, the deep-seated belief in a dualistic society of cultured (*gente culta*) and common (*gente cualquiera*) people living somewhat apart from one another has broken down substantially. Social change has been less in rural than in urban areas, where emerging middle classes have registered a strong impact, but nowhere in Venezuela is social change totally absent. Political power has also shifted perceptibly, and the leadership of middle-class politicians, based in large part upon popular support from the lower class, has decimated the traditional omnipotence of the propertied oligarchy.

Urban society has changed most rapidly in Caracas, Maracaibo, Valencia, Maracay, Barquisimeto, and San Cristóbal. Social change and new individual attitudes have marked life in these centers. A growing and highly self-conscious urban proletariat has come into being, while the influx of migrants from the countryside has aggravated living conditions, has overtaxed employment capacity, and has played havoc with orderly social life. Political agitators capitalize to the maximum extent on the situation, and the 1963 elections were significant in that none of the leading organized parties received major support from Caracas itself. While the rather heterogeneous upper class has adapted to shifting demands of political necessity, the burgeoning middle class has developed in little more than three decades. Although defying easy definition, the latter includes small merchants and businessmen, civil servants, white-collar workers, professional people, and teachers. Upward mobility does not end with the achievement of middle-class status, and many aspire to upper-class standing and perquisites. Moreover, as a class without a lengthy history or experience, the commitments of the middle class to a particular social order are diffuse. Only within the last decade has the existing state of affairs begun to attract significant support from the middle groups. The lower classes have come to include not only servants and manual laborers, but also labor workers, sales personnel, and the unemployed squatters in the large cities. The desire of the lower classes for advancement is great and is usually seen in terms of education and academic training.

Society in the countryside has not undergone the abrupt wrench from colonial practice which has disoriented the urban classes. However, change has by no means been absent. The predictable inequity of the land tenure system and the handicaps to productivity by primitive technology are both receding before the concerted effort by recent administrations through the agriculture ministry and the national agrarian institute. Total lack of education and broad social immobility have also been attacked by a variety of programs although final solution is many years removed. The great majority of peasants cannot readily be distinguished from one another and in a sense are classless. Distinctions do exist between the rural worker and the resident of the small village. For the latter, living standards are slightly higher, educational experience and literacy is greater, and there is at least a modicum of political power, something largely unknown to the *campesino*. The third important ingredient of the rural sector is the large landholder, who only infrequently lives on the land himself. Although changing dynamics are diminishing his role somewhat, he still plays a significant role in the course of agricultural life. The gradual mobilization of the peasants into the national *campesino* federation may change substantially the structure of the agricultural society, but, although class consciousness is arriving for many on the countryside, that mobilization is at the present time far from a monolithic or easily manipulated force. In political terms, the agricultural sector has achieved but a small part of its full potential.

Prevailing political attitudes have corresponded with the various elements of national transformation which have evolved since the 1930s. A broad commitment to orderly representative government and to the regularization of political power seems to have emerged with considerable clarity. Much of this commitment is reflected in an enlarging national consensus, which is discussed below. Clearly the programs of the major political parties reflect a growing area of national policy in which there is substantial concord, and the limited appeal of extremist terrorists further underlines public solidarity with elected popular government. National pride has grown with the dynamism of the contemporary period. Growing prosperity, industrialization, urbanization, and improved educational standards are but a few of the manifestations which are seized upon. A strong strain of nationalism has somewhat less xenophobia than is customarily found in Latin America, although there is a small minority to whom only the most aggressive and exaggerated expositions of national greatness are adequate. There is an awareness and no little pride in the stereotype many Latin Americans apply to Venezuela—a courageous and outspoken if somewhat rough bellicosity that makes of the Venezuelan an obvious extrovert. This stereotype is more of a caricature than a true image, especially as the average citizen is becoming more conscious of his nationality at the expense of his regional background. Interest in neighboring Republics and in the spirit of Americanism is not weak, yet appears far less obvious than elsewhere in the hemisphere. Venezuelans are engrossed in the difficult but promising course of modernization upon which they have embarked, and it is such a major focal point that continental or global relationships bear far less significance.

POLITICAL STRUCTURES AND ROLES

The contemporary Venezuelan political system can be analyzed and understood within the terminological framework of modern political science. The growth of stability, the proliferation of political organization, and the gradual institutionalization of national politics all help to facilitate a discussion of structures, roles, and of functional and dysfunctional processes. Here it is appropriate to approach the topic under the rubrics of input and output groups and of systemic regulating and enforcing mechanisms. Of fundamental importance are the major components of input groups; among these components, political parties are the most important ones, though organized labor and lesser pressure groups are also operative. Currently more functionally specific than are the output groups, input groups play a major role in the articulation of public interests. The growing complexity of political life, the increasingly broad range of responsibility, and the construction of a significant national consensus are all primarily a result of input-group activities.

Input Groups

Notwithstanding the historically embattled elements which claimed to be either "Liberal" or "Conservative," the development of political parties is of recent date in Venezuela. Not until the decade of the 1940s did party activity begin to assume a significant place in the legal order of things, although the forerunner of today's Acción Democrática can be traced back to 1928 student demonstrations against the tyrant Gómez. Indeed, many senior party leaders in the 1960s received their political baptism of fire in anti-Gómez activities. Only during the brief *trienio* (1945–48) under the dominance of Acción Democrática did additional democratic parties begin to organize and take shape, and the subsequent decade of military Caesarism proscribed party activity. Thus, today's party system in Venezuela is, for all but Acción Democrática, a phenomenon of but a few years' duration. Given this fact, it is all the more remarkable that the multi-party arrangements have become solidified as the most significant and influential of all the input groups. While many splinter organizations have enjoyed a brief existence, four major parties can be identified as playing a major role in the national approach to a viable political consensus: Acción Democrática (AD), COPEI, Unión Republicana Democrática (URD), and the Partido Comunista Venezolano (PCV).

First and foremost is Acción Democrática, one of the great political parties of Latin America. Historically Venezuela's first genuine popular movement, the party spent years of clandestine existence before being permitted to register under its present name on September 13, 1941. Organized by such men as Rómulo Betancourt, Valmore Rodríguez, Luis B. Prieto, and Raúl Leoni, the AD increased popular support by gaining the participation of such intellectual leaders as the novelist Rómulo Gallegos and the poet Andrés Eloy Blanco. After banding together with young military dissidents to mount the October Revolution in 1945, the AD attempted to implement its progressive reformism on a crash basis, first under the provisional leadership of Betancourt and then with the elected Presidency of Gallegos. In the absence of well-organized party opposition and buttressed by the country's first effective grass-roots organization, the party swept a series of elections in which the AD majority was never less than seventy percent. The subsequent ten years of persecution by Pérez Jiménez dealt the party several crippling blows, but it nonetheless returned in 1958 from the long exile with easily the soundest popular base on which to rebuild a representative system. Challenged by rival parties since 1958, Acción Democrática has remained the leading vote-getter in the country although the strength of the party has decreased substantially. Rómulo Betancourt led the party in 1958 elections with 49.2 percent of the vote and when, in 1963, his old compatriot Leoni was elected as his presidential successor, the party's share of the vote was down to 32.8 percent. Upon assuming office in March 1964, therefore, Leoni found that his legislative strength had to be erected upon a multi-party coalition. The success of that effort is indicated below as representative of the consensus which, under AD leadership, has gradually been taking shape.

Until recently Acción Democrática was the only Venezuelan organization to meet the criteria for a "modern" Latin American party. These criteria are effective national organization, a clearly identifiable program, and popular support distributed nationally over a period of time. In addition to a detailed pyramidal organization, which functions with a high degree of articulation, the party has set forth its programmatic plans over the past generation, with its leftist reformism—always framed by a constitutional setting—including agrarian reform, economic nationalism, revision of petroleum relationships, eradication of illiteracy, improvement of health and sanitation, social legislation, and the establishment of effective central economic planning. Thus the party has only recently reconsidered its earlier assumption of electoral omnipotence. The 1958 victory was followed in 1961 and 1962 by a pair of factional splits, costing the AD and President Betancourt a legislative majority. The further drop in the 1963 returns indicated that, although the AD had overcome internal differences and annihilated party rebels at the polls, the huge landslides of earlier years were gone forever. Given the increasing complexities of a competitive multi-party system, Acción Democrática now finds itself embattled as never before in retaining its position of leadership.

The major challenge to the AD has been mounted by the Christian Democratic COPEI, which was originally named the Comité por Organización Política y Electoral Independiente. Its genesis dates from a 1934 International Congress of Catholic Youth held in Rome, at which a youthful Rafael Caldera was in attendance. Later organizing a Catholic student organization to combat the anticlerical national student federation, Caldera eventually gathered together the "electoral committee" that took up the fight with Acción Democrática following the October Revolution. Relations during the *trienio* were acrimonious, with the AD viewing COPEI as a weak but bothersome political extension of the Roman Catholic Church. Ties between the Church and the party were actually slight and informal, although COPEI was initially Conservative and rested on a regional base of strength in the Andean southwest. Caldera himself was pledged to the implementation of social reforms suggested by papal encyclicals, but many in his party disagreed. Even ten years later, his party was regarded by many voters in 1958 as representing clerical and landholding interests. Caldera polled 16.2 percent of the presidential vote and ran last. However, the experience of the next five years brought about a virtual metamorphosis in the party.

In 1959 Rómulo Betancourt established a three-party coalition; the eventual departure of one member left COPEI as junior partner in the Government. Remaining throughout the Betancourt administration, COPEI thereby gained from direct governmental experience and from the sharing of patronage while extending party organization and underlining its public image as a responsible, social-minded entity. This apprenticeship helped to prepare the party for the 1963 elections, in which it rose to second place with Caldera polling 21.2 percent of the vote. Support was drawn from the ranks of labor for the first time, and COPEI was the only democratic, nonviolent party to score significantly with university students. An astute campaign enabled COPEI to claim credit for government accomplishments while disavowing failures, which were pinned to the AD. Despite logical ambiguities in such a campaign, it proved eminently successful. Buoyed by the rise of strength and already convinced that victory in the 1968 elections would be theirs, COPEI ultimately broke off negotiations with President-elect Leoni by refusing to join his coalition. The party's present stance of independent opposition, symbolized by the slogan AA, standing for "autonomy of action," leaves the party out of office, but *Copeyanos* are sanguine about future prospects. Having achieved "modern" party status through effective organization and national rather than regional popular appeal, the *Copeyanos* anticipate victory at the next elections. Their political position meantime is both articulate and responsible, its social reformism differing from that of the AD in only details of implementation.

While COPEI has joined the AD in becoming a "modern" party, the same cannot be said of the Unión Republicana Democrática. Founded in 1945, it soon became the personal preserve of Jóvito Villalba, who was a former student leader and colleague of Betancourt and Leoni and who had rejected the AD's determined party discipline. With a flair for oratory that rivaled Betancourt's organizational ability, Villalba had been prominent for several years; during the *trienio* he used the URD as a vehicle for vituperative attacks on the Government; the substance of these attacks was more personal than political. In 1952 Villalba seemingly won the military-controlled elections, in which the AD was prohibited from participation, only to have the results annulled. In 1959 he led his party into the Betancourt coalition Government, but by 1960 personal abrasions and political differences resulted in the URD withdrawal from Government. The party remained a vocal critic of the Government and entered the 1963 elections with a campaign which in essence promised to duplicate the AD program but to implement it more efficiently, honestly, and at less cost. A potential rift already existed as the result of strong *Fidelista* loyalties from younger members of the party's left wing. Following the vote, in which Villalba ran third with 18.9 percent, he purged the party of its extremist element and, a short time later, agreed to join the *Ancha Base,* or broad based, Leoni coalition. Organizational squabbles continued to plague the URD, and in early 1966 the party's leading younger figure, Alirio Ugarte Pelayo, was expelled from the URD along with other capable men. Shortly thereafter, in May, Ugarte shocked the nation with his suicide, and the repercussions within the URD itself were potent in their impact. With the URD relationship to the Government somewhat uneasy, and with Jóvito Villalba remaining the only nationally prominent party leader, the future remained doubtful. Traditionally strong on oratory and weak on organization, the URD has offered little new in the political field. In Venezuela's multi-party system, the survival of the URD cannot be assumed. The same is true of several small splinter groups which have been active in recent years. When the 1963 elections included the participation of an "independent" organization under Arturo Uslar Pietri, its relatively strong showing and subsequent creation as the Frente Nacional Democrático (FND) suggested the possibility of another effective party. Uslar Pietri, a well-known historian, essayist, and sometime politician, directed the party in carving out a moderate position somewhat to the right of the AD, COPEI, and the URD. But despite becoming a member of the Leoni coalition for a time, the FND soon suffered internal factionalism and in early 1966 withdrew from the Government amidst serious internal bickering. The approach of national elections in December of 1968 saw the FND active in an effort to create a multi-party opposition organization to contest against Acción Democrática.

Venezuela's Communist party is actually the oldest in the country. Formally created in 1931, the party's fortunes have fluctuated during the intervening years. Often in exile but occasionally a legal party, it has been consistently defeated in its continuing contest with Acción Democrática. Failing to control the covert movement of the 1930s, the PCV next lost in the effort to organize labor in the 1940s. Not until recent years, however, have the Communists attempted a revolution by violent means. Although the terrorists of the Fuerzas Armadas de Liberación Nacional included Communist elements, a rift existed over several issues. The Moscow-Peiping split, the appeals of *Fidelismo,* and differences over alternate tactics of armed revolution or of parliamentary maneuver, all contributed to the diffuseness of communism in recent years. While many of the younger members still prefer the methods of armed violence, the resultant wave of public disgust has tended to weaken whatever appeal the PCV itself might have had. Unable to participate in 1963 elections, it must now choose whether to continue occasional outbursts of terrorism from a clandestine existence, or to accept the rules of the political game and limit activities to those of an electoral and parliamentary nature.

Organized labor in Venezuela has, like the parties, assumed much larger proportions in recent years. Effectively stifled under military rule, organized labor first emerged during the heady days of the *trienio,* when the pro-labor AD Government actively promoted unionism and organization. The Confederación de Trabajadores de Venezuela (CTV) was directed by organizers such as P. B. Pérez Salinas, Valmore Rodríguez, and José González Navarro, all prominent *Adecos,* while Labor Minister Leoni extended paternalistic encouragement. Although. the Pérez Jiménez interlude was debilitating, the return of constitutionality in 1958 also saw the resurgence of labor, a movement which now ranks among the most effective in Latin America. Slightly more than fifty percent of Venezuela's labor force of 2.9 million is unionized, and the growth of agricultural bodies and peasant leagues is especially striking. The farmers' Federación Campesina de Venezuela (FCV), a member of the CTV with some 800,000 members, is providing an increasingly effective organizational drive for the first time.

The CTV has continued to enjoy strong support from all major political parties, most significantly Acción Democrática, whose members still constitute a majority within the directorate of the confederation. CTV strength thus cannot yet be divorced from that of the AD, although the trend in that direction is apparent. COPEI has become active in labor, and several of the directing posts of the CTV are now held by *Copeyanos.* The pattern of labor-government relations has only recently begun to assume clearer collaborative overtones, as labor support for democratic government and opposition to either *Fidelista* or military intervention is granted in return for continuing official assistance. Labor has consequently been much less extreme and vocal in its demands than might otherwise be expected, while the union member himself, to all appearances, is loyal both to union leadership and to the political system. Increasingly cordial labor-management relations have also developed, further strengthening labor's claim as a major component of the national political consensus.

The interests of labor are contested in various ways by a large number of pressure groups, only a few of which can be listed briefly in passing. Most concerned with economic policy is FEDECAMARAS (Federación de Cámaras de Comercio e Industria), representative of the private business sector. With increasing frequency an amicable collaborator with the CTV in labor-management discussions, FEDECAMARAS represents business and industry on the highest level. Its activity also includes occasional consultation with the Government and numerous economic studies of various sorts. FEDEAGRO (Federación Nacional de Asociaciones de Productos Agropecuarios), the organization of farm and livestock producers, has worked for the implementation of agrarian reform and the increase of productivity in recent years. A somewhat different organization created in 1962 is the Asociación Venezolana Independiente (AVI), which is a group of financiers and industrialists interested in public affairs. Support for Uslar Pietri's candidacy in 1963 was temporary, and it is uncertain whether AVI will continue as a means of giving public shape to the political views of its members.

Output Groups

The constitutional setting within which Venezuelan output groups operate has been relatively unchanging through the years, notwithstanding the fact that the country has enacted over two dozen separate documents—more than any other Latin American Republic. The bewildering number of Constitutions has not represented an absence of continuity, however, for the legal changes have been minor. There has been since 1945 a deference to popular elections and to national responsibility for social and economic welfare of the individual; otherwise, the long succession of charters has been broadly consistent. The present Constitution of 1961 is clearly similar to those which preceded it, and the legitimacy of the regime continues to rest as much on extra-constitutional political values and beliefs as upon the basic document itself. The form of government is described as federal although only narrow powers are set forth in explicit terms. State governors are appointed by the national Executive, and within the purview of state affairs are dominant over the state legislative assemblies. If the system is less highly centralized than most of the unitary Latin American Republics, that is not to say that the authority of the national Government can ordinarily be challenged by state or local officials. The only powers reserved for the states are those not specifically allocated to municipal or national government. The national Congress may cede additional matters to the states by a two-thirds vote, a practice designed to encourage greater administrative decentralization.

The systemic outputs in Venezuela are most frequently the result of presidential action, and the President himself is undeniably dominant in the policy-making process. Required to be Venezuelan by birth, over thirty years of age and not a member of the clergy, the President is elected by a plurality through direct and universal suffrage and serves a five-year term, after which he may not be re-elected until two more terms have passed. In the absence of a vice-president, the president of Congress stands next in the line of succession. For the President of Venezuela, powers of both rule-making and rule-application are sweeping. In the first instance he may summon special congressional meetings, arrange the introduction of administration legislation, and subsequently fill in the details through executive decrees. The legislative power of the Venezuelan President has not, in practice, been as great as in most other Latin American countries, but it is nonetheless significant. He is further empowered to negotiate national loans, to draft and issue administrative regulations, and to take special measures in economic and financial affairs. With congressional authorization he may also expend funds in addition to those provided by the budget, granting credits to the ministries. The power of appointment includes the thirteen Cabinet ministers, state governors, diplomatic assignments, officials of the growing number of semiautonomous state agencies, and assorted posts which are not regulated by civil service authorization.

If the President enjoys both rule-making and rule-applying functions, his comparative domination of national politics is further enhanced by the direction of foreign affairs, his position as military Commander-in-chief, and most importantly his authority to declare a state of emergency. In the latter instance he may suspend certain constitutional guarantees in the event of serious turmoil or national conflict. Proclamation of the state of emergency and the listing of suspended guarantees must be countersigned by the Cabinet and authorized by either the full Congress or, when it is not in session, the permanent Steering Committee. Such powers are extensive, although perpetual or indefinite imprisonment without trial are among the rights which cannot be waived. The President may also adopt sweeping powers in the event of a disturbance to public order, but here again, although prior congressional action is not necessary, there must be legislative agreement within ninety days, or else the measures are automatically terminated. Rómulo Betancourt was forced on several occasions to adopt such measures during the height of terrorist violence in 1962–63 but scrupulously sought and gained congressional approval or else halted the activities within ninety days. Such powers may well be abused by an impatient or power-seeking individual, but at the same time they can be highly useful to a representative, popular government fighting for survival, as was the Betancourt Government during much of his administration.

The public bureaucracy has swelled tremendously in the last twenty years and certainly provides ample opportunity for the exercise of presidential patronage. In addition to the thirteen national ministries, there are subagencies which are also part of the executive branch. The Ministry of Interior Relations includes the national police (DIGEPOL), while that of Justice embraces the Technical Judicial Police (PTJ). Semiautonomous government agencies, many of them created in recent years, include the Agrarian Reform Institute (IAN), the Venezuelan Petroleum Corporation (CVP), the Agricultural and Livestock Bank (BAP), and the National Institute of Educational Co-operation (INCE). Although there have been cries from all sides for the creation of a merit system, the proposal is still awaiting concerted government action, notwithstanding the establishment of an advisory commission on public administration by the provisional junta in 1958. A number of individual ministries have instituted their own internal administrative systems, with a rational and specified policy on hiring and firing, promotions, seniority, tenure, and related issues. But the public bureaucracy suffers from the lack of any standardization, and the power of patronage remains important. Discussions leading to the formation of coalition governments in both 1958 and 1963 necessarily devoted much time and care to the allocation of available posts for political appointees.

Venezuelan legislative power is the duty of a two-house body which is principally responsible for evaluating presidential initiative and passing judgment on the budget. The upper house is composed of two senators for each of the twenty states, plus the addition of a few others through an electoral quotient. Representation in the Chamber of Deputies, where the term is also for five years, is allotted on the basis of one per 50,000 population. It is the lower house which enjoys the constitutional right of initiation in budgetary and tax matters as well as the right to censure ministers (although the latter need not resign). Otherwise, ordinary legislation can be introduced in either chamber, though after a bill is introduced, it must have two hearings in each house. Once differences between the houses are ironed out, bills are forwarded to the President for action. The political function of the legislative branch has acquired new meaning since the 1958 restoration of representative government. While handicapped by many of the weaknesses of other Latin American Congresses—lack of expertise, inadequate technical advice, unduly small staffs, unwieldy committees, and so forth—the activities of many legislators within either a party or an active interest group have contributed to their knowledge and experience. Moreover, organizational affiliation has contributed to a more structured and rational pattern of legislative behavior. Congressional approval has also become increasingly important to the policy-making processes. When divisions within AD cost Betancourt his majority in the Chamber, he found himself seriously handicapped; later, President Leoni negotiated a multi-party coalition in order to assure himself of the congressional support that he felt obliged to seek. The gradual increase of functional specificity in national government seems to promise a congressional future of increasing political significance. Certainly its contemporary contribution to the political outputs of the system is much greater than was traditionally the case.

Regulatory and Enforcement Mechanisms

As in any political system, certain regulatory and enforcement mechanisms are needed for its stability and continuity. The degree to which Venezuelan political life has been disorderly and disruptive in the past has been in substantial part a reflection of weak rule-adjudication and regulation, coupled with erratic enforcement by security forces and political hyperactivity by the armed forces. The formal constitutional regulatory function is assigned to the judiciary, historically the weakest and least influential of the three branches of national government. Only the Supreme Court is described in the Constitution; lesser courts are left to the dictates of organic law. At the apex of the judicial pyramid, the Supreme Court of Justice is elected by joint sessions of Congress for nine-year terms, with one-third of the Court's body renewed every three years. The former Federal Court and the Court of Cassation were combined functionally into the present body in 1961; customarily it meets in three committees, or *salas,* which are a political-administrative section, an appeal division for civil cases, and an appeal division for criminal cases. Only in the most important cases does the Supreme Court meet in plenary session. The Supreme Court stands as final arbiter in cases of constitutionality and has the power to nullify either partially or totally the law in question. At state levels, courts of ordinary or special jurisdiction are responsible for justice, which in the village or community falls within the purview of the local authority, customarily an *alcalde,* or mayor.

While the sovereignty of the judicial branch has grown since the fall of Pérez Jiménez, this branch by no means plays a major role in the system; informal regulation is sometimes as effective as the legal when emanating from the moral authority of the Church. Venezuela itself is overwhelmingly Catholic; over ninety percent of the baptisms are recorded in that faith. Nonetheless, Catholicism as both a social and political force is not as dominant as in many other Latin American countries. The determined anti-Church warfare of Guzmán Blanco virtually decimated the moral and material position of the Church, and its activity has revived significantly within only the last generation. The Church is developing a greater public consciousness and is entering into social action for the first time, although much less so in the countryside than in urban regions. A comparable rise in prestige has accrued in recent years, while both religious and national pride was served when Caracas Archbishop José Humberto Quintero was named to the college of cardinals. Political pronouncements are rare, although the Church did speak out in the protest immediately preceding the overthrow of Pérez Jiménez. Individual priests still tend to draw greater respect from the populace than does the Church as a whole. Relatively weaker in wealth, manpower, and resources than in other Republics in the Western Hemisphere, the Church is not only undermanned but still relies heavily upon foreign priests, of whom the largest number are

Spanish in nationality. If the overall contribution of the Church is uneven at best and varying widely in impact, its generally forward-looking approach has contributed at least slightly to the formation of attitudes and political values. In all probability this contribution will become more impressive in the years ahead.

The systemic activity of enforcement and security agencies is intended, at least in idealized theoretical models, as a supporting factor in the maintenance of the overall system. In Venezuela, however, the decisive voice in the resolution of major conflicts has often been that of the armed forces, which at present continue to exercise a near veto power over policy decisions believed to affect their own interests. Few nations have experienced a longer history of military involvement in national politics. At the same time, Robert Gilmore has appropriately and perceptively remarked that militarism in the modern sense is a relatively recent phenomenon, with the era of the unlettered, undisciplined, regional *caudillo* gone forever. Only within the past quarter-century have the armed forces attempted to establish and to maintain high military standards, emphasizing professionalization and technological modernization. Military participation in the October Revolution of 1945 was the first instance in which a modern and corporate-minded military intervened in politics. The military has subsequently done so in 1948 and again in 1958. During the past decade the military has concentrated on the discouraging of uprisings by rightist officers, the control and eradication of urban terrorism, the countering of guerrilla activity, and defense of the constitutional system.

The military establishment presently includes the three service branches plus the national guard, with a combined membership of some thirty-five thousand. The Minister of Defense, ordinarily an officer himself, is directly responsible to the President, while commands from the ministry are passed through the Chief of the Joint Staff. The armed forces have generally enjoyed a favored position and have been pampered by successive administrations, including the present one. While the plush years for the military occurred as Pérez Jiménez attempted to buy its loyalty through extravagant expenditures, treatment by elected governments has scarcely been less generous. Under both Betancourt and Leoni the expenditures for the military have been from nine to ten percent of the total budget. Both the navy and the air force have added to their general prestige in recent years, which was abetted in part by the prominence of the brothers Larrazábal, both admirals, and by General Antonio Linares Briceño, the air force commander who served for several years as Betancourt's Minister of Defense. Indeed, the armed forces in general have recovered substantially from the disfavor that ensued from their identification with Pérez Jiménez. Military recruitment is being progressively democratized, and the officer corps is largely filled by men of middle-class and lower-class origins. It is probably accurate to describe military leadership as increasingly representative of society through sharing a broadly democratic political outlook. However, many officers retain the basic belief that as defenders of the constitutional order, it is ultimately the judgment of the military itself that must pass on the legitimacy of any government and its policies. While the political acumen of both Betancourt and Leoni has been dedicated to the courting and retention of military support, much energy is now channeled into a variety of nation-building civic action programs.

In addition to the regular military, security affairs are the responsibility of the national guard and assorted police agencies. Public order and safety have been plagued since 1958 by inefficient law enforcement as well as the periodic onslaught of extremist terrorism. Popular revulsion against the dreaded public security forces of Pérez Jiménez had encouraged the concerted decentralization of all such bodies. As a result, in addition to the Guardia Nacional, which operates under the Defense Ministry, three additional organs were created: DIGEPOL, a police force under the Minister of Interior, the PTJ, a technical investigative body under the Minister of Justice, and the traffic police, controlled by the Minister of Communications. Such a proliferation of organizations and a low level of competence contributed to the high crime rate in the cities as well as the political violence which plagued Venezuela in the 1960s. Co-ordination has progressed but slowly, and in the 1963 campaign the opposition derided the ineffectiveness of peace-keeping agencies and promised broad improvement if elected. The existence of state and local police alongside those already mentioned has added to the generally unsatisfactory handling of peace and public order. The national guard is widely regarded as having dedicated itself unflinchingly to its responsibilities, but the regular police forces are held in scorn, especially by cynically weary city-dwellers. The enforcement of domestic peace, although recovering from the depths reached in 1961 and 1962, still remains a subject for both governmental and public consternation.

PROCESSES OF FUNCTION AND DYSFUNCTION

In terms of functional analysis, a number of political forces have contributed in a negative fashion to the overall political process. Until the restoration of political democracy in 1958, for instance, the electoral system had been historically and consistently dysfunctional, with the exception of 1947–48. The same evaluation is relevant for the role of the State in socio-economic affairs, especially under Marcos Pérez Jiménez. More currently, the alienation of many young Venezuelans from the present political system is a dramatic indicator of dysfunctionalism. Notwithstanding the many advances initiated under the Betancourt and Leoni administrations, given the inordinately difficult and complex panoply of problems which had accumulated by 1958, it is not surprising that some features of the residue from years of Conservative rule still remain. But as the following will suggest, the overall record seems to be clearly positive. Perhaps the single most striking monument to the progress of representative government in recent years has been the breadth of popular participation and the emerging national electoral accord.

Elections and Political Representation

Basic electoral reforms were first instituted by the provisional Government of 1945–47 with the elimination of indirect elections and limited suffrage. Following the Pérez Jiménez interruption, universal suffrage for all citizens over eighteen years of age was reinstituted, with balloting secret and compulsory. The eligible voter who does not cast his ballot is subject to the suspension of various civil rights; this law is rarely enforced, however, and the generally high level of electoral participation has rendered the application of legal sanctions unimportant. Congressional membership is based on the D'Hondt system of proportional representation with the additional application of a national electoral quotient. The latter provides a degree of representation for the minor parties, which frequently fail to win seats by direct election. Congressional candidates are placed in order of preference on a party-list ballot; this method is true for both the *principales* and the *suplentes,* the latter being potential substitutes for the former.

In the presidential competition the winner is chosen by simple majority. National, state, and municipal elections are all held under national election laws, directed by the thirteen-member Consejo Supremo Electoral (CSE), which is chosen every two years by Congress. The CSE stands at the apex of a structure which includes Juntas Electorales Principales on the state level and then district and municipal juntas. The CSE directs the national registration period which precedes elections, operates polling places on election day, oversees the tabulation of the ballots, and decides all controversies over the use of party labels, mottoes, and symbols in the campaign.

Going beyond the mechanics of the electoral system, the degree of political representation gives practical substance to the creation of an electoral consensus. Notwithstanding the effect of a five-year interval between elections, during which time no direct test of public opinion is possible, participation is high. On December 1, 1963, in the face of an extended campaign by urban terrorists culminating in a promise of death for those who might vote, ninety-one percent of all registered Venezuelan voters went to the polls in support of the constitutional system. Block-long lines formed as early as an hour before the official voting began, and the psychological blow dealt the extremists by their failure has minimized their impact ever since. Whatever the distribution of party support, all candidates and organizations stood firmly behind the continuation of the existing system, and the popular commitment to democratic processes could scarcely have been outlined more vividly. The concomitant rejection of extremist pressure and alien ideological appeals was symbolized by the unprecedentedly high rate of participation. Furthermore, the nature of the national consensus had become increasingly clear as a result of the preceding electoral campaign. The similarity of programmatic appeals during the campaign was striking. While critics may point to the exclusion of the Communists and *Miristas* from political participation since the fall of 1963, this exclusion is not startling in view of the unrelenting and irresponsible violence which even today has not been renounced by the far Left. At no time in the past have the Communists and their supporters won more than five to six percent of the vote in Venezuela, and there is no evidence to suggest otherwise today. Especially under the peculiar and unique conditions of the 1963 vote, the functionalism of the electoral system strengthened both the subsequent Leoni coalition and the overall vitality and resiliency of Venezuelan politics.

Political Socialization and Recruitment

As in all modernizing nations, patterns of socialization and recruitment are of basic importance. Educational and social influences contribute at an early stage, while a subsequent impact is registered as the result of party, military, and labor activities. Overlying the environmental framework is the flow of political information and the state of communications development. Statistical measures of both quantitative and qualitative change cannot be detailed although it is appropriate to repeat the fact that the population in twenty-five years has been transformed from roughly two-thirds rural to two-thirds urban, while the mobility of the population has also increased. A middle class has been created from almost nothing in the space of a generation. Despite the imbalances created by such circumstances, the family continues most commonly to exercise the earliest socializing force, and the life of the family remains generally patriarchal. For well-to-do families, traditional patterns of relationships and of kinship solidarity are strong, and the young Venezuelan is socialized much as he was in earlier years. The situation is more varied for both the urban and rural lower classes, where common-law marriage is as much the rule as the exception. Families at all levels tend to be large; recent figures showed that sixty percent of all families had five members or more. Children customarily tend to be treated permissively. In lower-class families children are cared for by older sisters as well as by adult members of the family, while at higher levels there is usually supervision by nursemaids or by private tutors. Discipline is relatively unknown to the child until he enters school; where attendance is impossible or difficult, an artificially protective environment may last for several years more. With the proliferation of urban slums and of broken homes with almost nonexistent family ties, abandonment of infants is by no means uncommon, contributing in both obvious and subtle fashions to maladjustments in the emerging younger generation.

The educational experience brings much more direct politicization to many young Venezuelans. While many lower-class children still receive inadequate and irregular schooling, overall enrollment figures have risen phenomenally. Since 1958 attendance has more than doubled, as has the number of schools and teachers. By the end of the Betancourt administration, some eighty-five percent of the elementary-school-age children were enrolled. Illiteracy has also been halved, now standing at some twenty-five percent. Education has always been esteemed by the Venezuelan upper class; more recently, others have also come to recognize the importance of education. The traditional Hispanic concept of intellectual accomplishment has receded before the onrush of popular education and the commitment it has engendered. The upward social mobility gained from educational accomplishment has become well-known and thus provides renewed impetus to education. Rural attitudes still tend to question the lasting importance of an education, but in an increasingly urbanized nation this tendency is becoming less significant. Direct classroom activity, especially at the elementary school, centers entirely upon the teacher, for parental involvement is slight. Classroom socialization has therefore become a major factor and is increasingly reflecting the general improvement in the quality of teachers.

At a somewhat higher level, socialization and recruitment become functions served in various ways by organized labor, the military, and of course, political parties. In the first instance, with the CTV dominating labor affairs, its relationships to the Government and to management are of critical importance. The somewhat paternalistic attitudes of governmental and political leaders have in part choked off any rapid evolution of labor leadership, so that the rank-and-file members still tend to be controlled by a relatively small handful of leaders. Much of the power of labor leaders lies in their influence within labor bureaus of the leading parties rather than in the role of union officers. True democratic trade unionism is still underdeveloped in Venezuela. The broad socializing influence as young Venezuelans join a union and develop a sense of community and of mutual interests is important, but added to this influence is the fact that even the more active unions tend to enjoy strong leadership from the top, with individual personal relationships of utmost importance. Present trends suggest that the labor movement is becoming characterized by a greater degree of internal activity at all levels. As this development continues, and as labor-party-government affiliations gradually weaken, the heightened degree of independent trade unionism can be expected to nourish greater activism and involvement on the part of the membership.

Just as organized labor deals with incoming members of limited educational background and fairly primitive political ideas, so does the military in Venezuela contribute to the socialization process. Approximately half of the military conscripts must be taught to read and write before progressing beyond the most rudimentary kind of training. While traditional military activities are not designed to give the young soldier much sense of either responsibility or of participation, the present military activities are beginning to do so. The Venezuelan military, given impetus both by the inclinations of post-1958 governments and by the advice of North American military advisers, has turned increasingly to an assortment of civic action programs. These not only include the orthodox kind of public works construction, with improvement of communications and the amplification of transportation facilities, but also such things as staffing the series of night schools developed for the anti-illiteracy campaign. The growing emphasis on self-help in community development has on numerous occasions brought about a constructive and mutually supportive collaboration between rural citizens and soldiers from the ranks.

These programs mean in the long run a positive socialization for the usual conscript, who after his tour of duty returns home taking along the knowledge, experience, and sense of participation enjoyed during active service.

The political recruitment by parties has been important, for their year-round, day-to-day politicking over an extended period of time can scarcely be overestimated. In earlier years Acción Democrática dominated the country almost completely, but the party rivals of AD have learned well their organizational and publicizing lessons; as a consequence, activity is almost continual, and even the small communities can expect the frequent appearance of local as well as national political leaders. There has been a concerted effort to increase the sense of public participation. Once again the AD led the way in the drive for greater citizen involvement. Social gatherings, weekly party meetings, discussion groups, *fútbol* leagues, and many other activities have evolved as a means of bringing the membership into contact with one another as well as with the leaders of the party themselves. This daily involvement, interspersed occasionally with regional or even national conventions of various sorts, has heightened the sense of commitment on the part of many Venezuelans and has given them a self-identification which was historically weak if not nonexistent. Predictably, the degree of participation becomes highest during national election campaigns, but the conclusion of the campaign by no means signifies an interruption of the process. And when, as was the case in December 1963, nearly all Venezuelans feel that something is genuinely at stake, the resultant turnout has major political and socializing implications for the citizenry at large.

All of the above activities take place within the framework of communications, and this framework needs to be sketched for a satisfactory overview of the entire matter of politicization. There are in Venezuela roughly three dozen newspapers, with a total circulation approaching one million. There are an additional 150 journals and reviews, as well as 100 radio stations and a half-dozen television stations. The national pattern is uneven, with Caracas and other urban centers almost saturated with available news media, while outlying rural areas are, except for radio, far removed from ordinary channels of communication. Widespread rural illiteracy is also an obvious factor, although the anti-illiteracy campaign has reduced its potency. Caracas newspapers dominate the field of daily journalism, notwithstanding the existence of important papers in a few other cities, notably Maracaibo. Roughly one-third of those now published in Venezuela originate in Caracas, with the rest scattered broadly throughout the nation. The impact of newspapers, as well as other printed matter, is inordinately strong in Caracas and other population centers but weakens rapidly as one leaves these areas. Radio provides an almost universal means of communications, however, since nearly every Venezuelan can and does listen with some regularity. Television is also becoming important in the urban areas; the Venezuelan system is one of the best developed on the continent. The year 1963 marked the first time that television became significant in elections; the major candidates relied upon it substantially. One of the highlights of the campaign was a debate between presidential candidates Caldera and Uslar Pietri. For those who chose not to appear, there were widespread charges of concern over the vulnerability of an unfavorable television "image."

Public Policy

The administration of public affairs in Venezuela follows the customary Latin American pattern of major state involvement. A vast array of political, social, and economic powers are possessed either implicity or explicitly by the national Government and its affiliated agencies. To the broad Latin American preference for a large and relatively all-inclusive governmental machinery, then, can be added the major commitment to a social welfare state. While the early organizational impetus in this direction came from Acción Democrática and its forerunners, other important components of the political system have come to share the same view. Electoral and programmatic accord clearly includes a belief that governmental action should be exerted in major sectors of national life. Recent years have even seen a grudging but perceptible acceptance by business and commerce of such a view; by the time Raúl Leoni succeeded to the Presidency, it was felt that wide-ranging governmental activity was generally desirable. The broad adoption of reformist goals in the socio-economic as well as the political field has led to the conclusion that enlarged governmental activity is the only means of dealing with such matters. The policy-making organs are therefore large, prolix, and frequently have overlapping authority, which leads to occasional confusion if not outright bureaucratic war. To the basic institutional mechanisms mentioned above should be added CORDIPLAN, the Central Office of Co-ordination and Direction, which is widely regarded as the best and most effective national planning agency in all of Latin America. Attached to the presidential office and concerned more with the co-ordination and implementation of existing plans than with initiating programs of its own, CORDIPLAN has assumed major policy-making responsibilities, supported and strengthened as it has been by the Chief Executive himself.

A quick survey of Venezuelan public policy can for taxonomic purposes be categorized under three broad rubrics: economic development, social welfare, and foreign relations. While changes in party control may alter many of the details, it seems probable that the basic guidelines laid out and pursued by Betancourt and more recently by Leoni will not be fundamentally revised. In the area of economic development, there is a general recognition that, although estimates vary from twenty-five to fifty years or more, the rich supply of petroleum will eventually become depleted. However long this may take, the Republic will eventually be unable to capitalize upon such resources, and thus a more diverse economy needs to be developed. Where petroleum itself is concerned, there has been reluctance to permit further long-term concessions. While Venezuela's share of the profits has risen to some seventy percent, a national petroleum corporation (CVP) was established in 1960 and is gradually extending its operations. In time it will presumably be in a position to assume control of the nation's subsoil resources. Venezuelan leadership in the five-nation Organization of Petroleum Exporting Countries has increased its own flexibility in operating on the international level. The presence of a veritable mountain of iron ore in the interior near the confluence of the Orinoco and Caroní Rivers has led to a major development project that includes the quite literal creation of a new city, Ciudad Guayana, and the construction of what is becoming one of the major heavy industrial complexes in Latin America. Venezuelan participation in the Latin American Free Trade Area (LAFTA) may become especially lucrative with the further development of such industry.

The effort toward industrial diversification is not dissimilar from that elsewhere in the hemisphere, although again more adequately financed as a result of the wealth earned from petroleum. Major state intervention is the responsibility of the developmental organization known as the Corporación Venezolana de Fomento (CVF), which encourages expansion within the framework of broad national economic planning programs. Such regional entities as the Corporación de Guayana, which holds direct responsibility for the Guayana, further extend the degree of governmental involvement. The state-owned sector also includes a major electrical system and various lending agencies for the stimulation of native industry, both heavy and light. The gradual reduction of reliance upon the outside world for processed goods, combined with the economic rationality with which oil income is being applied, is reflected in the broadening prosperity which followed the depression brought about at the end of the 1950s by earlier Pérez Jiménez policies. An unrefined but significant indicator is the gross national product; rising from 5.8 percent in 1963 to 8.2 percent in 1964, by the beginning of 1966 the gross national product had exceeded 10 percent, the most phenomenal such growth in Latin America. Industrial production rose 8.7 percent in 1963, nearly doubled in 1964, and by 1965 was moving toward 20 percent. The national gold reserve was over $800 million by mid-1966, again far larger than any other country on the continent.

The second major area for economic development is the agricultural, and here again there is broad national agreement on the need for truly effective agrarian reform. Espoused by Rómulo Betancourt and his co-workers as early as the 1930s, it was introduced as legislation in late 1948 but failed to survive the overthrow of the Gallegos Government. The 1958 return of constitutionality brought general agreement by all parties, and the present agrarian reform law was passed in 1960. The Instituto Agrario Nacional (IAN) was created to oversee the program, the only one in Latin America which included significant compensation for privately held lands appropriated for redistribution. Assisted by the Banco Agrícola y Pecuario for the administration and financing of parts of the program, the IAN by the end of the Betancourt administration had distributed 57,000 families on some 3.75 million acres. Betancourt's successor promised in the next five years to increase governmental support for the program. With agricultural diversification as well as increased production among the major goals of the program, the Government reported that while output had risen five percent during the Pérez Jiménez years, it was up to more than seven percent during the first half of the 1960s. Venezuela has recently become self-sufficient in several basic foodstuffs which for many years had been imported to meet domestic consumption.

Welfare programs have been extensive in scope and ambitious in goals. Health, housing, education, and social security have all been subject to government policy. The eradication of malaria under the *trienio* presaged the frontal attack of recent years on disease, and the Ministry of Health has received eight to nine percent of the annual budget. The diversity of policies includes free lunches for school children, a series of clinics and rural health centers, and funds for postgraduate medical studies abroad and for existing programs of medical research. Housing has become something of an associated area, as it was estimated in 1964 that the shortage of 700,000 homes would in five years grow to one million. Campaign commitments in 1963 included specific promises; the victorious AD pledged the construction of 75,000 houses annually, while COPEI confidently raised the ante to 100,000 per year. Educational policy continues to support the eradication of illiteracy, while the budget for that ministry has risen perceptibly, permitting the development of extensive adult, vocational, and teacher-training programs, along with the more orthodox enterprises. Additional programs are in many cases operated under the Institute of Social Security, which receives funds directly from the treasury for the financing of health insurance. Separate arrangements exist for such matters as child welfare, while private social work is conducted by a variety of groups, including most prominently the Roman Catholic Church.

Foreign relations only intermittently draw particular attention from the public at large; ordinarily routine matters are conducted without great notoriety. One major historical boundary dispute continues to be unsettled, at least in Venezuelan eyes. As early as 1814 there was disagreement with England about the eastern border with what became British Guiana. A clash of border guards in 1895 triggered a reaction which drew upon the mediatory powers of Grover Cleveland. The final settlement is even today contested by Venezuela, which alleges partiality on the part of several arbiters. With British Guiana gaining its independence in 1966, the yet unresolved conflict apparently lessened somewhat. More traditional relations include those with the United States, with which Venezuela is presently amicable although less warmly cordial than when based upon the personal friendship of Presidents Betancourt and Kennedy. Within the hemisphere Venezuela, threatened continually by the clandestine aggression of Cuba, has been among those to combat the Castro regime most steadfastly. The explicit venom of Cuban propaganda attacks has added fuel to a popular reaction; the vast majority of Venezuelans are avowedly hostile to the Cuban revolutionary Government. At the same time the Venezuelan Government, largely as a result of traditional AD views on hemisphere affairs, has refused to maintain diplomatic relations with dictatorial or nonconstitutional regimes. Under the Betancourt Doctrine—really a modern version of the familiar Tobar Doctrine—such overthrows of government call for a diplomatic break. Among the most recent examples is the refusal of the Leoni Government to recognize the Brazilian military regime of Castello Branco, which led Venezuela to absent herself from the special foreign ministers' conference held in late 1965 in Rio de Janeiro. Distinctions between representative and nonrepresentative governments can be expected to continue as a basic criterion within the foreign ministry. Growing interest in the potentialities of possible regional integration, including membership in the Latin American Free Trade Area, can be anticipated for some time. Support of the Organization of American States continues, but the general view holds that either the OAS should be structurally and functionally strengthened, or else it should divest itself of its more ambitious goals and objectives on the grounds of inadequacy.

Political Alienation

The kind of agreement which has been evolving in the decade of the 1960s should not for a moment obscure the very real alienation which has been felt by some elements, especially the nation's youth. Both the regulars of the PCV and the more radical *Miristas* contributed to the violent antigovernment campaign of the extreme Left. Drawing inspiration from Fidel Castro, pledging themselves to a guerrilla campaign reminiscent of the Sierra Maestra, and bitterly attacking moderate leaders for their unwillingness to undertake an immediate national transformation, the two groups organized and supported a band of irregulars, which became the Armed Forces of National Liberation (FALN). The FALN first planned for a massive peasant uprising which would have paralleled what they believed had transpired in Cuba during the anti-Batista struggle. When *campesino* support for the Betancourt Government thwarted their efforts, they turned instead to a campaign of urban terror, which continued through most of 1962 and 1963. Hoping that the attendant chaos and disorder would compel the military to seize power, the FALN further reasoned that the inevitable deterioration into dictatorship would ultimately permit the far Left to lead a massive popular uprising culminating in the establishment of a "Socialist people's republic."

Havana's commitment to the exportation of the Cuban Revolution coincided with the Venezuelan extremists' decision to launch unlimited attacks in the urban centers, and waves of irresponsible mutilation and death periodically swept the city streets. The terrorists envisaged not only military intervention in politics but also the frightened withdrawal of major foreign investment. Such enterprises as Sears were attacked by arson, while petroleum pipelines and facilities were destroyed when possible; the theft of French art paintings from the Caracas Museum, the hijacking of the Venezuelan freighter *Anzoátegui,* and the kidnapping at various times of both a visiting Spanish soccer star and an officer in the U.S. military mission were all intended to win international headlines as well as youthful adherents. The planting of bombs and the machine-gunning in city streets proved more serious, however, and public opinion turned sharply against the FALN shortly before the December 1963 elections, when an excursion train was attacked and five national guardsmen died at an assassin's hands. The reluctant decision of the Betancourt Government to suspend the congressional immunity of Communist and *Mirista* representatives while further banning their party activities was accepted without serious protest from even the most outspoken members of the Democratic opposition. With the abject failure of the FALN to block 1963 elections, the far Left retreated to reconsider its position and eventually reversed policy once again to pursue the tactics of rural guerrilla fighting. Claiming that the rapid victory envisaged by urban violence had been unrealistic, the FALN promised to conduct a decade-long battle in the interior. There were few signs by 1967 that their prospects were any less dim than they had been earlier.

The membership of the FALN included certain criminal elements but was in large part composed of young Venezuelans, many of them university students. Moreover, much of the leadership in student organizations was transferred to Communists and Marxists following the MIR defection from Acción Democrática. While the degree of enthusiasm over Marxism is comparable to that among students elsewhere in Latin America, it is also true that large numbers of Venezuelan students have rejected the tactics and objectives of the far Left. While many students are politically apathetic, others have preferred to oppose the extremists in political competition. Student elections in recent years have seen the extremists generally winning only slightly greater support than pro-COPEI students, who draw most of the moderate vote. There have also been occasions on which strikes and protests by the more radical student leadership at Caracas' Universidad Central de Venezuela have not been supported by those at the other universities. It is not surprising that many Venezuelan student leaders feel a deep duty and responsibility for future progress in the country. This feeling has been a youthful trait in much of the world and has certainly been the rule historically in Latin America. It is also predictable that many, impatient with evolutionary progress and unrealistic about political and social experience, are blindly following paths which have a disruptive rather than a constructive influence. The dysfunctionality of extremist student leadership has both harassed freely-elected government and has occupied time and money which might more appropriately be applied toward other channels.

The alienation of many young educated Venezuelans from the political system is largely indirect in that their own substantive and material positions are relatively free of deprivation. Moreover, the majority have the promise of careers in which the often elusive combination of major responsibility and personal gain will be experienced. It is this latter fact which has been largely responsible for the gradual diminution of the influence of extremist student leaders. Judged on both psychological and material grounds, several sectors of society should with greater justice feel estranged from the ongoing system.

However precisely one may define political alienation, its components in Venezuela should include elements of both the urban and the rural lower classes. In the latter case, however, the perceptible if slow rise in productivity, the redistribution of land, with the technical assistance and personal contacts established by and through agents of the National Agrarian Institute, have all tended to draw the *campesino* into the existing system more effectively than before. There is greater uncertainty where the urban proletariat is concerned. The moderate, pro-AD leadership of the national labor movement has lost ground recently, with both *Copeyano* and extreme leftist leaders chipping away at the once monolithic AD control. With unemployment still a basic national problem, with urbanization adding to social dislocation in the city slums while the gap in housing and health remains, it is impossible to deny the existence of bases for various types of political alienation. And while the probability may not be great, it is by no means inconceivable that, if new legislation fails to promote the alleviation of such conditions, the lower classes in the cities, and notably organized labor, may for the first time in the past generation play a dysfunctional role.

DIMENSIONS OF SYSTEMIC CHANGE

Few countries of Latin America have undergone such a major and extensive set of alterations in a relatively short span of time. Political institutions have been democratized, public participation expanded, labor unionism encouraged, social reforms initiated, foreign relations rationalized, and economic structure diversified and improved. No single social class or subgroup has been insulated from change although the impact has naturally varied from one to another. The long-range ramifications of this national development are in many instances subtle and complex. While the present political leadership is devoting its energies to the rationalization and implementation of policy goals which have been articulated in earlier years, a new array of problems has emanated from the material accomplishments of the past twenty years. Dysfunctionalism has been typical of certain segments of social and political life. Psychological dislocations, the shifting of party allegiances, and the reformulation of economic conditions have not yet been fully recognized or studied. Concomitantly, the relative degree of stability within a system committed irrevocably to change is presently uncertain. Underlying possible developmental and modernizing trends, however, is the widely accepted accord which has sprung forth.

A Broadening National Consensus

An obvious and basic indicator of national agreement is represented electorally by the December 1963 vote. Although the campaign was the most heated in national history, there was little basic dispute on policy issues. The respective party bids for support were far more than mere personalistic peroration; public questions were debated across the countryside, with conflicting views aired at great length by the major communications media. The general acceptance of policy objectives as described above stood forth as one of the campaign's most striking characteristics. With six visible presidential challengers and a host of congressional contenders differing only on details of implementation, it was clear that responsible leadership had charted its basic course and was committed to a continuation along existing guidelines. While some voters undoubtedly found no candidate or party slate to their liking, their numbers were few. Only avowed sympathizers or supporters of the far Left were unable to register a vote for their own political preferences. While this inability reveals in part that the national consensus is by no means complete, it does not alter the fact that an overwhelming predominance of Venezuelans registered basic approval for existing public policies.

With Acción Democrática polling one-third of the vote and COPEI following with twenty percent, over half the electorate indicated satisfaction with the government coalition, notwithstanding the inevitable disillusionment and erosion of support that comes naturally over a period of time. The URD and its leader, Jóvito Villalba, won a fraction less than nineteen percent of the vote, with the then independent Arturo Uslar Pietri following with sixteen percent. The shape of the Leoni coalition following his inauguration in early 1964 bears further witness to the relative similarity of major political organizations. With COPEI choosing to remain outside the administration, Leoni was faced with the task of constructing a viable congressional majority. In so doing, he succeeded in embracing all major parties except COPEI. Of particular note is the fact that he was able to include Uslar Pietri's newly organized FND. Long one of the most articulate and outspoken critics of Acción Democrática, still mindful that the AD ouster of the Medina Government in 1945 had dissipated his own hopes for a subsequent Presidency through *Medinista* sponsorship, Uslar had been in greater disagreement with administration policies than any other leading politician. Although no arch-Conservative, he stood clearly to the right of the three major parties on economic and social matters. Nonetheless Leoni accomplished the feat of drawing Uslar Pietri into his coalition though the FND later fragmented and, in early 1966, formally withdrew.

The enunciation of national issues, then, presently reflects a high degree of accord on the part of political leadership. While differences may be sharply framed, they continue to focus attention on detail rather than on basic objectives. The achievement of such a consensus augurs well for the nation's future. The striking endorsement in 1963 elections also indicated an undeniable repudiation of violence and extremism. The evolution of the consensus suggests the prospect of an even fuller agreement in the years ahead. There are no indications that the radical proposals of the far Left have gained significant popular support, although the ill-advised reliance on urban violence has undoubtedly harmed the advocates of revolutionary action. It is not impossible, of course, that the present trends might be reversed. For a time, the existence of Raúl Leoni's "national unity" government provided the administration with a comfortable political position, but that situation changed in 1966. Since that time, the determination of opposition forces to defeat Acción Democrática in 1968 elections has heightened political antagonisms. The result has been a perceptible increase in systemic stresses. Today's consensus therefore can by no means be taken for granted. If political leadership acts within an atmosphere of insular self-satisfaction, the consensus will prove to be transient. In this event, presently alienated or dissatisfied elements might swiftly assume dominant roles. This new leadership would bring radical transformation, with a new consensus being articulated and reformulated only after the most disruptive of transitional periods.

Stability and Change

The occasional theoretical dichotomization of the terms "stability" and "change" is not uncommon in the Latin American literature, yet that dichotomization grossly oversimplifies the nature of social and political modernization in a region of dynamic forces. The very distinction between "revolutionary" and "evolutionary" is illustrated by the AD experience. The Venezuelan revolution precipitated in October of 1945 was radical, sweeping, turbulent, and ultimately doomed to failure. The post-1958 AD leadership, sharing for extended periods its power and responsibility with other parties, found a gradualistic approach more conducive to the modernizing process. Stability becomes a cherished value in a country such as Venezuela, where in the absence of stability, significant socio-economic progress can be seriously jeopardized for a period of years. Stability does not stand as a symbol of the Conservative forces committed to preservation of the *status quo;* what stability does imply is a modicum of regularity through which rational and orderly development may be achieved. It is the stability of this framework that is based upon the innate resiliency and durability of the national consensus.

The basic responsibility for the maintenance of the consensus is obviously that of the Leoni Government. There are small pockets of dissatisfaction which could provide the nucleus of dissent and opposition if existing grievances are not aired and remedied. The problems of Venezuelan youth have been cited already. Without explaining away the situation on the simplistic grounds of mere youthful exuberance and alienation of the younger generation from its elders, it is nonetheless true that the politically radical student leaders cannot be assured of unwavering support from the rank and file. To many who have matriculated, the attractive career opportunities after graduation beckon like a Circe. And in the long run, the sympathies of many young Venezuelans have not been involved by existing political forces. In this area the potential for change is enormous; in 1963 alone, more than half the electorate was voting for the first time. With Venezuela's population explosion one of the greatest in the entire world, the figure by the time of the 1968 elections will be even higher. In a very real sense the fate of the nation will rest ultimately in the hands of these citizens, and yet in many cases their loyalties have not yet been politically engaged, either by moderate or extremist forces. The challenge of Venezuelan youth is a major one for all of the parties, and the outcome of the response will play a large part in shaping the course of future events.

Existing party leadership must also deal with the urban dweller. One of the major conclusions drawn from the study of recent elections is the extent to which none of the major parties attracted truly significant support in Caracas and its environs. The so-called Metropolitan Center, which includes the Federal District plus the states of Miranda and Aragua, constituted twenty-eight percent of the estimated population in 1963, yet the presidential candidates of the three major parties drew only forty-three percent of its vote, while the "independent" Uslar Pietri and Wolfgang Larrazábal compiled well over half. Thus, what in 1958 had been regarded as the AD's "Caracas Problem" by 1963 became serious for the URD and COPEI as well, when the latter two trailed the AD in the area. Uslar Pietri, campaigning as an independent and deriding the selfish partisanship of existing parties, polled one-third of the Metropolitan Center vote while gathering a full forty percent in the Federal District itself. The relative dissatisfaction of those in and around Caracas thus constitutes a message of warning to each of the leading parties. And again, undue inactivity on the part of the present Government could well lead to a greater disaffiliation with these parties, which would leave the city voter ripe for the picking by some as yet unknown political leader or organization, which might fully and resoundingly shatter the electoral consensus.

Sources of class conflict and the problems attendant upon increased social mobility cannot be ignored. To these must be added the potential threat of a rural-urban cleavage. The Pérez Jiménez decade saw the interests of the interior totally overlooked, while money from the sale of oil was poured into gaudily extravagant construction projects in Caracas. Under Rómulo Betancourt the effort to redress this imbalance drew inevitable criticism from the *caraqueños,* aided in no small part by the obvious political advantages of courting *campesino* support. Similar charges have been directed toward the Leoni Government, although urban problems of housing and slum conditions have received somewhat greater attention. In any event, the threat of a rural-urban division offers another possible basis for conflict. Notwithstanding improving social and economic conditions generally, the potential for either organized or irregular violence exists. Whether or not this violence may evolve depends upon the pace and progress of modernization. The dimensions of change have been great, and they are not likely to diminish in the foreseeable future. Although the ultimate verdict for Venezuela must lie years ahead, the almost unlimited endowment for progress and change provides ample grounds for informed if cautious optimism.

9 / Colombia

L. VINCENT PADGETT

ENRIQUE LOW MURTRA

L. VINCENT PADGETT, Professor of Political Science at San Diego State College, received his Ph.D. from Northwestern University in 1955. He has received Doherty and Social Science Research Council grants for research in Latin America, and served in 1965–66 as Special Staff Assistant for the Rockefeller Foundation; he worked in the university development program at the Universidad del Valle in Cali, Colombia. Besides writing several articles on Mexico, he was the author of The Mexican Political System *and edited* Community Development in the Western Hemisphere.

ENRIQUE LOW MURTRA has been an economics professor at the Centro de Investigaciones de Desarrollo Económico of the Universidad de Valle, and in 1966–67 pursued advanced work at Harvard University under a Rockefeller grant. His research stresses international trade and fiscal policy, especially as these matters relate to Colombia.

INTRODUCTION

Colombia is a country with Hispanic antecedents which is located in the northern half of the continent of South America and borders on both the Atlantic and the Pacific Oceans. Because Colombia is a mountainous country with three major ranges, which run north and south, it has a wide range of climate—very tropical in some areas, moderate in others (of greater altitude), where crops are raised which are similar to those of countries of the Northern Hemisphere. There are rich river valleys and fertile high plains used for agricultural purposes. There is also relatively abundant mineral wealth. In part because of the mountainous character of Colombia, the culture of the country is highly regionalized; for example, it has only been in the last twenty or thirty years that leading families of one area have considered intermarriage with those of other regions.

Much of Colombian culture stems from the period of Hispanic colonization, although a few Indian tribes, such as the Chibcha, left cultural legacies. The high concentration of Negroes in the Valle del Cauca and on the coast around Cartagena indicates the inability of the original Indian inhabitants to do the kind of work that the Spanish conquerors demanded. Although there is a considerable Indian and Negro admixture in some areas, most upper-class Colombians show relative purity of the Caucasian strain.

HISTORICAL BACKGROUND

The Spanish, led by Gonzalo de Ojeda, landed in 1501 in the northern part of Colombia on the coast of what is now called the Guajira. They founded the town of Santa Marta in the present Department of Magdalena on the Caribbean coast.[1] In 1538 the present capital, Bogotá, was founded on the high plains by Gonzalo Jiménez de Quezada. This area then became a dependency of the Viceroyalty of Peru. Later a new viceroyalty, that of Nueva Granada, was formed, of which Colombia was a part. This was the administrative situation at the time the first standards of independence were raised against Spain in 1810.

In 1819, Colombian independence emerged from Bolívar's triumph on the battle of Boyacá in a mountainous area about a hundred miles from Bogotá. Within a few years Bolívar had also obtained the independence of other areas of the former Viceroyalties of Nueva Granada and Peru, such as Venezuela and Ecuador.[2] In the struggle for independence, especially in the area that is now the Republic of Colombia, Bolívar's foremost lieutenant was Francisco de Paula Santander.

Unfortunately for Colombia at the beginning of its independence, Santander and Bolívar fell into a disagreement, and each formed factions which eventually evolved into the two major political parties which Colombia has had since that time.[3] Despite Santander's opposition, Bolívar had himself declared dictator of the new Gran Colombia, which included Ecuador, Colombia, and Venezuela, and which broke apart with the decline of Bolívar's health and his death in 1830. Santander's faction drafted a Constitution in 1832,

---

[1] Colombia is a unitary state, and its major administrative subdivisions are called departments. These departments frequently but not always follow basic lines of regional and cultural patterns.

[2] The Capitanía de Venezuela was under the Viceroyalty of Nueva Granada. Ecuador, on the other hand, was part of the Viceroyalty of Peru.

[3] Eduardo Santa, *Sociología política de Colombia* (Bogotá, Tercer Mundo, 1965), pp. 25–45.

which referred to the area we now call Colombia as Nueva Granada, and Santander became President. Santander's group incurred the enmity of the Church in various ways, especially in education and in constitutional orientation. This anticlerical bias lasted throughout the nineteenth century and became a major source of dispute between Liberals and Conservatives. Proclericalism coincided with preference for greater centralization. Anticlericals tended to espouse the cause of federalism.

By the middle of the nineteenth century, the rival political groups were clearly delineated as the Conservative and Liberal parties. Apart from issues of centralism and clericalism, there was the slavery question, which was resolved in the 1850s, when the Liberals freed the slaves. In the seesaw struggle for power, the Liberals found a strong leader in Tomás Cipriano de Mosquera and were able to frame a Constitution in 1863, which reflected their federalist and anticlerical position. In succeeding years all Presidents were Liberals until Rafael Núñez, a Liberal turned Conservative, and Miguel Antonio Caro rebelled and wrote a new Constitution in 1886, which provided for a unitary government, but with some allowances for administrative decentralization. This is the Constitution (with many changes) which is the basis of Colombian law and governmental organization today.

The Conservatives controlled Colombia without major difficulties until the Liberals began an uprising in 1898. The ensuing struggle is now referred to as the Thousand Days War. The most important consequence of this bloody civil conflict was the hardening of long-standing rivalries and feelings of hatred between the two parties. In some respects the political history of Colombia until 1957–1958 revolved around these deep feelings of antipathy. The old issues of federalism versus centralism and clericalism versus anticlericalism became less important than the general feeling of hatred, which lasted for generations after this armed conflict.[4]

After the Thousand Days War the Conservatives were on top, and they completely controlled the Presidency until 1930. However, this dominance did not prevent the introduction of new ideologies which formed new bases of conflict. The question of rights for labor was introduced by Rafael Uribe Uribe, who was assassinated in 1913. Later, the Liberal Jorge Eliécer Gaitán returned from a trip to Europe, where he was much influenced by Socialist doctrines. With Gaitán's outstanding personal appeal, these ideas of the Left began to have popular roots. At the same time Conservative leaders, especially Laureano Gómez, began to be attracted by new Fascist concepts, especially as developed in Spain and Italy. It was these new ideological complications which were in part responsible for the Conservative split and the Liberal victory of 1930. However, the leftward drift of Liberal thought did not really begin to affect Colombian government and society until the Liberal Alfonso López was elected Chief Executive in 1934.

---

[4] It was in the aftermath of this civil war that the Colombians lost Panama through United States intervention in 1903.

Under López new reforms to the Constitution were pushed through. One of these made it possible for persons to get title to land if it could be proved that the land had not been used by the owner within a period of five years. This law provided a basis for the agrarian reform measures which Colombia was to adopt later. Another reform made it possible for the first time for unions to have legal personality. Labor was permitted the right to strike and the right of collective bargaining. Other provisions established the right to severance pay, limitations on the work day, and recognition of the norm of a minimum wage. Another measure provided for a progressive income tax, which, by augmenting public funds, permitted the construction of such public works projects as the campus of the National University and the expansion of highways and railroads. The latter were handled as public enterprises.

After López' four-year term, Eduardo Santos, representing the conservative part of the Liberal party, became President, and the impetus for the López reforms was lost. It was not regained after López was re-elected in 1942. The second López administration suffered greatly from dissension within the Liberal party, and his regime actually collapsed temporarily in July 1944. This collapse was in part the result of disputes springing from López' relatively favorable position towards labor, though his position on all reforms had become more conservative. After a period of twelve days, López was again able to assume control, but his administration had been so weakened that he felt it advisable to resign the following year and left the *designado,* Alberto Lleras Camargo, to carry on pending the advent of a new President in 1946.[5]

By 1946 the right wing of the Liberal party, led by Gabriel Turbay, and the left wing, under Jorge Eliécer Gaitán, were badly divided, whereas the Conservative party, under the leadership of Laureano Gómez and Mariano Ospina Pérez, had achieved a new unity around the candidacy of Ospina, who was elected President. It appeared that Ospina would have sufficient popular support to govern the country without difficulty, but in April 1948 Gaitán was assassinated in Bogotá at the time of the Eighth Inter-American Conference. The assassination set off days of violence in Bogotá and laid waste to the center of the city. The violence then spread to the countryside, and Colombia embarked upon what was perhaps the worst wave of fratricidal war in its history. Thousands of persons were massacred in the villages as Liberals and Conservatives attacked each other, and many hideous atrocities were committed. The consequences of *la violencia* were still being felt in 1966, long after the major trouble had subsided, because so many peasant children practically grew up in a school of village warfare, crime, and assassination. Some of these children became bandit marauders who evaded the Colombian military for a decade or more. The worst of this internecine struggle took place during the last two years of Ospina's term and the succeeding Presidency of Laureano

---

[5] The *designado* is elected by the Congress for a term of two years and succeeds the President if the latter dies or for some other reason vacates the office.

Gómez. The situation became so bad that Gómez was unable to avoid a successful *coup d'etat* under the direction of General Gustavo Rojas Pinilla in June 1953.

Rojas Pinilla began his military dictatorship with great popular support because he promised the tired and bloodsoaked country that it would have "peace, justice and liberty." There seems little doubt that the vast majority of Colombians in both the cities and the rural areas at first believed that Rojas could provide these conditions. Reports in the foreign press gave a favorable impression of the new Government, and the American observer Vernon L. Fluharty wrote on this period a widely distributed book that was very favorable to Rojas.[6]

Rojas inaugurated a series of policies which at first seemed to hold promise for the future. First of all, he succeeded in getting most of the warring bands on the eastern plains, where the violence had been extremely cruel, to lay down their arms under the motto, "The country above parties." Secondly, Rojas initiated popular housing programs through the Instituto de Crédito Territorial (ICT). Persons with small incomes were particularly favored, and the scope of the effort was planned to include not only the cities but the rural areas as well. Some 4,200 units were constructed in Bogotá in 1954, and though other areas did not benefit as much, there was wide popular support among the masses for this effort. Rojas also formed a new agency known as SENDAS (National Secretariat for Social Assistance), through which aid was distributed to poor and often homeless children in various regions of the country and which provided help in such emergencies as the explosion of a munitions train in Cali in August 1955. Finally, economic development received a new stimulus in the early Rojas years. Employment was high, the Colombian coffee crop was widely purchased on the world market and brought premium prices, and the peso was stronger in relation to the dollar than it had been for years.

In light of these conditions, how does one explain the fact that the Rojas Government lasted only four years? One answer is that a number of negative factors were at work alongside the positive ones. Although the violence had been all but eliminated on the eastern plains, it had not been eradicated in other areas. Bandits became active in Villa Rica and in Cunday to the east of Tolima in the mountains. The army began to carry out increasingly ruthless raids against peasant villages that were thought to be harboring the marauders and killed the innocent with the guilty and executed the adults of entire villages without benefit of trial. In addition, the SENDAS activities, which had begun with so much fanfare, gradually became less and less substantial. Programs were starved for funds, and the oratory of government officials served only to emphasize the lack of effectiveness in this sector. Hospital and medical services which had been promised did not expand significantly, and

---

[6] Vernon L. Fluharty, *Dance of the Millions* (Pittsburgh, University of Pittsburgh Press, 1957). For a contrasting view see John D. Martz, *Colombia* (Chapel Hill, The University of North Carolina Press, 1962), pp. 173–245.

programs for orientation of mothers in nutrition and basic hygiene remained limited to a very few centers in some of the larger cities. Moreover, Rojas did not significantly enlarge opportunities for the multitude of urban and rural poor to achieve at least a primary education.

The deficiencies of the Rojas Government in solving basic social problems were highlighted by careless handling of precious foreign exchange. Dollars and other hard currencies earned by the favorable situation of Colombian coffee in the world market were allowed to slip out for the purchase of unnecessary foreign products. Particularly irritating to many Colombians were the expensive benefits granted to the armed forces in the form of military hardware, and even more damaging to Rojas' reputation were the commissariats, where officers could obtain luxury items at the cost of purchase in the country where they were produced. The importation on a large scale of automobiles, often luxury models, became notorious. This profligate treatment of precious foreign currency reserves gave Rojas no margin when coffee prices began to fall.[7]

Rojas also had little regard for the usual basic civil liberties. During his four years of government, he managed to violate almost every guarantee in Title III of the Colombian Constitution. For example, he shut down Colombia's three leading newspapers, *El Tiempo, El Espectador,* and *El Siglo.* He broke up student demonstrations, and one such event in June 1954 involved sending troops into the supposedly sacred ground of the National University campus with the result that one student was killed and others badly injured. Attendance at public spectacles was jeopardized when police and troops on one occasion fired into crowds at Bogotá's bullfight stadium.

Corruption also appeared when Rojas took over the rich Verástegui sugar enterprise in the Department of Córdoba. Moreover, it was widely thought that he used public funds to develop his *finca,* located at Melgar in the Department of Tolima, for which he imported thoroughbred cattle without paying import taxes. Suppression of rights, mass killings, and errors in economic policy combined to bring about a steady diminution of his popularity. His Government finally fell before a nationwide protest on May 10, 1957. Even after his fall, however, the country remained for approximately a year and a half under the government of the military men Gabriel Paris, Deogracias Fonseca, Ruben Piadreahita Arango, Rafael Navas Pardo, and Luis E. Ordónez, who had been close collaborators of Rojas.

Like Perón in Argentina, Rojas left a large body of admirers whose devotion has seemed to increase in direct proportion to the amount of time since he has left office. The approximately 700,000 votes that were cast for the Rojas candidate, José Jaramillo Girardo, in 1966 bore witness to the fact that many people remembered very little about the negative aspects of the Rojas Government. These people simply recalled that, under Rojas, prices

---

[7] Coffee prices hit a new high in the history of the country when in 1954 a pound of Colombian coffee on the world market was worth ninety-eight cents (U.S.), but by 1966, the price dropped to fifty cents (U.S.).

were roughly four times lower and that there was less unemployment than in 1966.

In order to get the reins of government out of the hands of the military junta, Laureano Gómez of the Conservatives and Alberto Lleras Camargo of the Liberals worked out a sixteen-year agreement to divide positions equally, called *paridad,* in the major bodies of government, including the national ministries, the Congress, the departmental assemblies, the municipal councils, and all judicial tribunals. The Presidency was to alternate between Liberals and Conservatives every four years (known as *alternación*). To implement this agreement, the two parties agreed to carry out the first plebiscite in Colombian history; the result of this plebiscite vote would ascertain whether or not this pact, which excluded all but Liberals and Conservatives, should be written into the Constitution. On December 1, 1957, ninety percent of those voting approved the new arrangement. Thus was constituted what has come to be called Frente Nacional (National Front).

At first the leaders of the Frente were in agreement that a Conservative should be President. However, they could not settle on which Conservative it should be. The Liberals favored Guillermo León Valencia, the son of a former President, but the dominant Conservative leader, Laureano Gómez, would not accept Valencia's candidacy. When the *Laureanistas,* or the Gómez faction of the Conservatives, won a majority of Conservative seats in the congressional elections preceding the presidential election, Laureano Gómez suggested that the terms of the agreement be changed to allow the first President of the Frente to be a Liberal. Consequently, Alberto Lleras Camargo, who gained four times the vote of his opponent, Jorge Leyva, became President of Colombia in 1958.

With widespread popular support at the beginning of Lleras' Presidency, he called for fundamental systemic changes: The vast powers of the Executive, which had been greatly expanded during the Rojas period, should now be limited, and congressional power, waning from as early as Ospina's Presidency, should be strengthened. Not only did Congress assume a stronger posture in making laws, but it acquired the right to call itself into session when a state of siege would be invoked. Lleras also endeavored to foster a career civil service, to be nurtured by a National School of Public Administration. Unfortunately, this plan was thwarted by opposition from congressmen who preferred to award their supporters with appointments under the spoils system and by a growing unemployment problem, which many governmental leaders believed should be met by more rather than fewer bureaucrats. The idea of a career civil service finally died during the subsequent Presidency of Guillermo León Valencia, who concentrated entirely on avoiding difficulty among factions within the Conservative and Liberal parties by distributing, in an exaggerated form of *alternación,* all administrative posts, even down to the most menial janitorial tasks, in accord with the strength of these groups in Congress and in the departmental assemblies.

Apart from the failure of the career civil service program, other factors detracted from the record of the Lleras administration. New outbreaks of violence in the Quindío region in the Department of Caldas and in the northern part of the Department of Valle in the Cauca River Valley were blamed by many on the Minister of Justice's program for the rehabilitation of captured bandit leaders. A number of former bandits were released from prison without any measures being taken to prevent their obtaining firearms. Three major bands, *"Chispas," "Sangre Negra,"* and *"Tiro Fijo,"*[8] began to harass the countryside. The cost of this wave of violence was high not only in human life but in terms of the necessity of expanding army operations. This financial cost in itself detracted significantly from funds available to the Lleras administration for implementing economic and social development projects.

The Lleras reform program also fell short in its new tax laws. The project was supposed to graduate income taxes more sharply so that a lesser burden would fall upon middle-income employee groups and a greater one upon the high-income groups. However, the administration of tax collection under the National Tax Division of the Ministry of the Treasury was not improved in accordance with the plan, and many big industrialists and land owners followed the traditional practice of paying off to intermediaries, sometimes termed *manzanillos,* instead of sending the full sum of their taxes into the national treasury.[9]

As if all this were not enough, the Lleras administration also lost heavily on income because of unfavorable market conditions for the all-important Colombian coffee crop. During this period coffee prices dropped to thirty-nine cents (U.S.) per pound. This drop amounted to a disaster, since year in and year out the Colombian Government has depended upon coffee to provide seventy to seventy-two percent of its foreign exchange.

The drop in coffee prices, the tax reform failures, and the renewed violence made it necessary for the Lleras Government to cut back upon funds for development; however, even with reduced programs, the Government found itself with successive deficits in 1961 and 1962 which came to more than a billion pesos, or no less than thirty percent of the normal budget. Many economists consider that for a developing economy a deficit of only three to five percent is customarily acceptable if inflationary effects are not to be damaging.[10]

The Lleras Government added to its financial difficulties when it allowed the importation on a large scale of 1961-model cars from the United States

---

[8] As of June 1966, only one of the major bandit leaders, *Tiro Fijo,* was still at large, and his zone of operation had been reduced to a small area of mountainous country known as the Marquetalia region, in the Department of Huila.

[9] The Colombians use the word *manzanillo* in several ways. It can refer to a quack politician, to a down-at-the-heels lawyer or to the pay-off man in tax collection cases. In the instance of tax collection, *manzanillo* represents a cultural pattern of tax avoidance. The beginning of mechanization in the tax division in Bogotá indicates that Colombian policy-makers are becoming more aware of the gravity of this problem.

[10] Departamento Administrativo de Planeación y Servicios Técnicos, *Plan general de desarrollo económico y social* (Bogotá, 1963), Chapter 4. See also Laughlin Currie, *Accelerating Development* (New York, McGraw-Hill, 1966), pp. 188–90, 232.

and other countries. For example, during the year of 1960–61, Colombia imported 8,878 automobiles for a total value of $15,548,143 (U.S.), whereas in 1957 Colombia only imported 858 automobiles, which cost $1,879,660 (U.S.).[11]

The difficulties encountered by Lleras were magnified during the Presidency of Guillermo León Valencia (1962–66). The deficit in the balance of payments continued, and in an effort to correct this problem and give the economy a new stimulus, the Valencia Government tried devaluation. The grave error was made of announcing the devaluation two weeks in advance so that all persons in a position to buy dollars did so, causing still further difficulties in the balance of payments. This error, in conjunction with the new monetary issues authorized by the Government at this time, aggravated the inflation already underway. Within two years the cost of living index increased 96.3 percent.[12] Valencia's financial errors caused the International Monetary Fund, the International Bank for Reconstruction and Development, and the Inter-American Development Bank to cut off Colombian credit from the fall of 1964 until July 1965. With the continued dollar shortage, factories were frequently unable to secure the necessary foreign exchange for the purchase of raw materials. Consequently, many plants had to shut down or cut their operations significantly, and thus further exacerbated the already grave unemployment situation. The pattern of balance of payments deficits, inflation, and unemployment finally drove the Valencia Government to seek a new Minister of the Treasury who could persuade the international lending agencies to open up credit facilities again. The new treasury minister, Joaquín Vallejo, was successful in this respect, but none of the basic problems had really changed as the Valencia Government drew toward the close of its term.

As Valencia entered his last year of government, he stated that his administration had dealt effectively with the perennial problem of *la violencia*. There was some basis for this claim since, of the major bandit leaders, only *"Tiro Fijo"* remained at large. However, there were at least three bands of guerrillas, distinguished from bandit gangs, or *bandoleros,* by a political orientation toward social revolution, operating in the mountains. It was in a brush with one of the former that the one-time Catholic priest Camilo Torres Restrepo was killed.[13] His death caused great consternation among university

---

[11] Departamento Administrativo Nacional de Estadística (DANI), *Anuario del comercio exterior* (Bogotá, 1957), pp. 522–523; (Bogotá, 1960), pp. 647–649. After an International Monetary Fund loan was secured in 1966, there were signs that the pattern of mass importation of automobiles would once again be established.

[12] Universidad del Valle, Centro de Investigaciones de Desarrollo Económico (C.I.D.E.), *Compendio Estadístico* (Cali, 1966), Table 14.

[13] Camilo Torres Restrepo was an intelligent and widely liked young priest from the highest social stratum of Bogotá. After being ordained, he became both chaplain and teacher at Universidad Nacional. With his sociological bent, he became increasingly identified with the plight of Bogotá's poor. His emotional identification with the poor and their problems eventually led him to attempt to influence public policy, and in so doing he alienated the Catholic hierarchy. Torres joined the guerrillas after encountering insurmountable obstacles to the public meetings he tried to hold to present his views.

students all over the country and especially among former students of the Universidad Nacional, among whom he had gained almost universal respect. Official sources said little about the number of guerrillas in existence, but rumor put them anywhere from 150 to over 1,000.

Valencia paid a high price for his attempts to pacify the country. He found it necessary to declare a state of siege, and after the kidnapping and death of Harold Eder, the outstanding member of an extremely wealthy Valle family, Valencia turned over all kidnapping cases and associated crimes to trial by military tribunals instead of using the existing court system. The Ministry of Defense encouraged members of wealthy Colombian families to form a civil defense association and, in doing so, stimulated the acquisition of firearms for private use. The effects of this abdication of the Government's proper role in the maintenance of public order was reflected in uneasiness and in additional episodes of violence. For example, in March 1966, in the Department of Valle, a group of private citizens tried to assume the responsibility for maintaining public order by attacking students at the public high school in the town of Buga. When one of the students was killed, students in other institutions went on strike. Thus, the citizens' defense associations can be considered dysfunctional in that they have represented an abdication of an essential function of government.

On the 17th of August, 1966 Carlos Lleras Restrepo was inaugurated as President of Colombia. He had promised sweeping changes in economic and social arrangements within a short time. However, as the months passed it became clear that he would encounter difficulties in surmounting the obstacles which had confronted his predecessors. Perhaps his most serious problem stemmed from a steep drop in the price of coffee. By the end of 1966 the value of Colombian exports in dollars reached only $280 million, whereas estimates by the International Monetary Fund (IMF) had placed the dollar value of Colombian exports for the year at $360 million. A second major difficulty centered around increasing activity on the part of the National Liberation Army, a guerrilla movement in the Castro style.

The drop in coffee prices created difficulty in the Colombian balance of payments which in turn involved difficult decisions both in Washington and in Colombia. The IMF recommended a devaluation of the peso, but this was greeted by strong protest from various sectors of Colombian society. The difficulties with inflation which had arisen subsequent to the devaluation by the government of Valencia (discussed above) had caused many Colombians to think of such a policy as an instrument of exploitation by the wealthy. Moreover, it was quite clear that devaluation in the past had resulted in a flight of capital with the usual adverse effect on the balance of payments. These considerations led Lleras Restrepo to reject the recommendation of the IMF and in turn the IMF and the Agency for International Development (AID) suspended all loans which had been promised to the Colombian government. In his struggle to resolve the dilemma posed by domestic and external political pressures, Lleras Restrepo came up with two measures which permitted him to avoid the domestic onus placed upon devaluation, while at the same time reestablishing his government as an acceptable risk for IMF and AID decision-makers. One measure provided the sanction of imprisonment for persons who had been sending their capital out of the country for security reasons. Colombians reacted by returning an estimated $200 million, according to a report in *El Tiempo,* January 8, 1967. While this sum was probably not so high as the estimate, the results were clearly positive. And a second measure taxing sales of dollars to the Colombian government on the part of Colombian exporters also appeared to be having positive results. The international lending crisis was then temporarily alleviated when the IMF and other agencies in May, 1967 decided to authorize approximately $130 million for Colombia.

Solutions for the second major problem were not so easily forthcoming. A new pattern of violence seemed to be emerging. The old *violencia* which plagued Colombia from the time of the *Bogotazo* of 1948 had largely been carried on in recent years by *bandoleros,* i.e., raiders with little or no political orientation. Episodes such as the bombing of the United States Information Service in Bogotá in August, 1966, and an attack upon a railway train in the Department of Santander in March, 1967, along with a number of less spectacular incidents pointed up the shift to violence with a political orientation. To deal with the new type of violence, the Lleras government moved at various points to curtail the activities of political assemblies and demonstrations directed against Colombia's ruling groups. The difficulties in forming a policy for dealing with the problem in a restrained yet effective way was pointed up in October, 1966, when students of the National University demonstrated against the government, and the government retaliated with numerous arrests and trials by military courts which extended to the conviction not only of students and intellectuals directly involved, but also to many who were simply presumed to have been involved. Not only the acts by the National Liberation Army but also the method of retaliation on the part of the government underlined weaknesses of long standing with respect to the Colombian political system and the total system environment in which the political subsystem must be maintained.

However, the first year of Lleras' presidency also had its positive aspects. One of these was the abolition of the legal sanction for an old share-cropping institution, known as the *aparcería*. In removing the legal guaranties for this practice in December, 1966, Lleras pointed out that many abuses in the countryside could now be alleviated or abolished since the contract binding a peasant to give service to some landowner in return for cultivation rights could no longer be abused. In another area of affairs involving all classes of governmental capabilities, Lleras acted to rationalize selection and management of personnel over a wide range of governmental agencies. Much was made of the intent to select more technically qualified personnel and many persons holding public jobs were released from service. The long term effect of this effort to improve public administration, however, was not at all clear since personnel changes of this sort in the past had often been merely a reflection of political preferences rather than the institutionalization of achievement criteria. It would be a mistake, however, to write off this new thrust in the direction of improvement in the efficacy of government without a longer period to observe the results. These and other changes helped to offset some of the dimmer prospects as 1967 drew to a close.

THE SOCIAL ENVIRONMENT OF THE POLITICAL SYSTEM

It may be said that there are three major social strata in both the urban and the rural sectors, though it is possible to identify various substrata within these divisions. At the bottom is a poor class, the exact number of which would be difficult to determine, but which could be conservatively estimated as between sixty and seventy percent of the population. Components of this class range all the way from the omnipresent beggars in the city streets to the relatively privileged groups of organized workers and peasants whose earnings sometimes reach as high as 30 pesos a day or 750 to 800 pesos a month (as of June 1966).[14] At the bottom of this stratum are those who are in what J. A. Lebret calls the "destitute" category. A person belonging to this category is lucky to have an average income of five pesos per day. Sometimes a person with such an income must be relied upon to feed and house five or more persons. Even for the relatively privileged group in the lower stratum, opportunities for upward mobility are extremely limited. This limitation is particularly true of education, a major avenue for advancement. The illiteracy rate has remained close to forty-two percent since 1951.[15] Moreover, it seems to be well understood among Colombians who work with these statistics that the figures tend to obscure the magnitude of the problem. It appears to be the practice to include as "literate" almost anyone who can barely sign his name. Other considerations are perhaps more indicative of the problem of achieving social mobility through education. In the mid 1960s only about four percent of the Colombians in the relevant age groups could hope to complete high school, and probably less than one percent could expect to acquire a university degree. Difficulty in obtaining some education as a springboard for upward mobility is increased by the tendency of those in the lower social stratum to produce more children than do families in the middle sector or in the upper class; it is not unusual to find ten to twenty children in families of the upper lower stratum.

---

[14] Perhaps the most thorough study of Colombian society that has been published was done by a French priest and social scientist, J. A. Lebret. See his *Estudio sobre las condiciones del desarrollo de Colombia* (Bogotá, Cromos, 1958), p. 28. Lebret estimated that more than 80 percent of the population had incomes lower than three-fourths of the average per capita income and accounted for only about 30 percent of the total national income.

[15] According to the 1951 census, the illiteracy rate stood at 42.5 percent. See D.A.N.E., *Anuario general de estadística* (Bogotá, 1955), p. 23. In 1963, the illiteracy rate stood at 42.08 percent. See D.A.N.E., *Anuario general de estadística* (Bogotá, 1963), p. 206.

Among the poor peasants one frequently finds families of seven or more persons living on small farms, or *minifundia,* which cover five acres or less. The produce of these parcels may bring as little as four hundred pesos per year, or about one and one-half pesos daily. *Minifundia* of this type are especially noticeable in the Departments of Boyacá and Nariño. The total number of people living in these conditions cannot be estimated from existing statistics, but the sources available do indicate that this problem is one of national scope.

The second major social stratum is composed of middle-income groups, whose span of earnings reaches somewhere from 1,000 to 1,500 pesos a month at the lowest all the way to 10,000 pesos at the top. As of June 1966, it can be said that any family with an income of over 10,000 pesos per month has such a different way of life that such a family can only be considered to belong to the upper stratum. The upper middle stratum is characterized by concern for intellectual achievement and particularly for interest in philosophy, literature, and the humanities in general. The level of interest in these subjects even among persons with only a high-school education, or *bachillerato,* often compares favorably with that of university graduates from more developed countries. Moreover, this group is much more desirous of achieving educational advantages for their families than was the case a few generations ago.

Most predominant in the upper sector of the middle stratum are persons in the professions. However, some members of this upper sector are owners of small industries or shops, and others are those who without a university education have managed to achieve minor executive positions in banks or commercial and industrial firms. Also included in this sector are persons who have acquired some urban properties or stock shares and live primarily from this kind of income. In the rural areas upper-middle-class agriculturalists have holdings which can range all the way from twenty to a hundred hectares, depending upon the fertility of the land where their *fincas* are located.[16]

The majority of those at the lower level of the middle stratum occupy either the less important positions in the official bureaucracy or the corresponding levels in private firms. Here is found the majority of Colombia's white-collar workers. In the mid-1960s the monthly income of these people varied all the way from one thousand to three thousand pesos per month; thus the lowest in this group earned little more than the privileged organized worker or peasant. The social prestige of those in the upper middle class, while higher than that of a laborer, creates certain frustrations. For example, on a relatively small income members of the lower middle stratum are obliged

---

[16] See Dale Adams, *Landownership Patterns in Colombia* (Bogotá, Centro de Interamericano de Reforma Agraria, 1965), p. 3. See also INCORA, *Informe de Actividades en 1962* (Bogotá, 1963), pp. 49–50. According to Lebret's analysis, about 4.6 percent of the population accounted for 40 percent of the national income. The middle stratum probably amounted to no more than 16.4 percent of the population and had about 30 percent of the national income. Lebret, p. 28.

to spend money on dress clothes, which is not a problem for the blue-collar workers. The white-collar worker also has social obligations, such as the fiestas that must be given for all daughters when they reach fifteen years of age. In addition, white-collar workers usually want to give their children at least a high-school education and perhaps a university education, the costs of which are often beyond the financial means of these families. There are two principal barriers to achieving this ambition. One is the large size of the families, which stems in part from ignorance of effective methods of birth control. The other involves the scarcity of public school facilities, which do not meet the needs of the school-age population. Private schools, which educate the majority of high-school students, are often too costly for the large lower-middle-stratum family. Another pressure that weighs heavily upon the lower middle sector is its determination to live in *barrios,* or neighborhoods, apart from those of the upper stratum of the poor. Thus, lower-middle-class families incur significantly higher rentals or property costs than those of upper-lower-class families, whose incomes are not much lower.

These norms and patterns of behavior in the lower middle sector create conflict in the individual between the reality of his income and his conception of the correct style of life. The subsequent frustration, which often leads to alienation from the system, is aggravated by the still limited opportunities for upward social mobility. In this frustration is the basis for the frequent strikes of bank employees, teachers, and bureaucrats since the end of the Rojas Pinilla Government. This frustration is probably also one of the explanations for the relatively low voter turnouts under the *Frente* system. This substratum more than any other seems to provide leaders supporting extreme political views.

Colombians and most foreigners are well aware of an upper social stratum which is rather clearly defined and represents only a small percentage of the population. This segment can be divided into at least two groups. One of these is the managerial and entrepreneurial elite, which consists of those in charge of large commercial, industrial, and banking enterprises or of great industrialized haciendas, such as those producing sugar and sugar by-products. In some cases coffee *fincas* could also be included. People in this group are not necessarily descended from the other upper-class subgroup, which may well be termed the old aristocracy.

Within the upper stratum the managers and industrialists in general play the more dynamic role in the economy and in the society. The group as a whole is characterized by a desire to create new wealth, and often their creation of it is accomplished through a certain intuitive capacity rather than formal preparation for business administration. The people of the Department of Antioquia are particularly outstanding in this respect and have expanded their influence beyond their capital, Medellín, to other great cities, such as Bogotá, Cali, and Cartagena. It is the managerial and industrial group which has created the highly effective ANDI (National Association of Industrialists) and FENALCO (National Merchants Federation). Through these organizations great influence is exercised in not only the economy but politics and education as well. In education, for example, officials of ANDI and FEN-ALCO are found on the governing boards of all public universities and most private ones. Both these organizations were highly instrumental in bringing about the resignation of Rojas Pinilla in May 1957. These groups are also more influential in affecting government tax structure than any others. This substratum and its organizations have been the backbone of financial support for the Frente and include members of both the Liberal and Conservative parties.

The other subgroup in the highest social stratum is composed of persons whose socio-economic position depends upon extensive landholdings. The *latifundia* system in Colombia, as in many other Latin American countries, is still intact. In the Departments of Valle del Cauca, Cauca, Cundinamarca, Bolívar, and Huila, the system is particularly in evidence. In these departments the great landholders, whose possession of the land often dates back several centuries, consider holdings of twenty thousand hectares too small. For this group mere possession of the land is a symbol of high social standing.

Many of the great *latifundistas* prefer to live in town rather than in the country. These *latifundistas* leave their great estates in the hands of stewards and return infrequently for a weekend to hold a fiesta or a hunt for guests. Although there is a trend toward greater interest in improving cultivation and in livestock-raising, the majority still concern themselves very little with these matters. As long as these people have sufficient funds for their social commitments in the city of their residence and for lengthy excursions abroad, problems of maintaining or increasing production scarcely interest them. Often they lease their land for sharecropping under contracts that allow twenty percent or less of the income to those who seed and harvest the crops.

Especially in the Department of Bolívar, but also in the other departments mentioned above, there is a marked tendency to use fertile, level land as pasture for cattle and other livestock, perhaps because cattle-raising seems to present fewer problems than cultivation of the land. Moreover, the owners feel that raising cattle and fine horses is more a "gentleman's" concern. As cattlemen and as descendants of great horsemen, these *latifundistas* seek to reincarnate the ancient values of the *caballero* which have been handed down from the Spanish conquistadores. Following this system of values requires large amounts of leisure time.

The values of the old aristocracy influence the aspirations of other sectors of the upper stratum and of the upper middle sectors as well. Among the latter a major goal is to own a *finca* to which one can invite one's friends for a weekend. Many find it preferable to invest in land rather than in some industrial enterprise or co-operative. Thus the old landed aristocracy enforces the ancient *caballero* ideal, a state of mind little suited to the creation of new sources of capital and of employment for Colombia's burgeoning population.

Perhaps the great landholders of the Department of Valle del Cauca as a group constitute an exception to this overall pattern. In Valle sugar culture has become a predominant factor overshadowing livestock raising, and unlike many areas where cane is grown, the climate and soil make it possible to employ field workers the year around. However, there are Colombian economists as well as experts of the International Monetary Fund who wonder where the expansion in sugar culture will lead, since the demand on the world market is limited.

Because of the failure of many landholders to exploit their resources in an optimum way, the Lleras Camargo Government finally decided that some means of encouraging production in the rural areas as well as providing hope for enterprising but landless people should be attempted. Out of this decision came the agrarian reform legislation of 1960, which established the governmental agency INCORA, the Colombian Institute of Agrarian Reform. INCORA was assigned several tasks: to carry out studies of land tenure with a view to the redistribution of some of the unexploited privately-held land; to encourage the formation of co-operatives in order to integrate economically unproductive *minifundias;* to facilitate lending to small farmers; and to promote colonization of public lands in such unsettled areas as the Amazon forest region and the plains of the Orinoco River. However, progress in implementing these goals has been slow, and the redistribution of lands has been minimal. One of the reasons for this delay is that the law establishing INCORA called for detailed studies before any steps could be taken. Another reason is that private land when distributed has often been the least useful for the purpose, for example, in the Roldanillo region, in the Department of Valle del Cauca, estates were broken up which had provided high employment for rural workers, while great landholdings in the Department of Cauca, devoted to cattle-raising but rich enough for productive small farms, were not touched.

Another shortcoming of agrarian reform has been the failure to distinguish the cultural and geographic differences in working out land redistribution programs. The same regulations have been applied in Nariño—which is mountainous and is without a readily accessible water supply but which has a very industrious population—as have been applied to Bolívar, which has a none-too-energetic population and flat, fertile land used largely for cattle-raising.

INCORA has also been weak in the administration of credit. Here the lack of a skilled staff has been of key importance. Administrative red tape and lack of trained personnel, the result of a small budget, have also slowed down other aspects of the operation. Finally, colonization of public lands has usually affected inhospitable rain forest and savannah areas far removed from main transportation arteries and having an unfavorable environment for humans, crops, and animals.

In summary, INCORA and agrarian reform have changed very little, if anything, in Colombia. The social and economic structure in the rural areas remains intact and with it the traditional attitudes, affecting all of the upper class and some of the middle sectors, toward the land and the gentleman farmer. The old aristocracy has not been changed to any degree in either the extent of its holdings or its attitude toward cultivation of the land. Moreover, the high hopes which were raised in some sectors of the peasantry when INCORA was first established have turned to disillusionment, creating a further problem in the mobilization of support for the political system. Indeed, the *caballero* is still in charge, and the position of the masses continues to provide the basis of alienation, which requires only a spark to turn into an outburst of violence.

Clearly there exists great social distance between each major social stratum in Colombia. The families in the upper stratum enjoy a style of life beyond the wildest dreams of the people in the poor city *barrios* and on the *minifundia*. The distance is almost as great for lower segments of the middle stratum. Moreover, those on top act in such a way as to make explicit to those below their inferior status, especially those in the lowest stratum, where one encounters an attitude of humility, resignation, and obedience. Many observers feel, however, that this attitude is merely a facade hiding a profound hatred of the privileged groups. This underlying hatred is sensed throughout all the higher social levels, where conversation often reflects fear of sudden mass uprisings.

IDEOLOGICAL TRENDS IN THE POLITICAL ENVIRONMENT

During the nineteenth century, when the Liberal and Conservative parties developed their roots in popular loyalties, certain ideological differences were in evidence. In this period the Liberal party was characterized by its affinity with the doctrine of French and English liberalism; the party stood for the separation of Church and State, individual liberty, free enterprise, and federalism. The Conservative party of the epoch was highly pro-clerical and particularly supported intervention of the Church in education and matrimonial affairs, governmental guarantees for ecclesiastical properties, special clerical privileges, or *fueros,* such as tribunals for judging matrimonial problems and secret judgments on criminal acts committed by members of the clergy, as well as centralization of governmental power in Bogotá.[17]

Most of the ideological differences between the Liberal and Conservative parties of the nineteenth century were resolved in favor of the Conservatives by the end of the Thousand Days War at the turn of the century. By the 1930s, however, new bases for ideological conflict arose, which in part stemmed from

---

[17] See Gustavo Samper Bernal, *Breve historia constitucional y política de Colombia* (Bogotá, Litografía Colombiana, 1957), pp. 151–158. See also José Joaquín Caicedo Castilla, *Derecho internacional privado* (Bogotá, Editorial Temis, 1961). An important illustration of the continuing power of the Church in ordering people's lives lies in the fact that the so-called *Ley Concha* of 1924 is still in effect. Under this law a Catholic is apostate in his faith when he desires a civil instead of a Church marriage. A decision of the Supreme Court interpreting the law declared null a civil marriage of a Colombian Catholic which took place abroad because such a declaration was absent.

the growth of industries and the new preoccupation with what Colombians sometimes refer to as the "social question," or rising social aspirations. Leaders within the Liberal party such as Rafael Uribe Uribe, Alfonso López, and Jorge Eliécer Gaitán were particularly prominent in articulating these new aspirations, although the sentiment in that party was by no means unanimous, as the split between the followers of Alfonso López and those of Eduardo Santos indicated. In recent years there have also been divisions in the Conservative party, as the mass appeal of *Rojaspinillismo* has demonstrated.

These relatively new ideological differences were less apparent during the period of the latter 1940s and most of the 1950s, when everyone was preoccupied with *la violencia.* However, no sooner was the Frente formed than splinter groups of Liberals and Conservatives began to proclaim once again the necessity of basic social change. The *oficialistas* in both Liberal and Conservative parties who formed the coalition of the Frente accepted without qualification the importance of economic development, but they assumed that there was no need to disturb the existing social hierarchy in order to achieve that development. Those who wanted to move rapidly ahead with legislation for social change more or less radical in nature had their most powerful stimulus when Fidel Castro's victory exploded upon the Latin American scene. This stimulus is in part the reason for the success of the Movimiento Revolucionario Liberal (MRL), led by Alfonso López Michelsen and located to the Left of the Liberal party, during the period of 1960–62. However, the MRL has been greatly weakened by the charismatic appeal of Rojas Pinilla in the last few years. The shift in loyalties was clearly evident in the elections of 1966. In contrast to the weakening of the MRL, it is worth noting that the Frente showed recognition of the widespread desire for social change when the organization altered its name to Frente [de Transformación] Nacional at the time of the 1966 elections.

POLITICAL STRUCTURES AND ROLES

The Associational Articulation of Interests

In Colombia there exist various patterns for expressing demands and interests for consideration by public decision-making groups.[18] The most easily observable pattern operates on the basis of organized groups, often recognized under law, which have explicit ends and a bureaucracy of their own to help achieve those ends. Among these groups, perhaps the strongest in Colombia are ANDI, the National Association of Industrialists, and FENALCO, the National Merchants Federation. The key role of these groups is easily observed in three major areas. In the first place, these two groups are able to decisively influence legislative initiatives and executive decrees which affect the economy. In the second place, most of the Government's finance and

---

[18] The discussion of interest articulation is based upon Almond's format in Gabriel A. Almond and James S. Coleman, *The Politics of the Developing Areas* (Princeton, Princeton University Press, 1960), pp. 33–38.

development ministers are persons who have been supported by these two structures. The third area of influence in which these groups are prominent involves the selection of *oficialista* Conservative and Liberal candidates for the Frente.

Both ANDI and FENALCO represent business interests; the policies of the two are made by businessmen at the highest level and are motivated by a desire for economic growth so long as no attack is made upon the existing stratification arrangement. In their views on organized workers, ANDI and FENALCO stand against any legislation or decree providing for higher salaries and are not yet fully reconciled to certain legal arrangements in favor of the organized worker, such as minimum wages and fringe benefits. The two groups also oppose some tax laws which provide charges on corporation profits and are supported in this opposition by the powerful, though less active, Association of Agriculturalists and Cattlemen and the organization of the sugar growers, Asocaña, which is especially strong in the Department of Valle.

Articulating labor's aims are the CTC, the Confederation of Colombian Workers, and the UTC, the Union of Colombian Workers. These two confederations have had considerable success in creating better working conditions for their members. Perhaps one of the best examples of the influence of these confederations is seen in connection with the general strike planned for January 25, 1965. Before the strike could take place, the primary demands of these two great *centrales* were granted by the Government. The first demand was that the recently established sales taxes, particularly those on foodstuffs, be rescinded. The second demand was for a change in the labor code which would help to assure employment unless the employer could show just cause, such as proven bad behavior or inefficiency, for firing his employee. Up to this time the employer was often able to fire an employee without giving any justification. Finally, the *centrales* demanded that the Government use more effective means to control prices of foodstuffs and of transport. In practice this last demand turned out to be the least effective.

The strength of the *centrales* in dealing with individual firms has been demonstrated on several occasions. Two recent cases are outstanding. One of these involved the Compañía Tubos Moore, and the other concerned the El Arado Sugar Plantation and Mill. In both cases the workers had asked for a salary raise, and when it was denied, they went on strike. The employers resorted to a lockout. Since Colombian law provides no arrangement for dealing with this problem, the workers moved in, took over the administration of the enterprises, and carried on with production. At the same time the workers set aside profits in a special account for the owners. In the case of Tubos Moore the management brought a criminal indictment before the Superior Tribunal of Bogotá. The court completely absolved the workers of any violation of the statutes. In the case of El Arado, the owners, with the precedent of Tubos Moore in mind, sat down to a conference with labor leaders, and an arrangement satisfactory to labor was worked out.

In spite of the capacity to influence government and employers, the *centrales* have not had significant success when they have tried to enter the electoral lists. In the congressional elections of March 1966, the *centrales* presented lists of candidates under the Liberal party in both Cundinamarca and Antioquia. In both cases the *centrales* were badly defeated although these departments are generally considered strongholds of organized labor. Perhaps these defeats were the result of the relatively narrow scope of labor's social and economic aims.

As indicated above, the two confederations have sometimes cooperated though they tend to act independently for the most part. The CTC was the first confederation to appear and gain legal personality in Colombia. This appearance was in the years of the first Presidency of Alfonso López, and the orientation of the CTC at that time was clearly leftist; a number of leaders were avowed Marxists. To offset the CTC, the other confederation was formed during the Presidency of Ospina Pérez. This group, the UTC, has always had a close relationship with the Jesuits, particularly with Vicente Andrade Valderrama. The ideological basis for the UTC has been the encyclicals *Rerum Novarum, Quadragesimo Ano, Mater et Magistra,* and *Pacem in Terris.*

Although the two confederations are in many ways different and act independently most of the time, both use the same basic methods, which are strikes, collective bargaining, and arbitral tribunals. In recent years ideological differences between the two have tended to lose importance. The CTC has lost its originally Marxist orientation, and the Jesuits advising the UTC have become more closely identified, in the limited sense of labor-management negotiations, with the cause of labor. The UTC now surpasses the CTC in membership in part because of the Jesuit training of the UTC leaders, which has made them stand out as persons with more educational background and better administrative capacity. Their ability to present their case to the Government, to management, and to the workers has become superior.

Still other organized groups which are able to influence government are the National Federation of Coffee Growers and the Colombian Association of Small Industrialists. The coffee growers' goal is to improve the exchange position for coffee under Colombian law. They also seek to encourage the Colombian Government to work through diplomatic channels for special privileges for coffee exports. In this latter goal, the coffee growers have had some success. Under the International Coffee Agreement of 1963, signed in London by most of the coffee-producing countries, Colombian coffee growers have been able to obtain a higher price for their product than had previously been the case in the Free World market. Furthermore, the Government has granted them low-interest loans for coffee storage, has aided them with advertising abroad, and has permitted them to have representation on the National Exporting Council, which sets exchange rates on imports and exports. On the other hand, the *cafeteros* suffer from the rate of exchange, which brings them eight and one-half pesos on the dollar, while the government sells dollars to importers at the rate of thirteen and one-half pesos to the dollar, a rate constituting a coffee tax, which the coffee growers continue to protest. In all these negotiations, the growers rely less upon strength in numbers than upon the quality of their organization and their ties with the upper strata.

The Colombian Association of Small Industrialists (ACOPI) is another organization which sometimes makes its weight felt in government circles. In overall orientation, it is much like the ANDI but is not as strong. Membership in ACOPI is perhaps more varied than is the case with ANDI, because members of ACOPI range all the way from owners of small mechanic shops to owners of enterprises with a working capital of around one million pesos. As in the case with the *cafeteros,* ANDI, and FENALCO, it is not the number of members that makes ACOPI important but rather the effectiveness of organization and the connections with influential persons in the Government. ACOPI has been successful in reducing a number of taxes on imports, on finished products, and on raw materials which its members need to carry on their businesses. The major strength of ACOPI is to be found in Bogotá, Medellín, and Cali, although there are lesser chapters in other cities.

The university student groups in Colombia should also be considered as organized groups. The success of these student groups in influencing governmental policy is usually the result of demonstrations or of the threat of them. Very seldom do the students have a concrete goal in mind. Their orientation is more of a general ideological nature which frequently has as its basis protest against the *status quo, imperialismo yanqui,* and police action. Students suffer from the vagueness and ambiguity of their demands, the fear which they excite in the upper stratum, and their tendency to break into splinter groups. Perhaps one of the students' most important successes took place in 1957, when a student strike contributed to the resignation of Rojas Pinilla. Students have a tradition of political action, which causes them to feel the necessity of striking to change governmental policies, but the immediate, concrete achievements of the students have been few.

The Church

A very powerful institutional interest structure in Colombia is the Roman Catholic Church, which has been designated in the Preamble of the Constitution of 1886 as "an essential element of the social order." This provision and others emphasizing the importance of the Church were removed from the Constitution during the first Presidency of López but were reinstalled in 1945 and ratified again in the plebiscite of 1957 with even stronger emphasis. Under the Constitution, freedom of conscience for all religious sects is provided, but these provisions are qualified by statements that no sect may be permitted which opposes Christian morals. Other constitutional provisions give the Government the right to make agreements with the Vatican concerning relations between government and the Church. Finally, priests are not supposed to hold public positions, but this provision is qualified by permitting them to hold offices handling education and charitable activities.

For the most part the position of the Church in relation to government has been based upon the Concordat of 1887. In education the Church approves programs of instruction which are themselves enforced by government inspectors. Clerical authority covers not only the mandatory courses in religion and philosophy, which all schools must provide from the first grade on through high school, but also subjects such as history and even the natural sciences. Practically all the texts in both primary and secondary schools are written by Dominicans, Jesuits, Franciscans, or Christian Brothers. Some of the clerical writers treat all kinds of materials. For example, Brother Justo Ramón has published texts in history, geography, and biology.

The Church in Colombia remains very conservative. In Chile pastoral letters written by Monsignor Larraín are circulated which justify government seizure of private property without indemnification when this act is for the common good. But such a stand among Colombian clerics is most unlikely.[19] Part of the conservative clerical pattern, though not unique to Colombia, is the failure to take into account the social and economic problems stemming from the population explosion. Another aspect of clerical conservatism in Colombia is the tendency of parish priests to rely upon superstition to enforce the loyalty of their parishioners. These priests particularly encourage pilgrimages to the shrines of saints for miraculous cures of both body and soul. Often extremely poor people save all their lives in order to make just one of these pilgrimages. This emphasis upon myth has great social and economic importance in that it tends to work against rational solutions for the problems of poverty. This same emphasis also obstructs the growth of a sense of necessity for saving for either investment or one's old age.

Finally, and probably most important, is the fact that the Church has never thrown its great influence into the struggle to provide more adequate public-education facilities. The authors know of no major statement by an important Colombian cleric in support of the expansion of public education. In a country that is attempting to deal with the political demonstrations and the new vaguely stirring aspirations which they imply, the apparent prejudice of the Church in favor of private rather than public education increases the frustration of those in the lower strata, who are unable to pay the necessary fees, and adds to their belief that the community offers them little opportunity for improvement.

The clergy sometimes makes use of its institutional role to present demands which are basically alien to that role. One outstanding example of the tendency of the clergy to mix in government and influence policy occurred during the Presidency of Lleras Camargo. The Minister of Education, Abel Naranjo Villegas, undertook to fix tuition for all primary and secondary schools, whether private or public, throughout the country. His major opponent was Bishop Wilches, the spokesman for the clergy in this matter. In contrast to what one would expect in Mexico, Argentina, possibly in Brazil

---

[19] Manuel Larraín, *Pastoral* (Santiago, Editorial Arniz, 1965).

and Chile, and in any English-speaking country, the minister was forced to resign. Later, during the Government of Valencia, when certain Jesuits had set up a workers' university in Cali, the bulk of the clergy as well as certain leading citizens of the community worked through the local archbishop and succeeded in having the original Jesuits removed from the region because it was said that they were instructing the workers in leftist doctrines.

Still another example, somewhat similar, took place in Bogotá when the clergy delivered an ultimatum and attacked Padre Camilo Torres Restrepo because of his efforts to secure policies which would radically alter the distribution of wealth in the country. The public speeches of Torres alarmed members of the upper strata, and Monsignor Luis Concha Córdoba, Cardinal of Bogotá, articulated the upper-class point of view in a series of reprimands, which finally resulted in the defrocking of the ill-fated young priest.[20]

The Armed Forces

Another important area of institutional interest articulation in some Latin American countries has been the military. Under Colombian constitutional and legislative provisions, members of the armed forces are not allowed to vote, to hold political gatherings, or to participate in other political activities. Officers are not supposed to correspond with civilian officials except in matters concerning the effectiveness and morale of the service. However, these regulations do not mean that political considerations have not touched the armed forces. For example, everyone, from the highest officers to the lowest ranking enlisted men, was expected to identify with the Liberal party from López' first administration until 1945. When the Conservatives won office in 1946, they immediately began working to change the situation. From Gómez' Presidency on through the Rojas Pinilla period, the Colombian intelligence service checked carefully to weed out officers and enlisted men with strong Liberal tendencies, and newly commissioned officers had to be Conservatives. When the Frente came to power, an effort was made to strike a balance between Liberal and Conservative sympathies. Clearly, civilian politicians have been unable to ignore the tactical importance of the military in times of political crises, such as the coup of Gustavo Rojas Pinilla in 1953 and the threat of a coup by Alberto Ruiz Novoa in 1965.

Nonetheless, the military has been far less significant as an articulator of institutional interest than the clergy has been. Several factors explain this phenomenon. Up to the present time the academies which train officers have not been generally respected for their standards of academic achievement, and the professional military man, perhaps for this reason, does not have a particularly high status except in those rare cases when he is related to one of the leading families. In contrast to high-ranking churchmen, most officers are recruited from the middle stratum, and thus possibilities of alliance with the upper class are limited. Among the leading families the youth who chooses a

---

[20] *El Tiempo,* June 29, 1965, p. 1; *La Nueva Prensa,* July 1965, pp. 4–6.

military career has usually been regarded as a second-rate person who would do the family's interests little good in civilian life. Colombians often label military men, including the highest officers, as *chafarotes,* a word that carries the connotation of little intelligence and crude mannerisms. In light of this attitude, it is not surprising that seldom in recent history has the professional military held any other ministry than that of defense and that, except in the Rojas Pinilla era, officers have acquired few avenues to other branches of the decision-making process. However, the civilian leaders must depend upon the military to handle problems of banditry in the rural areas, guerrilla activity in the mountains, and urban demonstrations which tend to get out of hand. Consequently, budgetary allowances for the military are relatively generous, usually consuming about sixteen percent of a national budget that grants education only about ten percent. Nevertheless, the less prestigious position of the military in Colombia limits to a greater extent the capacity of the generals to act unconstitutionally than would be the case, for example, in Argentina.

Anomie and Nonassociational Interest Articulation

A third possible pattern in the articulation of interests involves the spontaneous groups and is related to the extent of anomie in the society. One group of this type would be the one which results when widespread discontent explodes at a given moment in the form of public demonstrations that are essentially unstructured and violent. That these demonstrations have no permanent structure does not mean that they have no leaders but simply means that the structure of leadership is not explicit and is hard to detect. The classic example of this kind of group in Colombia is the *Bogotazo,* which began on April 9, 1948, when masses of people poured out into the streets ostensibly to protest the assassination of Jorge Eliécer Gaitán. Although the violence lasted several days and destroyed the center of the city, this violence did not immediately result in important policy changes or in a significant change in ministerial posts. Actually, this pattern has not been frequent in Colombia in recent years apart from this one outbreak, which was reflected in lesser cities and triggered a long period of violence in the countryside.

More important than the anomic-group pattern has been that of the nonassociational, or the informally constituted, group, in which kinship, common social status, and economic interests result in a kind of identification among the persons and families involved. This kind of interest articulation has been most significant among privileged groups. The contacts among people of the same social and economic level at elaborate social gatherings, intimate dinners, luncheon engagements, informal conversations at exclusive private clubs, and weekends at someone's *finca* are central to this phenomenon; so, also, is the sense of identification among members of the graduating classes of universities, the private ones in particular. It is out of close friendships and family ties, not themselves identifiable in terms of formal organization, that there emerges a pattern of "understandings" that later result in policy. Meetings and agreements are not public. Instead, informal contacts result in consensus and subsequent application of pressure to secure desired ends.

POLITICAL PARTIES, COALITIONS, AND FACTIONS

The Frente Nacional

The traditional two-party nature of Colombian politics has already been discussed. It seems certain that the major contemporary dividing factor is largely emotional insofar as Liberals and Conservatives in general are concerned. Although the Frente was organized to alleviate and perhaps eliminate the old hatreds that had grown up during the nineteenth century, the two-party rivalry has not yet disappeared. People still think of themselves as Liberals or Conservatives even though they are identified with the Frente, and rivalry among leaders to some extent still follows the old divisions.

Under the plebiscite of 1957, which changed the Constitution, the Liberals and Conservatives were the only two parties recognized as having a right to hold government posts. As indicated above, the distribution of these posts was to involve alternate Conservative and Liberal Presidents and equal representation in all government bodies. However, the historical and sociological factors which contributed to the rivalry existing before the creation of the Frente are still operative, though less so than before. Colombian children continue to be taught allegiance to one or the other of the parties. The leaders of the Frente also continue to be regarded as either Conservative or Liberal instead of as all members of a new party, the Frente. The old leaders who still remember *la violencia* occasioned by the two-party rivalry continue to head the respective organizations; on the one side, Mariano Ospina Pérez and Alvaro Gómez Hurtado, the son of Laureano Gómez, lead Conservative factions, and on the other side, Alberto Lleras Camargo and Carlos Lleras Restrepo lead the *oficialista* Liberals. These are the men who in the end set the tone for the national and departmental directorates of their parties while members of younger generations continue to await their opportunity to take part in important decisions. It needs to be emphasized that men in their fifties and sixties continue to dominate the various national, departmental, and municipal levels throughout the country. That domination by this age group is particularly important in a country where between forty and fifty percent of the population is fifteen years of age or younger. The domination means that the old leaders who remember the times of bitter rivalry between Liberals and Conservatives are still in charge of the country's politics and that the alliance of the Frente will remain at best uneasy until these leaders are replaced by younger persons, who have not experienced the bitterness aroused by earlier struggles. Finally, that these older men are still in charge means that the newer generations chafe impatiently waiting their turn.

In spite of existing divisions, one cannot overlook some possible tendencies toward an essentially one-party system. Particularly important here is the large number of ballots which go to candidates of the Frente. For example, in 1958, 1962, and 1966, the presidential candidate of the Frente received more than double the votes of any other candidate. Further, major legislative measures of the Frente on agrarian reform, tax reform, and the petroleum code have received majority approval in the Congress. Moreover, groups in opposition to the Frente have not shown continuity in increase of strength; that is, one group may be strong at a particular time and lose strength to another at a different time. In 1958 Jorge Leiva, whose ideas constitute the doctrine *leivismo,* was the major opposition to Lleras Camargo. In 1962 the MRL faction of Liberals presented the major opposition to Valencia, and in 1966 principal opposition to the Frente's candidate came from ANAPO, the National Popular Alliance, which is the Rojas Pinilla organization.

On the other hand, there are tendencies toward a multi-party system. There is the split between the "official" line and MRL Liberals, and even within the MRL there is a split which involves the "soft line," led by López Michelsen, the "hard line," and the "hardest line," which is essentially Communist-led and goes under the name of MRL of the People. On this radical side is also a group, ANAPO Liberal, which retains its position within the Liberal party but which supports Rojas Pinilla.

There are also splits in the Conservative camp, the *Ospinistas* sometimes support the Frente and sometimes do not, the *Lauroalzatistas* sometimes support the Frente and sometimes do not, and the ANAPO Conservadora of Rojas Pinilla has always opposed the Frente. In certain regions of the country, such as the Valle del Cauca, the officialist Liberals have split and have presented their own independent lists for candidates to the Congress. Outside the Liberal and Conservative borders are the Christian Democrats, who are not allowed to participate in elections and who still lack technique in mobilizing voters.

Basically, it would seem that these divisions reflect a political culture which has become more and more heterogeneous and fragmented as the great problems of the country continue to remain unsolved. For example, the success of the MRL in 1962, or of the Rojas Pinilla group in 1966, appears to reflect the importance of appeals to the unanswered aspirations of large numbers of Colombians.

When Valencia became president in 1962, he tried to unite factions of the Frente by offering both Conservative groups positions in his Government, but in 1966 the *Lauroalzatistas,* the lineal descendants of Gómez, once again stood aside from the Frente by opposing the candidacy of Carlos Lleras Restrepo, while at the same time saying they were in favor of the Frente in general. Thus the Frente has periodically varied in composition and leadership. The organization has certain characteristics of a dominant, official party, yet it lacks the continuity of leadership which such a party might offer to the country.

Opposition Groups

The MRL and the ANAPO have been referred to as groups opposing the Frente, though they have continued to call themselves Liberals or Conservatives in order to fulfill the existing constitutional requirements. The MRL was organized at the time of the fall of Rojas and enjoyed considerable popularity among intellectuals, middle groups, and organized labor during the Government of Lleras Camargo. This popularity was in part the result of the personal characteristics of Alfonso López Michelsen, the son of ex-President López. López Michelsen was widely admired for his intellectual capacities and his "sincerity," though he never became a very successful orator and crowd-pleaser. In part the success of the MRL in those years was caused by its emphasis upon reform and social change. The organization attacked the privileged position of the upper class, especially the big industrialists. Secondly, the MRL accused the Frente of stifling the democratic process and providing a monopoly of power for elderly leaders. The MRL also criticized the provisions for alternating Liberal and Conservative Presidents within the framework of the Frente itself.

The success of the MRL continued through 1962, though the party still fell far short of defeating the Frente's presidential candidate in that year. By 1966 MRL strength had been cut in half. Of the major leaders who helped López, none is still connected with the MRL. Luis Alfonso Barbarena and Rafael Rangel died. Alvaro Uribe quarreled with López and formed the hard line in the MRL, and Felipe Salazar, who defected to the Frente, accepted a position offered him by the Valencia Government. López Michelsen himself moved toward a center position in the political spectrum. His former, relatively radical stand was taken over in large part by the followers of Rojas. In 1966 the appeal of Castro was no longer so significant in building support for the Colombian Left, and criticism of the alternating Presidency did not appeal as much to Liberals, since the Frente's candidate in 1966 was Lleras Restrepo, a Liberal of long standing. Moreover, López made no systematic effort to procure regional leaders for the 1966 campaign, and the MRL broke into factions. Particularly damaging to López was the way he favored his personal friends when he formed lists of MRL congressional candidates. Typical of the new López was the attempt to pass over his one remaining strong leader in Valle, Ramiro Andrade, without heeding Andrade's wishes regarding the composition of the MRL lists.

The other important opposition movement which has developed in recent years is the ANAPO, led by Gustavo Rojas Pinilla. When he was deposed in 1957, Rojas first fled to Spain but returned in 1958 to be judged by the Congress. He was charged with abuse of authority, corruption, and general malfeasance. The Congress deprived him of civil and political rights, a deprivation which meant that, so long as the Frente was in power, he could never become a presidential candidate. Nevertheless, he set about organizing a political movement, which gathered strength to the point that in 1966 his group presented the principal opposition to the Frente. The organizational level which ANAPO has achieved is indeed formidable, and Rojas has shown a great capacity for arousing masses of people by using a style which is extremely belligerent toward the upper strata but which has no systematic ideological orientation.

Typical of Rojas' style is a speech at Barranquilla attended by about twenty thousand persons. At this rally everyone knelt, pledging allegiance to their leader. At another major rally Rojas produced a goose at the high point in his speech, cut its throat, and then proclaimed, "This is the way we will cut the throats of the oligarchs." At almost all of Rojas' political gatherings, a series of basic foodstuffs was shown the people while he asked what the prices of these were when he was in power and thus invited comparisons with the much higher prices in 1966.

A lesser element opposing the Frente is the Christian Democratic organization. This group has so far appealed mainly to university students and persons of the upper-middle stratum. The organization has a doctrinal position which makes it impossible to infiltrate Conservative or Liberal parties, and its orientation is taken largely from liberal papal encyclicals. The group has close ties with the Christian Democratic movement in Chile, Venezuela, and Peru but still lacks the capacity to develop a significant popular following. The leader of the Colombian organization, Alvaro Rivera Concha, is not very well known throughout the country and has suffered from opposition among certain sectors of the high clergy, particularly Cardinal Concha Córdoba, who revoked Rivera's license to act as a lawyer under canon law. The movement received less than two thousand votes for all its lists in the congressional elections of March 1966.

Finally, another opposition group is the Communists, who have infiltrated the far Left of the Liberal party and who have set up various front organizations. In 1959 the Communists formed MOEC, the Colombian Student Worker Movement of January 7. Two years later they organized MAC, the Colombian Anarchist Movement, which succeeded in bringing about several important strikes at the National University. The Communists also established a Communist Youth organization, which undertakes the task of embarrassing the Government and the upper class by writing certain types of slogans on buildings and fences. Prominent among these inscriptions have been such phrases as "Down with the Oligarchs" and "Where is Camilo?", which refers to the death of Camilo Torres Restrepo.

It would be a mistake to underestimate the quality of Communist leadership, though the rank and file does not appear to be numerous. Gerardo Molina, for example, has been rector both of the National University and of the Universidad Libre in Bogotá. Diego Montaña Cuéllar has been a professor of sociology at Universidad Libre for a number of years and has published various articles and books. In large part the Communists recruit from among organized workers who belong to neither the CTC nor the UTC and from among university students. The Communist-led union, FEDETAV, the Independent Federation of Workers of Valle, still dominates one of the major sugar enterprises in that department, the Manuelita of the Eder family, and has organized workers in several other important enterprises. In 1960–61, there were many disastrous strikes at the sugar *ingenios* and in various industrial establishments in Cali, but the extreme intransigence of FEDETAV probably cost the Communists some victories. There have also been some

Communist successes in Santander. At Barranca Bermeja, the petroleum companies have been unable to push out Communist-dominated unions largely because of the extraordinarily capable leadership of Diego Montaña Cuéllar. The politically oriented guerrillas in the sierras are connected with the Communists.

In the elections of March 1966, the Communist party, masquerading as a fragment of the Liberal party, proposed lists of candidates in almost all departments of the country, but the success of the Communists was minimal; only about five thousand votes for them were cast throughout the entire Republic. Nevertheless, the Communists continue to be a threat because of the guerrillas in the sierras and because of the sympathy of some student groups. As long as there remain difficulties in upward social mobility for poor students and acute misery among small farmers and in the destitute *barrios,* the Communist threat must be taken into account. It appears that the Christian Democratic and the Communist movements, although clearly small minorities at the present time, may be more permanent than either ANAPO or the López MRL, since the latter two have depended so greatly upon personal leadership.

THE THREE BRANCHES OF GOVERNMENT

Colombia has a presidential system of government. Under the Constitution, the executive branch, which Colombians refer to as "the Government," is made up of the President and his ministers, the governors and their heads of departmental ministries, and mayors and their secretaries at the local level.

The President is elected every four years by a direct vote of the people; there is no electoral college. Several formal bases of presidential power are worth mentioning. The President has authorization to *"reglamentar"* statutes, which involves implementing orders for legislation. The President is Commander-in-chief of the armed forces, and he names his ministers as well as the governors of all the departments. He has the capacity to reject laws passed by the Congress on either the grounds that they are unconstitutional or that they are "inconvenient." He also has the ultimate authority in the conduct of international relations.

It is possible for Congress to delegate powers. These delegations enable the President to promulgate regulations in certain specified areas without consulting the Congress. For example, in 1964 the President ordered a reorganization of courts and judicial processes on the basis of power delegated by Congress. Should the President and his Cabinet consider that a political crisis exists in the country, the President can place the nation under a state of siege. In this situation he has power to issue decrees having the force of law, "providing the decrees tend to re-establish public order."

During the Governments of Laureano Gómez and Rojas Pinilla, all new laws were promulgated as presidential decrees under the state of siege. Many Colombians felt that there were unwarranted abuses of this power at the time, and the Constitution was amended after the Frente came to power in order to limit such executive authority. But the power of the President to issue decrees continues to be very broad. When President Valencia invoked the state of siege in 1965, he was able to change the entire process used in criminal proceedings by placing most crimes in the hands of military tribunals. Again in September 1965, when confronted with an economic crisis, Valencia decreed new taxes, changed customs procedure, and altered some aspects of labor law—all by executive decree. The sweeping power of decree law under Valencia would undoubtedly have been more dramatically demonstrated had there been in office a person of stronger convictions. Unquestionably the presidential role is the most important one in Colombia, although there is room for variation in accord with individual personality and existing situations.

Aside from the President, the most important persons in the executive branch are the ministers. In a certain sense the ministers have collegiate responsibility, especially under the state of siege. At such times no executive decree can become law without being signed by all the ministers. Among the ministers there are perhaps four of outstanding importance: the Ministers of Foreign Relations, of Defense, of "Government," and of the Treasury. The Minister of Foreign Relations stands high in status not only because of the normal importance of such an office but because, in Colombia, he is the first minister in the line of succession after the *designado*. The Minister of "Government" is important because he consults with the President in selecting the departmental governors and serves as liaison between the governors and the President. The Minister of Defense is important because he has at his disposal the armed forces and is for this reason in a position to avoid or carry out a *coup d'etat* against the Government. Finally, the Minister of the Treasury plays an important role in forming economic policy. He coordinates agencies involved in economic planning, and he serves as the nation's tax collector. He also generally heads Colombian efforts to procure loans from international lending agencies.

One of the most controversial policies inaugurated by Colombian Presidents in recent years was Valencia's policy of *milimetria,* which sought to apportion ministerial posts in accord with the representation of various Frente political groups in the Congress. The experience gained by the Valencia administration would seem to indicate that such a precise effort to achieve proportional representation in the Cabinet weakened the executive branch rather than strengthened it.

Legislative bodies in Colombia include the bicameral national Congress, which is composed of the Chamber of Representatives and the Senate, departmental assemblies, and municipal councils. The Chamber of Representatives is composed of persons elected on the basis of 1 for every 90,000 inhabitants, or 1 for every fraction no less than 45,000 inhabitants. As of 1966 there were 184 representatives, and there will probably be more as a result of the population explosion unless the law is redrawn. Senators are chosen on the basis of 1 for every 190,000 inhabitants, or of a fraction no less than 95,000; as of 1966, there were 92 senators.

Laws may be initiated in either house with the exception of tax laws, which have to originate in the lower chamber. Impeachment proceedings may be brought against the President through a procedure which closely resembles that in the United States Constitution. Aside from the lower chamber's capacity to originate tax legislation, that body has certain other special powers: electing the Attorney General, the Comptroller General, and being entitled to examine fiscal items in the executive branch. Apart from these powers, there are no significant differences between the powers of the two houses except that a senator is popularly considered to outrank a representative.

Most Colombians believe that the Congress has been less effective in recent years because of the provision in the plebiscite of 1957 which required a two-thirds vote of all present in both houses for the approval of a given law, in contrast to the majority vote formerly necessary. Because decisions are so difficult to obtain under this procedure, the Congress has tended to delegate more decree power to the executive branch. In fact, in the last few years the Congress has become more a debating society and a sounding board for political beliefs than a legislative body. Absenteeism is rife, and only tax and budgetary proposals seem to bring out a majority of members. Legislators devote much of their time to securing bureaucratic posts for their friends or supporters. President-elect Lleras Restrepo has proposed elimination of the two-thirds arrangement.

Apart from the formal powers of the Congress, it is important to note that certain individuals in both houses have very close ties with regional and national governing boards of the major political groups. Such individuals not only attempt to reward their supporters with bureaucratic posts but also act as spokesmen for important pressure groups. The President and his ministers pay attention to such individuals not only because outspoken criticism can damage the prestige of the executive branch, but also because these are the people who are most capable of mobilizing support for the regime.

Organization and operation of the judiciary is always important for the sense of legitimacy which holds up the system. Of course, there are other channels by which justice is distributed or denied, but the courts retain the primary responsibility in this domain. In Colombia the organization of the regular judiciary is divided into three basic levels. At the lowest level are the municipal courts; above them are circuit courts, which range in number from one to five according to the size of the department; and finally, at the national level is the Supreme Court of Justice. In addition, there exist courts in administrative law. Most important is the Council of State at the national level, but there are also departmental administrative courts. Cases coming before these courts involve pleas that officials of the executive branch have exceeded the functions legally attributed to them.

When issuing a judgment, Colombian judges must consider a hierarchy of judicial norms that comprises no less than nine levels, from the Constitution at the apex on down through national, departmental, and municipal statutes, decrees, and ordinances. Thus the hierarchy of law is quite complex, and administration of justice must take into account for every level of law whether or not it conflicts with a superior level. When parties to a court proceeding claim such conflicts, the final decision must be made by the Council of State. This regulation is unilaterally applicable except in cases of claims of conflict between lower levels of law and the Constitution; such constitutional cases are decided by the Supreme Court.

High court judges, appointed for life, seem to feel little pressure from the Presidency and actually enjoy considerable independence of action. However, autonomy is far less certain at lower levels of the court system. At these levels a number of problems in the administration of justice exist. Cases often remain undecided for years at a time as a result of the insufficient number of judges, and sometimes a person spends three or four years in prison on "preventative" grounds before his case is actually heard in court. Moreover, there appears to be considerable discrimination between rich and poor, since commentators on penal law point out that the wealthy suspect usually goes free on bond prior to the time of his trial, while suspects from the poorer classes await their trial in jail. Such difficulties are compounded by the fact that judges are poorly paid ($300 a month in 1966 for Supreme Court justices; $150 monthly for circuit judges; and $50 to $150 for municipal judges), and often consider their judgeships as simply a steppingstone to a more profitable career in private practice. Thus, judges are reluctant to hand down decisions unfavorable to the powerful, who can help them later on.[21]

One can readily conclude that the development of effective administration of justice has not been given high priority in Colombia and that there are many irregularities and administrative bottlenecks, particularly at the lower levels. Most important, people in the lower socio-economic strata have felt these abuses for so long that the attitude of these people toward justice and the law constitutes a kind of smoldering frustration which inhibits the growth of mass support and legitimacy for the judicial system and creates a sense of alienation in the lower-middle and lower strata.

PROCESSES OF FUNCTION AND DYSFUNCTION

Elections, Problems of Representation, and Alienation

According to the Constitution, all Colombian citizens over twenty-one years of age (women acquired the vote in 1957) are entitled to participate as voters. Voters directly select town councilmen, members of departmental assemblies, representatives, and senators of the national Congress, as well as the President of the Republic. There are no literacy or property-ownership restrictions to voting. The basic unit in the electoral mechanism is the department, of which there were nineteen in 1966. Within each department an equal number of Conservatives and Liberals are chosen as representatives, senators,

---

[21] Vicente Laverde Aponte, *Motivos de la reforma judicial.* This is a report given by the Minister of Justice in 1961 which points up discrimination in the administration of justice.

departmental assembly deputies, and town councilmen. In these elections there may be several groups in either party which propose candidates, the lists being drawn up by the various executive committees, or *directorios* or *politicos,* of the participating groups.

The lists are cleared with the municipal executive and the representatives of the National Office of Registrations in every municipality. There are no official arbiters or criteria for determining whether the lists which are claimed to be Liberal or Conservative actually fall within these categories. Furthermore, splinter groups can propose lists with ease because these groups do not have to show a certain number of signatures or votes in the last election. Thus there are no safeguards limiting the proliferation of new groups which claim to be either Liberals or Conservatives. Any candidate can be entered in any of the races for electoral posts as long as he is willing to call himself a Liberal or a Conservative.

Lists of candidates are printed at the expense of the committees supporting them, and these committees then distribute the ballots in front of the building where the voting is to occur. The only check is that those voting must have their names on the eligible voter list before they can deposit their ballot. The Government is obligated to provide protection against violence, to appoint election judges, and to count the votes.

The system makes it impossible to split votes between lists of candidates for any electoral collegiate body. For example, suppose that in a given department the size of the population warrants ten senators. Of these, five are supposed to be Liberals, the other five Conservatives. Let us also suppose that there are three Conservative lists and that the total number of Conservative votes is 200,000; there then will be a ratio of 40,000 votes per senator. Thus, if List A receives 100,000 votes, there will be two senators from this list. If List B receives 65,000 votes, there will be another senator from this list. List C will have the remaining 35,000 votes and will get another senator because of its high residual value. The fifth senator will go to List B because it has a higher residual value than List A.

List A	$\dfrac{100,000}{40,000}$	=	2 with residual of 20,000
List B	$\dfrac{65,000}{40,000}$	=	1 + .[1] residual of 25,000*
List C	35,000	=	1 (considered a sufficiently high residual)

* This is the higher residual of Lists A and B and warrants one more for List B.

The system has some of the defects and very few of the advantages which one might expect. In practice, the arrangement is relatively closed. Neither ANAPO nor the MRL has any significant impact on Frente decisions, yet the agreement to divide offices has made it difficult to achieve consensus and develop long-range programs. Moreover, many Colombians, especially students and professional men, feel that their opportunities for political participation have been curtailed. For example, the Christian Democratic organization, which has had considerable success in Chile, has no chance in Colombia under the existing Frente agreement. It is a paradox that this agreement, while excluding the relatively moderate Christian Democrats, permits the Communists to participate in elections because they have no moral scruples in calling themselves Liberals. In addition, politics in this system creates a widespread impression of *continuismo* among younger people who feel that the Frente benefits go almost exclusively to the old political bosses who have roots in the 1930s or earlier. Thus, many young economists and lawyers feel that their hopes for political office are doomed to frustration for many years. This sense of frustration has been greatly strengthened by unfilled promises made in 1965 and 1966 that there would be new names on the electoral lists of *oficialista* Liberals and Conservatives. Moreover, the disappointments of young would-be politicians extended to many others in the middle and poorer strata who had no political ambitions for themselves but did have a desire to see young blood injected into the Frente in the hope that new solutions could be found for endemic problems.

By and large, the older generation of politicians continues to think in terms of mobilization of voters along the old lines by using a hierarchy of caciques which reaches from the lowest level, the *vecindad* and the *barrio,* through municipal and departmental levels to the Congress and the ministers of the executive branch. Tendencies in voting indicate that there may be better ways to broaden support for the system and overcome apathy and alienation among the masses. For example, voting participation ranged from 69 to 39 percent in congressional elections and from 58 to 42 percent in presidential elections between 1958 and 1966. The tendency is generally downward and may be used as an indicator of apathy and alienation. Among those who did vote, the Frente gained overwhelming majorities in the presidential elections and even had the best of it in congressional elections. These facts sometimes obscure the pattern of abstention and its causes but do not eliminate the existence of certain dysfunctional elements in the Frente electoral arrangement.

CONCLUSION

The plebiscite creating the Frente has produced a dysfunctional factor in the two-thirds majority rule, which limits legislative effectiveness, in the cumbersome administration of justice, and in the privileges for the upper class, which are more easily obtained because of the low pay of judges and of court employees. Young university graduates find many opportunities, especially in politics, closed to them both because the society lacks sufficient complexity and because older generations insist upon viewing themselves as indispensable. This low rate of circulation in elites is even more serious in the light of the inefficiency of Colombian government in the economic sphere since the 1950s.

The great social distance between each of the social strata, and especially between the highest and the lowest, is conducive to a low rate of turnover in the decision-makers, which embitters both those who want to move upward from their present position in society and those who hope for better conditions in their present state. Conspicuous consumption by the upper strata—including the purchase of luxury automobiles, the construction of palatial residences, and the holding of grandiose celebrations of festive. occasions—further aggravates the sense of frustration and alienation among the less fortunate. The rich isolate themselves from the poor in order to protect themselves from the horrifying impact of the poverty that surrounds them and thus increase social distance and alienation. Inflation, balance of payment difficulties, and widespread unemployment in the major cities make their own vital impact upon the attitudes of Colombians on the legitimacy of the present system. The Church is a major instrument for reducing alienation and legitimizing the regime in all its aspects—social, economic, political, and religious—but it is not at all certain that this vital social structure can save the *status quo* if pressing needs for change in the society are not met.

In summary, there exist in contemporary Colombia many stimuli to mass alienation which do not augur well for either prospects of a more democratic Colombia or even the continued stability of the existing system. It seems certain that the Government of Carlos Lleras Restrepo (1966–70) will be crucial for the future. Unless the Lleras Government is able to ameliorate some of the conditions that cause alienation and to give concrete evidence of a new governmental effectiveness, crisis and violence can hardly be avoided. From the standpoint of global politics, it is not inconceivable that, five years from now, policy-makers in the United States will be faced with a difficult situation as they view the strategic location of Colombia, astride the continent and fronting on two oceans. In fact, the United States may be faced with the serious dilemma, similar to several erupting since World War II, of either sending troops to bolster a system whose leaders have alienated their people or of accepting an anti-American and possibly Communist dictatorship in this vital area. The problem for the non-Communist world is that of discovering alternatives which will prevent the crystallization of this dilemma.

10/Ecuador

JACK B. GABBERT

JACK B. GABBERT, Associate Professor of Political Science at Washington State University, served with the U.S. Foreign Service from 1949 to 1958, including two Latin American posts and an assignment as Intelligence Research Specialist for Ecuador and Peru. He also acted as an instructor in a Peace Corps training program for Ecuador during the summer of 1964.

In the classic understatement of four-time President José María Velasco Ibarra, "Ecuador is a very difficult country to govern."[1] Since its establishment as an independent Republic in 1830, Ecuador has had fifteen Constitutions and over seventy changes in the control of the executive power. In fact, only about a dozen Presidents have served out their full terms.

As to the underlying causes of these outward manifestations of instability, Ecuador presents a typical case of the syndrome characterizing political underdevelopment. A partial listing of the factors contributing to this instability indicates their complex, interrelated nature. Ecuador has a backward economy dependent on a few export crops, principally bananas, but is striving to industrialize. Ecuador has crowded cities unable to absorb adequately a rapidly growing population and the influx of rural migrants. Ecuador has an unbalanced social structure and an illiterate Indian subnation. There are bitter regional rivalries and massive geographical barriers to national integration. The political parties of Ecuador are weak and still hampered by personalism. The armed forces of Ecuador have renewed their direct interventions into political affairs. And the political structure, long dominated by an upper-class

---

[1] Quoted in George I. Blanksten, *Ecuador: Constitutions and Caudillos* (Berkeley and Los Angeles, University of California Press, 1951), p. v.

elite, has failed to satisfy the expectations of a majority of the population, and has thus resulted in a mounting sense of frustration and political alienation. What follows in this chapter are illustrations and elaborations of the basic theme that Ecuador has been, and remains, a "very difficult country to govern."

POLITICAL ENVIRONMENT

Geography and Demography

Taking its name from the equator which passes through the northern half of the country, Ecuador's total area, including the offshore Galápagos Islands is about 105,000 square miles. Approximately the size of Colorado, Ecuador is the smallest Republic in South America except for Uruguay. Having lost some two-thirds of its claimed territory to its neighbors, principally Colombia and Peru, Ecuador is sometimes referred to as the Poland of the Western Hemisphere.

Ecuador's dominant geographical feature is, of course, the towering Andean mountain range. It poses a major obstacle to transportation and splits the mainland into three distinct regions. On the west is the hot, humid coastal plain, which produces the principal export products. In the middle is the cool highland plateau, or Sierra, located between two ranges of the Andes and subdivided by crosswise ridges into a series of basins. The Sierra produces cereal crops and livestock mainly for the domestic market. The third region, called the Oriente, consists of the eastern Andean foothills and the tropical lowlands of the upper Amazon basin. This region is an undeveloped, heavily forested, and largely inaccessible area inhabited by such primitive tribes as the Jívaros and the Aucas.

The most important regions, therefore, are the coastal and the highland areas, which differ not only in their topographies and climates but also in their economies, cultures, and political orientations. These contrasts are symbolized in the long and bitter rivalry between coastal Guayaquil, the principal seaport and commercial center, and highland Quito, the nation's political capital, each dominating its respective region. The more liberal, worldly, and businesslike *guayaquileños* resent Quito's political domination. The more conservative, provincial, and agrarian-oriented *quiteños,* on the other hand, tend to be suspicious of Guayaquil's "rabble" as well as of the financial influence of the coast's commercial and banking interests. Instead of furnishing the stable equilibrium which an accommodation between such countervailing forces might provide, this regional antagonism has been a disruptive factor contributing to the pattern of instability.

According to a 1965 estimate, Ecuador's population is in excess of 5 million, ranking in ninth place among the twenty Latin American Republics.[2]

---

[2] United Nations, *Monthly Bulletin of Statistics,* XIX, No. 12 (December 1965), 2; and Robert C. Kingsbury and Ronald M. Schneider, *An Atlas of Latin American Affairs* (New York, Frederick A. Praeger, Inc., 1965), pp. 4–5.

The annual rate of population growth is about three percent, which means that the population of the country can be expected to double in twenty to twenty-five years. The population movement is to the cities and to the coastal region. Well over a third of the people already live in urban areas, and fast-growing Guayaquil's population of over 500,000 is a 100 percent increase over the 1950 figure, compared to Quito's population of about 350,000, representing only a 50 percent gain.

Social Structure

Ethnically, Ecuador is an Indo-mestizo nation. While the statistics vary widely, a fair estimate seems to be that ten percent of the population is white, about thirty percent is mixed (*cholo* and *montuvio* are the highland and coastal terms, respectively, for the mestizo or mulatto), over half is Indian, and a small percentage is Negro and other races. However, since such cultural attributes as language and type of dress are regarded as more significant than purely physical characteristics in determining race, the mestizo element in Ecuador has been estimated as high as sixty-six percent. Hence, race in the strict sense is no absolute bar to social mobility, since a pure-blooded Indian who leaves his community and takes on the ways of the non-Indian world is considered a *cholo*.

Although race, culturally defined, is a principal determinant of class status, race is not the exclusive determinant; economic and occupational criteria are also relevant. While it may be convenient to equate Indians and Negroes with the lower class, mestizos with the middle class, and whites with the upper class, such a simple classification scheme fails to take account of the mestizo who has achieved a high professional position, for example, or of the white who has been reduced to a salaried clerical job. One estimate of class divisions in Ecuador based on socio-economic factors places only one percent in the upper class, twenty-four percent in the middle range, and seventy-five percent in the lower class.[3]

In whatever light the class structure is viewed, it is evident that a vast social and cultural gap exists between the educated, urban, upper-class elite and the rural Indian peasant. Such wide social disparities are but another dimension of the divisive elements which retard the achievement of national unity and contribute to the tensions underlying Ecuador's political instability.

Historical Background

Although Spanish rule in Ecuador ended in 1822, the Ecuadorians were part of Simón Bolívar's Confederation of Greater Colombia for the next eight years. Juán José Flores, a Venezuelan-born general who acted as Bolívar's military representative at Quito, led a secessionist movement which established Ecuador as a separate Republic on May 13, 1830, "the last day of

---

[3] Bureau of Labor Statistics, United States Department of Labor, *Labor Law and Practice in Ecuador,* BLS Report No. 242 (Washington, D.C., U.S. Government Printing Office, 1963), p. 13.

despotism and the first day of the same thing," according to a well-known Ecuadorian saying.

General Flores, the Republic's first President, was a crude despot who dominated the political scene for fifteen years. In part he was able to maintain his dominance because he shrewdly allowed his chief rival, Vicente Rocafuerte, a cultured creole Liberal from Guayaquil, to occupy the Presidency for one term (1835–1839). Flores' ouster in 1845 was the product of a growing nationalistic resentment against all "foreign" elements, military as well as clerical.

The subsequent interlude between national *caudillos* was a highly unstable period of another fifteen years. Six Presidents, several juntas, and three Constitutions later, Ecuador was on the verge of disintegrating when Gabriel García Moreno, a militant Catholic Conservative, imposed his stern rule on the country in 1860. Ecuador's first outstanding statesman, García Moreno was essentially an authoritarian who used Catholicism as a disciplining force to restore order and reunify the nation. Ecuador became a virtual theocracy with the educational system and the power of censorship in the hands of the clergy. The Constitution of 1869 (the Republic's eighth) restricted citizenship to practicing Catholics, and in 1873 the Congress solemnly consecrated the Republic to the Sacred Heart of Jesus. But greater economic and cultural advances were made than during any other comparable period of the nineteenth century. The García Moreno era ended with his assassination in 1875.

Control by the highland Conservatives did not end with their leader's death, however. It was not until 1895 that the Liberals, under the leadership of General Eloy Alfaro, finally won out in a revolution which had originated in Guayaquil. Alfaro, generally regarded as Ecuador's other leading statesman, also met a violent death. He was killed by a Quito mob in 1912 after an unsuccessful attempt to seize the Presidency for a third term.

During the alternating administrations of Alfaro and General Leónidas Plaza (1895–1916), the program of the new urban elite from the coast was carried out. Church and State were formally separated, education was secularized, and divorce was legalized. The Constitution of 1906, one of the most liberal in Latin America for its time, remained in effect until 1929 and was reinstated from 1935 to 1945—a longevity record yet to be equalled by any other Ecuadorian charter. In the economic field the railway link between Guayaquil and Quito was completed, and with profits from the export of cacao, a "chocolate boom" got under way.

The Liberals remained politically dominant for nearly half a century (until 1944) but did little to alter the country's basic economic or social structure. Economic difficulties contributed to the mounting political and social unrest beginning in 1925. From that date through 1947, there were twenty-seven Chiefs of State (including four in one month) and three new Constitutions—an all-time record of instability in Ecuador.

From the standpoint of a pattern of stability and instability, the significant dates in recent Ecuadorian history are 1948 and 1961. These dates encompass a remarkably stable era during which four orderly presidential elections took place, and for the first time since 1924, Presidents—Galo Plaza Lasso (1948–1952), José María Velasco Ibarra (1952–1956), and Camilo Ponce Enríquez (1956–1960)—all completed their full terms. Velasco Ibarra was re-elected in 1960, but disputes with his vice-president, Carlos Julio Arosemena, and riots over the decreeing of new taxes, among other things, led to renewed military intervention and Velasco's ouster in November 1961. Thus ended the exceptional thirteen-year period of political stability.

After a brief dispute between the army and the air force over the succession issue, Vice-President Arosemena assumed the Presidency. Veering from left to right, and finally acceding to pressure from the armed forces to break relations with Cuba, Arosemena was no more successful than Velasco Ibarra had been in consolidating a firm political base. This failure, compounded by Arosemena's addiction to alcohol (with resulting embarrassments at official functions) and by charges that he was "soft" on communism, prompted a unanimous move by all three military services to remove him in July 1963.

For the first time since 1937, the armed forces assumed power directly with a four-member junta, headed by naval captain Ramón Castro Jijón. The junta announced that it would remain in power only two years, just long enough to carry out its promises to root out corruption and leftist influences and to implement basic reforms ranging from a new Constitution to administrative, tax, and agrarian reforms! The junta outlawed the Communist party, "purged" university faculties, revamped the tax structure, decreed a moderate agrarian reform law, secured international financing for a previously formulated economic development plan, and initiated a variety of other changes. The junta did not relinquish power at the end of two years (that is, by July 1965), but instead hinted that it might stay in office for a full four-year term. One member of the junta explained that Ecuador's political parties were still too weak and divided to provide stable government.

Several of the parties responded by organizing a National Patriotic Front, which staged during July 1965 a series of demonstrations demanding an immediate return to constitutional government. There was also mounting opposition, particularly from Guayaquil, to increased customs duties and other tax measures. Ex-President Ponce, briefly jailed for his part in the riots, denounced the "caveman mentality of the military despotism that considers civic dissent a crime against authority."[4] The junta survived this test of strength, but the political honeymoon was clearly over. In a mood of appeasement, the junta reshuffled Cabinet posts and, most significantly, promised to hold general elections no later than July 1966. These conciliatory moves gave the junta only a brief respite, for in March 1966 there was a renewal of intense political agitation including student demonstrations and a strike by merchants. Under pressure from the high command of the armed forces, the junta bowed

---

[4] *The New York Times,* July 12, 1965, p. 10.

out as gracefully as possible by resigning on March 29, 1966. Thus ended thirty-three months of military rule in Ecuador.

Responding to demands for a return to civilian rule, the military high command requested political party leaders to designate a provisional President. Accordingly, Clemente Yeroví Indaburo, a wealthy businessman and plantation owner who had served as Economics Minister during the Galo Plaza administration, agreed to head a caretaker government. Although the presidential election scheduled for July 1966 was cancelled, elections were held in mid-October 1966 to choose members of a Constituent Assembly. A rightist coalition succeeded in winning majority control of the Assembly, which then proceeded in November 1966 to select Otto Arosemena Gomez to serve as interim President until a regular presidential election could be held, probably in "about a year." Arosemena Gomez, a lawyer who was relatively unknown politically at the time of his selection, thereby became Ecuador's fifth Chief of State since 1960. As desirable as the return to civilian rule may be in principle, there is no evidence at the moment of this writing to suggest that Ecuador's ruling oligarchy has developed a positive program for guiding the nation through the painful process of modernization.

POLITICAL STRUCTURE AND ROLES

Before discussing Ecuador's formal governmental structure, a wider perspective should be provided by first considering the major action groups which supply the dynamics of the system: political parties and significant interest groups. As we shall see, in certain respects the group approach to politics has been institutionalized in Ecuador through the device of "functional" senators, who represent designated group interests.

Political Parties

The kindest thing to say about Ecuador's political party system is that it has been in a virtual shambles since 1944. Their programs now largely anachronistic and their great leaders long gone, the traditional parties have found it necessary to form temporary coalitions with other groups for electoral purposes. Yet no vigorous new parties capable of capturing popular imagination have emerged. José María Velasco Ibarra, an enigma of Ecuadorian politics, has been unable to build a political organization on any foundations more enduring than his charisma and his election-year promises. In effect, Ecuador's weak political parties have not only mirrored regional rivalries and class divisions but have also contributed to Ecuador's basic instability by their narrow concern for partisan advantage and their collective failure to respond to the needs and expectations of a society in transition.

The Traditional Parties: Conservatives, Radical Liberals, and Socialists   Oldest of the traditional parties, the Conservatives were dominant until eclipsed by the Liberals in 1895. However, the Conservatives made something of a comeback in 1956, when Camilo Ponce Enríquez won the Presidency by a plurality vote. Although Ponce campaigned under the label of his own Social Christian Movement, he was regarded as essentially of Conservative leanings. Conservative candidates also registered gains in the congressional and municipal elections of 1962 and, as already noted, a rightist coalition elected a majority of members to the Constituent Assembly in 1966. The Conservative party has remained primarily a Catholic party with its principles based on Church doctrines, on the inherent right to private property, and on the values of order and tradition. Thus, the party continues to advocate state subsidies for Church schools but, in response to the new social consciousness of the Church, announced in 1963 support for social and economic measures including agrarian reform and the integration of the Indian into the national community. The party is intensely anti-Communist, and its leaders allegedly encouraged the armed forces to oust President Arosemena in 1963 because they believed he had not acted vigorously enough against Communist influences.

The main Conservative stronghold continues to be in the highland region, particularly in Quito and Cuenca, where the principal supporters of the party come from the large landowners, other upper-class members, and the Church hierarchy. García Moreno is still the party's greatest hero.

The Radical Liberal party likewise has its martyred hero, Eloy Alfaro, and also must look backward to its days of glory. Dominant for nearly half a century (1895–1944), the Radical Liberals have not elected a President in their own right since 1940. Galo Plaza, son of Liberal ex-President Leónidas Plaza, won election in 1948 not as a Liberal but as the candidate of an *ad hoc* coalition, the National Civic Democratic Movement.

Founded on the anticlerical issue, this party of the urban business elite still emphasizes the issues of religious tolerance and free public education. As early as 1923, the party advocated agrarian reform and the rehabilitation of the Indian. More recently the party announced its support of labor and of a constitutional amendment prohibiting more than one presidential term. However, the Radical Liberal party continues to be identified as the party of the coastal commercial and banking interests. In fact, there are few real differences between them and their traditional rivals, the Conservatives. Once the Church-State issue was settled, their opposition amounted to a coast versus highland, business versus landowner split within the elite governing group. As Galo Plaza expressed it, the Liberal party has found itself "about on a par with the Conservatives in matters of social programs."[5]

Out of power since 1944, the Radical Liberals remain subject to factional splintering. Some have supported Velasco Ibarra's periodic candidacies; some have joined the Socialists in coalitions; each of two factions nominated

---

[5] Galo Plaza Lasso, *Problems of Democracy in Latin America* (Chapel Hill, University of North Carolina Press, 1955), p. 29.

presidential candidates in 1952; and in 1963 two rival executive councils, arising out of a disagreement over whether or not to collaborate with the Arosemena administration, each claimed to represent the party.

The Socialist party, founded in the mid-1920s by middle-class intellectuals and professionals, has retained its doctrinaire opposition to capitalism and its espousal of the cause of the Indians of Ecuador. The Socialists have never approached electoral victory on their own. However, in coalition with the Communists, the Socialists won a congressional majority in 1938, and individual members have frequently held Cabinet posts. Also faction-ridden, the Socialists have often collaborated in recent years with the Radical Liberals in center-left alliances.

Other Parties and Political Movements   The Communists split from the Socialists in 1928 and formed a separate party, which has consistently taken an anti-U.S. stand. Never a numerically large group, the Communists have split into Moscow and Peking wings, the latter calling itself the Socialist Revolutionary party (PSR). Both were outlawed in 1963 by the military junta, as was the Unión Revolucionaria de Juventudes Ecuatorianos (URJE), a Cuban-inspired youth movement.

Two minor political movements of rightist orientation are the Social Christian Movement (MSC) and Acción Revolucionaria Nacional Ecuatoriana (ARNE). The Social Christian Movement (not to be confused with the Democratic Christian party, a small left-of-center group) is a Conservative party supported largely by Catholic intellectuals. It partakes somewhat of the nature of a personalist party, since it was founded by Camilo Ponce Enríquez as a campaign vehicle for the 1956 elections. ARNE is a small, aggressive youth movement on the extreme right. Its readiness to use violent methods parallels that of URJE on the extreme left.

Personalism persists as a divisive force in virtually all Ecuadorian political groups, but two so-called parties are predominantly personalist in nature: the National Federation of Velasquistas (followers of four-time president Velasco Ibarra); and the Concentración de Fuerzas Populares (CFP), founded by Carlos Guevara Moreno.

The *Velasquistas* have no consistent program except loyalty to their *caudillo,* who in turn has no clearly identifiable political orientation except perhaps a vague populism. Variously called "the Great Absentee" (because of his prolonged residences abroad in exile), "the National Personification" (because of his mystical identification with the masses), and "the Crazy One" (because of his often erratic conduct once in office), Velasco Ibarra has accepted support at one time or another from almost every political group in Ecuador. But his impressive electoral victories (he won more votes in 1960 than his two opponents combined) derive from a variety of factors which make up his magnetic popular appeal: his reputation for honesty, his spellbinding oratory, his demagogic promises, and his scorn for partisan labels. Perhaps, as Professor Needler has suggested, such a "demagogic *caudillo"* is supported by the Left because "he speaks to the mobs in the words they wish to hear" yet also attracts support from the Right because Conservatives "can hope that he will provide the 'strong hand' that will discipline the people to obedience."[6]

The CFP, or Concentration of Popular Forces, originated in the 1940s as the political vehicle for the ambitions of a leftist *caudillo* from Guayaquil, Carlos Guevara Moreno, one-time protegé of Velasco Ibarra. With Guevara's resignation from the party's helm in 1964, the CFP's future seems highly uncertain.

As indicated earlier, recent Ecuadorian politics have been marked by transitory coalitions of various regular parties and splinter groups under a variety of meaningless labels. Typical of such arrangements is the Democratic Institutionalist Coalition (CID) formed in early 1965 and reportedly led by *Velasquistas*.[7] The proliferation of such *ad hoc* groups is symptomatic of the virtual bankruptcy of Ecuador's political party system.

Politically Significant Interest Groups

Ecuador's political underdevelopment is further indicated by the fact that the historic trio of army, Church, and large landowners remains a major component in the country's governing elite. If to these we add the commercial, industrial, financial, and professional groups, the composition of Ecuador's traditional power structure is reasonably complete. Two of these traditional groups, both of an institutional nature, are singled out for further discussion: the armed forces and the Catholic Church.

The Armed Forces Historically, the military establishment has furnished almost one-third of Ecuador's Presidents. In contrast to the earlier period of military *caudillos,* the pattern of military intervention during most of the twentieth century has been sporadic and temporary, with the armed forces acting primarily as guardians of the system rather than as direct holders of power. In this respect the 1963 takeover was a break with precedent, since the last outright military government in Ecuador had been in 1937–1938. Nevertheless, the all-services junta has been careful to maintain an image of political selflessness, even to the extent of ousting one of its own members, Air Force Colonel Guillermo Freile Posso, because of his ill-concealed presidential ambitions.

In assuming power in 1963, the military junta presented itself as having intervened not only to save the nation from an "irresponsible" civilian regime but also to institute necessary reforms. In an early manifesto the junta declared its intention of enacting social laws and other "modern legislation" as had been done "in that other historic moment, 1937–1938, in which the

---

[6] Martin C. Needler, *Latin American Politics in Perspective* (Princeton, D. Van Nostrand Company, Inc., 1963), pp. 110–11.

[7] *El Comercio* (Quito), January 1, 1966, p. 13.

Armed Forces took action in defense of the most unprotected sectors of the community. . . ."[8] Consistent with this conception of its mission, the junta denounced the "oligarchy," particularly for tax evasion, and expressed undisguised contempt for the existing political parties.

How does one explain the apparent anomaly of highly privileged, professionalized officers turning into social reformers and critics of the oligarchy? As complex as a total explanation might be (including, perhaps, the changing class origins of the officer corps), it is suggested that part of the answer may lie simply in the military's elemental instinct for corporate self-preservation. That is, Ecuador's military leaders may have been prompted by a kind of unformalized Burkean conservatism in that, by intervening to enact timely reforms, these leaders sought to preserve the basic elements of the *status quo* in the face of the possibility that the entire system, themselves included, might be destroyed in a Cuban-style revolution.

To view the basic purpose of the 1963 coup in this light is an attempt to explain that coup, not to approve it. Justifiable motives do not legalize an illegality, nor can assertions of a higher obligation excuse the junta's political naïveté in assuming that fundamental reforms can be quickly effected merely by assigning experts to write new laws. But it would seem quite likely that the incidence of future interventions by the armed forces in Ecuador will depend upon their appraisal of the ability of succeeding governments to maintain order.

The Church   Although the political power of the Catholic Church in Ecuador declined considerably after the Liberals gained control in 1895, its influence continues to be as strong as anywhere in Latin America. As already noted, the Conservative party and certain rightist movements are openly pro-Catholic. Its interests are also represented through a "functional" senator for private (that is, Catholic) universities. Like the Conservative party, the Church's principal stronghold is in the Sierra. Albert B. Franklin has noted that even the *teniente político,* the political lieutenant, of the rural parish "must never forget that there is one power which can always make his tasks impossible, and that is the local priest."[9] Although the Church was long considered as one of the most conservative in Latin America, the Ecuadorian hierarchy placed the Church on the side of reform just prior to the 1963 coup. The Church publicly advocated agrarian and tax reforms and stressed the social obligations of businessmen and property owners toward their employees.

Other Politically Active Groups   Groups outside the traditional power structure which contend for political influence are the labor unions and university students. Given the country's modest industrial development and

---

[8] Translated and quoted in Martin C. Needler, *Anatomy of a Coup d'Etat: Ecuador, 1963* (Washington, D.C., Operations and Policy Research, Inc., Institute for the Comparative Study of Political Systems, 1964), Appendix B, p. 51.

[9] Albert B. Franklin, *Ecuador: Portrait of a People* (Garden City, N.Y., Doubleday, Doran & Company, Inc., 1944), pp. 137–38.

the fact that most agricultural workers are unorganized, the estimated union membership as of 1960 was only eighty-five thousand, or roughly five percent of the economically active population.[10] By far the largest labor organization is the leftist-oriented Confederation of Ecuadorian Workers (CTE), although both a Catholic workers' group as well as a moderate non-Communist confederation organized in 1962 are challenging CTE's predominance. Despite organized labor's numerical weakness, the concentration of labor in urban areas and its susceptibility to manipulation by a few leaders gives the CTE a disproportionate weight when it comes to the use of strikes and demonstrations as political weapons.

A similar disproportion characterizes student organizations. Students in Ecuador are politically powerful far beyond their actual numbers; there are only some nine thousand students at five public and two Catholic universities. Student demonstrations in Ecuador have contributed to the downfall of Presidents, and the annual patriotic parade to protest the Rio Protocol of 1962 (by which Ecuador lost most of its claimed territory in the Oriente to Peru) affords an opportunity to demonstrate against the government in power. Following such a demonstration in January 1964, the junta temporarily closed Central University in Quito, dissolved the Federation of University Students, and reduced the degree of student participation in university administration. Student agitation during 1965 resulted in the loss of about sixty percent of classroom time at Central University alone and forced the rector and the vice-rector to resign.

Institutions of Government

While the Constitution of 1946 (Ecuador's fifteenth)[11] remained technically in effect throughout the changes in government which have occurred since the 1963 coup, the operative features of the Constitution have been ignored in practice since that time and probably will continue to be ignored until the Constituent Assembly, elected in October 1966, has drafted a new charter. Nevertheless, it seems unlikely that any very drastic changes will be made in the basic structure of government; that is, Ecuador will probably remain a unitary state with a presidential system. Therefore, the institutions discussed below are those provided by the Constitution of 1946 although by the time these lines are published, Ecuador may have a new organic law.

Let it be noted that it has not been for lack of imaginative constitutional experimentation that Ecuador's problems of instability have continued to defy solution. On the contrary, the constitutional system of the country contains

---

[10] Bureau of Labor Statistics, *Labor Law and Practice in Ecuador*, p. 27. Robert J. Alexander estimates union membership in Ecuador at only seventy-five thousand in *Today's Latin America* (Garden City, N.Y., Doubleday & Company, Inc., 1962), Table III, p. 95.

[11] Ecuador has had sixteen Constitutions (the figure sometimes cited) if the unenforced Constitution of 1938 is counted. Summaries of the fifteen "official" Constitutions are given in Dr. Francisco Zevallos Reyre, *Lecciones de derecho constitucional* (Guayaquil, Ecuador, Universidad de Guayaquil, Departamento de Publicaciones, 1947), pp. 341–436.

more unique features than that of perhaps any other Latin American Republic. The various devices for interbranch co-operation as well as the provision for "functional" senators, which is discussed below, are cases in point. This is not to say that constitutional formulas are irrelevant but simply to underscore the truism that constitutional tinkering in and of itself will not solve the underlying political problems.

The 1946 Constitution contains several noteworthy departures from the conventional separation of powers doctrine. The three branches of the central Government are not designated as coequal "powers" in the customary fashion, but rather as "functions," thereby connoting that only the Legislature possesses "power" in the legal sense. And rather than emphasizing a rigid separation of functions with each balanced by the others, considerable attention is given to devices for facilitating co-ordination among the branches. This attention is particularly apparent in the mixed membership provisions for the Legislative Commission and the Council of State.

The five-member Legislative Commission is clearly intended as a co-ordinating agency, since it includes representatives from all three branches plus the dean of Central University's law faculty as *ex officio* member. The functions of the commission are primarily those of a super drafting committee, as it proposes major bills and constitutional amendments for submission to joint sessions of Congress. The commission is also charged with codifying and editing existing laws.

The other important co-ordinating agency, the Council of State, is a heterogeneous body composed of eleven regular members and, as nonvoting participants, the nine Cabinet ministers. Among the regular members are included two congressmen, an armed forces representative, the presiding Justice of the Supreme Court, the heads of various independent agencies, and two private citizens selected by Congress. The functions of the council combine those of an interim legislative committee to perform necessary duties on behalf of Congress between sessions and those of a "watchdog" group to call the public's and the Congress's attention to violations of the Constitution or laws. Hence, in contrast to the usual conception of a Council of State as an advisory body to the President, in Ecuador its functions are intended to be supervisory.

The Legislative Function   The bicameral Congress meets annually for a sixty-day session extendable for an additional thirty days. Members of the lower house, or Chamber of Deputies, are elected by a system of proportional representation for two-year terms and may be indefinitely re-elected. Since there is a fixed ratio of 1 deputy for every 50,000 inhabitants, with each province guaranteed at least 2 deputies regardless of size, the total membership increased from 68 in 1958 to 73 in 1960, an increase which reflects population growth.

Senators serve four-year simultaneous terms and also may be re-elected. Senators are elected in two categories: provincial and "functional." The former are popularly elected, two from each of the nineteen mainland provinces and one from the Galápagos Islands.[12] The twelve "functional" senators are selected by electoral colleges representing certain cultural, occupational, and economic interest groups. (See the section below on suffrage, elections, and representation.)

In addition to the usual powers granted to legislative bodies, it should be noted that the Congress, acting alone, names judges of the Supreme Court and of the superior courts and that the Congress has the sole authority "to interpret the Constitution . . . and to decide the questions that may arise over the meaning of any of its terms."[13] The most unusual procedural feature is the provision for joint sessions whenever such important matters as enacting the budget, electing Supreme Court justices, or declaring war are under consideration. A two-thirds vote of those present is required for the approval of most actions taken in joint session. This provision seems to be an attempt to combine the advantages of bicameral structure with unicameral procedures, at least for certain high-priority functions. For the introduction of bills, the sponsorship of at least three congressmen is required. In addition, the executive branch, the Supreme Court, the Legislative Commission, and the National Economic Council may submit legislative proposals.

Although the legislative function was accorded theoretical supremacy over the other branches of government, Congress has rather consistently failed to live up to these expectations. Apart from the unreality of such expectations in a culture which has been conditioned to strong executive leadership, the Ecuadorian Congress has reflected the weakness of the political parties themselves. For example, no single party won a majority of seats in the lower house in 1958, 1960, or 1962. The inevitable result has been bickering and the pursuit of purely partisan advantages. Despite the polemical flavor of the junta's manifesto of July 1963, it undoubtedly echoed a general sentiment when it charged that Congress had failed to fulfill its function, "since the legislators, year after year, wasted their time in empty and trivial discussions. . . ."[14]

The Executive Function   The President of Ecuador is directly elected for a four-year term and, according to the Constitution of 1946, may be re-elected after an intervening term has elapsed. To win election, only a plurality of the votes cast is required. Thus, President Ponce was elected in 1956 even though he received only about thirty percent of the total number of votes. In the remote chance that the popular vote should result in a tie, Congress in joint session decides the outcome by majority vote, and if that

---

[12] Prior to a 1960 amendment, only the fifteen coastal and highland provinces were entitled to two senators, with the four Oriente provinces electing only one each. The cancellation of the 1964 elections prevented the implementation of this amendment. See *Methods of Electing National Executives and National Legislatures in South America*, Special Memorandum No. 21 (Washington, D.C., Operations and Policy Research, Inc., Institute for the Comparative Study of Political Systems, n.d.), pp. 15–18.

[13] Article 189, "Political Constitution of the Republic of Ecuador," as translated in Russell H. Fitzgibbon, ed., *The Constitutions of the Americas* (Chicago, The University of Chicago Press, 1948), pp. 323–65.

[14] Needler, *Anatomy of a Coup d'Etat,* p. 51.

vote should also be a tie, the matter is decided by lot. The new President assumes office on September 1 following the quadrennial June elections.

The President's various administrative, legislative, diplomatic, and military roles are similar to those of the President of the United States except as will be noted. The Ecuadorian President alone appoints and removes his Cabinet officers but plays no part in the appointment of judges. Promotions to high military ranks, however, require the approval of the full Congress, and diplomatic appointments require senatorial assent. The President may veto legislative bills on either or both of two grounds: "inexpediency" or unconstitutionality. If he objects on grounds of the bill's inexpediency, Congress in joint session may override by a two-thirds vote. If, however, a constitutional question has been raised and the Supreme Court concurs, the bill automatically dies. The President may issue emergency economic decrees with the approval of the National Economic Council although Congress may disallow such decrees at its next session. Like other Latin American Executives, the Ecuadorian President may exercise a broad range of additional powers during national emergencies, provided approval is granted by the Congress or, during its recess, by the Council of State.

Since Ecuador is a unitary rather than a federal State, this centralization of power enhances the President's predominance. He has the unrestricted authority to appoint provincial governors and, on nomination of the respective governors, also appoints the administrative heads of the cantons and parishes. The only exceptions to this pervasive control over local levels of government are the autonomous municipalities, which popularly elect their own mayors and councils.

Officials called Ministers of State head the nine administrative departments and assist the President in his role as Chief Executive. Although Congress has no direct voice in the appointment of ministers, Congress can demand that they submit reports, attend congressional sessions to answer questions, and even resign their posts if Congress passes a motion of censure against them. However, the frequent turnover of Cabinet officers has not been a result of the use of these quasi-parliamentary devices, which are rarely invoked, but rather of the general instability of the political system. Even the military junta had to play the game of musical chairs with Cabinet posts. As part of the effort to placate the restless political parties, the junta replaced seven of the nine Cabinet officers in mid-1965 and increased the number of civilian members in the Cabinet from six to eight.

With admirable zeal, the junta tackled the problem of modernizing Ecuador's archaic administrative and tax structure. An example of the magnitude of the problem was the fact that literally hundreds of autonomous and semiautonomous agencies had been allowed to proliferate, many with their own earmarked revenue sources. These agencies among them absorbed nearly sixty percent of all tax revenues. The junta abolished a number of these agencies, and, over loud protests, centralized the collection and distribution of the agency revenues. The junta also revised the general tax code, tightened the income tax laws, and improved the collection of customs duties. The junta further sought to rationalize the structure and procedures of the national bureaucracy, but it remains to be seen just how permanent these administrative and tax reforms will prove to be in face of the entrenched interests affected.

Brief note should be taken of the second elected official in the executive branch, the vice-president. This office was resurrected by the Constitution of 1946 after the abandonment of the office in 1906. As in the United States, the Ecuadorian vice-president presides over the Senate and stands by in case the presidential office should become vacant. It is alleged that Vice-President Arosemena did more than simply stand by, however, as he apparently was involved in the maneuverings which ended with President Velasco Ibarra's ouster in 1961. In a closer parallel to United States experience with the office, it also serves a useful political purpose in Ecuador in that the existence of the office allows the political parties to "balance the ticket" regionally by nominating one of their candidates from the Sierra and the other from the coast. However, since presidential and vice-presidential candidates are voted for separately, it is possible for a vice-president to be elected from a different party slate than the winning presidential candidate. This happened in 1948 when the vice-presidential candidate from the opposing Conservative ticket was elected to serve with President Galo Plaza.

The Judicial Function   Ecuador's judiciary is generally regarded as the one branch of government with a consistently high reputation. The judiciary has remained largely immune from the unstabilizing forces which have ousted Presidents and have rendered Congress ineffectual. By the same token the courts have had only peripheral effect on the central problems of the political system.

There are five levels in Ecuador's judicial structure: a Supreme Court; superior courts, which are equivalent to the United States circuit courts of appeal; provincial courts; cantonal courts; and the political lieutenants of the rural parishes, who, among their other duties, act as judges in minor cases. The fifteen Supreme Court justices are appointed by Congress for six-year, renewable terms and must have had twelve years of legal experience prior to appointment. As a matter of practice, the Court's membership is balanced between coast and Sierra, a practice which illustrates again the efforts to maintain a regional equilibrium. A somewhat unusual feature of the Supreme Court's operation is that cases are assigned by lot to each of its three chambers, or *salas,* rather than each chamber specializing in a particular category of legal disputes. This system is defended as contributing to impartiality and, of course, as guaranteeing an evenly divided workload.

Since the Constitution of 1946 endowed Congress with the sole authority to decide questions of constitutional interpretation, the Supreme Court's power of judicial review is virtually nonexistent. The Court has the authority to void a law only if prescribed procedures were violated in the law's enactment. And, as previously noted, if the President vetoes a bill on grounds of unconstitutionality, the Court's concurrence ensures the death of the measure.

The Supreme Court enjoys the privilege of directly introducing bills into Congress, and a member of the Court is entitled to attend congressional sessions and take part in discussing such bills. Furthermore, the presiding justice personally delivers an annual message to the Congress on the subject of the administration of justice in the nation. Such judicial involvement in the legislative process is a further example of the attempt to facilitate co-operation among the three functions of the central Government.

POLITICAL PROCESSES

Suffrage, Elections, and Representation

According to the 1946 Constitution, only literate nationals at least eighteen years of age are citizens and may vote. Women's suffrage was introduced in the Constitution of 1929, making Ecuador the first Latin American Republic to grant equal voting rights to women. Voting is optional for women, however, while it is theoretically obligatory for men. Members of the armed forces are specifically excluded from voting although their collective interests are assured a political voice through a "functional" senator, as noted below.

The literacy requirement automatically disenfranchises over forty percent of the population, principally among the Indians. Thus, this requirement has had the purpose and effect of helping to preserve middle-class and upper-class rule. Despite a number of ambitious literacy campaigns launched since 1945, little noticeable progress has been made in reducing the overall percentage of illiterates.

Direct popular elections are the rule except in the case of "functional" senators. A system of proportional representation is used whenever two or more seats are to be filled. Because the complex operation of the system is not understood by most voters, proportional representation as it has operated in Ecuador "has contributed to the political apathy of the people."[15] The system has also probably contributed to the multiplicity and the weakness of Ecuador's political parties.

General control over elections is assigned by the Constitution to a special electoral tribunal, whose members are selected by each of the three branches of the national Government. Since 1948, at least, Ecuadorian elections have been relatively honest and generally peaceful.

The representation system in the Ecuadorian Congress is based on a combination of factors—population, political units, and interest groups. Population is the primary basis for representation in the Chamber of Deputies except as this proportionality is skewed by the provision that every province, no matter how small its population, is guaranteed two deputies. Political units, the provinces, are the basis for representation in the Senate except for the provision that there shall be an additional twelve "functional" senators. Four

---

[15] Blanksten, *Ecuador: Constitutions and Caudillos,* p. 76.

of the twelve represent national groups: the armed forces, public universities, private universities, and a combined professional and cultural grouping, composed of journalists as well as members of scientific and literary societies. The other eight "functional" senators are distributed on a regional basis, four each for the highland and the coast, who represent the agricultural, commercial, industrial, and labor interests of each area. Each "functional" senator is selected by a separate electoral college for the respective interest groups. These electoral bodies are variously constituted; that for the armed forces, for example, consists of a delegate from each base and installation.

In effect, this unusual provision for "functional" legislators not only institutionalizes an interest-group approach to politics but also helps to maintain a regional balance of power. In this respect the provision is a realistic if inexact reflection of the actual power structure within Ecuador's political system.

The Political Decision-Making Process

The formal machinery for governmental decision-making in Ecuador has already been described. On occasion this machinery has operated more or less in accordance with constitutional prescription, that is, with Congress fulfilling its legislative role as occurred most notably during the Galo Plaza administration (1948–1952). But even President Plaza resorted to his power to issue emergency economic decrees in order to circumvent congressional refusal to enact a civil service law (which, as the next Congress pointed out in annulling it, was not exactly an emergency economic measure).[16] The more usual pattern of executive-legislative relationships, therefore, has been far more competitive than co-operative. At times even routine matters have been stymied, as when Congress once adjourned without acting on an armed forces promotion list. When the formal decision-making machinery reaches the point of a virtual breakdown, the very notion of parliamentary democracy is discredited.

Even in smoothly functioning democratic systems, of course, much of the decision-making process takes place on an informal, behind-the-scenes basis and involves the complex interaction of the decision makers and influential groups. Given the predominance of the executive branch and the weakness of Congress in the Ecuadorian system, it can be assumed that most policy proposals originate with the Chief Executive or his advisors; that these proposals are acted upon, or perhaps even canceled, following a complex procedure involving persons and groups having access to the Executive; and that various pressures, such as strikes and demonstrations, will be brought to bear, even by those without direct access to the decision makers. Such interaction is most obvious in the area of purely executive decisions. Thus, President Arosemena was quite obviously pressured by the armed forces into breaking

---

[16] Lilo Linke, *Ecuador, Country of Contrasts,* 3rd ed. (London, Oxford University Press, 1960), p. 57.

relations with Cuba and other Communist-bloc nations in 1962. Even the military junta did not remain immune from certain pressures regarding its decisions. Public demonstrations and riots in July 1965 sparked by demands for a return to constitutional government undoubtedly influenced the junta to announce shortly afterwards that it would step down in 1966 rather than in 1967, as earlier indicated. And it was the renewal of these public pressures which brought about the junta's downfall in March 1966, several months ahead of its re-scheduled relinquishment of power. In short, when a significant number of people agitate for changes, this agitation can be a factor in the decision-making process under even a military government.

Allegiance and Alienation

"Allegiance" normally refers to a feeling of national identification and loyalty on the part of members of a nation-state. National loyalty, in its most rudimentary form, is expressed as patriotism, or participation in certain rituals involving the symbols of sovereignty. Politically conscious Ecuadorians are unquestionably patriotic and never more so than on the annual occasion when they are as one in protesting the terms of the Rio Protocol of 1942. But in spite of the superficial cohesiveness furnished by patriotism, there still seems to be no real national identification, no operational acceptance of the interests of the nation as a whole which override regional, class, or group interests. There is perhaps no more telling evidence of this failure than the persistence of the bitter rivalry between Guayaquil and Quito.

"Allegiance" has a more precise meaning, however, especially when the term is used in conjunction with the concept of political alienation. In this usage, allegiance (or an "allegiant situation") exists when there is congruence between political attitudes and political structure; conversely, alienation exists when there is incongruence between political attitudes and political structure.[17]

But for a person to be either an allegiant or an alienate, he at least has to be aware of the political system and have some feelings about it, whether positive or negative. When a person is either unaware or only vaguely aware of the political system, Almond and Verba term him a parochial. "If they are aware of the impact of government but are dissatisfied, we can call them alienated subjects. If they are not aware at all or only dimly aware, we can call them parochials."[18]

To attempt to apply this typology to Ecuador without benefit of extensive research data is risky; nevertheless, certain observations may be ventured. The great bulk of the Indian population, illiterate and voteless, certainly falls into the parochial category. Perhaps only the isolated tribes of the Oriente are "pure" parochials, since the highland Indians are at least vaguely aware of the Government in the person of the *teniente político*. Many of the rural mestizos

---

[17] Gabriel A. Almond and Sidney Verba, *The Civic Culture* (Boston and Toronto, Little, Brown and Company, 1965), pp. 20–21.

[18] Almond and Verba, pp. 51–52.

would also have to be classified as parochials. For example, Albert B. Franklin tells the story of a mestizo subsistence farmer who "had not heard of the last three Presidents of Ecuador."[19]

Among the literate, politically conscious citizenry the predominant attitude appears to be one of alienation. It is not unreasonable to assume that the complaints about governmental neglect and corruption which Almond and Verba found among alienated Mexican respondents would be even more evident among Ecuadorians.[20] In fact, the complaint about neglect is almost endemic among *guayaquileños,* who point out that they contribute seventy-five percent of all national tax revenues but receive relatively few benefits in return. And the junta undoubtedly was playing to popular sentiment in its frequent attacks on "corrupt politicians" and "economic oligarchs." Indeed, the disjunction between the norms of democratic equality and the obvious reality of social inequality in Ecuador cannot but foster a sense of alienation.

Among the various identifiable means for expressing alienation, the one most evident in Ecuador is a tendency toward "identification with a charismatic leader."[21] Even Velasco Ibarra's demonstrable inability, with the sole exception of his 1952–1956 term, to stay in office once elected, seemingly has not dimmed his popularity with the electorate at large.

In summary, then, it can be assumed that the vast majority of Ecuadorians are either indifferent to the political system or else alienated in one form or another in that they feel they do not have a rightful or meaningful role in the political process.

ASSESSMENT OF STABILITY AND INSTABILITY

In making the implicit assumption that political stability is desirable, it should be made explicit that this assumption is made within the context of democratic values. That is, stability as a desired goal is not meant to connote either the static condition of an hierarchically ordered traditional society or the suppressive order of a totalitarian regime. By definition a government's ability to maintain public order is essential to a stable system. But equally important in a democratic system, and indeed a prerequisite for order-keeping, is the system's degree of responsiveness to the expressed needs of the population as a whole. Thus, the key to democratic political stability is the system's capacity to adapt to change in order to satisfy popular demands and expectations. Conversely, instability results when the system is either too rigid to adapt to change or else so weak and vacillating that attempted adaptations fail to fulfill social needs.[22] Ecuador's recent history indicates that the country

---

[19] Franklin, *Ecuador: Portrait of a People,* p. 200.

[20] Almond and Verba, pp. 50–51.

[21] For a discussion of the methods of expressing alienation, see Murray B. Levin, *The Alienated Voter* (New York, Holt, Rinehart and Winston, Inc., 1960), pp. 66–68.

[22] See Lucian W. Pye, *Aspects of Political Development* (Boston and Toronto, Little, Brown and Company, 1966), p. 75.

falls primarily into the category of weak, vacillating systems in which attempts to adapt to change either have been blocked or have proved inadequate. The result, as noted above, has been widespread frustration and political alienation.

Before attempting the highly speculative exercise of assessing Ecuador's chances for achieving stability, it may be helpful to examine the extent to which certain factors which promote instability are applicable. For analytical purposes we may utilize three general categories of interrelated factors which contribute to instability in Latin America: (1) entrepreneurial deficiencies which hinder economic development and hence the capacity of the economy to meet rising demands; (2) a lack of role specialization among politically relevant groups leading, for example, to military and clerical roles in political affairs; and (3) rapid population growth, especially in urban areas, leading to heightened frustrations as the cities prove unable to provide minimum facilities or adequate employment for the migrants from rural areas.[23]

Ecuador's low level of economic development reflects the failure to overcome certain entrepreneurial deficiencies—the reluctance to invest risk capital, the prevalence of tax dodging, the Government's chronic financial straits, and the sinecurism of much of the bureaucracy, to name only a few of the continuing problems. There is some hope for eventual improvement in this area, however, with the approval in 1965 of Ecuador's ten-year economic development plan under Alliance for Progress guidelines. A consortium of international lending agencies and foreign nations expressed sufficient confidence in Ecuador's economic future to agree to furnish investment funds or technical assistance for carrying out the plan.

The continued lack of role specialization is more apparent in Ecuador in the interventionist proclivities of the armed forces, the political influence of the Church, and the political activism of university students. While the renewals of military interventionism in 1961 and 1963 were more in the nature of effects than causes of the instability of the period, it is also pertinent to note that the very precedent of military interference tends to become a self-perpetuating factor, which further unsettles the constitutional order. Ecuadorians have not yet fully accepted the notion that the armed forces should confine themselves to a military role, students to an educational role, and the Church to a spiritual role.

As to the third general factor leading to instability, Ecuador's population explosion, accompanied by an even faster urban growth rate, tends to compound the problems flowing from the now familiar "revolution of rising expectations." The inability of either the political or the economic system to gratify the growing wants and expectations of the population—of the urban populations in particular—exacerbates the feelings of political alienation and helps create seedbeds of potential violence.

---

[23] These factors are analyzed in Kenneth F. Johnson, "Causal Factors in Latin American Political Instability," *The Western Political Quarterly,* XVII, No. 3 (September 1964), 432–46.

Hence, Ecuador furnishes an almost classic case of a country in which the causal factors of instability are still present in ample measure. If we add to these some of the special problems which Ecuador faces in achieving integrated nationhood (that is, regional rivalries and an unassimilated Indian population), we cannot lightly dismiss the possibility that the Ecuadorians, out of frustration, may opt for extreme solutions.

In short, Ecuador seems ripe for a shattering revolution if efforts at evolutionary changes are thwarted or move at too slow a pace. If a new political grouping which is genuinely committed to change should emerge from the disarray of fragmented political parties; if that grouping should find an able, popular leader; and if it is able to make an accommodation with the armed forces, then some degree of optimism might be justified.

In order to brighten the bleak prospects presented above, one last note of cautious optimism should be voiced. To this author at least, it is encouraging that the leaders of Ecuador's military establishment have demonstrated their commitment to reform and change. This is not to suggest that military authoritarianism or repeated interventions will furnish the solution to Ecuador's complex problems. But it is to suggest that a popularly-backed civilian government, supported by a solid party organization, may well find that the cooperation of a reform-minded military establishment is the key to the maintenance of public order while a transitional society undergoes the wrenching stresses brought on by political, social, and economic restructuring.

11/Peru

MARVIN ALISKY

MARVIN ALISKY, Professor of Political Science and Mass Communications and Director of the Center for Latin American Studies at Arizona State University, has been a Smith-Mundt professor at the Universidad Nacional de Nicaragua, United States Delegate to UNESCO (Quito, Ecuador), and consultant to numerous private and public agencies. In addition to being the author of Uruguay *and the co-author of two books on politics, he has written some eighty monographs and articles dealing with Latin America.*

Wide and Alien Is the World, the title of a twentieth-century novel by the distinguished Peruvian writer Ciro Alegría, offers a cryptic summary of political life in this Andean nation. To the average Peruvian citizen, however, life's "world orbit" has more often been alien than wide, given the environment in which he must function.

In recent decades, Peruvian politics have gradually changed from control by an oligarchy of traditional values to a system of multiple forces in which military guardianship of the peace appears to be the dominant influence. In fact, during the past two decades, probably more socio-economic adjustments have occurred than during the entire century and a quarter preceding those decades. That so many changes have occurred within so short a time makes Peru one of Latin America's most dynamic contemporary political systems.

THE ENVIRONMENT OF POLITICS IN PERU

Peru is divided into three parts: the narrow sea coast, the Andes mountains, and the eastern jungle. Running from northwest to southeast, the Andes cut Peru into these distinct geographical areas, each somewhat sealed off from easy land travel to the other by rugged ravines interlaced with some of the world's highest peaks. This rugged topography looms as a barrier to rapid development of the nation's natural resources as well as to socio-economic integration.

Between the Pacific Ocean and the steep escarpments of the Andes lies the coastal strip, Peru's western fringe. Hugging the shore for the entire 1,400-mile length of the nation, the coastal plain ranges in width from eight to seventy-five miles. This coastal region comprises only ten percent of the Republic's area but contains thirty percent of its population.

The Humboldt Current lowers the sea temperature below that of the land and thus prevents rain from the west, whereas the Andean range robs south-eastern winds of their moisture; these factors combine to produce a dry coast. Yet despite its naturally arid climate, the *costa* possesses agricultural and industrial oases. Fifty-two rivers emptying into the Pacific supply the irrigation waters for several valleys yielding cotton and sugar crops, and the cold Humboldt waters nearby make possible a lucrative fishing industry. In these same irrigated river valleys can be found much of the Peruvian industrial output.

Rising sharply from five thousand to ten thousand feet above sea level, the western edge of the Andes demarcates the *costa* from the *sierra,* or highlands region. Comprising thirty percent of the total area of Peru, the *sierra* contains sixty percent of the country's population. The setting for much of the Inca Empire of pre-Spanish days, the Andean region still contains most of Peru's Indian population, which ekes out an impoverished livelihood in agriculture and mining. Air transportation and radio link the cities and towns of the *sierra* to Lima and other coastal urban centers, but railroad and highway facilities have been inadequate though they are slowly improving.

Sloping sharply eastward from the Andean highlands, the remaining sixty percent of the national territory, the *selva,* or *"montañas,"* a tropical forest and jungle stretching to the Amazon basin, contains only ten percent of the Peruvian population. Few roads lead westward out of the *selva* across the Andes to the coast. In terms of total land area, Peru appears to be a large country, totaling almost a half-million square miles, or an area about the size of Alaska, or double the size of Texas. But when we subtract the *selva,* devoid of population and thinly marginal to the national economy, ecological Peru covers an area under 200,000 square miles, twenty percent larger than the state of California.

Integrating the three physically divided regions of Peru into an economic and social entity has proved a staggering venture for Peruvian leadership throughout the mountainous nation's history. Only since 1963 has a Peruvian government projected specific plans for incorporating large groups of isolated Indians more into the national way of life.

In 1940 the Peruvian population totaled 7 million, and by 1950 it had risen to 8 million. Estimates based on the 1961 census place the 1967 population at 12.5 million.[1] Peru now faces the pressures of a population increase of 3 percent annually, an explosion which threatens to nullify recent economic gains.

Peru's population can be characterized as young, forty-five percent being less than fifteen years of age. Many of the youths, for the first time since the pre-Inca migrations, have joined other segments of the Peruvian people who are moving westward. Indians are moving to the edge of cities and are swelling slums in the Andean and coastal urban areas. Greater Lima had a population of 1.2 million in 1958, but by the end of 1965, it had risen to almost 2 million. The national capital is increasing in population by approximately 5 percent annually; this increase is in part the result of the *barriadas,* or new slum areas of migrants from the mountains. Despite this urban pull, 60 percent of the economically active population is still employed in agriculture.[2]

Racially, Indians make up 44 percent of the population, white and mestizo (Indian-Spanish hybrid) groups combined make up 55 percent, and Orientals and Negroes make up 1 percent. Racial intermixture has been extensive enough to prompt census officials to avoid distinguishing between Caucasians and mestizos; both groups are placed in a single category. The term *cholo* denotes a composite Spanish-Indian culture which can apply to a hybrid social group independent of actual ethnic classification.

Linguistically, six out of ten Peruvians are Spanish-speaking, and the remaining four consider Quechua or Aymará to be their principal tongue. Census officials have not been able to determine accurately how many of the Indian-language Peruvians are bilingual in a genuinely functional sense. Only half the population fourteen years of age or older can read.

Peru is one of the few Latin American countries which has achieved meaningful diversification of its economy. This diversification saves Peru from the instability of monocultural economies. Unlike the banana or coffee Republics, Peru has become a nation whose payrolls vary from agricultural to mining to industrial to commercial activities.

Of those segments of the total population economically active, 60 percent work in agriculture, 20 percent in industry, 5 percent in commerce, 4 percent in personal services, 3.5 percent in government, 2 percent in mining, and the remaining 6.5 percent in miscellaneous pursuits. Within key segments of the economy, diversification has also set in. Peruvian mining for years was symbolized by copper, still very much a major export. But Peru also ranks second among nations of the world as a producer of silver and fifth in both lead and zinc production. Moreover, Peru ranks twelfth among the world's petroleum producers.

Major exports, in descending order of importance, are fish products,

---

[1] Ministerio de Hacienda, Dirección Nacional de Estadística, *Anuario estadístico del Perú* (Lima, 1958), p. 2; Ministerio de Hacienda, *Censo nacional, 1961,* printed press release of July 1965.

[2] Banco Central de Reserva del Peru, *Actividades productivas del Perú* (Lima, Banco Central, 1961), pp. 18–19, 21.

cotton, copper, and sugar. The fishing industry in recent years has been Peru's dynamic new source of wealth. By January 1961, most of the fishing and fish-products industry had been brought into the Consorcio Pesquero del Perú, a marketing agency with a global network of sales agents.

Encouraging as the Peruvian economic diversification has been, the regional distribution of productive activity still spells out a situation of political and social tensions in the face of a growing population. The greatest economic activity still clings to the coast. Only through mining does the *sierra* remain important to the Peruvian economy. National income in the 1960s has been increasing by 4.5 percent annually, but per capita income has been increasing by only 2.5 percent, partly because of the less productive *sierra* and the unproductive *selva*.

Steadily improving living conditions center in Lima, Callao, Arequipa, Trujillo, and a few other cities. In 1965 almost one million television sets were in use in homes, businesses, and public institutions in Lima, Callao, and Arequipa. Yet two-thirds of all Peruvians do not consume a balanced diet or live in homes with modern plumbing. In the 1950s half of the population lived at or slightly above the subsistence level.[3] After a decade of marked economic progress, Peru still had not reduced this proportion by more than a few percentage points. Unlike the rapid economic changes in Mexico, those in Peru have not been built upon a genuine social revolution.

Dramatic evidence of the growth of the middle sectors can be found in the rise of retail sales of merchandise geared to middle incomes. The Lima Chamber of Commerce estimated an increase in middle-income purchases from 1964 to 1965 of fifteen percent. Geared to middle-income and lower-income groups, the Peruvian Savings and Loan League, an organization of nineteen savings and loan associations, now operates in every major city of the Republic. A key member of the league, Mutual El Pueblo, founded in 1961 with just 1,900 savings accounts, by 1964 had 13,020 accounts, and was making plans for low-cost housing in several urban areas.[4]

In 1965, Ford, General Motors, and Chrysler announced plans for automobile assembly plants in Peru which will create hundreds of new jobs. The General Motors plant, which began operations in March 1965, by the end of the year already had an annual production quota of five thousand vehicles, one-fourth of the total number Peru had been forced to import during 1964. Bolstered by technical and financial assistance from the United States and the United Nations, Peru's national ministries have begun to develop new economic sectors, ranging from seaweed production to textiles. Programs of highway, school, and housing construction have been accelerated since 1963.

---

[3] Inter-American Development Bank, *Institutional Reforms and Social Development Trends in Latin America* (Washington, D.C., Government Printing Office, 1963), pp. 261–72; Thomas R. Ford, *Man and Land in Peru* (Gainesville, University of Florida Press, 1955), pp. 116–17.

[4] *Por un Perú mejor* (Lima, Federación Nacional de Cooperativas de Crédito del Perú, 1964), pp. 10–12.

Although the Peruvian social structure has not been radically changed, the impact of economic growth, both public and private, has spurred the semblance of new middle sectors. And a small amount of social mobility has multiplied the voices now being heard in the political arena.

THE POLITICAL SYSTEM OF PERU:
A DEVELOPMENTAL SKETCH

Until recent years, a few powerful national leaders have dóminated political action with little regard for whatever few mass demands were articulated.[5] Most of the period from 1821, when Peru became independent of Spain, to 1945, near the end of the first term of President Manuel Prado, found political conflict punctuated by the violence of a bipolar struggle between the "ins" and the "outs" among the economic elite.

For two decades after 1821, the political leaders were the generals who had helped win independence. From time to time, public-spirited civilians from the wealthy families managed to attain high office, but even after the military leaders of the independence wars had died, a new generation of army generals inherited most of the key governmental posts. From the military came most of the nineteenth-century Presidents, including several dictators, but few of them managed to retain power for any considerable length of time. One exception was Ramón Castilla, who served as President during 1845–51 and again during 1858–62. A benevolent autocrat, he helped anchor Peruvian law to the Napoleonic Code and promulgated the Constitution of 1860, which remained in force until 1920.

In the mid-nineteenth century, the economic and political elite, the "forty families," began their hegemony by controlling large portions of the land being cultivated or mined. Peru's loss of territory to Chile in the War of 1879–83 reinforced the tendency of the forty families to utilize military leaders to dominate the nation. Many high-ranking governmental officials continued to be supplied by the army.

One prominent exception to generals in the Presidency was Manuel Pardo, who served from 1872 to 1876. Pardo was the first Peruvian President to be elected by popular vote. Through his Civil party, he achieved various moderate legal reforms. The Constitution of 1860 called for a concordat on Church-State relations which would give the Peruvian Government national patronage in choosing bishops and in approving other ecclesiastic promotions. From the time of independence on, popes had refused such patronage to Peruvian governments. In 1874 President Pardo negotiated with Pius IX a modified form of patronage, which gratified Peruvian nationalistic feelings.[6]

During Pardo's civilian regime a faculty of political history at the Univer-

[5] Emilio Romero, *Historia económica del Perú* (Buenos Aires, Editorial Sudamericana, 1949), pp. 346–58, 424.

[6] J. Lloyd Mecham, *Church and State in Latin America* (Chapel Hill, University of North Carolina Press, 1934), pp. 2–6.

sity of San Marcos to train civil servants, several public schools, and teacher-training colleges were created. Peruvians began to discover their national heritage, and Italian-born geographer Antonio Raimondi ushered in a serious study of the Inca era.

General Andrés Cáceres, one of the few Peruvian heroes in the war with Chile, led the nation from 1885 to 1890, one year longer than the four-year term allowed by the Constitution of 1880. Nevertheless, Cáceres organized the Constitutionalist party, which did engender wider respect for lawful norms.

Nicolás de Piérola, President during 1895–99, organized the Democratic party, a token contribution to group identity against a backdrop of personalism. With improvement in the economy, Peruvian leadership shifted from military to civilian personalism. In the 1900s the Civil, Constitutionalist, and Democratic parties each grew, though the personal power of individual leaders still meant more than party affiliation.

José Pardo, son of the civilian President of 1872–76, held the Presidency during 1904–08 and during 1915–19. Pardo encouraged foreign investors to expand the copper industry, and he doubled the number of public schools during his first term. But after World War I ended, his second term saw the demand for copper, cotton, and guano diminish. Prices plunged and labor strife rose. Elected to improve economic conditions was a strong-willed Executive, Augusto B. Leguía.

For the next eleven years, 1919–30, Leguía occupied the Presidency. His dictatorship avoided the militarist image. He promulgated the Constitution of 1920, which lasted until 1933 and which replaced the Constitution of 1860. The 1920 charter increased the presidential term from four to five years and allowed immediate re-election.

To create a non-militarist facade, Leguía declared that his *patria nueva,* or new fatherland, would be based on new social guarantees to be found in the Constitution. He made a token gesture towards decentralized power by creating three regional legislatures to deal with provincial matters. But in terms of actual power, these bodies were not permitted to enact any laws of consequence, just a few minor regulations.

During his eleven years in office, Leguía multiplied the national debt tenfold by printing bonds for New York bankers to sell to American investors. Money flowed into Peru but did not substantially contribute to economic growth. Only after the New York Stock Market crashed in October 1929 did Leguía have any difficulty in acquiring large sums of dollars with which to reward his trusted associates and subordinates. Bribes to his political enemies and bonuses to his army and police officers kept Leguía's political machine thriving until the great economic depression sent shock waves from New York to Lima. In 1930 Peru faced its political realities; Leguía was ousted and sent to prison, where he died two years later.

Leader of the forces which overthrew Leguía was Luis Sánchez Cerro, a lieutenant colonel in the Peruvian Army. This provisional President had himself fraudulently elected to a regular presidential term in October 1931, but within a year and a half he was assassinated. Violence still marred Peruvian political life.

The early Leguía era saw the rise of a young political reformer named Víctor Raúl Haya de la Torre. Forced into exile in 1923, he created the American Revolutionary Popular Alliance, or Alianza Popular Revolucionaria Americana (APRA). Haya actually founded APRA in Mexico in 1924 but did not import the party into Peru as a full-scale political force until the fall of Leguía in 1930. When *aprismo* arrived in Peru, the nation had just suffered an eleven-year period of governmental repression and corruption. White-collar workers, manual laborers, school teachers, and university students drawn to APRA wanted political and social reforms.

Unfortunately, APRA did not become a party with pragmatic goals but rather adopted a doctrine of difficult and often unrealistic aims. For example, in 1931 the first APRA platform called for separation of Church and State in a country where the Catholic Church had been a constitutional part of the Government since independence and at the time was a pillar of the power structure. This platform demanded punishment for corruption in government in a nation whose entire public administration was based on patronage and spoils.[7] The *Apristas* soon alienated those in power and those most likely to acquire power, ranging from the military, the Church, the landowners, and the governmental elite, to the foreign business investors.

Since 1931 the *Apristas* have become much more politically astute, even to the extent of winning sympathy from younger priests, especially American Catholic missionaries, who have begun to temper the rigid postures of the Church. After taking part in the Government themselves, APRA leaders found that corruption is difficult to eliminate and that improvement would come more smoothly through a gradually professionalized civil service than through reprisals taken against the spoilsmen.

At first, APRA embraced Marxist principles, but the party broke sharply with the Communists and rejected the Soviet Union as the leader of revolutionary change for Latin America. As a new phenomenon on the Peruvian political scene, APRA represented a highly organized popular force and became a threat to the Communists. Relations between APRA and the Communists have been characterized by bitterness and hostility since the late 1930s. The APRA slogan, "Only *aprismo* will save Peru," was not dropped until 1961 and then only to give the party a less dogmatic image.

Since 1930, most Peruvian political struggles have to some extent involved the *Apristas*. At times suppressed, at other times able to operate freely, APRA has been a vital force at the polls, in labor-management bargaining, at rallies and demonstrations, and in Peruvian political life generally. During adverse years APRA developed a party discipline in sharp contrast to the older personalistic followings with political-party labels. For more than thirty-

---

[7] John E. Fagg, *Latin America: A General History* (New York, Macmillan Company, 1963), pp. 868–69. Also see Harry Kantor, *Idealogy and Program of the Peruvian Aprista Party* (Los Angeles, University of California Press, 1953).

five years, Haya de la Torre, the APRA presidential candidate in 1931, in 1962, and in 1963, enjoyed the loyalty of the movement.

In little more than the year between Leguía's resignation in August 1930 and Sánchez Cerro's inauguration in October 1931, APRA spread rapidly among the workers and peasants, throughout the labor movement, and among those farmers who were politically articulate. After his fraudulent victory, President Sánchez Cerro forced Haya de la Torre once again into exile. Even the promulgation of the Constitution of 1933, still in force today, wir'ı its theoretical norms of democratic government, did not spare the *Apristas* from suppression.

The successor to Sánchez Cerro, President Oscar Benavides, also an army officer, continued to exile or imprison his chief political opponents. A puppet Congress extended the term of President Benavides into 1939 with vague instructions to "call a new election when convenient." Paradoxically, while keeping the *Apristas* out of public life, Benavides did institute by decree a system of social security in 1936 and thus implemented one basic feature of the APRA program.

Though the election of Manuel Prado in 1939 again meant that the forces of traditionalism were to continue in power without radical changes in public life, near the end of his term in 1945, the *Apristas* found themselves free to enter fully into political action. The 1945 election and inauguration of José Bustamante, jurist and diplomat, brought an end to the legal ban on APRA. In January 1946, *Apristas* at last entered the top echelons of government. They were given three Cabinet ministries, those of Agriculture, Public Works, and Finance.

An *Aprista* attempt at municipal reform in 1946 was at first aimed at municipal elections but was soon cut down to increased subsidies voted by Congress to the centrally appointed municipal boards. These subsidies had been opposed by President Bustamante, who by mid-1947 had broken with the *Apristas* and with the moderate groups which made up the Democratic Front. A year later, Bustamante was governing without a functioning Congress and was openly relying on the army to enforce his decrees.

In October 1948, the *Apristas* revolted unsuccessfully against the Bustamante regime and once more found their party outlawed. A military junta then ousted Bustamante, and General Manuel Odría, who became President, sent his police out to seize Haya de la Torre. In January 1949 Haya received asylum in the Colombian Embassy in Lima, where he remained until May 1954. After four years of bickering with Colombia over whether or not the APRA leader deserved an exit permit as a political refugee, President Odría finally allowed Haya to leave the country.

This celebrated captivity of Haya in the Colombian Embassy helped dramatize the persecution of APRA during the Odría era. After eight years of authoritarian rule, Odría did agree to an orderly transfer of the Presidency to a popularly-elected Chief Executive, Manuel Prado, whose second term ran from 1956 into 1962.

Once again, APRA was free to function as a party and as an important element in Peruvian political life. President Prado made use of *Aprista* strength in Congress and among working classes while keeping *Apristas* out of the top governmental posts. During his first term (1939–1945), Prado had represented Conservative tradition, but during his second term (1956–1962), he modified that traditionalism into a pattern known as the *convivencia,* or agreement of mutual convenience, between the *Apristas* and the military guardians and Conservative groups supporting the President. Thus, in June 1962 the election found three major candidates in a free electoral struggle. Haya de la Torre was the presidential candidate of the *Apristas,* supported by the Prado forces under the Democratic Alliance banner. Former President Odría was the candidate of his own *Odríista* National Union. And Fernando Belaúnde, an architect from a wealthy family, who had been heading the Popular Action reform movement since 1956, was the third candidate.

The current Constitution provided that a presidential winner must receive at least one-third of the total popular votes cast for the office. The army not only policed the election and guaranteed its honesty but also protected the National Election Jury from outside pressures. Although Haya won the largest number of votes, he failed by a small margin to receive one-third of the total number of ballots cast because of the existence of minor-party candidates.

No alliance of interests among the three major candidates could be arranged within Congress. Military leaders again asserted their guardianship of the nation by annulling the election and installing a junta. Keeping its promise to hold elections one year later, the junta promised a free contest in June 1963. The same three major candidates ran again, but the minor candidates of 1962 did not. This time the percentages in the close contest between Haya and Belaúnde changed just enough for the young architect to win. After three decades of struggle, the *Apristas,* close to winning, had failed in a last desperate fight to capture the Presidency.

THE CONTEMPORARY PARTY SPECTRUM

Peruvian electoral law requires that a party be recognized if it has a list of at least twenty thousand qualified voters. An alliance of parties gains recognition with forty thousand signatures of voters. The law bans parties which are international bodies and thus keeps the Communist party off the ballot. Communists have been able to participate in Peruvian political action by joining other leftist groups. A continuing supply of minor parties abounds, inasmuch as Peruvian political groups tend to arise as personalistic followings of a dynamic leader and disappear after that leader has lost an election.

There are five major parties: The Partido Aprista Peruano, Acción Popular, Unión Nacional Odriísta, Movimiento Democrático Peruano, and the Partido Demócrata-Cristiano.

The Peruvian *Aprista* party, or Partido Aprista Peruano (PAP), is the nationalistic name which the *aprismo* movement adopted to comply with the legal ban on internationally-oriented parties. After more than three decades of on-again-off-again persecution, in the 1963 election the PAP emerged as the largest single political party in Peru. Through the PAP, the *Apristas* gained some influence with the 1956–1962 Government of President Prado and are important in the coalition Government of President Belaúnde for the 1963–1969 period.

PAP strength centers in coastal cities, such as Lima, Callao, Trujillo, Chimbote, Ica, Pisco, and Huacho. The PAP has grown in the urban areas of the *sierra* where labor unions have flourished, as well as in the port cities. For example, in the Andean cities of Cerro de Pasco and Arequipa, as well as in the ports of Callao and Chimbote, the increases in union and in PAP memberships have tended to correlate. Since 1958, in the areas where workers at the Chimbote Steel Mill live, union rolls and PAP membership have also tended to coincide.[8]

PAP maintains its own daily newspaper, *La Tribuna,* in Lima. The party is a special target for criticism by the Conservative daily *El Comercio,* which has consistently maintained an anti-*Aprista* editorial position.[9] Even the PAP's anti-Communist stand has failed to quell criticism by *Comercio;* PAP remains a Liberal reform party.

The Popular Action party, or Acción Popular (AP), became a major party in 1956 under the leadership of Fernando Belaúnde and grew again in 1962, when he became the first presidential candidate in Peruvian history to campaign in all twenty-four departments of the Republic. With the election of Belaúnde in 1963, the AP found itself a reform movement with the support of a substantial portion of the emerging middle class, moderates among the professional men, and even some Conservatives who saw the need for reform in the face of Communist and Castroite pressures. On some public issues, the AP has also drawn support away from the *Apristas,* though the *Accionpopulistas* in general do not attract leftist followers as easily as do the *Apristas.*

The National Odriist Union, or Unión Nacional Odriísta (UNO), remains as a party forged for the Presidency of General Odría during 1948–1956 and for his 1962 and 1963 campaigns. Since 1956, the UNO has held onto some congressional seats and has remained a home for many Conservatives.

Despite General Odría's crackdown on *aprismo* during his Presidency, some UNO and PAP congressmen have worked together. Odría ran third to Haya and Belaúnde in both the 1962 and 1963 presidential elections and by 1969 may no longer be a serious presidential hopeful. Nevertheless, in 1965 his followers avowed that the UNO would live on as a genuine political party dedicated to the economic growth of Peru.

The Peruvian Democratic Movement, or Movimiento Democrático Peru-

---

[8] *Noticiario Sindical* (organ of the Chimbote Regional Labor Federation), January 12, 1961, p. 8; *La Tribuna,* June 1, 1961.

[9] Marvin Alisky, "The Peruvian Press and the Nixon Incident," *Journalism Quarterly,* Fall, 1958, pp. 411–19.

ano (MDP), was created in 1956 to support the successful candidacy of Manuel Prado for his second presidential term. Though the *Pradistas* are Conservatives, they did agree to work with the Liberal *Apristas* under the *convivencia,* or mutual convenience agreement. In return for PAP support in Congress and in the lower echelons of the executive branch, the MDP agreed to back the 1962 PAP candidate, Haya de la Torre. Without its own presidential candidate, the MDP in the late 1960s had to find one or face the possibility of shrinking to a minor party or even of disappearing by the 1970s.

The Christian Democratic Party, or Partido Demócrata-Cristiano (PDC), is a haven for those in the political center. Echoing some of the Catholic liberalism of Western European and Chilean Christian Democrats, the PDC stresses moderate economic reforms and social justice as expressed in the encyclicals of Pope John of the early 1960s. With Hector Cornejo Chávez, a professor of law, as its 1962 presidential candidate, the PDC drew urban support from Lima and Arequipa in sufficient numbers to classify the *Democristianos* as the fifth major party. A barrier to the growth of the PDC is the fact that many of the moderates the party could best attract are already *Apristas* or *Accionpopulistas.* Only if the PDC, the PAP, and the AP could merge into one party—and these three parties so far have not indicated a strong desire to do so—would Peru have a left-center party which could dominate the nation as the Institutional Revolutionary party does Mexico.

Inasmuch as the *Apristas* have kept the labor unions in general leftist though anti-Communist, the political leaders of the far Left have had few groups other than dedicated Marxists from which to recruit. With support from university students and Andean Indians, the National Liberation Front, or Frente de Liberación Nacional (FLN), has spawned violence since 1962 and has thereby become the best known of the minor parties. In 1962 the FLN had its own presidential candidate, General César Pando, a radical-left army officer, a rarity in Peruvian military circles. By 1965 the FLN's best-known orator was a pro-Communist priest, Father Salomon Bolo, who was suspended from parish duties because of his political activities. Several of the clashes between *sierra* Indians and government troops in 1965 were attributed by the Government to the initiative of the FLN.

Another minor party of the far Left, the Movement of the Revolutionary Left, or Movimiento de Izquierda Revolucionaria (MIR), has sometimes co-operated with the FLN. From time to time influenced by Cuban Castroites, the MIR wavered between Moscow and Peking but by 1965 seemed to favor the hard-line Chinese Communist doctrine of violence. The Peruvian Communist party, or Partido Comunista Peruano (PCP), remained a pro-Moscow group and found itself overshadowed, among far leftists, by the FLN and the MIR. By late 1965, the weekly newspaper *Unidad,* organ of the PCP, was clearly losing its younger readership to the rival weekly, *Bandera Roja,* organ of the MIR and other pro-Peking groups.[10]

---

[10] *El Comercio* (Lima daily), October 3, 1965.

Besides the five major political parties and a half-dozen minor parties, interest groups engaged in political action include other segments of society working partly within political parties and partly outside them and often in conjunction with friends and associates in two or more parties. For instance, labor unions, especially the Peruvian Labor Confederation, or Confederación de Trabajadores Peruanos (CTP), are *Aprista*-oriented. Yet some local labor leaders maintain continuing dialogues with Popular Action, the Christian Democrats, and the MDP.

INSTITUTIONAL FORCES AND TRADITION

Deeply rooted institutional forces in Peruvian life, the military and the Roman Catholic Church, are the guardians of traditional social values. While the oligarchic remnants of the "forty families" of great wealth can still make their interests known and carefully considered by the Government, the social elite no longer possesses the seeming unanimity that for decades symbolized the Peruvian upper class. Differing economic views among aristocrats in a nation whose economy is diversifying has shifted some of the guardianship of traditional values from large landowners to their allies of long standing, top military and Church leaders. Yet the generals and the bishops themselves have become more the voices of moderation and speak in favor of social progress. The ancient tripod upon which traditionalism rested—landlords, army, Church—itself has changed the steepness of its perch to a level accommodating larger segments of society.

Peru has felt the revolutionary stirrings of the twentieth century. In the 1960s, the leaders of the country began to listen to the demands of its poorest sectors for economic and social emancipation. Not only the civilian administration of President Belaúnde but also the leaders of the Peruvian army and navy indicated in public statements that their understanding of the nation's major economic and social problems was far deeper than it had been even two decades before.[11]

In 1948 the Peruvian army directly re-entered politics to halt the presumed leftward trend of government. After eight years of authoritarian rule by General Odría, military leaders in 1956 decided to withdraw from direct involvement in running the nation and to remain in the background as keepers of the peace during the regime of President Prado (1956–1962). Even the military intervention of 1962 showed signs of self-restraint; the ruling junta put a one-year time-limit on its own term of office.

With the return of civilian government in 1963, the Peruvian generals displayed differing opinions within their own ranks. To be sure, a majority of the generals still wanted to resist any governmental evolution towards a labor-leftist posture. But a sizable minority of the generals, pointing to the failure of men in uniform in other Latin American nations to resolve social

---

[11] *La Prensa* (Lima daily), August 27, 1965.

crises, did indicate a desire to leave politics to the civilians. A third group of Peruvian military leaders, smaller in number than the other two groups, actually began to identify themselves with the causes of reform.

In the 1940s and 1950s, the annual Peruvian governmental budget earmarked for the armed forces approximately twenty-five percent of the total expenditures. Certainly this proportion did not approach the excessive fifty percent allotted in Venezuela during the rule of General Pérez Jiménez during the same time period, nor did the Peruvian amount match the modest ten percent found in the annual budgets of Mexico, where a successful social revolution had reduced the armed forces to a severely limited constabulary role.

Since 1963, higher percentages of the annual Peruvian budget have been used for social services and developmental investments and not for costly armament. Yet the military leaders do not see their personal privileges put in jeopardy; the leaders more and more feel comfortable in the background of public life as constabulary enforcers of presidential authority in outlying areas where impoverished peasants resort to violent outbursts.[12]

As for the moral guardians of society, the Church leaders, like the military, enjoy a legal relationship whereby promotions and other benefits are dispensed by the Government under constitutional provision. Religious freedom for other sects exists in Peru, but the Constitution gives the State *patronato nacional,* or national patronage, whereby the President of the Republic nominates bishops and archbishops for any vacancies in Church leadership.

After decades of identifying itself with the *status quo,* Church leadership in Peru in the 1960s began to embrace moderate change in the socio-economic life of the nation. To perceive the change in ecclesiastic public posture, one could contrast 1948 with 1962: When General Odría seized power in 1948, he provoked no public criticism from the Church. But when the presidential election of 1962 was nullified by a military junta, the newly-elevated Cardinal Landázuri, Primate of the Peruvian Church, publicly demanded a resolving of the political crisis by constitutional means.

ELECTORAL SYSTEM

Suffrage in Peru extends to men and women at least twenty-one years of age if single or eighteen if married. Voters must be able to read and write; the literacy requirement thus keeps almost half of the adult population from being eligible to vote.

A national electoral registry, with offices in all the provinces, is maintained. The registered voter receives a *libreta electoral,* or electoral credential, a valuable means of identification in Peru for many activities. A voter uses his *libreta* not only to receive a ballot for any election, but also when applying for

---

[12] Reuters News Service interviews released November 5, 1965.

a marriage license, a driver's license, a passport, a governmental job, and many other vital documents. A Peruvian adult who has not registered—and therefore does not have a *libreta*—finds even rudimentary modern life full of obstacles. At every turn he needs his voter credential for identification. Thus a compulsory voting law exists *de facto*. All literate adults do not actually cast ballots at election time, but most of them do register as voters.

Administering the electoral process, the Jurado Nacional de Elecciones or National Electoral Jury, supervises the inscription of candidates and political parties, the administration of balloting, and the canvassing of the votes after elections. The seven-member body also administers departmental-level electoral juries.

Polling stations provide for marking ballots in secret. Presidential candidates appear on one ballot; congressional candidates from a department appear on a separate ballot. After the voter marks his choice on these ballots, he deposits them in an envelope supplied by the departmental jury and puts the envelope in a box at the voting table manned by officials from all recognized political parties. A polling precinct official then dips one of the voter's fingers into indelible ink to prevent him from voting more than one time.

Peru is at a stage of modernization where a voter can be reasonably sure that his vote will be counted honestly. Given the multi-party political system of this economically underdeveloped nation and the commitment of many Peruvian leaders in the 1960s to some degree of social and economic reform, Peruvians have an incentive to articulate political demands via the ballot box and can be expected to do so increasingly in the near future, barring of course a resurgence of military dictatorship.

GOVERNMENTAL STRUCTURE

The Presidency

The most powerful institution in the Peruvian political system is the Presidency. According to the Constitution, Congress can and frequently does summon the ministers of the presidential Cabinet to account for governmental policies. Though Congress from time to time has forced ministers to resign, this legislative power serves as a counterbalance to presidential initiative but never as a substitute for it. The Chief Executive engages in policy-making by promulgating authoritative decrees on a wide range of issues.

The President's appointive powers alone give him the central role in Peruvian public decision-making. Peruvian civil service remains skeletonized; a majority of governmental jobs are still being filled by the system of patronage. Job hunters are numerous, and their friends and relatives total sizable blocs of voters. The President also appoints and promotes those filling the higher positions in the armed forces, in the Catholic Church, in the Cabinet ministries, and in the various entities of the executive branch, though congressional approval is needed for confirming the appointments of generals and bishops. Though Congress can force Cabinet ministers to resign, they are primarily responsible to the President, who selects them.

The President is elected by a popular vote for a term beginning on July 28, the national Independence Day holiday, marking the date of Peruvian independence from Spain in 1821. Presidential inaugural ceremonies take place before a joint session of Congress. The presidential term extends six years. The President cannot be immediately re-elected; a six-year term must intervene before a President is eligible to seek the office again.

To take office as President of Peru, a candidate must be at least thirty-five years of age, a native-born Peruvian, and a resident of the Republic for at least ten consecutive years. Cabinet ministers and officers of the armed forces are not eligible for the Presidency unless they resign their posts one year before the election takes place. A return to inactive duty has been interpreted as satisfying this requirement for military men who are not officers.

A first vice-president and a second vice-president stand in line of succession to the Presidency. They must meet the same age, residency, and citizenship requirements as the President. Neither vice-president is given by the Constitution any duties to perform, such as presiding over a chamber of the legislative branch.

Theoretically, the vice-presidents might go without any governmental assignments, but in practice, the President appoints them to diplomatic or other executive agency posts. For example, in 1963, elected along with President Belaúnde, First Vice-President Edgardo Seoane was named Peruvian ambassador to Mexico. The system of having two vice-presidents also accommodates the Peruvian political reality of party coalitions. Belaúnde was elected President as the coalition candidate of the Popular Action and Christian Democratic parties. Like the President, the first vice-president was a member of the AP, whereas the second vice-president, Mario Polar, was from the PDC.

The twelve-member presidential Cabinet is officially known as the Council of Ministers and includes a council president, who commonly has the title of Premier. If the President of the Republic so wishes, the Premier may also serve as head of one of the regular ministries, as occurred in 1959–1962, when President Manuel Prado singled out Pedro Beltrán to act as both Premier and Minister of the Treasury and Commerce. It should be understood, however, that the office of President of the Council is not a premiership in the European parliamentary sense of the term but is rather the office of an administrative presidential assistant, a post similar to the Ministry of the Interior in many other Latin American Republics.[13]

With the inauguration of President Belaúnde in 1963, a sub-Cabinet post, the Director of the Comisión Interministerial de Cooperación Popular, or Interministerial Commission of Popular Co-operation, began to grow in

---

[13] For example, this post in the Mexican presidential Cabinet is the Secretaria de Gobernación.

importance. This post was created by Belaúnde as the Peruvian equivalent of the U.S. Office of Economic Opportunity. The head of the commission has directed a domestic Peace Corps in a Peruvian war on internal social ills.

Involving the co-operation of the various Cabinet ministries, Cooperación Popular has supervised engineers on road projects, public health nurses and technicians in Indian clinics, teachers at adult literacy centers, and student volunteers building community centers in the *sierra*. Like the Premier, the Director of Popular Co-operation must co-ordinate many diverse offices and services in order to carry out presidential policies.

Congress

Peru's bicameral legislative branch consists of a Senate and a Chamber of Deputies. In each house, the term of office is six years, which coincides with the presidential term, but unlike the President, senators and deputies are eligible for immediate re-election.

To select members of Congress, an "incomplete list" type of proportional representation is used. Geographically and administratively, the Republic is divided into twenty-four departments, and the exact number of senators and deputies for each department is fixed by law. Under Peruvian proportional representation, every participating political party is assured of congressional seats if it obtains a minimum predetermined number of votes in a given congressional district.

For the 1963–1969 period, the Peruvian Congress had a Senate of 45 members and a Chamber of Deputies of 140. In terms of political parties, the composition of the Senate for 1963–1969 was the following: the Popular Action–Christian Democrat coalition had 20 seats, the *Apristas* 18, and the *Odriístas* 7. In the Chamber of Deputies, the Popular Action–Christian Democrat coalition had 52 seats, the *Apristas* 58, the *Odriístas* 24, and minor parties 6.

To qualify as a deputy, a candidate must be at least twenty-five years of age, a native-born Peruvian, and either a native of the department from which he is elected or a resident of that department for three continuous years. To qualify as a senator, a candidate must be at least thirty-five years of age and a native-born Peruvian. Not eligible to run for Congress are members of the clergy and officials of the judicial and executive branches of the Government. However, officials of the executive and judicial branches become eligible by resigning their posts six months before the election in which they run.

Beginning on July 28, annual sessions of Congress last 120 days, though special sessions can be called by the President of the Republic or by petition of an absolute majority of the congressmen. Each house selects its own president. Even though during 1963–1969 the President of the Republic, Fernando Belaúnde, was a member of the AP–PDC coalition, the PAP–UNO coalition held a majority of seats in each house of Congress. Therefore, an *Odriísta* presided over the Senate and an *Aprista* over the Chamber of Deputies.

The Constitution gives Congress a degree of authority found often in parliamentary systems, which makes the Cabinet ministers partly responsible to Congress. From time to time, Congress has summoned before it members of the Council of Ministers, collectively and individually, to account for policies of the executive branch. But even when Cabinet members have been forced to resign, the President of the Republic does not find his Government undermined. He appoints new ministers, for ministerial selection remains his prerogative. During the summer of 1965, Communist-led guerrilla bands launched a series of attacks on army posts in Andean towns. When the Ministers of the Army, of Labor and Indian Affairs, of Justice and Worship, and of Agriculture were criticized by Congress for their handling of the affair, President Belaúnde accepted the resignation of his entire Cabinet rather than allow it to appear before the Senate and Chamber for prolonged questioning. The members of the legislative branch considered the outbreaks of violence as evidence that various governmental reform policies were not being carried out correctly. The President felt that the skirmishes, incited by Communists, reflected age-old inequities of Andean life, not the policies designed to redress some of the grievances. Therefore, he did not wish a prolonged congressional investigation of his Cabinet, whose job it was to carry out the reforms. To avoid the probing, Belaúnde selected an entirely new Cabinet. Except for the heads of the armed forces ministries, he chose his ministers from the ranks of veteran deputies and senators who had rapport with the congressional leaders. Thus a second congressional investigation of the Cabinet was avoided at a time when ministerial energies were needed to execute policies.

According to the Constitution, one important function given to the Congress is the duty to sit as an electoral body and select a president if no candidate for the Presidency receives one-third of the popular vote cast in a regular election. When such a stalemate did occur in the 1962 presidential election, however, the taking over of the Government by a military junta prevented Congress from carrying out this duty.

The Judiciary

At the apex of the Peruvian judicial system is the Supreme Court of Justice, made up of eleven justices. They are selected by Congress from a list of nominees sent to the judiciary committees of each house by the President of the Republic. Supreme Court justices have life tenure. Qualifications are that prospective justices must be native-born Peruvians of at least forty years of age and have a minimum of either twenty years of legal practice or five years of experience on the bench of a lower court.

The Supreme Court has original jurisdiction in cases involving the highest officials of government and appellate jurisdiction over litigation from the lower courts. The Supreme Court submits to the President of the Republic the names of prospective judges for vacancies in the lower courts. From several nominees for each vacancy, the President then selects the new judge.

The Supreme Court chooses its own president, or Chief Justice. For some cases, the Court sits as a single body but under the law can also divide into two chambers, one civil and the other criminal, to consider appeals.

Internal Administration

Peru is a unitary Republic, its centralized administrative system geographically consisting of twenty-four departments varying greatly in area and population. Each department is governed by a prefect, appointed by the President of the Republic, and has a Departmental Council, popularly elected on the basis of proportional representation. Departmental councilmen serve four-year terms and are not eligible for immediate re-election, a factor further strengthening the position of the prefect, who makes all of the important decisions for the department. Only minor departmental matters are left for the councils.

Every department is divided into several provinces, which are governed by a subprefect. Each province is subdivided into districts, administered by a governor. The more populous districts are further subdivided into subdistricts, headed by lieutenant governors. Prefects, subprefects, governors, and lieutenant governors are the delegated assistants of the President of the Republic, who selects and who can dismiss them. Law enforcement depends on a national police force, answerable to the Minister of Justice in Lima.

The Organic Law of Municipalities provides for elected municipal councils. In each provincial capital is a Concejo Provincial, and in each district capital is a Concejo del Distrito. Municipal councils were elected bodies from 1892 until 1923, when the President of Peru by decree abrogated them as popularly-chosen entities and replaced them with appointed councils. Forty years later, in 1963, President Belaúnde restored their status as popularly-elected councils. To be eligible to serve as a councilman, a candidate must be of voting age, able to read and write, and a legal resident of the district he would represent. Councilmen are eligible for re-election every two years.

Throughout the provincial areas of Peru, elected officials and public administrators suffer from low salaries and the corresponding personal pressures to have a second job (or to participate in graft) in order to meet family expenses.

CONTEMPORARY POLICY ISSUES

As in most other nations of the world, in Peru millions of impoverished people are caught up in the demand for a better life, the dynamic factor of rising expectations. Even able administrators cannot in a few years redress the social and economic inequities of centuries, especially in the face of a population explosion. For Peru, like the other Latin American nations, in recent years has seen its death rate go down as the total population has gone up; consequently, thousands upon thousands of men and women in their teens and twenties are stalking a job market which cannot expand fast enough to absorb them.

That Peru has had a diversified economy has spared this Republic the crises faced by one-crop or few-crop nations. But great problems confront the Peruvian nation; expansion of industry, improvement of agricultural techniques, construction of a truly national transportation system, reduction of adult illiteracy, and incorporation of several million Indians fully into the national way of life are all problems to be solved.

In the face of the social unrest of millions of Peruvians impatient with their impoverishment, Peru's political leadership must put through reforms which require larger expenditures of funds than ever before, while at the same time encouraging both the public and private sectors of the economy to utilize developmental capital efficiently.

First the Prado administration and then the Belaúnde administration encouraged industries to settle in areas away from Lima in order to engender true nation-wide economic expansion. To a modest degree, other urban centers have begun to share the industrial growth with Lima and have thus given Peru, for the first time in its history, a semblance of some genuinely national industrial development.

Since 1963 the National Merchants Association, or Corporación Nacional de Comerciantes (CONACO), has spoken of not only Peru's continuing goals of economic development but also the national need for social welfare. The association's concern has brought the public dialogues of some sectors of management more into harmony with those of labor and government. Nevertheless, in another vital segment of the economy, banking management and bank employee unions have for a decade engaged in numerous brief strikes and in public argument via paid advertisements in the newspapers. Even with the good offices of high-ranking governmental decision-makers, banking labor-management relations have remained strained.

Recent years have seen the start of projects for the reclamation of forest land in the Apurímac and Urubamba Valleys, the building of a highway into eastern areas which in the future will link Bolivian and Peruvian hinterlands, and low-cost housing projects in several cities. The highway is a major showpiece for the Belaúnde regime.

One big Peruvian issue in the 1960s has been the question of foreign development of oil reserves. The International Petroleum Company, a subsidiary of Standard Oil of New Jersey, has extensive operations at La Brea and Pariñas and elsewhere in northern Peru. The IPC developmental concessions became such a public issue in the 1960s that the Congress created the La Brea Pariñas Commission to study the situation and negotiate new agreements with IPC.

A difficult task of the Belaúnde regime has been to pressure the IPC for a larger share of the profits from petroleum produced in Peru while not frightening off the foreign capital needed for Peruvian economic development. Both political opponents and some allies of Belaúnde in and out of Congress and other governmental circles have long debated the merits and demerits of nationalization of the foreign-owned oil companies. President Belaúnde has held in check nationalization demands without diminishing his own program of tax reform, which would channel more foreign profits back into Peruvian industrial development.

Burdensome as the economic policies toward foreign investors have been, even greater pressures have been placed upon the Belaúnde administration by the feeling of alienation of hundreds of thousands of Indians, impatient that publicized reforms have yet to touch their Andean homes. Outbursts of violence in the *sierra* have added to the presidential dilemma: Both developmental investments and social services must be expanded; which gets priority?

Judging from patterns of decision-making since 1963, the answer seems to be that priorities are established for different activities in various geographic regions. Each issue large enough to provoke public concern is analyzed by relatively pragmatic administrators. Many of the current socioeconomic reforms, translated into public policies, are consonant with the general aims of the Alliance for Progress. As a sugar producer, for example, Peru has been able to adjust its yield to the United States quota and has thereby attained a more favorable annual balance-of-trade status.

CONCLUSIONS

Violence, according to James L. Payne's recent analysis, is the most salient characteristic of political life in contemporary Peru.[14] During periods of non-dictatorial, or "free" government, Payne sees three principal forces converging in the political arena: the President and his supporting entourage, the opposition out groups, who are usually Communists and extremists of the Left, and the Peruvian military establishment, principally the army. In times of dictatorship—frequently the case, as has been shown in the foregoing pages—the military establishment commands the political arena and is confronted by a heterogeneous array of out groups, many of whom are forced into exile in nearby countries. Opposition forces during periods of constitutional government view politics as a bitter, often death-like struggle, in which the Presidency is a prime target for attack. Only seldom have Peruvian out groups functioned as a constructive and loyal opposition. The methods employed to express opposition range from words to guns, but strikes and demonstrations by labor groups are among the most frequent manifestations of violence.

A high level of conflict intensity is usually maintained between out groups and the Presidency. Payne explains this circumstance in terms of three basic conditions. First, political and governmental decision-making powers are highly centralized, and the President performs many functions that are reserved in the United States for the legislative and judicial branches. As a result, the President is held responsible for nearly everything, good or bad, that occurs in the Republic, whether it be a national issue or a strictly local affair. Second, the President controls a vast amount of patronage, and it is

---

[14] James L. Payne, *Labor and Politics in Peru* (New Haven, Yale University Press, 1965).

traditional in Peru that little or none of this largesse goes to opposition groups. The civil service, therefore, is staffed on what is largely a Jacksonian spoils basis. Finally, cleavage in the body politic is accentuated by rigid communication barriers erected on a partisan basis between competing political groups. The exclusiveness of these groups extends throughout the cultural spectrum; according to Payne, "the *Apristas* have their own cafeteria and barbershop, their own medical assistance staff, soccer teams, and party newspaper, *La Tribuna*."[15]

Because an intense bipolar conflict is generated between the "ins" and the "outs" over control of the Presidency, the Peruvian army has become a defender of the peace, and according to Payne, military intervention has occurred only in times of acute crisis in which the potential for violence was high. Members of the armed forces are exclusive guardians of the Presidency. But when the incumbent of that office becomes an object of popular disrespect, the armed forces as well take their share of the abuse, and pressures mount to a point at which the army coup becomes an almost predictable feature of behavior.

Out groups that are motivated to violence are commonly inspired by the issues and the agitation tactics of worker organizations. Labor-management disputes have an especially dangerous potential for triggering opposition violence, and the President is frequently driven to the position of dictating settlements that must, of necessity, favor the interests of the workers above those of management. Linkages between political parties and labor organizations stress the ideological cleavage between labor and management. This stress serves to further alienate both groups from the President.

If Payne's analysis is correct, Peru is then a partially unique political system within the Latin American community of nations. The Peruvian uniqueness would be defined largely in terms of the seeming ambivalence of her armed forces, in confrontation with competitive political groups and also in terms of the instrumentality of the Chief Executive in resolving conflicts that occur during periods of "free," or constitutional, government.

As a legacy of the turbulent political history of the past century, there have never been two successive presidential elections in this century which peacefully determined the transfer of power. Instead, military intervention has marked all but a few elections, though in the 1960s the military guardians have been caretakers who relinquished political power to civilians as soon as orderly processes had replaced civic disruption and threats of violence.

In terms of the United States model of constitutional democracy, the Peruvian Republic harbors much political instability. The constitutionally-created fundamental law of Peru rests on a document dating back to 1933, in contrast to many recently-written Constitutions in other Latin American nations. Yet Peru's transfer of power still relies on a military guardianship. With the Peruvian governmental operations highly centralized in the

---

[15] Payne, p. 7.

Presidency, political conflict often becomes intensely polarized between the "ins" surrounding the President and the "outs" coveting the Presidency. Some important communication, therefore, takes place between interest groups, such as labor unions and business enterprises, and the top echelons of the executive branch without consistent meaningful intercession by the political parties in their own right. Political party struggles within Congress, however, do temper presidential and ministerial decisions on important public policies.

The field of labor-management conflicts in Peru gives many examples of a breakdown in communication between opposing groups, with the Cabinet ministry having to resolve the impasse. The bank strike of 1958, which began at Easter in April and lasted into June, almost brought the entire Peruvian economy to a halt. Bank employee unions placed large advertisements in the newspapers, as did the bank owners, but neither group seemed to aim its messages at either the general public or the adversary. Rather, these public statements repeated original demands and charges with little variation.

In the United States, labor unions and management have adhered to collective bargaining, which is encouraged by the internal political stability of a broadly-based democracy. In contrast, political turbulence has prevented collective bargaining in Peru and has substituted instead political action which sometimes includes violence. The minimum wage provisions of an industry-wide contract in Peru may be honored by managers in some cities yet violated by branch managers in other cities. This inconsistency forces the Government to bring the full weight of the President and the Cabinet ministers to bear upon the everyday operation of the law. Therefore, the concessions actually received by workers in Peru may tend to be proportional to the degree to which labor unions can threaten the security of the executive branch if the President and his ministers do not enforce labor-management agreements.

The strike by the National Federation of Public School Teachers in October 1961 is a case in point. When the Ministry of Education and the union could not agree on increases in teachers' salaries, teachers left their classrooms on October 5. On October 17, demonstrations in Lima led to hunger strikes by some teachers. On October 23, a demonstration march by teachers in Lima ended with sympathetic university students joining the teachers' ranks and then attempting to enter the halls of Congress. When guards stopped the students, one demonstrator was killed. Mourning demonstrations for the dead student, which were organized by political extremists, prompted the Government to suspend constitutional guarantees of free assembly, thereby ending further demonstrations. On November 2, member unions of the federation voted to end the strike and accept the plan of the Ministry of Education for pay increases smaller than what the unions had originally proposed. During the prolonged strife, opposition parties within Congress attacked not only the Ministry of Education but also the position of the entire executive branch of government.

As other incidents of violence have erupted in the rural and semirural regions of Peru since 1963, an increasing number of Congressmen have voiced support for the President in his use of troops to end riots. The major efforts of the Belaúnde administration have not been confined to the negative actions of policing trouble spots. The emphasis has rather been on providing bank credit for farmers' co-operatives, sending specialists into the field to upgrade agricultural and livestock-producing techniques, encouraging public and private low-cost housing, and promulgating many other basic reforms to help raise the Peruvian standard of living.

Armed insurgency inspired by the Communist Left is a problem of major proportions throughout Peru. An organization known as MIR, Movimiento de Izquierda Revolucionaria, which polled approximately three percent of the total vote in the 1962 elections, has shouldered the Maoist hard line in fostering violence and terror in the face of Belaúnde's reformist drives. Working along with MIR is the FAR, Fuerza Armada Revolucionaria, which has incited peasant uprisings around the country. Much of the terrorist activity was centered in the Department of Cuzco, in which an estimated two thousand guerrillas were based late in 1965. Cuban-trained and carrying weapons of Czech manufacture, the guerrillas posed a severe threat to the Belaúnde Government in its stability-oriented programs of socio-economic reform. In 1966 and 1967, the army successfully captured most of the rebels, and ended the threat.

"In the provincial and municipal elections of November 13, 1966, the Popular Action-Christian Democrat coalition won 46.1 percent of the total votes, the *Aprista-Odriísta* opposition 45.5 percent. In 1967, with the 1969 presidential campaign two years away, the Belaúnde regime retained an edge over its chief opponents in terms of vote-getting."[16]

The Peruvian political system centers in the Presidency, yet in the latter half of the 1960s, the Congress has been able to influence the President on some policies as basic as restoring the death penalty for convicted terrorists. As Peru has begun to modernize and industrialize, the President has had to delegate more of the daily administrative duties. And with such duties goes decision-making as well. Although the inner circle of Peruvians who make the major decisions for the nation has broadened only moderately, the politics of recent years augur strongly for wider participation in the policy-making process and, perhaps, for increased stability as well.

---

[16] "Peru: Elections," *Latin American Digest* (ASU bimonthly), January 1967, pp. 5–6.

12 / Bolivia

ROBERT E. HUNTER

ROBERT E. HUNTER, Associate Professor of Political Science at Trinity University, has carried out research throughout most of Latin America. During 1960–61, he undertook field investigations in Bolivia as an H. B. Earhart Fellow of the Relm Foundation.

THE POLITICAL EVOLUTION OF BOLIVIA

That area of South America now known as Bolivia was called Upper Peru during the Spanish period. The richest silver mine ever known was discovered in Alto Perú by the Spanish conquerors in 1545. Within fifty years 400,000,000 pesos of silver were taken from the mountain in Potosí. Toward the end of the colonial period, over 60,000,000 troy pounds of silver had been shipped to Spain from Alto Perú. By the middle of the seventeenth century, Potosí was the largest city in the entire New World and a wealthy settlement boasting a fine theater and extravagant palaces. At the time of independence, the silver depleted, Potosí had shrunk to a village of a few thousand, but it helped to perpetuate Spanish power and customs in the area.[1]

For the first two hundred years of Spanish rule, Alto Perú was governed by the Audiencia of Charcas under the viceroy of Lima. During this period the Presidency took to itself practically sovereign powers. At times it even set itself in opposition to the will of the viceroy. As the cities of the area matured, they tended to become more independent of the viceroy; a community of

---

[1] Hubert Herring, *A History of Latin America from the Beginnings to the Present* (New York, Alfred A. Knopf, Inc., 1961), p. 199.

interests, common traditions, and a vigorous sense of regional unity developed. The capital city of the Audiencia, Chuquisaca (now Sucre), was perhaps the most fruitful center of liberal ideas on the continent. The University of San Francisco Xávier, founded in 1623 as the seventh university established by Spain in the New World, came to be recognized as one of the best institutions of learning in the Americas. Even though the university followed the limited curriculum of the Spanish educational system, this school developed superior intellectual qualities, and its graduates were members of the highest circles in colonial America. In the same city in 1776, the legal profession formed the Academia Carolina, which came to be of great importance as a school of theoretical and practical politics. From these two institutions the most advanced political doctrines radiated out to the rest of Spanish America, and many of the men who became the intellectual leaders in the independence movement were trained in the University or the Academia.

The combined power of the Audiencia, San Xávier University, and the Academia Carolina prepared the way for independence. When the Spanish general ordered the arrest of the Royal Audiencia judges, only one, Jaime Zudáñez, could be found and jailed. The people of Chuquisaca gathered in the Plaza Mayor, forced Zudáñez' immediate release, arrested the army commandant, and forced other officials loyal to Spain to flee for safety. The *chuquiseños* then proceeded to set up their own government and appointed Alvarez de Arenales to administer the Presidency. The Audiencia furnished the people with arms and sent missions to other cities in order to urge them to take similar action. The movement was in favor of complete independence from Spain, and the honor of the first overt gesture of independence in Latin America belongs to the *chuquiseños*. May 25, 1809, is the celebrated inaugural date for the independence movement. On July 16, 1809, the people of La Paz revolted and overthrew the Government, as did the people of Cochabamba on September 14, 1810. This action was in accord with many years of agitation by intelligent men connected with the University, the Academia, and the Audiencia for a share in government.[2]

While Alto Perú was the first to declare independence in the Spanish colonies, it actually was the last to obtain independence in South America. The actions of the *chuquiseños* was followed by the Guerra de Quince Años, which left an enduring impression on the people of the country. The plateaus and valleys of the area were subjected to the worst possible ravages of war. Four revolutionary expeditions from the south and seven Spanish expeditions from the north fought back and forth, defiling the countryside for fifteen years. No other portion of the continent was so battered by armies, and no other endured more through the devastation of crops and commerce.

Independence was finally achieved in 1825 after revolutionary leaders

---

[2] For a more complete survey, see Mariano Batista Gumicio, *Revolución y universidad en Bolivia* (La Paz, Ediciones "Juventud," 1956); Alcides Arguedas, "La fundación de la república," *Obras completas,* II (Mexico City, Aguilar, 1959), 24–36.

Kundt. And, although Paraguay had a population of only one-third that of Bolivia, Paraguay was led by a first-rate military strategist, Marshal José Félix Estigarribia, had shorter supply lines, and was more familiar with the territory. Bolivian troops were put to rout at every confrontation in a losing war, which lasted for three years.[3] When a truce was agreed to in 1935, it was estimated that Bolivia had lost sixty thousand men and Paraguay forty thousand. Moreover, Paraguay retained the greater part of the Chaco, and Bolivia lost an outlet to the Atlantic via the River Paraguay.[4]

The impact of the Chaco War on all sectors of Bolivian society was enormous. Carlos Montenegro describes the country as "groaning with pain and rage" and states that now an "aroused people" gained "a definite feeling of nationality" from the defeat. He further says that

> in the Chaco the stupidities of the press, of oratory, of the law were useless to perpetuate the fiction of a rich Bolivian civilization. The jungle without roads and the misery of the popular economy in the rear guard spoke the truth, contrasting it to the opulence of the mine owner immune to the pain and the needs of war, that is to say, immune to the fate of Bolivia. The catastrophe . . . exposed to the eyes of the people for the first time since the days of Santa Cruz, Ballivián and Balzu, the real and intimate image of the Bolivian spirit that had been covered up to the year 1935 by foreign trappings.[5]

Probably the most significant result of the Chaco War was the putting in motion of fundamental changes in the status of Indians; these changes would acquire deep meaning in the revolutionary efforts of the 1950s. The Indians have always constituted a majority of the Bolivian population (in 1966 Indians comprised seventy percent of the nation's 3,650,000 people), but they have known only the most abject poverty throughout the history of the Republic. In most cases, prior to 1952 the Indians had no rights against any person of higher social standing. Living mostly outside the cities, he was usually a part of some landowner's estate. Although the arrangements differed somewhat from province to province, Indians were usually required to provide free labor for a specified number of days a year for the landlord, in exchange for which they had small plots of land for their own use. The conditions under which they lived were disastrous. Leprosy, yaws, trachoma, malaria, malnutrition, and parasitical infestation were not uncommon. Death rates during the first year of life ran as high as 500 per 1,000 in the mining communities, and only one-third of the infants born reached the age of five. Average life expectancy was 30 to 40 years. The Keenleyside Mission found that the typical Indian in the city "possesses no stable habits and traditions and little

---

[3] Pablo Max Ynsfran, *The Epic of the Chaco: Marshall Estigarribia's Memoirs of the Chaco War 1932–1935* (Austin, University of Texas Press, 1950).

[4] Merwin L. Bohan estimated that 156,000 square miles were lost by Bolivia to Paraguay. See his *Report of United States Economic Mission to Bolivia* (MSS in United States State Department Library, August 1942), Appendix A, p. 1.

[5] *Nacionalismo y coloniaje* (n.p., Talleres Gráficos Bolivianos, 1953), pp. 209–10.

social discipline and cohesion." The mission reported that the instability of the family contributed to the high incidence of alcoholism and venereal disease and that the "most rudimentary notions of domestic hygiene are lacking."[6]

The belief of the dominant group in the incapability of the Indians inhibited the absorption of the Indian masses into the life of the nation. During four hundred years the Indians lost all battles: the judges were subservient to the *latifundista,* the local government was a creature of the provincial landlords, and the national Government was nearly always on the side of the *blancos.* The Indians had little hope of redressing their wrongs by violence, for the whites, constantly in fear of an uprising, would bring in the *carabineros* (police) or even the army at the slightest indication of a threat from the Indians. Those who tried to resist were killed or jailed.

For years the *Pensadores* decried the Indians as brutish, bestial, subhuman in intellect, impervious to education, an economic liability, and a drag on the development of the country. Alcides Arguedas wrote in 1909 that the large number of Indians plus the mixing of the races resulted in such a variety of evils—psychological, social, political, and economic—that he believed Bolivians were a "sick people."[7] Fernando Diez de Medina wrote of the Indian as a sphinx, "an inhabitant of a hermetic world," one who "does not allow himself to be understood. . . . Retiring, silent, immutable, he inhabits a closed world. The Indian is an enigma."[8] Federico Avila believed that the Indian possesses the "fatalistic characteristic of the Orientals"; he is "passive, servile, pessimistic," and "tranquil in spite of injustice, oppression, and death."[9]

One of the few voices raised against the traditional attitude and the orthodox opinion that the Indian was degraded, degenerate, and beyond rescue was the voice of the great mestizo Franz Tamayo. Son of a Spanish hidalgo and a native Indian woman, Tamayo is the one writer in Bolivian history who can with certainty be called a genius. In a series of editorials in *El Diario,* he made a daring attack on the accepted opinion. Calling the Indian the true depository of national energy, Tamayo insisted that "Bolivia is sick because of nothing less than bad and absurd thinking in conceding power and superiority to those who do not have it."[10] He deplored the fact that Indians were judged stupid and pointed to the political, social, and religious organization of the Inca Empire. Tamayo believed that the Indian morality was superior to that of the white man and pointed out that 20 million bolivianos

---

[6] H. L. Keenleyside, *Report of the United Nations Mission of Technical Assistance to Bolivia* (New York, United Nations, 1951), pp. 106–07.

[7] "Pueblo enfermo," *Obras completas,* I (Mexico City, Aguilar, 1959), 396–617.

[8] *Thunupa* (La Paz, Librería "La Universitaria" Gisbert y Cía., 1947), p. 177.

[9] *El drama de la sangre* (La Paz, Imprenta "Artística," 1944), pp. 82–104.

[10] This and the following quotations of Tamayo are taken from his *Creación de la pedagogía nacional* (La Paz, El Ministerio de Educación, 1944), pp. 70, 136, 140–41, 36–39, respectively.

worth of goods, all carried by Indians, changed hands between La Paz and the Yungas. Without a piece of paper, millions of dollars worth of merchandise moved "with no guarantee but the word of illiterate Indians." Tamayo said that much could be learned from Indians "about respect due parents and respect of parents for children, patience, respect for one's word, obedience to the law, reverence for tradition, preservation of life." Tamayo believed it was useless to try to explain the nation's difficulties in terms of such exterior conditions as geography and ethnography. The real culprit, he thought, was national self-doubt, which debilitated and depressed the national will and caused the country to suffer from what he called "racial doubt." The remedy was "to awaken national consciousness."

The Chaco War succeeded in arousing the national consciousness. Thousands of Indians were mobilized by the war efforts and were thus introduced to new clothes, new ways of housing and living, radios, and such ideas as getting pay for services. The idea of salary was introduced in the Cochabamba area after the war and was followed in some other districts. The owners of some *fincas* eliminated the *pongueaje,* or compulsory personal services, for the Indians.

The soldiers returning from the Chaco became aware of other ways of life and would no longer be satisfied with conditions as they were; these men wanted change. The whites found the experience of being dependent on an army made up largely of Indians to be disturbing. The Indians, serving the nation beside the whites and not as *indios,* began to comprehend Bolivia as a nation.

As the military had generally refrained from taking an active role in politics since 1883, the Chaco defeat had the effect of discrediting the civilian political parties that had so long led the nation. The army itself suffered a split; the junior officers blamed the older officers for the defeat. The backlash of the army against the civilian government quickly led to changes.

Colonel José David Toro was the first of five Chaco War army officers to hold the office of President during the tumultuous next ten years. Toro gained power by a coup in 1936. He established what he called military socialism and expropriated the Bolivian holdings of the Standard Oil Company. He then attempted to extract higher taxes from the tin companies—an act which led to his overthrow in 1937.

Colonel Germán Busch, thirty years old and another Chaco War veteran, replaced Toro. Busch also pressed for larger payments from the tin companies and decreed that all foreign exchange from the mining operations be turned over to the Government. He promulgated a new Constitution, which nationalized subsoil rights, provided schools for all children, gave labor the right to organize and bargain collectively, and declared human rights to be supreme over property rights. But before the Constitution could be put into effect, Busch was found shot to death in 1939.

Conservative officers and traditional parties took control after the death of Busch, and General Enrique Peñaranda was elected President by a small margin. Peñaranda was a man of little education who had proved to be a poor commander in the Chaco War. The tin interests made him their puppet and forced him to use strong tactics in checking the mine workers and in using the army to put down strikes. The Catavi massacre in 1942, in which scores of men and women were killed by the army during the Catavi mine strike, paved the way for his eventual fall.

Major Gualberto Villarröel led a coup that overthrew Peñaranda in 1943. Villarroel was the leader of a coalition between an army lodge, the RADEPA, the Razón de Patria, and a civilian group, the MNR, Movimiento Nacionalista Revolucionario, headed by Víctor Paz Estenssoro. The philosophy of the RADEPA was copied from fascism, which most of the MNR leaders rejected. They were opposed by the leading tin operators, landowners, bankers and manufacturers, all together popularly called La Rosca. "La Rosca" in colloquial Bolivian usage has no English translation, but the Bolivians use the term as meaning "a glazed doughnut of which the tin corporations and feudal land-owners are the dough and the icing, and the masses are the hole." La Rosca was not a formal organization or a political party but a sort of informal council for managing politics from behind the scenes. "For decades, they have constituted the unseen government of Bolivia."[11]

President Villarröel challenged the control of La Rosca by bringing the tin industry under greater government control, tried to force the tin magnates to deliver all foreign exchange to the Government except for a small percentage, and required the banks to increase reserves as an anti-inflation measure. He ordered a reassessment of the large haciendas, strengthened the powers of Yacimientos Petrolíferos Bolivianos, the Government's oil corporation, so that it could exercise tighter control of the oil industry, created a chain of cooperatives to compete with food speculators, and supported expansion of social security. Villarröel also signed a law fixing the minimum wages for farm labor and limited the authority of landowners to remove or transfer sharecroppers. Finally, he sponsored the establishment of a strong labor union movement in the mining areas.

In *Un pueblo en la cruz,* Alberto Ostria Gutiérrez paints a vivid picture of the rough treatment given the opposition by Villarröel when the author describes the brutality of physical torture at Panoptico, the federal penitentiary on Plaza San Pedro in La Paz.[12] Many of Villarröel's supporters were impatient with the cautious way he handled political crises. These supporters engineered the kidnapping of mine owner Mauricio Hochschild and of the leaders of an abortive revolt in 1944. The MNR leaders disclaimed all knowledge of these activities and said that the Oficina de Control Político, the

---

[11] Ernesto Galarza, "The Case of Bolivia," *Inter-American Reports,* No. 6 (May 1949), p. 16.

[12] *The Tragedy of Bolivia* (New York, Devin-Adair Company, 1958), translation by Eithne Golden of *Un pueblo en la cruz.*

secret police, was responsible for the reign of terror, torture, and concentration camps and that the Control Político was Communist-dominated.[13]

At least two serious attempts were made to overthrow Villarröel. The first one was in 1944, and afterwards its ringleaders died under mysterious circumstances. The other was in June of 1946, and after that one, *La Razón* and *Ultima Hora,* both opposition newspapers owned by the mining interests, were closed. Bitterness, discontent, and violence broke out in La Paz. The immediate cause of the violence was a teachers' strike in July, which the MNR claimed was Communist-inspired. Efforts to suppress the strike resulted in protest strikes by students and workers. The army officers' loyalty was divided between the younger men, who looked to Villarröel as their intellectual and political leader and the older officers, who were opposed to his Government. The latter insisted that Villarröel resign on July 20, and when he refused, they succeeded in winning over enough regiments so that at the end the President's own guard had been reduced to less than fifty officers and men. On July 21, 1946, the palace was stormed, the President shot, his body thrown out a second-story window to the sidewalk, and then hung from a lamp post in the Plaza Murillo. The week of street fighting which preceded these events found 163 persons killed and 313 wounded.

Enrique Hertzog, a physician and professor, was elected President. Relaxing the pressure on the big tin companies, the new Government curtailed trade unions and jailed union leaders, and used army troops to prevent public meetings of railroad workers and to occupy any struck tin mine. Hertzog used force against the Indians and destroyed most organized peasant opposition. Opposition leaders were forced to flee the country or were jailed, and pressure was applied to any newspaper that did not support the administration. A state of siege, under which all constitutional liberties and civil rights are suspended, was frequently invoked. The conditions that had existed prior to 1943 were effectively restored.

President Hertzog resigned because of ill health; the vice-president, Maneito Urriolagoitia, succeeded him. The coalition continued on in an unstable manner, marked by frequent Cabinet changes, constant pressure from the workers' syndicates, and persistent efforts of the opposition to overthrow the Government. It was in this atmosphere of uneasiness that the elections of 1951 were held. Those forces that had been associated with the Government since 1946 were split, and several of those parties named candidates, while the opposition to the ruling regime concentrated their efforts in the MNR even though their principal leaders, including the presidential candidate, Víctor Paz Estenssoro, were in exile.

---

[13] Various aspects of the MNR during the Villarröel Presidency are discussed in Pedro Zilveti Arce, *La hora de la verdad* (La Paz, "Exilio," 1958); Armando Arce, *Los fusilamientos del 20 de noviembre de 1944 y el Movimiento Nacionalista Revolucionario* (La Paz, Talleres Gráficos Bolivianos, 1952); José Fellman Velarde, *Víctor Paz Estenssoro: El hombre y la revolución* (La Paz, Editorial "Don Bosco," 1954).

The National Revolutionary Movement

The Movimiento Nacional Revolucionario gradually evolved, beginning around 1936, from the association of a group of young intellectuals, veterans of the Chaco War. In that year Armando Arce y Céspedes founded a paper, *La Calle,* which protested against the abuses of the tin barons, Patiño, Aramayo, and Hochschild; concentrated on examples of the plight of the Indians and miners; and denounced the role of La Rosca. Intellectuals contributed to *La Calle,* and it became the center of MNR ideas. In 1940 the group, now thinking in terms of political organization, held a series of formative meetings at the home of Hernán Siles. The result of these discussions was to intensify the group's political activity, which led to the election of two congressmen, Hernán Siles and Alberto Mendoza, under MNR auspices in 1942. At the same time, the MNR issued its "Principles and Actions of the National Revolutionary Movement," which gave high priority in its program of action to nationalizing the tin mines and breaking up the large landholdings.

During the period from 1942 to 1951, the movement became increasingly involved in the political affairs of the nation. MNR was instrumental in the ousting of Peñaranda. Several of the members served in the Cabinet of Villarröel, where they obtained their first experience in government and consolidated the party's position in the labor movement. From this experience the MNR became the leading political force in organized labor. Juan Lechín Oquendo, one of the early MNR members, headed the labor federation from 1945 on. In the 1947 congressional elections, the movement showed unusual strength and carried a number of mining districts where jailed union leaders were elected. With the ascendancy of Hertzog to the Presidency, party leaders who did not leave the country were jailed. The movement continued, however, for

> they were men who could not be intimidated in their determination not to submit to the Rosca, nor the "anticulture of tin." In the same manner they fought the encroachment of the Stalinists and Trotskyites. They were men who assumed the function of agents of the historical dialectic of Bolivia rousing the people from their social and intellectual ambivalence.[14]

The MNR formed "Groups of Honor," Grupos de Honor, ten people with a leader. Groups were established in all sections of La Paz, in Oruro, and at the mines. "Commandos of Workers" were also organized. Each commando group was assigned to specific spots to take over with violence at the proper time. Sra. Tejada, an organizer and member of both types of groups, claims that these organizations "made possible the popular uprising of 9 April 1952."[15]

---

[14] Agusto Céspedes, *El dictador suicida* (Santiago, Editorial Universitaria, 1956), p. 246.
[15] Lydia Gueiler Tejada, *La mujer y la revolución* (La Paz, n.p., 1959), p. 57.

The 1952 Uprising

The actual outbreak of the revolution occurred when Paz and Siles, having won the elections of 1951, were not permitted to take office. The Government claimed that, although the Paz ticket received far more ballots than any other, Paz and Siles had not received the required fifty-one percent of the vote. President Urriolagoitia, however, did not hand the matter over to the Congress, elected at the same time, as provided by the Constitution. Instead, he resigned, turning the Government over to a military junta, which lasted from May 1951 to April 1952. The fighting which was to bring about the downfall of the junta broke out on the morning of April 8, 1952. Sra. Tejada describes how her "Honor Group," after meeting all night on April 8, was surrounded in the early hours of April 9 and taken to the police station. But to their amazement the members of the group were told, "You are free to go to your posts." They went to their "central barracks," where they received arms and orders to march but not to shoot at the *carabineros,* or police, because "they are on our side." "There were many secret missions," she wrote, and "three revolutions": one the civilians like herself, another the *carabineros,* and the third the unions, especially the miners. "The idea was always to co-ordinate the three revolutions."[16]

Son of Former President Hernando Siles, Hernán Siles, who had returned secretly to the country and directed the movement as executive secretary, was chief of the National Revolutionary Committee, which succeeded in overthrowing the junta in three days of fighting. Juan Lechín headed the labor sector, and General Antonio Seleme, Minister of Government in the military junta, who had defected to the side of the revolution, provided the arms and the police for the MNR. Several members of the committee wanted Siles to be provisional President for at least six months as a necessary period of preparation before the party chief, Paz, could take over. Siles insisted "in an act of unprecedented political loyalty" in bringing Paz back from exile in Argentina for the Presidency.[17] Siles took over as vice-president, and Paz returned as President in about two weeks. A Cabinet was formed consisting of leading MNR figures and three labor ministers, including Lechín as Minister of Mines.

The Program of Revolutionary Change

Nationalization of the Tin Mines The mining industry had been the backbone of the country ever since colonial times; the mines were always the chief source of public revenue and the main support of commercial and industrial activities. A modern Bolivian writer who has been active in the political affairs of his country published a book called *Metal del Diablo*

---

[16] Tejada, pp. 68–71.

[17] Alfredo Ovando Candia, *Un experimento comunista en la América* (La Paz, Talleres Gráficos Bolivianos, n.d.), pp. 50–51.

shortly after World War II. Tin is referred to in the book as the Devil's metal because the mortality rate is extremely high in the tin mines; most of the miners who spend some time in tin mines die from either tuberculosis or silicosis. Other harsh circumstances in the miners' working conditions also contribute to the high mortality rate. And yet tin is absolutely essential to the country.[18] Considering this importance of tin mining plus the aid given by the miners to the MNR in ousting the junta, it is not surprising that the first action of the new Government concerned tin.

Within a month after taking office, President Paz appointed a commission of economists, lawyers, and engineers to study the problems of the nationalization of the tin mines.[19] Recommendations of the commission were studied by the Central Obrera Boliviana, the national labor organization. The Trotskyites in the COB demanded, unsuccessfully, confiscation without compensation. La Corporación Minera de Bolivia, organized by decree on October 2, 1952, was established as an autonomous governmental agency with the power to explore and exploit mineral deposits assigned to the corporation by the Government. Seven directors were named, five by the President of the country and two by the workers of the Federación Sindical de Trabajadores Mineros.

The next step, the nationalization of the tin mines, was carried out with great ceremony at the mining camp of María Berzola at Catavi. The mining decree, Decreto Supremo No. 3223, October 31, 1952, starts with a long preamble giving the reasons for the issuance of the decree and a stinging indictment of the three mining companies. The substance of the law follows and declares the mines belonging to Patiño, to Hochschild, and to Aramayo to be national property and sets forth the tentative amounts to be paid the companies. The properties were turned over to COMIBOL for operation, and an agreement was reached to pay the companies a percentage, varying with the price of tin, on the exports.

Of the popularity of the *decreto* there can be no doubt. Even some elements opposed to the MNR approved. Much justification of the nationalization, ranging all the way from the Communist doctrines of Ricardo Anaya to the more rational *White Book,* published by the Government,[20] was written. *The White Book* stresses the interference of the companies in governmental affairs. Quoted in the book is a speech that ex-President Tejada Sorzano made before the Senate in 1919. In this speech he described the laborer's condition as being the "saddest one could see" and pointed out that, having just completed a tour of the mining centers, he was upset at finding that "in the

---

[18] Agusto Céspedes, *Metal del Diablo* (Buenos Aires, Editorial Palestra, 1960).

[19] The decree setting up this commission and all decree laws concerning tin properties can be found in Isaías Pancheco Jiménez, *Derecho minero de Bolivia* (La Paz, Empresa Editora "Universo," 1954).

[20] *Nacionalización de las minas de Bolivia* (Cochabamba, Imprenta Universitaria, 1952); Departamento de Publicaciones, *El libro blanco de la independencia económica de Bolivia* (La Paz, Editorial del Estado, 1952).

twentieth century . . . there exists a twenty-four hour shift," so that a man must remain in the mines for a full day. He said that all efforts to solve these serious social problems were blocked by the mining companies and that even in the attempt to pass an accident law, "we were faced by the same firm and dedicated opposition of the great industrialists [and] Bolivian millionaires who speed their money to foreign lands."

Also quoted is Dr. Bautista Saavedia, who tells of the interference he received as President in 1923 from "Don Simón Patiño." Saavedia said that he had in his possession many written and verbal proofs of mining companies' interference: "I knew who had advanced money, who had been the intermediaries and the sums they had subscribed." He also delineated efforts by Patiño agents to kill him. It came to be his firm conviction that the MNR could do nothing less than nationalize the tin mines "or leave its super-state with its power intact in Bolivia and in 6 or 8 months have a new revolution financed by them."

Many other charges against the companies were enumerated in *The White Book*. They were accused of gross mistreatment, including mass murder, of the miners; evasion of taxes by exporting bismuth in the tin ore without cleaning it; exporting concentrates of low assay when company machinery was capable of producing a much higher concentrate; and of inflating their own stock. The Government complained in the book that the companies bought up all the principal mining zones to keep other capitalists out and prevent competition. Because of the country's great dependence on tin, the monopoly could not be allowed to continue.

In spite of the popularity of the tin nationalization, it probably could not have happened at a more inopportune moment, for the reserves were nearly depleted. Warnings of the serious situation of tin mining were sounded by the Bohan Mission as early as 1942. The mission report found that the mine veins seldom contained more than 3 percent tin and that the ores were in narrow veins that prevented the use of machinery to lower costs. The study found that from 1936 through 1940, 94 percent of the nation's exports came from minerals, of which tin constituted the bulk (73–80 percent). The study warned of the serious consequences that would develop if major minerals became exhausted (indications are that they will) or if prices drop (as happened after the war). The mission praised the three largest companies for their excellent technical organization, with staffs superior to any "which the government of Bolivia, alone or with American assistance, could put into the field."[21] The report noted that the cumulative lack of maximum co-operation between government and industry resulted in the reduction of new capital investments and the closing of marginal properties.

The United Nations Mission in 1950 came to essentially the same conclusion. This mission also criticized the lack of training facilities for geologists, metallurgists, and mining engineers and the dearth of laws regulat-

---

[21] Bohan, Part IV, p. 4.

ing operating and working conditions in the mines. Concerning nationalization, the U.N. report stated:

> Even if nationalization of the mining industry were theoretically desirable, it would be wholly impracticable in Bolivia under present conditions. The government has neither the financial resources nor the technical and administrative competence to undertake any such task.[22]

Nevertheless, the *decreto* was made effective. Lechín established the Control Obrero, a labor group to "advise" management at each mine, and he increased the miners' pay and created jobs which had no function. The working force at the national mines increased from 17,990 in 1949, to 28,998 in 1952, to 34,500 in 1955. Meanwhile, production decreased from 34,662 fine tons in 1949 to 23,484 in 1955, and production per shift showed a decline in labor efficiency of from 15 to 20 percent during the same period. Working days were reduced, so that in 1955 there were 80 paid holidays, which added 8 percent to the production costs.[23] One report stated that, "according to official statistics only 119 days were worked during 1954 in the mines."[24] It was estimated that 65–70 percent of the management and technicians left when the mines were nationalized. This exodus resulted in a serious staff deficiency in operating the mines to the best economic advantage. Instead of producing 60 to 70 percent of the Government's revenue, the mines became a major drain on the Government.

There were many other problems over the mining industry which had serious economic effects. The mining companies naturally withdrew their working capital when the mines were nationalized. The Government had no capital and therefore found it necessary to print more money, which added to the already runaway inflation. The *pulpería,* or general store, selling essential articles at a loss, added to the deficit from operating the mines. In addition, low efficiency in the mines derived from excessive political patronage; labor interference in management; workers' lack of discipline, stemming from a breakdown in respect for the law; inflation, food shortages, and work stoppages due to unstable political and social conditions; and excessive red tape, resulting in lack of materials, equipment, and supplies. The Ford, Davis, and Bacon Report noted "that most of the problems in the final analysis are social ones and to a much lesser extent, technical ones."[25] The MNR had little success in dealing with these problems, and the tin mining deficits were covered by United States aid.

---

[22] Keenleyside, p. 50.

[23] Ford, Bacon and Davis, Inc., *Report Mining Industry of Bolivia, Ministry of Mines and Petroleum,* III, "Nationalized Mines of Bolivia" (La Paz, Unpublished, 1956). The entire nine-volume report is the most comprehensive study ever made of the Bolivian mining industry.

[24] Demetrio Canelas, *Bolivia After Three Years of Revolutionary Dictatorship* (n.p., n., 1955), p. 5.

[25] Ford, Bacon and Davis, Inc., III, 2.

Oil and Other Minerals   While the output of tin and most other minerals was declining, economic conditions in the oil industry were brighter. In fact, Bolivia seemed to experience much more success, right from the start, in regulating the oil industry. As far back as 1916, Bolivian oil deposits were nationalized, and the granting of oil lands in perpetuity was forbidden. In 1921 the amount of petroleum land any one company or individual could exploit was limited to 100,000 hectares. The law restricted oil concessions to 55 years and required a minimum royalty of 11 percent of the oil produced to be paid to the Government.[26] The government corporation Yacimientos Petrolíferos Fiscales Bolivianos was established in 1936 to administer the interests of the State in petroleum and other hydrocarbons and their derivatives. The Standard Oil Company's concession and properties were taken over by YPFB in 1937, but very little was done in the development of oil until the MNR administration. Then a contract was signed with the Gulf Oil Corporation, and pipe lines were constructed. YPFB was able to increase its investments by 24 million dollars in four years, whereas the total amount invested prior to that time was only 22.9 million dollars. YPFB increased its production by 600 percent in the same period. The country became self-sufficient in oil and was even able to export 3,000 barrels by 1957.

The MNR Government encouraged the extraction of other minerals. The Government granted a twenty-five-year concession to the South American Gold and Platinum Company, a United States firm, for gold-dredging along the tributaries of the upper Beni River. The agreement allowed all gold bullion to be sold on the free market with the Government to get a substantial part of the profits. No duties were to be levied against machinery which the company imported. Despite such favorable developments, the overall picture of the progress of the mining industry has been discouraging.

Land Problems and Agrarian Reform   Although Bolivia is known chiefly for its minerals, a vast majority of its people are tillers of the soil. From primitive times the inhabitants of this area were farmers. Farming activities directed laws, religion, and customs. Such pursuits as mining and fishing were only incidental. So it is today; the bulk of the population lives off the land. The country possesses vast agricultural resources, including tropical forests of immense wealth, nearly all of which are untapped.

The country may be thought of as being divided into three agricultural zones: The first, the west, consists of two massive mountain chains having peaks of more than 21,000 feet. Between the mountains is the *altiplano,* a high level plateau, which lies at an average of 13,000 feet above sea level and covers about 38,000 square miles. La Paz is located here. The second zone, the eastern slopes of the Andes, includes the Yungas, an area which drops down steeply to about 4,000 feet. It produces lush vegetation; sugar cane, tobacco, cacao, coffee, and fruit thrive there. Other high, fertile valleys, such as Cochabamba and Tareja, are located in this zone. It comprises about

---

[26] Pacheco Jiménez, Chapters 33, 34.

one-tenth of the area and contains one-third of the population of the country. The third zone, the Oriente, consisting of the whole of Bolivia east of the Andes, makes up about 70 percent of the area of Bolivia but contains very few people. The altitude varies from 1500 to 600 feet or less. The climate is tropical with high but seasonable rainfall, which drains into the Amazon basin to the north through thick tropical forests.

Although most of the Bolivian people are employed on the land, where the production potential is very great, Bolivian agriculture has been depressed for many years. It became constantly necessary to increase imports of agricultural products after 1930. By the outbreak of World War II, Bolivia was dependent on Peru for sugar, Argentina for beef, the United States and Peru for rice, and Peru and Brazil for lumber. In 1949, the Keenleyside Mission observed that Bolivia was using precious foreign exchange for agricultural products. The amount spent was 4 million dollars each for wheat and refined sugar, 1¼ million dollars for rice, 2½ million dollars for meat, and over 1 million dollars for cotton fabrics.[27] Each succeeding study showed additional quantities of these items being imported despite the fact that all agricultural needs could be produced within the country if it were not for the stagnancy of Bolivian agriculture, which had a tendency "to impede—if not arrest—the ordinary course of economic development." If the earnings from exports could be used for expanding industrial and overall social investments, such as highways, then a growing urban population would create a larger market for farm products. At the same time the growth in the agricultural income would create "new purchasing power and effective demand for the products of the local industry." This development would permit the gradual investment of capital in a variety of manufacturing enterprises, and "a mature economy [would be] attained." The whole economy would then be "transformed into an integrated market system with interlocking, partly new, circuits of exchange."[27]

Prior to the 1952 revolution, the Bolivian Government had no agricultural policy, and the nature of land ownership as well as the ready availability of virtually limitless Indian labor provided no incentive to modernize or even to increase agricultural production. The nature of Bolivian agriculture also kept nearly three-fourths of the population completely out of the economic stream of the nation, as the Indians took care of practically all of their own needs and obtained the rest by barter in the villages.

Land reform was one of the principal objectives of the National Revolutionary Movement. On January 20, 1953, President Paz appointed an Agrarian Reform Commission with Vice-President Siles as its chairman.[28] The Central Obrera Boliviana, the Communist party, the Trotskyites' Partido Obrero Revolucionario, and the MNR all presented their versions of how agrarian reform should be carried out. The proposals were widely discussed in

---

[27] Pacheco Jiménez, p. 86.

[28] Wálter del Castillo Avendaño, *Compilación legal de la reforma agraria en Bolivia* (La Paz, Editorial Fénix, 1955), pp. 27–32.

the Cabinet and in the press and culminated in the eagerly awaited Decreto Ley No. 03464, which was presented to the public at Ucurena on August 2, 1953.

The agrarian reform law starts out with a short history of land uses from the Inca period to the date of the decree. Then setting out the distribution of land ownership according to the 1950 census, the law claims that the inequitable division prevents the production of enough food for the people. Finally, the six objectives of land reform are announced to be: (1) distributing the arable land to the peasants on condition that they work it; (2) restoring to the Indian communities the land taken from them; (3) freeing the'agricultural workers from their condition of serfdom; (4) stimulating increased productivity and the commercialization of agriculture; (5) promoting internal migration of the rural population from the *altiplano* to the eastern part of the nation; and (6) conserving the natural resources of the country.

The act exempts four types of holdings from being taken over or split up by the Government. One is the small property worked by the owner and his family. Another is the medium-sized property using wage labor or mechanization and producing largely for the market. The third type is the co-operative, which might be either an Indian community holding its original land or a newly formed agricultural association. Finally, there is the agricultural enterprise, the *empresa agrícola,* a large holding which is characterized "by the investment of supplementary capital on a large scale, the system of wage labor, and the employment of modern technical methods." The law was intended to authorize the takeover and redistribution of only the feudal holdings, the *latifundio,* property "which remains unexploited or insufficiently exploited," or one in which the return depends on the production of peasants in a "condition as serfs or *colonos.*"

Landlords losing all or any part of their land were to be paid in two-percent, twenty-five-year bonds based on the assessed value of the property. The securities were nontransferable but could be used for payment of accrued taxes, debts to the agricultural bank, or for new land in the frontier areas of the east. Those who received the *latifundio* lands were to pay the assessed value over a twenty-five-year period at two percent interest. Actually, if the provisions for payments by the peasants were strictly enforced, very few would retain their land. Consequently, this provision has been ignored.

On paper, the agrarian reform decree had a great deal of merit, but the implementation of the decree threw the country's agriculture into a state of paralysis. The administrative problems involved in parceling out the large estates were tremendous. For example, there were only about three hundred topographers to do the surveying and dividing of property. Then, in numerous cases endless litigation occurred, and many people were reluctant to plant on land that might not be theirs. Often the landlord had furnished tools and management—both of which were lost when the land was broken up. There was also a severe shortage of credit to enable the new owners to obtain seeds and tools. Nonetheless, land redistribution continued, and the President reported in 1958 that the revolutionary Government had not only carried out its promise of agrarian reform, "but it [could] now announce a five-year study for the termination of the agrarian reform program altogether."[29]

The most important provision of the decree and one that took immediate effect was that "from today the service system of unpaid labor is abolished forever." Every *campesino* understood that he was no longer obliged to give unpaid service. The breaking up of the *latifundias* also eliminated the large landowners as a social class. This impact on the social structure, with its change of long established patterns of human relationships, marks land reform as the most revolutionary aspect of the National Revolutionary Movement's program.

The MNR immediately set out to arouse the interests of the *campesino* in political affairs. *Sindicatos* with free membership and many privileges, including cheap tools and coupons permitting purchase of goods at very low prices, were formed. The *sindicato* members were armed, and a *caudillo*-type government of strong leaders was superimposed on the Indian population.

Education   The National Revolutionary Movement had also promised to concern itself with the education of the nation. Education had always been restricted to the upper class, who generally feared educating the masses. The 1950 census reported that seventy percent of the people could not read or write and that there were 12,409 university graduates in the entire population. There were only 55 secondary schools, all but 8 located in the cities, with only 1 in every 29 persons between the ages of 15 and 20 in school. Only a very few of the school buildings were built to serve as schools. There was also a general shortage of desks, chairs, libraries, and teachers. Some of these problems were recognized in earlier years, and a growing awareness of the need for additional educational facilities resulted in the doubling, between 1939 and 1943, of the percentage of the national budget to be spent for education.

The MNR soon launched a program to completely reorganize the educational system. Paz appointed a commission headed by Fernando Diez de Medina and containing representatives of the education and agriculture ministries, the miners' union, the Bolivian Labor Central, the University Council, the University Confederation, and the private colleges. The commission reported that public education must be free and obligatory in fact as well as in theory; pointed out the need of the country for more educated people; set forth the principle that education is the right of all Bolivians and not just of the minority; and placed the MNR squarely behind "equal opportunity for education for all as the problems of the country cannot otherwise be solved."[30]

The new educational code established the *nucleo escolar* as a basic school in the rural school system and placed the rural system under the Ministry of Rural Affairs. Urban education was left in the Ministry of Educa-

---

[29] Hernán Siles Zuazo, *Mensaje al Honorable Congreso Nacional* (La Paz, Editorial del Estado, 1958), p. 35.

[30] Ministerio de Educación, *Código de la Educación boliviana* (La Paz, Departamento de Publicaciones, 1956), pp. 11–16.

tion. The code required teaching the illiterate about health and sanitation as well as teaching them reading and writing. A great deal of emphasis was placed on the need for training applied scientists and engineers. Institutes to teach new farming methods, animal husbandry, social and legal rights, and arts and crafts were to be established. Servicio Cooperativo Interamericano de Educacíon was established with the United States in order to help extend vocational training and to train teachers.

By 1957, 4,097 rural schools had been established; a year later, 1,183 were added to the system. By 1960, 61 percent of the population between 7 and 14 years of age were in school in comparison to 32 percent in 1951. But even then, 64 percent of the population remained illiterate. President Siles announced in 1958 that his Government wished to place a major portion of its spending in the improvement of education and that he was studying ways and means of "providing schools for the half-million children now without schools."[31]

Universal Suffrage   Another of the changes to which the MNR was committed was a revision of the election code. As Bolivia is a unitary Republic with elected officials, whoever is permitted to vote largely determines who will be represented. Prior to 1952, registration was limited to those who were able to read and write; there were 205,000 registered for the 1951 elections. Early in the first term of President Paz, the vote was extended to the miners and the *campesinos*. Moreover, under a new rule, all Bolivian citizens (with certain exceptions) residing within the country who are 21 to 70 years old are now required to register and vote. Registration is voluntary for citizens over 70 and for those who are married and between the ages of 18 and 21. The MNR made every effort to inform the citizenry of their newly won voting privileges. By 1956, 958,016 people had registered. This figure increased to 987,730 for the 1960 elections and to 1,324,203 for the 1964 elections.

The President and vice-president are elected by a direct vote of the people for a four-year term. The senators are elected for six-year terms (there being three senators from each of the nine departments). One-third of the membership stands election every two years. Deputies serve four years, with one-half of the Chamber elected every two years. The capital city of each department is allowed five deputies plus one additional deputy for every 50,000 people or fraction over 30,000 in the districts outside the capital. The present Chamber consists of 102 members. As in most Latin American countries, the executive branch in Bolivia greatly overshadows the legislative and dominates the country.

THE POLITICAL PROCESS

The MNR dominated politics and ruled Bolivia from the 1952 revolution until the overthrow of the party in November 1964. To be sure, it was not without foes, but most opposition was from within the party, and the Govern-

---

[31] Guillermo Bedregal, *La ruta histórica de la Revolución Boliviana* (La Paz, Editorial de Estado, 1958).

ment did not hesitate to use force or curtail freedoms whenever it felt it was necessary to control groups outside the party. The party's first elected Chief Executive, Víctor Paz Estenssoro, left the Presidency at the end of his first term in accordance with a constitutional prohibition against immediate re-election. His vice-president, Hernán Siles Zuazo, was elected President. For the first time in many years, a constitutionally elected President had served his full term and turned over the Government to another constitutionally elected President. Paz returned from London for the 1960 campaign and prevented for the second time the candidacy of Wálter Guevara Arze, one of the founders of the MNR. Guevara was expelled from the party, and Paz was nominated by the MNR. Upon his election as President, Paz pushed through a change in the Constitution allowing for a second consecutive term of office.

During this period (1960–64), Vice-President Juan Lechín, the most powerful leader of the miners and workers, came to believe that he would follow Paz as President. However, various charges were brought against him, he was expelled from the party, and Paz was again selected as the MNR candidate in 1964. While it is true that up to this time the government had made no headway in solving the tin-mining problems, it had had moderate success in controlling inflation and in reducing the importation of food; the nation was now self-sufficient in sugar and rice. The Government was also successful in moving about a quarter of a million people off the *altiplano* to new farms in the lowlands and in building roads, hydroelectric facilities, and factories. These programs were carried out and the MNR maintained in power by means of massive aid from the United States. In addition to direct aid of nearly 400 million dollars since 1952, the United States supported Bolivia's applications to the World Bank, the International Monetary Fund, and the Inter-American Development Bank.

For a time it appeared that the promises of the MNR revolution would be realized and that civilian democracy had arrived in Bolivia. However, that interval was before Paz shattered the MNR through his personalism. He won his third term in 1964, and the MNR obtained about ninety-eight percent of the vote. But it must be remembered that Paz was the only candidate running for the Presidency, and only two parties, the Bolivian Anti-Communist Front and the National Civic Union, both partly financed by the MNR, had legislative candidates. All other parties abstained. The military was once again evident in politics, for the military forced Paz to accept General René Barrientos as running mate. As it turned out, it was Barrientos who forced the resignation of Paz and established a military junta in November 1964.

CONTEMPORARY POLITICS

Political Parties

Bolivian Revolutionary Front   Soon after the 1964 coup, the Popular Christian Movement (MPC) was formed to support General Barrientos for President. The MPC is now a member of the Bolivian Revolutionary Front

(FRB), an organization of four moderate-left parties and one interest group. Besides the MPC, the FRB includes the Authentic Revolutionary party, the Social Democratic party, the Leftist Revolutionary party, and the Chaco War Veterans Confederation. The Authentic Revolutionary party (PRA) is an offshoot of the MNR and was founded by Wálter Guevara Arze, a highly respected leader and one of the original men in the MNR. The PRA is organized territorially and functionally, and its membership includes factory workers, miners, *campesinos,* teachers, and youth groups. The program of this party is very similar to that of the MNR. The Social Democratic party (PSD) was formed in 1945 as an organization of university people and became a political party in 1946. It is organized only in La Paz and Sucre, and its membership includes some of the country's most distinguished intellectuals. The PSD is concerned with the ethical standards of government and advocates more effective use of United States aid and more highly qualified public officials. The Leftist Revolutionary party (PIR) was originally formed about 1940 by a group of Marxist intellectuals. This party early organized labor unions and worked with the *campesinos.* It elected several deputies in the 1940s, and although proposing a number of radical reforms, the party supported the Conservative governments after the fall of Villarröel. Following the 1952 revolution, many of the PIR members joined the MNR, and the PIR did not participate in any of the elections between 1952 and 1964. Its platform calls for industrialization and diversification. The party has some support among miners and railroad workers, but its chief strength is in La Paz and in the universities. The Chaco War Veterans Confederation was established after the Chaco War in order to seek and protect veterans' benefits. This party registered as a political group and joined the FRB, but the strength and influence of the confederation are uncertain. The FRB won the 1966 elections and its candidates, General René Barrientos and Luis Adolfo Siles Salinas (President of the PSD and half brother of Hernán Siles Zuazo), were installed as president and vice-president, respectively. It remains to be seen whether the FRB can maintain the dominant position once held by the MNR.

Moderate Left-of-Center Parties   Altogether there were fourteen parties registered for the 1966 elections, though three were more important than the rest. The Revolutionary Socialist party (PSR) supported Barrientos but did not join the FRB. The PSR was founded in 1965 by former members of the Falange and is a left-of-center party differing from the others in its benign attitude towards the military.

The Bolivian Socialist Falange (FSB), formed in 1937, participated in numerous attempts to overthrow the MNR between 1952 and 1962. The FSB successfully challenged the Communist control of the universities and is the major party of the academic community. Urban middle sectors also tend to support the Falange. Its program is almost identical with the other left-of-center parties, though because the Falange believed that Barrientos did not fulfill promises made to it before the 1964 ouster of Paz, the party opposed Barrientos' candidacy.

The Christian Democratic party (PDC) was organized as the Social Christian party. The PDC advocates a more strict morality and is supported mainly by college professors and students with growing support from urban youth of the middle class. This party did not participate in the 1966 elections.

Conservative Parties   Two parties can be classified as conservative. The Liberal party (PL) was formed in 1883 and controlled the Government from 1899 to 1920. This party is opposed to the nationalization of the mines, to universal suffrage, and to land reform. The PL supported the 1964 junta but not Barrientos as a presidential candidate. The program of the Socialist Republican Union party (PURS) is closely allied to that of the PL. PURS and PL formed the Democratic Institutionalist Alliance (AID) for the 1966 election. They have little electoral importance.

Extreme Left Parties   There are several parties of the extreme Left. The Bolivian Communist party (PCB) was founded in 1950 by some dissident members of the PIR. After the 1952 revolution some of the PCB followers joined the MNR. At present the party is divided into a pro-Moscow and a pro-Peking faction. The party has a limited following in the universities.

The Revolutionary Workers party (POR) was organized in 1920. The party is not satisfied with the progress of the revolution under the MNR and wants much more radical changes. The POR is very anti-United States in its propaganda. It is strong in the mining areas and has some following among industrial workers.

The National Leftist Revolutionary party (PRIN) was created by Juan Lechín upon his expulsion from the MNR in 1964. Most of the left wing of the MNR joined Lechín in forming the party. Mine and factory workers, students, and teachers constitute most of. its membership. The PRIN was strongly opposed to the military junta, and the violent opposition of PRIN-controlled labor unions caused the junta to crack down on the party and exile Lechín.

The National Liberation Front (FLIN) was organized in 1964 in opposition to Paz' bid for a third term. This party is very similar to the Communist party except that FLIN is nationalist and rejects Moscow and Peking control. FLIN has opposed the junta, the United States, and the Alliance for Progress.

Interest Groups

Students and Workers   The two most active groups in Bolivian political life are the students and the mine and industrial workers. The students have often exerted an important influence on government activities by means of hunger strikes, marches, and actions of that nature. This is especially true in La Paz. In recent years the students have tended to support the Christian Democrats and the Socialist Falange.

Though very small in number, the industrial workers and miners can bring the country to a standstill by a strike. The country is still dependent on the tin mines for most of its foreign exchange and thus for the importation of supplies the country must have to survive. In addition, the miners are armed and have long used violence to obtain their ends. The Barrientos' Government has forced reforms on the miners in reducing wages and personnel, but only with troops and planes. Many persons have been killed and leaders jailed or exiled. The miners can be counted on to express their dissatisfaction in any movement to overthrow the present Government.

Campesinos   The most important segment in any Bolivian election is the *campesinos* as they compose seventy to seventy-five percent of the voters. Mostly illiterate, they follow *caudillo* leaders who have complete control over their various areas. The leaders also have armed *campesino* militias and can even control who is permitted to enter their territory. The *campesinos* are generally not so violently active as students and workers between elections, but *campesino* support is almost essential for any group seeking to gain or retain power in Bolivia. Politically, they will probably become a much more important force than they have been thus far.

The Army   Subjecting the army to civilian control was one of the first objectives of the MNR in 1952. Toward this end, eighty percent of the officers and noncommissioned officers were retired after the revolution. In 1953 the army was re-established and the military academy reopened. New cadets were to be accepted on the basis of their social background (fifty percent were to be from the peasant and worker class) and political beliefs. By 1956 there were eight thousand men in the army, and two thousand of these were employed in building roads and in clearing the land on the frontier. The armed forces were of little political significance until the United States' Military Assistance Program again built them into a powerful organization. This new strength was brought about through modern equipment of all kinds and in abundant amounts. The new influence was first demonstrated in the 1964 MNR convention, when Paz was forced to dump Federico Fortún Sanjinés, chosen by the convention to be Paz' running mate; the choice of Chief of Staff General Alfredo Ovando Candia was General René Barrientos Ortuno of the air force. Moreover, just before the election the army demanded the removal of Wálter Revuelta as Prefect of the Department of Cochabamba, even though Revuelta was a Paz man with a large following among the *campesinos*. The new influence of the army was also demonstrated by numerous appeals made to it by opposition leaders to intervene in the 1964 election.

Paz was inaugurated for his third term on August 6, 1964. Public disharmony between Paz and his vice-president, Barrientos, erupted on October 6, when the general released to the press a critical telegram he had sent to Paz which protested newspaper censorship. Paz released his own answer, in which he suggested that the place for Barrientos to criticize was in the Cabinet meetings in La Paz instead of from Cochabamba, where the general was spending most of his time. Barrientos' reply reminded Paz of the military's role in Barrientos' nomination and election. Student demonstrations, strikes, and various difficulties followed one after the other in October, and Barrientos suggested that Paz resign from the Presidency. Paz turned to the Chief of Staff, and after a number of talks between the two, Ovando informed his President, late at night on November 3, that he could no longer control the armed forces. Paz and his family left for Lima the next day and left the military once again in charge of the country.

A prognosis for Bolivia's future is illusive at this time. President Barrientos shows little understanding of the country's problems or of the need for discussing possible solutions with leaders of the various segments of the economy. He seems more interested in hunting down and removing the old union officers, actions which may only make way for younger, more radical leaders. There is no evidence to suggest that Barrientos grasps the complexities inherent in integrating the nation; rather, he appears bent upon dividing Bolivia by setting *campesino* against miner. Barrientos was elected President in July 1966 as the candidate of the Bolivian Revolutionary Party.

Bolivia is a sort of South American heartland bordering five other countries. Its boundaries cannot be defended against encroachment, and the country could easily become a spawning ground for guerrillas of the Castro type. Nevertheless, the fact remains that there has been in Bolivia a national revolution which significantly altered traditional socio-economic relationships through land reform and which instilled a sense of national identity in the minds of the people. Events of the last few years measurably slowed down the revolutionary process, but so many changes have been put in motion that it cannot be halted.

13 / Chile

BEN G. BURNETT

INTRODUCTION

Students of Latin American politics have long been drawn to Chile. Its outgoing and genuinely hospitable people, its spectacular and varied scenery, and its deserved reputation as one of the few stable, democratic constitutional systems in the hemisphere must be included among the reasons for that attraction. Early in the nineteenth century the old aristocracy implanted the stabilizing influences, and in the early decades of this century, the middle sector opened the system to stronger democratic tendencies and to limited social reforms. Unfortunately, the working classes remained almost entirely on the fringes of political control until the 1960s. Their claims were poorly articulated, and on those occasions when members of the working classes did reach policy-makers, they were customarily ignored. Recently, a few reformist and radical political parties recognized these inequities and endeavored to aggregate such group needs. This action in turn heightened political activism among the working classes. As a consequence, the 1960s seemed to constitute a decisive period in the unfolding of Chile; either the reform-minded administration installed in 1964 would find a way to satisfy the impoverished urban and rural laboring segments or a growing political alienation could very well strike at the foundations of Chile's political system.

THE POLITICAL ENVIRONMENT

The long sliver of land constituting Chile spans some 2,600 miles from the Peruvian border in the north to Tierra del Fuego in the south and is so pinched between the massive Andean range to the east and the Pacific

Ocean on the west that the width of the country averages only about 110 miles. Beyond these territorial boundaries Chile looks to island possessions in the Pacific—the Juan Fernández group and Easter Island—as well as to Antarctic claims. However, these still await some hoped-for, though undefined, future importance.

Chile's elongated continental expanse encompasses some of the most varied terrain and climate to be found in Latin America. Although geographers define numerous topographical-climatic categories, four general regions stand out. The first is the dry northern desert, which is sparsely populated and has little vegetation but which contains great quantities of copper, iron ore, and nitrates (though the value of nitrates has been declining in the international market) as vital contributors to the national economy. The second region, northern middle Chile, stretching from Coquimbo to Concepción and containing most of the population, is the economic, political, and social heartland. The third, southern middle Chile, with its giant forest stands and largely agricultural and pastoral economy, halts at the Island of Chiloé. The rugged frontier region, known simply as the south, is the fourth region, where nature has been inhospitable to colonization to such a degree that most of the hundred thousand people of this area are to be found in and around Punta Arenas, where they gain a livelihood from pastoral pursuits, interocean commerce, and more recently and significantly from the new oil industry. Another way to illustrate Chile's great diversity is to transpose the country onto North America. When placing the southern tip of the country in the Arctic territory of Canada, the opposite end of Chile lies in Northern Mexico; in many ways the variances are comparable—from the harsh climate of Tierra del Fuego through rain forests equivalent to those in the Pacific Northwest, then changing in central Chile to a Mediterranean climate similar to southern California and terminating in Atacama's mostly rain-free desert.

Geography has also contributed measurably to Chile's insularity. The Andes inhibit an easy flow of population between Chile and its Argentine and Bolivian neighbors, and the northern deserts slow traffic to Peru. By the same token, boundaries with the three neighboring Republics, despite periodic grumblings from Bolivia over its loss of access to the sea after the War of the Pacific (1879–83) and occasional differences of opinion with Argentina regarding Andean borders (for example, the Palena dispute that festered between 1963 and 1966), have been sufficiently secure for a long enough time to provide an air of comfort to the Chilean in so far as the extent of his national territory is concerned. Moreover, Chile remains at a considerable distance from most of the world's great trade centers. Noting that Valparaíso, located in central Chile and the country's leading seaport, is only slightly north of Cape Town, South Africa, helps to emphasize the nation's remoteness—5,300 statute miles for a steamship to reach New York (only 200 less by air), 7,200 to Melbourne, Australia, and almost 9,000 to Hamburg, Germany. All of this, then, served to create an atmosphere of relative peace and isolation for a long enough period to permit the development of a Chilean ethos, which includes a deep pride of country, but a nationalism that is rather quiet and not subject to the irrational and aggressive features characteristic of certain other peoples whose nerve ends seem to be exposed and ready for a combative response to real or imagined slights. By the turn of the century, Chile turned more and more outwardly to participate in international conferences and offer its voice on matters of wide-ranging import in world councils. Throughout, the nation has tended to display a general consistency of purpose—maintain its own security, comply with international legal forms, search for hemispheric co-operation, and request nonintervention in the international affairs of nations. Frequently, especially in modern hemispheric relationships (for example, in relations with Cuba), that consistency leads to Chile's opting for an independent line of foreign policy that does not always follow that of the United States.

Population and Social Structure

Chile's particular insularity, along with historical and natural challenges, helped to mold a remarkably homogeneous populace. During the long colonial period, the indigenous people either blended in with the conquering Spaniards, retreated south into remote areas to try to escape extermination, or slipped over into Argentina in order to survive military campaigns directed against them by the Spaniards in reprisal for Indian uprisings. As a consequence, an Indian population thought to have numbered between 500,000 and 1,500,000 in the 1500s has been reduced to the approximately 130,000 living on reservations today.[1] This figure is only about 1.6 percent of all Chileans, and while traditionalist influences remain in certain of the Indian social and religious ways, most Indians speak Spanish and live like the other Chileans who make up the peasant economy.

Immigration has not been quantitatively significant. In the entire history of the Republic of Chile, it probably admitted only about 100,000 immigrants. Germans began to arrive in the 1850s and can claim especial importance in developing southern middle Chile; people from the Middle East appeared in the 1860s, though most of them in time became integrated into the Spanish culture even to the extent of converting to Roman Catholicism; and a sprinkling of Italians, Swiss, Yugoslavs, French, and British reached Chilean shores at various times, particularly right after independence and again at the turn of the century. Many of these immigrant families achieved the highest leadership positions in virtually every aspect of Chilean life; such names as O'Higgins, Edwards, Mackenna, Yarur, Subercaseaux, Alessandri, and Frei stand on a par with Aguirre, Ibáñez, Balmaceda, Pérez, and Sanfuentes. Furthermore, the old Chilean elite did not close its doors to these newcomers, so that by the end of the nineteenth century, intermarriages between the two elements were commonplace. This amalgamation of races and nationalities resulted in a

---

[1] Julian Steward and Louis C. Faron, *Native Peoples of South America* (New York, McGraw-Hill Book Co., Inc., 1959), p. 268; Oscar Kaplan C., *Geografía de Chile* (Santiago, EDIGRAF, 1963), p. 89.

relatively unified culture, ethnically European (about thirty-five percent) and mestizo (with a heavy European side to the mixture) and linguistically Spanish.

On the other hand, social strains do exist in Chile which have been conducive to manifestations of political alienation. In no small measure these are a result of the population pressures plaguing much of Latin America. Chile's annual population growth of 2.5 percent falls behind only Brazil, Venezuela, and Ecuador among the South American nations and ranks above the world total of 1.8 percent. When translated into total population figures, the rate of increase is even more striking:

1920	3,785,000
1930	4,365,000
1940	5,063,000
1950	6,073,000
1960	7,340,000
1970	9,800,000 est.

But the real gravity of population pressures can be observed in the dizzying numbers of people flooding the cities. In 1940, Chile passed into a stage in which a majority of its inhabitants were urban dwellers; twenty-five years later, more than two-thirds of all Chileans comprised the urban population—a figure only a little less than those for the United States and Canada and as high a percentage as can be found anywhere in the rest of the hemisphere. Regrettably, the bulk of urbanization affects the already crowded national capital and has caused one author to refer to Santiago as "a head too large for the country."[2] In the middle 1960s, over one-third of all Chileans resided in Santiago, whereas only sixteen percent of the nation lived there in 1920.

For a tourist visiting Santiago for a brief stay, putting up in a modern hotel, and relying upon taxis for his transportation, the city offers an attractive picture of orderliness replete with neat parks, smart shops, and generally well-dressed people. Such an initial impression will be at least partially borne out by a longer residence, but that impression belies the multitude of problems besetting this great metropolitan center in the functioning of transportation, communication, utilities, sanitation, and housing. Because of the acute shortage of buses, upon which most *santiagueños* rely, the round trip once or twice a day from home to work can be an unnerving and grueling experience. The telephone system is inadequate and chaotic. Pollutants fill the air from the ubiquitous burning of trash and mark the city as one of the world's most smog-ridden. Potable water is often in short supply and occasionally unsafe for drinking; it is said that sewer and water pipes are laid side by side in the same trenches, reducing costs and permitting a more rapid extension of the lines but raising a danger of leakage. Gas piping, made of light metal and thin construction, frequently breaks and fills the air with obnoxious and sometimes

---

[2] Pedro Cunill, *Geografía de Chile* (Santiago, Editorial Universitaria, S.A., 1963), p. 98.

noxious fumes. Still, except for transportation difficulties, these problems are little known to the approximately 650,000 (of Greater Santiago's 2,400,000 people) whose slum dwellings circle the city. The *poblaciones callampas,* or "mushroom settlements," sprout up in vacant lots, in river beds, and along train tracks. A noted professor of geography at the University of Chile, Pedro Cunill, describes them in the following manner:

> The mushroom settlements are unwholesome, constructed with discarded materials, such as boards, cardboard, metal, cans, etc. In their interior state they appear poor, without sanitary services, without potable water, without electric lights. The acervation and promiscuity reach infrahuman degrees in these living sectors. A low level of culture, malnutrition, and illiteracy complete the picture previously described.[3]

Such living conditions, resulting from the unceasing immigration, which exceeds the capacity of the economy to employ and shelter such a burgeoning population, produce demands upon the political system which have not been satisfied. Thus, alienation is deep and widespread. This development creates considerable concern among those responsible for maintaining order, for so large an alienated segment of the population coiled around Santiago like a serpent, when activated, could spew its venom of discontent over the heart of the metropolis. Besides endeavoring to satisfy the basic needs of the poor, it has been proposed that a concerted effort should be made to relocate them in small groups throughout the city. Not only would this relocation reduce the problem of keeping the peace, but it should help to give the poor something of a neighborhood orientation and, more important, integrate them into the community.

The reasons for urbanization, and especially the movement of people to the capital (only one-third of its citizens were born in the province of Santiago), are manifold, but three reasons stand out. First, there is an overabundance of political, economic, and social power concentrated in Santiago. Local governments are so weak that almost any claims on the decision-making process demand the attention of national government officials. The headquarters of most managerial and labor associations as well as a high percentage of industrial, commercial, and financial institutions are located in the capital. And most social and cultural services and activities fan out from Santiago as well. Second, Chile has been tragically prone to countless natural disasters in the form of earthquakes, tidal waves, and volcanic eruptions, all of which destroy homes and eradicate jobs. With each new crisis another stream of displaced persons finds its confluence of hope in the nation's capital. Finally, the never-ending search of the even more destitute rural populace for better opportunities for securing a livelihood lures countless thousands of them to the metropolises.

Of course, the net result of this perennial migration only further compounds the chronic difficulties facing the cities—above all, Santiago. At the

---

[3] Cunill, p. 94.

same time, the provinces find themselves depleted of some of their best laborers, the most vigorous segment of their working population. Studies by the University of Chile's Economics Institute tell some of the story.[4] Unemployment in metropolitan Santiago held at a rate of 5.1 percent of those classified as in the working force in the middle 1960s, whereas in the Concepción region unemployment averaged more than 8 percent, with the rate in the impoverished coal mining area of Lota-Coronel just south of Concepción rising as high as 12.3 percent. (These statistics are more than a little misleading since a far greater percentage of workers in both Santiago and Concepción are gravely *under*employed.) The loss of working-age people can be observed in the fact that in Lota-Coronel more than 44 percent of the population is under fourteen years of age, while only a little over 33 percent of the *santiagueños* can be found in that category.

To a degree, the excessive population growth of Santiago and of certain other urban centers is caused by a vicious circle, rural peoples enter the city, which in turn spreads out into what were farmlands and thus displaces agricultural workers, who then turn to the urban centers for jobs, which further augments the city's need to consume more agricultural property for housing and industrial sites. Furthermore, the haphazard nature of the urban extension encourages the swallowing up of chunks of land which at one time were small farms, but now, being cut off from irrigation canals, remain vacant lots.

Nonetheless, the bulk of the cities' immigration from rural regions derives from the culture of poverty there. Living and working conditions persist at substandard levels for most of the landless. A brief description of one, though not atypical, farm may point up something of this situation:

> The [Fulanos] work on a *fundo* or farm which is owned by a wealthy landowner who also owns a large pigsty as well as acres of land on which are grown vegetables and fruits of all kinds. These are canned in a factory owned by him. Mr. [Fulano] receives the equivalent of $1.00 to $1.80 a day for his labor. The money must reach to feed and clothe a family of eight, so they must live almost totally on bread and tea. Their home, provided by the landowner, is about three yards away from an immense pigsty which is built in the form of a square and is open two-thirds of the way from a low wall to the roof, a breeding place for thousands of flies. . . .
>
> The inside of the house represents a barn but is much cruder with a rough stone floor in the dark crowded bedroom where the whole family sleeps. To the right is a small room serving as a dining room. Its only boast is a low table without chairs to sit on. To the left of the bedroom is another small room serving as a kitchen. The fireplace is nothing more than a heap of wood on the floor toward the center of the room. There is little cooking outside of heating water for tea.
>
> These people must use muddy ditch water or go a long distance to a center where there is a fresh water faucet. They then lug the water home in pails or cans only to find it does not go very far with a big family. The manager of

---

[4] These were extensively reported in *El Mercurio,* October 30, 1963, and April 25, 1964.

the *fundo* does not provide fresh water for most of the families, and even keeps a special man on duty to try to keep the people from using the dirty water of the irrigation canals.[5]

By and large, agricultural workers, or *inquilinos,* who live on the farms receive partial payment for their services in cash, and the remainder is doled out by the landowner in "perquisites." The latter take the form of shelter, perhaps a ration of food, a small plot of land to plant, and the right to keep some animals. Consequently, it could be pointed out that the actual income of these resident laborers is far greater than just their cash income. Still, critics of this system argue that both the cash and the "perquisites" prove to be inadequate for a family's most basic needs. At any rate, beginning in 1961 the cash portion was annually increased at legal insistence—in 1962 cash being 25 percent of the total, in 1963, 35 percent, in 1964, 50 percent, and so forth. It was hoped that this increase would remove the clouds covering rural income as well as give the farm worker more economic flexibility. Whatever the merits of these changes, the Government's failure to increase minimum wages for agricultural workers generally reduced their real income.

Besides the *inquilinos,* other categories of farm workers are the share-croppers, or *medieros,* who often do not live on the farm; migratory laborers, or *afuerinos,* who, along with those laborers working part-time on the farms and spending the rest of their working day in other economic pursuits, rank in income at the bottom of all Chilean occupational elements; and a number of technical, clerical, and other specialized help—including a great number of watchmen who guard the property and its produce as well as tend to the irrigation system. Finally, there exist countless proprietors of lands too small to care for their families who must seek outside employment. The agricultural census listed the nonpropertied, economically active, farm working class as follows:

Administrators	10,094
Technicians & Office personnel	2,570
Watchmen	19,499
Specialized laborers	13,808
Inquilinos	82,367
Medieros	26,861
Full-, part-time, & migratory workers	179,779
TOTAL	334,978

After World War II, Chile experienced a certain agricultural growth stimulated by price and production increases. Still, the improved situation

---

[5] This description is excerpted from a letter to the author from a friend providing medical help to these agricultural workers. For obvious reasons, the person must remain anonymous.

only favored the landowner, whose real income grew by more than 48 percent in the 1950s; labor income actually decreased by 5.3 percent in that decade. In addition, the labor cost of agricultural production declined between 1950 and 1959 from one-half to one-third of the total, and only to a small extent could that decline be attributed to mechanization or improved labor productivity.[6]

Although by 1967 there was some optimism over the Christian Democrats' efforts to help the destitute farm worker in acquiring his own property, the concentration of land ownership in a few hands still prevailed as a nagging problem. Of the total land area, 87.38 percent is held by large farms or *fundos* (those over 200 hectares), 7.60 percent by medium-sized estates (50 to 200 hectares), and 5.02 percent by small plots (under 50 hectares). More meaningfully, .4 percent of the estates—all over 5,000 hectares—comprise 54 percent of Chilean farm land. By enlarging the number of *fundos* to 2 percent of the total, the extent of land area held by this minority reaches 72 percent of all occupied farm property. Naturally, a portion of this is unproductive or minimally productive. On the other hand, most of the small *fundos* (two-thirds of Chile's 151,000 farms) encompass marginal land as well, and 85 percent of them can be classed as possessing almost no cash resale value.[7]

In its desire to upgrade the poor farmers' status and create a rural middle class, the Chilean Government initiated a land reform program more than thirty years ago. Periodically, new legislation was promulgated to strengthen agrarian reform. The most liberal of these laws appeared in 1962–63. However, the rural poor enjoy little opportunity to take advantage of the opportunities ostensibly granted them. For example, a twenty-five-acre truck farm with good soil in the Santiago area costs about $5,500. The down payment of $275 is close to the average annual per capita income, and since agricultural workers have almost no ability to save money, it is virtually pointless for them to aspire to land ownership. Any who can qualify to purchase such a *fundo* must repay the Government $300 a year for thirty-nine years, or including interest, about double the original price. Thus, almost no progress has been registered in distributing land to the impoverished Chilean peasants. By contrast, Mexico in 1962 alone settled two times the total amount of land parceled out in Chile over a thirty-year period.[8]

Because of the difficulties continuously harassing the rural and urban classes, there have been numerous manifestations of their discontent—from occupying land illegally to chronic street demonstrations and strikes. Being the largest stratum of the population and expanding at the fastest rate, the sheer numbers of these underprivileged and the fact that they are rapidly obtaining

[6] Corporación de Fomento de la Producción, *Geografía económica de Chile* (Santiago, Talleres Gráficos "La Nación," 1962), III, 83–88; Kalman H. Silvert, *Chile: Yesterday and Today* (New York, Holt, Rinehart and Winston, Inc., 1965), pp. 125–26.

[7] Center of Latin American Studies, *Statistical Abstract of Latin America: 1964* (Los Angeles, University of California Press, 1965), p. 56; Cunill, pp. 110–11.

[8] *South Pacific Mail,* December 6, 1963.

political awareness and activism marks them as a powerful political force now awakening from their long slumber.

The remaining one-fifth to one-quarter of Chileans, constituting mostly the middle and upper classes, enjoy the fruits of the best the country has to offer. As Kalman Silvert suggests, they are the ones who live in modernity:

> . . . They are educated, they can aspire to higher position for their children without being unrealistic, they can talk and meet and write and read freely, they can make a fairly wide occupational choice, they have access to government and can be assured of equality before the law, they can enjoy a wide array of the material fruits of industrial life, they can belong to unions and political parties and pressure groups and professional societies, and they can assume that their vote has some real significance.[9]

But they, like the working classes, know the pernicious influences at play in the economy. More than eighty years of recurring inflationary spirals stand at the top of these influences. In the last decades prices rose at a dangerous pace: between 1930 and 1940 by 94 percent, from 1940 to 1950 by 412 percent, and during the 1950–1960 period by 2,089 percent. Of course, workers suffered from wage increases customarily lagging behind price jumps and found themselves devoting an ever-larger proportion of their salaries to basic necessities. Inflation also contributed to entrepreneurial deficiencies. The middle and upper sectors felt compelled to conceal assets from taxation and to contribute to the flow of capital from the country by sending profits abroad and engaging in black market money dealings. And many private safes contained hordes of hard currencies.

Recent presidential regimes sought solutions to Chile's vexing problems, and although some reforms attracted general support, too many appeared too late, were qualitatively and quantitatively too limited, and thus failed to satisfy the rising expectations of large segments of the population. Hence, social strains not only largely remained but proliferated, and group pressures and clashes in the political system became pervasive.

POLITICAL STRUCTURES AND ROLES

At the center of any political system is the relative ability of the members of society to communicate with each other. The flow of information from sender to receiver can be limited by government restrictions, linguistic variances, inadequate media, low literacy, and a host of other inhibiting influences. Chile is fortunate in possessing a highly penetrative communications process largely devoid of such circumscriptions. Spanish serves as the language of practically all Chileans, and more than eighty percent of those past ten years of age are classified as literate. Even admitting to the low literacy level of many of these, the proportion capable of perceiving political information is outstanding for Latin America.

---

[9] Silvert, p. 26.

The openness of the polity admits a free expression of the widest range of political views. Publications from western and Communist nations vie for attention on the newsstands with a domestic press representative of Chile's broad political spectrum. This broadness is especially exemplified by the newspapers of Santiago, among whose dailies are *El Siglo* (Communist), *Las Noticias de Ultima Hora* (Socialist), *Clarín* (independent leftist), *Tercera de la Hora* (Radical), *El Mercurio* (Liberal), *El Diario Ilustrado* (Conservative), and *La Nación* (government). Numerous weekly, fortnightly, and monthly periodicals augment this coverage. The combined circulation of the nation's daily newspapers alone (approximately 1,100,000) and their distribution to 134 of every 1,000 people ranks Chile third in Latin America (behind Uruguay and Argentina) in newspaper dissemination. While provincial newspapers tend to be conservative, they are supplemented by leftist (as well as other rightist) dailies from the capital. Radio broadcasting blankets the country though natural obstacles do limit reception in several areas. There are no national broadcasting systems as such, but from time to time, the Government takes over a select number of radio stations for simultaneous, nation-wide broadcasts. It is estimated that more than a million receivers are in use. However, this figure probably falls considerably below the actual number since it is based upon electric power use, and many poor people illegally tie into electrical lines and thus escape detection, and countless transistor radios (a large proportion of which are smuggled into the country) cannot be counted. One study concluded that in the Santiago area seventy-seven percent of workers and ninety-eight percent of the upper class owned radios.[10] While radio performs significantly as a communications medium, television remains in a retarded stage of growth; television is confined to Santiago and depends upon a couple of low-funded and usually poorly programmed educational channels.

In short, groups of all sorts can find some outlet in the mass media for issuing claims into the political system. This is not to say, however, that all the communications instruments are open to all types of structures. Obviously, the Left and Right will not be receptive to providing extensive coverage of opposite opinions. And some groups, especially the democratic trade unions, who are opposed by conservative management as well as by leftist unions and political parties, must often fall back on paid announcements (a severe strain on their small budgets) in order to attract public attention to union needs. Still, the flow of information is generally good; the style of information presented is vigorous (at times too unrestrained in the minds of some), the citizenry hears competitive viewpoints, and the sources of information are quite open. One final strength of the communications process in Chile needs to be mentioned. While Chile can be classed as one of the more modernized nations of Latin America and hence is growing in complexity, the country has

---

[10] Ralph Marienberg F., *Algunas sugerencias respecto a combinaciones de medios de propaganda de Chile* (Santiago, Universidad de Chile, Lic. memoria, 1960), p. 94.

still not lost the function of personal persuasion. Most leaders are accessible to each other and, by and large, can be approached by the ordinary citizen. Furthermore, inasmuch as most of the leaders can be located in downtown Santiago, whatever the other problems this creates, the ease of personal contact is definitely enhanced.

Interest Groups

One of the most remarkable features of the Chilean political system is the comparatively high degree of role differentiation among several interest groups. That is to say, that whereas in most of Latin America such structures as the Roman Catholic Church and the military compete for political favors and power along with labor unions and management associations, in Chile this type of influence is minimal. Power clashes by so many types of interest groups cause many societies in the Western Hemisphere to be prone to chronic instability. Certainly this is not the only reason, but when in addition there is an absence of a rule of law and of behavioral political ground rules, these power clashes are a major contributing factor.

In Chile the Church cannot be considered the great land proprietor or the intervener in politics which it is elsewhere. Such properties as the Church held have been going through a voluntary redistribution program. And under the leadership of the cardinal archbishop of Santiago, Raúl Silva Henríquez, policies on economic and political matters have been made amply clear to all. The cardinal offers strong support to economic reforms that will benefit the working classes, but the clergy is not to endorse candidates or enter the electoral process in any way. In the 1964 presidential campaign, when several priests exhorted parishioners to vote for a Roman Catholic (a barb aimed at the Socialist-Communist candidate), the cardinal reminded those priests that he and all his bishops were in agreement that the Church must remain apolitical.

However, there is no doubt that the Church generally favored the Christian Democrats over the Socialist-Communist coalition. When the Christian Democrats came to power in 1964, many young priests began to work among the urban poor as part of the Government's social and economic program; it seems very probable that in this capacity, the clergy also exert some political influence over their parishioners. Moreover, Roger Vekemans, a Jesuit priest at the Catholic University, serves as an important adviser to President Eduardo Frei. In short, the Church's contemporary social policies are openly progressive, while its political activities tend to be performed more subtly behind the scenes.

The military and police perform a variety of undifferentiated roles, including teaching and providing first-aid attention to those in lower economic strata, especially in the more inaccessible regions, as well as supervising elections, building roads, and pursuing other basically nonmilitary functions. But the two groups have rarely been drawn into politics. Indeed, the roots of a professional and apolitical military go back deep into the nineteenth century, and only in exceptional crises that enveloped the nation, such as in the middle 1920s, has this pattern been reversed. One of the causal factors of this situation stems from a long-honored arrangement whereby the military is assured of a given percentage of the budget and goes about its own way. This arrangement is not the same thing as genuine civilian control but has worked surprisingly effectively in divorcing the military from political activities.

Students penetrate the political system often, but without the virulence characteristic of their counterparts in some neighboring countries. All of the universities maintain student directorates, composed of officers with stated political leanings. In the middle 1960s, those with Christian Democratic affiliations dominated the executive boards, the only exception being the Socialist-Communist control of the University of Concepción. Frank Bonilla found that the history of the student federation of the University of Chile (FECH), far and away the most important student group politically, indicated it to be most operative in periods of economic and political tension, in response to oppressive governmental actions, or in order to fill a void created by the decline of a government opposition party. But students' political achievements have been uneven, their efforts ephemeral, and their organizational apparatus unstable. Only a very few students participate in any way in federation activities.[11] For all their weaknesses, student structures in Chile should not be ignored; on occasion, as when they are in league with political parties and trade unions, the federations can exert a measurable pressure on decision-making councils.

The usually apolitical nature of the military and the intermittent and generally moderate styles of clergy and student political action narrow the pressure field primarily to economic interest activity. Above all, this narrowing has meant competition between the agricultural-manufacturing-commercial-mining elite and trade unions, with the former usually carrying the day.

Management Groups

Managerial structures in Chile have matched their powerful and centralized dominance of the economic system with a virtual monopoly control of political resources during most of the nation's history. Beginning as early as 1838 with the founding of an agricultural association, in later years industrial, mining, and commercial organizations joined to form a great economic elite, often competing with each other but eventually closing ranks to maintain their predominant economic and political position when challenged by newer structures appearing in the twentieth century.

Each of these management groups articulates the claims of most of those engaged in its particular economic endeavor: Sociedad Nacional de Agricultura for agriculture, Sociedad de Fomento Fabril for manufacturing, Sociedad Nacional de Minería for mining, and Cámara Central de Comercio de Chile for commerce. All are centered in Santiago within walking distance of each

---

[11] "The Student Federation of Chile: 50 Years of Political Action," *Journal of Inter-American Studies*, II, No. 3 (July 1960), 311–34.

other, and in fact, today they enjoy generally harmonious working relations on matters affecting all of them. Furthermore, all four are merged into the Confederación de la Producción y del Comercio, a single great economic unit which can bring enormous pressure to bear on the political system.

In addition to a long organizational history and a high level of structural cohesion, management also benefits measurably from able leadership and strong financial reserves. But there remain two especially meaningful dimensions of managerial strength that more adequately define its economic and political roles: economic concentration and institutionalized governmental representation.

In a classic study, Ricardo Lagos has developed a convincing thesis that a few great families and a small number of economic structures hold sway over every aspect of the economic system.[12] Basically, these structures are composed of some inordinately wealthy families who, by means of interlocking directorates, form eleven "supergroups" that govern the economy. Originally, they developed their economic power through banking institutions and by the turn of the century were accused of having converted Chile into a plutocracy. Even today, of the eleven supergroups, eight are banking houses which spread out into the directorates of every conceivable type of enterprise. It is estimated that the eleven together hold in their hands 70.6 percent of all Chilean investment capital. Thus, the same names keep cropping up time and again on boards of directors. By the same token, these names appear as congressmen, Cabinet members, and Presidents of the Republic. To mention just one, Gabriel González Videla, who served as Chile's President from 1946 to 1952, continued to exercise great power in the Radical party as well as heading the Democratic Front electoral coalition for a time and also sat on directorates which controlled or influenced six banks and 116 companies.[13]

The other management strength, institutionalized governmental representation, can be observed in legal enactments passed over the years by the economic oligarchy which grant to its members seats on the governing boards of countless public and semipublic agencies. These include national banks, the development corporation, labor and social welfare agencies of vital concern to labor (but in which labor's role is usually minimal), educational institutions, customs, and many others. For example, the Banco Central, which manages the entire monetary policy for Chile, is administered by a directorate, of which three are appointed by the country's Chief Executive, four appointed by stockholding groups, one jointly determined by the Sociedad Nacional de Minería and the Sociedad de Fomento Fabril, one whom the Cámara Central de Comercio and the Corporación de Ventas de Salitre y Yodo appoint together, and one from labor. Customarily, labor's sole representative on the Central Bank (and on other agencies) has not truly been from organized

---

[12] *La concentración del poder económico* (Santiago, Editorial Pacífico, 5th ed., 1962), pp. 93–177.

[13] For a detailed discussion of this subject, see *Vistazo,* March 20, 27, 1962; March 30, August 6, 13, 20, and 27, 1963.

labor, but recently Chile's main central confederation found a technicality which enabled the confederation to place its man on the bank's directorate—the only instance where this occurred.

To conclude, then, management has tended to stand united as a relatively small segment of the economic community and has been able to utilize its massive resources to great political advantage. In one sense, management's tight reins on the political system contributed importantly to the early establishment of Chile's famed political stability. Later, during the 1920s, the rising middle class forced the traditional elite to widen control of decision-making to cater to the middle sector's needs and even to enact progressive legislation favorable to the urban working class. However, the implementation of progressive measures was sporadic at best, depending as it did upon the temperament of the regime administering the laws. Indeed, in the three decades prior to the Christian Democrats' ascendancy to political power, only the brief Popular Front Government of Pedro Aguirre Cerda (1938–41) could be labeled as friendly to the working classes.

Labor Groups

Unlike the history of management associations, the unfolding of organized labor's history is marked by incredible obstacles which prohibited any orderly and regularized expansion.[14] Mutual benefit societies came into being as early as the 1850s, and the Anarcho-Syndicalists formed their militant, anti-capitalist "societies of resistance" beginning in the 1890s. Most of these lived ephemeral lives as a result of the inexperience of their leadership and the consistent opposition of management. Bloodshed characterized the relationships of labor and management, and the latter frequently called upon the coercive arms of government to put down workers' organizational efforts. In 1903 the navy was ordered into Valparaíso to halt a maritime workers' strike which had broken out into rioting. Four years later one of the most shocking pages was written in a long history of labor grievances when striking nitrate workers, upon being commanded by management to leave their company-owned homes, flocked to the center of Iquique only to be decimated by soldiers' rifle fire. Such events were duplicated repeatedly in the early 1900s, and literally hundreds of workers died in the struggles.

Chile's first national labor central, the Gran Federación Obrera de Chile (GFOCH) evolved out of this decade of violence. Although formed at the behest of a Conservative attorney of the railroad workers' union who sought a political base, the nature of the central altered greatly during World War I, when it fell under Socialist hegemony, dropped the "Gran" from its title, and became more centralized in its organizational makeup. Luis Emilio Recabar-

---

[14] Studies of Chilean trade unionism can be found in Moisés Poblete T. and Ben G. Burnett, *The Rise of the Latin American Labor Movement* (New York, Bookman Associates, 1960); Robert Alexander, *Labor Relations in Argentina, Brazil, and Chile* (New York, McGraw-Hill Book Company, Inc., 1962) and *Organized Labor in Latin America* (New York, The Free Press, 1965).

ren now led FOCH, and in 1921 he moved it into the international Communist orbit. The stimulus given to trade unionism in Chile during World War I and the effectiveness of several strikes attracted ever more workers to trade unionism. A further spurt of growth occurred once President Arturo Alessandri promulgated a labor code in 1924.

The story of Chilean trade unionism is a cyclical one, and the next decade saw labor's fortunes more or less on the downgrade. A schism in Communist ranks and governmental persecution by the Ibáñez dictatorship (1925–31) bankrupted FOCH. Other confederations, trying to fill the void in labor leadership, came to the forefront. This only created a proliferation in unionism that weakened it, and when the depression struck, organized labor all but collapsed. True, a number of labor centrals held on during this era, but they merged and split with bewildering repetition until 1936, when the Socialists and the Communists could finally get together. The Confederación de Trabajadores de Chile (CTCH) resulted, though the two principal founding groups constantly fought between themselves and even broke the CTCH apart for a short period in 1939. Moreover, the Anarcho-Syndicalists stayed away in their own central, the Confederación General del Trabajo (CGT).

And yet at that time unionism experienced some of its best years, under the sympathetic policies of President Pedro Aguirre Cerda. Legislation which had been on the books for a dozen years or more was administered in labor's behalf; unions could collectively bargain and strike without fear of government coercion. In this unprecedented context of freedom, trade unionism flourished. During the Popular Front, labor's rolls swelled from 125,000 to 173,000, and the number of unions leaped from 932 to 1,919.[15] This impetus sustained labor after Aguirre Cerda's death, and a very large proportion of organizable workers (that is, excepting government and agricultural laborers) possessed union cards by the end of World War II.

The old Socialist-Communist rivalry erupted once again in 1946 and this time proved irreparable as far as the CTCH was concerned; each camp went off with its own components. The Socialist CTCH declined especially, and the Socialist party itself divided; Communists suffered renewed governmental antagonism when the González Videla administration sponsored the Law for the Defense of Democracy, which outlawed the Communist party. Actually, Socialists and others in the labor movement fell under the net of this law and came to know harassment as well.

The contemporary phase in trade unionism's evolvement coincides with the voters' decision in 1952 to bring Carlos Ibáñez back to the Presidency. Efforts to resurrect a confederation predated this event, though the election itself spurred labor to act quickly out of concern for the new Government's social policies. The result of deliberations was the establishment of a central, the Central Unica de Trabajadores de Chile (CUT), amalgamating

---

[15] John R. Stevenson, *The Chilean Popular Front* (Philadelphia, University of Pennsylvania Press, 1942), pp. 129–30.

Communist, Socialist, and moderate federations. By this time the two Marxist groups seemed to have learned the bitter lessons of dissension; in this period the two built a more solid organizational base, brought in white-collar workers along with laborers, and rallied a dominant percentage of organized labor under their aegis with the appeal that only with unity could trade unionism sustain itself. Nevertheless, unity remained a tenuous thing, as the Communists with their weaker partners, the Socialists, controlled a central whose largest single element in fact was the Christian Democrats. Clashes between Marxists and Christian Democrats occurred frequently, particularly because of the former's propensity to drag CUT into political activism. Other threats to unity stemmed from management opposition and its ability to capitalize on weakened labor areas to break unions, a wide current of distaste by many workers for the politicized nature of unionism, and the refusal, for a variety of reasons, of important segments to affiliate with CUT. Thus, while perhaps close to a half-million workers are union members, probably only a little more than 300,000 are in CUT. The most significant hold-outs are the maritime workers' Confederación Marítima de Chile (COMACH) and the white-collar workers' Confederación de Empleados Particulares de Chile (CEPCH), each with about 40,000 members.

Undoubtedly, lack of cohesion and the politicized nature of much of union leadership stand out among labor weaknesses, but they also derive from, and in a sense contribute to, deeper problems in economic and political processes which disrupt and at times even destroy legitimate labor practices. First of all, unions and particularly union leadership are often badgered by antagonistic employers, who utilize a host of weapons to inhibit labor's organizational efforts. These weapons range from subtle coercion to the devastating effects of the black list, that unfortunate invention which circulates the names of labor "agitators" among a management group that will refuse to hire any name so listed. (It must be pointed out here that countless employers in Chile maintain harmonious working relations with unions and that frequently union leaders bring abuse upon themselves for their own untoward and irresponsible acts. Still, there persists a sufficient number of anti-union practices among employers to warrant mention here.) More important in some ways, though, than the threats from management in the economic realm are legal limitations, which circumscribe trade unionism. Workers desirous of setting up a union must file a formal petition to this effect with the employer and the labor inspector. This procedure involves a good deal of red tape and usually a delay, which may introduce the coercive influences of management to discourage the union's formation. Once established, unions are subjected to multitudinous restrictions affecting their internal organization, financial procedures, and elections. Although in theory these are aimed at controlling unscrupulous union officials, the restrictions do militate against all types of leaders and their groups. For example, white-collar workers may not create a union shop; check-off of members' dues is not permitted, causing most unions to suffer extremely weak financial bases; strike funds may not be legally formed;

union revenues must be banked and cannot be withdrawn except with permission of the labor inspector (cash on hand is confined to the ridiculously low amount of fifteen cents, necessitating "pocket banking"); and excepting the highly privileged copper workers, no union leaders may be salaried by their organizations. The last restriction imposes unusual hardships on labor officials, who generally must work full-time elsewhere and then lend their services to the union in their free time. Interestingly, this last restriction redounds to the Communists' favor inasmuch as they have been the best organized of the political groups and draw upon their resources to underwrite their labor leaders' salaries, thus freeing them for full-time union activity.

Before 1965, agricultural workers lived in an atmosphere making unionism almost totally prohibitive. Only about ten percent of all the farms in Chile had the minimum number of workers required in order to try to set up a union, and even fewer farms had the requisite ten literate male adults that an agricultural union was required to include in its membership. Should by some unbelievable good fortune a farm become unionized, it could not federate with counterparts on other farms. Agricultural workers were precluded from striking during planting or harvesting—the only times when their voices might be heard. Not surprisingly, these and other restrictions kept labor-management relations at the feudal level, and only a paltry handful of all farm workers, less than 2,000 out of 300,000 total, were in unions.

In short, prior to the Frei administration, Chile's working classes, who carry the heaviest burden resulting from grave deficiencies in the economic system, found it the most difficult to articulate their needs through formal associations. Legal, managerial, and internal challenges frustrated those trade unions that did exist and severely confined their performance roles. Relative to the rest of Latin America, Chilean trade unionism appears strong because of its long history, the viability of many of its organizations, and the large number of urban workers unionized (though the total in Chile is less than twenty percent of the working force because of the farm situation and because of a primitive associational development in certain fields, such as textile and service industries). Still, in a society with high educational and political literacy among its citizenry and the presence of the revolution of rising expectations that is pervasive in so much of the world, the Chilean worker increasingly demands a larger share of the nation's income. He is frustrated as a wage earner, and he is frustrated in his union. He has come to be alienated from governments that talk but do not act. Such conditions increase the interaction of pressure groups and political parties; the latter seeks votes and electoral help from the former while in return the pressure groups seek satisfaction of claims upon the political system.

POLITICAL PARTIES

A multi-party system such as Chile's must often endure a certain immobility of the decision-making process and periods of stalemate and inaction.

The inability to put together working coalitions can reach serious proportions; even so large a support as the Christian Democrats boasted in the middle 1960s experienced their proffered reforms being debated almost to death by recalcitrant minorities. And yet on the positive side, the many political parties contesting for achievement of goals does offer a lively dialogue of fundamental doctrinal differences that not only brings forth critical issues for full public purview but also supplies opposing solutions wherein the voter can ascertain real choices. Such a span of views now depends primarily upon six agglomerations: on the right, the Conservatives and Liberals; in the center, the Radicals and Christian Democrats; and to the left, the Socialists and Communists (whose coalition is known as FRAP). To dispel any danger of misclassification at this juncture, it should be made clear that the spread of opinion in each of these parties is quite broad; hence, any concept of the traditionalists completely tied up in one neat package, the moderate reformers in another, and the revolutionaries in still a third is simply a distortion of fact.[16]

The Political Right

The present-day Conservative and Liberal parties owe their nineteenth-century origins to a political climate then common throughout Latin America. Personalized factions would agglomerate the few politically involved elements of the citizenry and carry on their competitive search for political resources above the heads of most of the population. During most of the first thirty years after independence, two vague groupings took form, the *pelucones,* or bigwigs, and the *pipiolos,* or greenhorns. By the middle of the nineteenth century, the two divided on the Church issue, and this issue orientation in turn helped to institutionalize the earlier factions into Conservatives and Liberals, respectively. Although other political structures were to appear, the Conservatives or Liberals controlled national political offices during most of the period up to 1920. However, throughout the parliamentary era (1891–1920), both parties divided and merged and needed to coalesce with other political structures in order to obtain majorities. The Conservative party counted upon landowners and urban supporters of the Church in the central provinces for membership; the Liberal party drew its components from mostly banking and commercial interests.

Long-established membership bases and programs largely carry down to the present day. Both parties depend heavily upon upper-class backing, continue to hold steadfastly to private enterprise, and yield to reform aiding the working classes only as a last resort. The proper role of the Church, the ancient issue splitting the two parties, no longer holds much substance. (Until 1966, the Conservative party limited its adherents to practicing Roman Cath-

---

[16] Among several helpful studies of political parties, see Sergio Guilisasti Tagle, *Partidos políticos chilenos* (Santiago, Editorial Nascimento, 1964); Donald W. Bray, "Chile: The Dark Side of Stability," *Studies on the Left,* IV (Fall 1964), 85–96; Peter G. Snow, "The Political Party Spectrum in Chile," *The South Atlantic Quarterly,* LXII, No. 4 (Autumn 1963), 474–87; Federico G. Gil, *The Political System of Chile* (Boston, Houghton Mifflin Company, 1966).

olics and hence was a confessional party.) It favors religious education in the public schools but speaks to this point so softly as not to endanger the party's alliance with the Liberals. Of the two, the Liberal party reflects a slightly more flexible stance, which permits it to perform the pivotal role in periodic coalitions encompassing Conservatives and center groups. The bulk of this rightist leadership can also be located in the powerful managerial associations, that is, in the Confederación de la Producción y del Comercio and its commercial, agricultural, mining, and manufacturing components. In 1966, the Conservatives and Liberals joined together as the Partido Nacional (PN, or National party).

The Political Center

Two of the most interesting political parties in all of Latin America are the Chilean Radical and Christian Democratic parties, the former for its historical role and the latter for its contemporary significance. Beginning in the 1860s as an offshoot of the Liberal party, the Radical party was mostly made up of wealthy provincials lacking social prestige and resenting the Santiago-controlled nature of the Liberal group. They were soon followed by elements of the middle sector, especially school teachers, and as the middle class expanded, the Radical party benefited from an enlarging electoral base, while the traditional parties experienced a proportional decline. To some extent the party garnered working-class sectors through its early reformist programs. The Radicals started to make an imprint on the political process in the 1920s, when they participated in the alliance underpinning the Arturo Alessandri regimes. The party finally saw Radical Presidents in power between 1938 and 1952.

From its founding, the Chilean Radical party emulated many aspects of its French namesake and served as a major instrument for change. The Chilean party's doctrine was secularist and "socialist." In fact, though, it was never truly socialist but simply favored emoluments and protection for its middle-class businessmen (and thus some government intrusion in the economy) and enlarging governmental functions, which necessitated greater numbers of government workers (most of whom were Radicals). Other planks in the Radical party's platform, which were government resting upon political parties, public education, the equality of women with men, wider freedoms, generally became part of Chilean political life, at least for the middle class. But an inherent incompatibility in membership created a disenchantment among workers and intellectuals with the pragmatic, bargaining nature of the party's more moderate elements. The wide umbrella which had sheltered urban and rural, middle-class and lower-class sectors no longer held sufficient meaning for those demanding immediate and profound changes in the economic and political systems. By 1958, when the Radicals entered the aristocratic regime of Jorge Alessandri, they had fallen into a measurable decline, and symptomatically, just as they coalesced with the old oligarchical Conservative and Liberal parties in that regime, the Radicals had to recognize an overwhelming loss of workers and students to the more liberal Christian Democrats and Marxists.

Christian Democracy took up the mantle of reform within a democratic context where the Radicals left off. Actually, the Christian Democrats started in the 1930s as the left wing of the Conservative party's youth movement. Stimulated by liberal papal encyclicals, Christian mysticism, and the practical experience of European Christian Democracy, they soon realized that their parent group mouthed Christian social precepts while closing off all avenues to their fulfillment. Consequently, after a few years of operating within the Conservative party, in 1938 this group spun off as a full-fledged political party, the Falange Nacional. Remaining miniscule for almost two decades, it never accumulated more than five percent of congressional or municipal votes until 1957, when it merged with another like-minded group and renamed itself the Partido Demócrata Cristiano. Almost from that moment it knew a meteoric ascendancy to power.

The Christian Democrats' unprecedented success rests upon the best leadership of Chilean political parties, a dynamism that inspires attention and excitement, and a readiness to move into governance of the nation at just the right time. Along with these attributes Christian Democracy offers an answer for Chile's ills in the form of a coherent and all-encompassing ideology that attracts those middle sectors desirous of fulfilling their "social conscience" and the politically alienated anticipating the satisfaction of their claims upon the political system. By the time Eduardo Frei led the Christian Democrats into the Presidency in 1964, he had expounded this ideology in more than a half-dozen books and countless articles and speeches.[17] Six principal currents reappear throughout: (1) Christianity is the moving spirit, but this is not to suggest that Christian Democracy is only for one sect; instead, it welcomes Catholics and non-Catholics, believers and nonbelievers. (2) Authentic democracy must replace the traditional paternalistic system so characteristic of all Latin America. Thus government must not only "formally guarantee rights, but it has to structure them in a form so as to permit all the citizens the plain exercise of them." (3) Humanism will strengthen man's political performance in such a pluralistic society by giving him dignity and a sense of individual worth. (4) Nationalism is to be reinforced in the Chilean people. However, this will not be a "nationalism of surrender" which upholds United States investments and all other actions as good for Chile, nor will it be a "nationalism of strategic hatred" against the United States that only stifles the possibilities for economic growth. Instead, Frei prefers the "nationalism of constructive co-operation," permitting Chile to seek harmonious relationships with the United States as long as those relationships are in Chile's best interest. (5)

---

[17] Two important statements in English are "Christian Democracy in Theory and Practice," in *The Ideologies of the Developing Nations,* ed. Paul E. Sigmund (New York, Frederick A. Praeger, Inc., 1964), pp. 309–20; "Paternalism, Pluralism, and Christian Democratic Reform Movements in Latin America," in *Religion, Revolution, and Reform,* ed. William V. D'Antonio and Frederick B. Pike (New York, Frederick A. Praeger, Inc., 1964), pp. 25–40.

For the completion of the ideal society, the only means to be considered is revolution, a fundamental alteration of the fabric of society. Nevertheless, it must be a "revolution in freedom." (6) Communitarianism marks the final stage in the emancipation of Chilean society. This phase is neither capitalist or socialist but a new way of life in which former antagonists, that is, management and labor, will be organized together "in the same hands." This goal will certainly occur in time, though if workers strive for it now (and it is they who must force the well-to-do to accommodate), the good life will be with them much sooner. Frei sums up his beliefs in the following manner:

> In Latin America we must today shoulder the responsibility of entering a new phase. The people wish to break with the old paternalism and ancient privileges, but do not wish to be led into dictatorships of any kind. They wish to progress and create new forms of social life. Latin Americans will not copy formulas that may have been suited to others but that are of no avail to them. I dream of a synthesis of justice and freedom in an economy that is based entirely on man's ability, not on inherited factors of money, class, or race. In Latin America it is man that must be made great.[18]

More specifically, the Christian Democrats called for "Chileanizing" foreign investments, breaking monopoly control of the economy, protecting and fostering trade unionism among rural as well as urban workers, instituting genuine agrarian reform, expanding and democratizing educational facilities, bringing about vastly improved working and living conditions for the impoverished, and broadening diplomatic and commercial relations with any and all nations that will promote Chile's welfare.

The Political Left

For the moment, Christian Democracy has been able to capture a vast following from among most classes because of the answers the movement seems to possess for the nation's chronic problems and because it came onto the scene at a time when the Conservatives, Liberals, and Radicals appeared bankrupt and unable or unwilling to face these problems. Frei and his coterie brilliantly capitalized on the majority's wishes for basic change within the democratic context. On the other hand, should they fail, the Socialists and the Communists stand ready to wrench the nation all the way to the left, even to destroying present political forms, in order to bring about the revolution sought by the massive, politically alienated, unemployed and underemployed, destitute portion of the population. The leftists almost had their opportunity in 1958, when their candidate, Salvador Allende, lost by less than 34,000 votes, out of a total of 1,250,000 cast for the presidential candidates.

The history of Marxist parties in Chile is one of confusion, countless vicissitudes, and deep cleavages. As has been noted, Luis Recabarren led the first national confederation of labor, FOCH, into the international Communist

---

[18] "Paternalism, Pluralism, and Christian Democratic Reform Movements in Latin America," pp. 39–40.

movement in 1921. Earlier, in 1912, he established the Socialist Labor party, which he also converted into a Communist vehicle in 1921. Communist fortunes experienced governmental antagonism during part of the following decade, and their own house split between Stalinists and Trotskyites, a breach that was not resolved until 1937, when the Stalinist camp came forth as the official Communist party. Meanwhile, a number of Socialist groupings made their appearance and sought to seize leadership from the struggling Communist factions. In 1933, the Socialists merged into the Socialist party of Chile and pushed their way into a majority control of the labor classes. This trend reversed in the 1940s, when the Communists jumped into predominance. Then a restoration of Socialist hegemony appeared in the ten years following the outlawing of the Communist party in 1948. By the 1960s the Communists were moving to the front once again. The Communists' strong organization, financial base, and leadership provided them with built-in advantages and a consequent resiliency that helped the party to bounce back after each crisis.

Chilean Communist doctrine is an intriguing mixture of the usual Soviet ideology and an adjustment to the Chilean context. Thus, the Chilean Communists typically support the Marxist-Leninist line, stressing dialectical materialism with its class-struggle concept and the certitude of the eventual workers' revolution. Along with their stand against feudalism, monopoly, and imperialism, the Communists seek to nationalize foreign ownership of Chilean natural resources as well as to place domestic monopolies and the *latifundia* under state control. This objective proves, the Communists insist, that they are the most nationalist of Chilean political parties, since they will return control of Chile's resources to the people of Chile. However, because of the political tradition of democracy in Chile, the Communists reject the idea of dictatorship and repeatedly insist that they will preserve the open society while making it much more pluralistic. This goal is to be accomplished by governing with several great mass parties that more truly reflect the will of the Chilean people than those ruling the nation to date. Finally, the present Communist leadership, especially through the voice of Secretary General Luis Corvalán, prefers the *vía pacífica,* or peaceful road, to achieving the Communist revolution. This preference brands the official Communist party as being on the side of the Soviet Union in the Moscow-Peking dispute and at the same time presents a more attractive methodology for change to most Chileans today than the violence advocated by *Pekingistas.* On the other hand, the failure of FRAP, the Communist-Socialist electoral coalition, to win the 1964 presidential election strengthened the claims of the small pro-Peking sector in the Communist orbit and of a much larger group in the Socialist party that the *vía pacífica* will never bear fruit.

Just as the Liberals are not really liberal and the Radicals not very radical, the Chilean Socialist party bears little resemblance to most Socialist parties in the so-called Western World. Their theoretical foundation is Marxist-Leninism, and they adhere to the usual belief in dialectical materialism. This belief includes the class struggle, the installation of the dictatorship of the proletariat, the socializing of the means of production and exchange, and the inevitability of a classless society. At first glance, one might assume a remarkably harmonious arrangement with the Communists. In fact, this is not the case at all. The two Marxist groups coalesce for expediency while engaging in an often vitriolic debate and contending for control of working-class associations. The Socialists have attacked their *Frapista* partners as championing Russian direction of international Marxism; the Socialists evince sympathy for the Yugoslavian example, which permits each nation to work out its own way to socialism. Socialists also rebuked Soviet-imposed military blocs as adding to international hostilities at a time when popular movements needed international peace to attain their goals. Moreover, the Socialists rejected the Communists' slavish devotion to Marxism as being dogmatic and often divorced from reality; the Socialists embraced Marxism as a scientific way of recognizing what is happening in society but not as a liturgy or an inflexible dictum. Of course, the Communists countered with arguments of their own. Actually, the Socialists exhibited a more extreme nationalism and a far greater freedom from outside controls. This freedom has permitted the Socialists to affiliate themselves variously with non-Soviet Communist movements. However, the Chilean Communists have found it perfectly possible to work within the parliamentary system, while the Socialists oppose it and persistently maintain that the existing political system is simply a tool of the oligarchy. This particular point of contention became manifest at the Communists' Thirteenth National Convention in October 1965, when Communist leaders proposed supporting progressive Christian Democratic legislation and the Socialists totally repudiated this policy line. Furthermore, the pro-Peking Socialist wing called for a hard line in contrast to the Communist official *vía pacífica*.

Conclusion on Political Groups

To summarize, then, political parties range over a wide doctrinal offering, from unfettered free enterprise to pro-Peking Marxism. The Conservatives and Liberals agglomerate managerial interest groups and, with the resultant vast economic and political resources, have succeeded in moderating and even halting occasional reform efforts. The Radicals suffer from a split personality; originally catering to the growing middle sector and staking an early claim to some labor-class support, especially among governmental workers, the Radicals tried to identify with disparate and increasingly antagonistic elements. More and more, the old oligarchy co-opted Radical businessmen onto managerial boards of directors and hence converted them to upper-class values if not always upper-class status. Both students and erstwhile Radical workers' groups flocked in ever greater numbers to the Left, and even opportunistic maneuvers failed to save the Radical party from declining in the 1960s.

At the same time that the traditionalists, often making common cause with the Radicals, blocked change, the demands for a radical transformation of society spread to larger numbers of Chileans, particularly as a result of endemic economic problems, which Christian Democrats and Marxists recognized with extensive programs of reform. The causes of these two groups were strengthened by their ability to activate such formerly quiescent elements as the impoverished farm population. The strains building up gave the first clue to the extent of political alienation in a congressional by-election held in March 1964. Then, in the almost completely rural district of Curicó, where politics had always been controlled by the landowning few, the *Frapista* candidate registered a surprising victory. The rightist coalition tumbled into disarray as the next months presaged the movement of Chilean politics to the left with the Christian Democrats and Marxists dominating the ensuing presidential and congressional elections.

PROCESSES OF FUNCTION AND DYSFUNCTION

Groups in society penetrate the political system with the goal of expressing their needs and then endeavoring to transfer their claims into policy. Toward this end the groups may utilize a variety of methods, from lobbying to street demonstrations, in order to bring pressure to bear on the decision-making process. Most important, in a representative system the citizenry must be able to reflect its wishes through regular and meaningful elections. One of the most compelling reasons for the very limited response of most Chilean governments to working class needs—in addition to the inherent associational weaknesses already noted—is to be found in the electoral process. Certain dysfunctional patterns have simply precluded the lower economic classes from finding full expression at the polls until very recently.

The Electoral System

The Chilean voter is called upon to express his electoral choice for four types of office-holders: municipal councilmen (*regidores*), national congressmen (both deputies and senators), and the nation's President.[19] The President is chosen by direct popular vote every six years (for example, 1958, 1964, 1970). However, if no candidate obtains an absolute majority of the ballots cast, the decision on who the winner is falls to Congress, which assembles in a joint session with each deputy and senator voting as an individual. Then the Congress chooses between the two candidates who secured the highest popular pluralities; historically, this procedure has always meant that the leading candidate received congressional approval. In 1964 the *Frapistas,* who had a definite minority of congressional seats, claimed that, should their nominee win a plurality but not a majority of the popular votes, the center-right would violate tradition and pick the second man on the list. Numerous Marxist labor

---

[19] Mario Bernaschina G., *Cartilla electoral* (Santiago, Editorial Jurídica de Chile, 1958); Ricardo Cruz Coke, *Geografía electoral de Chile* (Santiago, Editorial del Pacífico, S.A., 1952); *Chile: Election Factbook* (Washington, D.C., Institute for the Comparative Study of Political Systems, 1963); Federico G. Gil, *The Chilean Presidential Election of September 4, 1964* (Washington, D.C., Institute for the Comparative Study of Political Systems, 1965).

and political leaders threatened to "go to the streets" if that should occur. Since the Christian Democrats' Eduardo Frei actually carried an absolute majority, the issue did not arise.

Municipal councilmen and congressmen are selected by direct popular vote on the basis of the D'Hondt type of proportional representation. Thus, each electoral district produces several office-holders for the representative bodies. Commonly, most municipal councils are composed of five *regidores*, but departmental capitals have seven, provincial centers nine, and Valparaíso and Santiago twelve and fifteen, respectively. The electoral districts for the Chamber of Deputies select a more varied number, with three to five being the most common, though rising to eighteen in Santiago's first district. Senators are elected from nine districts, each having five Senate seats. All deputies and approximately half the senators stand election every four years (for example, 1961, 1965, 1969); elections for *regidores* used to occur in three-year intervals but beginning in 1967 take place every four years. Since the municipalities are virtually powerless, elections for councilman posts attract primary interest as a bellwether of political party strength.

Generally, electoral procedure has evolved into a democratic and meaningful process in modern times. Still, it has not been completely devoid of problematic aspects. Under the 1925 Constitution literate males twenty-one years or more were obligated to register and vote though the compulsory feature was largely ignored. In 1949, women gained the franchise. One grave shortcoming of the registration process reduced the citizenry's voting capacity; registration offices were open for only a very few hours. During the 1950s, offices were open for only about four percent of the average work time in Chile. This proved to be a particular handicap for the working classes, who found it difficult to obtain a release from their employment in order to register. If there was a line-up, they often had not been granted sufficient time to complete the registration process.[20] This difficulty affected as many as twenty-six percent of those legally entitled to vote. Improvements in the system were finally enacted in 1962 which created permanent registration, and at about the same time a longer period to register was ordered.

For the most part, the balloting process itself is conducted under fair and impartial boards of scrutiny, and vote-counting is carried out honestly. Any political party can list its candidates on the ballot once that party has filed the necessary information with electoral authorities. The principal requirement, that a party must be endorsed by a signed petition of 10,000 registered voters, is not a serious deterrent to such groups. Only independent candidates at times find it difficult to acquire the requisite number of signatures, of which 2,000 for a deputy, 5,000 for a senator, and 20,000 for President are needed. Violence is not unknown but is uncommon. Certain coercive techniques have been part of the stock in trade of traditionalist elements. In the rural areas especially, landowners ordered qualified voters on their estates to cast ballots

---

[20] *Ercilla,* August 22, 1956.

for conservative candidates, and frequently votes were purchased. Similar practices could be found in some urban-management situations. As recently as the Curicó by-election of 1964, the conservative electoral front banked a large sum of cash with the intent of spreading the largesse for vote-buying. On learning of this move, the Christian Democrats joined with the Marxists to keep the rightists physically from entering the bank to make a withdrawal. Such techniques are rapidly becoming passé as reformist parties play upon working-class needs for fundamental change instead of on just a bread and circus approach at election time.

An intriguing electoral phenomenon in recent years has been the expanding number of citizens expressing their wishes at the polls. The proportion of those who registered grew from roughly one-eighth of the total population in the 1940s to more than a third in the 1960s. This increase can be explained partly by the addition of women's votes after 1949 and partly by improved registration procedures. In addition, swelling alienation from do-nothing regimes undoubtedly had its impact on election turnouts. Statistics on the percentage of the total population who actually voted in the last four presidential elections dramatically substantiate this trend: in 1946, 8.73 percent voted, in 1952, 15.95 percent, in 1958, 17.90 percent, and in 1964, 31.82 percent.

The 1964 presidential election was remarkable from the opening of the campaign to the announcement of the voters' decision. In Chile the formal campaign process may not begin until six months before the date of the presidential election (two months in the case of congressional and municipal elections), but by that time many things have already transpired. Shortly after the April 7, 1963, municipal elections were concluded, four candidates actively sought support for their presidential aspirations. Right-wing elements of the Radical party succeeded in carrying the Radicals into an electoral alliance with the Liberals and Conservatives. Calling itself the Frente Democrático (FD, or the Democratic Front), the alliance nominated the right-wing Radical Julio Durán, who had come up from his party's youth movement to be a deputy and then a senator since 1957. Durán demonstrated excellent stage presence and youthful vigor (he was forty-six years old in 1964), and the fact that the Front's three component groups had won slightly over forty-six percent of the votes cast in the 1963 municipal elections engendered optimism among FD members that their candidate held the inside track to victory.

The Socialists and Communists, along with the small hanger-on PADENA, Partido Democrático Nacional, had coalesced into FRAP, Frente de Acción Popular, or Popular Action Front, and now renominated their 1958 standard-bearer, Salvador Allende Gossens, a physician and Socialist senator who only narrowly lost to Jorge Alessandri in 1958. Allende at fifty-six was the oldest of the candidates and, though a Marxist, came from the professional upper class. Some critics considered him rather foppish, an image he sought to dispel by shaving off his mustache and appearing in a less flamboyant manner. Still, his followers prized him as one of their own, a man of means with a genuine social conscience.

The logical choice of the Christian Democrats for their presidential nominee, Eduardo Frei Montalva had helped to found the Christian Democratic party (known as the Falange Nacional in earlier times) when a number of youths broke away from the Conservative party. Frei had alienated the upper class by this act. Moreover, he continually attacked the upper class as well as the conservative regime of Jorge Alessandri (1958–64). Undoubtedly his background as a law professor and senator helped Frei to gain a reputation as a notable opponent in debate and, together with a stately appearance and manner, marked him as a formidable campaigner. He had been the first member of his party to gain a seat in the Senate, had received twenty-one percent of the vote in the 1958 presidential election, and now at fifty-three years of age would become Latin America's first Christian Democratic President.

The candidacy of the far rightist Jorge Prat Eschaurren held only nuisance value for the campaign. A follower of the *caudillo* Carlos Ibáñez, in whose administration Prat had served as Minister of Finance, his posture was personalist and independent, against politics, big business, and the United States. Some concern existed that the forty-six-year-old candidate might cut into one of the other three front-runners' voting strength.

The campaign unfolded in typical Chilean style as the candidates scurried throughout the Republic in developing organization, seeking financial aid, and talking to anyone who would listen. All the media were filled with their wanderings, charges and countercharges, and estimates of their relative standing among the voters. Then, in the otherwise minor special election for deputy held in the rural district of Curicó in March 1964, the tone of the campaign altered. All three major candidates staked a great deal on the outcome of the Curicó race and converted it into a micropresidential election. Durán announced that, if the Democratic Front did not win, he would withdraw his candidacy—seemingly a safe statement, since the Front had previously accumulated almost as many votes as the total of Frapist and Christian Democratic ballots. Meanwhile, FRAP had been increasingly registering strong inroads in the rural areas, considered the Frapist chances to be very good in Curicó, and so accepted it as a welcome proof of superior national strength. The Christian Democrats unwillingly entered a candidate of their own in the contest as well; Prat refused to do so and, standing on the side lines, attacked the entire process.

When the last ballot was counted, the Democratic Front's pre-election claim of 56 percent of the votes proved absurd, as it received only 32.5 percent. The Frapist candidate won with 39.5 percent. Now the Democratic Front collapsed. Durán resigned though was later compelled to re-enter the campaign in order to try to hold the Radical party together. The Liberals and Conservatives faced a critical dilemma. They disliked Frei but feared that, if they backed Prat, they might permit Allende to sneak into the Presidency by a small plurality. Hence, they ended up throwing their weight to Frei, and Prat stepped out of the running—effectively reducing the race to a contest between Frei and Allende.

The most important change in the campaign in subsequent months was the increasing emphasis on Allende's being controlled by the Communists and the recurring propaganda asking Chileans if they wanted to go the way of Cuba. This propaganda evoked images of dictatorship, executions, and children being taken from their mothers and sent off to the Soviet Union. Actually, the two candidates' programs possessed elements of great similarity; both candidates attacked the incumbent, do-nothing Alessandri regime and demanded the deepest political, economic, and social reforms. Indeed, both insisted that only revolution would answer Chile's needs. However, Frei denounced the Frapist revolution as being "with dictatorship" and instead offered his own "revolution in freedom." Allende countered with the claim that the Christian Democrats would really bring "exploitation in freedom," the Frapists planning a "revolution without blood."

Most significant here is the stress upon revolution. The conservatives had to support Frei as the lesser of two very unpleasant evils, more of the conservatives probably liked Allende but were fearful of his Marxist beliefs and Communist ties. This alliance left the Christian Democrats comparatively free to pursue their reformist program and capture the allegiance of the poor, among whom dissidence was ubiquitous.

In line with Chile's generally unbroken democratic tradition, the Government remained scrupulously impartial, election day passed devoid of improprieties, and the voting process was carried out in total honesty. In the end Christian Democracy recorded a clean sweep: Frei garnered 56.1 percent of the vote (1,409,012 votes), Allende followed with 38.9 percent (977,902 votes), and Durán could only pull in 5 percent (125,233 votes). Frei carried nineteen of Chile's twenty-five provinces, narrowly lost in five of the remaining six, overwhelmingly won in Santiago and Valparaíso (Allende's district), and captured 60.5 percent of the women's vote (compared to Allende's 35.7 percent). Unexpectedly, the Christian Democrats defeated FRAP among rural workers, did exceedingly well in the urban slums, found a large following among northern miners (a long-standing leftist stronghold), and even mustered a majority in Valdivia, which the *Freista* hierarchy had viewed in advance as a certain loss. Frei's magnetism, strong organizational base, doctrinal dynamism, and, very importantly, the Communist issue—all contributed to the extraordinary Christian Democratic victory.

From another viewpoint, the 1964 election seemed to manifest widespread and growing insistence upon change. For one reason or another, ninety-five percent of Chileans voted for revolution—either Christian Democratic or Marxist. This move to the Left was repeated in the equally incredible and perhaps more revealing congressional elections held in March 1965. The popularity of Christian Democracy continued to climb to precedent-shattering heights. The Christian Democrats won 82 of 147 deputies' seats—strikingly more than their own most optimistic prediction of 60. Christian Democracy was the first political party to hold a majority in the Chamber of Deputies in well over a century. The party only put up candidates for twelve senatorial seats and won all twelve. Unfortunately, including a carry-over of one senator, the party controlled but 13 of the Senate's 45 seats—a minority situation that would act as a serious barrier to Christian Democratic reform efforts. Meanwhile, the Socialists and Communists survived the election in an even stronger position with 33 deputies, compared to 28 in the previous congressional election. Of course, the recipients of the voters' wholesale rejection of old styles and outdated solutions were the former partners of the Democratic Front. Their combined representation in the Chamber of Deputies toppled from 84 to 29; the Radicals had only half of their former strength, and the Liberals-Conservatives had one-fifth. Clearly, Chile had shifted to the Left. Now the remaining question hinged on what Frei could do with such an obvious mandate in the way of translating his programs into action.

The Decision-making Process

The structural framework in which the decision-making and decision-enforcing process operates in Chile depends upon a separation of powers at the national level. The relationships of the three branches, and especially of the executive and legislative, were redefined at various times in history. In 1830, after several years of great political turbulence, Diego Portales molded a governing mechanism based upon the authority of the Executive and impersonality, regularity of procedures, and legitimacy. Three Presidents, each holding office ten years, heeded Portales' prescription and brought stability and order to Chile. This era, often referred to as the Autocratic Republic, was succeeded by another thirty years, the Liberal Republic, when Presidents still wielded enormous authority but rested upon political party support. The Parliamentary Republic, which followed (1891–1920), saw the implanting of a semiparliamentary government and the total dominance of political parties. Executive authority passed into legislative hands manipulated by shifting coalitions of political parties, and "systematic disorder" characterized their dealings.[21] Nevertheless, during these years literacy increased with the expansion of public education, freedoms of speech and assembly were generally respected, and while the Radical party grew with the enlarging middle sector, new political parties and trade unions also came forth to speak for the workers. In 1920 the middle and working classes elected Arturo Alessandri Palma President and for the first time reduced the oligarchy's monopoly of political power. The Alessandri-sponsored Constitution of 1925 ensured this transformation by restoring powers to the popularly elected President at the expense of the oligarchy-controlled Legislature.

Although the Constitution of 1925 strengthened the position of the Executive, it also rimmed him with circumscriptions to inhibit his ability to become tyrannical or abusive. He serves a six-year term to ensure him time to develop policy, but Chile pioneered in forbidding no immediate re-election (as early as 1871, the one-term rule became a part of the constitutional system).

---

[21] Francisco Frías Valenzuela, *Manual de Historia de Chile* (Santiago, Editorial Nascimento, 1963), p. 561.

The President employs wide appointive powers and need not cater to the military by drawing from that group for members of his Cabinet or other high offices though his selection of major military, diplomatic, and sub-Cabinet administrative officers require senatorial approval; he is Commander-in-chief of the armed forces, issues pardons, calls special sessions of the Legislature, and employs great budgetary authority. He also promulgates decrees that augment and sometimes even alter legislative enactments. In periods of especial crisis, the President may declare a state of siege, but this power is more closely defined and restricted than in the rest of Latin America (that is, Congress must approve the declaration and, if not in session, must be convened within sixty days to decide whether to continue or halt this condition). Contrary to abusive practices elsewhere, the President may not imprison political offenders. In order to qualify for the Presidency, a person must be a native-born Chilean, thirty years old or more, and possess the right to vote. Most Chilean Presidents manage their powers with restraint and offer a picture of decorum and integrity. Ordinarily they are quite accessible and informal. Jorge Alessandri daily walked from his bachelor apartment the several blocks to his executive offices in La Moneda, was unaccompanied by guards and chatted with passers-by; he was an aristocrat performing democratically, in line with the preferences of his compatriots.

There is no vice-presidential office in Chile. A 1942 decree ranks members of the ministry in order of precedence, beginning with the Minister of the Interior, to succeed the President. Should such a succession occur, new elections for President must be held within sixty days. The Chief Executive appoints his own ministry, comprising twelve portfolios and, because of the multi-party system, often enlarges the Cabinet in order to provide representation for the several parties in his coalition. The President also appoints with Senate consent, but does not control, a particularly significant and unique officer, the Comptroller General, who oversees all nonlegislative financial matters. Undoubtedly the controllership general, which acts as a powerful check on the executive branch of government, is one of the most important reasons for the relatively higher level of official deportment found in Chile, especially in comparison to that in most of Latin America.

As has been implied, the President can call upon extensive authority to govern, and he holds the most significant position among the three governmental branches. By the same token, he is closely guarded by restrictions imposed upon him by the Constitution as well as by other institutions in order to delimit usurpatious tendencies. Contrary to Latin American practices generally, the Congress acts as the most important of these checks. Indeed, the Chilean Congress ranks as the most influential in Latin America. A bicameral body, it contains a Senate of forty-five members elected for eight years, of whom roughly half stand election every four years, and a Chamber of Deputies of 147 representatives, all selected at each four-year election. Both benefiting and suffering from the parliamentary era, the Congress gained a sense of individuality and jealousy of its authority, while its frequent directionlessness created a certain popular disenchantment over the inability of Congress to cope with problems by enacting laws. Still, it has stood up to the President on many occasions and in many ways through exercising its impeachment power, refusing to grant exceptional powers to the President, not ratifying treaties negotiated by the executive branch, and often declining to pass legislation requested by the President. As a carry-over from parliamentary experience, ministers appear in Congress to debate in behalf of their proposals. On the other side of the coin, deputies and senators occasionally challenge a minister so vigorously as to leave him no alternative but to resign from his post. Congress establishes rules to govern itself and passes on the qualifications and conduct of its members; congressmen are protected by broad immunity when acting in their official capacity; and, rare for the hemisphere, the Chilean Congress maintains adequate bill-drafting services, including what is almost certainly the outstanding congressional library in Latin America.

The Chilean judicial system acquired a certain stature almost by default. In the seesaw power struggle between the executive and legislative branches, both tended to leave the courts alone. As a consequence, while the judicial branch is the weakest of the three, for the most part judges have been independent, apolitical, and capable. A rule of law permeates the Chilean political system, and constitutional law carries great weight. The Supreme Court, or Corte Suprema, at the apex of the judiciary, is composed of thirteen members who are self-perpetuating with presidential approval. Usually they sit *en banc* and, among other functions, may produce decisions of a quasi-judicial review nature—that is, passing on the constitutionality of the enforcement of given laws but not invalidating the law itself. In time, a law so challenged several times becomes invalid. High-court jurists must have been practicing lawyers for at least fifteen years. Three levels of courts of appellate and original jurisdiction adjudicate below the Supreme Court. Of particular interest are innumerable special courts, dealing with real property assessment, mining, communications and transportation, patents and trademarks, customs, military, juvenile (Chile is in the forefront in Latin America regarding the handling of problems affecting youth), and other matters. The large number of these courts permits the development of expertise among those dealing with specialized law. Although Chilean court procedure generally can be credited with meting out justice, it sometimes is criticized for its costliness and slowness.

The relationship of the national and local governmental units is not only unitary but also highly centralized. In fact, many observers appraise local institutions as virtually useless. The governing officials of most local governments (that is, from largest to smallest: provinces, departments, subdelegations, and districts) are appointed and controlled by the Minister of the Interior. Only municipal councilmen are popularly elected, and their acts are subject to the veto of an intendant chosen by the Interior Minister. The frustrations of local officials over their inability to act upon their own affairs and over alleged rebuffs from Santiago to pleas for attention to their needs has engendered widespread dissatisfaction at the local level. Indeed, local officials in one northern town went so far as to raise the Bolivian flag over the city hall in order to demonstrate their irritation with national disregard for their problems. In the 1960s, such dissatisfaction accentuated an old political issue and gave it new import. Nonetheless, more basic problems in the decision-making process needed resolving before an invigoration of local authority would be possible.

CONCLUSION: A PROGNOSIS OF STABILITY AND INSTABILITY

The endemic social and economic problems outlined in this chapter in large measure owe their perpetuation to inadequacies in the political system. Paradoxically, perhaps, these political deficiencies are not too closely related to the political shortcomings characterizing most other Latin American nations; that is to say that, while much of the hemisphere is still at a primitive level of constitutional political development, Chile has achieved an enviable state of democracy and stability. Instead, the challenges of dysfunctionalism in Chile reside primarily in the inability or unwillingness of successive administrative regimes to convert campaign promises into functioning policy. In short, a serious current of immobilism marks the decision-making process.

During 1963 and 1964, Santiago's leading universities sponsored a series of conferences which sought to root out the causes of this immobilism. By and large, the participants concluded that the 1925 Constitution was probably due for an overhaul and in particular that the office of the President should be granted greatly augmented authority. Certainly, many of Chile's Chief Executives found it all but impossible to deal with a chronically recalcitrant Congress. The nation's traditional multi-party system—almost purposely emulative of pre-De Gaullist France and suffering from similar inadequacies— survived the 1925 constitutional transition from a parliamentary to a presidential form of government. Thus, despite his relatively stronger constitutional role, the President still had to try to manipulate diverse interests represented in Congress by the numerous political parties. Usually he could not pull together a workable majority coalition. For example, President Carlos Ibáñez was not able to budge Congress during a particularly grave economic crisis in the 1950s, though he tried both coercion and conciliation. On the one hand, he established a constitutional commission to find ways to strengthen the President's hand in his dealings with the Legislature. Congress balked, and the commission failed. Moreover, Ibáñez' attempts to find a working coalition by reshuffling his Cabinet (nineteen times in four and a half years) also came to naught.[22] Jorge Alessandri, who followed Ibáñez in the Presidency, expressed dismay over precisely the same difficulties and proposed that, when an execu-

---

[22] Robert E. Scott, "Legislatures and Legislation," in *Government and Politics in Latin America,* ed. Harold E. Davis (New York, The Ronald Press Company, 1958), p. 298.

tive-legislative impasse occurs, the citizenry should be consulted, either by means of a plebiscite or by the dissolution of Congress and calling for new congressional elections.

To a lesser extent, but still an important causal factor in the overall problem of immobilism, the bureaucracy also impedes policy effectuation. On the positive side, the bureaucracy is comparatively honest and in such agencies as the Office of the Comptroller General and CORFO, the Development Corporation, is very professional. Still, the number of civil servants is excessive, and the nit-picking nature of countless jobs reduces the effectiveness of administration. Too many bureaucrats enjoy sinecures protected by political interests, especially by the Radicals, who dominate the civil service. But above all, the *trámite,* or system, is fraught with ponderous procedures that inhibit the quick and effective application of rules. (This writer still shudders on recalling the daily negotiations necessary to acquire a visa in a few weeks instead of in the usual months-long period.)

But again, congressional inaction remains the single greatest deterrent to satisfying group claims on the political system. And rarely in Chilean history did the nature of this problem become as strikingly apparent as during the first years of Eduardo Frei's Presidency. Out of the hotly contested campaign of 1964, Frei carried an absolute majority of the votes to win the Presidency with the enthusiastic or reluctant support of virtually every segment of the Chilean populace. But his Christian Democrats remained a minority in a lame-duck Congress that refused even to listen to presentations by Cabinet members on proposed reforms. Because of a congressional rule that legislative matters defeated in one session must wait until the following year for reconsideration, Frei was forced to withdraw his programs or see them defeated and put off for a full year. Rightists attacked his measures as moving too fast, and leftists simply followed their practice of generally opposing anything they did not propose themselves. Meanwhile, President Frei and his ministers put in eighteen-hour working days seven days a week to bring about changes which could be made by presidential decrees and to be ready for a hoped-for enlarged congressional delegation. The March 1965 congressional victories vindicated those efforts to the extent of gaining an absolute (and almost completely unprecedented) majority in the Chamber of Deputies. Since the Chamber is the stronger house of the Legislature and since even a one-third plurality is ordinarily considered a sufficiently large base for bargaining successfully with other parties, it was generally held that nothing now existed to keep the program from being implemented. Unfortunately, the Senate alone persisted in its obduracy. Slightly less than half of the Senate seats (21 of 45) were up for election in 1965, and the Christian Democrats erred in offering candidates in only a dozen districts, all of which the party won, but which with an additional carry-over still left the Christian Democrats with far less than a majority.

Thus, Frei's most earnest and dedicated efforts to answer the nation's needs with a dynamic, vigorous, and coherent program of reform, his "revolution in freedom," faced the opposition coalition in the Senate. He inflamed the right-wing parties by demanding the highest taxes in history and a completely re-evaluated property assessment base, by insisting on authentic agrarian reform with a removal of the constitutional restriction necessitating immediate cash payment for expropriated estates, and by countless other social and economic policies that would disrupt the aristocracy's favored position. The Leftists fought hard to defeat the Christian Democratic program because it did not go far enough or because they were not the authors of it. Still, against incredible political odds that were compounded by natural disasters, Frei pushed ahead on a broad front. Labor laws were liberalized and even agricultural workers could now organize quite freely into unions. A somewhat watered-down version of Frei's copper bill passed into law and hence gave the nation a greater share of its most valuable natural resource. Educational facilities and public housing expanded at an exceptional pace, and significant advances in combatting the galloping inflation were observable. Chile expected to end 1967 with the impressive economic growth rate of 7.5 percent and an increase in per-capita income of five percent. President Frei sought to achieve additional economic gains with effective land reform and greater agricultural production; through the expansion of steel, oil, and other industrial sectors; and by working with other Latin American nations towards the creation of a vigorous common market for Latin America. In his efforts to bring about the formation of a common market, Frei scored personal triumphs at economic conferences in Bogotá in 1966 and in Punta del Este in 1967.

In 1967 Frei undoubtedly stood out as the most popular and admired of Chilean leaders; but his regime never really enjoyed a political honeymoon, and each month in office brought new difficulties. Copper workers had gone out on strike some twenty times during Frei's first sixteen months in office. Ostensibly, these work stoppages were economic, but the Government labeled them political, solely aimed at destroying reforms by reducing revenues from the mines, an amount that already reached almost 60 million dollars.

In a Valparaíso by-election in March 1966, the Christian Democratic candidate won but with a lesser margin than the party had carried in that district a year earlier. Moreover, the Christian Democrats slipped in strength in the April 1967 municipal elections, while the Radicals and Communists experienced gains. However, the election's long-range meaning is uncertain. Municipal elections usually impinge more on local personalities than on national politics and a certain letdown in the ruling regime's support in off-year elections is not surprising. Moreover, the voter turnout of fourteen percent was the lowest in three decades and so could not be construed as an accurate measurement of the parties' national strength. On the other hand, Frei had personally called upon the Chilean voters to renew his mandate by giving a large vote to the Christian Democratic candidates; in this sense he suffered a loss. Indeed, some alleged that Frei's popularity was on the downgrade and that this presaged even more serious days to come.

Whatever the case, Frei's Promoción Popular seemed caught up in a false dilemma. The oligarchy supported him as being preferable to the Marxist Allende but largely frustrated Frei's reforms. (Some of the upper class and many of the middle class did, however, underwrite his programs enthusiastically.) The Left demanded revolution but would not co-operate in enacting even statutory measures they themselves were already on record as favoring. Frei sought to make operable programs which most of the working classes demanded, but the immobilist features of the political system checked the fulfillment of those programs and consequently increased the likelihood of additional working-class alienation and possibly conflict.

As has been noted, the Senate remains the most serious single obstacle to Frei's program of reform and at times it has acted in the most irresponsible manner. For example, in January 1967 Frei requested the Senate's permission to leave the country in order to visit the United States. Usually, this is only a perfunctory matter; but in this case both the Left and the Right joined to refuse his request. Nevertheless, some shifts in political allegiances may be in the offing which could accrue to Frei's ultimate advantage. Most importantly, the unity of the *Frapista* coalition appears to be in jeopardy. For while the Socialists continue to oppose any law which the Government proposes, the Communists have begun to demonstrate a more flexible attitude. In some instances, such as an agrarian reform, the Communists have favored the principle, if not all of the details, of the proposal; at other times, as occurred in the vote against Frei's trip to the United States, the Communists have followed the Radical party's lead. Hints of a possible dissolution of FRAP could also be observed in student elections at the University of Chile, when the Socialists and Communists offered separate lists of candidates, as well as in the Communists' rather conciliatory attitude toward the Government in their Thirteenth Party Congress at a time when the Socialists tried to push the Communists into a far more militant stand.

It is still much too early to evaluate the ultimate impact of Christian Democracy on Chile. However, one factor seems certain: Most Chileans want, indeed demand, change, and if Christian Democracy cannot override institutional inadequacies to answer that demand, the probability of any other *democratic* groups being able to do so is very slight.[23]

[23] The author is indebted to the Social Science Research Council for a grant to Chile in 1963–1964 which enabled him to interview Eduardo Frei, Salvador Allende, and scores of other Chilean leaders. Also, he would like to express his appreciation to Luis Quirós-Varela, Jaime Undurraga Matta, and Steven Hughes for their helpful comments.

14 / Paraguay

PAUL E. HADLEY

PAUL E. HADLEY, Professor of International Relations and Dean of University College and Summer Session at the University of Southern California, served with the U.S. Department of State as Director of the Centro Cultural Paraguayo-Americano in Asunción, Paraguay (1942–44) and as head of the Cultural Institutes Unit (1945). He was the first regular chairman of the Pacific Coast Council on Latin American Studies. His publications include "Cuba and Co-existence," "Internal Institutions and External Assistance: Some Political Implications of the Alliance for Progress," and "Tensions of Development in Latin America."

POLITICAL ENVIRONMENT

Geography and Demography

Although the people of Paraguay have fought heroically to preserve their national identity, it is an irony of history that they have not succeeded in populating their land. Today their country still remains almost a classic illustration of the hollow frontier concept. In each of the last three centuries, the progress of Paraguay toward stability has been frustrated by cataclysmic events. In 1767, before independence, the suspension of the Jesuit order brought an end to the Guaraní reductions and left the borderlands exposed. A century later, the War of the Triple Alliance ended with the literal decimation of the people and a second return to helplessness. Biological and political reconstruction was again frustrated in the 1930s, when the effort of the Chaco War sacrificed thousands of the country's capable young men. Almost miraculously, however, instead of returning to negativism, the nationalistic spirit of

Paraguay has built upon the success of the Chaco. A century after the catastrophe of 1870, the nation may at last be in the process of becoming a viable nation-state with an effective deployment of its population throughout its 157,000 square miles of territory. The present population increase, at the rate of 2.65 percent per year (estimated 1964), has brought the total to 2 million, the largest in the country's history, but still one of the smallest in the hemisphere; in Paraguay there are fewer than 13 persons per square mile, and the population is still largely concentrated in the environs of Asunción, the capital city, which has a populace of 300,000.

Large areas of the country remain completely unpopulated even in the zone of rich land to the east of Asunción. Although the land is Paraguay's chief resource, less than 2 percent is at present under cultivation.[1]

The national territory is divided into two contrasting zones. To the west of the Paraguay River lies two-thirds of the country: the Gran Chaco, which has an inhospitable, unstable climate and an equally forbidding landscape of irregular plains and marshes extending almost to the foothills of the Bolivian Andes. The Gran Chaco is used only in part for cattle raising, and oil explorations in the area have been unsuccessful. Only 4.2 percent of the population lives in the Chaco. To the east lies the smaller but better region, which has a fairly steady subtropical climate, rich arable soil, and a potentially remunerative stand of virgin hardwoods.

Paraguay is an impoverished country. The national budget is about 40 million dollars per year, and per capita income is less than two hundred dollars. Fifty-two percent of the active inhabitants, many of them at the subsistence level, are engaged in agriculture and livestock-raising. Gross domestic production (GDP) is increasing slightly faster than the population, but poverty cannot be relieved for many years. After the expulsion of the Jesuit masters of the Guaraní mission reductions in 1767, the majority of the population became squatters upon the land. They are proud and egalitarian in a unique way, desperately needy yet inherently resistant to organized change.

Lack of internal and external communication has contributed to the national frustration of Paraguay. Until recently, only one interior center, Villarrica, a town of 35,000, was readily accessible from Asunción. Reaching Concepción, in the north, required a two-day journey by boat, and Encarnación, in the southeast, a painful trip by an antiquated railroad. During the 12 years of the present administration, however, the highway mileage has been quadrupled to a total of 8,000 miles, of which 1,000 are hard surface. With major assistance from the United States and some help from Brazil, a network of roads has been developed which will not only connect all the major towns but will effectively reach the borders of Brazil and Bolivia as well as Argentina. A national military airline, which also carries civilian passengers and goods, is contributing to national integration. The Central Railroad, recently

---

[1] Perhaps the best description of the data on the demographic and economic situation of Paraguay in 1965 is found in Inter-American Development Bank, *Social Progress Trust Fund, Fifth Annual Report, 1965*, pp. 490–512.

transferred from British to national ownership, runs the 275 miles from Asunción to Encarnación.

Although Asunción, which was founded in 1537, represented the first Spanish settlement in the River Plate area, it was inevitably superseded in importance by the estuary port of Buenos Aires. From colonial policy, as well as geographic determinism, then, the Paraguayans developed a feeling of claustrophobia. Located 1,000 miles from the sea, they have faced logistic problems, commercial discrimination, and interference with navigation rights in efforts to export agricultural products. The undoubted paranoia of the first dictator of Paraguay, Dr. Gaspar Rodríguez de Francia, was in a way only an extreme manifestation of the national psychology. Even today the Ministry of Foreign Affairs is devoting much of its energy to lifting Argentine interference with traffic on the Paraná and protesting Brazilian encroachment in the Guairá Rapids section of the Alto Paraná.

Social Composition

The Paraguayans are a remarkably homogeneous people. Introverted because of their external frustrations, they have been thrown more upon each other than is the case in most modern societies; a sometimes fierce xenophobia has created bonds of nationalism which transcend the continuous internecine party strife. The catastrophic reduction of the male population in the 1860s and in the 1930s tended to obliterate genealogical niceties along with social distinctions. Class discrimination has inevitably risen again somewhat as a few of the original great families have re-established their position and as a new aristocracy has been created out of financial, military, or political success. For decades, however, there have been unifying privations which have made comrades of the poor and the not-so-poor. Aristocratic lines tend to be flexible, and there is a commonness of touch which gives pride to the serving class and informality to the masters. The workman carries a threadbare coat as a forlorn symbol of gentility, and the dean of the university speaks Guaraní, the tribal language which makes ninety percent of the people bilingual. Only a handful of *criollos* can boast pure Hispanic parentage, and hardly twenty thousand Indians remain unassimilated. Negroes are few, and the rare sight of a black-skinned workman on the street provokes profane reference to the Brazilian occupation of 1870.

Educational facilities have been developed fairly rapidly in recent years. Perhaps three-quarters of the people have had some schooling and, speaking loosely, may be called literate. The level falls off rapidly. Only fifteen percent finish elementary school. Perhaps one-tenth of these enter one of the two universities in Asunción. The National University accommodates between five and six thousand students, and Our Lady of Asunción Catholic University has an enrollment of 1500. Secondary and normal schools serve about 30,000; not more than 5,000 students are enrolled in technical institutions.

The majority of the people are at least nominally Catholic, and the Church remains established. Its services are, however, inadequate for the needs of the rural population. There are a few Protestant and foreign Catholic missions.

Historical Perspective

For the nationalist Paraguayan the past is indeed here to stay. The mastheads of most of the newspapers follow the lead of the government publication *Patria* in carrying the legend, "Centenario de la Epopeya Nacional de 1864–70," and even the relatively cosmopolitan, apolitical *La Tribuna* runs a daily feature recounting the events of the heroic war of 1865, when Paraguay, under Francisco Solano López, fought Argentina, Brazil, and Uruguay. Modern political history begins with the founding of the Liberal and Colorado parties out of the wreckage of the "National Epic." The Liberals are not allowed to forget their origin in the Paraguayan "Legionaries," who formed a government-in-exile in Buenos Aires during the López regime. The *Colorados* date from the nationalist general Bernardino Caballero, who founded the Asociación Nacional Republicana in 1887.

The present era of Paraguayan politics dates from the end of the Chaco War with Bolivia, when, in 1936, a group of army officers led by Colonel Rafael Franco overthrew the constitutional Liberal Government of Dr. Eusebio Ayala. From this period stems the third political party of today, the Partido Revolucionario Febrerista. Its social experimentation resulted in confusion, however, and the Liberals returned briefly to power with the successful candidacy in 1939 of the war hero and well-educated statesman General José Felix Estigarribia.

Making a futile effort to serve as a constitutional Chief Executive, the general attempted to work with Congress in passing needed legislation. Opposition soon began to grow, however. Student strikes broke out; newspapers began to attack the new President; conspiracies were formed in the barracks. Estigarribia then dissolved Congress and issued a manifesto in which he stated that,

> after six months of fruitless efforts . . . I must confess . . . with deep regret . . . that political disturbances . . . have reached the point of degenerating into anarchy. . . . [Opposing factions] aspire to seize the government through force alone. Hate separates Paraguayans. Respect for the constitution and law have been lost. . . . A simple change in personnel would not satisfy the exigencies of these historic moments. . . . Democracy must demonstrate that it is able to assure the peace and tranquility so needed by the country. . . .[2]

President Estigarribia's council of co-operative members of the Liberal party obediently drafted a new, authoritarian Constitution, under which, in princi-

---

[2] Cited by Philip Raine, *Paraguay* (New Brunswick, New Jersey, Scarecrow Press, 1956), p. 255.

See also Amos T. Peasley (ed.), *Constitutions of Nations,* III (The Hague, Martinus Nijhoff, 1956), 115–125. Following the text of the Constitution of 1940 is a six-page commentary by President Estigarribia, in which he rationalizes the institution of a strong executive as necessary for the furtherance of democracy in Paraguay.

ple, the country is still governed. (A new Constitution was to be written in 1967 by a Constituent Assembly chosen in public elections.) Soon thereafter, the President was killed in an airplane accident, and political parties effectively disappeared from the scene for six years.

Estigarribia's defense minister, General Higinio Morínigo, ruled the country throughout the World War II period and governed without a Congress and with few trappings of democracy. In conformity with the general wave of relaxation after the war, President Morínigo liberalized his Government by admitting a contingent of civilian *Colorados* to his Cabinet, along with some reformist *Febreristas*. The latter resigned in January of 1947, however, and later provoked a bloody, five-month civil war. Following this conflict, the *Colorados* staged a single-ticket election and, after a brief interregnum under the administration of Chief Justice Juan Manuel Frutos, installed the distinguished author J. Natalicio González, a member of the conservative Guión Rojo, as President. Six months later, however, González was charged with financial irregularities, and his place was provisionally taken by General Raimundo Rolón. The Guión Rojo staged another coup and installed Dr. Felipe Molas López, a dentist, who had the support of both the army artillery division and the cavalry. There was another one-ticket election to confirm Dr. Molas López' position, but after only three months the more radical Democratic *Colorados* chose old-time party luminary Federico Chaves as Chief Executive and again had him elected in July of 1950. (Small wonder that there is a certain cynicism in Paraguay on the intrinsic value of the electoral process!) Chaves established a severely authoritarian regime and consolidated the position of the Colorado party. In 1953 he stood for election again (unopposed, of course) and permitted the election of a Congress, the first since the Chaco War. Only *Colorados* were chosen. In his inaugural address, Chaves promised the "spiritual pacification" of the country.

However good his intentions may have been, Chaves' pacification methods were more heavy-handed than spiritual, and again, as unrest mounted, the army took over. Once more the constitutional formalities were invoked, as the Colorado party president served provisionally until another one-party election could be held. General Alfredo Stroessner received 98 percent of the votes, the only evident opposition consisting of 3,180 blank ballots. Stroessner has proved to be more skillful, more durable, and more powerful than his predecessors. He united the armed forces behind him through skillful use of patronage and was re-elected in 1958. Thereafter he survived both guerrilla invasion and internal uprising by his political antagonists. By 1963, he had stabilized the country enough to permit token opposition. An opportunist wing of the exiled Liberal party, the Revolutionary Directorate, was allowed to present a presidential candidate (later appointed Ambassador to Great Britain) and to win the one-third of the congressional seats reserved for minority representation.

Since 1963, considerable relaxation has occurred. Dissident parties, except the Communists, have been invited home to publish their newspapers, to hold supervised meetings, and, within bounds, to criticize the *Colorado* regime. In October of 1965, municipal elections, the first in forty years, were held throughout the country. The *Colorados* campaigned in earnest, with speeches, broadcasts, dedication of public works, handing out of deeds to rural properties, and some repression of the opposition. They won handily, of course.

The Liberal splinter group again presented lists to the electorate in the fairly orderly balloting. In the municipalities of the interior, where members of the group enjoyed preferential treatment from the *Colorado* officials, these Liberals retained their second position in receiving one-seventh of the votes cast. The *Febreristas,* allowed to campaign quite actively, opened their lists to members of the original Liberal party and achieved the second position in the capital by garnering nearly one-fourth of the votes. According to Paraguayan electoral law, the winning party receives two-thirds, or six-ninths, of the seats; the second party, two-ninths; and the third, one-ninth. The other active group, the Christian Democratic Movement, advised its supporters to turn in blank ballots (contrary to electoral law). This group achieved some modest success in a few country areas where Christian Democratic peasant leagues had been well organized. It appeared that, for the time being at least, the *Colorados* had chosen sophistication rather than brute force as a means of preserving their dominance. The process of accommodation and stabilization continued throughout 1966 and well into 1967. The authentic Liberal Party, renamed *Liberal Radical,* accepted conditions offered by the Administration so that it might participate openly in politics. Elections were called for late May 1967 to choose delegates for a National Constituent Assembly. Only the Christian Democrats remained intransigently in opposition.

One might question the statement of the president of the Colorado party, Dr. Juan Ramón Chaves that "The first lesson which we receive from the municipal election of October 24 is the proof that the country is marching on the road of democracy and liberty."[3] A *Colorado* editorialist was, moreover, theoretically correct in writing that

> The first healthy effect of the Colorado governmental action is that it has succeeded in establishing a dialogue among Paraguayans who hold different political thoughts. . . . The presence of the opposition in the Municipal Councils or in the Parliament . . . is to exercise co-government, which is the essence of democracy.[4]

Political Ideologies

As can be inferred, political differences in Paraguay tend to be based on other than ideological grounds. The traditional Colorado and Liberal parties, like most in Latin America, are personalist and opportunist in their orientation. Their cleavages are the result of historical position and attitude rather

---

[3] *Patria,* October 27, 1965.

[4] *Patria,* October 29, 1965. This and other translations are mine.

than philosophical distinction. At the present time, however, the ruling *Colorados* are assiduously trying to establish an interventionist, welfare-state philosophy, to be distinguished from the aristocratic legalism of the Liberals. The *Febrerista* revolution of the 1930s was the first effort to establish a political ideology. The contemporary Christian Democratic Movement may be the second. Communism has been kept underground by constant and severe repression. Both liberalism and "coloradism" claim to be democratic, but the evidence which Liberal and *Colorado* leaders present is likely to be in terms of personal behavior patterns and advantages bestowed upon the people rather than in terms of philosophies or sophisticated party credos. The only meaningful ideology remains the all-pervasive nationalism deeply rooted in Paraguay's introverted past.

POLITICAL STRUCTURES AND ROLES

Political Parties

As noted above, political parties in Paraguay have served historically more as vehicles to convey personalist leaders to power than as organizations to promulgate ideas. The California anthropologist Frederic Hicks stated the case harshly but accurately when he was interviewed for an Asunción newspaper in October of 1965:

> My impression is that today the Colorados have leaders who understand their people and know how to gain their confidence to a greater degree than the other parties. It is clear that they have many advantages and also that many of them abuse that capacity and that they use it to their own interest. But if some workers or farmers receive some benefits, too, those leaders have much more influence than an intellectual of another party who, in spite of his lofty concepts, does not know how to overcome the disadvantages he has and how to win the confidence of the masses.[5]

Colorado Chaves gives evidence of his understanding of this position in the following statement, which he made after the election of October 24, 1965:

> "Another important lesson is the one which emerges from the people themselves, alert people, who think and vote for officials . . . who have placed at the service of the colléctivity essential public works such as running water, streets, electric lights, asphalted pavements, plazas, gardens, television, sports and general culture. . . ."[6]

Colorado Party   Between 1950 and the contemporary period of limited political dialogue, the only significant political input group in Paraguay has been the Asociación Nacional Republicana, the Colorado party. Its leaders have used every device at their disposal to pacify and organize the country,

---

[5] *Comunidad* (Christian Democratic paper), first week in October, 1965. (Original in Spanish.)

[6] *Patria,* October 27, 1965.

including police control, propaganda, financial rewards, public works, land reform and housing projects, improved transportation and communication, public health programs, expanded educational facilities, and economic stabilization. With major external assistance from multilateral agencies and from the United States, the *Colorados* have given the country much material progress and internal stability if not democracy. Paraguay is a benevolently authoritarian, one-party State. The party has functioned as the nationalistic, aggressive, economically progressive grouping within the essentially conservative framework of twentieth-century Paraguayan politics. The "key-concept of co-religionist" (*correligionario*) has dominated *Colorado* public vocabulary. In the context of Paraguayan political psychology, this domination means a preferential form of relationship among the members of the organization itself. In the words of J. Natalicio González, "No *Colorado* should be poor."[7] Lest this remark seem unduly parochial, it should be pointed out that *Colorados* have thought in the larger concept of the party-state as a unity.

As would be expected, *Colorado* writers have taken particular pains to outline their principles in favorable comparison with those of their traditional Liberal rivals. González writes that a "State of Law," which the Liberals profess, is "in the light of modern constitutional doctrines . . . governed by coercive norms, alien to the misery or grandeur of the people. It is a typical police state."[8] And again: "Another distinctive characteristic of the law, apart from its coercive, obligatory, and punitive nature, is its absolute lack of goals. The law does not pursue an ideal, does not seek either the happiness or the misfortune of man, it is indifferent to misery and wealth, alien to justice and injustice. . . . It has to be a legalized police state."[9] *Colorado* principles, on the other hand, offer a "platonic just state" (p. 23), the "political state," "which has goals, which has been instituted to serve as an instrument for the protection of the social body and to work for the happiness of man" (p. 17). Or, as another *Colorado* writer states, "Liberalism trusts in the power of conformance, harmonizing and regulating liberty in the social and political milieu."[10] In contrast, "the State in *Colorado* doctrine contemplates in terms of justice the interests of the collectivity as much as those of individuals, respecting liberty and the equality of opportunity for all" (p. 197). "The State should *intervene* if not *direct*. And it should intervene only when there is a just cause, felt by society, which demands this action" (p. 200).

There is also an exiled branch of the party, the more radical Movimiento

---

[7] *Paraguay* (Montevideo, Instituto de Estudios Políticos para América Latina, 1964), pp. 16–17.

[8] J. Natalicio González, *El Estado servidor del hombre libre* (Mexico, D.F., Editorial Guarania, 1959), p. 12.

[9] González, pp. 14–15. González seems to suggest that an authoritarian state is to be condoned if its actions are essentially for the popular welfare.

[10] Bacón Duarte Prado, *Fundamentos doctrinarios del Coloradismo* (Asunción, El Arte, 1959), p. 195.

Popular Colorado. Its leader, Epifanio Méndez, has considerable Castro-like charisma, gives four-hour impassioned speeches by radio from Argentina, and is admired by many young people.

Liberal Party Liberal-party leaders have not written extensively in recent years on their own party principles but have devoted their essays to polemics on the police methods and the corruption of the *Colorado* rulers. Traditionally, however, the Liberals would claim to be in the Manchester tradition. They tend to represent the aristocratic-conservative segment of the political spectrum. Their membership includes some land owners and, especially before their disbarment, many of the genteel, well-educated professional people of the capital. The ideas of the Liberal party have not always been parochial, however. Its leaders, smarting under the charges that Liberals helped to draft the authoritarian Estigarribia Constitution of 1940, point to glorious stages in Paraguayan history when there was "an Electoral Board with participation by the opposition party, full administrative responsibility in managing public affairs, participation by the opposition in government, freedom of the press, and normal functioning of the National University."[11] Another Liberal claims for his party credit for originating the ideas of modern reform movements. He wrote that statutes passed by a Liberal Congress in 1916 sought "the establishment of a regime which would permit and facilitate a just distribution of wealth, stimulate the economic education of the people, encourage by all possible means the stability and growth of small property, and organize the legal defense of the farmer's interests."[12] Such writers charge that the Stroessner Government has no moral right to receive assistance from the Alliance for Progress. In general, however, when the Liberals have been in power, they have promoted political democracy among the upper classes but have not been greatly concerned with social or economic reform movements.

Febrerista Party The Partido Revolucionario Febrerista was born out of the traumatic experiences of the Chaco War. The not always harmonious components of this party derived from the camaraderie of the conflict and the restless reformism of the young intellectuals who reacted against the outmoded institutions of the old regime. The party membership today is still split between rather radical political activists and idealistic intellectuals.

The first governing efforts of the *Febreristas* after their coup of February 17, 1936, were disastrous. The Instituto de Estudios Políticos states harshly,

It was a confused socialism born of the problems of the war and of the socialist currents inspired by the Mexican Revolution and Peruvian *aprismo*. While the ideological content of the traditional party platforms has never ab-

[11] Walterio Mercado Alder, "Paraguay y el plan Kennedy," *Combate,* número 18, septiembre y octubre, 1961, p. 30.

[12] Jose Antonio Ayala, "Cooperativismo, clave económica del Paraguay," *Combate,* número 15, marzo y abril, 1961, pp. 44–45. It will be noted that Liberals as well as *Colorados* profess today the concepts of economic and social as well as political development.

sorbed many outside influences, *Febrerismo* has taken unto itself exotic tendencies which are most difficult to reconcile: marxism, fascism, nazism, all crowned by an orientation toward a cohesive democracy.[13]

These inner conflicts could not be resolved in the 1930s by the inexperienced *caudillo* Colonel Rafael Franco, and the Government collapsed. To a certain extent they still pursue the party today.

Essentially purged of its military and violent elements, *Febrerismo* belongs to the *"Aprista* family," the parties of the democratic Left in Latin America. They send their students for training at José Figueres' political institute in Costa Rica and are reported to accept financial assistance from the German Social Democratic party. The party proclaims that "the State shall always be at the service of man, and not man at the service of the state."[14]

In synthesis, *Febrerismo* is proclaimed to be:

1) a party which in the political, economic, and social field proposes the uplifting of individual liberalism as a plan for the solution of our national problems;

2) a new figure of citizenship, structured in the form of a political party, faithful to the principle that these groupings constitute the natural organs of democracy;

3) a political party which presents to the Republic a programatic plan by means of which we seek the liberation of the oppressed, the dignification of the working masses, the farmers, and the middle class in a harmonious consolidation of ideals and united action, all for a national renascence. . . . (p. 9)

Although the *Febreristas* are a minor party, effectively shorn of the military power they exercised in 1936 and again in the civil war of 1947, their ideas of social and economic reforms have been evident in the recent activities of the *Colorado* Government. The party in turn, has absorbed both the policies and the programs of the more successful groups. Its current position seems to be typically ambivalent: the strongest criticism permitted of the *Colorado* regime and at the same time a not irresponsible political opposition.

The Christian Democratic Movement   Admittedly a part of the international Christian Democratic Movement, transferred from Eastern Europe in the post World War II period, and now successfully established in Chile and Venezuela, the Paraguayan Christian Democrats are a small and struggling organization. Their program of action is patient and long-range. They receive a modicum of international financing, publish a sophisticated and moderate weekly newspaper, *Comunidad,* represent themselves as vigorously patriotic

---

[13] Instituto de Estudios Políticos, *Paraguay,* p. 18. It is interesting that the *Febrerista* party has recently requested membership in the Ninth Socialist International. (See *Boletín del Buro Coordinador de la Internacional Socialista en América Latina,* Segunda época, V, No. 9 [primer trimestre de 1966], 170.)

[14] Partido Revolucionario Febrerista, *Ideario, declaración de principios del programa de gobierno* (Segunda Edición publicada por la Secretaria General, Comité ejecutivo nacional, 1959), p. 20.

on international issues, and indulge in attacks on the *Colorado* government. The statements of the party members reflect a somewhat closer attachment to the Roman Catholic position than does the platform of their associates in Chile, but the Paraguayan Christian Democrats do not hesitate to take the same reformist postures. The political activity of the party is perhaps most easily perceived in the country districts where it has organized Agrarian Leagues with considerable success, as indicated by the 1965 municipal elections. The Instituto de Estudios Políticos reports that there are 22 Ligas Agrarias now functioning, with some 45,000 farmers as members, some 6,000 or 7,000 of whom are effectively affiliated. (Instituto, *Paraguay,* p. 26.)

The Christian Democrats, very much an intellectual organization, have taken interest in university reform, not only in the Catholic university, but also in the National University; several members of the party serve on the two faculties. The Christian Democrats issue voluminous materials which echo the international ideals of the movement enunciated especially by the Chilean leaders.

Although Paraguayan government leaders criticize the Christian Democrats harshly, particularly for their decision to boycott the 1965 municipal elections, the government does not interfere noticeably with the movement's activities and has indeed allowed it to redesignate itself as the Christian Democratic Party of Paraguay.

A pamphlet issued by the party in Asunción on June 30, 1965 [no publisher] synthesizes the party program:

> The PDC does not appear as just another party. It is not a question of a new and sterile division of the Paraguayan community, already so much divided. It arises as an instrument of liberation of our oppressed people and as a decisive and efficacious advanced guard of the Paraguayan and Latin American revolution. . . .
>
> . . . Once and for all the anachronistic and unconstitutional state of siege . . . must be lifted. . . .
>
> The PDC recognizes the family as a fundamental of society. . . . The defense of its spiritual, moral, and economic unity is a primary and fundamental duty of the State.
>
> .   .   .
>
> The PDC will work boldly for the freedom of labor unions. It repudiates the demogogic use of the workers and especially the present enslavement of the Paraguayan Confederation of Labor by an immoral and conniving clique. . . .
>
> .   .   .
>
> A true agrarian reform is required which shall be radical and at the same time integrated into a general plan of the restructuring of rural life.

In the publications of the Christian Democrats, they also stress the need for comprehensive national planning in the field of education and administration as well as in agriculture. They call for continental Latin American integration, with a major reorganization of the Organization of American

States. The party members profess a strong anti-Communist position, whether the type of communism be Soviet, Chinese, Cuban, or native in origin. Finally, they indicate their confidence that the necessary changes can be accomplished politically without violence.

Any success of the Christian Democrats of Paraguay will depend, first, upon a progressive liberalizing of political repression in the country and second, upon the models offered by Christian Democratic participation in government in other Latin American countries. The influence of the party is likely to be greater than its numbers, since it is working at long range for the general political development of the Paraguayan masses rather than for immediate party strength.

Communist Party   Because of the effective control measures of the *Colorado* Government, the Communist party has been kept underground. Of its 5,000 members, 4,500 are in exile. The Sino-Soviet split is reflected in the establishment of two factions; the Partido Comunista Paraguayo, based in Montevideo, follows the Russian line, and the Paraguayan Leninist Communist party, based in Buenos Aires and Montevideo, follows Peking. Both groups advocate violent tactics against the Stroessner regime. A so-called United Front for National Liberation seems to attract some non-Communist support.

Interest Groups

Private Enterprise   The primitive industrialization of Paraguay has obviously limited the roles of both capital and labor as political forces. Under the general influence of the Alliance for Progress and of the activities throughout the continent of the Economic Commission for Latin America, the Paraguayan Government has in recent years encouraged the formation of associations of businessmen and industrialists. In October of 1965, President Stroessner himself appeared before the Second Congress of Private Economic Organizations of Paraguay. He asked for the continued co-operation of these private organizations in the national plans for development and at the same time promised a continuation of the government support necessary to their interests.[15] The industrialists, in their turn, issued a declaration of principles, which reaffirmed the joint responsibility of the State and of the affluent social classes to improve the health, liberty, and education of the people. The industrialists agreed that the "prosperity of the Nation requires understanding and harmonious co-operation between National Government, private enterprise, and the workers. . . . The right of ownership of the land and of the instruments of production recognizes no other limitations than the primacy of the superior and legitimate interests of the collectivity."[16]

While this expressed harmony of interests does not reveal any great independence of action on the part of Paraguayan private enterprise, the

---

[15] *Patria,* October 2, 1965.

[16] *La Tribuna,* October 7, 1965.

declaration does indicate another step in the program of the Colorado party to harmonize national interests and to continue the development of the economy. It is significant that, for the first time in recent history, the Government has found it desirable to enlist the active collaboration of the private sector.

Labor   Labor organizations are not new in Paraguay. The same slow industrial development, however, which has limited the role of management has also inhibited the development of labor. Not more than thirty thousand workers could properly be called proletarian. The highly centralized nature of politics has, moreover, limited the initiative available to workers. Management and labor have no history of resolving disagreements by direct negotiation. The Government has settled conflicts through the mechanism of the Ministry of Justice and Labor. The Paraguayan Workers' Confederation is the only large labor organization, and it is essentially controlled by the Government. Social welfare programs for labor are fairly extensive, but little initiative has been left to the union itself.

The Church   The relationship between Church and State in Paraguay has not changed appreciably as other political developments have taken place. The input of the Church in politics has normally consisted of an endorsement of the Government's position so long as the latter has maintained a conservative line, although the archbishop has spoken strongly of the need to improve the status of the poor. Only a few members of the Church hierarchy have endorsed the radical platform of the Christian Democrats, and these prelates have often been relegated to obscure posts. This close co-operation between the Church and the Government has, of course, strengthened the position of the Colorado party and has tended to maintain the stability of the regime.

THE STRUCTURE OF GOVERNMENT

The Executive

The Constitution of 1940 provides that the role of the executive branch shall be exceedingly strong. The President is the "supreme head of the State and is responsible for the general administration of the country. . . . He participates in formulating the laws in accordance with the Constitution, approves them, and promulgates them. . . . He exercises the rights of National Patronage of the Republic in the presentation of archbishops and bishops. . . . He opens the sessions of the House of Representatives each year . . . ; he extends the sessions of the House . . . or convokes this body into special sessions; in the latter case, the House shall deal only with those matters submitted to it for consideration by the Executive Power."[17]

The President has other, even more significant, powers: He may declare a state of siege. He may transfer persons suspected of subversion from one part of the country to another, "unless they prefer to leave the country"

---

[17] *Constitution of the Republic of Paraguay, 1940* (Washington, Pan American Union, 1963), Article 51.

(Article 52). Any bills which the President submits to the House must be acted upon during the course of that year, or they become law *ipso facto*. While the House is not in session, the President may issue decrees having the force of law, provided that they are submitted to the House during its next session (Article 54). Finally, "the Executive Power shall adopt plans for redistributing the present population for economic, social, public health, or national defense reasons" (Article 56).

Next to the President the most influential unit of government is a quasi-executive body, the Council of State. It shows a certain amount of Italian fascist influence, combining the Cabinet ministers with corporate representatives of business, the agricultural and livestock industries, manufacturing, the National University, the Church, the national bank, and the armed forces. The President appoints the members of the Council of State. During the years when there was no Legislature, the Council exercised the normal functions of that body. Since the reconstitution of the Legislature, the council still exercises great influence (Articles 62–65).

As in most Latin American countries, the Ministers of State are appointed by the President without the need for legislative approval. They are, of course, members of the Colorado party who are very close to the President, and clearly responsible to him for their administrative actions.

The Legislature

The duties of the unicameral House of Representatives are clearly subordinate to the will of the President. The Constitution states clearly that their legislation with reference to money matters, industrial concessions, legal amnesties, military ordinances, and "contentious-administrative questions" depends upon his initiative (Article 76). Certain responsibilities remain with the House. It may legislate upon municipal organizations, duties, taxes and assessments, the banking system, and river and air navigation. The House may authorize the President to make war or to negotiate peace (Article 76) and has the right to initiate any law which is not deemed the "express responsibility of the Executive Power." The President has the right of complete or item veto. In theory, the House may pass a bill over the President's veto (Article 79), but since two-thirds of the House are members of the President's party, this is not likely to occur.

The Judiciary

The judicial structure of Paraguay is remarkably simple. There is a Supreme Court of three members appointed by the President with the approval of the Council of State. Other magistrates are appointed by the President with the approval of the Supreme Court (Article 82). Lower courts include justices of the peace, primary courts, and courts of appeal. Special divisions include chambers for civil and commercial, criminal, and labor cases. There is also a Tribunal of Accounts (Court of Exchequer), which hears damage suits by individuals against national or municipal administrative units, that is, cases in administrative law. This court also re-examines and approves actions involving the investment of public funds, including the administration of the budget (Article 85).

The Supreme Court has both original and appellate jurisdiction. The Court also supervises the lower courts and justices, including the Tribunal of Accounts.

Trial by jury ended in 1940, and there seems to be no plan to re-establish it. The judicial process on all levels is entirely in writing. A case is usually initiated in a primary court, where the opposing lawyers present their written interpretations of the code. The appellate courts accept appeals against the decisions of the justices of the peace, and the Supreme Court considers complaints against both the original decisions of the secondary courts and judgments of these courts which modify or overrule decisions of the primary tribunals. Sentences which impose the death penalty or prison terms of more than fifteen years must be reviewed by the Supreme Court.

The Department of Justice includes the Ministry of the Attorney General, with subdivisions corresponding to the chambers of the court system. Finally, there is a Ministry for Public Defense, with sections to assist minors and the incapacitated, poverty-stricken and absentee defendants, and the poor who may be charged with criminal acts.

Although the Constitution unequivocally guarantees the independence of the judicial power (Article 87), the courts have never succeeded in freeing themselves from their partisan origin. Members of the Supreme Court and other magistrates hold office for only five years and are, of course, subject to presidential controls. The institution of the state of siege (Article 52), imposed almost continuously in part or all of the country, means that the power of the judicial branch may be subordinated to that of the executive.

Municipal Government

Municipal authority in Paraguay has hardly advanced beyond the colonial structure. The power remains in the hands of representatives appointed by the President of the country; those representing him in the sixteen departments are called *delegados,* and those functioning in the 152 smaller units, or *comunas,* are called *interdentes.* These administrators are nearly always military governors, whose function is essentially maintaining order and supervising the work of the necessary civic offices. The town councils, nonexistent for several decades before the elections of 1965, are largely of an advisory nature and have little power to make important decisions. It is to be hoped, however, that the reinstitution of these local bodies will, in the general process of relaxation, lead to wider participation by the capable citizenry in its own affairs.

The Military Establishment

The Paraguayan army is traditionally the strongest force in the Republic. No President can remain in power without the support of the army, and only the present Chief Executive, General Alfredo Stroessner, has so effectively controlled the armed forces as to stabilize his own position. The army, composed of approximately twelve thousand well-disciplined men, is deployed throughout the nation, both to present a show of force at the frontiers and, more importantly, to control the population. Universal military service brings nearly all the young men of the country into the armed forces and provides them with both discipline and a modicum of practical education. The navy and air force are small but well-integrated segments of the military. There is a large national police force, which contributes to the effectiveness of population control. In recent years the Stroessner regime, through this highly centralized military arm, has successfully pacified the country. Neither civilian nor military opposition has showed itself since 1964, nor have invasions by exiled opponents of the *Colorado* Government had any success. Ruthless suppression of any antigovernment moves has permitted a relaxation of control sufficient to give at least an appearance of domestic tranquility.

This era of relaxation has permitted the military to turn to other types of endeavor. Most obvious is a broad program of Civic Action. Colonel (now General) Ramón C. Bejarano has described the multifarious activities of the Paraguayan military in a classic, ingenuous example of role substitutability. Career military men in Paraguay are educators, bridge and road builders, well-diggers, medical practitioners, museum curators, and geographers; these men play their role for civilian as well as military purposes.[18] The military officer in Paraguay is convinced of his own unique discipline, capability, and probity. What Bejarano could not discuss are the activities which are really the continued abuses of the nineteenth century: arbitrary arrest, imprisonment, and brutality. He could not, of course, analyze the charges of financial manipulation, of brazen self-aggrandizement, nor could he from his posture examine the psychological and sociological problem of praetorian authority, or analyze whether the development of civilian entrepreneurial skills is inhibited by the concentration of development in the hands of a semimilitary government.

In endorsing Bejarano's book, General Stroessner writes, "The institutions of the State are perfected, and democracy opens its normal channel . . . to give full life to desires for *justice* and *liberty,* when the Armed Forces constitute and guarantee the peace of the Nation. . . ." One may be permitted, however, to suggest that Simón Bolívar's analysis of 135 years ago was more astute: "Are the military always to rule, sword in hand? Will not the military population complain of the despotism of the Army? I admit that the existing Republic cannot be governed except by the sword; and yet at the same time I must concede that the military spirit is incompatible with civilian rule."[19]

---

[18] Ramón C. Bejarano, *Contribución de las FF.AA. al Bienestar y Progreso del País* (Asunción, Editorial Toledo, 1959). For a brief outline of the activities of the army in the field of Civic Action, see *Alianza para el Progreso en el Paraguay,* 1965, Unidos de América en Asunción, pp. 15–18.

[19] Vicente Lecuna (comp.), *Selected Writings of Bolívar* (New York, The Colonial Press, 1951), II, 740. Letter to General Daniel O'Leary from Guayaquil, September 13, 1829.

POLITICAL DEVELOPMENT

The tranquility of Paraguay at the time this article is written, the effective functioning of the Government and of the economy, give superficial evidence of a mature State. In many respects Paraguay is endeavoring to keep pace with modern times. In co-operation with the institutions and in at least lip service to the spirit of the Alliance for Progress, the *Colorado* Government is increasing its sophistication and apparently transferring controls to civilian administration. With the assistance of the United States, a variety of administrative reforms and improvements are taking place. The Center for Training in [Civil] Service has given practical and theoretical education to more than 2,500 government employees. A Secretariat for Social and Economic Planning has been set up; a Housing Institute has been created; the Institute for Agrarian Reform has undertaken various projects; several new banking institutions have been developed in an effort to make domestic and foreign loan funds available to both industrialists and large and small landholders. As observed above, elections have been held with considerable regularity to the extent that they have served as the formal, if indeed somewhat artificial, device for the maintenance of political power. More than 700,000 Paraguayans are registered to vote. In the presidential election of 1963, 460,000 of them actually cast their ballots. Women received the vote in that year and outnumbered the men at the polls.

Internal communication is more open than in any period in recent history. Six newspapers are allowed to publish in the capital with only occasional interference, and there are a few provincial publications. There are fourteen radio stations, also generally free, although individual programs may be arbitrarily canceled at the moment of broadcast. There are 160,000 radio receiving sets. Libraries, even in the capital, are small and generally dependent upon foreign assistance. There is a fair number of book stores in Asunción, very few in the interior. There is no general publishing house in the country, except for the several print shops which publish the newspapers, government documents, and a considerable number of informal items. While the literacy rate has increased notably in recent years, it would not be accurate to state that the average citizen is a reader. Newspaper circulation is less than 100,000. As in any country, however, there is an increasing number of well-educated intellectuals who participate in the normal current of international communication.

Several agencies are working energetically to expand the level of political socialization in Paraguay. Obviously, the most active politicizing force is the Colorado party, working through its Government. The party has a widespread organization throughout the entire country, directs propaganda toward all of the people, and provides an increasing number of services which tend to identify the party and the Government with the daily lives of the citizens. The small labor unions are carefully supervised. This does not mean that civic organization is becoming noticeably more widespread. Although the Colorado party may be traveling the same road as the Institutional Revolutionary party (PRI) of Mexico, it is years behind in its effort to serve as an instrument of political education for the masses. The Colorado party does not yet feel itself sufficiently secure in power to permit too rapid a diffusion of decision-making.

The Christian Democratic party, with no political power to lose, is moving in a much more disinterested way to spread political sophistication among the people. With the organization of Agrarian Leagues, the Christian Democrats are deliberately beginning to develop the civic and political consciousness which is basic for genuine participation by the people in their government. These activities are, however, small and not yet widespread. It would require years of this kind of effort to open the Paraguayan society to political pluralism.

The effect of United States programs cannot be ignored in any estimate of the political socialization of Paraguay. Although North Americans have endorsed the existing dictatorships since the time of President Morínigo, the United States has succeeded in initiating scores of institutions—educational, cultural, public health, agricultural, and informational—which have brought thousands of Paraguayans into decision-making roles. These catalytic efforts, supplemented by Brazilian and United Nations activities, have brought Paraguayan governments into an attitude of compliance. Paraguayans of all levels have had a taste of what it means to participate in the political process. If Paraguay is in a state of transition from a "fused," nonspecialized, or closed society to a more open, specialized or "refracted" social system, the United States must receive a considerable share of the credit.

In spite of the accomplishments of the Paraguayan Government with its outside support, many Paraguayans remain alienated from the present regime. Alienation may be an essentially static condition, "the state in which individuals feel no sense of belonging to their community or nation. Personal contacts are neither stable nor satisfactory."[20] Alienation may also be a more overtly negative frame of mind, indicating an active estrangement or antagonism between an individual and the government toward which he feels unfriendly. At least half a million Paraguayans are in exile today. They constitute perhaps a fourth of the entire population and are certainly much more than a third of the members of the educated class who would be capable of entrepreneurial or bureaucratic leadership. Some, perhaps most of these, have left home for economic advantage. The Minister of the Interior, Edgar L. Ynsfrán, insists that "there are not more than 50 authentic political refugees who could not return if they wanted to do so."[21] Some refugees have returned since 1961, but countless Paraguayans remain in exile, and land colonization plans to repatriate them are so far quite inadequate. Hundreds, perhaps thousands, of Para-

[20] Morton Grodzins, *The Loyal and the Disloyal* (Chicago, University of Chicago Press, 1956), p. 137.

[21] Edgar L. Ynsfrán, *Crisis de crecimiento* (Asunción, Imprenta La Humanidad, 1961), p. 9.

guayans have experienced whippings and more painful torture. Although the notorious political concentration camp, Peña Hermosa, in the Chaco, has been closed, there are still political prisons, and other antagonists of the regime are maintained in an informal state of confinement in interior towns. Neither they, nor the survivors of torture, nor their families can easily accept bygones as bygones and come home to peaceful political campaigning. Violence breeds retaliatory violence, and Oresteian revenge becomes a matter of family and personal obligation. Although the Government may be quite sincere in its efforts to lead the country toward pluralism, those efforts may be frustrated. Minister Ynsfrán dramatized the dilemma when he complained somewhat petulantly, "This is no party dictatorship. . . . We recognize . . . the existence of other parties; the lamentable thing is that they will not recognize the existence of the Colorado party and they resist it because they see the success of our efforts."[22]

Very few Paraguayans are alienated in the sense of anomie; that is, only a handful of citizens are unaware of their Government or feel essentially isolated from civic activities. There are a few, mostly Indians living a secluded and deprived existence, who are unaware of the kind of government they have. And, of course, there are in the slums of the capital itself many whose existence is so painfully circumscribed that they have no comprehension of what goes on about them. Essentially, however, the Paraguayan is politically aware. To the extent that this assessment of belonging to the Paraguayan nation is correct, the greater are the perils of retrenchment from dictatorship. Having come thus far, the Stroessner Government can hardly again revert to totalitarianism without arousing even more resistance than it encountered during the bloody 1950s.

The strongest single aspect of Paraguayan society is extreme nationalism, which permeates all levels of the people, both resident and exile. Nationalism is stronger than hatred of the Government, stronger than resentment of the military severity and the financial machinations by which its leaders maintain themselves in power. Universal pride in the unique national language, Guaraní, binds the people together. Under President Stroessner, *Colorados* have stressed their nationalism in the strongest terms. Of all the peoples of Latin America, the Paraguayans are certainly the most parochial.

PROSPECTS FOR POLITICAL CHANGE

Active alienation from the State is, therefore, a less significant factor in Paraguay than might be expected. There is some possibility that the *Colorados* may be able to follow the Mexican model and achieve stability through a continuous diffusion of authority and a healthy moderation of the party's practices. The strongest factors indicating such success lie in the economic

---

[22] Edgar L. Ynsfrán, *Tapejuasa* [Guaraní word meaning "Crossroads"] (Asunción, Facultad de Filosofía, 1961), p. 11.

field. It may be true that the relative prosperity which seems to be coming to Paraguay is limited to Colorado party members and supporters. However, the numbers of those who are benefiting from the Government's program of development are increasing. If the regime should maintain its tenure for another decade and at the same time continue its policies of relaxation, the number of satisfied citizens might reach something resembling a majority. A critical test of the stability of any state is, of course, its capacity to transfer political power peacefully from one ingroup to another. This transfer is a sophisticated exercise in which the Paraguayans have little experience. The Paraguayan people are capable, however, they are adaptable, and they are relatively homogeneous. By character they are orderly and disciplined in their behavior. They are proud and highly educable. Few underdeveloped states have the same human potential for progress. The political observer may nevertheless be permitted some sympathetic skepticism. Stability is not inevitable. The traumas of Paraguay's past are severe. Hatreds are deep. Dictatorships, like princes, are not likely to perpetuate themselves by liberal practices. Seldom in history have dictatorships transformed themselves into free societies.

15 / Argentina

PETER G. SNOW

PETER G. SNOW, Associate Professor of Political Science at the University of Iowa, held a Doherty Foundation grant for research on Argentine political parties. Among his many publications on Latin American politics, several are specifically devoted to Argentina: "Argentine Radicalism: 1957–1963," "The Evolution of the Argentine Electoral System," "El político argentino," and Argentine Radicalism: The History and Doctrine of the Radical Civic Union. *His book* Government and Politics in Latin America: A Reader *appeared in 1967.*

THE POLITICAL ENVIRONMENT

Argentina, with an area of slightly more than 1 million square miles, comprises about one-sixth of the South American continent. Stretching from the tropics of Misiones to Tierra del Fuego in the south, Argentina is a nation of geographical contrasts. The bleak and forbidding region south of the Colorado River, usually referred to as Patagonia, occupies more than a fourth of the national territory but contains less than three percent of the population. This dry and windy plateau was populated by only a few Indians prior to the 1860s; since that time it has been taken over by sheep ranches of enormous size. While there is some petroleum and coal there, the great distances from the nation's population center and the poor transportation facilities have discouraged the development of those deposits. The Andean region of the northwest comprises another fourth of the nation's land area. Here the relatively sparse population is concentrated in a few small river valleys, where irrigation makes possible the raising of sugar cane and several types of fruit. The smaller region of the northeast contains both the tropical, lowland plains known as the Gran Chaco and the land between the Paraná and Uruguay Rivers.

In the remaining region, the pampas, almost three-fourths of the Argentines live on one-third of the land. In the minds of many, this is Argentina. Here an immense, fertile plain extends from the nation's capital in a semicircle, whose radius is about five hundred miles. The southern section is devoted to the breeding of a very high grade of sheep and cattle, the west is used primarily for wheat and alfalfa, while the part nearest the city of Buenos Aires has been developed to supply the capital with fruit, vegetables, and dairy products. This last area is also the nation's industrial center. It accounts for about ninety percent of the national industrial product, of which thirty percent is concentrated in the capital alone.

Society and Class Structure

According to the 1960 census the Argentine Republic had just over twenty million inhabitants, a population second only to Brazil on the South American continent. As is the case in most of the nations of this hemisphere, the people are distributed quite unevenly across the country. The federal capital alone has almost 3 million inhabitants, 14.8 percent of the total. When the eighteen suburbs are added, the total for greater Buenos Aires reaches 6,762,629, which is more than a third of all Argentines. This concentration does not stop here, for the city and province of Buenos Aires together contain 48.5 percent of the population, and if the adjoining provinces of Santa Fe and Córdoba are added, the total reaches 66.6 percent. This concentration means that 19 of the 22 provinces contain only one-third of the population.

While the country's population is growing, it certainly is not doing so at nearly as rapid a rate as that of many of the Latin American nations. For example, some of the Caribbean and Central American countries have growth rates which are among the highest in the world, while that of Argentina is only 1.7 percent per year, and it has been declining steadily for half a century. Within Argentina the rate of population increase varies greatly from one area to another. In recent years the most striking increase has been in the Buenos Aires suburbs, which more than doubled in size between 1947 and 1960 (from 1,700,000 to 3,800,000). This tremendous increase is part of an overall trend toward urbanization. The magnitude of that increase becomes apparent when one realizes that, at the time of national consolidation in 1862, the country was about 75 percent rural, while it is now almost 70 percent urban.

For many years now, Argentina has been an almost completely "white" nation. Most of the Indians were killed during the nineteenth century in order to push the frontier to the south, and at the same time mestizos were absorbed by waves of immigrants, primarily from Italy and Spain. Negroes were never numerically significant. Today probably no more than 10 percent of the population could be classified as mestizo; there remain perhaps 100,000 Indians and 5,000 Negroes.

In spite of trends toward urbanization and industrialization, agriculture still provides the livelihood for about one-fourth of the economically active population. In Argentina, as in most of the other Latin American nations, the dominant characteristic of land tenure is the existence of both *latifundia* and *minifundia* with little in between. About half the rural population owns only 2 percent of the land devoted to agriculture, while 1.5 percent of the population owns 45.2 percent of the land. Concentration of ownership of livestock is equally pronounced; over 70 percent of the cattle is raised on about 9 percent of the cattle ranches.

About 30 percent of the population is engaged in the industrial sector of the economy. The largest share of these work in the food processing, construction, textile, and metal industries. The last industrial census (1946) listed almost 90,000 industrial establishments. Most of these were very small, however; 56 percent employed less than ten workers. Industry is concentrated in the city and province of Buenos Aires, which have 57 percent of the industrial plants, 69 percent of the industrial workers, and 74 percent of the gross industrial product.

The remaining 40–45 percent of the economically active population is engaged in commerce and services. The largest groups within this sector are businessmen, public officials, and domestic servants. It is this sector that is growing in relative size, while the percentage of the population engaged in agriculture is declining and the industrial sector remaining relatively constant. A major part of the growth of this sector is the result of the ever-increasing size of the bureaucracy.

The proportion of the population in each of these three sectors in any given province depends largely upon the degree of economic development obtained by that province. In the pampas the largest percentage of the population is engaged in commercial or service occupations, with industry second and agriculture third. In most of the remainder of the country, the greatest portion of the people are employed in agriculture, with commerce second and industry last.

As can be seen in Table 1, the often repeated bromide about the lack of a middle class in Latin America is simply not the case in Argentina. While it is true that the upper class is quite small, the two middle sectors amount to almost forty percent. However, in spite of constant enlargement of the middle groups during the last several years, the class pyramid remains broad at the base and very narrow at the top. The lower and lower-middle classes still amount to more than ninety percent of the population.

One more feature of the Argentine populace, its level of education, needs brief mention. In comparison to the rest of Latin America, the Argentine educational system is quite advanced though in comparison to that of the United States, the Argentine system is quite backward. While over two-thirds of the school-age population attends primary schools, only one-fifth of it follows this with secondary schooling, and less than one percent attends college. Today the average Argentine has 3.9 years of formal education; for all Latin America the average is 2.2 and for the United States 9.0. In spite of what sounds like a rather poor educational system, only 13 percent of the

TABLE 1
Argentine Class Structure*

Class	Composition	%	acc.%
Upper Class	Large landowners (over 5,000 acres)	0.3%	
	Owners of large industries	0.1%	
	Owners of large commercial and service enterprises	0.1%	
	Upper-level administrators in all sectors	0.2%	0.7%
Upper Middle Class	Middle-sized landowners (500 to 5,000 acres)	1.0%	
	Owners of middle-sized industries	0.9%	
	Owners of middle-sized commercial and service enterprises	1.4%	
	Lower-level administrators in all sectors	1.9%	
	The liberal professions (lawyers, doctors, engineers, etc.)	1.2%	6.4%
Lower Middle Class	Small landowners (less than 500 acres)	7.4%	
	Owners of small industries	2.3%	
	Owners of small commercial and service enterprises	4.8%	
	Employees in industry, commerce, services, and government	15.0%	
	Pensioners	2.4%	31.9%
Lower Class	Agricultural workers	16.0%	
	Industrial workers	21.9%	
	Workers in commercial and service enterprises	19.5%	
	Unclassified workers	2.5%	59.9%
	Unclassified	1.1%	1.1%
		100.0%	

* Gino Germani, *La estructura social de la Argentina* (Buenos Aires, Editorial Raigal, 1955), pp. 196–197.

population is illiterate, and as might be expected, these persons are concentrated in rural areas.

A Historical Sketch

The first half-century of Argentina's national history is characterized by a bitter struggle between the interior provinces and Buenos Aires. The main issue was what form of government the new nation would have. The political leaders of the interior, calling themselves Federalists, equated federalism with liberty and democracy; they remembered the high degree of centralization of the colonial period and wanted no part of a continuation of a unitary system. (Many of the local *caudillos* who clamored for provincial autonomy were primarily interested in the ability to exploit their own areas as they saw fit.) On the other hand, the Buenos Aires Unitarians were convinced that only a unitary system could weld the warring provinces into a united nation. This group wanted to form a strong national government, but one run by and for the people of Buenos Aires. This issue was not permanently settled until 1862, and then it was resolved on the battlefield.

The next half-century was almost as peaceful as the first had been stormy. Between 1862 and 1916, the Conservatives gave Argentina constitutional government and at least a degree of democracy. However, while the masses of the people had many civil and political rights, the masses were almost completely removed from the political process. Governmental machinery revolved around the person of the President. In the provinces, legislatures were usually subservient to governors, who in turn were almost the personal agents of the President. It was not too difficult for him to keep them in line with the use—or just the threat—of his power to intervene in their provinces. The system was self-perpetuating; the President and the governors managed to keep each other in office.

Until the formation of the Radical Civic Union (UCR) in 1891, the Conservatives reigned almost unchallenged. At that time, however, the land-owning elite was for the first time confronted with an opposition party representing groups other than the upper class. The UCR represented the new middle class, which had been formed to a great extent by European immigrants. This group was not willing to accept the passive position of the native lower class and wanted a voice in the Government, yet the only political party of importance represented the aristocracy almost exclusively. Faced with economic ruin by the financial crisis of 1890, the middle sectors formed their own party.

For the next fifty years Argentina had what was essentially a two-party system. The Conservatives, representing primarily the large landowners, were convinced that only the upper class was capable of governing. Restricted suffrage and fraudulent elections were considered a positive good, for otherwise the uneducated masses might gain political power and ruin the country. The Radicals represented a very nebulous liberalism; they were opposed to the Conservative regimes and were in favor of reform but lacked a concrete program.

Conservatives continued to dominate the political scene, on both the national and the provincial level, until 1916. The real turning point came in 1912 with the passage of a new election law. This law, bearing the name of President Roque Sáenz Peña, who sponsored it, provided for universal and compulsory male suffrage, a secret ballot, permanent voter registration, and minority representation in Congress. The honest administration of this law almost immediately cost the Conservatives their monopoly on political offices.

By 1916 the UCR had attained the Presidency, although the party still had no real program. The Radicals represented liberalism and the middle class instead of conservatism and the upper class, but they had no idea how to put into effect the "national renovation" about which they had been talking for a quarter-century. The UCR held power for fourteen years, but although there were some relatively minor reforms, no structural changes were even attempted. The economic power of the Conservatives remained intact. In 1930 the economic crisis, the ever increasing corruption in the administration, President Hipólito Irigoyen's senility (at eighty he was serving a second term), and the general disillusionment with the UCR led to the forceable ejection of the Radicals and the establishment of Argentina's first military Government. The nation, which had experienced only Conservative rule prior to 1916, expected miracles from the Radicals, and miracles were not forthcoming.

The second Conservative period (1932–1943) differed markedly from the first. The men who governed Argentina between 1862 and 1916 were extremely capable politicians who were dedicated to good, if not democratic, government; the same cannot be said of the administrations following the 1930 revolt. During this period the Radicals, although practically leaderless and completely devoid of a real program, could have won virtually any honest election. However, there were no honest elections. These oligarchic administrations could claim as their only accomplishment the discrediting of democracy in Argentina.

In 1943 the Argentine armed forces again became the keeper of the national conscience and deposed the Conservative Government. While the 1930 revolt involved many civilian politicians, the coup of 1943 was completely military in character. After a relatively lengthy power struggle within the armed forces, there emerged a single dominant figure, who was to control the destiny of Argentina for a decade. This man was Juan Domingo Perón.

With the armed forces and organized labor as his main bases of support, Perón became a virtually absolute dictator. He purged the judiciary, intervened in the universities, and jailed critics. Yet at the same time a genuine social and economic revolution began. Between 1946 and 1951, great strides were taken toward industrialization and complete economic independence. The industrial worker, and to a lesser extent, his agricultural counterpart, gained a degree of economic security and a voice in the Government which were both unknown until this time. By 1951, however, the sources of Peronist strength were beginning to be eroded. Emphasis upon industrialization had led to neglect of the agricultural sector, which retrogressed badly; economic difficulties led to the freezing of industrial wages; and the administration's anticlericalism cost it the support of the Church. In September 1955, Perón was overthrown by segments of the armed forces—the same group that had been largely responsible for his rise to power.

After a three-year period dedicated to "de-peronizing" the nation, elections were held in February 1958, and the Government returned to civilian control. With the support of the Peronists, who were denied the right to nominate their own candidates, Arturo Frondizi and the Intransigent faction of the UCR scored a clean sweep in the elections. In the attempt to combat some of Argentina's multitudinous economic problems, Frondizi accepted the recommendations (including an austerity program), of the International Monetary Fund, granted foreign petroleum concessions, and in general reversed the nationalistic position he had taken prior to 1958. While the administration's policies may have been economic necessities, they were also political liabilities.

In the congressional and gubernatorial elections of March 1962, Peronists were allowed to nominate their own candidates for the first time since the 1955 revolution. Supporters of the ex-dictator won almost one-third of the total vote, forty-one seats in Congress, and control of ten of the nation's twenty-two provinces (including all-important Buenos Aires). This victory was the beginning of the end for President Frondizi, who was ousted by the armed forces less than two weeks later. Another provisional government, under the titular leadership of José María Guido but actually controlled by the military, held power until the fall of 1963, when elections were once again held. This time Peronists were denied the right to nominate candidates for executive office. In these elections the other faction of the old UCR obtained a majority of the seats in the Senate, a plurality in the Chamber of Deputies, and placed Arturo Illia in the Presidency. As Joseph Barager states,

> A wave of relief seemed to sweep over the country as it became clear that Argentina was to be returned to constitutional civilian government. President Illia thus began his term in office with a great deal of popular good will, amid a revival of business confidence. It remained to be seen how long the mood of optimism would continue to be warranted.[1]

GOVERNMENTAL STRUCTURES AND FUNCTIONS

While there are those who would argue that governmental structures are relatively unimportant and that attention should be focused upon functions, the former is here described first if for no reason other than the fact that it serves a backdrop against which the entire political process moves.

The Structure of Government

The formal structure of the Argentine Government is quite similar to that of the United States. That these similarities are not accidental can be seen in the words of the men who wrote the Constitution of 1853 (which except for the period between 1949 and 1955 has been in effect ever since). The committee which actually drafted the document is reported to have said, "This project is modeled in the form of the Constitution of the United States," and the convention itself declared, "The nature of the Confederation will be comprehended more readily if one understands that it is the same as the United States."[2] Most of the basic principles which underlie the American Constitution—popular sovereignty, separation of powers, federalism, limited

---

[1] Joseph R. Barager, "Argentina: A Country Divided," in Martin C. Needler (ed.), *Political Systems of Latin America* (Princeton, D. Van Nostrand, Inc., 1964), p. 432.

[2] Juan A. González Calderón, *Derecho constitucional argentino,* 3rd ed., I, 278, as translated in Austin F. MacDonald, *Government of the Argentine Republic* (New York, Thomas Y. Crowell Company, 1942), p. 128.

government, national supremacy, and the rule of law—are equally basic to the Argentine fundamental law.

Federalism   The Constitution divides power between a national government and twenty-two provinces. In general, the former has only those powers explicitly delegated, while the provinces retain "all powers not delegated by this Constitution to the Federal Government. . . ." More specifically, there are some powers delegated exclusively to the national Government, and some are to be exercised concurrently by nation and province; certain powers are denied to each, and all others are reserved to the provinces.

The range of delegated powers is much broader than in the United States, and thus the residual powers of the provinces are limited in number and importance. To begin with, the national Government is given complete jurisdiction over the entire fields of civil and criminal law through the power of Congress to enact the civil, commercial, penal, mining, labor, and social security codes. Congress thus has the power to define and provide penalties for all crimes without the need to show that the crimes have some relationship to other delegated powers.

The exclusive powers of the national Government are similar to those of the United States: coining money, declaring war, conducting foreign relations, and regulating both foreign and interprovince commerce. Concurrent powers include taxation, education, the right to borrow money, and the promotion of industry, trade and immigration. Powers denied the provinces fall into three broad categories: conduct of any phase of foreign relations, regulation of certain aspects of the economic system, and interference with uniform national standards set by Congress. Within the realm of these limitations, all other powers of government are reserved for the provinces.

Even within that limited sphere, the Argentine province is not sovereign. Provincial autonomy is constantly threatened, and often destroyed, by the use of the power of national intervention. The Federal Government may intervene in the territory of a province in order to guarantee the republican form of government, or to repel foreign invasions, and at the request of the constituted authorities, to support or re-establish those authorities, should they have been deposed by sedition or invasion by another province. Thus the Congress, or the President if Congress is not in session, may remove all government officials in a province and replace them with a federal appointee responsible only to Congress or the President. The use of this power in case of invasion or rebellion would cause little comment. However, a very large number of interventions have been ordered to "guarantee the republican form of government." And since the judiciary has refused to define "republican," the one who decides upon intervention is empowered to define republicanism. One might well argue that it is only the formal structure of the Government that is federal, for provincial autonomy is at the mercy of the national Government at all times.

The President   Even without consideration of his extra constitutional prerogatives, the Argentine President is far more powerful than either the

Congress or the judiciary. The framers of the 1853 Constitution were determined to create a strong Chief Executive, and they succeeded.

The President is formally chosen by an electoral college somewhat similar to that used in the United States. The federal capital and each of the provinces are entitled to twice as many presidential electors as they have congressmen. These electors are chosen directly by the qualified voters by means of a two-thirds incomplete list; that is, each voter may vote for only two-thirds of the number of electors awarded his province. (In 1963 only, electors were chosen by means of proportional representation.) In order to be elected, a candidate must receive an absolute majority of the electoral votes; otherwise, the Congress will choose from among the top two candidates (to date, no presidential election has ever gone to Congress). As is the case in the United States, the presidential electors very rarely exercise any discretion in the casting of their votes; they simply vote for the nominee of their own party.

The executive powers of the President are more than ample. For example, he is authorized to appoint almost all members of the national administration, and with the exception of judges and members of the diplomatic corps, who must be confirmed by the Senate, he is the sole judge of the qualifications of his appointees. His removal power is virtually unlimited. The President is also Commander-in-chief of the armed forces (at least nominally) and is in complete charge of the conduct of foreign relations. While he may not formally declare war, he can use his military and diplomatic powers in such a manner as to virtually force Congress to do so.

The President also has a great deal of legislative power, even beyond that usually held by Chief Executives. His right to introduce legislation in Congress is explicitly sanctioned by the Constitution, and he frequently sends to Congress final drafts of bills he feels essential to the national welfare. His veto power is almost identical to that held by the American President, except that the Argentine President does not have a pocket veto. The President's most important legislative power is probably his ability to issue executive decrees which have the force of law. In Argentina, as in most of Latin America, this power has been carried to the extreme.

The judicial power of the President revolves around his ability to appoint, subject to senatorial confirmation, members of the federal judiciary and to grant pardons and commute sentences. Much more important is his power to declare a state of siege. This power goes far beyond the United States congressional power to suspend the writ of habeas corpus; the declaration of a state of siege would be more closely analogous to the suspension of our entire Bill of Rights plus the procedural guarantees of the Fourteenth Amendment. The state of siege may be declared only in time of foreign invasion or internal disorder, but the latter may be defined in such a manner as to impose no real restriction.

Congress The Argentine Congress is bicameral in order to attempt to give representation to the people as a whole in one house and to the individual provinces in the other. The Senate is composed of forty-six members, two from each province, who are chosen by local legislatures, and two from the federal capital, who are indirectly elected by the people. Senators serve nine-year terms with one-third retiring every three years. The Chamber of Deputies at present has 192 members with the provinces and the capital represented on the basis of their own population. Deputies are directly chosen by the people for four-year terms with half the members elected every two years. Between 1916 and 1963, deputies were elected by means of the two-thirds incomplete list—in about the same manner as presidential electors—but since that time the D'Hondt form of proportional representation has been used.

With a few exceptions, the constitutional prerogatives of the Argentine Congress are identical to those of the Congress of the United States. Twenty-eight powers are enumerated, the last of which is "to enact all laws and regulations that may be necessary to carry out the foregoing powers. . . ." The two major exceptions to the similarities of powers have already been mentioned: the Argentine lawmakers have the power to enact complete civil and criminal codes which are uniform across the nation and can declare a state of siege in all or parts of the nation.

The procedure used in the enactment of legislation is also quite similar to the practice followed in the United States. Bills may be introduced in either house; they are sent to appropriate standing committees for consideration and amendment, then returned to the floor of the house for debate and a final vote. In order to become law, the bill must be approved by both houses; however, in case of disagreement between the two chambers, there is no conference committee but rather a complicated system whereby the bill is shuttled back and forth between chambers for a considerable period of time.

The Judiciary   The organization of the judiciary has been primarily the work of the Congress, for the Constitution says only that "the Judicial Power of the Nation shall be vested in a Supreme Court of Justice, and in such lower courts as the Congress may establish." Congress almost immediately divided the national territory into several judicial districts, each of which was assigned a single justice (since that time the number of justices in the more populous regions has been increased). These districts are the courts of original jurisdiction, comparable to the district courts of the United States. For a half-century all appeals were carried directly to the Supreme Court, which soon became greatly overburdened. In 1902 an intermediate level of courts was established. These appellate courts serve basically the same function as the American circuit courts.

In general, the jurisdiction of the federal courts is dependent upon the subject matter of cases and the persons involved. For the former, the federal courts have jurisdiction over all cases involving the Constitution, laws or treaties of the nation, and cases in admiralty and maritime jurisdiction. Within the sphere of the latter, these courts have jurisdiction over all suits involving foreign diplomats, suits in which the nation is a party, suits between two or more provinces or between one province and the citizens of another, and suits between citizens of different provinces. In those cases concerning foreign ministers and in those to which a province is a party, the Supreme Court has original jurisdiction; in all others its jurisdiction is appellate.

Although the Constitution does not specifically grant to the federal courts the power of judicial review, the Supreme Court in 1887 declared an act of Congress unconstitutional. The court justified its action with reasoning quite similar to that of John Marshall in *Marbury vs. Madison*. Since this time the power has not seriously been questioned. However, it has been used quite sparingly, and the judiciary itself has imposed several restrictions upon the use of that power: refusal to grant advisory opinions, willingness to hear only cases and controversies, refusal to decide political questions, and so on.

Provincial Government   Each of the Argentine provinces has adopted the separation of powers doctrine, and within each province it is the governor who is given most of this power. The gubernatorial qualifications, terms of office and methods of election are remarkably similar in the various provinces. Everywhere the minimum age requirement is thirty years, and the term of office four years; nowhere is the governor eligible for immediate re-election. In a large majority of the provinces, he is chosen by a direct vote of the people, but in a few provinces there are electoral colleges similar to that used to select the President.

The powers of the governor are analogous to those of the President but on a smaller scale. The governor is the provincial chief executive with almost unlimited power of appointment and removal, the commander-in-chief of the local militia, and the negotiator of treaties with other provinces. Within the legislative sphere he has the power to call special sessions or extend the normal ones, to introduce bills, and to veto them (including in some cases an item veto). Also of importance is his power to issue executive decrees. In most of the provinces he has the power to pardon offenders of provincial laws. In addition, he sees to the preparation and execution of the provincial budget and is the direct agent of the national Government who is charged with the enforcement in his province of all national laws.

The organizational structure of legislatures varies a great deal from one province to another. Almost two-thirds of the legislatures are unicameral, the remainder bicameral; this variance is primarily a result of population, for with the exceptions of Catamarca and the Chaco, the provinces with less than half a million people have a single legislative chamber, while those with populations in excess of this figure have two chambers. The number of members of these chambers varies from thirteen in the Corrientes Senate to eighty-four in the Buenos Aires Chamber of Deputies. The term of office is usually four years in the lower house (and in the unicameral bodies) and six in the upper, with terms frequently staggered to insure some continuity of membership. Most of the provinces use some form of proportional representation to choose legislators although the incomplete list is certainly not unknown. Most legislatures meet annually for four or five months.

The powers of the provincial lawmaking bodies are quite restricted. To begin with, the division of power between nation and province is heavily weighted in favor of the former, and then within the individual province, it is the governor who has received the bulk of the residual powers. The major prerogatives of the legislatures include taxation, approval of the budget, and promotion of education and health.

Provincial court systems are, on the whole, modeled upon the federal judiciary, with a supreme court, several trial courts, and in some instances an intermediate level of appellate courts. Most justices are appointed by the governors for fixed terms of office; life tenure is still a rarity. The appellate courts ordinarily have three members and supreme courts five. In a very few instances the judiciaries have the power to declare provincial laws unconstitutional. The courts are the weakest branch of weak provincial governments.

Municipal governments are the creatures of the provinces. These governments possess very little authority, and that which they have is a gift which may be taken back at any time. Executive power is held by an *intendente,* not infrequently chosen by the governor; city councils, on the other hand, are popularly elected. The power of municipal administrations is limited primarily to budgetary matters and even this power is severely restricted by provincial constitutions. In addition, the provincial authorities are empowered to intervene in the cities in much the same manner as the national Government intervenes in the provinces.

The Authoritative Functions of Government

From the above description of the organizational structure of the Argentine Government, one might well come to the conclusion that rules are made by Congress and the provincial legislatures, applied by the President and governors, and adjudicated by a dual judiciary. Such a picture is more than slightly misleading, for it greatly overemphasizes the functions of the legislative and judicial branches, while underemphasizing those of the executive.

Rule-making　　The Argentine Constitution explicitly delegates the rule-making function to Congress (and to a lesser extent, to the provincial legislatures), but in fact this function is exercised to a greater extent by the President and by the leaders of the armed forces. In no period of Argentine history has Congress acted as the nation's major rule-maker. Instead Congress has adopted altogether different functions, chief of which is the legitimizing of rules made by others. In the enactment of major legislation, for example, seldom is the initiative taken by Congress; that body will usually await the introduction of an administration bill and then give the President's rules legitimacy by means of the formal legislative process. The Congress also serves as a forum for the expression of hostilities and aggressions, and to some extent it performs a representational function. Congress does not, however, serve as the nation's main rule-making body.

Prior to 1930 the making of authoritative rules was the almost exclusive domain of the President. Since that time, however, this function has been shared with the leaders of the armed forces. On occasion the military has completely assumed the rule-making function and at other times has delimited a sphere within which the President was allowed to make rules subject to a military veto. At present it would appear that most of the authoritative rules are made by the President—although some of them may require military approval—and are then sent to Congress for legitimation.

(In at least one respect the rule-making function in Argentina differs from that of its sister Republics. In much of Latin America, constituent assemblies play an important role in rule-making since Constitutions are changed with amazing frequency. This is not the case in Argentina, where only two constitutional conventions have met during the last century, and both served legitimizing rather than rule-making functions.)

Rule Application   The application of rules is primarily a function of the Presidency. Here there exists much less difference between the formal structure and the authoritative functions of the Argentine Government. The Constitution gives the President primary responsibility for the application of rules, and he does in fact exercise this function although it is not his exclusively.

During the last several years the leaders of the armed forces have also played an important role in the application of rules; this is especially true of the rules which were made by the military establishment. A striking example of this power took place in April 1962, when President Frondizi was deposed. The major rule *made and applied* by the military is that Peronists must not be allowed to regain any appreciable amount of political strength.

To a lesser extent, the Church also plays a role in the application of rules. As George Blanksten stated, "Here the function of the clergy is to endow the rules with legitimacy and provide them with moral and political sanctions."[3] It should be emphasized that in the rule-application function the role of the Church is decidedly secondary to those played by the President and by the armed forces.

Rule Adjudication   Although the rule-adjudication function is formally given to the judiciary, it is not the courts, national or provincial, which in actuality perform this function. Instead, primary responsibility falls to the President, and again it is the military which plays a major role and the Church a somewhat minor one. There does appear to be a trend toward the creation of a truly independent judiciary; nevertheless, in important controversies final adjudication does not take place in the courts.

While the adjudicatory functions of the President and the armed forces are relatively apparent, it should be pointed out that the Church has the ability in some controversies to endow one side or the other with legitimacy. It is not entirely coincidental that Perón was overthrown shortly after his excommunication. The final arbiter is, of course, the military; several of its leaders tend to think of themselves as a sort of repository of the national will.

---

[3] George I. Blanksten, "The Politics of Latin America," in Gabriel A. Almond and James S. Coleman (eds.), *The Politics of the Developing Areas* (Princeton, Princeton University Press, 1960), p. 526.

In conclusion it may be asserted that the making, applying, and adjudicating of rules are all functions which have traditionally been performed by the President. The Church has always performed those functions but within a rather limited sphere, and since 1930 the role of the armed forces has become important, at times even dominant. This should not be taken to mean that the legislative and judicial branches are meaningless in the Argentine political system, but rather that they perform functions which differ appreciably from those described in the nation's fundamental law.

INTEREST GROUPS

While there is a multitude of interest groups of some consequence in the Argentine political system, three of them, the armed forces, organized labor, and the Catholic Church, are of far greater importance than all the others combined.

The Armed Forces

From the time of national consolidation in 1862 until 1930, the Argentine military remained in the background. However, beginning in the latter year and continuing to this time, the military has been an active political force. As Robert Potash said, "The role the military has played during this period [1930–1958] has varied in terms of the specific objectives sought, the methods used, and the intensity of its action, but at no time did it cease to be a political force, at no time have the governing authorities whether military or civilian been able to discount its desires or demands."[4]

At different times since 1930, the armed forces have played three distinct roles. First, they have acted as a strong influence upon policy formulation. This was the case between 1946 and 1955, when one of their own was in power. During the Perón period the military received just about all it wanted within a not-too-limited sphere: appropriations for modern, expensive equipment; rapid promotion; pay increases; and so on. In addition, the armed forces were consulted on most important issues and thus had a hand in the development of many nonmilitary policies. Second, it has been a wielder of an absolute veto, as was the case during the 1958–1962 Frondizi administration. With a few important exceptions, the military did not actually formulate policy but instead vetoed policy proposals to which it was opposed.

Third, and most important, on four separate occasions the military has forcibly ejected Presidents and assumed power itself. In 1930 and 1943 a segment of the armed forces—with the approval or acquiescence of the remainder—deposed civilian regimes. In each case there followed brief periods of complete military rule, but civilians were soon brought into the Government and elections held within three years. In 1955 the armed forces again

---

[4] Robert A. Potash, "The Changing Role of the Military in Argentina," *Journal of Inter-American Studies* III, No. 4 (October 1961), 571.

assumed power but this time not without appreciable opposition. However, elections were again held within three years and the Government returned to civilian control. In 1962 the armed forces removed still another President but with somewhat different results. The constitutional successor was allowed to take office, and almost all formal government positions continued to be held by civilian politicians. Nevertheless, the military held effective control; policy decisions were made by the heads of the three service branches and not by the provisional President. General elections were held in 1963, and the armed forces returned to the barracks, though for how long it would be foolish to predict.

At the time of the 1930 revolt, the military was probably composed of no more than 50,000 men; by 1943 this number had doubled, and by 1955 it doubled again. During the last decade it has been cut somewhat and is scheduled for further reduction as part of an overall modernization scheme. At present, the army has about 80,000 to 85,000 men, of whom 60,000 to 65,000 are draftees, 15,000 career noncommissioned officers, and 5,000 officers. There are perhaps 35,000 men in the navy and 20,000 in the air force, each of which has about 1,250 officers.

Neither the draftees nor the noncommissioned officers figure in political action to any real extent, nor do officers in the professional services, such as medicine and law. It is the Command Corps that makes the news, and within this group are the hundred or less generals, admirals and brigadiers who have power (the time when field-grade officers were a strong political force appears to have passed). Much has been written about these men, their social backgrounds, their goals and values, but very little of it has been based upon empirical evidence. For example, it often has been asserted that most of the upper echelons of the armed forces come from the traditional landowning elite of the northwest. Yet it can be demonstrated that far more generals are born in Buenos Aires and its suburbs than in the older provinces and that between 1936 and 1961 almost half of them were born of immigrant parents. If one examines the occupations of the fathers of these men, it becomes apparent that almost all could be labeled middle class.[5] It would thus appear more reasonable to assume that the basic conservatism of the leaders of the armed forces comes not from an aristocratic social background but from contact with the elite and gradual adoption of many of its ideals.

At least since 1955 there has been a great deal of factionalism within the Argentine armed forces. This is seen in rivalry among the three branches and within each branch, especially the army. The political role of the navy was minor prior to 1955. Then, with the army divided, the naval fleet turned the balance against Perón and assured victory for the rebels. The navy gained a great deal of prestige and some real power from this action; for example, the navy's leader, Admiral Isaac Rojas, was provisional vice-president between

---

[5] See José Luis de Imaz, *Los que mandan* (Buenos Aires, Editorial Universitaria de Buenos Aires, 1964), pp. 52–61.

1955 and 1958. Since the fall of Perón, the navy has remained the most violently anti-Peronist branch of service; it has some basis for its claim to be the only service not even tainted by Peronism.

The air force has had only two decades to build a tradition of political action and has moved slowly and extremely cautiously in this area. This branch has seldom tried, and never succeeded, in instigating political action. The main concern of the air force seems to be to end up on the winning side. This it almost always manages to do but waits so long to commit itself that very little is accomplished by the action.

It thus is the army which has traditionally been the instigator of political action, and it is the army which is most riddled by antagonistic ideological factions. This factionalism became apparent during the military administrations of 1955–1958, when one of the major concerns was the holding of elections and the return to constitutional government. In this regard there were three main factions: *quedantistas,* who wanted to remain in complete control until the last vestiges of Peronism were eliminated; *continuistas,* who favored the holding of elections but at the same time making sure that the victors were sympathetic to the goals of the military; and the "fair play" group, which wished to hold honest elections (although with a continuance of the ban on Peronist candidates) and respect the results.[6] The third group emerged victorious by 1958, in no small part the result of the position of General Pedro E. Aramburu, who was then provisional President.

By 1962 these and other groups has gradually coalesced into two main sectors, which to some extent cut across service lines: *gorilas,* or *colorados,* and legalists, or *azules.* The *gorilas* are the hard-line anti-Peronists who emerged during the Aramburu administration. They see the 1955 revolt as a fundamental revolution whose primary goal is the elimination of the conditions which allowed the growth of Peronism. Convinced that Argentina is still not ready for democracy (the large Peronist vote in 1962 is cited as proof of this conviction), the *gorilas* demand military rule for an indefinite period— ostensibly to prepare the way for "real" democracy. Their strength appears to have been centered in the navy, the infantry and the engineers.

The legalists, a much more moderate group, look at the 1955 revolt as a simple act of resistance to tyranny. The general position of this group has been that the military should stay out of politics unless the alternative is chaos or dictatorship. The legalists appear to draw most of their support from the cavalry, which includes all mechanized forces, and especially the huge Campo de Mayo garrison, which is strategically located just outside the Federal District.

In March 1962, there was general agreement among the armed forces that President Frondizi must be removed. The *gorilas* had always hated him. They were angered by his attraction of Peronist support in the 1958 elections

---

[6] James W. Rowe, "Argentina's Restless Military," *American Universities Field Staff Reports Service,* East Coast South America Series, XI, No. 2 (May 1964), 12.

and by his attempt to bring Peronists into his party; his legalization of Peronism prior to the 1962 elections was intolerable as far as this group was concerned. At this time even the legalists were somewhat worried about the possibility of the establishment of a regime of the Peronist sort and quite upset with the approaching power vacuum. After the removal of Frondizi, however, there was little or no agreement between *gorilas* and legalists. For several months there was an apparent power struggle, which seemed likely to lead to virtual civil war. Finally, in September of 1962, the legalists emerged triumphant, and since April 1963, when an attempted coup on the part of *gorila* naval officers was put down, the legalists have been firmly in control. Their present position is contained in the much publicized Communique 150 of September 23, 1962, which contains three main points: subordination of the military to civilian control; a return to constitutional government; and reincorporation of Peronists into national political life, while making sure that there is no return to the days of 1946–1955.

Organized Labor

It is only during the last quarter-century that organized labor has attained a significant position in the Argentine political system. Although there were trade unions formed as early as 1853, it was during the 1880s that the movement gained its original impetus. (It is not coincidental that this was also the period in which Argentina was receiving waves of immigrants from Spain and Italy.) Under the leadership of Anarcho-Syndicalists until 1910 and of Socialists for the next thirty-three years, organized labor was unable to obtain even legal recognition.

This situation changed radically after the 1943 revolt. Perón used his position as Secretary of Labor and Social Welfare to bring pressure upon employers to grant large wage increases and other concessions long demanded by labor; he also enacted by decree a considerable body of labor legislation. In return it was organized labor which forced the reinstatement of Perón in October 1945 after he had been overthrown by some of his fellow army officers. For the next decade labor was one of the major pillars of the Peronist regime. Peronist domination of the labor movement was accomplished primarily through reorganization and control of the General Confederation of Labor (CGT), which by 1952 had affiliated almost all the nation's important unions and a large majority of the labor force.

Immediately after Perón was overthrown the revolutionary government intervened in all the nation's unions, replacing Peronist leaders with military men. However, when elections were held a few months later a majority of the unions reverted to Peronist leadership; a few were captured by the Communists, while others reverted to the Radical, Socialist, and anarchist leadership of the pre-Perón period. These political sectors soon came to be referred to by the number of individual unions they controlled. Thus "the 62 organizations" referred to the Peronist dominated group, "the 19" was the Communist group, and "the 32" was the non-communist, anti-Peronist sector which was also referred to as "the democratic unions." By 1958 there had appeared an "independent" sector formed by unions which formerly had belonged to the "62" or the "32." This division along political lines has consistently frustrated attempts at CGT unity.

During the Frondizi administration a combination of honest elections and government intervention cost the Communists most of their former power. When reduced to the control of a half dozen small unions this group reorganized as the Movement of Syndical Unity and Co-ordination (MUCS). Fraudulent elections allowed "democrats" to retain control of several unions, but the "32" virtually disintegrated as most of its component unions passed into the "independent" camp. Most of the honest elections held in this period resulted in victory of the "62"; however, it was at this time that the "62" began to have serious internal problems. Several Peronist labor leaders co-operated with the Frondizi administration, and others attempted to remove the CGT from the realm of party politics—both of which ran counter to the orders of Perón, then in exile in Madrid.

In January 1963 the CGT held its first National Congress since 1955. The "independents" and "62" divided the seats on the Secretariat, but real control of the CGT fell to the Peronists, as one of the "62" leaders, José Alonso of the Clothing Workers Union, was chosen as Secretary General. Neither MUCS nor the "32" received representation on the national governing body. By this time the former had been reduced to a few small unions, and the latter had virtually ceased to exist.

At about the same time that the Peronists regained effective control of the CGT, the split within the "62" widened appreciably. A so-called "orthodox" faction led by José Alonso was unconditionally loyal to Perón; it was opposed by a more moderate group under the leadership of Augusto Vandor of the Metallurgical Workers Union. The *alonsistas* have been in violent opposition to the administrations of Frondizi, Guido, and Illia. On the other hand, the *vandoristas,* while claiming to be loyal to Perón, have been more prone to negotiation than to open struggles with the government, and have attempted at almost any cost to avoid renewed government intervention in the CGT. The possibility of intervention does not seem to bother Perón or Alonso; in fact, at times they seem intent upon provoking it.

Throughout the first two years of the Illia administration, conflicts within the CGT were intensified, not just within the "62," but also between that sector and the "independents." The latter conflict reached a peak in 1964 when the Peronist controlled CGT Secretariat decided to embark upon a "Battle Plan" which included general strikes and the occupation of factories. The "independents," who consistently have opposed such political action, responded by withdrawing completely from the CGT, leaving the two factions of the "62" to fight for control of that organization.

The struggle between Vandor and Alonso was resolved in favor of the former in February 1966 when the executive council of the CGT removed

Alonso from his post of Secretary General. Three months later a provisional council was established with Francisco Prado of the Light and Power union as Secretary General. The "orthodox" Peronists immediately took their unions out of the CGT, leaving in that organization only the *vandorista* unions and four then controlled by MUCS. With Vandor thus left in control of the "62" as well as the formal apparatus of the CGT, Alonso created a "62 organizations which stand up for Perón" (usually referred to simply as the "62 *de pie*").

At present over 70 percent of Argentina's organized labor force belongs to Peronist-dominated unions. About 15 percent of this Peronist group is non-aligned, while the rest are divided equally between Vandor's "62 organizations" and Alonso's "62 *de pie.*" Communists control four unions which together have perhaps two percent of the CGT membership. Virtually all the rest belong to at least nominally "independent" unions.

The Catholic Church

The history of Church-State relations in Argentina has been much more serene than in many of the other Latin American Republics. Most major conflicts were resolved, and relatively amicably, during the nineteenth century, and on the whole the Church stayed out of the political arena between about 1890 and 1943. However, as was true of so many aspects of the Argentine political system, this neutrality was radically changed during the Peronist period.

The revolutionary Government of 1943 set out at once to gain the support of the Church. This objective was accomplished in a variety of ways, the most important of which was an executive decree of December 31, which re-established religious instruction in the public schools for the first time since 1884. The first Peronist Congress soon converted this decree into law. Church support for the regime took various forms, not the least of which was a pastoral letter of November 1945, which in effect asked all Catholics to vote for Perón.

While the Church can claim some credit for Perón's rise to power, it can also claim some credit for his fall. By about 1951, Church support had changed to neutrality and by 1954 to open hostility toward the regime. On June 15, 1955, after Perón had discontinued religious instruction in the schools, legalized divorce and prostitution, and jailed or exiled several leading clergymen, Pope Pius XII excommunicated "all those who have trampled on the rights of the Church." Although Perón was not named, there can be little doubt that he was included in the decree.

Catholic nationalists had some influence in the short-lived Lonardi administration in 1955, but since that time the Church has returned to the political background. While two Catholic political parties were formed about the time of the fall of Perón, neither has been able to attract any appreciable electoral following. The Federal Union, composed primarily of right-wing ultranationalists, has virtually disappeared. The more moderate Christian

Democrat party has a small following spread rather evenly across the nation. The party has for several years been attempting to enlist the support of "soft-line" Peronists but has had no real success.

Other Groups

In addition to the above, there are a number of associational interest groups which at least deserve to be mentioned. The most important agricultural group is probably the Rural Society, which represents the nation's largest landowners, especially those in the province of Buenos Aires. Formed in 1866, the group now has over nine thousand members, among whom is almost all the top echelon of Argentine society. A virtual subsidiary of the Rural Society representing the cattlemen is the Argentine Meat Producers Corporation.

Among the leading industrial and commercial organizations are the Industrial Union, the Argentine Chamber of Commerce, and the General Economic Confederation (CGE). The Industrial Union represents the larger, older industries, which are quite anti-Peronist, and which support complete free-trade policies. On the other hand, the CGE unites the newer and smaller establishments, many of which collaborated with the Peronist administration. This group is more inclined toward state regulation.

THE POLITICAL PARTY SYSTEM

Throughout most of its history, Argentina has had two major political parties and a large number of minor parties. Prior to 1862, when the most important political issue was what form of government to adopt, Federalists and Unitarians dominated the scene; for the next eighteen years it was Nationals and Autonomists who argued over the establishment of a federal district at Buenos Aires. With this issue settled in 1880, there no longer remained real issues to divide the ruling elite, and it was united politically as the National Autonomist party (PAN). For a decade the PAN was virtually unchallenged, but with the formation in 1891 of the Radical Civic Union (UCR), Argentina returned to what was basically a two-party system. Between 1891 and 1943, several new parties were formed, but none could even approach in importance the Conservatives and the Radicals. During the era of Perón, the power of the Conservatives was broken, and only the Radicals were able to offer meaningful opposition to the Peronists.

The Contemporary Party Scene

The Radicals   With the overthrow of the Peronist dictatorship in 1955, the UCR once again became the nation's strongest political force. The only group capable of effective opposition to the Radicals was the Peronists, but the revolutionary Government immediately banned all political activity by this group. The UCR, however, was not the same party it had been in 1943. Since the 1930s it had been badly split between Conservative and Liberal factions, each of which was itself divided. The right wing of the party talked a great deal about political democracy, especially free suffrage and strict adherence to the Constitution, but was not as interested in social and economic reform as was the left wing. That sector was more intent upon welfare legislation than upon the right to vote or upon provincial autonomy.

By 1956 it was obvious that, if the military regime allowed free elections, the Radicals would have little effective opposition. However, the party seemed determined to provide this opposition within its own organization. The conflict between the conservative Unionists and the left-wing Intransigents became more and more bitter until March 1957, when the UCR formally split into two separate parties. In addition to the general conflict between liberalism and conservatism, there were two main issues separating the two groups: Who was to receive the UCR presidential nomination (and thus be virtually assured of election), and what position the party should adopt in relation to the illegal Peronist movement. In general, those favoring the candidacy of Arturo Frondizi and looking for an electoral alliance with the Peronists, formed the Intransigent Radical Civic Union (UCRI); the opponents of Frondizi, who were also quite anti-Peronist, established the Popular Radical Civic Union (UCRP).

The original program of the UCRI is easier to determine than that of the UCRP, for the former had one acknowledged leader, Arturo Frondizi. The party was formed to a great degree around the personality of this one man. His virtually absolute control of the party might be compared to that of Hipólito Irigoyen from 1900 to 1922. Thus one would not be far afield if one assumed that the program of the UCRI was that of Frondizi.

According to Frondizi, there should be three elements in the socio-economic revolution he felt was necessary to bring Argentina into the community of world powers. The first was to be agrarian reform. He was somewhat hesitant about the shape this reform should take. On the one hand, he felt that "it is necessary to give access to the land immediately to whoever works it," yet he was worried about the inefficiency of a multitude of small farms. He seemingly would have preferred large co-operatives, which should greatly increase production, but he did not want them forced upon the populace. The second step was to be industrialization. This, he thought, was the only way Argentina could defeat the designs of the imperialist nations, which were trying to keep Argentina a producer of raw materials and a market for their industrial products. The third step Frondizi labeled "democratization of the economy." He wanted immediate nationalization—with just compensation—of all the nation's public services and all monopolies. Except for these two areas, however, he did not favor indiscriminate nationalization. In general, the program advocated by Frondizi and the UCRI prior to 1958 was quite similar to that of Haya de la Torre, the Peruvian *Aprista* leader, whom Frondizi once referred to as the number one citizen of America.

While the program of the UCRI can be obtained from the writings of its single leader, this cannot be done in the case of the UCRP. About the only conclusion one can reach is that the early UCRP had no explicit program. The party was, for the most part, composed of all the sectors of the old UCR which had opposed Frondizi. Even within the three main components of the party (the Movement of Intransigence and Renovation, the Movement of National Intransigence and Unity Nucleus, each of which was virtually a party within a party), there was a wide divergence in ideology. The members of the MIR and MIN had more in common, ideologically, with the UCRI than with the Unionists within their own party. The members of the latter group were by far the most conservative of all Radical factions and seemed to have had only one thing in common with the other segments of the UCRP— opposition to Frondizi.

After his election to the Presidency in 1958, Frondizi acted in a manner almost diametrically opposed to his earlier writings and speeches. In general, candidate Fondizi talked about statist solutions to economic problems, retention of the *status quo* in religious questions, a nationalistic program in regard to the development of natural resources, and greater freedom of union activities. Yet President Frondizi championed free enterprise, forced through Congress a bill allowing the establishment of Catholic universities, granted oil concessions to foreign companies, and used the army to break strikes. Frondizi's control over the UCRI was shown in 1960, when the party's national convention amended its platform to bring it into line with the actions of the administration. Dropped were planks calling for a state-planned economy, for opposition to Catholic universities, for nationalization of petroleum and electricity, and for immediate and profound agrarian reform. These were replaced with a promise of respect for private property, co-operation between state and private education, and acceptance of foreign capital for the development of natural resources.

Between 1958 and 1962, the UCRP and the UCRI virtually switched positions. Originally the former was considered the more moderate and less nationalistic of the two. However, after Frondizi and the UCRI-dominated Congress signed agreements with the International Monetary Fund and with United States oil companies, the UCRP seized the banner of nationalism. By 1963, Popular Radicals were claiming, with some justification, that they comprised the liberal and nationalistic sector of Argentine radicalism. During the 1963 election campaign, it was the UCRP that promised to annul the petroleum concessions granted by the Frondizi administration and return the sacred cow of Argentine nationalism to total government control. The UCRI, forced to defend the record of its past administration, continued to espouse the inviting of foreign investment to aid in industrialization. The UCRP, or at least most of its sectors, promised more immediate prosperity through the exploitation of natural resources and of agricultural products in exchange for money and goods.

Both Radical parties have been ambivalent in their policies toward Peronism. In 1958 the UCRP supported the revolutionary Government of General Aramburu and promised continued prohibition of Peronist political activity. On the other hand, the UCRI openly sought, and obtained, the electoral support of the Peronists in the 1958 elections. Frondizi probably promised immediate legalization of the Peronist party as the price of this support; however, it was 1962 before the followers of the ex-dictator were allowed to run for election. Here again the positions of the UCRI and UCRP have been reversed to some extent. The UCRI continued the legal proscription on Peronism during most of the party's tenure in the executive office, and when Frondizi did allow Peronist electoral participation in 1962, he intervened in the provinces won by Peronists and kept them from assuming office. In the 1963 campaign it was the UCRP which promised the Peronists full legal equality if the party gained power. It is quite probable that the UCRP presidential nominee received a great many Peronist votes as the least of several evils.

The Peronists With the Peronist party prevented from entering elections between 1955 and 1962, several "neo-Peronist" groups were formed. That these were not then Peronist parties, strictly speaking, is seen in two facts: Both the provisional Government of Aramburu and the Frondizi administration allowed them to nominate their own candidates in the elections of 1957, 1958 and 1960, and these parties refused to obey Perón's directives on how to vote. (Perón ordered his followers to cast blank ballots in 1957 and 1960 and to vote for UCRI candidates in 1958.) With the complete legalization of Peronism in 1962, several new Peronist parties were formed. As a result of the continued ban on the use of the term *"Partido Peronista,"* these organizations have today several different names; they include Labor party, Three Flags, Popular Union, and Social Justice.

The current program of the Peronists is almost impossible to define. During election campaigns the Peronists offer only vague promises of a return to the good old days of 1946–1955. However, it can be said that Peronism today is primarily a movement of the urban laborers with its greatest strength in the General Confederation of Labor, which Peronists dominate. Between 1946 and 1955, Peronism gained the support of not only the urban working class but also the middle classes of the interior provinces and the new industrialist upper class, which had prospered during the war but needed protection thereafter. However, the latter two groups were, to a large extent, wooed away by Frondizi and the UCRI and thus left Peronism almost completely a working-class movement.

Today Peronism is splintered into several quarrelling groups. Each of the various neo-Peronist parties has a leader who considers himself subordinate only to the exiled leader in Madrid. This in itself makes co-ordination among the several groups quite difficult. In general, the Peronist movement might be divided into two sectors, which are frequently referred to as the hard line and soft line. The former, concentrated in the federal capital and the province of Buenos Aires, is the more militant and is tied directly to the trade unions, which have their greatest strength in this area. The leaders of the hard-line sector still talk of the return to power of Perón; they envision a government almost identical to that of 1946–1955. Despised by the leaders of the armed forces, this group's chances of peaceful acquisition of power are virtually nonexistent.

The soft-line sector is dominant in several of the interior provinces. It appears to be willing to work through the democratic channels of government and take its chances at the polls. In spite of Perón's demands for the casting of blank votes in 1963, this group nominated its own candidates, several of whom were successful. These parties will be much easier to reintegrate into the national political arena because of their at least partial separation from Perón. One of their leaders has recently said, "Perón is now history," a statement of heresy as far as the hard-line group is concerned. This is the much-mentioned "Peronism without Perón."

The Conservatives   Since 1955 the Conservative vote has been split among several parties. Although completely dominant on the political scene prior to 1916 and again between 1930 and 1943, the Conservative party disintegrated rapidly during the Perón era; between 1943 and 1955, only three Conservatives were elected to Congress. To make matters even worse, in 1956 the party divided into two separate groups, which took the names Democrat and Popular Conservative Democrat (PDCP). The fragmentation did not stop there; in several provinces splinter groups left the PDCP and thus further weakened the Conservative cause. The main difference between the Democrats and the PDCP members lies in their views toward Peronism. The former is quite anti-Peronist, but the latter calls for the restoration of full political rights to Peronists and openly appeals for their electoral support. (In 1963 Vincente Solano Lima, the PDCP leader, was for a short period the Peronist presidential nominee.) Late in 1958 the Democrats united with several small provincial conservative parties to form the National Federation of Parties of the Center (FNPC); this is today the main voice of Argentine conservatism. Thus far the PDCP and its splinter groups have refused to join this coalition in spite of the fact that joining would certainly enhance their electoral prospects.

The Socialists   The Socialist party, which had gained some strength during the 1930s, lost most of its support between 1943 and 1962. (The party did not elect a single congressman during this period.) Since its founding about seventy years ago, the Socialist party has commanded a great deal of respect. It has been one of the very few parties completely removed from the many scandals the nation has witnessed, and the calibre of the party's leaders, including such men as Juan B. Justo, Alfredo Palacios, Nicolás Repetto, and Enrique Dickmann, has been as high as that of any Argentine party. Argentine socialism has been much more moderate than in most other Latin American nations, and this moderation proved to be detrimental between 1943 and 1955, when the Peronists won over most of the unskilled and semiskilled labor vote. In 1959 the Socialists split into two parties, one retaining the original Argentine Socialist party (PSA) label and the other calling itself the Democratic Socialist party (PSD). The PSA, led by Ramón A. Muñiz, Carlos Sánchez Viamonte, and David Tieffenberg, is primarily the left wing of the old party; however, it is difficult to generalize here, for this group is itself split into several antagonistic factions. The PSD, under the leadership of Américo Ghioldi, Juan Antonio Solari, and Luis Pan, is so moderate as to be Socialist in name only; in 1964 its congressmen voted most often with the members of UDELPA and of the FNPC.

Christian Democracy   In 1955 Argentina's first important Catholic party, the Christian Democrat party (PDC), was formed. It was originally a moderate center party much like its Italian counterpart of the same name. At the time of the founding of the Argentine party, it was somewhat to the right of the Chilean PDC, yet to the left of the Venezuelan Christian Democrats. Espousing a middle position on most economic issues, the founders of the Argentine PDC favored neither state ownership nor absolute free enterprise. Early platforms stressed the need for a strengthening of Congress in relation to the President, the adoption of a system of proportional representation in the selection of congressmen, and the right of private organizations to operate educational facilities. During the last few years the Argentine PDC has moved appreciably to the left. Since about 1960 the party's leadership has been split on the question of whether or not to attempt to gain the support of the more moderate sector of the Peronist movement. In an effort to obtain this support, the now dominant faction, led by Horacio Sueldo, is advocating a program that some say is more similar to the Peronism of 1946–1955 than that offered by the Peronists today. Since 1961 there have been frequent rumors of the formation of a Social Christian Union embracing large sectors of these two groups, but no such coalition has taken place to date.

Other Parties   Another of the nation's traditional parties which survived the Peronist period is the Progressive Democrat party (PDP), a moderate, left-of-center, somewhat anticlerical organization. The PDP was formed early this century as a union of Lisandro de la Torre's League of the South and other small provincial parties. Originally the PDP was meant to voice the interests of the small farmers of the interior provinces, but today it appears to appeal mainly to intellectuals and professionals in Santa Fe. Dying a not-so-slow death, the Progressive Democrats gained new life in 1963 with the nomination of Pedro Aramburu. as their presidential candidate.

The Argentine Communist party (PCA) is among the largest in Latin America but has never elected a congressman. The party retained legal recognition during the provisional Government of 1955–1958, was prohibited from engaging in political activities during the Frondizi administration, and was completely outlawed by President Guido in 1963. The Communists nominated their own candidates in 1957, supported Frondizi in 1958, cast blank ballots in 1960, and aided the Peronist candidates in 1962.

In January 1963, a new political party, the Union of the Argentine People (UDELPA), was formed to back retired General Pedro E. Aramburu for the Presidency. This party is obviously quite personalistic, with very little ideological content. Any effort to determine what the party stands for must begin with an examination of the ideas of General Aramburu. Yet during the

1963 campaign Aramburu refused to espouse a definite program. Realizing that many Argentines looked upon him as the strongman who could bring order to the chaotic national scene, Aramburu was willing to run as a sort of Argentine De Gaulle. Some persons have equated the ideals of UDELPA with those of the PDP since that party also gave Aramburu its nomination; however, during the special session of Congress in 1963–1964, the UDELPA and PDP congressmen appear to have voted on opposite sides of an issue more often than not. UDELPA has supported the Illia administration, while the PDP has refused to do so. From the actions of Aramburu between 1955 and 1958 and from the voting record of the UDELPA congressmen, one is forced to the conclusion that this party is basically a Conservative organization.

In 1964 the Intransigent Radicals split into two separate parties, one faction retaining the original UCRI label and the other calling itself the Movement of Integration and Development (MID). This split was precipitated by a conflict between Frondizi and Oscar Alende, former UCRI governor of Buenos Aires, over participation in the 1963 elections. Frondizi wanted the Intransigent Radicals to boycott the election in protest of the Government's refusal to allow Peronists to nominate candidates for executive office; on the other hand, Alende insisted that the UCRI nominate a full slate of candidates with his own name at the head of the list. In addition to personalistic antagonism, there are some ideological differences between the two groups. In general, the UCRI of Alende supports the pre–1958 party platform, which is quite nationalistic and somewhat left-of-center, while Frondizi's MID advocates a continuation of the policies followed by its leader between 1958 and 1962. It might be added that the MID seems intent upon an alliance with the Peronists at almost any price, while the UCRI, although not at all opposed to such a coalition, puts the interests of the party above any alliance.

An Assessment of Party Strength   An accurate estimate of the electoral strength of individual parties in Argentina is complicated by the fact the Peronists cast blank ballots in 1957 and in 1960 and voted for UCRI candidates in 1958; at the same time, both Peronists and UCRI members cast blank ballots in large but unmeasurable numbers in 1963. Nevertheless, some general comments can be made.

First, it should be noted that from the time of the fall of Perón through 1963, there were four political sectors of roughly equal strength: Peronists, Intransigent Radicals, Popular Radicals, and what might be labeled "minor parties." In the five national elections held between 1957 and 1963, the UCRP vote fluctuated very little, ranging from a high of 25 percent in 1958 and 1963 to a low of 20 percent in 1962. The UCRI vote also remained between 20 and 25 percent in the elections of 1957, 1960, and 1962 but was inflated to 42 percent in 1958 (as a result of the number of Peronist votes the party received) and declined to 16 percent in 1963, when many of Frondizi's supporters cast blank ballots. The number of blank ballots (the vast majority of which were cast by Peronists) reached 25 percent in 1957 and 1960, and the legalized Peronist movement received 32 percent of the vote in 1962. The total vote received by minor parties has fluctuated between 20 and 30 percent. This picture was somewhat changed by the elections of 1965. The vote for Peronist candidates was up to 35 percent, and the UCRP, probably supported by minor-party members, received an all-time high of 29 percent. Hurt the most by this polarization of the electorate were the UCRI and MID,

TABLE 2

Argentine National Elections: 1957–1965*

Party	1957	1958	1960	1962	1963	1965
UCRP	2,016,929	2,229,244	2,119,094	1,875,578	2,419,269	2,727,216
UCRI	1,847,583	3,778,561	1,832,248	2,301,397	1,541,902	413,916
FNPC	499,400	290,200	786,442	556,622	538,425	494,402
PDC	419,630	327,744	347,316	212,605	436,935	253,294
PDP	263,865	164,532	241,611	158,114	555,991	290,001
PSA			398,127	168,578	310,739	180,886
PS	524,311	520,830				
PSD			348,623	259,246	306,650	172,354
Peronist				2,999,146	665,376	3,305,330
UDELPA					656,124	184,566
MID						602,406
Others	998,730	857,446	610,569	598,100	418,604	627,029
Blank	2,132,806	808,651	2,228,014	262,020	1,668,170	172,449
Totals	8,703,254	8,977,208	9,389,725	9,518,185	8,912,044	9,423,849

* These are the official results as published in mimeograph form by the Electoral Department of the Interior Ministry in *Resultados electorales comparativos* and *Elección de Diputados Nacionales 14-III-1965.*

who together received only 11 percent of the total, perhaps relegating these groups to the category of minor parties.

Party Membership and Organization

Political party affiliation in Argentina differs appreciably from the practice in the United States, where one becomes a Democrat or a Republican by simply proclaiming himself as such. Membership in an Argentine political party is a much more serious matter. It is somewhat difficult to describe the exact procedure by which one becomes a member, for it varies from party to party and even within some of the parties which leave this up to their local organizations. The Democratic Socialists have a single national policy, which is illustrative of the general method used. In order to be eligible for membership in the PSD, one must be a registered voter and have "an honest means of making a living." Anyone meeting these requirements may go to the local PSD headquarters to pick up an application form, which must be filled out in quadruplicate. The form merely asks for personal data, such as age, occupation, and address, and for a sworn pledge to uphold the ideological principles of the party. After being countersigned by two persons who have been Democratic Socialists for at least two years, the application is returned to the local party office. If approved there, the application is forwarded to the PSD National Executive Committee. Approval by that body means admittance. (If there is no local party office in the candidate's locality—as is often the case with the PSD—application may be made directly to the National Executive Committee.)

The highest organ within each party is the national convention. Delegates are apportioned among the various provinces in differing manners: The Radicals give each province the same number of delegates as it has congressmen; the Conservatives apportion delegates according to the number of party votes cast in any given province in the last national election; and the Christian Democrats simply give each province five delegates. In all cases the delegates are chosen at the local level by party members casting a secret ballot. There are usually provisions for minority representation within each provincial delegation. Most parties require that delegates have the same qualifications as members of the Chamber of Deputies and that they are not deputies.

The national conventions usually meet each year although some parties have biennial meetings. The functions of the convention are basically those of the Democratic or Republican conventions in the United States. The convention (1) writes the party platform though not infrequently the platform of the previous year is readopted; (2) amends the party constitution, an activity which takes place about as often as the adoption of new platforms; (3) decides whether or not the party will enter into electoral alliances at the national level and approves or disapproves of alliances at the provincial level; and (4) in presidential election years, chooses the party's nominees.

Between meetings of the national convention, the parties are directed by national committees, which may be called national executive committees or national juntas. Membership on the national committees varies from eleven in the case of the PDC to four per province in the UCRP; in any case, members are chosen at the local level and not by the national convention, which has very little control over them. In addition to carrying out the day-to-day duties of the party, the national committees direct national election campaigns, control the party's finances, and, if necessary, call for special sessions of the national convention. Within each party it is the President (or Secretary General) of the National Committee who is *the* party leader.

Organization within the various provinces depends upon local rules, but in general these provincial organizations are simply miniatures of the national one. There are usually provincial conventions, which write local platforms and nominate candidates for governor and for the Chamber of Deputies. Provincial executive committees normally have the same functions—at a lower level—as the national committees do. Most parties also have municipal or district conventions, which nominate legislators and municipal councilmen.

Each of the national parties is highly centralized, with each organ having almost complete disciplinary power over its subordinates. Discipline usually takes one of four forms: private admonition, public condemnation, suspension, or expulsion. Members are most frequently disciplined for departure from the ideological principles of the party. A private member might be admonished or condemned for publicly disagreeing with the party's platform or statement of principles. A congressman might even be expelled from the party for refusing to vote in the manner directed. For example, in September of 1960, President Frondizi introduced in Congress an extremely controversial bill to allow the Chief Executive to grant to domestic and foreign private companies concessions for the exploitation of power resources. Facing the certain negative votes of the opposition parties, the bill needed the support of 97 of the 110 UCRI congressmen. At first many of the UCRI deputies joined the opposition in boycotting sessions at which the bill was discussed, but upon the threat of disciplinary action, most of the deputies returned and voted for the bill. Nine members refused to do so; the next month the UCRI National Committee removed three of them from the party and suspended the other six.

The power of expulsion is frequently used to settle intraparty disputes. In the Socialist party, for example, a bitter ideological conflict raged from the time of the Liberating Revolution until 1958. In July of that year, the leftist faction of the party gained a majority of the seats on the National Executive Committee and almost immediately expelled all the right-wing members of the committee. This soon led to the formation of two separate Socialist parties. Virtually the same thing had happened the year before in the Radical Civic Union and had the same results.

Centralization of power is accomplished primarily through the disciplinary powers mentioned above and through the power of any party organization to intervene in any lower echelon. For example, the Christian Democrat National Executive Committee might decide that the PDC organization in the Province of Córdoba was not following the correct ideological line. The committee could remove all the party's officials in that province, annul the local constitution and program, and send in someone from the national office to run the party there single-handed. Eventually elections for new officers would be held and programs written. Prior to this time, however, recalcitrant PDC members might find themselves removed from the party rolls.

The power of the national organizations of the parties to intervene and to discipline counteract all the long provisions in party constitutions which guarantee local autonomy. Parties in Argentina are no more federal in nature than the nation itself.

A TENTATIVE PROGNOSIS

Only the very brave or the very foolish would attempt to predict the future of Argentine politics. The solution of each problem seems to be accompanied by the creation of another one—or two. President Illia has now completed one-third of his six-year term, and much of the atmosphere of crisis that was so pervasive in 1962 and 1963 has been alleviated. However, the problems that remain are of such a magnitude as to allow only very cautious optimism.

The problems facing Argentina are both economic and political. There are many who claim that the political crisis will remain until the major economic problems are solved, but an equally large number of observers insist that political stability is a prerequisite to solution of these economic problems. The Illia administration seems determined to attack both at the same time but quite cautiously.

Heading the list of the nation's economic problems are fiscal deficits, a large foreign debt, and rampant inflation. The fiscal deficit is now running about three-quarters of a billion dollars a year; a very large part of this is attributable to the enormous losses sustained by the state-owned railways. As is so typical of the current situation, solution of this economic problem by reducing feather-bedding, increasing rail fares, and so forth, might well lead to political complications of even greater magnitude. Another example of this sort of vicious circle may be seen in the large foreign debt, which is consistently aggravated by an unfavorable balance of payments. One of the first acts of the Illia administration was the cancellation of the foreign petroleum contracts granted by Frondizi in spite of the fact that Argentina was then on the verge of self-sufficiency in petroleum products. This often repeated campaign promise had become a political necessity, yet in 1965 Argentina had to use about 100 million dollars of its precious dollar reserves to import oil. Much of this drain of hard currency could probably be halted by granting new petroleum concessions, but such an act would be sure to have dire political consequences.

About the best that can be said for the economy is that inflation is being "held" to 25 or 30 percent per year, and the gross national product is now increasing at the rate of about 7 percent. However, many wages are going up at a much slower rate than the cost of living, and the recently increasing GNP has not yet made up for its decline in preceding years.

The current political situation looks slightly better. Bitter anatgonism between Peronists and anti-Peronists has abated somewhat although this conflict is still far from a permanent solution. Throughout 1964 there was a great deal of talk about the return to Argentina of Perón; finally, on December 2 the ex-dictator flew from Madrid to Rio de Janeiro, presumably on his way to Argentina, but the Brazilian authorities quite predictably refused to allow him to continue his journey. This attempt to return, if it was that at all, was rather half-hearted; it was prompted perhaps by the belief that Perón's mere proximity would set off a rebellion that would lead to his return to power. Nothing could have been further from the truth, as Argentina remained surprisingly calm throughout the episode. The year 1965 was to have been one of reorganization and reuniting of the Peronist movement, but this was just as great a failure as Perón's return. There remained differences between the labor, the political, and the female sectors of the movement, in addition to the split between the Popular Union, which is the main Peronist party, and the provincial neo-Peronist organizations.

The elections of 1963 and 1965 have helped at least to begin the reincorporation of Peronism into Argentine political life. In the former year Peronists were denied the right to nominate candidates for executive offices, and Perón responded by ordering his followers to cast blank ballots. Many of the neo-Peronist parties of the interior ignored this order by running candidates for legislative positions. These groups won sixteen seats in the lower house of Congress and several seats in provincial legislatures, including pluralities in four. The highly responsible actions of these Peronist congressmen and legislators went a long way toward dispelling the illusion of Peronism as a bunch of rabble-rousers intent upon monopolizing power by force. In the March 1965 congressional elections, the Peronists were given complete electoral freedom. Fifty-two Peronists were elected to the Chamber of Deputies and took their seats with a minimum of opposition.

The election victories of Peronism in 1962 were the primary cause of the military coup of that year, yet the leaders of the armed forces made no attempt to cancel the Peronist victories of 1963 or 1965. There are probably two main reasons for this. First of all, in 1962 Peronists won the governorships of ten provinces, including all-important Buenos Aires, in addition to legislative positions. Military leaders might have allowed the Peronists to assume their legislative seats but were adamant that Peronists not be admitted to major executive offices. In 1963 Peronists were not allowed to nominate candidates for executive office, and in 1965 only legislative positions were at stake. Second, the composition of the top echelons of the armed services changed drastically between 1962 and 1963. In the former year a great many *gorilas* held important positions, but a year later the legalists, under the leadership of General Juan Carlos Onganía, were firmly in control.

Argentines are already looking ahead to the elections of 1967, when half the membership of the Chamber of Deputies, almost all governors, and many provincial legislators will be elected. Peronists are being extremely cautious not to give the administration or the military any excuse to prohibit, or even limit, their participation in these elections. Given complete electoral freedom, Peronists could gain control of several provinces and perhaps obtain a plurality of the seats in the Chamber of Deputies (the new proportional representation law makes the Peronists' chances of obtaining a majority there very slim). Illia's Popular Radicals have already begun their campaign to enlist the support of the minor parties for UCRP candidates in order to forestall such a

Peronist sweep. Such an attempt was only partly successful in 1965; how it will fare two years later is an open question.

POSTSCRIPT[7]

On the morning of June 28, 1966, General Julio Alsogaray walked into the office of President Illia and announced, "Dr. Illia, sir, you must leave this office in the name of the armed forces." Thus for the fifth time since 1930, the military removed the nation's constitutionally elected President.

The official reasons for the coup were: a growing lack of order, authority and discipline; advances made by communism, especially in the national universities; the type of election campaigns waged by the UCRP, and the sterile electoral option of Peronism or anti-Peronism; the unrepresentative character of the Illia administration; deterioration of the national economy; a bad foreign image; structural defects in the political system; and a general need for modernization. While these factors (real or imaginary) were probably disturbing to many of the leaders of the armed forces, it seems unlikely that they were the main reasons for the coup.

Throughout most of the Illia administration there was friction between the President and the leaders of the armed forces. The military wanted to send troops to the Dominican Republic at the time of the "constitutionalist" uprising, and it wanted intervention in the national universities "to clean out the Communists," but in each instance Illia refused. The President did not share the enthusiasm of the military for the creation of an Inter-American Peace Force, nor did he react to the Chilean border clash as forcefully as the military leaders wanted. None of these attitudes endeared Illia or his administration to the armed forces; however, in themselves they would probably not have led to a coup—nor could they be used as a public justification for breaking of the constitutional order.

The single overriding factor appears to have been fear of Peronist victories in the gubernatorial elections scheduled for March 1967. The military leaders were willing to accept Peronism as a minority party in the Congress, and even willing to tolerate a few neo-Peronist governors in the smaller provinces, but the thought of a Peronist governor of Buenos Aires was by no means acceptable. For a year and a half Illia had been subjected to pressure from the military to demonstrate how Peronists would be kept from winning the 1967 elections; this he could not do.

In spite of the demand of the armed forces that Peronists be denied major executive posts, the military leaders did not want to be in the position of having to annul an honest election, as was the case in 1962. The only alternative was to see to it that the elections were not held, yet this could not very well be the announced reason for the coup. Thus the coup took place well

---

[7] The above was completed before the coup. This postscript was written in Buenos Aires in May 1967.

in advance of the scheduled elections, in fact before the campaign had even begun. Still, it was necessary to explain the causes of the coup in a manner which could gain popular support for the new regime. This led to the claim that the June 28 coup was just the beginning of a "real revolution" which would bring about fundamental changes in the social, economic, and political systems.

In spite of all this, the announced causes and goals of the coup should not be considered as complete hypocrisy. The military had witnessed the failure of two civilian administrations to solve "the Peronist problem" (and these were the administrations of the only two political parties in Argentina with popular support even approaching that of the Peronists). Also the nationalism of many military leaders led them to demand that Argentina greatly accelerate its rate of economic development. In addition, there appear to have been some influential leaders of the armed forces who supported the coup in order to put an end to the "need" for coups. To this must be added the fact that by June 1966 the Illia administration was almost totally lacking in popular support.

President Illia was originally replaced by a junta composed of the commanders-in-chief of the three service branches: General Pascual Pistarini, Admiral Benigno Varela, and Brigadier Adolfo Alvarez. This junta immediately dissolved congress, the provincial legislatures, and municipal councils, removed from office all governors, mayors, and the members of the Supreme Court, and dissolved all the nation's political parties. Next the junta issued the *Acta de la Revolución Argentina,* named as President retired General Juan Carlos Onganía, and then dissolved itself.

General Onganía first gained public attention in 1962 when he became the acknowledged leader of the legalist faction of the armed forces. With the victory of the legalist forces in September of that year, Onganía became commander-in-chief of the army, a position he held until November 1965 when he retired from active duty as a result of a disagreement with President Illia. The naming of Onganía as President seems somewhat paradoxical because he could easily have assumed dictatorial powers at any time between September 1962 and July 1963, and could almost surely have been elected to the Presidency on the latter date had he so desired. Also it should be noted that it was Onganía who was responsible for the issuance of Communique 150 which called for subordination of the military to civilian control, and for a resumption of constitutional government.

About a month after his inauguration Onganía issued a statement entitled "Policies of the National Government" which was meant to explain the future course of action of his administration. In the realm of foreign policy this declaration includes a statement of friendship for all the nations of the Americas, Spain and the other European nations with a western Christian culture. The section on domestic policy promises the re-establishment of representative government (without mentioning how or when these representatives are to be chosen), the restructuring of the educational system, the neutralizing of Marxist influence and action by Communists and other extremists, and prevention of any action which would impede the ends pursued by the decree dissolving political parties. The section on economic policy promises to reverse the trend toward statism by returning to a system of "private enterprise through the competitive mechanism." This section contains statements such as "private property will be considered as basic to the preservation of individual liberty," yet it also promises that the state will play an active role in the nation's economic life instead of remaining a mere spectator. The section on labor policy says that there will be a minimum of government control over labor organizations and that the unions will not be subject to intervention as long as they obey the law and pursue only those ends for which they were created. The last two sections offer vague promises of improvements in the fields of social security, public health and national security.

There is one type of statement which has been conspicuously absent during the first year of the Onganía administration; this is a declaration of the provisional nature of the government and a promise of early elections. Quite to the contrary, Onganía calls himself President of the Argentine Republic and not provisional President. He has assumed legislative as well as executive power, and is issuing laws, not decrees. The same is true of the men he has appointed to provincial governorships—and they are referred to as governors, not interveners. All this is quite unusual for revolutionary governments in Argentina. Also unusual is the fact that the present administration is essentially civilian in character. The President, the members of his cabinet, and the provincial governors are all civilians (although several of the last mentioned are retired military men). In fact, in the entire administration the only two positions held by officers still on active duty are the President of the State Railway System, and the Secretary of the National Security Council.

It has always been very difficult to predict the future course of Argentine politics. Predictions are especially hazardous today for at least two reasons. As pointed out above, this is not a typical revolutionary government, and, more importantly, the present administration has steadfastly refused to adopt any coherent political program.

Immediately after the military coup Onganía seemed intent on following a completely apolitical line. Virtually none of his original appointees could be identified with the nation's major political parties; the only common denominator seemed to be the fact that a large number of them were quite reactionary Catholics. Within three months there appeared a slow but steady drift toward something approaching a corporate state. It seemed as though the President was still opposed to any definite political orientation, while many of the members of his administration—especially his Interior Minister—wanted to establish a regime resembling that of Franco's Spain.

The revamping of the cabinet in December 1966 resulted in the replacing of most of the reactionary corporativists with relatively moderate Catholic nationalists—primarily those belonging to Mario Amadeo's *Ateneo de la República*. This group soon gained almost complete control over the political ministries and secretariats; however, before their influence could be expanded, most of the important economic positions were turned over to the conservatives. Within the last few months, the picture has been further complicated by the rise of a social christian group centered in the Ministry of Social Security. As of May 1967 it is virtually impossible to say which, if any, of these groups will be able to impose its philosophy upon the revolutionary government.

One thing seems relatively clear at this time. If President Onganía can remain in power for another three or four years—as now seems quite possible, barring a severe economic crisis—the future course of Argentine politics should differ appreciably from that of the period prior to June 1966.

16 / Uruguay

DONALD W. BRAY

DONALD W. BRAY, Associate Professor of Government at California State College at Los Angeles, has visited all twenty of the Latin American Republics. He spent 1959–60 in Chile on a Fulbright grant and has written "Chile: The Dark Side of Stability," "Latin American Political Parties," and other articles dealing with politics in the hemisphere.

THE POLITICAL ENVIRONMENT

Uruguayans have a saying, "There is nothing like Uruguay" (*Como el Uruguay no hay*). One of their writers has half-jokingly urged that the aphorism be changed to "There never was an Uruguay" (*Como el Uruguay no hubo*).[1] He means to suggest that the common perception of what Uruguay is like is fiction. It is true that the country has often been idealized by both nationals and foreigners. Yet it also remains true that there is really nothing quite like Uruguay; it is an interesting and unique political culture.

The Land

The smallest of the South American states, Uruguay is the only one in which the entire national territory has been effectively occupied. Settlement has been facilitated by the absence of physical barriers and by a moderate climate throughout the nation. The predominant surface feature is rolling, grass-covered hills, which nowhere exceed 2,000 feet in elevation. There are approximately 16 acres of land suitable for livestock-grazing or cultivation for

---

[1] Mario Benedetti, *El país de la cola de paja* (Montevideo, Ediciones Ciudad Vieja, 1961), p. 76.

each inhabitant. The land is overwhelmingly used for grazing; sheep number around 23 million and cattle about 8 million. Crop-growing is largely confined to the southern third of the country, partly because of proximity to urban markets and partly because topsoil in other regions is often thin and rainfall less dependable.

Mineral resources are modest, being chiefly marble, granite, talc, and small deposits of iron ore and manganese. Hydroelectric power has been developed by damming the Río Negro and thus creating a large lake in the heart of the country.

One important natural advantage is produced by the magnificent beaches which stretch the length of Uruguay's Atlantic coast. Since the area of Buenos Aires is devoid of such endowments, Argentines stream to Uruguayan coastal resorts during the summer season.

Transportation

Uruguay is the only South American state aside from Argentina which has a national railroad network. Uruguay's total rail mileage, 1,828 miles, is of uniform gauge. British-built, the network is now wholly state-owned. Road transport is today offering severe competition to the railroads even though most roads in the interior are unpaved. A national airline, PLUNA, provides regular service to the principal interior towns and international service to Brazil, Paraguay, and Bolivia.

The People

Despite its agriculture-based economy, Uruguay is one of the most urbanized of nations. Only twenty-one percent of its population lives on ranches and farms. Just under forty-six percent of the total lives in the "suction pump," Montevideo. This is the most extreme case in the world of what demographers call the "primate city" problem, that is, dominion over a nation by a single, outsized city. Montevideo, the capital, with its 1.2 million population, dwarfs the second largest city, Paysandú, with its mere 60,000.

The people of Uruguay are, relative to most of Latin America, healthy and literate. Epidemic diseases have been brought under control, average calorie intake is 3,100 per day, and life expectancy is a remarkable sixty-six years. An estimated eighty-five percent of persons over fifteen years of age are literate, and approximately three-fourths of the population enjoys adequate housing.

Those on the bottom of the social and economic heap are found among (1) underpaid and underemployed workers of the *estancias,* or ranches; (2) some 60,000 inhabitants of the *rancheríos,* or rural shanty towns; (3) 10,000 residents of the *cantegriles,* urban shanty towns corresponding to the *barriadas* of Lima or the *favelas* of Rio de Janeiro; and (4) the 10,000 dwellers in the *conventillos,* the old slums of Montevideo.

Uruguay's rate of population growth, 1–3 percent per year, is extremely low for Latin America. Although the birth rate is higher in rural than in urban areas, migration to the cities is causing a decrease in rural population, both in percentage terms and in absolute figures.

Chronic underemployment is to be found in the rural areas. A recent study found that, of 179,000 rural workers, only 14,000 enjoy year-round employment.[2] This lack of employment derives, in part, from the extremely low labor demands of livestock-raising and the prevalence of *latifundia*. Six hundred families control thirty-four percent of all the exploitable land in the country.

The Social Class System

The Uruguayans are predominantly Caucasian, chiefly of Spanish and Italian descent. Only about ten percent have Indian blood. Though a population breakdown according to social class is always somewhat arbitrary since it depends upon what criteria are used to assign persons to designated classes, an approximate breakdown for Uruguay would be the following: upper class, two percent; middle class, 31 percent; and lower class, 67 percent. These figures represent quite a "modern" class distribution, similar, for example, to that of Great Britain. Uruguay was the first Latin American country to modernize politically, and the explanation lies in part in the fact that, as early as 1908, 25–30 percent of the country's population was already in the middle class.[3]

An Uruguayan sociologist makes the following categorization of the classes in terms of their geographic distribution:[4]

	Upper Class	Middle Class	Lower Class
Montevideo	9,000	360,000	531,000
Rural Areas	11,080	160,660	383,260
Provincial Communities	34,380	275,040	836,580
	54,460	795,700	1,750,840
Total Population	2,601,000		

POLITICAL HISTORY

The history of Uruguay merits special study because the country has been a laboratory of political innovation and accommodation. In addition to being the first Latin American country to undertake modernization, Uruguay has been the only one to adopt a plural executive branch and, prior to the Cuban Revolution, was the one with the most extensive welfare system.

---

[2] Carlos M. Rama, *Sociología del Uruguay* (Buenos Aires, Editorial Universitaria de Buenos Aires, 1965), p. 73.

[3] Aldo E. Solari, *Estudios sobre la sociedad uruguaya*, I (Montevideo, Editorial Arca, 1964), 119.

[4] Rama, p. 94.

The task of the student of political science is, of course, to go beyond the acquisition of knowledge of formal institutions of government and to explore the underlying social processes out of which these institutions emerge. Such an analysis of Uruguay is a particular challenge because of the seemingly sharp break with tradition which occurred early in the twentieth century. A norm of political instability was replaced by one of constitutionalism within the space of a few years. The year which divides the period of political disorder from the subsequent one of relative stability is 1903. One writer points out,

> Of the twenty-five governments that guided the Uruguayan ship of state from 1830 to 1903, nine were forced out of power, two were liquidated by assassination and one by grave injury, ten resisted successfully one or more revolutions, and three were free of serious disturbance during their periods in office.[5]

The Period of Instability

Frequently in the nineteenth century Uruguay was a battleground. Before independence, the Banda Oriental, the left bank of the Uruguay River, had been a neglected province of the Spanish viceroyalty of La Plata and a habitat of the gaucho and wild cattle. Portuguese (later Brazilians) fought for the province on one side, and Spaniards (later Argentines) on the other. The Portuguese, who became Brazilians after 1821, ruled the area from 1816 to 1828. After 1825 Argentina fought Brazil to reclaim the area, but neither side was able to win a decisive victory. Great Britain, seeking to protect its commerce with Brazil and Argentina, was able to convince the two combatants that the Banda Oriental should become an independent buffer state. Thus did Uruguay gain its independence, which became effective with the Constitution of 1830. Almost immediately civil strife developed. The warring factions were called *Blancos,* or Whites, those who followed Manuel Oribe, and *Colorados,* or Reds, those led by Fructuoso Rivera. Political contenders have identified themselves as *Blancos* or as *Colorados* ever since. Beginning in 1843, Oribe, assisted by the dictator Juan Manuel de Rosas of Argentina, besieged Montevideo, defended by Rivera, who was supported by England and France. By the time this siege was ended by compromise nine years later, a sense of party affiliation had become engrained in the national consciousness. Hatred and chaos continued. *Blanco* and *Colorado caudillos* fought for supremacy, often with the assistance of Argentina or Brazil. Then, after 1875, professional soldiers replaced *caudillos* in the Presidency. Beginning in 1890, civilians came to power but failed to bring order. By 1903 a *Blanco caudillo* in the interior, Aparicio Saravia, was ready to lead a showdown battle against the *Colorado* President elected in that year, José Batlle y Ordóñez. In a climactic and final civil war, Saravia was killed, the *Blancos* defeated, and President Batlle was in a position to undertake the political transformation of Uruguay. Although every President between 1865 and 1959 was nominally a

---

[5] Simon G. Hanson, *Utopia in Uruguay* (New York, Oxford University Press, 1938), p. 3.

Colorado, the practice developed of making cash payments to buy off *Blanco* opposition, of entering into compromise agreements with them (see below), and even of granting *Blanco* control over designated interior provinces. Manipulating elections from Montevideo, *Colorados* selected candidates for offices in the interior and often made fraudulent vote counts. Until 1903 Uruguayan politics remained in the hands of political bosses and their more wealthy supporters.

Economic development, retarded by civil strife during most of the nineteenth century, began in earnest in the 1870s. Protective tariff legislation beginning in 1875 led to the establishment of national food processing and other light industries. Foreign capital, largely British, developed railroads, other public utilities, and a meat-extract industry. Wool products became the chief item of export, and production increased threefold between 1876 and 1900. In the southern provinces, production of foodstuffs for the growing Montevideo population was expanded.

These economic changes meant a new pattern of interest groups and political alignments. Although the greatest concentration of wealth remained in the hands of *estancieros,* or ranchers, with their vast tracts of land, these men were willing to allow political power to flow to Montevideo and to an opposition party (the *Colorados*) so long as the *estancieros* controlled their own local regions. Those men often disliked and withdrew from the national political process. The *Colorados,* who originally were also dominated by *estancieros*, came to be the party of the newer forces. These forces were immigrants, the overwhelming majority of whom either stayed in Montevideo or became dirt farmers; the new industrialists and businessmen created by the protectionist policies of *Colorado* regimes; and the growing numbers of government workers, professionals, and members of the nascent trade-union movement. These were the groups to which President Batlle turned for support of the radical measures he proposed. "To counteract the influence of the conservative classes, Batlle did not organize a rival class coalition; instead, he united the colorados."[6]

The Batlle Program

Few political figures have left their stamp on the political institutions of their country to the extent that Batlle has in Uruguay. He served two presidential terms, 1903–07 and 1911–15, and remained until his death in 1929 the most influential politician in Uruguay. His influence continues among his followers, who seek to assume his mantle and who regard many of his ideas about government as sacred writ. What might be called the Batlle system—a given set of approaches to public life—has furnished Uruguay with political goals with which the majority of the population could and still do identify. The identification with his system has been an important basis for political consen-

---

[6] Milton I. Vanger, *José Batlle y Ordóñez of Uruguay* (Cambridge, Mass., Havard University Press, 1963), p. 274.

sus in the society, and without that consensus the political stability which Batlle yearned for probably would not have been attained. Batlle, like certain other statesmen of his era, such as Roque Sáenz Peña in Argentina, Francisco Madero in Mexico, and Woodrow Wilson and Robert La Follette in the United States, did tend to overestimate the efficacy of the formal political machinery of democracy as a means of bringing about democratic government. If Batlle had not advocated changes such as his plural executive scheme which were beyond mechanistic and constitutional alterations, chances are he would have failed to promote political stability as Madero failed in Mexico. But Batlle, a thoughtful journalist and student of government, made proposals affecting almost all social problems.

The principal features of the Batlle system are the following:

1. It opposed the secular power of the Church and succeeded in separating Church and State, in secularizing public education, and in legalizing divorce. In attacking the Church, *Batllismo* took on a foe that had always been weak in Uruguay. The country is today one of the most nonreligious in the world.

2. The system opposed foreign enterprises. Batlle gave early expression to the sentiment, now common among Latin American leaders, that, "From the point of view of the national economy a wasteful administration by the State is always preferable to the efficient management of an industry by foreign enterprise."[7] Acting upon this assumption, Uruguay has over the years nationalized several foreign enterprises. These nationalizations culminated in the purchase of the railroads from British interests in 1949 and of the Swift and Armour packing plants from U.S. interests in 1958.

3. The Batlle system promoted state enterprises. He believed that the public interest was better served by public than by private ownership in many sectors of the economy. Between the time of his first government and 1952, when the last government company to date was established, public corporations were organized in the fields of banking, insurance, light and power, telephones, cement, alcohol, fuel, petroleum, refining, meat packing, tourism (hotels, casinos, travel services), chemicals, railroads, milk production, and others.

4. The system opposed dictatorship and authoritarianism. With military strongmen discredited by Batlle's decisive victory over Saravia in 1904 and with the rallying of majority support to the program of the *Colorado* President, Batlle and his successors were able to overcome the nineteenth-century Uruguayan practice of overthrowing the constitutional government. Only two coups have occurred since, one in 1933 and another in 1942. These have not taken the form of the overthrow of a government, but rather the form of the President in office assuming dictatorial power for a brief period.

5. Batlle's system supported the growth of the trade unions and protective legislation for labor. He secured the right of labor to organize and to bargain collectively. Legislation providing for an eight-hour working day was

---

[7] Hanson, p. 24.

passed in 1915, far in advance of most of the industrialized world. During Batlle's second administration, 1911–15, some Uruguayan legislators came to regard their country as the world leader in labor legislation and sought to outstrip their nearest competitor, New Zealand.

6. The system promoted educational and social welfare programs. Basic social security legislation was passed in 1919. Today nearly everyone of retirement age is legally entitled to a pension. The country is strongly committed to the ideal of free public education for all even though the goal has not yet been reached.

7. The system was not threatening to the *latifundia,* prevailing in most rural areas, or to private property in general. Batlle did not regard concentration of land ownership as a social evil, nor was he opposed to capitalism itself. There has never been a serious legislative drive against *estancieros,* and even today Uruguay does not have an effective personal income tax.

8. *Batllismo* advocated perfecting representative government by means of a plural executive, proportional representation, and "co-participation." These aspects of the ideology are discussed below.

With minor exceptions the Batlle system has essentially been continued by his successors, even by the *Blancos,* who came to power in 1959, after ninety-three years of *Colorado* rule. "In a number of important respects, it can be argued that the thinking of the country has not progressed substantially since the death of Batlle."[8]

Recent Political Developments

Exploration of the remarkable return to power of the *Blancos*[9] between 1959 and 1967 and their frustration by deep-seated national problems is a fruitful point of approach to the political dynamics of contemporary Uruguay. In the 1958 elections the *Blancos* won in every province except one, Artigas, despite the fact that so many voters had a vested interest in the Batlle system. Twenty-eight percent of the work force was dependent upon the Government for a livelihood. Thirty percent of the population belonged to families receiving government pensions. Many business, labor, professional, and other groups had developed under the protective wing of *Colorado* politics.

The immediate causes of voter rebellion were economic dislocations caused by inflation, unemployment, and sluggish international trade. In addition, there was disenchantment with squabbling among the many *Colorado* factions and an impression of general inertia in government.

The nature of the government bureaucracy had long been an issue of public debate. In Uruguay, as in most developing countries, public employment is generally preferred to private employment for reasons of prestige, security, and working conditions. In such countries public employment usually has as one of its functions accommodating educated members of the middle

---

[8] Philip B. Taylor, Jr., *Government and Politics of Uruguay* (New Orleans, Tulane University, 1960), p. 22.

[9] The official name of the party of the *Blancos* is the *Partido Nacional.*

class for whom there is inadequate employment opportunity in the private sector. Such persons are normally hired in larger numbers than are actually required to perform a given public service. Ordinarily, Uruguayan government workers receive their positions on the basis of ascriptive norms, that is, who these workers are, whom they know, and what political relationships they enjoy, rather than on the basis of a system of impartial determination of competence. Overstaffing and inefficiency in government is joked about and denounced by Uruguayans. Both were undoubtedly voted against in 1958. Yet people often behave in one way politically as voters and in another way as members of a particular interest group. Those who voted for *Blanco* candidates advocating economy in government spending were not voting for austerity for themselves. Thus *Blancos* found it politically expedient not to undertake general economic reform for fear of alienating a number of interest groups sufficient to make the *Blancos* lose power in the 1962 elections. Although economic conditions actually grew worse during the 1958–62 period, the *Blancos* were re-elected to power in 1962.

Aside from the issue of whether or not the *Blancos* really wanted to redirect the national economy, they were confronted with the fact that the Batlle system, like its counterparts in many countries, has its own inner logic and defenses. These defenses, locked into the whole social and political structure, limit the possibilities for the *Blancos* or for any opposition party to effect major changes without resort to coercion. The Batlle system is a complex of protective mechanisms for the major urban interest groups and consists of such devices as tariff protection for industry, low borrowing but high lending rates for bankers, and job security for government workers. When the system failed after about 1955 to provide continued national economic development, *Batllismo* was rejected in the abstract by voters but remained in fact the social and political reality of the country. The system will, of course, change and evolve, but it will probably not be drastically affected by formalistic changes such as the return in 1967 to a single President instead of a plural executive branch.

POLITICAL STRUCTURES AND ROLES—PROCESSES OF FUNCTION AND DYSFUNCTION

The Plural Executive and the "Pacts of the Parties"

Two aspects of the Uruguayan political process which are particularly interesting to the student of comparative politics are the plural executive and the political party system. That between 1951 and 1967 the country was not governed by a President but by a national council of nine men is not primarily attributable to the idealistic appeal of such an arrangement, that is, the appeal of a power-dispersing, democratic, executive branch of government. This peculiar institution developed because of the special character and history of the struggle for power among competing parties and factions.

An extraordinary feature of Uruguayan political history is that leaders of the competing camps have time and again arrived at specific agreements to share the emoluments of power instead of fighting one another for an exclusive claim upon these emoluments. Uruguay's political leaders call this phenomenon *coparticipación,* or "co-participation." Among the more important *Blanco-Colorado* agreements, or "pacts of the parties," have been the following: In 1851 an agreement was reached to end the Great War (1839–1852). In 1872, after a civil war, the *Colorados* consented to *Blanco* control of four departments. In 1897, after another period of disorder, the *Blancos* were allowed control of six departments. The party lost this control after the civil war of 1904, but a new Constitution which went into effect in 1919 contained provisions which assured the *Blancos,* the minority party, control of three seats in the National Council of Administration, which shared executive power with the President. In 1933 a *Colorado* President, Gabriel Terra, reached an agreement with the *Blanco* leader, Luis Alberto de Herrera, that Terra would execute a coup and assume dictatorial powers. The Constitution of 1934, which abolished the National Council of Administration, provided that each party should have fifteen seats in the thirty-member Senate.[10] In 1951 *Colorado* President Andrés Martínez Trueba entered into an agreement with *Blanco caudillo* Herrera to abolish the office of the Presidency in favor of a nine-man plural executive. Herrera, who had always bitterly opposed the collegial executive scheme, now accepted it as a way of insuring an increased share of power for the *Blancos,* since the arrangement provided that the minority party would receive three of the nine council seats. President Martínez Trueba, a dedicated disciple of José Batlle, wished to implement Batlle's dream of a collegial executive and also saw the proposal as an opportunity to undermine a rival *Colorado* faction.

The pattern that emerges from this history of pacts is one of the two parties dividing political spoils within and between themselves with decreasing recourse to violence. The 1951 agreement, under which *Blancos* and *Colorados* reserved control of the plural executive to themselves on a 6 to 3 basis, is a somewhat similar phenomenon to the Liberal and Conservative parties in Colombia agreeing in 1958 to restrict the exercise of political power to themselves for 12, later extended to 16, years. Whereas in Colombia the understanding is that upper-echelon government positions will be divided between the two parties on an equal basis (though Valencia went beyond this), in Uruguay all government jobs are parceled out on a 3 to 2 basis—three for the majority party for each two for the minority party.

POLITICAL STRUCTURES AND ROLES

The Political Party System

An editorial in the independent Uruguayan weekly *Marcha* took the interesting position that in Uruguay there are no political parties.[11] This statement has a certain degree of validity insofar as the two traditional parties

---

[10] This provision was subsequently rescinded.

[11] *Marcha,* November 27, 1965.

are loosely structured, fractionated, and do not take the lead in developing and executing public policy.

The two traditional parties, or *lemas,* are divided into several *sublemas,* which are a kind of sub-parties. Electoral laws make it easy to organize *sublemas,* each of which may offer its own list of candidates for public office. The principal organizational entity of the sub-parties is community and neighborhood clubs. Clubs of the more enduring sub-parties function chiefly as places where people can go to seek jobs and other favors from the Government. Effective party-wide institutions for co-ordinating the aggregative activities of the various sub-parties do not exist. Therefore, the legislative and executive branches receive multi-focused demands from political parties as well as from interest groups. This circumstance tends to neutralize political parties as formulators of overall government policy.

The system tends to lead to the Government's avoiding or only partially facing up to issues of public policy but can be defended on the same grounds that any "western," pluralistic system can; it could be said that it prevents any single interest or faction from exercising tyrannical control over public power. However, the Uruguayan system is especially vulnerable to a major criticism of pluralism: If government policy is the product of a multitude of groups protecting their own interests, then what guarantee is there that any force will champion the public interest?

Even with the replacement of the plural executive by a President, there is little reason to anticipate that the single executive will be supported by a working majority in Congress. Results of the 1954, 1958, and 1962 elections

Election	Winning Lema	Winning Sublema
1954	*Colorado* with 50.5 percent of vote	"List 15" (Luis Batlle) with 28.9 percent of vote
	17 Senate seats of 31 51 representatives of 99	10 Senate seats of 31 31 representatives of 99
		6 of 9 seats on National Council
1958	Nacional (*Blanco*) with 49.6 percent of vote	"Luis Alberto de Herrera" with 24 percent of vote
	17 Senate seats of 31 51 representatives of 99	9 Senate seats of 31 24 representatives of 99
		6 of 9 seats on National Council
1962	Nacional (*Blanco*) with 46.6 percent of vote	Unión Blancà Demo- cráticà (U.B.D.)
	15 Senate seats of 31 47 representatives of 99	7 Senate seats of 31 22 representatives of 99
		6 of 9 seats on National Council

indicate that if the leader of the winning *sublema* had been President instead of merely a member of the National Council, his *sublema* would not have enjoyed a majority in Congress. Moreover, in the 1962 election not even the winning *lema* won a congressional majority.

The Ideological Parties

In addition to the much-divided *Blancos* and *Colorados,* there are three "ideological" parties in Uruguay. They are the Socialist party, the Communist party, and the Christian Democratic party. Although the ideological parties have a long history in Uruguay—the Socialist party was founded in 1910, the Unión Cívica (forerunner of the Christian Democratic party) in 1872, and the Communist party in 1921—they have never presented a major threat to the traditional parties. In recent elections the combined vote of the ideological parties has been about ten percent of the total vote. Using the general elections of 1954 as a base (=100), the growth or decline of those votes was as follows:[12]

Total Voters	Election	Unión Cívica	Socialist Party	Communist Party
		(Christian Democrats after 1962 election)	Headed alliance in 1962 called Union Popular	Headed alliance in 1962 called F.I.D.E.L.
100	1954	100	100	100
(879,242)		(44,255 votes)	(28,704 votes)	(19,541 votes)
114	1958	82	121	134
136	1962	82	90	207

These same trends continued in the 1966 election. The Communists continued to gain significantly, while both the Christian Democrats and the Socialists failed to win new adherents. Interesting questions are why other parties have not been able to challenge successfully the near monopoly position of the *Blancos* and the *Colorados* and why these three parties emerged and not others. Some of the factors explaining why the Catholic party, now called the Christian Democratic party, has had so little appeal in a nominally Catholic country are suggested by John J. Johnson in *Political Change in Latin America,* in which he accounts for some of the historical reasons underlying the Church's relatively weak position in Uruguay: the absence of Indians to convert, the establishment of Catholicism in Uruguay after the Church had passed its zenith of missionary zeal in Latin America, the organizational subservience of the Uruguayan Church to Buenos Aires, the absence of a ready source of wealth for the construction of churches, the influential

[12] Aldo E. Solari, *Estudios sobre la sociedad uruguaya,* II (Montevideo, Editorial Arca, 1965), 156.

Batlle's vehement anticlericalism, and the high degree of urbanization.[13] Perhaps it is a general attitude of religious indifference which accounts for the failure of Unión Cívica to increase its voter support when the party refurbished its image by adopting the Christian Democratic label—a name which has such demonstrable voter appeal in countries like Chile.

The Socialist party in Uruguay has also had little voter appeal and is currently in a state of decay. Perhaps one of the reasons for the weakness of this party is that the welfare-state policies of the *Colorados* have resulted in keeping within the Colorado party voters who might otherwise become Socialists. On the other hand, the Communist party has gained voters since 1954, but deteriorating economic conditions provide only part of the explanation for this growth. Students of Latin American politics soon come to appreciate that definitive answers for most political questions are not yet available.

Political Moderation

In general, the voting behavior of the twentieth-century Uruguayan has been that of a political moderate, a gradualist who rejects extremes of right or left. An Uruguayan sociologist stresses the influence of the moderate values of the middle class.

> Whatever the actual percentage of the middle classes in Uruguay may be, it is evident that they constitute the most important reference group that exists in the society. Their values, their expectations, their norms, their guides, tend to be the values, expectations, norms, and guides for the whole society. . . . The hypothesis is possible that the middle classes adhere, above all, to the values of security, moderation, absence of risk, and the prestige that comes, especially from consumption.[14]

Another Uruguayan, Carlos Maggi, describes the outlook of his countrymen in the following terms:

> The Uruguayan does not wish to be a very important, man, or an insignificant one. He just wants to live in freedom, without making any great sacrifice, and without forcing others to make them. Here is a country whose people do not aspire to greatness, or to anything absolute, but who desire that things shall be kept in good, human proportion and that the human values shall be treated with proper respect. With such a people one does not build empires or alter the course of history. Here, nothing is very rigorous. Everything is improvised, haphazard and rather ineffectual. In the end, everything is settled by conversation, and never completely.[15]

Another Uruguayan writer, Mario Benedetti, contends that a deterioration in the character and values of the upper class has occurred since World

---

[13] John J. Johnson, *Political Change in Latin America* (Stanford, Stanford University Press, 1958), pp. 46–47.

[14] Solari, I, 171.

[15] *Marcha,* November 24, 1961, quoted in George Pendle, *Uruguay* (New York, Oxford University Press, 1963), p. v.

War II. The new men of wealth, the *picucos,* are, he asserts, obsessed by the quest for comfort, material affectation, and Philistine social distractions.[16]

It is not enough to say that Uruguay is politically moderate because it is a political culture with predominantly middle-class or bourgeois values. After all, it is precisely the middle-class groups which are the disruptive, revolution-leading elements in many Latin American countries. Political moderation in Uruguay is a function of the kind of middle-class values and the kind of society in which they exist. Argentina has as high a rate of literacy, as large a percentage of its population in the middle classes, and as high a standard of living as Uruguay. Yet since 1930 the history of Argentina has as often as not been one of authoritarianism and militarism. The factors of relatively high literacy and newspaper circulation, of ethnic homogeneity and the compactness of national territory, and of urbanization are among those elements that are relevant to a theory of why constitutionalism has become rooted among the *Orientales.* Still, all of these conditions exist, partially or more widely, in Latin American countries where constitutionalism is not the norm.

The following considerations set Uruguay apart. (1) The political system enjoys a sufficient degree of legitimacy so that key groups are usually willing to seek their political goals within the bounds of a legal order and hence, allegiance to the system tends to override allegiance to individual politicians. (2) There is a relatively high degree of public consensus on political goals and on how they should be pursued. (3) The military is not regarded as a normal or licit instrument for altering power relationships.

A more challenging analytical task is to explain *why* these three conditions obtain. The legitimacy of the political system is related to the fact that, for special historical reasons, a majority of those who seek power and advantage from government do so under one of two banners, *Colorado* or *Blanco.* The two "parties" (they are better described as coalitions of parties) divide rather than monopolize political inputs and outputs. The political system has legitimacy, therefore, because the system is continuously open to the demands of the most powerful groups in the country, whether *Blanco* or *Colorado.* The cattle and sheep interests have not received as many direct payments from the Government as have urban interests, but the "payoff" of the rural interests has been in the freedom to dominate their local areas in such ways as being able to keep agricultural wages low. The welfare system has tended to retard middle-class and lower-class alienation and thus to increase further the legitimacy of the political order.

Legitimacy and consensus are interrelated and mutually reinforcing but not identical. The former denotes public acceptance of particular political institutions, and the latter denotes agreement on political means and ends. Whereas Argentines, for example, do not generally agree upon what direction political life should take, most Uruguayans, on the other hand, are together in

---

[16] Benedetti, pp. 107–15.

favoring the kind of welfare state policies with which they have become familiar.

The military has not been a political force of major consequence in Uruguay since 1904 and, even before that time was never well organized or well financed. Nineteenth-century military leaders were generally unimpressive when they assumed political roles. After Batlle overcame the last of the insurgent *caudillos,* Saravia, in 1904, Batlle laid the basis for a system in which political adventurism on the part of the military was effectively precluded. Military officers were subjected to close scrutiny by civilian superiors in the executive and legislative branches. Congressional approval was required for the military advancement of any officer. The coup of 1933 was headed by a civilian, President Terra, and an important supporting role was played by firemen. It is not probable that the military will overthrow governments in the future. On the basis of past experience, a coup might conceivably take place only if it had the prior consent of important factions of both traditional parties.

The Economic Crisis

Since about 1955, Uruguayan politics has been beset by serious national economic problems. The writers and artists who have emerged since the mid-1950s are sometimes referred to as the "generation of the crisis." The "crisis" has been one of economic stagnation accompanied by mounting unemployment and inflation. Per capita gross national product (about 500 dollars a year) did not increase during the decade following 1955 and in some years actually declined.[17] By 1966, unemployment had risen well above Uruguay's "fixed" unemployment rate of 10 percent, and the peso, which had officially exchanged for 2.06 dollars in 1952, had fallen to 65 per dollar in 1966.

Stagnation in Uruguay is not the result of transitory economic conditions but is deeply imbedded in the socio-economic makeup of the country. The growth impasse at which Uruguay has arrived raises profound questions about the future of any semideveloped, democratically governed welfare state which is a supplier of raw materials to the international market. What characterizes the situation within which the country finds itself is that its only important productive resource is land, upon which Uruguay must rely almost exclusively for acquiring foreign exchange. In order to increase the volume of trade, the country must increase agricultural output. However, the agricultural sector is stagnant. Ranchers are psychologically and financially unprepared to undertake the kind of long-term investment in winter livestock shelters, supplementary food storage facilities, pasture improvements, and the like, which, it is estimated, could double the present volume of livestock production. The Government is unable to grant substantial tax relief incentives to agriculture

---

[17] Herman E. Daly, "The Uruguayan Economy: Its Basic Nature and Current Problems," *Journal of Inter-American Studies,* VII, No. 3 (July 1965), 316.

because of the political resistance from urban groups. Industry, which has developed because of import substitution (that is, enabling domestic producers to replace foreign ones through protective tariffs), has exhausted available demand and cannot grow without an expansion in consumer buying power. Consumer demand cannot increase, of course, without growth in production. The average productivity of labor, however, has actually *declined* in recent years; it dropped by 3.2 percent between 1955 and 1961.[18] Low productivity of both labor and management in the private as well as the public sector relates in part to a national outlook which emphasizes consumption and leisure at the expense of industriousness and investment. Twenty percent of the entire population depends upon revenue from the Government for its livelihood. This dependence has the effect of providing employment for large numbers of people and of somewhat equalizing income distribution in addition to yielding health, educational, and other socially desirable results. However, the welfare system is plagued by mismanagement, inefficiency, favoritism (which Uruguayans refer to as *muñeca,* or "pull") and a good measure of *coima,* or corruption.

Some would argue that the expenditure on welfare is a serious drag on the economic development of the country because that expenditure diverts limited resources away from industry and business. One is tempted to conclude that Uruguay has a welfare system more appropriate to a developed economy than to a developing one. On the other hand, it can be argued that some Latin American countries without socially ameliorative welfare systems are also experiencing development impasses, often with a sizable portion of government revenue going into nonproductive military expenditures. The Uruguayan economy may be ailing, but unlike, for example, Brazil or Peru, a significant portion of the population is not slowly dying of starvation.

Political Leadership

Although Uruguayan politics is perhaps the least personalistic in Latin America today, it has been marked during the twentieth century by two outstanding leaders, José Batlle and Luis Alberto de Herrera. Batlle was a democratic strongman and Herrera, the long-time leader of the conservative wing of the *Blancos,* was often referred to as *el caudillo.* Herrera was a man of authoritarian bent who fought doggedly for power through a long political life. Ironically, he died in 1959 a few weeks after attaining the presidency of the National Council. Another *Blanco* leader who came to share power in 1958 was Eduardo Víctor Haedo, who also had subscribed to authoritarian doctrines. The third principal *Blanco* leader to emerge in 1958 was Benito Nardone, a political opportunist who was the leader of a movement called "ruralism." Nardone achieved his following as a radio broadcaster who claimed to esteem the values and folklore of rural Uruguay. Like the authors of nineteenth-century Gaucho literature, he pointed a finger of scorn at the

---

[18] Daly, p. 329.

corrupting influences of urban life. His movement, similar in many respects to "Poujadism" in France, played upon the frustrations of both urban and rural members of the lower class. He, like Herrera, died soon after the 1958 election.

Colorado leadership fractionated after the death of José Batlle. Two of Batlle's sons, César and Lorenzo, became the leaders of a *sublema* which sought to preserve and to extend the ideals of their father. A nephew of Batlle, Luis, has led a *sublema* known as "List 15," which has taken a generally more leftist and innovative course than that of the Batlle sons. "List 15" has sought the support of organized labor. Several other *Colorado sublemas* have risen and fallen, and new ones continue to appear.

With the death of Herrera and the division of the *Colorados,* "pacts of the parties" have become less feasible because individual leaders no longer command the major parties. The *Colorado* politician elected to a five-year presidential term, in 1966, Oscar Gestido, was a quiet, retired Air Force General chosen for his "common sense" and his favorable record as an administrator of government enterprises. He led "List 515," which splintered from "List 15" in March 1965. Electoral laws encourage the proliferation of candidates for public office and the launching of new *sublemas.*

There is, then, relatively easy access to the role of political leadership, and the exercise of such leadership is prized. Members of the upper class as well as the middle classes look with favor upon a political career. This attitude is partly the result of the rather limited opportunities that exist in the field of industrial management. Persons from the ranks of the lower class play a very minor leadership role in the national political process. This lack of participation by the lower class bespeaks of the still formidable social, psychological, and educational barriers to social mobility which exist in "socialized" Uruguay.

Legislative Process

In Uruguay, the bicameral parliament called the General Assembly has been the primary arena of political decision-making. The executive branch was unable to take a decisive lead in public policy because it was until 1967 a committee of nine—only six of whom were from the same party. In 1967, constitutional changes empowered the President to submit "emergency laws," which automatically become law if not overridden by a two-thirds vote in both houses of the General Assembly.

The development of parliamentary legislation usually follows a rather elaborate series of agreements within *sublemas,* among *sublemas,* and, finally, among *lemas.* A moderate degree of party discipline exists within *sublemas* but not within *lemas,* and thus the kind of political horse-trading which occurs in multi-party parliaments is necessary.

Although the ninety-nine-member Chamber of Representatives is elected on the basis of electoral districts (departments) and the thirty-one senators are chosen at large, the fact that representatives do not have to be residents of their districts has meant in practice that the members of both houses are mostly lawyers who make their homes in Montevideo and are urban-oriented.

Interest groups have relatively easy and direct access to individual congressmen, who are under constant pressure from seekers of jobs and of other favors. Their legislative function is hampered by the failure of the Government to provide them with staff assistants and office space. Power is diffused within the chambers among the leaders of the major *sublemas* and the chairmen of the standing committees. Very powerful individual legislators are not a regular part of the contemporary political process.

The parliament, in addition to its legislative function, plays a watchdog role over the national bureaucracy. The parliament has the power to conduct investigations and to question, to censure, and to impeach Cabinet ministers. Congressional interpellations and investigations are common, but impeachment of ministers is rare. An overall judgment on dysfunction in the Uruguayan legislative process would have to be based upon value preference. The existing system tends to allot "something for everyone," that is, for every organized and articulated interest, at the expense of an integrated and highly rationalized program of national policy objectives. This result of the system tends to be the price of pluralism everywhere: "the squeaky wheel gets the grease."

Interest Groups

Widespread government intervention has been answered in Uruguay by the organization of numerous pressure groups seeking to defend and promote special interests. The interests of the more wealthy men in agriculture are represented by the Asociación Rural and the Federación Rural, both dating from the nineteenth century. The Asociación Rural is today probably more dedicated to social snobbery than to political lobbying. The more militant and politically active Federación Rural has been quite successful in making its weight felt by the Government and has employed muscle-flexing techniques such as public demonstrations, boycotts, and even the promotion of smuggling live cattle and wool to Brazil in efforts to change public policy. A third group, the Liga Federal de Acción Rural, was organized by Benito Nardone, and its adherents have mostly been small landowners. The Liga has been regarded with resentment and suspicion by the two older agricultural societies.

Business and industrial groups are well organized to confront and to influence government. Enterprises are organized according to types into *gremios*, or guilds, which are confederated in the National Chamber of Commerce and the National Chamber of Industries. In addition, there are two "exceptionally effective," professionally run, business lobbying firms,[19] the Cámara Mercantil de los Productos del País and the Liga de Defensa Comercial.

Urban labor is highly unionized, but the unions have never been able to

---

[19] Taylor, p. 54.

join forces in a consolidated, generally inclusive confederation. Five efforts to launch a general confederation of labor, or *central,* between 1905 and 1951 ended in failure. The latest such attempt was the organization of the Central de Trabajadores del Uruguay in 1961. Uruguayan labor leadership can be characterized as pragmatic rather than doctrinaire and as only moderately militant. Nevertheless, strikes are fairly frequent.

Groups representing Government employees and pensioners are prominent among lobbyists. Public employees have sparked the drive for pensions, dependents' allowances, paid vacations, and other benefits. It is customary for government employees to work only half a day—in the afternoon in winter, when mornings are cold, and during the mornings in summer, so that the beaches may be enjoyed in the afternoon. This arrangement is less idyllic than it appears to be because many public employees must take a second job in order to support themselves. Pensioners' groups lobby not so much to increase pension payments as to seek payment of amounts to which persons are entitled but for which funds are not available.

Political Communication and Participation

There is a high degree of political awareness in Uruguay. This circumstance is facilitated by (1) the publication and wide readership of several daily newspapers (all of which are "political" in that they represent a specific point of view, usually that of a particular *sublema*), and (2) strong interest in political gossip and knowledge of political happenings, which quickly make the verbal rounds in the compact little country.

It would be misleading to suggest that there is grass-roots democracy in Uruguay, no more so than in most of the urban centers of North America. There is, however, general interest in and awareness of politics. Persons over eighteen years of age, male and female, literate and illiterate, may vote, and in the 1962 general election an impressively high seventy-two percent of eligible voters did cast ballots.

CONCLUSION

In the areas of freedom, civil liberties, and democratic government, Uruguay ranks near the top in the Western Hemisphere. As a society which provides a tolerable level of economic and social well-being for nearly all of its members, Uruguay ranks second to Cuba in Latin America and is probably the most "modernized" of the Latin American states. Evaluated by the standards of the European-North American cult of efficiency though, there is considerable deficiency in both public and private activity. If one does not find preoccupation with painstaking effort or the pursuit of excellence, one finds charm, pleasure-seeking, and advocacy of the just society.

17 / Brazil

JORDAN M. YOUNG

*JORDAN M. YOUNG, Professor of Social Science at Pace
College and former Visiting Professor of Government at New
York University, has held Doherty, U.S. Office of Education,
and Fulbright grants and has worked with the Special Public
Health Service in the northeastern and Amazon areas of Bra-
zil. He is the author of "Military Aspects of the 1930 Brazilian
Revolution," "The Brazilian Congressional Elections," "Some
Permanent Political Characteristics of Contemporary Brazil,"
and* The Brazilian Revolution of 1930 and the Aftermath,
published in 1967.

POLITICAL ENVIRONMENT

Unlike most nations of Latin America, Brazil boasts a political culture
which is unique and which cannot easily be generalized into broad cross-
national patterns of structure, style, and process. Brazilian political institutions are intimately tied to social structure in a way that makes it difficult to
separate the two for purposes of political analysis. Although the politics of
other Latin American nations are also intermixed with the social fabric, the
social and political union in Brazil has been more profound. The concept of
"patriarchalism," as developed in the works of Gilberto Freyre, goes far
toward explaining how a close-knit unity of family fits centrally into Brazilian
society and political dynamics.

A tightly structured society of families, Brazil is also a giant among
nations. Her 3,286,473 square miles make this country the fourth largest
nation in the world, and such a land mass has produced contradictory results
as far as the average Brazilian is concerned. Until the twentieth century, the
size of the country overwhelmed her population. All the ills of a great nation,

economic weakness, political discord, and administrative chaos were blamed on the dead weight of the impenetrable hinterland. Urban citizens were pessimistic about anything that was farther inland than two hundred miles. Added to the fear of the interior was the overriding fact that it was easier to survive and make a living along the coastal areas. Brazilians, similar to the Argentines, are people of plenty when compared to many other Latin American nations. Significantly, however, there were few obstacles to keep the Brazilians from penetrating the interior. No mountains or forbidding deserts blocked the way. Few warlike Indian civilizations existed. There were simply no roads and, perhaps more significant, no folklore of success stories of yeoman farmers or common people going into the interior, carving out a successful plantation, and returning wealthy and prosperous to the coastal civilized areas.

The twentieth century, however, brought about a change in attitude toward the Brazilian interior. As the scientific revolution swept the world and more technological advances were made, the backlands of Brazil suddenly became a garden of treasure rather than a burden to the nation. Instead of pessimism a surge of almost unrealistic optimism developed, along with an exaggerated sense of Brazilian self-sufficiency. Brazilians feel today that their nation is so rich and so well endowed with natural resources that, if they could only solve their transportation, communication, and distribution problems, they could wipe out the problems of starvation, hopelessness, and misery that exist in many areas.

Nevertheless, the vast size of the country has resulted in a "big nation" complex. Brazilians have no feelings of inferiority in their relations with the great powers of the world and have a definite feeling of superiority when dealing with the other Latin American nations of the Western Hemisphere. The internal political implications resulting from this situation are significant. Political leaders in Brazil have not built followings nor created emotionally charged situations by attacking the United States, Britain, or the Soviet Union for meddling in the internal affairs of the nation. Since the coup of 1964, which overthrew João Goulart, a slight change has occurred, and the United States Government has, in the minds of many, been overidentified with the military-oriented administration that took control of the country.

Internal politics has also been affected by the size of the country. Though Brazil has twenty-two states and four territories, it is still a country sharply defined by regions. There are basically two Brazils. The first is the modern, twentieth-century state. To locate this Brazil, one simply draws a line east to west at the Tropic of Capricorn, 23 degrees south of the equator. At this point, approximately where the city of Rio de Janeiro appears on the map and going due west, lies a rough dividing line of the two Brazils. Below this line is a relatively dynamic civilization. The political system that operates here is sophisticated and tends to reflect the demands that citizens make on their government. This area is also known as the "Establishment" of the nation. Most of the important political and economic decisions are made in this region of Brazil.

Before 1964, when civilian politicians still went to the people, the people meant the nearly 45 million Brazilians living below the Tropic of Capricorn. Brazil may be a nation of over 80 million people, but only 15 million voters appeared in the 1963 elections, and of those 10 million were in the south. The key states in the Brazilian political structure are São Paulo with 14 million, Minas Gerais with 11 million, Guanabara with 4 million, and Rio Grande do Sul with 6 million. These states had, and to some degree in the post-1964 period still have, a political life of their own. Most of the other states in Brazil are satellites of the Federal Government. To win elections in the period before 1964, Presidents had to win and win strongly in at least two of the four key states. There is a great degree of state loyalty, and prominent political leaders had an easier time identifying with the people if they came from one of the four major states.

The large cities located within the major states have all the luxuries (and miseries) associated with urban centers all over the world. Rio de Janeiro, São Paulo, Santos, and Porto Alegre have slums and residential palaces, wealth and poverty and, more important, a vast job market coupled with great pockets of unemployment.

The other Brazil, north of the 23rd degree line, is slowly but certainly entering the twentieth century. This part is the oldest settled section of Brazil. Tight family lines, fortunes built on landholding and sugar planting, resistance to change, are all hallmarks of northeastern and northern Brazil. This area is seldom regarded as part of the "Establishment." Brazilians from the other states often feel that their states have been the colonies of the southern Brazilian businessmen. Politics in the northeast and north is the politics of frustration. This other Brazil has neither the votes nor the economic power to make itself felt in national affairs.

Events of the 1960s resulted in a fresh start for the northeastern part of Brazil. The 1962 election of Marxist Governor Miguel Arrais in Pernambuco brought home to the *status quo* civilian and military leaders of Brazil the problems of the northeast, which were so deeply felt as to inspire middle-class citizens to vote for a politician allied with the Communists if he would only do something to improve conditions. The military, upon coming to power in 1964, took away the governorship from Miguel Arrais but have not ignored the area. There has been an accelerated government program of aid for the northeast through the SUDENE, the Superintendency of the Northeast, which is a Brazilian version of the TVA. Both the Government and private industry have extended financial credit to the northeast in an effort to establish light consumer industries. The United States has also been helpful with its allocation of Alliance for Progress funds in the northeastern sector. The Catholic hierarchy in Brazil has declared its awareness that the northeast must be aided quickly and drastically.[1]

Despite the existence of two Brazils, there is nevertheless the inescapable

[1] Stefan H. Robock, *Brazil's Developing Northeast: A Study of Regional Planning and Foreign Aid* (Washington, D.C., The Brookings Institution, 1963).

fact of a distinct Brazilian nationality. An Amazon rubber worker deep in the jungle of the upper Xingu River, an accountant rushing to catch the 6:37 evening ferryboat from Rio de Janeiro to cross the bay to Niteroi, and a suntanned cowhand on a ranch near the Rio Grande do Sul-Uruguayan border are all consciously Brazilian. They share something of a common culture, and its parts are varied. Among the more important cultural bonds is language unity. The Portuguese language, with variations in dialect, enables one to identify a northerner, a northeasterner, a resident of Rio de Janeiro and a gaucho from Rio Grande do Sul. Another factor lending itself to a Brazilian nationality is the religious ethic. Ninety-three percent of the nation acknowledges Catholicism as its religion. Brazilian Catholicism has tended to be tolerant and noncrusading and has become intertwined with the political mores of the country.

Social Structure

The political environment of Brazil demonstrates that there is mobility in the social structure. Brazil is going through a tremendous transition in the decade of the 1960s. There is a major dislocation of certain traditional groups, and important shifts are taking place. Though the pace is uneven and is swifter in certain areas where tools for mobility are more easily obtainable, change is a part of Brazilian life. The lower-income Brazilian does not see himself as frozen into one class. The mystique is that he is going to improve and better himself, but there is evidence accumulating from recent research to suggest that these changes are not as easy as expected.[2]

The lowest member of the social scale in Brazil is the northeastern rural worker. Up until relatively recent times, there was no manner in which these people could express their discontent except by migrating to the cities. Though numerous laws were passed during the Vargas dictatorship and the later democratic period, very little real progress was made in aiding the rural workers. President Goulart issued a decree on November 13, 1963, which provided for identification cards for rural workers, the observance of hygiene and security measures, adequate rural habitation, and health provisions.[3] But more important was the 1960 activity of an intelligent lawyer, Francisco Julião, who became prominent in Pernambuco when he defended a group of sharecroppers being evicted from a plantation where they were working. Julião later organized Peasant Leagues to defend the rights of rural workers. Pointing up his success is the simple fact that in 1958, when Julião ran for state deputy on the Brazilian Socialist party ticket, he received only 3,216 votes, which won him the title of Alternate Delegate to the State Assembly. In 1962, Julião ran for the Federal Congress and won easily with 16,200 votes.

---

[2] Joseph A. Kahl, "Social Stratification and Values in Metropoli and Provinces: Brazil and Mexico," in *América Latina*, January–March 1965. Latin American Center for Research in the Social Sciences, Rio de Janeiro, Brazil.

[3] Robert E. Price, *Rural Unionization in Brazil*, A research paper, No. 14 (Madison, Land Tenure Center, University of Wisconsin, 1964).

The rural peasants had found a spokesman. Also fighting for influence among the rural workers was the Catholic Church, which organized unions first in Rio Grande do Norte and then expanded into other northeastern states. The movement has been led by Bishop Eugenio Sales. The April 1964 coup stripped the political rights of Francisco Julião and also diminished the activity of some of the militant Catholic unions in the northeast. The rural workers in southern Brazil are in a better social and economic category than their northeastern counterparts. Wages and salaries are higher, and the percentage of literacy is higher, enabling these workers to participate in the political process.

In the cities, the *favelas,* or slums, of Rio de Janeiro and, to a lesser degree, of São Paulo, offer severe political problems. In Rio de Janeiro an estimated one-half million to 800,000 people live in the hills surrounding the city out of a total population estimated at just over 4 million. Here is one of the few areas where one finds a direct correlation between race and poverty; the majority of the people who live in the slums are Negro. By and large the slum dwellers are open to and respond to the appeals of demagogues and thus tended to identify with Getúlio Vargas as a father image for the poor. Politicians who invoke his name and make similar promises are frequently elected.

A vast and ever-growing middle class, however, is the key to the extremely mobile and flexible social structure of Brazil. The number of middle-class citizens is constantly increasing, and it is here that both the potential danger and the greatest stability for the nation is to be found. The danger lies in the fact that the pent-up frustration of the intellectuals, who are largely from the middle class, could lead the nation into a period of violence and turmoil. This possibility has not yet occurred. In search of administrative talent, ideas, and money, the Brazilian elite tends to draw continuously from the middle class.

The success symbols of the middle and upper classes are concrete and attainable objects. A Brazilian knows that these goals, a car, an apartment on Copacabana Beach, a home in the mountains, a trip to Buenos Aires, a visit to the United States, and membership in a country club, are possible. Many of these dreams are never realized, but despite one's social position in Brazil, the same dreams are shared. The result is a pliable social structure that theoretically holds out hope for success to all.

Political Evolution

The past hangs heavily over the political environment of contemporary Brazil. The events that have affected the nation's development are clear-cut and sharp. As far back as the seventeenth century, Brazilians developed a sense of nationalism when they removed the Dutch invaders from their country. Nearly two hundred years before the other Latin American countries had any glimmerings of nationalism, the northeastern Brazilians, without the aid of the mother country, had expelled a foreign intruder. Another historical episode which molded the Brazilians was the flight to Brazil of the Portuguese king in 1808 to escape Napoleon. The fact that Brazilians sheltered their king and were raised to the status of a kingdom equal with Portugal further enforced the growing sense of equality that the citizens exhibited toward the mother country and the rest of the world. When the Portuguese king reluctantly left Brazil in 1821, he felt that an independence movement was inevitable and advised his son, Pedro, to lead such a move lest undesirable elements capture control of the nation. Thus, Brazil in 1822 broke with Portugal and accomplished in fifteen months, with little or no bloodshed, what it took the rest of Latin America more than fifteen bloody years of fighting to achieve. The move from colony to independent empire was a peaceful transition. When the emperor, Dom Pedro I, granted a Constitution to the people in 1824, it included a special provision that was unheard of in the western world. The emperor reserved for himself the "moderating power." This gave him the right to override any action by the Parliament or the Supreme Court and, in effect, made him the conscience of the nation. When Dom Pedro I fell into disfavor with the social and economic elite of the country, he quietly resigned in 1831 and went into exile, leaving his son as the heir to the vacant throne. Brazil was governed by a variety of regents for nearly ten years until Dom Pedro II assumed the throne in 1841. All of these administrative changes were peaceful and nonviolent. Dom Pedro II governed from 1841 to 1889 with the aid of disciplined, elite-oriented Liberal and Conservative parties, which slowly broadened their political base to include a rising middle class. Profound economic changes took place in the 1870s and 1880s. Slavery was not popular with the business community of southern Brazil and was abolished in 1888. No violence accompanied the emancipation legislation.

The year 1889 was a watershed in Brazil's history. The aging Emperor Dom Pedro II had no male heirs and showed little interest in fighting for the continuity of his regime. The Brazilian Church had assumed an air of benevolent neutrality toward the rising wave of republican sentiment. Civilian political leaders in the important states of São Paulo and Minas Gerais were quietly making plans for a republic. A tiny and relatively insignificant Republican party was agitating for the immediate establishment of a republic. But the catalyst in the events that toppled Dom Pedro's Government was the military. A group of army officers protesting against what they considered discriminatory action directed against the Brazilian military triggered a chain of events that resulted in the establishment of a republic on November 15, 1889. No violence took place when the empire ended, and there was general acceptance from the social, economic, and political elite of the nation. The army may have moved more quickly than the civilian political leaders had anticipated, but in no manner could this be considered a clash between civilian and military authority. The civilian leaders of São Paulo, who were also planning a republic, did resent the fact that the Republic had been born with the aid of the bayonets of the Brazilian army.

The military governed Brazil until 1894, when presidential elections were permitted and civilian politicians took control of the executive office. In 1891 a new Constitution was prepared for Brazil and followed in general lines the United States Constitution. The famous "moderating power" of the emperor fell by implication and by tacit agreement into the hands of the Brazilian military establishment.

Brazil was governed almost exclusively by civilian politicians from the states of São Paulo and Minas Gerais from 1894 to 1930. For nearly thirty-six years, elections on national, state, and municipal levels were held at regularly scheduled periods, and Brazil slowly broadened her political structure. In the more wealthy states of São Paulo, Minas Gerais, and Rio Grande do Sul, a tiny opposition to the semiofficial Republican party was tolerated. In the seventeen other smaller states comprising the Brazilian union, the Republican party was dominant, permitted no opposition, and generally followed the orientation of the national Government. Whenever a challenge or a threat to the *status quo* developed, the Brazilian military establishment could be relied upon to support the Government. Actually, throughout the period from 1894 to 1930, there were few serious challenges to the existing political structure.

The old Republic fell apart in 1930, when civilian political leaders from the three states of São Paulo, Minas Gerais, and Rio Grande do Sul quarreled and could not unanimously agree on a candidate for the Presidency. In the March 1930 presidential election, politicians from Minas Gerais, Rio Grande do Sul, and the tiny northeastern state of Paraíba fought for the Presidency. Getúlio Vargas, Governor of Rio Grande do Sul, lost to the official Republican candidate, Julio Prestes, governor of the powerful and important state of São Paulo, who had the support of the Federal Government and sixteen other smaller states. Taking advantage of the uneasy economic conditions caused by the depression of 1929, politicians from Rio Grande do Sul, who were aided by the tacit approval of the professional army, annulled the election results of March 1930 by a revolution which broke out in October 1930. The revolution was genuinely popular, but before it could be successful, it had to have the approval of the army. Once again the people saw in the political process a rather abrupt change accompanied by little or no bloodshed and saw the military performing a decisive role in the events of the period.

Brazil was governed by a Rio Grande do Sul civilian, Getúlio Vargas, from 1930 to 1945. Shoring up the Chief Executive was the Brazilian military. There was no conflict between the two. Two dramatic incidents during the period point up the contradictory position of the mass of the people in relation to the political structure. In 1932 the people of São Paulo, who charged that Vargas had promised a new constitution and none was granted, rebelled against his Government. The *paulista* citizens joined the revolt with enthusiasm. The rest of Brazil viewed the rebellion in different terms and considered it more an attempt by the state of São Paulo to regain control of the national government which they had lost in 1930. But the decisive factor, as always in Brazilian affairs, was the military establishment, which remained loyal to Getúlio Vargas, and after a few tense months the rebellion collapsed. A new

Constitution was written in 1934, and the constituents elected Vargas President for a four-year term. A second incident occurred in 1937, when some interest began to be generated for the presidential elections promised for 1938. The army and Getúlio Vargas both decided against holding elections, and in November 1937 a dictatorship was formalized. The Brazilian population took this move apathetically, and only mild protests against the Government-army action were heard.

The fifteen-year Vargas era, basically an authoritarian period, resulted in both progress and setbacks for the Brazilian political environment. Vargas did incorporate the working class into the body politic by making sure that certain of the laborers' minimum requirements were taken care of by the Government; the urban working class was not systematically excluded from the political and economic process. The economic structure of Brazil was profoundly modified by government encouragement of both light and heavy industry. Regionalism was attacked by the Vargas regime with some degree of success. Regardless of this economic progress, the political setbacks meant fifteen years of cynicism toward the political process; anything could be accomplished if one knew the right people. Fortunes were made overnight, and along with a new elite, a new and more powerful middle class developed during the period. Behind all this was the Brazilian military, carefully keeping an eye on the political mechanism and guarding its own interests.

In 1945 the military establishment lost confidence in Vargas, who, bowing to pressures to return Brazil to a democratic state, began to build a larger personal following among the working class. In October of that year, the army requested Vargas to leave office, and he peacefully complied. The Brazilian citizens, pleased to hear that the country was returning to democratic norms, watched the events with detachment. From 1945 to 1964, Brazil was basically governed by civilian politicians operating under a new Constitution prepared in 1946. Presidential elections were held every five years. Political parties functioned, with the exception of the Communist party, which was outlawed in 1947.

There was a ripple of apprehension among the military leaders when Vargas announced that he would be a presidential candidate in the 1950 elections. The army was perplexed, as they had removed him in 1945 and now he threatened to return. Since the general public voted their approval of the Vargas candidacy, the military did nothing to block the former dictator from assuming office. However, they kept a watchful eye on his presidential activities, and when he began to rebuild the same alliance that he had started in 1945, mainly seeking support from the labor unions and the lower income groups in the cities, the military became more apprehensive. In August 1954, a crusading newspaper editor, Carlos Lacerda, exposed the tremendous graft that men around the President were engaged in, and became the target of an assassination attempt which resulted in the death of an air force major. When the gunman was caught and linked to the Vargas household, the military demanded that the President resign. To everyone's amazement, Vargas refused to heed the demand of the military and committed suicide on August 24, 1954, rather than leave the executive office, to which he had been legally and honestly elected. The citizens, stunned and incredulous at this unprecedented turn of events, had no leader to rally around. But after a few agitated days, political life returned to normal with the vice-president completing the last year of the Vargas administration.

The Vargas men came back with winning candidates in 1955. Juscelino Kubitschek, former governor of Minas Gerais and former Minister of Labor, and João Goulart from Rio Grande do Sul, were installed as President and vice-president for the term 1955–1960. The military forces were again concerned about the victory of a group of civilian politicians which the military did not completely trust but did nothing to block their control of the national Government. In the 1960 election the Brazilian military was extremely pleased when a reform candidate, Jânio Quadros, who was not connected or associated in any way with the Vargas clique, won the Presidency. His was a relatively easy victory, as the general public was tired of the men who had inherited the Vargas mantle.

However, Brazilian law permitted split tickets, and Jânio Quadros' vice-president came from the Vargas camp. Thus, João Goulart, one of the men most distrusted by the Brazilian military establishment, was inaugurated with Jânio Quadros in January 1961. The Brazilian public and the military, satisfied with the Quadros victory, confidently awaited the promised reforms. Instead of governing well, Quadros, who claimed that mysterious forces had toppled him, resigned unexpectedly in August 1961 and fled the country. It had been easier for Quadros to govern the rich state of São Paulo than the poor country of Brazil. Then, a stunned Brazil watched in amazement as the military establishment refused to accept João Goulart as President. When the army split, for the first time in Brazilian history, over the issue of Goulart in the Presidency, the door was opened to a compromise solution; the Brazilian Congress voted a constitutional amendment which theoretically transformed Brazil into a parliamentary government with great powers in the hands of the Congress and a Prime Minister. The President was to be a figurehead.

The system did not function, and the Brazilian Government was in a state of chaos from September 1961 until April 1964, when the military and the governors of the major states of São Paulo, Minas Gerais, Rio Grande do Sul, and Guanabara joined together to oust the João Goulart administration. This ouster was a popular action backed by the majority of the people; the military establishment did not move against the Brazilians but moved with them. From 1964 to 1966, however, a widening gulf developed between civilians and the military. The army assumed more and more of the authority to make decisions that was formerly in the hands of civilian political leaders. A gradual hardening of attitudes, among both the younger army men and the civilian political leaders, who were gradually being eliminated from participation in the political process, took place. By 1966, public involvement in the electoral process was reduced to selecting members of the national House of

Representatives, while political participation at the state and municipal levels in many cases fell under the close supervision of the military.

Ideology

Ideology in the Brazilian political environment reflects shifting, often pragmatic approaches to solving immediate problems and leaving for some future date the resolution of deeper needs. At least in this regard, Brazilians seem somewhat like North American citizens in that *ad hoc* solutions are often the most workable. Political leaders and parties do not feel at all restricted by platforms and programs. Politically, Brazilians live very much in the present. They manifest little patience for the past and, at least until the mid-1960s, showed enthusiasm and optimism for the future.

In an attempt to describe ideological leaders who have left their mark on Brazilian political thinking, it is necessary to mention briefly some historical figures who may contribute to the future direction of Brazilian political ideology. But again, Brazilians will not be strapped into or held prisoner by a well-thought-out or predetermined blueprint. A plan, a thought, or an idea will be molded and changed to fit Brazilian realities.

Benjamin Constant Botelho de Magalhães is the first of the historical leaders who influenced the young army men of the 1880s. A Positivist and professor at the military school, he grouped around him an amazingly dedicated young corps of officers, who felt that the chaos of the Brazilian Government under the emperor must be radically changed and that political order and progress must be substituted.[4] It has been suggested by some Brazilians that Benjamin Constant and his Positivist followers could be compared to the Alexander Hamilton faction in early American history, who favored law and order over any other attribute of government. This abhorrence of political disorder appears to be one of the paradoxes of Brazil: While yearning for law and order, the country has one of the most casual and disorganized political systems operating anywhere in the world.

One further contribution of Benjamin Constant was the fact that Positivism quietly eased many Brazilians away from tight, unquestioning attachment to Catholicism. Constant is not read or followed consciously by many in Brazil today, but one often feels the impact of this man's thinking behind statements by leading army officials and civilian economic advisers.

Rui Barbosa represents the other side of the Brazilian political coin. A brilliant, erratic, flamboyant, and almost reluctant republican leader, he continues to represent the Jeffersonian complex among Brazilian political thinkers. During the last decade of the empire, Rui Barbosa fought for abolition of slavery, extension of popular education, freedom of religion, and especially the concept of civilian power over that of the military. This last item has great appeal in the 1960s. Rui Barbosa was one of the most important men in the

---

[4] João Cruz Costa, *A History of Ideas in Brazil* (Berkeley, University of California Press, 1964).

writing of the 1891 Constitution. In 1910 he launched his campaign for the Presidency around the concept of civilian power and the freedom of the small Brazilian states from encroachment by the Federal Government and the army establishment. Rui Barbosa lost in 1910, but his ideas are still quoted despite a recent wave of criticism of his role in the early years of Brazilian republican history.

Euclides da Cunha's contribution lies in his attempt to get Brazil to come to terms with the mass of people who live in the backlands. An army-trained civil engineer, he was sent in 1896 by one of the country's leading newspapers to cover the military operations of the Federal Government against a fanatical religious and political leader, Antonio Maciel, who resisted both the state and the Federal Government in the backlands of Bahia. The heroic resistance of the *sertanejos* so impressed Euclides da Cunha that he began to speculate whether this backwoods Brazilian, an Indian-Negro-white mixture, was not the true Brazilian rather than the *paulista* or the *carioca* (that is, a resident of Rio de Janeiro). Influenced strongly by the French racist Gobineau, Euclides da Cunha's book, *Os sertões* (translated as *Rebellion in the Backlands*), a classic in Brazilian letters, implies that the reason Brazil made so little progress up to that time is the racial mixture, which produces a nasty, tough, backwards type of person who is really an impediment to progress. The author's approach to the problem seems to be ambivalent; he admires the toughness of the backland citizen while at the same time noting his generally unprogressive attitudes.

Monteiro Lobato was an important force in the late 1920s and early 1930s in arousing interest in the natural resources of the country. Lobato constantly charged that iron and oil resources were in danger of falling under the domination of the foreign speculators and imperialists. His book *The Scandal of Petroleum and Iron* is a classic study and demonstrates an extreme nationalism. Lobato, an outspoken critic of arbitrary government, fell afoul of the Vargas administration and spent many years in exile. His manner of writing conjures up images of Standard Oil geologists and oil specialists finding oceans of oil in Brazil and pouring concrete down the holes so that Brazilians could not gain access. As the Brazilian Government did not permit foreign firms to drill for oil, Lobato claims that there has been a gigantic plot on the part of United States companies to prevent Brazil from discovering the vast oil reserves that the huge land mass must cover. Should ultranationalism take wing in Brazil in the last decades of the twentieth century, Monteiro Lobato's works will be for the country one of the principal sources of reference.

A militant Catholic, Alceu Amoroso Lima, who writes under the pen name of Tristão de Ataide, has been well known for nearly forty years as a social critic of Brazilian society. A literary commentator and Professor of Philosophy at Catholic University, he has constantly called the attention of the middle class to its failure to do something about the problems of poverty, disease, and ignorance that exist in the urban slums. His political posture in the 1930s indicated that he considered authoritarian government more in keeping with Brazilian realities. Yet, in the 1960s, and particularly since 1964, he has become one of the most outspoken opponents of the Brazilian military. He has continually charged in the press that the army men have lost all sense of balance with their attacks on the Brazilian intellectual community. His continued friendliness to the United States has been important in counteracting the feelings of many Brazilian Catholic intellectuals who consider the United States civilization a threat to Brazilian values and mores.

Gilberto Freyre is another important figure in setting the ideological tone of the Brazilian political environment. More than a social anthropologist, he brings the enthusiasm of a skillful writer and polemicist to the current scene. Freyre's basic thesis that Brazilians are a new cosmic race, successfully blending Negro, white, and Indian and developing a new society, is an attractive and inviting picture. Much of what Freyre writes about race mixture reflects Bahia and Pernambuco plantation society rather than the situation of the states of São Paulo, Minas Gerais, and southern Brazil. Nevertheless, Freyre captures some of the optimism of the Brazilian about his culture, his society, and the fact that Brazil is developing into one of the first great modern societies to emerge in a tropical or subtropical area.[5] Since the 1964 revolution, Freyre has become more politically conservative and, much to the dismay of many Brazilian intellectuals, has defended the military.

The situation in Brazil since 1964 is difficult to describe, but it is clear that the vast bulk of the intellectual community has become greatly disenchanted with the army. The Brazilian intellectuals normally have had little dialogue or confidence in the politicians, left or right, who have governed the nation. But the alienation of the intellectuals from the military rulers has become total and complete. There is, of course, no one spokesman for the younger generation of intellectuals, but Helio Jaguaribe and Candido Mendes de Almeida can easily be considered as the most representative of the new group. Jaguaribe's books demonstrate an approach to the Brazilian economic and political process that seems to leave little to chance. His examination and description of the middle class is extremely pessimistic and expresses his feelings about Brazil's future. For Jaguaribe, there seems to be little likelihood that Brazil and the United States can work together peacefully and harmoniously. His approach to the Brazilian economic process indicates that United States capital can only play the role of a despoiler and not really be of aid to Brazil's development. After the military takeover in 1964, Jaguaribe left the country and has been teaching at Harvard in the Department of Government.

Candido Mendes de Almeida has been described as a Brazilian McGeorge Bundy. Formerly a foreign-policy adviser to Jânio Quadros and a close adviser to Dom Helder Camara, the left-wing archbishop of Recife, in northeastern Brazil, Candido Mendes' approach to the contemporary situation is less pessimistic than Jaguaribe's. The former appears impressed with the

---

[5] Gilberto Freyre, *New World in the Tropics* (New York, Alfred A. Knopf, Inc., 1945).

young technicians who have been attracted to the military Government and subsequently given a free hand to plan the economic future of the country. Without approving of their techniques in governing, Candido Mendes de Almeida gives the impression of quiet but grudging admiration for what the new technocrats have accomplished.

In summary, the ideological commitment of Brazil is difficult to pin down. No one spokesman has formulated an ideological blueprint for the nation. There is more conscious economic planning by the military since 1964. But, in contrast, the political style of the military men has alternated between toughness and some accommodation with civilian leaders—though always on the terms set by the army. The bulk of the population seems acutely disenchanted with the military, however, and continues to press for a return to constitutional rule.

POLITICAL STRUCTURES AND ROLES

Political Parties

The traditional Brazilian political parties were abolished by a decree issued by the present military Government on October 27, 1965. The junta ordered the creation of an official government party, which took the name ARENA, National Renovating Alliance, and at the same time requested that an opposition political party, the MDB, the Brazilian Democratic Movement, be organized. As both the two new political parties are composed of professional politicians from previously functioning parties, it is necessary to describe the role that these traditional parties occupied in the Brazilian political milieu before 1965.

When Brazil became a Republic in 1889, one powerful political party emerged, the Republican party, which was dominant from 1889 to 1930. Though organized nationally, it was mainly a state-level party which provided the organizational structure for candidates, platforms, as well as political expression for a relatively small minority of educated citizens. São Paulo, Minas Gerais, and Rio Grande do Sul had the most important Republican organizations in the country. The political leaders from the Republican parties of those three states dictated the name of the presidential candidate every four years, and the politician selected never failed in almost four decades to be elected. The President could generally dictate the terms of political life to the smaller states, so Brazil was basically a one-party State under the Republicans. In the three most powerful states, there were also tiny but ineffective opposition parties, though these groups never threatened the Republican party on either the national or the state level. Within these limits the "party system" functioned fairly well from 1894 to 1930. The franchise was generally broadened, and every national election resulted in an increase in political participation.

The revolution of 1930, which put Getúlio Vargas into the executive office, broke the power of the traditional Republican party. For fifteen years

Brazil was governed without consulting the Republican party, nor was there any attempt to form an official party. When the dictatorship ended in 1945, four new political units appeared. The most important were two which Vargas himself created. The first was the PSD, the Social Democratic party. Composed of wealthy landowners and political bosses installed during the period from 1930 to 1945, the party had a virtual political monopoly in the smaller states of the union and was also strong in Minas Gerais and Rio Grande do Sul. A second party organized with Vargas' blessing was the PTB, the Brazilian Labor party, which was aimed at maintaining the loyalty of the urban working class. A third party, the UDN, the National Democratic Union, was composed of middle-income and upper-income-group elements who opposed the Vargas regime. A fourth party, the PSP, the Social Progressive party, appeared and was the personal vehicle of São Paulo politician Ademar de Barros. The Communist party existed briefly from 1945 to 1947.

The four major parties and nine smaller parties played significant roles in the period from 1945 to 1965. They selected candidates, aired issues, stirred controversy, and provided opposition. In São Paulo, Minas Gerais, and Rio Grande do Sul, there were bruising struggles for power in which all manner of compromise had to be made in order for a candidate to win. No one of the four major parties dominated to the extent that it could ruthlessly dictate what it wanted.[6] Even the smaller states, which had no tradition of two-party power struggles, slowly became involved in this search for political consensus.

The period from 1945, when the PSD was virtually unchallenged in the nation, to 1964, when the party had lost power in every major state, reveals an interesting story of democratic development. It is true that the nation-wide parties were not disciplined on the national level and especially in their operation in the Brazilian Congress, where the scene was often chaotic. On the state level, every manner of political compromise occurred. Parties whose platforms seemed diametrically opposed to those of opponent parties would suddenly form an alliance with the opposition to elect a governor and then share in the spoils. In the smaller, less politically sophisticated states, rough and often bloody political battles frequently transpired on the municipal level. In the northeast and in the Amazon north, political operations were primitive, and terrorism, intimidation, and every form of coercion were brought into play.

The Brazilian military kept watch on the entire party system; so long as the major parties did not threaten the privileged position of the military, it seemingly had no quarrel with what the politicians were doing. The army could live with the PSD, the UDN, and the PSP. But when Goulart, in mid-1961, began to throw the entire mechanism of the Federal Government behind the PTB in an attempt to build a machine personally loyal to him and apparently dedicated to destroying all opposition, then and only then did the

---

[6] Themistocles Cavalcanti and Reisky Dubnic, *Comportamento eleitoral no Brasil* (Rio de Janeiro, Fundacão Getúlio Vargas, 1964).

army, the middle class, the Church, and all the other political groups literally close ranks to oppose the PTB and President Goulart.

When the 1964 coup removed Goulart, there was for a short time a close co-operation between the civilian political party leaders and the army. But gradually a split developed and the tough-line army men decreed their Institutional Act Number Two in October 1965, which abolished all the existing political parties in Brazil. When the shock of this action faded, many political professionals rushed to join the official government party, ARENA. The military men were embarrassed as friend and former foe alike sought to join them. What finally developed was that the strongest conservative politicians in the PSD, the UDN, and the PSP found homes in ARENA, while the moderate members of the PTB and some alienated politicians in the UDN and others from the smaller parties joined the MDB.

In mid-1967 the new party system continued to function precariously and its effectiveness is still in question. ARENA launched an official presidential candidate, who, as a former Minister of War and an important general, cannot be defeated. The MDB refused even to name an opposition candidate. The problem in part lies in the typical Brazilian fashion of the Government's not informing the opposition on how far it can go in criticizing the military. Should the arguments against the Government become too strong, the opposition congressmen would probably be removed and senators stripped of their political rights. As a result, in 1966 a rather dispirited opposition limped along with the government plans.

Interest Groups

The Military   In any assessment of the Brazilian political structure, the army must be given prominence. It is by far the best organized national force. It has the most effective political mechanism in that it does have programs and apparently may have the ability to carry them out. The army, which is the most significant part of the military establishment, is not, however, a tight, monolithic group representing an outmoded elite. The Brazilian army is in many areas of operation a highly sophisticated and subtle force.

Historically, the army has very carefully sounded out civilian political leadership before moving into the political arena. The army normally co-ordinates most of its moves with the traditional power sectors, which accounts for its high degree of success. Generally, the army is adept at taking a reading of the public pulse. It is doubtful whether the public would have supported the army if it had prevented Goulart from taking office in 1961, and the army men knew it, though in 1964 the general public supported the army's removal of President Goulart. Nonetheless, the political role of the army between 1964 and 1966 caused a deterioration in its popular image.

It is generally accepted that there are three basic army groups striving to direct policy. The first is composed of the hard-line men, who feel that the civilian political structure is absolutely and incontrovertibly corrupt. These men, many of them young colonels, believe that the bankruptcy of civilian politics makes it imperative that the army act for the good of the country. These men are not necessarily reactionary; that is, they do not speak for or represent the wealthiest elements in the country, since in Brazil many of the wealthiest elements support the most corrupt of the civilian administrations. The image that these young military men have of their country is that of an industrialized nation. This image inevitably brings them into conflict with the landowners in the northeast. The hard-line officials have been unable to comprehend the action of the other military men in permitting Congress to function, the Supreme Court to operate, the universities to remain open, the press to be relatively uncensored.

At the opposite end of the pole is a substantial block of officials who consider themselves the soft-line group. They regard the role of the army as that of the traditional "moderating force." These men favor stepping in to correct a critical situation and then returning to the barracks. Civilian leaders should be encouraged to manage the Brazilian political process. The soft-line element asserts that the young tough-line men have gone too far and that they may be creating the very conditions that will lead to a nasty and bloody civil war.

Oscillating between these two groups are officials closely connected with the Superior War College, the Escola Superior de Guerra, who have tried to steer a middle course between the opposing tendencies of the military. Many of these men are aware of the shortcomings of military solutions for complex economic and social problems and have tended to look to young economists for orientation and guidance in preparing plans for the slowing down of the inflationary trend and for promoting industrialization of the nation. The sensitive question of foreign capital participation in basic Brazilian industries is also one which is approached by this group with a great deal of caution.

The Superior War College officials have tried as much as possible to make accommodations with the civilian political chiefs wherever they did not seem to constitute a threat to the overall plans of the revolution. Thus, Governor Ademar de Barros, because he controlled São Paulo, was tolerated until the military was able to establish to its own satisfaction that he no longer commanded the support of vast numbers of *paulista* citizens and that the overwhelming graft of his administration and his opposition to the military were sufficient to result in his removal from office in August 1966. His disappearance caused hardly a ripple on the political surface.

The consensus that does emanate from the military seems to take the two-Brazils approach. In the northeast the military operates in a relatively rough manner. In this region one is living in a garrison state. There is relatively little redress against grievances, both real and supposed, for the civilian population. There is no mobilization of public opinion, and nothing counterbalances the military. Should an army major feel that the faculty of some university is too far left and a center of subversion, the offending professors can be removed. Should the mayor of a small town in the interior incur the wrath of an army officer, the mayor is removed. In general terms, this arbitrary use of power is kept to a minimum but does occur with some regularity.

In the other Brazil, the Brazil of the south, the military men proceed with a great deal of caution and care. The majority of the politicians who have been removed from office were undoubtedly deeply involved in graft and corruption. Others have worked closely with Marxist groups. In some cases reformers have been removed from elected posts by overzealous military men because those reformers opposed the army. But in the south the press, the radio, the television, the universities, the intellectual community, including the liberal wing of the Catholic Church, loudly and stridently protest. Yet this verbal opposition has not prevented the military from destroying the top civilian leadership in Rio Grande do Sul, São Paulo, and Guanabara in the years 1964–1966.

The military forces feel that they must be given more time to continue their cleaning up of the Brazilian political process. In part, this conviction explains their insisting on the candidacy of Marechal Costa e Silva for the presidential term beginning in March 1967. The top-ranking men think that for too long they have pulled civilian chestnuts out of the fire only to have to return to do the job over. Now they believe that they must dictate the terms and methods of political and economic reconstruction that are necessary for the nation.

Church   After the army, the Church is probably the best organized political force in Brazilian life. The operations of the Brazilian Church in the political arena in 1966, however, seem to resemble the role which the Church played in 1937 during the Vargas dictatorship period. The leaders of the Catholic Church in Brazil are realists and are not planning to enter into any power struggle with the military or with any government that promises stability and is anti-Communist. Though there are many radical elements in the Brazilian Church, they are marking time in the post-revolutionary period and not confronting or challenging the administration. There seems to be a general reciprocation at the moment, a situation which resembles the Mexican PRI's attitude toward the Church, though certain exceptions to this rule do exist in the northeast and in the interior.

Church and State in Brazil have always had a special relationship. One finds that politics, religion, and nationalism blend in Brazil; there are no violent clashes between Church and State in the history of the country. Representatives of the clergy are found on every level of political, economic, and social activity. Still, the Church's role in the political milieu of Brazil tends to be ambiguous. In the Vargas period the formation of the LEC, Liga Eleitoral Católica, or the Catholic Electoral League, was in part an attempt to mobilize middle-class citizens to take part in the political life of the country. A subtle power struggle began as the Vargas administration moved into the social welfare area and assumed some of the Church's functions. No open conflict developed, but the Church and the Vargas regime watched each other warily.

From 1945 to 1964, the Church in Brazil presented a novel pattern in politics. The top hierarchy tended to be conservative, with the exception of one cardinal, who took a benevolent attitude toward the Goulart regime and, after April 1964, was promptly transferred to a small diocese in the interior of the country. The lower Church officially tended to hold more liberal political attitudes. But the crucial factor was that the Church could not manipulate the vote. This continues to be especially true in urban areas. In the rural areas, where votes are fewer and less significant, the Church plays a more important role in establishing political attitudes.[7] In the 1962 congressional elections the Church-oriented Family Electoral Alliance backed seventeen candidates in Bahia, but only six were elected.

There is no Church political party per se, and as a result the various clergymen who go into politics join existing parties. In 1964 there were 7 clergymen in Congress; 5 were federal congressmen belonging to the UDN, PSD, and PTB parties, and 2 were senators. The Church does have youth movements, such as the Catholic University Youth organization, and before the 1964 revolution, the Popular Action group was operative and worked closely with the Marxist elements.

The number of priests in Brazil is estimated to be about 10,000 for a population of over 80 million. Of this number, only 4,000 are Brazilian; the remainder is divided among Spanish, French, Italian, German, and United States nationals.

The clergy in southern Brazil appears to take radical positions on social problems in the northeastern part of the nation. In the north itself, with the exception of Archbishop Dom Helder Camara, the upper clergy is relatively conservative. In the rural areas of the northeast, Bishop Eugenio Sales and Padre Antônio Melo are working with the dispossessed and attempting to improve their living and working conditions. The military has sometimes frowned on the positions and attitudes of the clergy, and in fact, Church activity in the area of social welfare has declined since 1964.

Economic Groups   The business community actively and openly entered the political arena in the 1960s when IBAD, the Brazilian Institute of Democratic Action, was organized. It financed the election of anti-Communist congressmen and senators throughout the nation. IBAD pressured business organizations for contributions. It was apparently fairly successful, as the Goulart Government turned the full force of the executive office against the group. A congressional investigation was ordered but came to no conclusion on whether or not the group was a threat to democratic institutions. Then Goulart outlawed IBAD by executive decree in 1963. The business community is not monolithic, and more often than not, conflict among the various entities arises over who is the true spokesman for the group and what its objectives really are.

---

[7] Belden Paulson, *Local Political Patterns in the Northeast: A Community Case Study* (Madison, Land Tenure Center, University of Wisconsin, 1964).

Middle-class Conservative groups present candidates and mobilize public opinion in support of the candidates the groups feel will carry out their objectives. Their relatively high degree of success indicates that they are making their appeals in terms that are significant for the average middle-class voter. What is more interesting, however, is the fact that the lower-income groups have not broken with the system but have tended to accept middle-class conservative platforms upholding the traditional structure of politics. Approval or disapproval is registered within traditional political norms. From the dangerous northeastern area, where the political structure seemed to be on the verge of breaking down, to the urban slums of Rio de Janeiro, one constantly encounters candidates going to the people with appeals directed to the lower class. From Francisco Julião, northeastern rural leader, to Leonel Brizola, urban demagogue and brother-in-law of João Goulart, the message to the voters is to cast their ballots and have confidence in their elected representatives. It is curious that after nearly twenty years (1945–1964) of political "normalcy" in Brazil, it was the middle class and the upper-income groups who were willing to back and gamble on an extralegal military move.

From the evidence of living standards and of feedback from the economic process, it would appear that the real support for drastic nontraditional change should have come from the lower-income groups. Apparently, however, the lower-income classes did not see themselves in such desperate straits as to consider increased militarism in government a panacea for their wants. In short, the masses probably saw little difference in the benefits they would receive should Goulart continue or should he go. Thus it was that the leadership to inspire his removal was left to the higher-income groups.

Finally, the upper-income groups have, of course, benefited from traditional political operations. The upper-income groups did well under the Vargas dictatorship, in the post-Vargas period, and continue to do well in the 1964–1967 period. There has been no specific threat to this income group, with the possible exception of the men who grouped themselves around Goulart in the last two years of his administration. But even in the Goulart period, the major thrust of criticism was against foreign interests working closely with Brazilian capitalists and with the large landholders of the northeast. Yet wealthy Brazilian capitalists, industrialists, and landowners from Rio Grande do Sul also supported radical elements in the Goulart administration. Many of them may have felt that they were buying insurance. One of Brazil's wealthiest industrialists consistently poured money into the Labor party and was elected as a senator from the northeastern state of Pernambuco. When the army moved in, taking away political rights of governors, senators, congressmen, and mayors, the military skipped over this senator, who probably had also contributed to the revolt against Goulart.

When the middle class was given a chance to select a reform candidate, Jânio Quadros in 1960, who promised austerity and clean government, they overwhelmingly voted him into office. Brazil in 1961 seemed to be on the threshold of a progressive movement. The middle classes had been subjected to fifteen years of Vargas' cliquish government and had come out of the decade and a half cynical and lacking confidence that they could manage political affairs by themselves. Slowly, after 1945, there was a rebuilding of public self-confidence throughout the middle sector.

Quadros' resignation in August 1961 discouraged middle-class confidence in the Brazilian political system. His action struck Brazilians in much the same manner that President Kennedy's assassination affected many Americans. Whereas in the United States the political process is so institutionalized that there was immediate continuity, in Brazil the political system is not old enough and stable enough to superimpose continuity upon an abrupt change in government. The middle classes watched the incoming vice-president, João Goulart, with distaste and distrust. The military surrounded him with advisers, and the Congress and the political parties were suspicious of every move that the President made. When he attempted to create a new political power base, the Brazilian political system faltered while the military slowly began to take over civilian political prerogatives.

Since 1964, middle-class political behavior has been in a critical stage. The army may not be skillful or sophisticated enough to interpret the demands and desires of the middle class, and economic reforms which may have hurt only the lower-income groups could begin to pinch the middle sectors. However, the middle groups are accustomed to complaining and having their complaints heeded. If the army does not listen to their demands and chokes off their ability to change and shift politicians, the middle class may resort to leading a movement to oust the military from control of the country.

The behavioral norms of the lower-income groups present a confusing picture. One could first dismiss the northeastern rural peasant as a force for radical change for a number of reasons. This group is too small and does not have effective leadership. Second, it appears relatively easy to placate the rural peasants. A few minor changes, a little food, a little attention, and they tend to become rather acquiescent. Another reason that there appears to be no threat to the body politic from the rural element is that those who have the desire to leave their destitute rural environment usually can find a way to migrate to cities, where it seems possible to improve living and working conditions. With such a safety valve, rural frustration can ordinarily be relieved before it explodes. Finally, it appears that the military, in contrast to its reluctance to use force in the urban areas, will use it quickly and effectively in the interior.

The largest question mark as far as the lower-income groups are concerned relates to the slum dwellers of Rio de Janeiro. Most of the people in the *favelas* feel that Vargas and the men who supported him really have wanted to do something for them. The slum dwellers are, however, becoming about as cynical as the middle class over their future in the entire political process. Perhaps Carolina de Jesus' *Child of the Dark,* in which Ademar de Barros is evaluated, probes the essential attitudes of the *favela* dwellers. The politicians, she writes, show up at election time and then disappear. Two concrete examples underline this practice. Leonel Brizola, brother-in-law of

President João Goulart, ran for federal congressman from Rio de Janeiro. Brizola campaigned on the memory of Vargas and promised to be the spokesman of the poor in the federal Congress. He received one of the greatest vote totals ever cast for any candidate in Rio de Janeiro history. His record in Congress was not, however, very auspicious. When the revolt broke out against Goulart in 1964, one of its principal civilian leaders was Governor Carlos Lacerda of the state of Guanabara, that is, the city of Rio de Janeiro. One might reasonably have expected the slum dwellers to become shock troops for the Goulart administration and be ready to die in the streets of Rio de Janeiro for politicians who were dedicated to the cause of the poor. Not one ripple of enthusiasm or desire to come out of the *favelas* and make common cause with the fleeing politicians was in evidence. The political behavior of the *favelados* may be passive, but it appears that most slum dwellers know that their needs are recognized, if not satisfied, and this knowledge seems to have reduced the proclivity for violence.

Elections and Representation

Brazilian elections and representation on the national level in the period from 1945 to 1964 generally reflect more the operation of dysfunction than of function. The Brazilian Congress did not function well during this nineteen-year period. In the aggregate, congressmen were petty, narrow, undisciplined, and corrupt. If any sector of the Brazilian political structure can be charged with failing to live up to its minimal responsibilities, it is the legislative branch. With some conspicuous exceptions in both the Senate and the Chamber of Deputies, the majority of the congressmen were guilty of absenteeism and flagrant abuse of their elected office. Any survey of congressional activity indicates that they were constantly the do-nothing branch of government. Reform legislation requested by the executive branch was persistently rejected. Tax changes, land reforms, basic structural reforms, and the discipline necessary to function through a parliamentary period were all unattainable from the Congress.

Southeastern Brazil sent to Congress a variety of legislators, ranging from some urban demagogues to a number of conscientious and hard-working lawmakers. On the other hand, two rather specific types represented the northeast in the federal Congress. The most powerful were the old professional politicians who were holdovers from the Vargas period. They had established political feudal states and were almost unbeatable. In the vast majority of cases, these men were conservative and defended the *status quo*. Opposing this element was a small but growing group of radicals, who made their appeals to the masses and underprivileged groups. But once in Congress, these men tended to look after their own personal interests. Not surprisingly, this tendency often created disillusionment among their constituents.

Congress's basic slowness and obstructionism was one of the prime targets of the military after the 1964 coup. New regulations demanded that Congress act on proposed legislation within a certain specified period of time.

If the congressmen failed to act, the proposed bills became law. Other procedural and structural changes, such as the artificial creation of two new political parties, ARENA and MDB, largely reduced Congress to the status of a rubber-stamp body.

Elections and representation at the state level were more successful and more sensitive than was the case in the national Legislature. A few important examples indicate this difference. The Pernambuco gubernatorial elections in 1962 demonstrated some of the basic resiliency of that state's political environment. Miguel Arrais, a shrewd and popular politician, ran for governor and solicited the support of any and all left-wing groups. The Communists backed him wholeheartedly, as did the national Government of João Goulart. Moreover, José Emirio de Morais, one of the nation's wealthiest industrialists, contributed vast sums of money to Arrais' campaign. Arrais won a narrow victory, and the army and middle-class elements waited nervously for changes in state personnel or drastic reforms to take place. Nothing spectacular happened, as the state legislature was conservatively oriented. But one move by the governor did result in his downfall. Arrais appointed as his chief officer in charge of security a regular army man who was known to be an ultranationalist and extremely sympathetic to Marxist elements. Thus, the governor was one of the first to be removed from office when the army took over in 1964.

In 1962, in Rio Grande do Sul, the reverse took place when Leonel Brizola could not elect the governor he wanted to follow him in office. Here was the power of the incumbent governor, the good will of the national Government, and yet the candidate could not be elected. Brizola charged that the Catholic Church was responsible for the defeat of his candidate—a charge rarely heard in recent years. In effect, then, the Rio Grande do Sul voters simply had chosen the man they felt would best serve them, regardless of the wishes of the governor and of the President of the country.

The 1962 São Paulo governor's race presented an interesting study in the crisscrossing of Brazilian political affairs. Jânio Quadros, former President and ex-governor of the state, was attempting a comeback after his disastrous seven-month term of office in 1961 as the nation's Chief Executive. His opponent was Ademar de Barros, also a former governor. Both men made strong appeals to the lower-income groups. Most of the working-class population expected Jânio Quadros to explain in detail why he quit the Presidency in August 1961. When he failed to make clear his reasons for resigning and staged a normal middle-class-oriented political appeal, the working class still voted for him but in vastly reduced numbers, while the middle-class vote went to Ademar de Barros. The *paulista* electorate would not accept the alleged threat of "mysterious forces" as sufficient reason for Quadros having quit the Presidency.

One further example of political function in the area of elections and representations took place in October 1965, when gubernatorial elections were held in eleven of the states. The military debated long over whether to permit these elections. The soft-line officials finally won out, declaring that the elections had been previously promised and therefore should be held. Also, the reasoning was that, even if candidates whom the military did not favor won, it could take away their political rights. Attention focused on the state of Guanabara, where a crucial election was to take place. Carlos Lacerda, the outgoing governor, sponsored a candidate. Since Lacerda had already broken with those leading the revolt, his support of a candidate could have been considered a demonstration of disapproval of many of the army's actions. But Lacerda is anathema to most of the extreme Left as well as to many in the Vargas machine, who consider him personally responsible for the suicide of Vargas and who view his attacks on João Goulart as having led to the army's seizure of power in 1964. The Vargas men shrewdly filed a candidate who, if he won, would not be considered a threat by the military. Lacerda was unable to extend the charismatic benefits of his personality to his own candidate for governor. At the same time, all the important men of the Vargas administration who had not been removed by the army after April 1964 joined to support the man running against the Lacerda choice. It appeared that a large segment of the army also seemed favorably disposed to the defeat of the Lacerda candidate for governor and thus weakened still further the influence of a man who was annoying and attacking the military. A strange misalliance occurred as certain administration men in the Castello Branco regime let it be known they would not oppose the man running against Lacerda's candidate. Thus an old Vargas politician won the governorship of the critically important state of Guanabara. Lacerda's influence declined, and the military emerged stronger as a result, though it was widely held among those who had voted against Lacerda's candidate that it would have been better if he had won. Unquestionably, Rio de Janeiro has fallen into decay since 1962. Many of Lacerda's public works programs were stopped, ostensibly for lack of funds. Nevertheless, public officials are paid promptly; since large numbers of *cariocas* work for the government, this development increased the popularity of the new governor among those elements.

In general, it can be argued that the electoral-representational function has operated fairly effectively on both state and local levels, though tighter discipline and a higher degree of dedication have been needed in Congress. Whether nineteen years was enough time for the proper spirit to permeate the lawmaking process at the national level remains an open question.

Political Socialization

The question of how and to what degree Brazilians are inducted into the political structure reveals some of the strength and the flexibility of the fabric of government. In the southeastern part of the nation, the so-called Establishment, the induction is notably effective.

From the moment a child or young adult goes to church, he finds that Brazil and God are closely interrelated. For those who have the luck and the opportunity to attend private or public primary schools, the geography courses, the history courses, and even the natural science courses pick up and emphasize national political awareness in countless ways. At a level that may be the most persuasive and penetrating, the sports arena, Brazilians of all classes are made to feel pride in their nation. Here, the emotion that the average Brazilian shares for his world champion soccer team is equal to what some North Americans feel toward their flag. That so many Brazilian teams have brought home world championship trophies has been crucial to the average citizen's sense of national consciousness and pride. This type of feeling even extends to middle-class intellectuals. When a Brazilian author is translated into English, when a Brazilian painter is exhibited at the Metropolitan Museum of Art, when a Brazilian movie wins the Cannes Festival award, when a Brazilian singer stars in the United States, Brazilians experience a strong emotional identification and forget class, race, and serious problems in their pride over the accomplishment of their compatriots.

The press, television, and radio all also contribute to political socialization. Brazilians resent magazines or newspapers that are written in other nations and translated into Portuguese. There is a tremendous drive to keep the great foreign press organizations from gaining footholds or dominating the information media of the nation.

On the other hand, patriotic rallies are seldom part of Brazilian political socialization methods. The Government does not call out the citizens to huge rallies where the people are exhorted by politicians. Even on September 7th, Brazil's Independence Day, when there are great parades and military displays, as many *cariocas* go to the beaches as line the streets to watch the bands, the tanks, and the marching soldiers go by.

Young men are drafted into the army and must serve as either enlisted men or officer trainees, depending upon their educational background. Military conscription is rigorously enforced, and one cannot avoid it because of family position or wealth. Conscription hits the middle class hardest; in the lower-income group, if the citizen is a migrant worker, chances are that by the time the government machinery catches up with him for the draft, he will either be too old or his physical condition will not enable him to serve. At any rate, enough youths are inducted into military training to significantly augment the inculcation of national values.

In short, from an early age the Brazilian is incorporated into the political culture. Political and nationalist values become interrelated in all of his activities, and though he may develop negative attitudes toward certain aspects of the political process, he cannot remain untouched. One of the things that the average Brazilian learns early is a deep cynicism about the governmental process. If you want something from the Government, it is best if you have a friend who knows someone; if you have "connections," you can get what you are looking for. Otherwise, any attempt to realize an objective through the Government is like jousting with windmills. What is amazing about this aspect of the Brazilian political process is that so many average citizens do have a friend or a relative who can open the way to a government office.[8]

Finally, the question of political socialization must also be viewed from a regional point of view. The process is most pervasive in the southeastern section of Brazil and least penetrative in the northeastern rural area.

Mobilization

One gets the impression from a study of Brazilian politics of the past twenty years that the concept of political mobilization has produced disastrous results, and that if at all possible, those in decision-making positions would prefer that the mass of the population remains inert, unresponsive, and uninvolved. In Brazil it appears that, if people are mobilized, that mobilization may bring the entire traditional political process down in pieces.

There are, obviously, limits on what kind of and how much mobilization political leaders want in Brazil. In general terms, mobilization means the lower-income groups, both urban and rural. Their mobilization would, in turn, mean a decided shift in the direction of government.

The Presidents of Brazil from 1945 to 1966 illustrate this aspect of the Brazilian political system very well. President Dutra (1945–1950) never went to the people, never sought to mobilize public opinion, and quietly went about his job as Chief Executive. Strangely enough, Getúlio Vargas, in his last years in the Presidency (1950–1954), did not dramatize his appeal to the people but claimed that he was more important than party, Congress, Church, or country. Even when he began his speeches to the workers of Brazil, Vargas would almost invariably use middle-class terminology. Even suicide notes were couched in conservative terms. Vargas' successor, Juscelino Kubitschek, cautiously courted public opinion, but in no way did he attempt to mobilize other than the traditional forces of the country. The same could be said about Jânio Quadros during his seven-month administration. By contrast, in Goulart's administration, one notes the first serious attempt by a President of Brazil to mobilize elements which, despite their great numbers, could be considered to be only on the periphery of political activism. President Goulart's attempt between 1961 and 1964 to appeal to the illiterates (more than one-half of Brazil's population falls into this category), to the landless rural laborers of the interior, and to the noncommissioned officers in the army all gave the appearance of a Brazilian Populist movement. The term, however, should be used carefully. The yeoman farmer of southeastern Brazil did not support Goulart in his attempt to stir popular support. Rather than a Populist movement, perhaps Goulart's popular support more clearly constituted a revolt of the most alienated members of Brazilian society who failed to obtain satisfaction of their expectations. In this sense those Brazilians were atypical

---

[8] Anthony Leeds, *Brazilian Careers and Social Structure* (Austin, Texas, The University of Texas, Institute of Latin American Studies, Off-Print Series, No. 15).

of most political participants of that era, who seemed to prefer the traditional ways and were content to see quiet, almost ineffective, leaders in power rather than the unpredictable popular Executives with their wider bases of power.

The question of who mobilizes public opinion gives some clues to the Brazilian situation. The press, obviously, is consciously in the arena of public-opinion mobilization. Though illiteracy is high in the crucial urban centers of the nation, literacy rates are substantially higher than the fifty percent average for the nation as a whole. The greater part of the press has been conservatively oriented. There are one or two journals which appeal to the working-class groups, but only during the Goulart period, when the national Government threw its weight behind these newspapers, did they have any impact on the people. Television and radio also tend to be conservative in their content, though some radio broadcasters have aimed their appeals at the poor, most of whom own or have access to the ubiquitous transistor radio. Since 1964, the military Government has exercised a subtle but efficient control over the communications media.

In another area of mobilization, the many sports clubs in Brazil are ot a conservative nature and unite people of all classes and all racial backgrounds. A great deal of emotion and excitement is generated, and often this relieves pressure in the political area. The same can be said of the famous Brazilian Carnival, when three days and three nights of dancing and singing direct the frustrations, especially of the lowest economic sectors, into nonpolitical activities.

The university community plays an important role in political mobilization. The students constantly criticize the Government and the conservative groups that control the nation. The most vocal of the student groups, the National Students Union (UNE), was ordered disbanded after the 1964 revolt. Generally, the student activities are so predictable that they have begun to lose some of their interest and appeal outside the small circle which uncritically approves of everything they do. The students are predictably anti-United States on every issue. They favored the Goulart Government and accepted large government grants, which limited their freedom to criticize the administration. The *paulista* students favor land reform in the northeast. The northeastern students agitate for reforms in the slum areas of Rio de Janeiro. But relatively few students become activists in the sense of doing something concretely to ameliorate conditions of the lower-income groups. Few Brazilian students are found in the slums. The students conceive of themselves as leaders of a national conscience that must reform Brazilian society. But their complete lack of interrelationship with the working class and the rural workers creates a feeling of mistrust between the two groups. Many worker groups feel that they are simply being used by the energetic, vocal university students, who will become venal politicians the moment they have power in their hands. The military Government operating in Brazil since 1964 has moved rather cautiously in the area of curbing student criticism of the administration. But it appears that the students have defeated themselves, and only some foolish move by the military might save them. Still, the army in Brazil is slightly more sophisticated in this regard than its Argentine counterpart and has not moved in as heavy-handed a fashion against the university community.

Labor unions mobilize their members, but since 1964 the major concern has been for wages to catch up with prices. The labor union movement in Brazil is artificial in that it has always been nurtured and fed by the Federal Government. Until the Goulart period, the movement played no really crucial and powerful role in the political process except to reinforce the existing structure. Between 1962 and 1964, the national Government poured an increasing percentage of the national budget into the labor unions in an attempt to make them a viable political force, but before they reached this position, the military moved in and halted such aid. In the vital industrial areas of Brazil, notably São Paulo and Minas Gerais and the outskirts of Rio de Janeiro, working and living conditions, though grave, have not reached the critical stage. If the military Government can control the prices which workers pay for food and lodging and can keep these costs within the grasp of the workers, the Government probably can forestall any serious threat in this area.

Parenthetically, it might be mentioned that, in dealing with Brazilian realities, one must learn to read between many lines for an approximation of the political and economic situation. When the Government announces a wage freeze, it must be read within certain workable guidelines. The Brazilian military, the economists, the politicians, and the labor union leaders are too pragmatic to take any government pronouncement as final or binding. More often than not, it is just the signal for an elaborate round of talks and discussion in which everything must be adjusted to new and overriding demands.

There is limited political mobilization in Brazil, and it would probably be unnecessary and undesirable to have total and constant mobilization of the mass of the population. On specific issues, it is a relatively easy task to arouse the necessary support for any single action, especially among middle-class, educated sectors, among which channels of contact are much more direct and widespread. This was illustrated in 1964 when a half-million women marched in the streets of São Paulo to protest against the Goulart administration.

Politically Relevant Decision-Making

The group that makes the important political decisions in Brazil is relatively small but is sufficiently sophisticated and accessible so as not to be out of touch with the desires and the necessities of the mass of the population. The military have, of course, dominated this position since the 1964 coup. What is also significant is that a relatively small group of men within the army have a unified point of view and are often able to influence and carry others who have far greater strength numerically but who are organizationally weak.

The same names appear over and over in military circles. Since 1945, first at the colonel level and in 1966 at the general-staff level are officers who have fought against the Vargas machine. They were active in the overthrow of Vargas in 1945, they signed manifestos that he resign in 1954, they led the silent revolt against Goulart's regime, and since then have openly emerged as the rulers of the nation. No one individual commands the unqualified loyalty of the group. The military at first selected a relatively unknown general, Humberto Castello Branco, to be their spokesman through the transition period. He was presented to the mass of the Brazilians as an intellectual, quiet, and soft-spoken man who had the interests of all of Brazil in his heart, but no great enthusiasm developed for him. For the five-year presidential term beginning in 1967, the candidacy of a much more flamboyant and "popular" figure, Marechal Artur da Costa e Silva, was launched. Most of the top men in the army who make the important decisions were in the same military class at school and have a close, informal, kinship type of relation to each other, such as being godfathers and best men at weddings. For the most part, they know what to expect from each other. The army, however, recruits broadly, and many a lower-income-group citizen has risen to the top of the military hierarchy. In contrast, few of the rich families in the nation have sons in the military.

Before 1964, most civilian leaders also were closely connected. Theirs was not an interrelationship built upon family ties but upon power and wealth. Many of the civilian leaders got their start in the Vargas period, and even when the dictatorship ended in 1945, in many cases they were able to expand their political and economic power base. Most of the really powerful civilian leaders who controlled parties and states were not from old elite families. Brazil is too huge and too much in transition for old-line families to be able to control completely. In the north, the northeast, or the interior, new elements had a better chance to assume power, but this was not the case in the tremendously important south.

A new group of civilians, who began taking important administrative posts in 1966, were some economists grouped around the Minister of Economic Planning, Roberto Campos. These young technicians, mostly in their late twenties and early thirties, handled economic theory and planning for the new State. They exuded a great amount of enthusiasm and *esprit de corps,* and the military gave them comparatively free rein to carry out their jobs.

CONCLUSION

The army has not only shown few tendencies to fragment but stands as the most cohesive force in the entire nation. This cohesiveness assures the political dominance of the army, and undoubtedly it will continue to govern as long as it is convinced that only it is able to provide solutions to Brazil's problems.

While large segments of the upper class support the military Government, few middle-class groups actively oppose it. In no small measure most members of the middle class are acquiescent because they can still accumulate economic resources that permit them to buy cars, send their children to school, and fill their homes with appliances. Obviously, even though middle groups may resent the Government's censoring newspapers or circumscribing university activities, these acts alone are insufficient to drive them to the barricades.

At first glance, it seems curious that the workers and the unemployed have not exhibited a more measurable alienation from the military regime— indeed, if not from the whole political system. Inflation, unemployment, underemployment, disease, and hunger plague millions of Brazil's poor. And yet, among the low-income groups in southern Brazil, many derive some rewards in health insurance, paid vacations, and maternity benefits from the Social Institutes, and the benefits are just enough to keep these people more or less quiescent. The most thoroughly dispossessed are in the shockingly desti- tute northeastern section. And it is a significant commentary on the Brazilian system that, while food rots on the docks and railroad platforms in one part of the country for want of organization and transportation, two thousand miles away children die of starvation on city streets and in rural hovels. But many of those who might turn to violence instead follow a migratory path to the comparatively more affluent south.

Above all, the absence to date of widespread anomic eruptions among the Brazilian poor seems to derive from a kind of traditional apathy and submission, which probably will not be substantially altered until organiza- tions and leaders come forth to fight for the lower class. Unless the military assumes responsibility for the lower class, it will not soon find a supporter. The military's actions soon after the coup to limit or cancel the political rights of hundreds of Brazilians caught up many leaders of working-class associa- tions. Since most trade unions and peasant associations were weak anyway, restrictions imposed by the military and the loss of leadership reduced the associations to virtually a moribund state.

Nor does there seem to be any real threat to the military from among the intellectuals, probably the most vocally alienated element. The intellectual community generally is antiestablishment without being able to define very clearly what it favors. The intellectuals are out of step with the pragmatic middle class, from which most of them come, but are still unable to enter into dialogue with the workers.

Brazil in 1967 lived in the shadow of a modified dictatorship similar to that of the 1937–1945 period. The military regime permits the exercise of civil liberties to the extent that the Brazilian does not become too disgruntled about restraints on such rights, but not to the point where he might endanger the regime. So many political leaders of nation-wide reputations (including ex- Presidents Kubitschek, Quadros, and Goulart) lost their political rights under the Institutional Act that very few politicians of a national stature remain as potential rallying points of opposition to the regime. (It strikes one as paradoxical to observe a Brasília monument saluting ex-President Kubitschek's contributions to the capital of a country which has canceled his political rights.)

As long as the military runs Brazil—and there is no important external counterforce presently observable—there will be increasing centralization of power in the Federal Government's hands. For the most part, this centralization will take place in order to facilitate a concentrated attack on Brazil's monumental economic problems. Some inroads have been made in improving taxation procedures and in putting a land reform program in motion. But a tremendous amount of work still lies ahead in co-ordinating and integrating the poverty-stricken northeast with the rich industrial south; Brazil can no longer afford to have colonial areas within the nation.

On October 3, 1966, marechal Artur da Costa e Silva, a native of Rio Grande do Sul was elected President of Brazil by a unanimous vote of 295 Congressmen. There was no opposition candidate. Direct elections for the Brazilian Congress held in November 1966 gave the government a solid working majority in both the Chamber of Deputies and the Senate. In January 1967 Congress voted a new conservative and highly centralized constitution for the country.[9] President Costa e Silva in his inaugural address in March 1967 took a conciliatory tone toward labor and other alienated sectors of Brazilian society. This action reduced the tension which former governor Carlos Lacerda had begun by attempting to form a third party in a strange alliance with ex-president Juscelino Kubitschek. In April 1967 Kubitschek quietly returned to Rio de Janeiro and the Brazilian political scene settled down while all groups watched the performance of the new president Costa e Silva. Pragmatism and unpredictability are still the hallmarks of political life of this giant among nations.

A Brazilian joke which sums up the nation's plight queries, "Brazil always seems to be wavering on the brink of an abyss but never falls in. Why?" The answer, "Because Brazil is bigger than the abyss,"[10] reflects the enormity of the national challenges. If the military can provide the kind of inspired leadership to pull together abundant manpower and rich resources, a peaceful, genuine revolution could result.

---

[9] Jordan M. Young, *The Brazilian Revolution of 1930 and the Aftermath* (New Brunswick, Rutgers University Press 1967), p. 118.

[10] Related in Charles Wagley, *Brazil: Crisis and Change* (New York, Foreign Policy Association, October 1964), p. 3.

18/ Latin American Political Thought: Some Literary Foundations

KENNETH F. JOHNSON

Each of the foregoing Latin American political systems has generated a body of literature which we shall tentatively label "political thought." Efforts by North American scholars to study this literature have generally been limited to the researches of literary specialists in the humanities or to annotated listings made occasionally by social scientists. In addition, several useful vernacular anthologies have appeared, such as Chang-Rodriguez and Kantor, *La América Latina de hoy,* 1961. In the present effort, the author promises, at best, to have superficially touched the surface of Latin American political thought in the hope that students will be encouraged toward more thorough analytic efforts. The selections included, while representative of a great body of literature, are not necessarily offered as being the most important contributions. An exhaustive sampling will be quite beyond the province of a chapter of this length.*

From the very beginning, the thrust of Latin America's political life was punctuated harshly by physical violence and ideological discord. Men rising to arms have since become traditional appendages to a culture that abounds with literary eulogies to human sacrifice and physical monuments to a legion of martyred heroes. In the eyes of many North Americans, our neighbors to the south have a puzzling capacity for violence and for what in our way of thinking is political chaos. The average Ladino will tell you for his own part, however, that violence is not akin to his *naturaleza,* or human nature, but rather that traditionally violence has been foisted upon him by imperialists and exploiters of one sort or another: copper companies in Chile, oil industries in Venezuela, sugar, coffee, and fruit interests in Cuba, Brazil, and

---

* The author is solely responsible for the limitations of this work but expresses profound gratitude to Paul E. Hadley, of the University of Southern California, for his criticism and guidance.

Central America, the United States armed forces in Mexico and Santo Domingo. Thus it is that the fruits of violence have been fused into national symbols of group attachment and honor, which serve to unite many Latin American peoples in the experience of a common historical development. The fruits of revolutionary violence are costly, as nearly all of Latin America's so-called *liberación* movements can ably testify.

Again from the standpoint of the North American, it will appear that violence is a central feature of Latin American psychology, indeed that tolerance of and the resort to violence may be an ideological constant in Latin American political thought. Let us consider one poetic sketch that seems to place the matter in bold relief.

Mitin relámpago.	A mob gathers as if by lightning
Gritan cuatrocientos obreros y estudiantes: Salarios!	Cries of four hundred workers and students: Wages!
El cobre para Chile!	The copper is Chile's!
Pan y Paz!	Bread and Peace!
Que escándalo!	Outrageous!
Se cierran los negocios, se oye un disparo, surgen de todas partes las banderas.	They are closing the shops and stores, a shot is heard, and flags surge forth from everywhere.

—Pablo Neruda
Oda a la calle San Diego

Many have been the times that a quiet *paseo* led into a threatening blind alley, a *callejón sin salida,* from which few could escape the imminence of harm. A single death in Colombia in April 1948 unleashed an horrendous bloodletting, whose lingering curse still plagues that struggling nation. Pages of castigation are now heaped upon the volatility of Latin American politics. Few, if any, have been offered up in its defense although, not infrequently, a distinguished novelist and social critic will glorify and dramatize the spontaneous violence of the downtrodden, as did Jorge de Icaza in his *Huasipungo*. Certainly it would be unfair to attribute violence as being the most salient characteristic of political life in Latin America. Violence is just one of many ideological themes which we shall consider in this chapter. Indeed, the only reason for emphasizing violence per se as an ideological theme is to stress an important distinction which is basic to this consideration of Latin American political thought, the difference between ideology and theory.

Let us say that political theory, at least where Latin America is concerned, is a body of prescriptive beliefs about how the body politic and its government *ought* to function, what should be the optimal preferred set of relationships between man and the State, and what values and goals ought to be organically central to the system. Theory also may consist of descriptive and analytical statements and hypotheses about the way the political system *does* operate in organic but nonprescriptive terms. Contributions to the political theory of a people or nation will commonly be found in published form, but frequently theory is expounded verbally in the statements of scholars and public officials. Political ideology, in comparison, refers to "the body of beliefs which are habitually evident in the actions of a political society."[1] The characteristic that distinguishes ideology from theory is that the former is a set of beliefs which are popularly held, shared, and acted upon. Theory may never be believed by anyone except its protagonist. However, theory may ultimately come to be ideologically embraced by a populace. Ideology, in its turn, may never receive formal promulgation as theory but may continue, nevertheless, to function normatively in the minds and the behavior of individuals.

The birth of Latin American nations, for the most part, did not occur under conditions so favorable to the rise of democracy as existed at the time the American colonies separated from Great Britain. Latin Americans inherited social and economic institutions that were largely feudal, the union of Church and State was complete virtually everywhere, and the countries were not so favorably endowed with climate, geography, or natural resources, although in the third respect the balance now seems to be improving. With environmental misfortune visited upon them at nearly every turn, Latin American intellectuals have grasped defensively for utopian panaceas and apocalyptic visions of revealed truth. Unfortunately, and unlike Hegel, these intellectuals have found difficulty in agreeing among themselves on just whose vision of "truth" would do most to advance the "march of God across this earth." Extremisms of Right and Left have therefore punctuated the history of Latin American political thinking and have colored its general orientation toward the North American colossus. Today, the polemic between these extremes seems for the most part to have yielded in favor of the Left. Hence, it is with some chagrin that the North American discovers a prominent Latin American scholar quoting, as his authority on the development of American capitalism, a one-time Communist aspirant to the Presidency of the United States.[2]

Although the dividing line between ideology and theory in Latin American political life is tenuous (often the two are in fact joined), we have organized this book in such a way as to allow ideologies to be treated as

---

[1] Thomas P. Jenkin, *The Study of Political Theory* (New York, Doubleday & Company, Inc., 1955), p. 10.

[2] Luis Cardoza y Aragón, *Guatemala: las lineas de su mano* (Mexico, Fondo de Cultura Económica, 2nd edition, 1965), p. 325.

implicit elements in the specific political movements that were described in the preceding chapters on the various Latin American nations.

The present chapter is primarily concerned with political theories, thought, and prescriptive and critical analyses, drawn from the published works of prominent Latin American intellectuals.

Several important caveats are in order here, especially for the student of Latin American politics who has a humanistic bent. Most Spanish-American vernacular literature has, unfortunately, been written without a general theoretic design. This is "unfortunate" only with respect to the practical dilemma of ponderously searching through many large tomes for glimpses of specialized political wisdom that are not readily found—indeed, which the author may never have intended. Latin American political theory is found in diverse sources; the political thinkers have had a well-demonstrated affinity for achieving brilliance in more than one literary medium. To be thorough, then, one must examine novels and poetry along with essays and more specialized treatises.

Emphatically, one does not read the political writings of Latin American theorists as one would the verbose and syllogistically structured formulations of Immanuel Kant or Ralph Barton Perry. Latin American theorists have largely been humanists, perhaps in the tradition of Jean Jacques Rousseau. Most of them have lived and struggled directly with the political relationships they have sought to remold. Because of highly personal and emotional involvements, the formulations of these theorists may appear eclectic and self-contradictory (as were Rousseau's) and not operationally viable. This will be understood and expected by those who gain some depth of substantive exposure to the political culture of Latin America. Moreover, what Latin Americans do or advocate publicly may be visibly corrupt while their private lives remain exemplary;[3] thus the schizoid nature of much Latin American political thought is not unexpected or unusual. It is the product of men who must function in a political culture that is "prismatic" or transitional and whose basic theoretic assumptions often get in each other's way.[4] Let us examine some of these ideas.

DEMOCRATIC LIBERALISM

The struggles for independence in the early nineteenth century left Ibero-America with an ideological heritage of French liberalism, American constitutionalism, and typically Spanish modes of political conduct. By the third element is meant an exaggerated and exploitive individualism that sharply distinguished Spanish, and perhaps to a lesser extent Portuguese, colonial policy from that of the British, the French, and the Dutch in North America.

---

[3] Cf. John A. Crow, *Mexico Today* (New York, Harper & Row, Publishers, Inc., 1957), p. 325.

[4] Cf. Kenneth F. Johnson, "Causal Factors in Latin American Political Instability," *The Western Political Quarterly,* September, 1964.

It has been contended, and with good reason, that liberal principles and operating structures were adopted at so early a time in the development of the new Latin American nations that no valid sense of national community existed to make democratic liberalism a viable doctrine with which to replace colonial rule.[5] Simón Bolívar's naïve hope was that an untutored body politic would eagerly embrace a self-perpetuating National Executive who would maintain cross-regional political allegiances. A crude and distorted miniature version of this ambition was still being pursued, however precariously, by François Duvalier in Haiti during the 1960s.

Following Bolívar, however, was a rising group of new intellectuals, who imported the thinking of the French *philosophes* into Latin America. Thus, the early systematic efforts to theorize about political relationships and to make organizational prescriptions for Latin America were carried out in the tradition of French liberalism. Argentina was among the first of the new nations to generate democratic liberal thought. Associated with this trend were Esteban Echeverría and Juan Bautista Alberdi. The former (1805–1851) had lived and studied in Paris, where he acquired a strong romantic bent that colored his later writing and public life. Echeverría's influence was subsequently reflected in the liberal unitarism of Mitre and Sarmiento, both of whom attempted to give Argentina the government in practice that Echeverría had championed in theory.

When the dictator Juan Manuel Rosas closed the literary salons of Buenos Aires in 1837, Echeverría and his followers organized a passive resistance movement called the Asociación de Mayo (referring to the Revolution of 1810) that was patterned after Mazzini's Young Italians. The code intended as the movement's bond of unity was the *Dogma Socialista,* a fragmented statement of political principles borrowing generously from the writings of the great Italian patriot. More important and representative of Echeverría's thinking, however (because it is more systematic), is his *Los ideales de mayo y la tiranía* which appeared around 1838. Whether influenced by Mazzini or not, this statement of theory clearly reflects the French *philosophe* bias.

Echeverría urges his concept of sovereignty by postulating that it resides in the people.[6] The people create the nation state through voting their individual wills into a collective whole, whose preservation becomes the task of elected magistrates. Before this delegation of wills takes place, there is an "atomization" of particular wills and no state sovereignty in the organic sense. Magistrates exercise power on behalf of the sovereign people, whose consent is requisite for legitimacy. Delegation of particular wills into a unified whole is done by means of representation in a decision-making forum. There are two

---

[5] Cf. Russell H. Fitzgibbon, "Political Theory vs Practice," in *The Caribbean: Its Political Problems,* A. Curtis Wigus, ed. (Gainesville, University of Florida Press, 1956), pp. 25–40.

[6] Esteban Echeverría, "Los ideales de mayo y la tiranía," in *Grandes escritores argentinos,* XXVII (Buenos Aires, El Ateneo, 1928), 52–81.

basic kinds of political representation: constituent and ordinary. Constituent representation is utilized when a constitution of government is to be drawn up; ordinary representation is invoked thereafter to preserve an existing order and to exercise the lawmaking function as may be required. Such parliamentary acts become social law and may be called a *pacto social* that unites the nation. Essential provisions of the *pacto social* are individual guarantees of person, property, and freedom of association, plus the creation of adjunct powers for administration. Echeverría specifies that when the magistrates do not uphold the *pacto social,* or if they act *ultra vires,* the people may justly rebel. These principles were endorsed by Juan Bautista Alberdi, who, although differing in certain aspects of emphasis, drafted Argentina's liberal, democratic Constitution of 1853.

Echeverría, especially, was steeped in the thinking of Jean Jacques Rousseau. Yet his *pacto social* is by no means a duplicate of Rousseau's treatise, an alleged handbook for the French Revolution of 1789. There are several doctrinal distinctions between the two theorists that are important. Echeverría does not lead himself into endorsement of an authoritarian majority that can stultify opposition by forcing everyone to be "free." He realistically expects and welcomes dissension and seeks only to channel it constructively. Rousseau's authoritarian majority would seem logically to lead into some sort of direct democracy on a small scale with loose confederations of communities ruled under legislative supremacy with only nominal executives. Echeverría, on the contrary, insists upon strong central leadership drawing upon the skills of a benevolent *caudillo.* Nor does he distinguish between a community or general will and a will of all (that reflecting any or several particular interests), as does Rousseau. Thus, Echeverría allows for leadership to lead and for followers to obey even if under protest. By making an accommodation for the play of private interests, he avoids that peculiar feature of Rousseau's "will of all," which produces the dilemma of how to allocate public resources without inadvertently serving someone's private interest (how, for instance, to locate a new public building without serving more the interests of users living close by than those of more distant dwellers).[7]

Finally, it should be pointed out that whereas Rousseau is quite clear about the nonexistence of inalienable rights (except possibly the right to rebel), Echeverría accepts as inalienable the right to life, property, and free association. He is in the latter respect closer to Locke's theory of contract government than to Rousseau's theory of the noble savage. Specifically, Echeverría contends,

> Tampoco puede el pueblo en ningún caso, por extraordinario que sea, conferir a un hombre una autoridad ilimitada que trespase los derechos individuales porque el hecho de hacerlo, enajenaría la soberanía, dejaría de existir

---

[7] This point is expanded in an interesting manner by Leslie Lipson in *The Democratic Civilization* (New York, Oxford University Press, 1964), pp. 53–55.

como pueblo y daría a uno el derecho de aniquilar los derechos de todos, de robar y matar a todos y de obrar contra el fin de la asociación.[8]

The people can never, no matter how extraordinary the circumstances, surrender to one ruler a power so unlimited as would violate individual rights. For in so doing, the people would be alienating themselves from their own sovereignty, ceasing to exist as a people per se, having delivered to one man the power to cancel the rights of all men, to rob and kill wantonly and to work against the goals of the people.

It is likely that the differences in theoretic construct between the two philosophers result from the fact that, although a romantic, Echeverría was still a practical man with an instrumentalist orientation, while Rousseau, as his *Confessions* reveal so vividly, was decidedly more romantic than practical.

Echeverría's contemporary statesman and political theorist, Juan Bautista Alberdi, wrote much of Argentina's Constitution of 1853, which has colored his country's political thought to the present day. Writing somewhat in the style of Alexander Hamilton, Alberdi argued the case for strong central government and protection for private property and commerce. He encouraged immigration from Europe in the hope of populating and developing Argentina's vast western frontier. Alberdi's *Bases y puntos de partida para la organización política de la República Argentina,* 1853, together with the works of Echeverría, are prominent examples of liberal democratic thinking in Latin America that endure to the present day. They illustrate some of the impact of French as well as North American ideas on Latin American political thought.

AUTHORITARIAN IDEALISM

The desire for popular adulation has been a frequent ideological feature of Latin American rulers. Disasters such as the Paraguayan War (1865–70), largely precipitated by Francisco Solano López, the age of Santa Anna in Mexico (roughly 1823–1853), or the more recent dictatorships of Trujillo in the Dominican Republic and Pérez Jiménez in Venezuela all reflect elements of an extremely personalized idealism that was used to justify authoritarian regimes. To single out one Latin American theorist as the father of what is clearly an antithesis of the liberal ideas of Echeverría and Alberdi would be presumptuous if not impossible. Certainly the responsibility cannot be Bolívar's alone. Yet just as surely, in the background of much contemporary idealistic thinking about Latin American politics, there lurks one towering figure, the Uruguayan writer José Enrique Rodó.

Rodó is best remembered for *Ariel,*[9] a charge to the youth of America to reject materialism in general and North American influences in particular.

---

[8] Echeverría, pp. 74–75.

[9] José Enrique Rodó, *Ariel* (Mexico, Nova-Mex, 1957). The title and principal characters are borrowed from Shakespeare's *The Tempest.*

Rodó sought wholesale derogation of commercial and materialistic values. He was fond of Auguste Comte's view that a materialistic life shrinks the human brain and eventually reduces a specialist to the lowest attribute of his specialization. His most fundamental principle is that the advancement of *naturaleza* ought to be man's first purpose. This advancement would promote the noble values of prudence, frugality, and purity of physical and spiritual morality. As for the chains in which man finds himself, there are two fundamental causes: the scientific revolution, which has divided labor and reduced men to functional automatons, and the triumph of democratic ideas.[10] The latter, says Rodó, has meant an elevation of mass goals at the expense of intellectual expertise. His argument could be a page out of José Ortega y Gasset's later work *The Revolt of the Masses*. Too much mass democracy and the concomitant stultification of a higher moral direction have left society without distinguished spokesmen, or at best, have driven intellectual sagacity into hiding. You will never replace the waste of one brilliant mind, wrote Rodó, by merely aggregating a host of vulgar spirits.[11]

Rodó's faith in a great spiritual leader borrows more of Bolívar's omnipotent Executive than of Echeverría's benevolent *caudillo* Executive. In this connection Rodó reaffirms the basic antagonism between democracy and a higher spiritual life.

> La oposición entre el régimen de la democracia y la alta vida del espíritu es una realidad fatal cuando aquel régimen significa el desconocimiento de las desigualdades y la substitución de la fe en el 'heroismo' en el sentido de Carlyle por una concepción mecánica de gobierno.[12]
> The opposition between a democratic regime and the higher spiritual life becomes fatal when the former regime means disrespect for the legitimate inequalities among men and the sacrifice of Carlyle's true hero leader in a mechanistic conception of government.

Rodó wanted an ideal leader, personified by Ariel, who would arise on a self-identifying basis. This leader would not be one of Nietzsche's supermen, nor one of Spencer's fittest competitors, but a benevolent dictator whose blessing would be a true reflection of *naturaleza,* and only Ariel's counterpart could accurately interpret this reflection to the people. *Naturaleza* would be preserved against imitation, which Rodó insisted could only result in a deformation of the original lines of its model. Clearly, one can detect a dangerous parallel between Rodó's argument and that of Ernst Rudolf Huber, who wrote one of the principal justifications for the interpretive *rapprochement* of the Nazi *Führer* with the German *volk* during the Third Reich.

Speaking through the omnipresent voice of Próspero in a final charge to the neophyte audience, Rodó places past, present, and future in their proper (nearly dialectical) perspective.

---

[10] Rodó, pp. 85–86.

[11] Rodó, p. 94.

[12] Rodó, p. 95.

El pasado perteneció todo entero al brazo que combate; el presente perte-
nece, casi por completo también, al tosco brazo que nivela y construye; el
porvenir . . . un porvenir tanto mas cercano cuanto mas enérgicos sean la
voluntad y el pensamiento de los que le ansian . . . ofrecerá para el desen-
volvimiento de superiores facultades del alma, la estabilidad, el escenario y el
ambiente.[13]

The past belonged almost entirely to the fighting arm; the present belongs,
almost entirely as well, to the strong arm that creates and builds; the future
. . . a future that grows closer with the volition of those who desire it . . .
will offer an atmosphere of stability that is conducive to developing the superior faculties of the human spirit.

Appearing at the turn of the twentieth century, *Ariel* coincides tempo-
rally with the rise to influence of Uruguay's great statesman José Batlle y
Ordóñez. It was in 1919 that Batlle made his first and partially successful
effort to institute the collegiate executive principle into Uruguayan political
life. Whether there existed any political affinity between Rodó and Batlle is
doubtful as a result of the latter's commitment to negotiation and compromise
and of the former's aversion to any appeasement of the forces of materialism.
It appears that Rodó made few pronouncements on governmental or political
organization apart from the content of *Ariel*. Perhaps it would not be unfair to
say that what remains today of Rodó is two influential ideas: the somewhat
Platonic philosopher-king mystique and a persistent tendency to condemn
material acquisition on the part of those who, paradoxically, must seek it just
the same. Although Rodó's theoretic impact is most often seen in terms of his
aesthetic appeal, he should not be overlooked as an early *raisonneur* for
authoritarianism in Latin American political thought.

THREE POLITICAL DIALECTICS

Whereas for Rodó intellectual change was a function of spiritual development, the Mexican philosopher José Vasconcelos saw that change more as a
function of ethnic or racial evolution. In his *La raza cósmica,* 1925, Vasconcelos outlined a theory of four basic human species and corresponding cycles of
power operative throughout time.

Tenemos entonces las cuatro'etapas y los cuatro troncos: el negro, el indio, el
mongol, el blanco. Este último, después de organizarse en Europa, se ha con-
vertido en invasor del mundo, y se ha creído llamado a predominar lo mismo
que lo creyeron las razas anteriores cada una en la época de su poderío.[14]

Thus we have the four stages and the four racial types: the black, the Indian,
the Mongol, and the white. The last of these, upon organizing itself in Europe,
has become the invader of the world and has proclaimed itself the master of
all peoples as did previous races each at the height of its power.

Vasconcelos believed that domination by the white race would be temporary.
The whites have had a different mission than their predecessors in dominance;

---

[13] Rodó, pp. 172–173.

[14] José Vasconcelos, *La raza cósmica* (Mexico, Austral, 1948), p. 16.

the whites have created a technology necessary for socio-economic development. The white and Indian races are destined to pass through a period of miscegenation, out of which will emerge a new fifth race. This race will be the final stage of the ethnic dialectic and will apply the technology created by the whites. Thus, the white race will have made possible the final development of mankind, which is cultural union in a fifth or cosmic race. *"El fin ulterior de la Historia . . . es lograr la fusión de los pueblos y las culturas."*[15]

At one point, Vasconcelos outlines a law of three stages, the *ley del gusto*, which is operative throughout history. The three stages are the material, or warrior stage, the intellectual, or political, and the spiritual, or aesthetic. In the first stage material wants and values are the goals of human behavior. The second finds reason prevailing over the human appetite for force and violence. The final period, yet to come, will see reason replaced as the sole arbiter of men's lives by a constant aesthetic inspiration.

> Y no se buscará el mérito de una acción en su resultado inmediato y palpable, como ocurre en el primer período; ni tampoco se atenderá a que se adapte a determinadas reglas de razón pura; el mismo imperativo ético será sobrepujado y más allá del bién y del mal, en el mundo del pathos estético, solo importará que el acto, por ser bello, produzca dicha. . . . Vivir el júbilo fundado en amor, ésa es la tercera etapa.[16]

> One should not look for the merit of an action in its immediate result, as was done in the first period, nor should one adopt hard rules of pure reason; the same ethical imperative will be surpassed and beyond good and bad, in the world of aesthetic pathos nothing will be important except that an act should result in beauty. . . . To live in the happiness of love is the third stage.

Vasconcelos goes on to reveal overtones of Comte, Spencer, Hegel, and Nietzsche. The ultimate synthesis—indeed, the very process of the *ley del gusto*—resembles the Hegelian ultimate idea, or final ideal state. The myth of inherent racial superiority is not unlike Nietzsche's Superman. Acceptance of necessary and imminent conflict and the sense of an always improving and increasingly complex social organism call to mind tenets of Spencer's *Social Statics*. In a loose sense, the *ley del gusto* resembles in substance and number Comte's law of three stages, which encompasses his evolutionary sociology of knowledge.

La raza cósmica was produced during the period when Vasconcelos served as Minister of Education in Mexico under President Alvaro Obregón (1921–25), one of the most productive and satisfying periods in the author's life.[17] The work is a serious and determined intellectual formulation seeking to explain an unjust social order. In the ethnic dialectic Vasconcelos offers Ladinos a cause for renewed confidence in the future of their culture. *La raza*

---

[15] Vasconcelos, p. 27.

[16] Vasconcelos, p. 40.

[17] In 1929 Vasconcelos was bitterly defeated in his bid for the Mexican Presidency by Pascual Ortiz Rubio.

cósmica was an optimistic call to faith which its contemporary social and political events did not always justify.

A more contemporary Mexican writer, Octavio Paz, wrote that solitude, the condition of thinking and feeling oneself alone, is the essence of the human condition. Solitude underlies man's natural state of change, which consists in aspiring to be what one is not. This concept is the foundation of an important essay, *El laberinto de la soledad,* 1947, in which the Mexican writer interprets life as flowing toward loneliness immediately upon birth. To live is to separate ourselves from what we were in order to enter into what we are going to be. Alone in the phenomenal world, man toils laboriously to steel himself against the fact of his being isolated. In self-defense he creates artifacts, one of which is the contractual concept of marriage, a co-operative human effort to defeat loneliness through love.

> El amor es uno de los mas claros ejemplos de ese doble instinto que nos lleva a cavar y ahondar en nosotros mismos y, simultaneamente, a salir de nosotros y realizarnos en otro: muerte y recreación, soledad y comunión.[18]

> Love is one of the clearest examples of this double instinct which leads us to withdraw and find refuge within ourselves, and at the same time, to go beyond ourselves for self-realization in another form: death and recreation, solitude and communion.

Largely concerned with metaphysical themes, Octavio Paz applies his formulations only peripherally to society and politics. In so doing, he holds that society collectively seeks to satisfy certain of its own organic needs, which are tied in with the individual's need to overcome solitude. One of these needs, order, may clash with special interests of particular classes and thereby induce social crisis and political instability. The dualism in society expresses itself in terms of the compatible and the incompatible, the good and the bad, the bourgeoisie and the proletariat. Such clashes at the collective level hamper individual struggles against solitude. Paz is a champion of the primacy of individual values.

Were all men able to contemplate their true existential selves, they would have no fear of loneliness, but only the exceptional few have this faculty of self-analysis. In his emphasis upon the basic factors of antagonism in society and upon the psychic content of personal behavior, Octavio Paz encompasses at once Marxism, surrealism, and existentialism. Despite his somber tone, he gives a tight causal nucleus, which can be used in many contexts for interpreting human situations relating to political behavior. The greatest utility of his dialectic, however, lies in interpretations of his own semi-industrial Mexico rather than for the less developed systems of other Latin American nations.

A final work in this genre contains little in the way of conceptual system but offers a coherent and easily understood analysis of political instability in Latin America. Colombia's prominent essayist Germán Arciniegas holds a

---

[18] Octavio Paz, *El laberinto de la soledad* (Mexico, Fondo de Cultura Economica, 1959), p. 182.

militant faith in the causes of democracy, Latin American culture, and progress. *Entre la libertad y el miedo,* which appeared in 1952, was dedicated to the downtrodden *campesinos* of Colombia. Arciniegas believed that, because of a rigidly controlled press, especially in his contemporary Colombia, and a widespread tolerance of authoritarian government, the people of Latin America were passing through cycles of popular attachment and servitude, which were polarized by the quest for liberty and the flight from fear. Lacking popular involvement, the people often fail to support a democratic regime when it appears. Hence a tottering democracy gives way to a temporarily stable but eventually precarious dictatorship. That is the cycle between liberty and fear, between ephemeral democracy and despotic tyranny.[19] Arciniegas attributes this blight largely to the joint factors of poor communications and a lack of popular involvement in public affairs; both are seen as conducive to political alienation. He therefore makes a basic distinction between two faces of the Americas, the official face of governments and the real face of the depressed populace; "... *este doble papel entre lo que se dice y piensa y lo que se hace. . . .*"[20] Arciniegas warns that the interests of the heretofore neglected masses must be served if the two Americas are ever to be united in a stable cultural whole.

DEMOCRATIC UTOPIANISM: THE VOYAGE TO IPANDA

Notions of obligation, accountability, legitimate authority, and order are central to broad political theories such as those of Hobbes and Locke. Latin American theorists have also dealt with these questions but by and large on a fragmentary basis. The imperative for having some minimal level of order and predictability in human relationships became a focal point for the ideas of the Guatemalan poet and novelist Rafael Arévalo Martínez. His literary and philosophic life spanned the era of Rodó through the first half of the present century. The utopian novel *Viaje a Ipanda,* 1939, best represents Arévalo Martínez' prescriptive thinking on political organization, while earlier works, especially *Concepción del cosmos,* develop an epistemology which underlies his political philosophy.

Arévalo Martínez' query of what is an indispensable requisite for making democracy work is central to the problem of maintaining a democratic politics. His answer, order and authority, is revealed in the following lines:

> El derecho es, ante todo, un orden, y bueno es cualquiera, aunque sea el de una cuadrilla de ladrones, antes que la anarquía. Cuando la democracia, en un pueblo no maduro para ella, falla, bueno es el caudillismo. El hombre no puede existir en el desorden. Y el orden es inseparable de la autoridad.[21]

---

[19] Germán Arciniegas, *Entre la libertad y el miedo* (Santiago de Chile, Editorial del Pacífico, 1952).

[20] Arciniegas, p. 341.

[21] Rafael Arévalo Martínez, *Viaje a Ipanda,* in *Obras escogidas* (Guatemala, Editorial Universitaria, 1959), p. 396.

Law is, foremost, a measure of order, and it is better to have some level of order, even that dictated by a band of thieves, than to have anarchy. If democracy fails in a country which is not mature enough for it, *caudillismo* would be the next best alternative. Man is not made to live in disorder. Order and authority are inseparable.

But if authority, in the sense of legitimized power through popular consent, is to be exercised democratically, who will superintend it, and does this require that the rulers of the state be continually subject to a popular or representative veto? Must a ruler's decisions have additional validation from some independent body such as a court of justice? And once democracy is established, will it guarantee a predictable order? All of these questions turn in circular fashion about the central dilemma that Arévalo Martínez poses: Must order precede democracy as a requisite condition, or would the reverse be true? His dictum is that order must come first. For countries which have not undergone a sufficient apprenticeship in the arts and skills of self-government, it will be necessary first to begin with the most effective authority available that can establish and guarantee an enduring order. Thereafter a transition to democratic forms becomes possible.

If order is to be the prime requisite for maintenance of a democratic politics, and if mere democratic practices themselves cannot always be relied upon for their own fulfillment, then wherein lies the secret to creation of a political structure that can be called a democracy? Arévalo Martínez' answer to this problem is essentially that no structure can ever be contrived that would assure Aristotle's eudaemonia, the good life. The goodness or badness of any political form will ultimately depend upon relative criteria, that is, upon whose pocket is being robbed or filled, whose home is being adorned or pillaged. The real danger lies in seeking utopia through refuge in panaceas. Such utopian visions Arévalo Martínez sought to expose in *Viaje a Ipanda*.

As a child, Arévalo Martínez abandoned the Catholic faith of his parents. Similarly, he became averse to any doctrine whose truth depended upon private revelation. He was strongly influenced by the existentialism of Schopenhauer. This influence may be somewhat paradoxical; the German philosopher had argued that philosophy can never be a science but is rather an art depending upon a special brand of revelation, of which only "great" men with genius could be capable. Notwithstanding, Schopenhauer's influence is clearly visible in Arévalo Martínez' idea of the will. For both men, will is the ultimate source of perceived reality. Will creates an outside order, which is then perceived.[22] What became crucial for Arévalo Martínez was how well, and for how long, men could perceive their environmental order with clarity. For without clarity of perception, how could one be sure that there was any order at all? This is a difficult notion to generalize, but we might say that, according to Arévalo Martínez, man exists only so long as he perceives what is taking place about him, which, in turn, his own will helped to create. Man's existence

---

[22] Arévalo Martínez, *passim.*

is at once a spiritual and intellectual experience, which postulates the assurance of a predictable and ordered social environment in which man can pursue self-realization under circumstances of the greatest liberty. The role of the State is to be a remover of barriers to human progress, as Thomas Hill Green might have put it. Or in Arévalo Martínez' terms, the State must guarantee such order as will be requisite for the development of innate human capabilities and the growth of democratic political institutions.

Therefore, he invented Ipanda, a mythical state whose authority relationships were so structured as to guarantee social order and predictability. So contrived, the scheme failed. Ipanda was formed out of an uneasy alliance of conscripted state labor and free trade unionism. Collectively owned property and private property were expected to live happily together. Government monopolies over basic goods maintained an unstable coexistence with the unhampered forces of a *laissez-faire* marketplace. No individual family's financial holdings were allowed to exceed 2 million *enandas,* a stricture that was easily violated with immunity through interfamily transfers of money and by primogeniture inheritances. Racial miscegenation was honored by law, but discriminatory practices and outright xenophobia were rampant in Ipanda.

Nominally, Ipanda was a member of the League of States, a transparent analogy to the old League of Nations. Members of the League of States saw themselves as being threatened by hostile external powers designed to represent the totalitarian states of Germany, Russia, and Japan. But the League did not degenerate into a fragmentation of its parts as had its real-world counterpart, the League of Nations. The League of States represented a truly supranational government, within which Ipanda remained as the only power whose sovereignty was not a paper myth. The League had dictated a lowering of tariff barriers among the member states, which, combined with population shifts and a militant trade unionism, was breaking down the socio-economic buttresses of Ipandese political independence.

There was also a crisis of leadership. In truly utopian fashion, perhaps through a combination of influences from Kafka and Orwell, Ipanda was administered under a unique presidential system and through a unitary administrative structure. Both were organically tied to Bolisario, the Head of State, whose engaging charisma united the Ipandese populace into a nation. As a gesture of his total immunity from subjective impulses in his service to Ipanda, Bolisario had put his own parents to the sword as a ritual of dedication. He ruled Ipanda as the benevolent authoritarian who might have inspired Rodó's vision of Ariel except for one fact: Bolisario had been offered the Presidency of Ipanda by its Congress and was supposed to remain accountable to its members for his actions. He was dramatically challenged before the Congress by a rival, Hofernes, over matters of economic policy and private love. The charismatic leader did not survive this attack, and power and prestige slipped from his grasp.

Ipanda dramatized three mistakes which a truly sovereign state could not commit and yet keep its independent being: such a state could not permanently confuse political liberalism and *laissez-faire* economics; it could not build its hierarchy of authority on the basis of a personal charisma that, in Weber's terms, was incapable of being "routinized"; finally, it could not surrender its political identity to an international government and still maintain the substance of independence within its own geographic boundaries.

Arévalo Martínez engineered the ultimate crash of his vision by having the League take advantage of Ipanda's internal political disorders. The League sent out "peaceful visitations" of armed forces for the ostensible purpose of a cross-national exchange of ideas and friendship. Perhaps Arévalo Martínez actually feared that the real League of Nations in his own day would become a bona fide supragovernment, although this is a moot issue. Nevertheless, the allegorical League took advantage of the weakness of Ipanda, its last remaining vestige of independent political sovereignty, and extended armed power clothed as a peace mission. The author tells us that "this was what the newspapers said."

> Esto decian los periódicos. Pero todo el mundo sabía que la verdad era otra. La Liga, órgano del Estado Universal, en el que desapareciéron las soberanias de todos los pueblos, había seguido con interés la situación política de Ipanda, había previsto la iminente caida de Bolisario, y ordenó la reunión en Roblanco de parte de su flota aerea de guerra y su jornada sobre Atlán. No era un triunfal paseo en conmemoración de un día de gloria. Era una amenaza a los Estados Centrales, en que fermentaba la rebelión y el nacionalismo. El gran Estado Policía Universal avisaba al mundo que debía vivir en paz, y celaba el orden.[23]

> This was what the newspapers said. But everyone knew otherwise. The League, organ of the Universal State, in which the sovereignties of all peoples were now disappearing, had watched the political situation in Ipanda carefully and, anticipating the downfall of Bolisario, had . . . (mobilized its air force to take advantage of the situation). This was no parade in commemoration of a day of glory. It was a threat to the Central States, in which the appeals of rebellion and nationalism were now fermenting. But the great Universal Police State proclaimed to the world that all should live in peace, and thus was order preserved.

And thus was order preserved, the primary requisite for human self-fulfillment. For Rafael Arévalo Martínez, any order, even that of the League, would be preferable to anarchy. But he knew that a democratic order would clearly be superior to a totalitarian one. Thus he demonstrated allegorically the dangers involved in utopianism as a path toward securing a democratic order. In so doing, he revalidated a familiar Aristotelian dictum, that the inherent goodness of ideal forms depends upon the natural roots from which they spring. We might conclude that in Ipanda, Arévalo Martínez blended the best of Echeverría and the worst of Rodó, and then invented a Bolívar to run the country. Upon reading *Viaje a Ipanda* the critical scholar will undoubtedly ask: But when does the price one pays for a stable order become too high? It is a major question that Arévalo Martínez does not answer.

---

[23] Arévalo Martínez, p. 439.

CONTEMPORARY DEMOCRATIC PROGRESSIVISM

In Latin America as elsewhere, the writings of great men must often endure a long passage of time to achieve recognition. This is particularly true of active statesmen whose ideas must be drawn together from speeches and articles which were presented on diverse occasions and which were devoted to a multitude of themes. Here we examine the thinking of one such contemporary statesman, a man who served his country twice in the Presidency and on numerous occasions in the diplomatic service. Alberto Lleras Camargo of Colombia is one of the truly distinguished statesmen of contemporary Latin America. Widely respected as an intellectual and national Executive, Lleras' ideas have received wide publication, which makes a comprehensive statement of the range of his thought impossible at this time. He has, however, always been preoccupied with questions basic to the partnership of economic system and government as institutions holding a joint responsibility for the upward mobility of Latin American societies. Many of these ideas were compiled in a volume that appeared in 1957, just before Lleras assumed the Colombian Presidency for the second time.

These writings, known as *Nuestra revolución industrial,* are based on a series of addresses given by Lleras shortly after he retired as rector of the Universidad de los Andes of Bogotá in October of 1955. A broad theme of his work is the growing dichotomy between western and eastern power blocs in the twentieth century, both in polemic and phenomenal terms, and the direction being taken by Latin America in the face of the two influences. Lleras expounded the basis for a political theory of development for his part of the underdeveloped world. No nation, he wrote, will ever be prosperous if its economy is based upon the servitude of seventy percent of its population. In the past, rural areas accounted for much of the servitude in Latin America. But with the coming of agricultural machines, men were rapidly displaced, and they migrated into the already crowded cities. Urbanization became an acute form of social change during the first half of the twentieth century in Latin America, but her cities obviously could not absorb this human input. Yet absorption of the displaced rural population is one of the primary tasks of a mature industrial economy. Certainly, the economy would be aided in this function by a controlled population growth, whether by natural or induced means. Lleras urged popular education as an integral facet of any program which would seek to deal with socio-economic development in rural areas.

The benefits of modernity, concomitants of urbanization and middle-class growth, have come late to Latin America. One of these benefits, seldom accorded the importance it deserves, is the political and economic liberation of women. Lleras saw the process as only partially completed in his native Colombia. There, many urban women had been "liberated" into the national political and economic life, at least enough so as to establish a visible precedent. The remainder were still slaves of men and were lower-caste members of a stratified society. Lleras recognizes free competition, within the framework of enforced controls against monopoly, as the correct road toward Western modernity in Latin America. He describes the "depauperization" of mankind as a more likely eventuality than the earlier predictions of Marx and Lenin. Lleras' optimism is much in the style of W. W. Rostow; the contribution of Lleras is clearly a "Non-Communist Manifesto."

But Lleras is no apologist for big business. He takes Latin American industrialists to task for their indifference to change. Lleras argues that Latin America's industrial base could not reach maturation so long as commercial interests were shamefully hiding behind tariff barriers and extorting from the populace high profits through controlled production. Only through expanded volume production, increased employment, and price reductions through an honest marketplace could industrial maturity be approached. An industrial economy is not mature unless it fulfills still another and basic social function, increased distribution of wealth through employment. Here Lleras speaks in the tradition of Galbraithean economics.

Lleras sees governments of Latin American states as political bureaucracies without adequate preparation to direct a planned national economy. These governments have never undergone the kind of patriotic experience which, as in the United States during two world wars, brought the best minds of private industry into the public service and thus laid the basis for a permanent *rapprochement* that would leave the two forces interdependent and not in a state of perpetual rivalry. He asserts that Latin American governments have adopted the practice of intervention in the private economy to an extent which and by means which are not theoretically compatible with even socialist doctrine. Lleras views much of the "patriotic nationalization" of industry in the present day more as the search for a whipping boy (what Ayn Rand would call looting) than as a genuine effort to redistribute wealth in a severely monopolized economy. A part of this thesis merits quoting directly.

> Intervenir en la indústria y en general en la economía privada, y dirigirla, es para el Estado latinoamericano a la vez, la continuación lógica de la reglamentación imperial de los Carlos y Felipes españoles, y al mismo tiempo, la manera de que el Gobierno sea cada vez más fuerte, por que ninguna cosa escape a su capacidad de mezclarse en las vidas de los ciudadanos y por que estos dependan cada vez más de sus decretos y disposiciones. No hay una tesis socialista ortodoxa en estos movimientos, aunque ocasionalmente se presente en la forma de una defensa de los intereses del consumidor o del obrero. Hay si una vieja tesis política, la misma que llevaba a los modestos golillas del Siglo XVI a pretender que no se moviera sin el consentimiento de sus oficinas de Madrid o Sevilla una hoja en el vastísimo bosque americano desconocido.[24]

> To intervene in industry and in the private economy generally, to direct it, is for the Latin American state a logical continuation of the imperial rule of the Spanish regimes of Charles and Philip and at once a manner of maintaining the strength of government by keeping the citizenry subservient to it. There

---

[24] Alberto Lleras Camargo, *Nuestra revolución industrial* (Bogotá, Aedita Editores Ltda., 1957), p. 50.

is no orthodox socialist thesis in these movements, although occasionally it presents itself in the form of a defense of consumers and workers. There is indeed an old political thesis, the same which led the minor magistrates of the sixteenth century to pretend that not a leaf in the vast, unknown American forest should move without the consent of the (colonial) offices in Madrid or Seville.

Such, unfortunately, remains the case today with respect to government encroachment on the private sphere. Lleras finds that today two types of bureaucracies are feeding at the public trough in a costly demonstration of Parkinson's Law. They are the political bureaucrats who live by exploiting the pariah capitalists, upon whom they anomalously depend, and the capitalistic bureaucracies, formed out of such polite forms of nepotism as *compadrazgo,* or extended family relationships. The latter bureaucrats thrive behind protective barriers where an inefficient "private" operation may survive as long as it keeps government policies on its side. In such circumstances, the industrial monopolists will probably be in control of the governing bureaucracy. Lleras lamented that such had been the case entirely too often in his native land, no matter whether an incumbent government was nominally Liberal or Conservative. It was a disease of government for which Colombians had paid dearly in material wealth as well as with their blood. Lleras indicts his culture for having compounded the original errors of the framers of the independence movements, who failed to see the possibilities of even regional union and cooperation, a part of Bolívar's grandiose dream of total Latin American unity. The creation of great regional groups, Lleras wrote, along with regional economic agreements, is the solution to the problem of underdevelopment in Latin America today.[25]

Lleras points emphatically to one area of reform that might be the starting point for others to come. Why is it, he asks, that North American industries are continually being revitalized with good minds that are capable of taking both a public and private view of industrial growth? He answers that North American industries gratuitously contribute to academic institutions in order to reap, ultimately, a harvest of new ideas and competent personnel. Lleras underscores the doctrine of external economies, long recognized by industrialists in the Western world and now gaining slow acceptance throughout Latin America. When an industry ceases to be just a family affair within a feudal model and becomes a social function although still in private hands, it then makes sense for that industry to grant funds to universities for scholarships and research. Eventually, some of the human offspring of those investments will return as productive supporters for the investing industry. These are truly external economies that benefit not just the donating industry but the society in general.

Unfortunately, Latin American universities generally do not receive in-

---

[25] Lleros Camargo, p. 102.

dustrial support, nor do they produce the personnel which industrial maturity demands. These institutions help to produce few such external economies. Usually the universities are under state control and constitute little more than training camps for future politicians and bureaucrats. Entirely too often, state control has meant student control. Unlike the North American state schools, which stay relatively nonpolitical and thus maintain objective achievement standards that lend value to the degrees conferred, most Latin American schools fail miserably in preparing young men and women for a life in which success comes through the rigors of submitting one's work to the judgment of impartial experts. Lleras had been rector of the Universidad de los Andes in Bogotá, one of the few Latin American universities in which relatively high and impartial achievement standards are maintained. It is also one of few Latin American universities in which faculties are not the helpless prisoners of a student "government."

Let us conclude, then, that in the thought of Alberto Lleras Camargo, one finds only a little of Bolívar (regionalism), much of Echeverría (democratic liberalism built out of a partnership of private and public forces), a slight dose of Arévalo Martínez (concern for bureaucracy as a political organism), and probably none of Rodó. Lleras is neither a utopian idealist nor a dialectician. Since his retirement from the Colombian Presidency in 1962, Lleras has become increasingly influential in currents of Latin American political thought. He has written a distinguished series of articles for *Visión,* one of the area's top vernacular journals for public consumption. During the spring of 1965, Lleras was called upon by the United States Senate to give testimony on approaches to the problem of population pressure in Latin America. In his outright advocacy of birth control programs as a step toward integration of social and economic growth, Lleras led the ranks of progressive statesmen who accept cultural change as an imperative for Latin America's long-range survival.

INVECTIVES AND VENDETTAS

Quite noticeably, there has been a tendency among Latin American intellectuals to look outside their own political milieu for assignment of blame for local ills and failures. It is appropriate that we survey some of these critics here immediately after an examination of the work of Alberto Lleras Camargo, who set an example for many of his contemporaries by directly indicting the Latin American culture for its own shortcomings. There is an important difference, however, between the broad cultural criticism of Lleras, who asks the citizen to reconsider his value premises, and criticism of a specific political ill. The latter, especially when it has one person, such as a dictator, as its object, lends itself well to highly emotive appeals. Here we will examine Latin American thought on the issue of tyranny, not as an exercise in introspection but in consideration of a phenomenon that has captured the attention of theorists from Machiavelli to Hannah Arendt and probably will never be laid to rest so long as men devise ways to enslave their fellows.

Of literary names associated with denunciation of Latin American tyranny, that of former Argentine President Domingo F. Sarmiento remains the epitome. His principal work, *Facundo* (1845), has forever burned the name of Juan Manuel de Rosas into the pages of Spanish-American literature as the prototype of things evil in political life. *Facundo* is a treatment of one of Rosas' rival *caudillos* as well as an attack upon the tyrant himself and seeks generally to denigrate totalitarianism in all its then known forms.

In reality, post-independence life in Argentina consisted of four distinct areas: the port-city area of Buenos Aires, the agricultural region along the Andes Mountains in the west, the northwest province of Santa Fe and the surrounding river country, and Buenos Aires province itself, extending south from the port city. Disunity and friction among the four provincial areas continually flared over the question of centralism (national unity under one government, directed from Buenos Aires) as opposed to federalism (continued provincial independence and rivalry). A succession of weak Presidents had failed to hold the country together. However, following the resignation of President Rivadavia in 1827, there appeared on the scene a *caudillo* from the province of Buenos Aires, Juan Manuel de Rosas, who knew how to build power and who could do so without seeming to be hungry for it. He maneuvered the provincial legislature of Buenos Aires into offering him unlimited dictatorial powers as governor. When the offers came, he refused them consistently until a plebiscite was held to give popular validation to his rule. Since he was thus cajoled into high place, no one suspected that Rosas would become one of the cruelest dictators in all Latin American history.

A federalist in name only, Rosas gave Argentina a degree of centralism theretofore unknown. He enforced decree law with his dreaded *mazorca,* a secret police whose organized terror rivaled even that of the Gironde days during the French Revolution. Supported by many of the clergy and wealthy landed classes, Rosas ruled through persecution, violence, and institutionalized rapine up until his resignation and exile to England after the defeat of his forces in the Uruguayan War following 1852. Domingo F. Sarmiento's treatment of Rosas breathes the embittered passion of a man who has suffered personally at the hands of a *caudillo* much like Rosas, Facundo, from whose name comes the title of the work.

Facundo es un tipo de la barbarie primitiva; no conoció sujeción de ningún género; su cólera era de las fieras; la melena de sus renegridos y ensortijados cabellos caía sobre su frente y sus ojos en quedejas, como las serpientes de la cabeza de Meduza; su voz se enronquecía y sus miradas se convertían en puñaladas.[26]

Facundo is the incarnation of primitive barbarity; he never knew subjection in any form; his rage was of the greatest fierceness; black-and-blue locks of

---

[26] Domingo F. Sarmiento, *Facundo* (Buenos Aires, Espasa Calpe, 1951), p. 69.

his curly hair tumbled over his forehead; his eyes were in sockets fringed by shaggy eyebrows whose serpentine shapes meshed tortuously as if from the head of the Medusa; his voice rasped while he cast about glances that were like daggers.

Unquestionably, one of the ironies that plagued Sarmiento and his contemporaries in the resistance to Rosas' tyranny was the anomaly of the tyrant himself. Unlike Juan Facundo Quiroga, Rosas was not the offspring of guerrilla warfare and personal deprivation. Why should a man who came into public office under popular duress then turn into the bloody assassin of his countrymen? Yet there he was. Here is Sarmiento's pledge of reform:

> Porque él ha hecho del crimen, del asesinato, de la castración y del deguello un sistema de gobierno; porque él ha desenvuelto todos los malos instintos de la naturaleza humana para crearse complices y partidarios, el nuevo gobierno hará de la Justicia, de las formas recibidas en los pueblos civilizados, el medio de corregir los delitos públicos, y trabajará por estimular las pasiones nobles y virtuosas que ha puesto Diós en el corazón del hombre para su dicha en la tierra, haciendo de ellas el escalón para elevarse e influir en los negocios públicos.[27]

> Because he has turned crime, assassination, castration, and the guillotine into a system of government; because he has released all the bad instincts common to man in order to make men his accomplices, the new Government will adopt Justice and civilized forms of administration to correct present crimes in the public sector; it will work to encourage the noble passions and virtues that God placed within the heart of man so that he can advance himself honorably in the realm of public affairs.

When Sarmiento was elected to the Argentine Presidency in 1868, he brought to that office a provincial background and self-education. He engendered great respect for sane human achievement. He was perhaps, as much the Abraham Lincoln of Argentina as was his contemporary Mexican counterpart, Benito Júarez, the educational godfather of that country. Sarmiento sought to correct public corruption through exciting the nobler human passions. Ignorance, and its chief sponsor, the *Gaucho-caudillo,* had to be overcome. Ironically, Sarmiento's contemporary, the poet José Hernández, was just then seeking to glorify the same disappearing Gaucho that the Argentine statesman was condemning. Hernández' epic poem *Martín Fierro,* while great poetry, was an unconvincing answer to the detailed charges spewing from *Facundo.*

A twentieth-century treatment of the tyranny theme is found in Jesús de Galíndez' *La era de Trujillo,* 1956. Galíndez' work earned its author a doctorate from Columbia University but probably cost him his life at the hands of the Dominican tyrant's paid henchmen. Born a Spaniard, Galíndez had lived in the Dominican Republic and was vitally interested in that country's political life. He saw the Trujillo dictatorship, indeed most Latin

---

[27] Sarmiento, p. 235.

American dictatorships, as distinguished from their European counterparts in the lack of a formal mystique that was claimed as the ultimate goal of the state. In the case of Trujillo, Galíndez noted the absence of any truly popularly based party structure to support and justify a totalitarian regime. Government under Trujillo was a family affair with only the most transparent facade of political democracy surrounding it. Thus Galíndez concluded that personal tyranny was a more appropriate term for describing the naked exercise of political power under regimes such as that of Rafael Leonidas Trujillo.[28]

Denunciation of tyranny as a theme in the vernacular literature of Latin America had received at once birth and perfection in Sarmiento's work. The literature thereafter is strewn with remnants of and variations upon that theme. Briefly, among the names which could be mentioned for the interested scholar to explore more fully is José Mármol, an Argentine poet who is said to have written his first poetry on the walls of a prison where Rosas held him captive in 1839.[29] The Venezuelan Rufino Blanco Fombona wrote a satire against the tyrannical regime of Juan Vicente Gómez.[30] Not until the death of the dictator Gómez in 1935 was Blanco Fombona able to return safely to his native land. From the same country a one-time President, Rómulo Gallegos, offered the novel *Doña Barbara* (1921) as a modern version of *Facundo* again satirizing the Gómez regime; the title *Doña Barbara* is derived from the word *"barbarie."*[31] Finally, Luis Antonio Eguiguren's *El ursurpador* decried the fraudulent election in Peru of Oscar Benavides in 1936.[32] In that election the author was himself a "defeated" candidate.

If tyranny can be said to mean temporary political stability that is achieved through arbitrary use of force, then the opposite evil would be anarchy, ensuing once the stabilizing force has crumbled. For Mexicans, the years 1910 to 1917 meant anarchy. The treachery of Victoriano Huerta (under the eyes of United States Ambassador Henry Lane Wilson) produced the murder of Francisco Madero and his vice-president, Pino Súarez, two men who personified the first breath of real hope for liberty that Mexicans had known since the beginning of the thirty-five-year tyranny, the *Pax Porfiriana*. The assassination of Madero triggered a horrendous bloodletting that ulti-

---

[28] Jesús de Galíndez, *La era de Trujillo* (Santiago de Chile, Editorial del Pacifico, 1956), pp. 445–46.

[29] Marmol's best known novel, *Amalia* (1851) is at once an autobiography and a scathing commentary on the Rosas dictatorship.

[30] Rufino Blanco Fombona, *El hombre de oro* (Madrid, Editorial America, 1916).

[31] Rómulo Gallegos, *Doña Barbara* (Barcelona, Araluce, 1929).

[32] Many critics might argue that the most profound and universal analysis of Latin American tyranny was done by the Guatemalan novelist Miguel Ángel Asturias, whose works are discussed elsewhere in this chapter but in another context. His novel *El señor presidente,* 1946, is said to have followed almost linearly in the tradition of *Facundo* and others and presents insights so generic as to be appropriate nearly everywhere (cf. Francis J. Donahue, *Miguel Ángel Asturias: Escritor comprometido* [Los Angeles, University of Southern California PhD Thesis, 1965], pp. 223–270).

mately produced one of Latin America's most stable contemporary political systems. His assassination also gave birth to a great tradition in Spanish-American literature, the revolutionary novel.

Undoubtedly the greatest of these novels, indeed a monument to the humanistic achievements of Latin Americans, is Mariano Azuela's *Los de abajo*, known in English as *The Underdogs*. Azuela, himself a disillusioned revolutionary, was appalled by the savage fury, the senseless anarchy of the Mexican fighting between 1910 and 1917. The actors in the revolution were discrete units in a tangled mosaic of conflict and were forced to fight without clearly defined goals, even intermediate ones. Within the revolution was an inertia which carried men with it into a nihilistic void. The *hombres de Macias* followed their leader, Demetrio, through debauchery and rapine without ever knowing why. One of their number, Luis Cervantes, an ex-medical student and journalist turned guerrilla, frequently piqued his leader by questioning the goals of their continued fighting. Some innate omnipresent force swept these men onward to their destruction. They could do nothing to control it. Few dared to think of what they were doing, and those who did became terrified at the prospect; it was less frightening simply to die.

> Que hermosa es la Revolución, aun en su misma barbarie, pronunció Solis conmovido. Luego, en voz baja y con vaga melancolía:
> Lástima que lo que falta no sea igual. Hay que esperar un poco. A que no haya combatientes, a que no se oigan mas disparos que los de las turbas entregadas a las delicias del saqueo; a que resplandezca diáfana, como una gota de agua, la psicología de nuestra raza condensada en dos palabras: robar, matar! . . .[33]

> How beautiful the Revolution, even in its own barbarity, declared Solis emotionally. Then, in a voice low and faltering with melancholy:
> How shameful that what remains should not be equally beautiful. Let us wait a while. Should not there be soldiers? We should be hearing shots other than those of the mobs that are reveling in the delights of pillage and looting; to some glittering transparency, like a drop of water, the psychology of our race condensed in two words: robbery, killing! . . .

In *Los de abajo* Mariano Azuela has given us a poignant view of anarchy surpassing all of the verbal gymnastics that philosophers could invent to analyze the same phenomenon. His criticism of anarchy is implicit in the telling of what it is. To Mariano Azuela, anarchy is a social state in which all men are rendered equally superfluous. Without knowing it, he had foreshadowed Hannah Arendt's definition of totalitarianism.[34]

As a prelude to his own death, the protagonist, Demetrio, returns to the arms of his woman and child after an absence of nearly two years. In a now-famous passage she beseeches him to tell her why he must still fight.

---

[33] Mariano Azuela, *Los de abajo* (Mexico, Fondo de Cultura Economica, 1958 ed.), p. 72.

[34] Hannah Arendt, *The Origins of Totalitarianism* (New York, Harcourt, Brace, and World, Inc., 1951).

Demetrio can only fling a stone down the steep side of a ravine and tell her that the stone too cannot stop moving . . . men, rocks, superfluity.

Another Mexican novelist, Rudolfo Usigli, specialized in social and political satire. His melodrama *El Gesticulador,* 1937, concerns a professor of history, César Rubio, posing as a famous revolutionary general by the same name, who had been assassinated years earlier. At first Rubio adopts the role of impostor to gain financial reward, but he later becomes an ardent supporter of the ideals of the revolution. Ironically the professor-impostor is assassinated by the same rogues who murdered his namesake. This is Usigli's way of exposing the deceit and intrigue of Mexican political life in the era prior to 1937.

Latin American intellectuals have from time to time adopted minority causes as subjects for invective and vendetta. Among the most celebrated of these is the cause of the Indian. The Ecuadorean novelist Jorge de Icaza became a major champion of the Indian's plight. His best known work, *Huasipungo,* 1934, protests the exploitation of the squatter Indians by their masters.[35] The title, in Quechua, means the plot of land which the landlords gave to the Indians in return for labor on the hacienda. The Indian had no tenure or expectation of permanence, and the land was frequently sold from under him. Icaza depicts the helpless terror of slum-dwellers being uprooted from their valueless but cherished piece of soil. The outcome is one of the most pitiful visions of anarchy that one could ever imagine.

Also well known for its championship of the indigenous people's cause is Ciro Alegría's *El mundo es ancho y ajeno,* 1941. The author, a native of Peru, was an active supporter of Haya de la Torre and his APRA movement, in whose cause Alegría spent many difficult years in prison and in foreign exile. The principal action of the novel takes place in the mythical community of Rumi, which was probably modeled after one of the actual communities in which Alegría was frequently forced to take refuge. Rumi was a community land-ownership arrangement (in one sense, and unintentionally, foreshadowing the more recent Vicos experiment in Peru), whose pattern followed that of the old Inca *ayllu.* Economic and agricultural functions were performed on a communal basis under the supervision of an elected and democratic local council. Privately-held garden plots and a meager barter-subsistence economy were the principal concessions made in Rumi to the principle of capitalistic enterprise. Rumi's democracy was its principal innovation over the *ayllu* tradition, which had featured local autocracy. Alegría stresses the virtue of this departure in governmental practice in terms of the measurable benefits which accrue to the local citizenry. Despite the advantage of political democracy and local identification, however, the community of Rumi is another microcosm for the study of Indian suffering and persecution, which is no less poignant than that depicted in Icaza's *Huasipungo.*

---

[35] *Huasipungo* carries especially useful insights for the theory scholar who is interested in local power structures.

Another contemporary defender of the Indian is Miguel Angel Asturias, whose novel *Los ojos de los enterrados,* 1960, closed a trilogy of writings about his native Guatemala. According to an ancient legend widely shared among the Indians of Guatemala, the deceased are buried with their eyes open and looking upward at the phenomenal world. Their eyes are to close only upon the imminent day of justice for those who were perpetually exploited and neglected by mestizos and whites. Through the eyes of the dead, one sees the rancors of life—a "banana republic" in a new and ethnically colored perspective. *Los ojos de los enterrados* followed upon *Viento fuerte* and *El papa verde,* the latter a well-known excoriation of the United Fruit Company and other foreign interests in terms of the helpless struggle of small banana-growers against the great company, whose president is the green pope, *el papa verde.* The same theme is dramatized in *Viento fuerte* as Asturias unleashes a savage hurricane in the hands of a mad sorcerer, who devastates the foreign-owned banana plantations with furious vengeance.

Latin America has not been without its reactionary traditionalists. Julio Ycaza Tigerino, a Nicaraguan Conservative, asserts that New Spain originally needed strong centralized administrative institutions to preserve stability. He charges that liberalism and Liberal institutions resulted in social instability, which subsequent dictatorial regimes could easily exploit. This Conservative point of view is relatively uncommon in Latin American vernacular literature, and Ycaza Tigerino's remarks merit special attention. Calling for a benevolent authoritarianism (not totally unlike Rodó), Tigerino says,

> La democracia liberal significó, pues, la destrucción de las bases del orden feudal americano, la incapacidad de substituir este orden feudal por un orden nacional adecuado a la realidad social de nuestros pueblos, y el consiguiente abandono del proceso de mestizaje étnico y cultural, con la consecuente liberación de las oscuras fuerzas primitivas latentes en el ancestro racial de indios y mestizos, fuerzas desatadas que dieron a la anarquía hispanoamericana un tremendo carácter de retrogradación histórica y cultural.[36]

> Liberal democracy meant the destruction of the bases of American feudal order, the inability to replace the feudal order with a national one which was adequate to the social reality of our people, and the consequent abandonment of the ethnic and cultural mixing then going on. The result of this was a liberation of dark primitive forces latent in the racial ancestry of Indians and mestizos, forces unleashed which gave Hispanic-American anarchy a tremendous character of historical and cultural degeneration.

But Ycaza Tigerino's conservatism is not one of reverence for the influence of the United States, either.

> Agentes diplomáticos Norteamericanos irían al Congreso de Panamá invitados por Santander, con instrucciones precisas del Secretario de Estado Henry Clay, enemigo personal de Bolívar, a quien odiaba cordialmente, de hacer

---

[36] Julio Ycaza Tigerino, "Las formas políticas anarquía y dictadura," in Chang-Rodriguez y Kantor, eds. *La América latina de hoy* (New York, The Ronald Press Company, 1961), p. 106.

propaganda al sistema democrático de gobierno y de sabotear todo intento de unidad continental oponiendose al grandiose proyecto del Libertador.[37] North American diplomats set out for the Congress of Panama invited by Santander but carrying precise instructions from Secretary of State Henry Clay, a personal enemy of Bolívar, to propagandize in favor of democratic forms of government and to sabotage any effort toward continental unity. They were completely in opposition to the Liberator's grand design.

Lurking behind Ycaza Tigerino's concern for the loss of strong centralized political institutions in Latin America is his fear of recurrent disorder and anarchy. His views are typical of contemporary Latin American Conservatives, many of whom would follow the earlier cited dicta of Arévalo Martínez in preserving order even at the cost of human liberty.

Inevitably, we must come to the topic which has preoccupied the invectives and vendettas of Latin American intellectuals more than any other. The theme, as the above quotations from Ycaza Tigerino might suggest, is that of the United States as villain.[38] Without excessive unfairness to proponents of this idea, one must say that many words have been written about it, but very little has really been said since Rodó and Cuba's José Martí championed the theme around the turn of the present century. Martí, whose *Nuestra América* appeared in 1878, admonished his countrymen against the temptation of imitating North American influences by saying, "Read to learn but not copy."[39] Martí's voluminous writings cannot be surveyed in a work of the present scope. He is best known to Latin Americans as the freedom-fighter in Cuba's drive for independence during the 1890s. Currently, Martí is claimed as an intellectual symbol of unity for the Castro-Cuban Revolution.

In Nicaragua, at approximately the same time, Rubén Darío mourned the loss of the Panama Canal venture to the United States because with the Canal went an opportunity for a truly French heritage, which he considered best for Latin America. His *Prosa política* is also an embittered reaction to the Nicaraguan exploits of William Walker during the 1850s, which Darío viewed as a foreshadowing of other things to come. Rufino Blanco Fombona, who was cited earlier for his criticism of tyranny, also contributed to the anti-American theme; in his *La lámpara de Aladino,* 1915, he lauded the assassination of President McKinley as a just reprisal for the humiliation and sacrifice of Latin Americans during the Spanish-American War. Blanco Fombona credited much of the evil intentions of North American politicians to the voracious influence of women in United States political life.

Perhaps the epitome of anti-Americanism, however, is to be seen in the work of a contemporary Cuban poet. Nicolás Guillén, a Negro and an avowed Communist, is often lauded for his poetic achievements and, like his Chilean contemporary, Pablo Neruda, has been recognized internationally. From the

---

[37] Tigerino, p. 107.

[38] Cf. Donald F. Fogelquist, "The American Villain in Latin American Literature," *Modern Language Journal,* March, 1949.

[39] José Martí, *Nuestra América* (Buenos Aires, Editorial Losada, 1939), p. 19.

standpoint of political criticism (in this case, of United States influence in Latin America), Nicolás Guillén's *El son entero,* 1947, and *La paloma de vuelo popular,* 1948, are milestones in the denigration of North American political images before the eyes of Latin Americans. Guillén writes of the bastardizing of *naturaleza* that comes from a cultural miscegenation now taking place in Puerto Rico under United States "occupation."

> masticas una jerigonza
> medio española, medio slang;
> de un empujón te hundieron en Corea,
> sin que supieras por quien ibas a pelear,
> si en yes,
> si en si, . . .
> si en mal,
> si en bad, si en very bad![40]

> you chew a gibberish
> half Spanish, half slang;
> at one shove they wipe you out in Korea,
> without knowing what you're fighting for
> si en yes,
> si en si, . . .
> si en mal,
> si en bad, si en very bad!

Guillén's revulsion for the Puerto Rican assimilation of North American influences is typical of contemporary resentment in Latin America toward other instances of such mixing, for example, Guatemalan attitudes toward Belice, Colombian feelings about their island San Andrés, and Brazilian chagrin over the mixing of their vernacular in the Guianas.

Throughout his writings, Guillén has maintained that his *poesía negra* reflects a profound national character of the Cuban people, that his work champions their determined resistance to the foreign invaders whose penetrations have occurred for three centuries. The following selection from *El banderón* stresses the polarization of Cuban aspirations as against the foreign agents of imperialism who have overrun the Cuban homeland.

> Como un punal, como un arpón,
> el banderón americano
> en tu costado de carbón.
> Sucio de sangre el banderón.
> Un yanqui allí, látigo en mano.

> Sé de la bala en el pulmón
> y del capitán inhumano
> y de la nocturna prisión.
> Arde el violento barracón.
> Un yanqui allí, látigo en mano.

---

[40] Nicolás Guillén, *La paloma de vuelo popular* (Buenos Aires, Editorial Losada, 1959), p. 31.

Será tal vez una ilusión,
tal vez será un ensueño vano,
mas veo rodar el banderón
y arder el viento tu canción,
puesta en el mástil por tu mano.[41]

Like a spear or harpoon
the American tyrant
in your coalblack side.
Dirty with blood the tyrant.
A Yankee there, whip in hand.

I know the bullet in the lung
and of the inhuman captain
and of the arrests by night.
Bursting forth the violent barracks master.
A Yankee there, with whip in hand.

It will be perhaps an illusion,
or maybe only a dream in vain,
but I see the tyrant destroyed
and your song burning across the wind,
flown from the masthead by your hand.

Guillén's is a guttural yet sensitive poetry, seldom free from preoccupation with the imminence of death but never losing hope for the deliverance of the poet's black people from their traditional bondage to foreign masters. In lesser degrees of severity perhaps, most Latin American political thinkers share Guillén's concerns.

Here as before, we must stress that the scholar of Latin American politics need not concern himself with the historical accuracy of any of the allegations contained in the above invectives and vendettas. In terms of contemporary Latin American political behavior, it is most important to recognize that such pronouncements were and are believed, acted upon, and now have come to rest as parts of functioning ideologies as well as in whole theories. These fragmentary views are directly relevant to the study of indigenous political thought in Latin America as premises, often inarticulate, that underlie theoretic formulations designed for translation into ideologies and actions.

POLITICAL IDEAS IN THE FRENCH IDIOM

Since Haiti's official independence in 1804, the "black republic" has been a glaring testimonial to the prevalence of human misery and injustice in Latin America. Not unexpectedly, this most underdeveloped of island states has never enjoyed an atmosphere conducive to creative artistry that might produce a fecund literature from which glimpses of political thought could be taken. The most easily accessible political works by Haitian authors are histories, usually of the "official" sort, limited to the mechanics of presidential successions and military events. A sad byproduct of Haiti's poor intellectual atmos-

---

[41] Guillén, p. 23.

phere has been the exodus of some of her best minds: For example, it is scandalously well known that numerous Haitian jurists are devoting their talents to service with the United Nations in Africa.

One of the few Haitians to achieve recognition as a writer notwithstanding these limitations is Jean Price-Mars. His *La Republique d'Haiti et la Republique Dominicaine* (1953) is generally of the "official" type mentioned above, yet he does point with insight to certain psychological facts of his island's society that help us to understand not only the crisis of ninety-five percent of Haiti's population but explain as well the paucity of her available theoretic works in the vernacular. In the introduction to a two-volume work, Price-Mars, placing the dilemma of Haiti's political life in bold relief, says,

> En effet, quand on étudie la psychologie du marron avec soin, on s'aperçoit qu'il n'était rien d'autre qu'une révolte dont la détermination de rompre avec le statut de l'opprime se manifesta dans sa décision de défendre ses privilèges inaliénables d'homme en se refugiant en quelque lieu inaccessible aux suppôts du conformisme social.[42]

> In reality, when one studies carefully the psychology of the slave, one finds that his revolt is nothing other than determination to break away from a regime of oppression and reflects his decision to defend his inalienable human privileges by taking refuge in some place where he will not be found out by the agents of social conformity.

Price-Mars recognizes the Haitian's craving for a refuge from the oppressive political order that rules him. He speaks of "revolt," however, more in the subtle context of psychological withdrawal than in terms of open insurgency for political goals. Such overt types of action have yielded not even the seeds of genuine social revolution in Haiti, nor have officially sponsored writers been permitted to express such ideas whenever they dared to hold them.

A contemporary of Price-Mars, Achille Aristide, has further developed the notion of stoic withdrawal among Haitian subcultures and has done so with an anthropological approach. In explaining the central idea of the Bantoue-Africaine philosophy which is prevalent in Haiti today, Aristide stresses the concept of *force vitale,* the essence of this spiritual discipline. *Force vitale* is the Haitian's faith in the transcendental value of his own being. He believes that, despite the chains in which he must live, his true self belongs to a superior being and will someday be recognized by society. The Haitian is accustomed to waiting for change to come. His greatest asset is time. Put under pressure, his existence threatened corporeally, he can always seek refuge in *bwanga.*

> Ils auront recours, le cas échéant, au bwanga, remède magique pour renforcer ou augmenter leur force vitale, la magie étant pour eux une force ou l'art de mettre en mouvement une des forces.[43]

---

[42] Jean Price-Mars, *La Republique d'Haiti et la Republique Dominicaine* (Port-au-Prince, Imprimèrie Held, 1953), p. 17.

[43] Achille Aristide, *Problemes haitiens* (Port-au-Prince, Imprimèrie d L'Etat, 1958), p. 15.

Always they have recourse, should such be the case, to *bwanga,* a magical remedy to bolster and strengthen their vital force, the magic being for them a force in itself, the skill of setting other forces in motion.

The *force vitale* is a universal law of supreme value. It steels its black practitioner against the acrimonious miseries of a hostile environment. The *force vitale* is maintained and propagated by the spirits of dead Haitian ancestors. It may assume animal, vegetable, or inanimate forms. Happiness is reserved for those who can know its ubiquitous presence; disease is for those who allow the *force vitale* to slip away or for those who have never achieved its blessing. For the downtrodden Haitian peasant, born into a land of never-ending slums, whose dwellers exist fearfully in the ever-present shadow of the *Ton-Tons Macoutes,* the Bantoue-Africaine mystique is a stoic ritual and, as such, is indispensable to their life.

The writings of Jean Price-Mars and Achille Aristide do not represent literary achievements in the same sense as the previously surveyed works from the Spanish-American tradition. There are few available Haitian works which do fit within this genre and which also yield insight into Haitian political thought. For the scholar who wishes to pursue this line of analysis, however, there is in the French vernacular a useful survey of Haitian authors, which was prepared in 1947 by Dantes Bellegarde.[44] The reader is reminded that Haiti has never been a land in which literary creativity, especially of the political variety, has received the level of encouragement and recognition that one encounters throughout the remainder of Latin America.

BRAZILIAN POLITICAL THOUGHT

One of the more important political critics of nineteenth-century Brazil was João Francisco Lisboa, an essayist whose best known work was *Ó Jornal de Timon,* 1852. Named after the fifth century B.C. misanthrope Timon, the work reflects the author's deep pessimism over the corruption of Brazilian political life which was prevalent in his day. Lisboa emphasized electoral fraud as the extreme of degeneracy into which his society had fallen, and he seems to have held to a strong faith in the mechanical aspects of political democracy. Like many Latin Americans, he felt more concern over whether the vote was counted honestly than for the validity of the alternatives being selected in a given election.

Spanning the turn of the present century was Joaquim Aurelio Barreto Nabuco de Araujo (1849–1910), the son of a politically prominent family in Pernambuco, who served in the Brazilian Chamber of Deputies. Known for his opposition to slavery, Nabuco wrote an autobiography, *Minha Formação,* in which he tried to depict Brazil's political life in its total social context and to stress some of the more sordid features then in need of reform. One of

---

[44] Dantes Bellegarde, *Ecrivains haitiens* (Port-au-Prince, Societé d' Éditions et de Librairies, 1947).

Nabuco's contemporaries, Rui Barbosa (1849–1923), was also a political critic who won fame for participating in actual political events in Brazil. His *Contra o militarismo* castigated the Brazilian military for its frequent interventions in the political arena, especially after the fall of the empire in 1889. In 1891 the election of Brazil's first republican President, Deodoro da Fonseca, was carried out under the aegis of a new liberal constitution, framed by a special constituent assembly that was dominated by Rui Barbosa. He is known in Brazilian annals as a great leader in the fight against militarism in government.

Probably the best-known recent theoretic achievement in Brazilian literature is one that is now more widely read in its English translation than in the original Portuguese. Gilberto Freyre's *Casa-grande & senzala* (1946) is recognized by literary critics as a vernacular masterpiece, and its English version, *The Masters and the Slaves,* is equally honored as a modern treatise in social research. The work is a treasure chest of intimate glimpses into Brazilian social life. The book offers something for nearly everyone, and probably no two scholars of Latin American politics will agree on what its most crucial contribution to political thought is. The work is not, of course, a political treatise per se. Freyre traces Brazil's growth from a cultural wilderness to a system of *latifundia* monoculture and slavery. The Big House, symbol of a manorial socio-economic system, and racial miscegenation ultimately produced what Freyre regarded as the most stable civilization in Latin America. The only Latin American nation to function as a truly monarchial empire after independence, Brazil has perhaps been among the region's more stable polities even though events in the twentieth century which have surrounded the era of Getúlio Vargas and subsequent changes in the structure of power do not necessarily confirm a strong thesis for Brazilian political stability.

The sixteenth-century Portuguese colonists found the Brazilian Indian ill-adapted to the rigors of building modernity out of a provincial and tropical life. Hence the colonists imported African Negroes in great numbers, with whom the Iberians freely interbred. Brazil's colonists brought with them a paganized Roman Catholicism drawn from an Iberian heritage of racial mixing with the Moors. According to the English version of Freyre, "The slaves that came from the more advanced areas of Negro culture were an active, creative, and, one might also add, a noble element in the colonization of Brazil; if they occupied a lower rung, it was due simply to their condition as slaves."[45] Significantly, they did not remain just slaves, nor were they relegated to roles of third-class citizenry, as occurred in the southern United States,

---

[45] Gilberto Freyre, *The Masters and the Slaves* (New York, Knopf, 1964 ed.), p. 270. A useful discussion of Freyre's later works and those of other Brazilian intellectuals in the contemporary scene is found in Frank Bonilla's chapter on national ideology in K. H. Silvert's *Expectant Peoples: Nationalism and Development* (New York, Random House, 1963). Bonilla does not distinguish between theory and ideology as we have attempted to do in this chapter, but his insights into such Brazilian concepts as *alienação* and *tomada de consciência* are valuable for the scholar who wishes to consider the two modes in their composite form.

indeed in many parts of Latin America as well. After the decreed abolition of slavery toward the end of the empire under Dom Pedro II in 1888, the process of racial blending that had begun with the sixteenth-century colonists now created a profoundly national Brazilian character, one that tempered the typically extroverted behavior of the African with the introversion of the Indian. The manorial system fostered assimilation of the Negro into a new mulatto culture that did not leave a vast social cleavage which someday would become politically dangerous. Reading Freyre, one gets a picture of social and political synthesis which is far different from that one finds in studying countries such as Peru and Bolivia, where a gigantic gulf separates the indigenous population from the national political life.

The reader of *The Masters and the Slaves* will delight at tales of human warmth as well as of violence and suffering; he will discover bizarre scenes of sexual orgies, superstition and magic, religous orthodoxy and witchcraft. Surely, however, he gains the conviction that Brazil is a truly unique Latin American nation, a society blessed with at least the roots of political stability if not with the knowledge to achieve it.

CONCLUSIONS

Were this chapter to contain an exhaustive survey of writings by Latin American intellectuals, it would become a book. Such a work is dearly needed, however, and it would behoove some rising group of postdoctoral scholars to undertake the task in comprehensive fashion. In the present survey, several names come to mind that were passed over in the interest of space. Among them are Andrés Bello, Erico Verissimo, José Figueres, Juan José Arévalo, Daniel Fignolé, Uslar Pietri, Eduardo Santos, Leopoldo Zea, and many others. Also deliberately excluded from consideration here is a body of political thought that may be lumped conveniently under the general rubric of constitutionalism and legal theory, a prodigious literature in itself, which has already been surveyed by Helen Clagett.[46] We have omitted ecclesiastical and propaganda works per se, and at the onset we presented a justification for opting in favor of separating theory from ideology, the latter being reserved for inclusion within individual chapters corresponding to the various Latin American Republics. Latin American political thought is an open and inviting field for the entrepreneurial scholar; emphatically, there is much to be done and learned.

Viewed across the temporal sweep of the nineteenth and twentieth centuries, Latin American political thought comes to us in clusters and fragments. Few, if any, are the broad or general theories. Latin America has not produced her own counterparts, say, to our William Graham Sumner, John Dewey, or perhaps even Walter Lippmann. In Latin American political

---

[46] See Helen L. Clagett, *Administration of Justice in Latin America* (New York, Oceana Publications, Inc., 1952).

thought, democratic liberalism and socialism have been more enduring. These ideas, considered by many North Americans to be "leftist," have been embraced ideologically, incorporated into numerous constitutions and legal structures, and comprise ruling norms in many Latin American political systems. The political thought of most Ladinos seems definitely committed to liberal varieties of social experimentation and reform, ranging from the progressive formulations of Alberto Lleras Camargo to the violent and full-blown Márxism of Nicolás Guillén.

Perhaps the most salient fact of political thought in contemporary Latin America is that the on-paper versions of progressive thinking may never come to fruition, being open to subversion by ideological norms which control the actions of public officials. As we noted in the opening of this chapter, behavior on paper and in fact are often quite different things in Latin America. One of her greatest challenges today is to narrow this gulf, to bring about a greater congruence of prescription and practice. The expression *mucha palabra y poco hecho* (many words, few deeds) typifies the genuine cynicism with which many Ladinos view the political theorist: Everyone can agree with progressive ideas on how to achieve reform, but few people can transport them across the gulf between theory and reality. Where the span is widest, tyrants, soothsayers, vendors of the apocalyptic have entered the breach and spread havoc. Had constitutional theories been erected upon a strong base of ideological conviction, which in turn was firmly rooted in a socio-economic system geared to broad distribution of wealth and material reward, it is doubtful whether men like Porfirio Díaz, Manuel Estrada Cabrera, Marcos Pérez Jiménez, and François Duvalier would have punctuated the political development of Latin America.

On the more positive side, Latin America was blessed with a number of genuine reformist thinkers, men like Benito Juárez, Bartolomé Mitre, José Batlle y Ordóñez, and some might even argue a case for *caudillos* like Augusto B. Leguía, Alfredo Stroessner, Juan Domingo Perón, all of whom tried in one way or another to reduce the polarity of theory and practice in their country's political life. Arrayed against them were complex legions of disunifying forces, agents of political instability. For now, suffice it to conclude that the incongruity of theory and operative ideology is a basic and perplexing dilemma of contemporary Latin American political life. Many Latin American intellectuals are acutely conscious of this dilemma and are desperately seeking to correct it. Unhappily, however, the forward steps of these progressive thinkers may often be emotionally glazed over by the slings and arrows of the vendetta peddlers, who thrive amid the chaotic maelstrom of Latin America's ongoing social and economic revolution.

19 / Stability-Instability in Latin American Politics

KENNETH F. JOHNSON
BEN G. BURNETT

The ever-enlarging mountain of political literature on Latin America contains a sizable section which deals with the prevalence of instability in most of the hemisphere's polities. Any listing of events in recent Latin American history underscores the validity of such attention to the instability theme. Just since 1950, nearly thirty events, both domestic and international, of a major nature threatened the political stability of one or more of these nations:

1950   Colombia seethed with rebellion and insurgency under the dictatorship of Laureano Gómez.

1952   Popular reform triumphed in Bolivia with a near social revolution that swept Víctor Paz Estenssoro to power; in Cuba, Fulgencio Batista overturned the Prio Socarrás government by means of a *cuartelazo*.

1953   In Colombia, General Gustavo Rojas Pinilla ousted Laureano Gómez.

1954   Castillo Armas successfully invaded Guatemala from the neighboring "neutralist" territory of Honduras; military pressure led to Vargas' suicide in Brazil.

1955   Perón's long rule in Argentina ended as a result of a military revolt; the Organization of American States narrowly averted a Nicaraguan invasion of Costa Rica; Panamanian President Remón was assassinated in public.

1956   Somoza died a violent death while campaigning for re-election in Nicaragua under a contrived plebiscite; in Cuba, Fidel Castro launched his guerrilla campaign against Batista's regime.

1957   Rojas Pinilla yielded power in the face of popular pressures in Colombia; Guatemalan President Castillo Armas died from an assassin's bullet.

1958   Vice-President Nixon and his entourage were mauled during their South American tour.

1959   Batista's stranglehold on Cuba collapsed, and Fidel Castro embarked on a collision course with the United States.

1960   General Trujillo organized a crude and unsuccessful plot to murder President Betancourt of Venezuela.

1961   United States-supported invasion of the Bay of Pigs failed disastrously; the Dominican strongman, Trujillo, was assassinated.

1962   The military pushed Frondizi out of the Argentine Presidency.

1963   In the epitome of political instability, the Presidents of the Dominican Republic, Ecuador, Honduras, and Guatemala were overthrown by military coups, and violence erupted in Panama over the burning issue of the Canal Zone.

1964   The subversive designs of Cuba against Venezuela resulted in diplomatic sanctions being imposed by all member nations of the OAS except Mexico; military forces deposed Presidents Goulart of Brazil and Paz Estenssoro of Bolivia.

1965   The United States invaded the Dominican Republic.

1966   A bloodless coup installed Clemente Yerovi Indaburo as Ecuador's Chief Executive; constitutional rule in Argentina ended abruptly with the military's seizure of power.

From this summary of political instability during more than a decade and a half, one gets a broad, albeit superficial, notion of the dimensions of the phenomenon. And even then countless anomic manifestations, such as street demonstrations and insurgency activities, have not been included. Nearly all of these events were concerned in some intimate way with militarism, military rivalries, popular attacks on military dictators, assassinations, and ever present in the background was some measure of United States support for the military guardians of the *status quo*. It can surely be said that much of the political instability in contemporary Latin America can be blamed on U.S. support for military dictatorships. Yet in many cases there has appeared to be no alternative for the United States. It has been argued, and convincingly, that the United States Military Assistance Program (MAP) to Latin American nations has simply exacerbated the propensity of military establishments to intervene in their respective political systems: "This may be the hidden price tag on the anti-communist security which the United States seeks in the Western Hemisphere through the MAP."[1]

It is always tempting to see a complex phenomenon like political stability-instability in Latin America in terms of black and white. By denigrating military establishments throughout the hemisphere, however, one is likely to assume that civilian-dominated political systems—indeed, civilian-dominated security forces—in Latin America are inherently less prone to instability. The issue is a moot one among policy-makers, diplomats, and social scientists. Not wishing to enter that controversy here, we have simply raised the issue because

---

[1] John D. Powell, "Military Assistance and Militarism in Latin America," *The Western Political Quarterly*, XVIII, No. 2 (June 1965), 388. See also Martin C. Needler, "Political Development and Military Intervention in Latin America," *The American Political Science Review*, LX, No. 3 (September 1966), 616–626.

of its continuing salience and criticality in the affairs of this hemisphere's family of nations.

Another assumption that should be made explicit in an analysis of political stability-instability in Latin America is the equation of stability and democratic practices. Such an assumption is highly tenuous. As indicated above, many dictatorships guarantee a high degree of stability; that is, there are no riots, there is little violence, and business goes on placidly even though enormous socio-economic inequities exist for the masses. Superficially democratic processes may bring to power a regime that will be toppled shortly by a military coup, often with ensuing violence; Guatemala, Argentina, and Ecuador are notorious examples of this occurrence.

Which nations of Latin America are the most stable, and which are the most unstable? Are these nations also, respectively, the most democratic and undemocratic? A study published in 1961 by Russell H. Fitzgibbon and Kenneth F. Johnson may perhaps shed some light on these questions. Fitzgibbon and Johnson compared results of a survey of forty Latin American specialists with previous survey data on the status of democratic practices in the twenty Latin American nations. The experts were asked to rate the countries according to fifteen substantive criteria, which were as follows:

1. An educational level sufficient to give the political processes some substance and vitality.

2. A fairly adequate standard of living.

3. A sense of internal unity and national cohesion.

4. Belief by the people in their individual political dignity and maturity.

5. Absence of foreign domination.

6. Freedom of the press, speech, assembly, radio, etc.

7. Free and competitive elections: honestly counted votes.

8. Freedom of party organization; genuine and effective party opposition in the legislature; legislative scrutiny of the executive branch.

9. An independent judiciary and respect for its decisions.

10. Public awareness of accountability for the collection and expenditure of public funds.

11. Intelligent attitude toward social legislation and the vitality of such legislation as applied.

12. Civilian supremacy over the military.

13. Reasonable freedom of political life from the impact of ecclesiastical controls.

14. Attitude toward and development of technical, scientific, and honest governmental administration.

15. Intelligent and sympathetic administration of whatever local self-government prevails.[2]

---

[2] Based on Russell H. Fitzgibbon and Kenneth F. Johnson, "Measurement of Latin American Political Change," *American Political Science Review,* CV, No. 3 (September 1961), 515–526.

TABLE 1

Correlates of Democracy in Latin America

	1945	1960
Uruguay	1	1
Costa Rica	2	2
Chile	3	3
Colombia	4	6
Argentina	5	4
Cuba	6	15
Mexico	7	5
Panama	8	11
Venezuela	9	8
Peru	10	9
Brazil	11	7
Guatemala	12	13
El Salvador	13	12
Ecuador	14	10
Nicaragua	15	17
Haiti	16	19
Honduras	17	14
Bolivia	18	16
Dominican Republic	19	18
Paraguay	20	20

Spearman Rank Correlation Coefficient: Rho = .88
Significant
at <.01

Table 1 shows the result of a rank order correlation of the countries' ratings, according to composite scores for the fifteen criteria, for the twenty Latin American nations as viewed by the experts in 1945 and 1960. The statistic Rho gives us a .88 correlation that is highly significant in terms of probability and tells us, in effect, that during that fifteen-year period, there was a very strong tendency for the most democratic, and the least democratic, nations to remain that way (assuming, of course, one is prepared to accept the testimony of forty experts in support of the contention). The nation whose image changed (in this case deteriorated) most radically was Cuba, unquestionably as a result of the combined impact of Batista and Castro.

For the first question posed above, whether democracy tends to correlate with political stability, our data, except for the cases of Uruguay, Costa Rica, and Chile, would suggest a qualified no. Because of the nature of ongoing internal events in each of the twenty Republics (notwithstanding the ostensible stability, that is, longevity, of governing regimes), prominent exceptions can be cited to the contention that the most democratic nations are also the most stable. Colombia, Argentina, and Cuba have been plagued with chronic instability for the reasons of, respectively, internal civil war, military coups, and violent social revolution. Peru, Brazil, and Guatemala are rated as moderately democratic but are also chronically unstable for the reasons of, respectively, indigenous social cleavage and insurgent warfare, military dominance of the political system, and military dominance coupled with indigenous social cleavage and insurgent warfare. Toward the bottom of the democracy ratings, the seven nations from Ecuador to Paraguay changed position only slightly over the fifteen-year period, and the consensus is that they are generally undemocratic nations. Ecuador, Honduras, Bolivia, and the Dominican Republic are clearly unstable political systems as a result of military dominance and coups and thus support the contention that instability goes along with the absence of democratic practices. But Nicaragua, Haiti, and Paraguay, all of which have highly undemocratic political systems, are nonetheless among the most stable in Latin America, at least ostensibly in terms of the absence of violent social cleavage and the relative permanence of the recent governments.

Therefore, where Latin American political systems are concerned, stability-instability is a continuum concept that is relative to a number of subfactors or causal factors which underlie many superficial events and appearances. Let us briefly consider some of these causal factors.

STABILITY-INSTABILITY AS AN INTERACTION SYSTEM[3]

Political instability occurs when the governing institutions of organized society are ineffective in gratifying popular wants and expectations. In that sense, governments are "maximizers," sending out streams of satisfactions. Failure of governments to gratify popular wants leads to political alienation in varying degrees of intensity. Alienation, in turn, is not a fixed quality but varies according to a number of causal factors. Political alienation may be defined as a deeply felt resentment toward social and governing institutions which is so intense as to be manifested in happenings which contribute to political instability. Political instability, accordingly, is defined as a state of conflict between governments and competing power groups which is characterized by overt acts of violence, by support for extreme political radicalism, or by apathy in the face of movements which are committed to extreme,

---

[3] This section is based on Kenneth F. Johnson, "Causal Factors in Latin American Political Instability," *Western Political Quarterly*, XVII, No. 3 (September 1964), *passim*. A stimulating discussion of the same theme is found in John D. Martz, "The Place of Latin America in the Study of Comparative Politics," *Journal of Politics*, XXVIII, No. 1 (February 1966), 57–80.

radical, or violent dislocations of the *status quo*. Thus, political alienation is seen as a widely shared attitude-potential, and instability is viewed as those phenomena proceeding from political alienation.

Since both political alienation and instability are dependent variables of a number of causal factors, an elaboration of these factors as an influence set becomes critical for a theory of political instability in Latin America. These causal factors exhibit varying intensities throughout time and occasionally approach thresholds of criticalness insofar as the causative aspects of stability-instability are concerned. It should thus be possible to develop fairly precise indicators (or thresholds) of criticalness for each of the major causal factors in the instability system.

Causal factors in Latin American political instability can be viewed as forces in a circular, or self-reinforcing, system. Their cumulative effect is a barrier to the drives of Latin American nations toward economic development and political stability. As a result of low socio-economic development, maldistribution of wealth reaches critical levels; frustration of socio-economic mobility expectations is widespread and produces popular and elite alienation, disaffection, and outright aggression toward the State.

Political instability in Latin America results from the circular interaction of three general categories of factors: (1) entrepreneurial deficiencies, which include passive and flight capital, social values and cultural influences, religious institutions, illiteracy; (2) high degrees of role substitutability among politically relevant performance entities; and (3) accelerated urbanization and overpopulation.

Entrepreneurial Deficiencies

As a human dynamic, entrepreneurship is defined as the function of perceiving and effectuating new combinations of factors of production in order to take advantage of existing or anticipated market situations. The commercial entrepreneur deals in ideas, supported by capital from credit or familial sources, in such a way as to realize a marginal profit. Governmental entrepreneurship relates largely to leadership expertise in problem-solving through public policy and administration. Both entrepreneurial forms require available active capital for effective functioning. The relative absence of entrepreneurship accounts for much of Latin America's backwardness and contributes to political instability.

Chronic in all underdeveloped countries is illiteracy, a tremendous entrepreneurial deficiency, which has been abundantly treated in the literature on Latin American political change and, requiring no further elaboration here, will be passed over in preference for other factors.

Social attitudes and values act to inhibit entrepreneurial growth in Latin America. Throughout the area is a general lack of individual preparedness to take big financial risks in order to capture lucrative gains. Although many Latin Americans are willing to invest in stocks, bonds, mutual funds, and securities, the majority of investors prefer something safer, such as land or independently issued credit at high rates of interest. One frequently hears stories of private money caches both great and small, and according to informal reports, one would expect fairly impressive sums to appear if all of these passive investors were to declare their resources.

Because a genuinely competitive and collaborative spirit is lacking, Latin Americans are suspicious of impersonal institutions which control and allocate capital. Investors prefer to keep their funds out of banks and government-sponsored lending institutions, where those funds might otherwise be available for entrepreneurial use as development capital. Reluctance to mobilize capital for entrepreneurship accompanies failure to achieve volume marketing conditions through increased unit output. There seems to be an ingrained notion that it is better to sell a few items at a high price than to improve one's total income through promotion of volume sales at a reduced price. Another entrepreneurial deficiency lies in the problem of excessive centralization of decision-making where allocation of credit for commercial development is concerned.

Still a further barrier to effective entrepreneurship is found in Latin American religious institutions. The general proposition may be made that the Roman Catholic ethic, being preoccupied with achieving and preserving grace in the sight of God, discourages the vigorous competitive spirit needed for accomplishment within an entrepreneurial value hierarchy. Besides Roman Catholicism, anthropologists have noted in certain Indian societies value systems which discourage capital formation for other than ceremonial purposes. The Maya Indians of Mexico and Guatemala accumulate capital for annual religious displays, which wipe out family savings.

Ultimately, in the deep recesses of Latin American culture, one comes to the inescapable conclusion that collusion rather than collaboration is the dominant characteristic of human enterprise. The absence of a truly collaborative spirit is an enormous entrepreneurial deficiency which Latin America cannot easily overcome.

Entrepreneurial deficiencies constitute a market imperfection which allows capital to flow into passive rather than active forms. The process is circular and jointly affects the public and private sectors of the economy. Exploitive tributary taxation and corrupt fiscal allocation by governments discourage private investment and capital formation. Public fiscal dishonesty inspires nonpayment of taxes and wastes much of whatever funds are collected. Accumulated capital is hoarded or invested in ritual and prestige items or in usurious investments with proceeds concealed from taxation or exported abroad. Public treasuries are thus impoverished, and public services remain at low levels. Controlling value systems sustain corrupt public officials and inhibit adoption of policies aimed at socio-economic betterment. Low entrepreneurial growth means that Latin American economies cannot absorb rapid population increase without hardship. Frustration of mobility expectations is therefore widespread and dictates to political alienation and instability.

Role Substitutability Among Politically Relevant Performance Entities

The prevailing lack of role specializations and interdependence among performance entities in Latin America is a continuing invitation to armies and government bureaucracies to usurp each other in a power grab. Similarly, the failure of Latin American universities to become specialized seats of learning has relegated student groups to extreme and radical political roles. The same may be said for trade unions which, in countries such as Bolivia, Venezuela, and Argentina, constitute veritable political parties in themselves and are frequently embroiled in extreme acts, which contribute to political instability.

The apparent ease with which performance entities have usurped each other in Latin America can be partly explained in terms of the relative absence of social pluralism within that political culture. Involving as it does a multiplicity of overlapping group memberships, social pluralism has a decidedly moderating effect upon political behavior; one's performance in a given membership context is certain to have restraint implications for other memberships as well.

Because of the relative lack of social pluralism in Latin America, performance entities become psychologically compartmentalized and politically semiautonomous. Vocational roles tend to circumscribe social attitudes and political attachments. Armies, bureaucracies, and legislatures, are found each with its own highly subjective *élan vital,* an aggressive expansionist force marked by the all-consuming lust for control and easily infused with a moral purpose to justify intrusion upon other roles. For many Latin Americans, a career in the army or government bureaucracy is the only way to socioeconomic mobility. The conscious and openly felt ubiquitousness of armies, bureaucracies, and legislatures therefore allows a substitutability of functional roles which has little rational justification but which can be accomplished by force. United States aid programs such as MAP are prominent underlying factors in this process.

Urbanization and Overpopulation

During the past several decades, urbanization in Latin America has taken on proportions of acute social change. Rural-to-urban migratory patterns complicate efforts to promote urban economic growth and to stimulate new agrarian entrepreneurship. Displaced peasants seek welfare and opportunity in great cities. Frustration of these people's expectations produces alienation, and thus urbanization exacerbates existing symptoms of political instability.

Causes of Latin America's accelerated urbanization, which eventually aggravates political instability, are the following: (1) Urban industrialization and the promise of a better life lures unemployed groups from the country; (2) exploitation of rural workers by *latifundistas* forces exodus, as does material impoverishment of *minifundistas;* (3) terror and violence perpetuated by bandit groups, especially in Colombia, Venezuela, and Peru, make rural life unbearable; (4) certain legal structures promote social and economic development of a capital or central city at the expense of the rest of the country; (5) many peasants are motivated to leave their farms because of exploitation by the bureaucracy of an agrarian reform program; and (6) in at least one country, Colombia, there is specific evidence that service in the military brings many young peasants into the city who are unwilling to return to an agrarian life upon completion of their duty. These motivational factors for rural-to-urban migration are relevant for the majority of Latin American nations. Urbanization has brought increased demands upon governments and socio-economic systems for accommodation of the expanding work force. Because of the entrepreneurial deficiencies discussed earlier, popular expectations for achievement and mobility are frustrated, and this frustration leads to political alienation and instability.

A concomitant of urbanization has been overpopulation in both urban and rural areas. Though government programs of disease control have sharply reduced infant mortality throughout Latin America, urbanization has not produced a significant decline in overall fertility rates. While rural populations have continued to grow, rural food production has not always kept pace with urban needs. This discrepancy keeps food prices high and militates against the already depressed and alienated social sectors. Migrants to the cities find that large families are no longer the asset they might have been in the country, as family incomes are dissipated by nonproducing members, who continue to consume. With children under fifteen years of age making up nearly fifty percent of Latin America's total population, the need to provide for these dependents heavily burdens the head of a household. He is at a major disadvantage in seeking to improve his level of living through accumulation of capital for investment or for family emergency.

As Latin American overpopulation continues, pressure mounts upon the already inadequate rural land and thus forces more and more people into the great cities, where entrepreneurial deficiencies make it doubtful that the wants of those people will be gratified. Growing popular frustration and alienation are manifest in popular support for aggressive radical movements which voice mistrust of government and hatred for the dominant classes.[4] At this point, opportunities for usurpation of governing roles may be seized upon by armies, bureaucracies, or other power groupings, and political instability moves across the continuum from latent to overt.

THE PRICE OF STABILITY

On the other side of the coin, stability may exist in a given polity when individuals and groups obey the established government. Such obedience obtains because (1) it does not occur to them to do anything else; (2) they have no power to change things; (3) the system gratifies needs they feel; or

---

[4] This theme is prominent throughout Oscar Lewis' study of the slums in Mexico City, *The Children of Sánchez* (New York, Random House, 1961).

(4) they believe it right to do so, even when they feel that they are not receiving any perceptible benefits through obedience.[5]

Obviously political regimes seek stability if only to keep themselves in power. And, unquestionably, a more or less stable political environment is essential if government is to provide basic services, offer direction to overall planning, and permit economic and social enterprises to get on with their normal pursuits.

However, stability may not necessarily always be a good thing in itself. As has been noted, Haiti represents one nation where stability has marked the political system for a number of years, but the existing Duvalier administration surely ranks as one of the world's most brutal dictatorships, and "Papa Doc's" seemingly maniacal behavior has stultified the social system— education, for example—and has all but bankrupted the economy. Trujillo in the Dominican Republic and the Somozas, who are still in Nicaragua, maintained stable political systems for decades and brought some economic benefits to certain segments of the population but all the while piled up massive fortunes, which drained the economies of capital that could have been better used to refurbish the economic system and open the nation's economic resources to a much wider percentage of the population. Similar episodes have been chronicled in the past and persist in the present in numerous other Republics in Latin America.

At times internal forces combine to ensure stability—as in the hegemony enjoyed by the traditional triarchy of Church-army-aristocracy, or in contemporary Brazil and Argentina, where the military's coercive force needed little help from other social groups in order to seize power and hold sway over national fortunes.

In many other instances, external forces have left an indelible imprint on several of the Latin American countries. Here, the role of the United States in private and public capacities stands out. Private U.S. investment has had its impact in most of Latin America and has, in the weaker polities especially, often buttressed conservative regimes sympathetic to such outside capital. U.S. military intervention in Nicaragua, Haiti, and the Dominican Republic undoubtedly helped to underwrite stability, but under durable dictatorial regimes. It can no longer be denied that money and agents from the U.S. were vital instruments in overturning the Arbenz Government of Guatemala in 1954 (as well as being participators in some less successful undertakings) only to install one more conservative executive and to halt a decade of revolution (in which Communists were significantly involved during its last years) without offering any reformist substitute. Indeed, the widespread intrusion of the U.S. Government in Latin American affairs is conducive to a pervasive belief among many if not most Latin Americans that U.S. foreign policy rests almost totally upon supporting conservative governments

---

[5] Martin Needler, "Stability, Instability, and Evolutionary Change: The Case of Latin America," paper presented to the Western Political Science Association meeting in Victoria, B.C., March 17–20, 1965.

whenever and wherever it can. Order, not reform, is the guiding purpose. Thus, it was widely held at the time that the Central Intelligence Agency organized the Brazilian military coup in 1964. An even more exaggerated form of this general attitude can be seen in a rumor widely circulated in Chile in 1964 that the C.I.A. controlled the Argentine army, which, poised on the frontier, was ready to invade Chile and seize power if the Socialist-Communist coalition should win the presidential election. Whatever the merits or absurdity of such rumors, United States government actions in Guatemala in 1954, in Cuba in 1961, and in the Dominican Republic in 1965 reinforce such beliefs.

Aside from the dictatorships and conservative, semiauthoritarian political systems, some questions can also be raised about the stable democracies. For example, Chile rates, through most of the past half-century, as a generally open society with a considerable respect for the freedom of the individual, for the prevalence of a rule of law, and for the maintenance of an orderly succession of Presidents. Stability has rarely been seriously threatened. And yet, at least before 1965, the political system almost totally failed to respond to the needs of the massive segment of urban and rural poor. The Alessandri era did strengthen the middle sectors, and Aguirre Cerda's brief Popular Front government gave additional attention to middle groups and aroused some hope among organized labor. But in the aggregate, a rather close-knit oligarchy of upper and upper-middle segments of the population have dominated scarce economic and political resources to the continuing disadvantage of the impoverished masses. The heavy vote going to the Socialist-Communist presidential candidate in 1958 and in 1964 served as an indicator of deep alienation and a demand for change, as did the nature of much of Eduardo Frei's support in 1964.

Thus, relative stability in Chile, as well as in certain other democracies and near-democracies, appears to have failed to provide the kind of an environment in which mass needs can be satisfactorily answered—though contemporary reformers in Chile, Venezuela, and Peru may offer some hopeful signs for enlargement of and more equalization of the control of economic and political resources. In short, while almost any observer of the Latin American scene can condemn stability of the Haitian sort as lacking in any redeeming virtue whatsoever, millions of people in an orderly polity of the Chilean sort argue against political niceties in a sea of socio-economic deprivation.

THE PROBABILITY OF STABILITY IN LATIN AMERICA

Many social scientists who study contemporary Latin America have infused their researches with a generic and highly subjective value assumption, that the coming of "modernity" implies as well the coming of political democracy and stability. In an excellent conceptual analysis of the problems of underdeveloped nations, Fred W. Riggs has urged that we challenge this assumption and suggests instead that instability is perhaps a permanent feature of "modernity" in some parts of the contemporary world. We should be prepared for the possibility that this may in fact be the case in Latin America.

Riggs' concept of the "prismatic society" is designed to accommodate this eventuality. A component of his formulation that goes far toward summarizing what may well be the nub of Latin American political instability is in his coined term the "clect." The clect is a ruling or controlling group whose roots reflect broad social cleavages—a sort of governing council, whose members have mutually incompatible aspirations and requirements. In the language of game theory, the members of a clect have interests that represent something of a "zero-sum game"; they are inversely correlated with each other. Thus, compromise is difficult if not impossible because satisfaction of one set of aspirations is usually accomplished at the expense of others. All may be prominent in the given structure of power. Specifically, Riggs writes,

> So long as each clect is busily seeking privileges for members of its community and opposing the extension of similar privileges to members of hostile communities, the underlying hostilities and fears which prevent assimilation into a single national community are deepened.[6]

This statement is a social, economic, and psychological fact that underlies much of Latin America's chronic political instability. A native Latin American, the Argentine sociologist José Luís de Imaz, has said, in a remark akin to that of Riggs,

> But the term "managerial elite" . . . [means] . . . the existence of a group of individuals who concertedly manage the community; they direct it toward specific ends, within reach of certain attainments, governing by normative standards that are more or less the same. This is what we fail to see in our own case. In this sense, Argentina does not have a "managerial elite." This is true notwithstanding that there may be a plurality of individuals who "command."[7]

Combining the two points of view into one, we might say that in Latin America today there are many powers and forces that give commands and make demands upon the political system, but there are few who really seek to govern.

If this psychological basis for Latin American politics continues to prevail, there is every reason to think that instability will prevail along with it. The ethic of the conquistadores championed an exaggerated primacy of individual values. Rosas, Díaz, and Trujillo plundered, killed, and died for it. At the turn of the twentieth century, José Enrique Rodó dedicated his *Ariel* to the

---

[6] Fred W. Riggs, *Administration in Developing Countries: The Theory of Prismatic Society* (Boston, Houghton Mifflin, 1964), p. 172.

[7] José Luís de Imaz, *Los que mandan* (Buenos Aires, Editorial Universitaria, 1964), p. 236. The original reads: "Pero el término 'elite dirigente' . . . [significa] . . . la existencia de un grupo de individuos que concertadamente conduzca a la comunidad, la dirija en vista a la obtención de determinados fines, al alcance de ciertos logros, se dirija por marcos normativos más o menos similares, eso es lo que no se percibe en nuestro caso. En este sentido, en la Argentina no hay una 'elite' dirigente. Aunque hay una pluralidad de individuos que 'manden.' "

downfall of such materialism but succeeded instead in becoming a *raisonneur* for other and equally extreme motives for exploitive individualism. Well into the twentieth century, Rodó's legacy is perhaps mirrored, albeit faintly, in the existentialism of Octavio Paz, whose *El laberinto de la soledad* yields psychological insight into why Latin America is characterized more by a "plurality of individuals" (as in the quote above from Imaz) than by what we in the United States recognize as a stabilizing social pluralism. That is the dilemma of the forces which shape Latin America's quest for political stability, if indeed there is a quest at all.

Glossary

abolengo distinguished family heritage

afuerino migratory worker

aguardiente a strong liquor

alcalde mayor local Spanish colonial official

alternación agreement between Colombia's Conservative and Liberal political parties to alternate control of the nation's presidency beginning in 1958

amparo a type of legal writ or remedy normally called *juicio de amparo*

audiencia an administrative and judicial subdivision of colonial New Spain

ayllú a Peruvian collective farm among the Quechua Indians

bachillerato high school diploma

barriada urban slum

barrio normally means neighborhood

Bogotazo an extended period of anarchy in Colombia that was precipitated by the assassination of Jorge Eliécer Gaitán in April 1948

botella "soft job"

bracero a contractual migratory Mexican laborer in the United States

campesino normally means peasant, but may mean "countryman" or farmer in a more honorific context

cantegril urban slum

carabineros police

casas brujas urban slum

caudillo the stereotyped Latin American strongman on horseback or army-backed dictator

chafarote a derogatory reference to a military man's lack of intelligence and crude manners

chef de section Haitian rural police officer

cholo person of mixed ethnic background or of mixed cultures

chombo   West Indian Negro living in Panama

Científicos   the "brain trust" of Mexican dictator Porfirio Díaz

coima   corruption or, as in Argentina, a bribe

compadrazgo   the extended family system of godparents

continuismo   the practice of succeeding oneself in office either directly in person or via puppet appointees who are often called *incondicionales*

conventillo   urban slum

convivencia   political agreement between Peruvian President Prado and the *Apristas*

co-participacion   political party agreement whereby the minority party shares in governing

corregidor   Spanish Colonial governor

corregimiento   governmental subdivision of a municipality

criollo   historically, a Spaniard born in Latin America; now refers to natives generally

Cristeros   Mexican pro-clericals who fought the anti-Church measures of Presidents Calles and Obregón during the 1920s

cuartelazo   barracks-based effort to seize political power

designado   official elected by Congress to succeed to presidency on the vacancy of that office

ejido   the Mexican system of state-supported collective farms

encomienda   a colonial land grant including limited rights to forced Indian labor

estancia   ranch

estanciero   rancher

favela   urban slum

favelado   slum dweller

finica or **fundo**   farm

fuero   special Church privilege

gachupín   Spaniard from the mother country

gente baja   the "common" or lower class people

gente decente   refined or "decent" people, often means upper class

gobernador   governor

golpe de estado   an illicit overthrow of a government with or without force; coup d'état

grand don   wealthy Haitian peasant

gremio   professional or occupational association

gros habitant   large landholders who are Haitian community leaders

Guardia Nacional   designation for the armed forces in several Latin American countries

hombres de Macias   protagonists of Mariano Azuela's novel of the Mexican Revolution *Los de Abajo*

inquilino   tenant farmer

intendente   official representative of the Spanish monarch in colonial America beginning late in the eighteenth century; he held wide administrative and judicial powers

jefe máximo   colloquial reference to the (perhaps charismatic) leader of a party or group

latifundista   great landowner

lema   political party electoral list

ley de hacienda   treasury law

ley fuga   an excuse for shooting hostages used during the *porfiriato* in Mexico

Ley Juárez   an integral part of the Mexican anti-clerical reform in the 1850s

Ley Lerdo   an integral part of the Mexican anti-clerical reform in the 1850s

libreta electoral   electoral identification card

mandamiento   land relationship whereby an Indian agrees to work out an advance payment from the landlord

masombo   Brazilian term for a European born in the New World; creole

mazorca   secret police

mediero   sharecropper

mezcal   a strong cactus liquor typical of Mexico

milimetria   Colombian President Valencia's practice of allocating government posts proportionate to the partisan composition of the Frente

minifundia   small (usually inefficient) landholding

montuvio   person of mixed ethnic background

mordida   corrupt practice of bribery

municipio   municipal subdivision normally combining the United States concepts of city and county

muñeca   governmental favoritism or "pull"

Oficina de Control Político   Bolivian secret police

Oriental   Uruguayan citizen

paridad   a parity type of agreement, especially in Colombia, in which two principal parties agree to divide power between themselves so long as they are able to present a winning ticket in popular elections

Patria Nueva   Peruvian President Leguía's social concept of the New Fatherland

patrón   may mean a landowner, or employer generally, or some sort of sponsor; "boss"

patronato nacional   authority of a nation's President to fill high Church appointments

peninsular   a person born on the Iberian Peninsula, either in Spain or Portugal

peón   serf, peasant, lower class salaried worker

pituco   newly wealthy man

población callampa   "mushroom settlement" or urban slum

pongueaje   compulsory personal service Indians must perform for landlords

porfiriato   the long dictatorship of Porfirio Díaz in Mexico

pulpería   general store

rancherío   rural shanty town

Reforma   the anti-clerical and anti-latifundia campaign in Mexico during the 1850s

regimiento   smallest administrative subdivision of a Panamanian municipality

repartimiento   colonial institution of forced Indian labor on landed estates

rurales   mercenary rural police who maintained order by terror during Porfirian Mexico

sertanejo   one who dwells in Brazilian backlands

sertão   Brazilian backlands

sublema   party faction, or sub-party, which offers its own electoral list

teniente político   local governmental official

Ton-Ton Macoute   "Uncle Bogeyman"; Haitian Dictator Duvalier's special police

unión de facto   marriage lacking a civil contract or Church vows

vodun houngan   Haitian voodoo priest

Selected Bibliography
Of Works in English

GENERAL WORKS

Adams, Mildred, ed. *Latin America: Evolution or Explosion.* New York: Dodd, Mead & Co., 1963.

Adams, Richard, and others. *Social Change in Latin America Today.* New York: Harper & Row, Publishers, Inc., 1960.

Alexander, Robert. *Communism in Latin America.* New Brunswick: Rutgers University Press, 1957.

————. *Prophets of the Revolution: Profiles of Latin American Leaders.* New York: The Macmillan Company, 1962.

————. *Today's Latin America.* Garden City: Doubleday and Co., Inc., 1962.

————, and Charles O. Porter. *The Struggle for Democracy in Latin America.* New York: The Macmillan Company, 1961.

Anderson, Charles W. *Politics and Economic Change in Latin America.* Princeton: D. Van Nostrand Company, Inc., 1967.

Blanksten, George. "The Politics of Latin America," in *The Politics of the Developing Areas,* ed. Gabriel A. Almond and James S. Coleman. Princeton: Princeton University Press, 1960.

Burr, Robert, ed. "Latin America's Nationalistic Revolutions," *Annals,* 334 (March 1961).

Busey, James L. *Latin America: Political Institutions and Processes.* New York: Random House, Inc., 1964.

Christensen, Asher N., ed. *The Evolution of Latin American Government: A Book of Readings.* New York: Holt, Rinehart and Winston, Inc., 1951.

Clagett, Helen L. *Administration of Justice in Latin America.* New York: Oceana Publications, Inc., 1952.

Crawford, W. Rex. *A Century of Latin American Thought.* Cambridge: Harvard University Press, 1944.

D'Antonio, William V. and Frederick B. Pike, eds. *Religion, Revolution, and Reform.* New York: Frederick A. Praeger, Inc., 1964.

Davis, Harold, ed. *Government and Politics in Latin America.* New York: The Ronald Press Company, 1958.

————. *Latin American Social Thought.* Washington, D.C.: University Press of Washington, D.C., 1963.

Edelmann, Alexander T. *Latin American Government and Politics.* Homewood: Dorsey Press, Inc., 1965.

Fitzgibbon, Russell H., ed. *The Constitutions of the Americas.* Chicago: University of Chicago Press, 1948.

————. "Political Theory vs. Practice," in *The Caribbean: Its Political Problems,* A. Curtis Wilgus, ed. Gainesville: University of Florida Press, 1956.

Gerassi, John. *The Great Fear in Latin America.* New York: Collier Books, 1965.

Gómez, R. A. *Government and Politics in Latin America.* New York: Random House, Inc., 1964.

Hirschman, Albert O. *Journeys Toward Progress.* New York: Twentieth Century Fund, 1963.

————, ed. *Latin American Issues: Essays and Comments.* New York: Twentieth Century Fund, 1961.

Johnson, John J., ed. *Continuity and Change in Latin America.* Stanford: Stanford University Press, 1964.

————. *The Military and Society in Latin America.* Stanford: Stanford University Press, 1964.

Jorrín, Miguel. *Governments of Latin America.* New York: D. Van Nostrand, Inc., 1953.

Lieuwen, Edwin. *Arms and Politics in Latin America.* New York: Frederick A. Praeger, Inc., 1961.

————. *Generals vs. Presidents: Neo-Militarism in Latin America.* New York: Frederick A. Praeger, Inc., 1964.

Lipset, Seymour M., and Aldo Solari, eds. *Elites in Latin America.* New York: New York University Press, 1967.

Maier, Joseph, and Richard W. Weatherhead, eds. *Politics and Change in Latin America.* New York: Frederick A. Praeger, Inc., 1964.

Martz, John. "Characteristics of Latin American Political Thought," *Journal of Inter-American Studies,* VIII, No. 1 (January 1966), 54–74.

————, ed. *The Dynamics of Change in Latin American Politics.* Englewood Cliffs: Prentice-Hall, Inc., 1965.

Masur, Gerhard. *Nationalism in Latin America: Diversity and Unity.* New York: The Macmillan Company, 1966.

Mecham, J. Lloyd. *Church and State in Latin America.* Chapel Hill: University of North Carolina Press, rev., 1965.

Needler, Martin C. *Latin American Politics in Perspective.* Princeton: D. Van Nostrand, Inc., 1963.

————, *Political Systems of Latin America.* Princeton: D. Van Nostrand, Inc., 1964.

Pierson, William and Federico G. Gil. *Governments of Latin America.* New York: McGraw-Hill Book Company, Inc., 1957.

Pierson, William W., ed. "Pathology of Democracy in Latin America: A Symposium," *American Political Science Review,* XLIV, No. 1 (March 1950), 100–49.

Pike, Frederick. *The Conflict Between Church and State in Latin America.* New York: Knopf, 1964.

Poblete Troncoso, Moisés and Ben G. Burnett. *The Rise of the Latin American Labor Movement.* New York: Bookman Associates, 1960.

Poppino, Rollie E. *International Communism in Latin America.* Glencoe: The Free Press, 1964.

Schmitt, Karl M. and David Burks. *Evolution or Chaos: Dynamics of Latin American Government and Politics.* New York: Frederick A. Praeger, Inc., 1963.

Schurz, William L. *This New World: The Civilization of Latin America.* New York: E. P. Dutton & Co., 1954.

Silvert, Kalman. *The Conflict Society: Reaction and Revolution in Latin America.* New Orleans: Hauser Press, 1961.

Snow, Peter G., ed. *Government and Politics in Latin America: A Reader.* New York: Holt, Rinehart, and Winston, Inc., 1967.

Stokes, William S. *Latin American Politics.* New York: Thomas Y. Crowell Company, 1959.

Szulc, Tad. *The Winds of Revolution: Latin America Today and Tomorrow.* New York: Frederick A. Praeger, Inc., 1963.

TePaske, John J., and Sydney N. Fisher, eds. *Explosive Forces in Latin America.* Columbus: Ohio State University Press, 1964.

Tomasek, Robert D., ed. *Latin American Politics.* Garden City: Doubleday & Company, Inc., 1966.

Veliz, Claudio, ed. *Obstacles to Change in Latin America.* London & New York: Oxford University Press, 1965.

Washington Foreign Law Society. *A Symposium on the Law of Latin America.* Washington, D.C.: George Washington University Law School, 1959.

Whitaker, Arthur P., and David C. Jordan. *Nationalism in Contemporary Latin America.* New York: The Free Press, 1966.

Zea, Leopoldo. *The Latin-American Mind,* trans. by James H. Abbott and Lowell Dunham. Norman: University of Oklahoma Press, 1963.

ARGENTINA

Alexander, Robert J. *The Perón Era.* New York: Columbia University Press, 1951.

Blanksten, George I. *Perón's Argentina.* Chicago: University of Chicago Press, 1953.

Gómez, Rosendo A. "Intervention in Argentina," *Inter-American Economic Affairs,* I, No. 3 (December 1947), 55–73.

Josephs, Ray. *Argentine Diary.* New York: Random House, Inc., 1944.

Kennedy, John J. "Accountable Government in Argentina," *Foreign Affairs,* XXXVII, No. 3 (April 1959), 453–62.

———. *Catholicism, Nationalism, and Democracy in Argentina.* Notre Dame: University of Notre Dame Press, 1958.

Macdonald, Austin F. *Government of the Argentine Republic.* New York: Thomas Y. Crowell Company, 1942.

Pendle, George. *Argentina.* London: Oxford University Press, 1955.

Potash, Robert A. "Argentine Political Parties: 1957–58," *Journal of Inter-American Studies,* I, No. 4 (October 1959), 515–24.

Potash, Robert A. "The Changing Role of the Military in Argentina," *Journal of Inter-American Studies*, III, No. 4 (October 1961), 571–78.

Rennie, Ysabel. *The Argentine Republic*. New York: The Macmillan Company, 1945.

Richmond, Leonard T. *Argentina's Third Position and Others Compared*. Buenos Aires: Acme Agency, 1949.

Romero, José Luis. *A History of Argentine Thought*. Stanford: Stanford University Press, 1963.

Rowe, James W. *The Argentine Elections of 1963*. Washington, D.C.: Institute for the Comparative Study of Political Systems, 1965.

Silvert, K. H. "The Annual Political Cycle in Argentina," *AUFS Reports*, VIII, No. 6 (December 1961).

————. "Economics, Democracy and Honesty: An Assessment of the Frondizi Regime," *AUFS Reports*, VII, No. 1 (April 1960).

Snow, Peter G. *Argentine Radicalism*. Iowa City: University of Iowa Press, 1965.

————. "Parties and Politics in Argentina: The Elections of 1962 and 1963," *Midwest Journal of Political Science*, IX, No. 1 (February 1965), 1–36.

————. "The Evolution of the Argentine Electoral System," *Parliamentary Affairs*, XVIII, No. 3 (Summer 1965), 330–36.

Weil, Felix. *Argentine Riddle*. New York: John Day Company, 1945.

Whitaker, Arthur P. "The Argentine Paradox," *Annals*, CCCXXXIV (March 1961), 103–12.

————. *Argentine Upheaval*. New York: Frederick A. Praeger, Inc., 1956.

BOLIVIA

Alexander, Robert J. *The Bolivian National Revolution*. New Brunswick: Rutgers University Press, 1958.

Andrade, Victor. *Bolivia: Problems and Promise*. Washington, D.C.: Embassy of Bolivia, [1956].

Arnade, Charles. "Bolivia's Social Revolution, 1952–59," *Journal of Inter-American Studies*, I, No. 3 (July 1959), 341–52.

————. *The Emergence of the Republic of Bolivia*. Gainesville: University of Florida Press, 1957.

Bohan, Merwin L. *Report of the United States Economic Mission to Bolivia*. MSS, Department of State Library, 1942.

Ford, Bacon & Davis, Inc. *Report Mining Industry of Bolivia*. 9 vols. La Paz: not published [copy in Library of Congress], 1955.

Galarza, Ernesto. *The Case of Bolivia*. Washington, D.C.: Inter-American Reports, No. 6, 1949.

Goodrich, Carter. *The Economic Transformation of Bolivia*. Ithaca: New York School of Industrial and Labor Relations, Cornell University, 1955.

Hewlett, John. *Like Moonlight on Snow: The Life of Simón Iturri Patiño*. New York: Robert M. McBride & Co., 1947.

International Labour Office. "Andean Indian Mission," *Industry and Labour*, X, No. 5 (September 5, 1953).

Keenleyside, H. L. *Report of the United Nations Mission of Technical Assistance to Bolivia*. New York: United Nations, 1951.

Leonard, Olen E. *Bolivia: Land, People and Institutions*. Washington, D.C.: Scarecrow Press, Inc., 1952.

Marsh, Margaret A. *The Bankers in Bolivia: A Study in American Foreign Investment*. New York: Vanguard Press, Inc., 1928.

Martin, Lois D. *Bolivia in 1956: An Analysis of Political and Economic Events*. Stanford: Stanford University, Hispanic American Studies, 1958.

Osborn, Harold. *Bolivia: Land Divided*. London: Royal Institute of International Affairs, 1958.

Patch, Richard W. "Peasantry and National Revolution: Bolivia," in K. H. Silvert, ed. *Expectant Peoples*. New York: Random House, Inc., 1963.

————. Series of *Reports* for the American Universities Field Staff.

Stokes, William S. "The Revolución Nacional! and the MNR in Bolivia," *Inter-American Economic Affairs*, XII, No. 4 (Spring 1959).

BRAZIL

Azevedo, Fernando de. *Brazilian Culture: An Introduction to the Study of Culture in Brazil*, trans. William R. Crawford. New York: The Macmillan Company, 1950.

Azevedo, Thales de. *Social Change in Brazil*. Gainesville: University of Florida Press, 1963.

Busey, James L. "Brazil's Reputation for Political Stability," *Western Political Quarterly*, XVIII, No. 4 (December 1965), 866–80.

Cardozo, Manoel. "The Brazilian Church and the New Left," *Journal of Inter-American Studies*, VI, No. 3 (July 1964), 313–21.

Cruz Costa, João. *A History of Ideas in Brazil*. Berkeley: University of California Press, 1964.

Fitzgibbon, Russell. "Federalism and Party System in Brazil," paper prepared for delivery at the 1961 annual meeting of the American Political Science Association, St. Louis, Missouri, Sheraton-Jefferson Hotel, September 6–9, 1961.

Freyre, Gilberto. *Brazil: An Interpretation*. New York: Alfred A. Knopf, Inc., 1945.

————. *New World in the Tropics*. New York: Random House, Inc., 1963.

Furtado, Celso. *The Economic Growth of Brazil: A Survey from Colonial to Modern Times*. Berkeley and Los Angeles: University of California Press, 1963.

Harris, Marvin. *Town and Country in Brazil*. New York: Columbia University Press, 1956.

Horowitz, Irving L. *Revolution in Brazil: Politics and Society in a Developing Nation*. New York: E. P. Dutton & Co., 1964.

Hutchinson, H. W. "Culture Change in Brazil: An Analytical Model," *Journal of Inter-American Studies*, VI, No. 3 (July 1964), 303–12.

Leeds, Anthony. *Brazilian Careers and Social Structure*. Austin: University of Texas Press, Institute of Latin American Studies, No. 15.

Lipson, Leslie. "Challenges to Constitutional Government: Brazil," paper prepared for delivery at the 1963 annual meeting of the American Political Science Association, New York City, Commodore Hotel, September 4–7, 1963.

Morse, Richard M. *From Community to Metropolis: A Biography of São Paulo, Brazil.* Gainesville: University of Florida Press, 1958.

Paulson, Belden. *Local Political Patterns in the Northeast: A Community Case Study.* Madison: University of Wisconsin Land Tenure Center, 1964.

Price, Robert E. *Rural Unionization in Brazil.* Madison: University of Wisconsin Land Tenure Center, 1964.

Robock, Stefan. *Brazil's Developing Northeast: A Study of Regional Planning and Foreign Aid.* Washington, D.C.: The Brookings Institute, 1963.

Schurz, William L. *Brazil: The Infinite Country.* New York: E. P. Dutton & Co., 1961.

Smith, T. Lynn. *Brazil: People and Institutions.* Baton Rouge: Louisiana State University Press, 1963.

————, and Alexander, Marchant, eds. *Brazil: Portrait of Half a Continent.* New York: Dryden, 1951.

Wagley, Charles. *An Introduction to Brazil.* New York: Columbia University Press, 1963.

Young, Jordan M. "Some Permanent Political Characteristics of Contemporary Brazil," *Journal of Inter-American Studies,* VI, No. 3 (July 1964), 287–301.

CHILE

Alexander, Robert J. *Labor Relations in Argentina, Brazil, and Chile.* New York: McGraw-Hill Book Company, Inc., 1962.

Bonilla, Frank. "The Student Federation of Chile: Fifty Years of Political Action," *Journal of Inter-American Studies,* II, No. 3 (July 1960), 311–34.

Bray, Donald W. "The Dark Side of Stability," *Studies on the Left,* IV, No. 4 (Fall 1964), 85–96.

Butland, Gilbert J. *Chile: An Outline of Its Geography, Economics, and Politics.* 3rd edition. London: Oxford University Press, 1956.

Cohen, Alvin. "Economic Change in Chile," *Latin American Monograph No. 11.* Gainesville: University of Florida Press, 1960.

Cope, Orville G. "The 1964 Presidential Election in Chile: The Politics of Change and Access," *Inter-American Economic Affairs,* XIX, No. 4 (Spring 1966), 3–29.

Cox, Isaac J. "Chile," in *Argentina, Brazil, and Chile Since Independence,* ed. A. Curtis Wilgus. Washington, D.C.: George Washington University Press, 1935, 279–414.

Daugherty, Charles H., ed. *Chile: Election Factbook.* Washington, D.C.: Institute for the Comparative Study of Political Systems, 1963.

Frei, Eduardo. "Christian Democracy in Theory and Practice," in *The Ideologies of the Developing Nations,* ed. Paul E. Sigmund, Jr. New York: Frederick A. Praeger, Inc., 1964, 308–20.

Galdames, Luis. *A History of Chile.* Chapel Hill: University of North Carolina Press, 1941.

Gil, Federico. *The Political System of Chile.* Boston: Houghton Mifflin Company, 1966.

————, and Charles J. Parrish. *The Chilean Presidential Election of September 4, 1964.* Washington, D.C.: Institute for the Comparative Study of Political Systems, 1965.

Halperin, Ernst. *Nationalism and Communism in Chile.* Cambridge: M.I.T. Press, 1965.

Hirschman, A. O. *Journeys Toward Progress.* New York: Twentieth Century Fund, 1963.

McBride, George M. *Chile: Land and Society.* New York: American Geographical Society, 1936.

Morris, James O. *Elites, Intellectuals, and Consensus.* Ithaca: Cornell University Press, 1966.

Pike, Fredrick B. *Chile and the United States, 1880–1962.* Notre Dame: University of Notre Dame Press, 1963.

Silvert, Kalman. *Chile: Yesterday and Today.* New York: Holt, Rinehart and Winston, Inc., 1965.

——. "Some Propositions on Chile," *American Universities Field Staff Report,* XI, No. 1 (January 1964), 43–57.

Snow, Peter. "The Political Party Spectrum in Chile," *South Atlantic Quarterly,* LXII, No. 4 (Autumn 1963), 474–87.

Stevenson, John R. *The Chilean Popular Front.* Philadelphia: University of Pennsylvania Press, 1942.

Subercaseaux, Benjamín. *Chile: A Geographic Extravaganza.* New York: The Macmillan Company, Inc., 1943.

Thiesenhusen, William C. *Chile's Experiments in Agrarian Reform.* Madison: University of Wisconsin Press, 1966.

COLOMBIA

Bernstein, Harry. *Venezuela and Colombia.* Englewood Cliffs: Prentice-Hall, Inc., 1964.

Fals-Borda, Orlando. *Peasant Society in the Colombian Andes.* Gainesville: University of Florida Press, 1955.

Fluharty, Vernon L. *Dance of the Millions.* Pittsburgh: University of Pittsburgh Press, 1957.

Galbraith, W. O. *Colombia: A General Survey.* London: Royal Institute of International Affairs, 1953.

Gibson, William M. *The Constitutions of Colombia.* Durham: Duke University Press, 1948.

Helguera, J. León. "The Changing Role of the Military in Colombia," *Journal of Inter-American Studies,* III, No. 3 (July 1961), 351–58.

Holt, Pat M. *Colombia Today And Tomorrow.* New York: Frederick A. Praeger, Inc., 1964.

Hunter, John M. *Emerging Colombia.* Washington, D.C.: Public Affairs Press, 1962.

Johnson, Kenneth F. "Political Radicalism in Colombia: Electoral Dynamics of 1962 and 1964," *Journal of Inter-American Studies,* VII, No. 1 (January 1965), 15–26.

Martz, John. *Colombia: A Contemporary Political Survey.* Chapel Hill: University of North Carolina Press, 1962.

——. "Political Parties in Colombia and Venezuela: Contrasts in Substance and Style," *Western Political Quarterly,* XVIII, No. 2, Part I (June 1965), 318–33.

Wilgus, A. Curtis, ed. *The Caribbean: Contemporary Colombia*. Gainesville: University of Florida Press, 1962.

COSTA RICA[1]

Biesanz, John and Mavis. *Costa Rican Life*. New York: Columbia University Press, 1944.

Busey, James L. "Foundations of Political Contrast: Costa Rica and Nicaragua," *Western Political Quarterly*, XI, No. 3 (September 1958), 627–59.

————. *Notes on Costa Rican Democracy*. Boulder: University of Colorado Press, 1962.

————. "The Presidents of Costa Rica," *The Americas*, XVIII (July 1961), 55–70.

Costa Rica Election Factbook. Washington, D.C.: Institute for the Comparative Study of Political Systems, 1966.

Goldrich, Daniel. *Sons of the Establishment: Elite Youth in Panama and Costa Rica*. Chicago: Rand McNally & Co., 1966.

Jones, Chester L. *Costa Rica and Civilization in the Caribbean*. Madison: University of Wisconsin Press, 1935.

Kantor, Harry. *The Costa Rican Election of 1953: A Case Study*. Gainesville: University of Florida Press, 1958.

Loomis, Charles P., and others. *Turrialba*. New York: The Free Press, 1953.

Sariola, Sakari. *Social Class and Social Mobility in a Costa Rican Town*. Turrialba, Costa Rica: Inter-American Institute of Agricultural Sciences, 1954.

Wagner, Philip L. *Nicoya, A Cultural Geography*. Berkeley and Los Angeles: University of California Press, 1958.

CUBA[2]

Burks, David D. *Cuba Under Castro*. New York: Foreign Policy Association, 1964.

Chapman, Charles E. *A History of the Cuban Republic: A Study in Hispanic American Diplomacy*. New York: The Macmillan Company, 1927.

Draper, Theodore. *Castroism: Theory and Practice*. New York: Frederick A. Praeger, Inc., 1965.

————. *Castro's Revolution: Myths and Realities*. New York: Frederick A. Praeger, Inc., 1962.

Fitzgibbon, Russell H. *Cuba and the United States, 1900–1935*. New York: Russell and Russell, Publishers, 1964.

James, Daniel. *Cuba: The First Soviet Satellite in the Americas*. New York: Avon Books, 1961.

International Bank for Reconstruction and Development. *Report on Cuba*. Baltimore: Johns Hopkins Press, 1951.

MacGaffey, Wyatt, and Clifford R. Barnett. *Cuba: Its People, Its Society, Its Culture*. New Haven: Human Relations Area Files Press, 1962; and re-

---

[1] This country is also discussed in general works on Central America listed under Guatemala.

[2] This country is also discussed in general works on the West Indies listed under the **Dominican Republic**.

published as *Twentieth Century Cuba: The Background of the Castro Revolution.* Garden City, New York: Anchor Books, 1965.

Nelson, Lowry. *Rural Cuba.* Minneapolis: University of Minnesota Press, 1950.

Phillips, Ruby Hart. *Cuba: Island of Paradox.* New York: McDowell, Obolensky, 1959.

Seers, Dudley, and others. *Cuba: The Economic and Social Revolution.* Chapel Hill: University of North Carolina Press, 1964.

Smith, Robert F. *Background to Revolution: The Development of Modern Cuba.* New York: Alfred A. Knopf, Inc., 1966.

————. *The United States and Cuba: Business and Diplomacy, 1917–1960.* New York: Bookman Associates, 1960.

Stokes, William S. "The Cuban Parliamentary System in Action, 1940–1947," *Journal of Politics,* II (May 1949), 339–364.

————. "The 'Cuban Revolution' and the Presidential Elections of 1948," *The Hispanic American Historical Review,* XXXI, No. 1, Part I (February 1951), 37–39.

————. "National and Local Violence in Cuban Politics," *Southwestern Social Science Quarterly,* XXXIV (September 1953), 57–63.

DOMINICAN REPUBLIC

Alexander, R. J. "After Trujillo What?", *New Leader,* XLIV (June 12, 1961), 3–4.

Anonymous. *Dominican Republic, a Study in the New Imperialism.* New York: Institute for International Labor Research, 1965.

Bosch, Juan. *The Unfinished Experiment, Democracy in the Dominican Republic.* New York: Frederick A. Praeger, Inc., 1965.

Crassweller, Robert D. *Trujillo: The Life and Times of a Caribbean Dictator.* New York: The Macmillan Company, 1966.

Fagg, John E. *Cuba, Haiti, and the Dominican Republic.* Englewood Cliffs: Prentice-Hall, Inc., 1965.

Goldwert, Marvin. *The Constabulary in the Dominican Republic and Nicaragua, Progeny and Legacy of United States Intervention.* Gainesville: University of Florida Press, 1962.

Kelsey, Carl. "The American Intervention in Haiti and the Dominican Republic," *Annals of the American Academy of Political and Social Science,* C (March 1922), pp. 166–199.

Knight, Melvin M. *The Americans in Santo Domingo.* New York: Vanguard Press, Inc., 1928.

Martin, John Bartlow. *Overtaken by Events: The Dominican Crisis from the Fall of Trujillo to the Civil War.* New York: Doubleday & Company, 1966.

Ornes, Germán E. *Trujillo: Little Caesar of the Caribbean.* New York: Thomas Nelson & Sons, 1958.

Pearcy, G. Etzel. *The West Indian Scene.* Princeton: D. Van Nostrand, Inc., 1965.

Rodman, Selden. *Quisqueya: A History of the Dominican Republic.* Seattle: University of Washington Press, 1964.

Welles, Sumner. *Naboth's Vineyard: The Dominican Republic, 1844–1924.* New York: Hasten and Clark, Ltd., 1928.

Wiarda, Howard J. "The Politics of Civil-Military Relations in the Dominican Republic," *Journal of Inter-American Studies,* VII, No. 4 (October 1965), 465–484.

Wiarda, Howard J. "The Changing Political Orientation of the Catholic Church in the Dominican Republic," *Journal of Church and State,* VII (Spring 1965), 238–254.

ECUADOR

Blanksten, George I. *Ecuador: Constitutions and Caudillos.* Berkeley and Los Angeles: University of California Press, 1951.

Blomberg, Rolf, ed. *Ecuador: Andean Mosaic.* Stockholm: Hugo Gerber, 1952.

Clagett, Helen. *Guide to the Law and Legal Literature of Ecuador.* Washington, D.C.: Library of Congress, 1947.

Collier, John, and Aníbal Buitrón. *The Awakening Valley.* Chicago: The University of Chicago Press, 1949.

Franklin, Albert B. *Ecuador: Portrait of a People.* Garden City, N.Y.: Doubleday, Doran & Company, Inc., 1944.

Linke, Lilo. *Ecuador: Country of Contrasts.* 3rd ed. London: Oxford University Press, 1960.

Needler, Martin C. *Anatomy of a Coup d'Etat: Ecuador, 1963.* Washington, D.C.: Institute for the Comparative Study of Political Systems, 1964.

Saunders, John Van Dyke. *The People of Ecuador: A Demographic Analysis.* Latin American Monograph Series, No. 14. Gainesville: University of Florida Press, 1961.

Urbanski, Edmund S. "Ecuador's Socio-Political Mosaic," *Current History,* XLVI, No. 269 (January 1964), 19–25.

EL SALVADOR[3]

Feuerlein, Willy J. *Proposals for the Further Economic Development of El Salvador.* New York: United Nations, 1954.

Hoselitz, Berthold F. *Industrial Development of El Salvador.* New York: United Nations, 1954.

Osborne, Lilly de Jongh. *Four Keys to El Salvador.* New York: Funk & Wagnalls Co., 1956.

Turner, George P. *An Analysis of the Economy of El Salvador, April 1961.* Los Angeles: [Limited ed.], 1961.

Vogt, William. *The Population of El Salvador and Its Natural Resources.* Washington, D.C.: Pan American Union, 1946.

Wallich, Henry C., and others. *Public Finance in a Developing Country: El Salvador—A Case Study.* Cambridge: Harvard University Press, 1951.

GUATEMALA

Adams, Richard N. *Cultural Surveys of Panama-Nicaragua-Guatemala-El Salvador-Honduras.* Washington, D.C.: Pan American Sanitary Bureau, 1957.

---

[3] This country is also discussed in general works on Central America listed under Guatemala.

Arévalo, Juan José. *The Shark and the Sardines,* trans. by June Cobb and Raul Osequeda. New York: L. Stuart, Inc., 1961.

Holleran, Mary. *Church and State in Guatemala.* New York: Columbia University Press, 1949.

James, Daniel. *Red Design for the Americas: Guatemala Prelude.* New York: John Day Company, 1954.

Johnson, Kenneth F. *The Guatemalan Presidential Election of 1966.* Washington, D.C.: Political Systems, 1967.

Jones, Chester L. *Guatemala: Past and Present.* Minneapolis: University of Minnesota Press, 1940.

Kalijarvi, Thorsten V. *Central America: Land of Lords and Lizards.* Princeton: D. Van Nostrand, Inc., 1962.

Karnes, Thomas L. *The Failure of Union; Central America, 1824–1960.* Chapel Hill: University of North Carolina Press, 1961.

Kelsey, Vera, and Lilly de Jongh Osborne. *Four Keys to Guatemala.* New York: Thomas Y. Crowell Company, 1961.

Lipp, Solomon. "Attitudes and Opinions of Guatemalan University Students," *Sociology and Social Research,* XLIV (May–June 1960).

Martz, John D. *Central America: The Crisis and the Challenge.* Chapel Hill: University of North Carolina Press, 1959.

Munro, Dana G. *The Five Republics of Central America.* New York: Oxford University Press, 1918.

Nash, Manning. "Political Relations in Guatemala," *Social and Economic Studies,* VII (March 1958).

Parker, Franklin D. *The Central American Republics.* London and New York: Oxford University Press, 1964.

Peck, Anne M. *The Pageant of Middle American History.* London: Longmans, Green & Co., 1947.

Rodríguez, Mario. *Central America.* Englewood Cliffs: Prentice-Hall, Inc., 1965.

Rosenthal, Mario. *Guatemala: The Story of an Emergent Latin American Democracy.* New York: Twayne Publishers, 1962.

Schneider, Ronald. *Communism in Guatemala, 1944–1954.* New York: Frederick A. Praeger, Inc., 1959.

Silvert, Kalman H. *A Study in Government: Guatemala.* New Orleans: Tulane University Press, 1954.

Whetten, Nathan L. *Guatemala: The Land and the People.* New Haven: Yale University Press, 1961.

Wilgus, A. Curtis, ed. *The Caribbean: The Central American Area.* Gainesville: University of Florida Press, 1961.

HAITI[4]

Davis, Harold Palmer. *Black Democracy: The Story of Haiti.* New York: Dodge, 1936.

De Young, Maurice. "Class Parameters in Haitian Society," *Journal of Inter-American Studies,* I (October 1959), 449–458.

---

[4] This country is also discussed in general works on the West Indies listed under the Dominican Republic.

Herskovits, Melville J. *Life in a Haitian Valley*. New York: Alfred A. Knopf, Inc., 1937.

Leyburn, James G. *The Haitian People*. New Haven: Yale University Press, 1941.

McCrocklin, James H. *Garde d'Haiti, 1915–1934*. Annapolis: U.S. Naval Institute, 1956.

Manigat, L. *Haiti of the Sixties: Object of International Concern*. Washington: Center of Foreign Policy Research, 1964.

Metraux, Alfred. *Haiti: Black Peasants and Their Religion*. London: Harrap, 1960.

Millspaugh, Arthur C. *Haiti Under American Control, 1915–1930*. Boston: World Peace Foundation, 1931.

Rodman, Selden. *Haiti: The Black Republic*. New York: Devin-Adair Company, 1954.

Simpson, G. E. "Haiti's Social Structure," *American Sociological Review,* VI(1941), 640–649.

Wingfield, R., and V. J. Parenton. "Class Structure and Class Conflict in Haitian Society," *Social Forces,* XLIII (March 1965), 338–347.

HONDURAS[5]

Checchi, Vincent. *Honduras: A Problem in Economic Development*. New York: Twentieth Century Fund, 1959.

Stokes, William S. *Honduras: An Area Study in Government*. Madison: University of Wisconsin, 1950.

Tower, Frederick J. *Basic Data on the Economy of Honduras*. Washington, D.C.: U.S. Government Printing Office, 1961.

U.S. Bureau of Labor Statistics. *Labor Law and Practice in Honduras*. Washington, D.C.: U.S. Government Printing Office, 1961.

MEXICO

Brandenburg, Frank R. *The Making of Modern Mexico*. Englewood Cliffs: Prentice-Hall, Inc., 1963.

Cardenas, Leonard, Jr. "Contemporary Problems of Local Government in Mexico," *Western Political Quarterly,* XVIII, No. 4 (December 1965), 858–65.

Cline, Howard F. *Mexico: Revolution to Evolution, 1940–1960*. London: Oxford University Press, 1962.

———. *The United States and Mexico*. Cambridge: Harvard University Press, 1953.

Garza, David T. "Factionalism in the Mexican Left: The Frustration of the MLN," *Western Political Quarterly,* XVII, No. 3 (September 1964), 447–60.

Glade, William P., and Charles W. Anderson. *The Political Economy of Mexico: Two Studies*. Madison: University of Wisconsin Press, 1963.

James, Daniel. *Mexico and the Americans*. New York: Frederick A. Praeger, Inc., 1963.

---

[5] This country is also discussed in general works on Central America listed under Guatemala.

Johnson, Kenneth F. "Ideological Correlates of Right Wing Political Alienation in Mexico," *American Political Science Review,* LIX, No. 3 (September 1965), 656–64.

Kling, Merle. *A Mexican Interest Group in Action.* Englewood Cliffs: Prentice-Hall, Inc., 1961.

Lewis, Oscar. *The Children of Sánchez.* New York: Random House, Inc., 1961.

Padgett, L. Vincent. *The Mexican Political System.* Boston: Houghton Mifflin Company, 1966.

————. "Mexico's One Party System: A Re-evaluation," *American Political Science Review,* LI, No. 4 (December 1957), 995–1007.

Schmitt, Karl M. *Communism in Mexico.* Austin: University of Texas Press, 1965.

Scott, Robert E. "Budget Making in Mexico," *Inter-American Economic Affairs,* IX, No. 2 (Autumn 1955), 3–30.

————. *Mexican Government in Transition.* Urbana: University of Illinois Press, 1964.

Stevens, Evelyn P. "Mexican Machismo: Politics and Value Orientations," *Western Political Quarterly,* XVIII, No. 4 (December 1965), 848–57.

Taylor, Philip B. "The Mexican Elections of 1958: Affirmation of Authoritarianism?" *Western Political Quarterly,* XIII, No. 3 (September 1960), 722–44.

Tucker, William P. *The Mexican Government Today.* Minneapolis: University of Minnesota Press, 1958.

Vernon, Raymond. *The Dilemma of Mexico's Development.* Cambridge: Harvard University Press, 1963.

NICARAGUA[6]

Busey, James L. "Foundations of Political Contrast: Costa Rica and Nicaragua," *Western Political Quarterly,* XI, No. 3 (September 1958), 627–59.

Cox, Isaac J. *Nicaragua and the United States.* Boston: World Peace Foundation, 1927.

International Bank for Reconstruction and Development. *The Economic Development of Nicaragua.* Baltimore: Johns Hopkins Press [1953].

PANAMA[6]

Baxter, Richard and Doris Carroll. *The Panama Canal.* New York: Oceana Publications, Inc., 1965.

Biesanz, John, and Luke M. Smith. "Panamanian Politics," *Journal of Politics,* XIV, No. 3 (August 1952), 386–402.

Biesanz, John, and Mavis. *The People of Panama.* New York: Columbia University Press, 1955.

Goldrich, Daniel. "Requisites for Political Legitimacy in Panama," *Public Opinion Quarterly,* XXVI, No. 4 (Winter 1962).

————, and Edward Scott. "Developing Political Orientations of Panamanian Students," *"Journal of Politics,"* XXXIII, No. 1 (February 1961).

---

[6] This country is also discussed in general works on Central America listed under Costa Rica and Guatemala.

———. *Radical Nationalism: The Political Orientation of Panamanian Law Students*. E. Lansing: Bureau of Social and Political Research, Michigan State University, 1962.

Metford, J. C. "The Background to Panama," *International Affairs*, XL, No. 2 (April 1964).

Republican Citizens Committee of the United States. *Panama: A Realistic Appraisal*. Washington, D.C.: Critical Issues Council, 1961.

Tate, Mercer D. "The Panama Canal and Political Partnership," *Journal of Politics*, XXV, No. 1 (February 1963).

Travis, Martin B., and James Watkins. "Control of the Panama Canal: An Obsolete Shibboleth?", *Foreign Affairs*, XXXVII (April 1959), 406–18.

PARAGUAY

DeRonde, Philip. *Paraguay: A Gallant Little Nation*. New York: G. P. Putnam's Sons 1935.

González, Juan Natalicio. *The Growth and Development of Paraguayan Culture*, trans. and ed. by Paul E. Hadley. Los Angeles: unpublished manuscript, University of Southern California, 1946.

Inter-American Development Bank. "Paraguay," in *Fifth Annual Report, 1965*. Washington, D.C.: Social Progress Trust Fund, February 28, 1966.

Pan American Union. *A Statement of the Laws of Paraguay*. Washington, D.C., 2nd ed., 1962.

———. *Constitution of the Republic of Paraguay, 1940*. Washington, D.C., 1963.

Pendle, George. *Paraguay: A Riverside Nation*. London: Royal Institute of International Affairs, 1954.

Raine, Philip. *Paraguay*. New Brunswick: Scarecrow Press, Inc., 1956.

Service, Elman R., and Helen S. *Tobatí: Paraguayan Town*. Chicago: University of Chicago Press, 1954.

Warren, Harris G. *Paraguay: An Informal History*. Norman: University of Oklahoma Press, 1949.

Zook, David H., Jr. *The Conduct of the Chaco War*. New Haven: Bookman Associates, 1960.

PERU

Adams, Richard N. *A Community in the Andes*. Seattle: University of Washington Press, 1959.

Alers, J. Oscar. "Population and Development in a Peruvian Community," *Journal of Inter-American Studies*, VII, No. 4 (October 1965), 423–48.

Alisky, Marvin. "The Peruvian Press and the Nixon Incident," *Journalism Quarterly* (Fall 1958), 411–19.

Belaúnde, Fernando. *Peru's Own Conquest*. Lima: American Studies Press, 1965.

Bennett, Wendell C., and J. B. Bird. *Andean Culture History*. New York: Museum of Natural History, rev. ed., 1960.

Bushnell, Geoffrey H. S. *Peru*. New York: Frederick A. Praeger, Inc., 1963.

Chilcote, Ronald H. "An Assessment of Peruvian Problems and Progress," *Journal of Inter-American Studies*, VI, No. 2 (April 1964), 181–86.

Fitchett, Delbert A. "Cadastral Systems on the Northern Coast of Peru," *Journal of Inter-American Studies*, VI, No. 4 (October 1964), 537–47.

Ford, Thomas R. *Man and Land in Peru*. Gainesville: University of Florida Press, 1955.

Gibson, Charles. *The Inca Concept of Sovereignty and the Spanish Administration in Peru*. Austin: Institute of Latin American Studies, University of Texas, 1958.

Hegen, Edmund E. "The Andean Cultural Frontier," *Journal of Inter-American Studies*, V, No. 4 (October 1963), 431–36.

International Labour Office. "Land Reform Act in Peru," *International Labour Review* (October 1964), 376–79.

Kantor, Harry. *Ideology and Program of the Peruvian Aprista Party*. Los Angeles: University of California Press, 1953.

Little, Arthur D., Inc. *A Program for the Industrial and Regional Development of Peru: A Report to the Government of Peru*. Cambridge: 1960.

Owens, R. J. *Peru*. New York: Oxford University Press, 1964.

Patch, Richard W. "The Peruvian Elections of 1963," *AUFS Report* (July 1963).

Payne, James L. *Labor and Politics in Peru*. New Haven: Yale University Press, 1965.

Pike, Frederick B. "The Modernized Church in Peru: Two Aspects," *The Review of Politics* (July 1964), 307–19.

Robinson, David A. *Peru in Four Dimensions*. Lima: American Studies Press, 1964.

United Nations Economic Commission for Latin America. *The Industrial Development of Peru*. México, D.F.: United Nations, 1959.

United Nations Food and Agriculture Organization. *The Agricultural Development of Peru*. Washington, D.C.: International Bank for Reconstruction and Development, 1959.

URUGUAY

Daly, Herman E. "The Uruguayan Economy: Its Basic Nature and Current Problems," *Journal of Inter-American Studies*, VII, No. 3 (July 1965), 316–330.

Fitzgibbon, Russell H. *Uruguay: Portrait of a Democracy*. New Brunswick, N.J.: Rutgers University Press, 1954.

———. "Uruguay: A Model for Freedom and Reform in Latin America?" in Frederick B. Pike, ed. *Freedom and Reform in Latin America*. Notre Dame, Indiana: University of Notre Dame Press, 1959, Chapter X.

Hanson, Simon G. *Utopia in Uruguay*. New York: Oxford University Press, 1938.

Pendle, George. *Uruguay*. New York: Oxford University Press, 1963.

Taylor, Philip B., Jr. *Government and Politics of Uruguay*. New Orleans: Tulane University Press, 1960.

———. "Interests and Institutional Dysfunction in Uruguay," *American Political Science Review*, LVII, No. 1 (March 1963), 62–74.

Vanger, Milton, I. *José Batlle y Ordóñez of Uruguay*. Cambridge, Mass.: Harvard University Press, 1963.

VENEZUELA

Alexander, Robert J. *The Venezuelan Democratic Revolution.* New Brunswick: Rutgers University Press, 1964.

Bernstein, Harry. *Colombia and Venezuela.* Englewood Cliffs: Prentice-Hall, Inc., 1964.

Friedman, John. *Venezuela: From Doctrine to Dialogue.* Syracuse: Syracuse University Press, 1965.

Gilmore, Robert L. *Caudillism and Militarism in Venezuela, 1810–1910.* Athens: Ohio University Press, 1964.

International Bank for Reconstruction and Development. *The Economic Development of Venezuela.* Baltimore: Johns Hopkins Press, 1961.

Lieuwen, Edwin. *Petroleum in Venezuela: A History.* Berkeley: University of California Press, 1954.

————. *Venezuela.* London: Oxford University Press, 2nd ed., 1964.

Luzardo, Rodolfo. *Venezuela: Business and Finance.* Englewood Cliffs: Prentice-Hall, Inc., 1957.

Marsland, William D. and Amy L. *Venezuela Through Its History.* New York: Thomas Y. Crowell Company, 1954.

Martz, John D. *Acción Democrática: Evolution of a Modern Political Party in Venezuela.* Princeton: Princeton University Press, 1965.

————. *The Venezuelan Elections of December 1, 1963.* Washington: Institute for the Comparative Study of Political Systems, 1964.

Morón, Guillermo. *A History of Venezuela.* New York: Roy Publishers, Inc., 1963.

Rourke, Thomas. *Gómez: Tyrant of the Andes.* New York: Pageant Press, Inc., 1956.

Watters, Mary. *A History of the Church in Venezuela, 1810–1930.* Chapel Hill: University of North Carolina Press, 1933.

Wise, George S. *Caudillo: A Portrait of Antonio Guzmán Blanco.* New York: Columbia University Press, 1951.

Index

absolutism: 175
Academia Carolina: 314
Acción Católica Mexicana: 42
Acción Democrática party (Venezuela): splits in, 106; history, 203, 208; power of, 204, 221, 227; program, 209, 224; domination in, 221; support of, 228, 230; opposition to, 229; mentioned, 102, 211, 214, 222, 226
Acción Democrática Popular (Costa Rica): 105 Table 1, 107 n.12
Acción Popular (Peru): 297, 298, 300, 303, 304, 311
Acción Revolucionaria (Dominican Republic): 161
Acción Revolucionaria Nacional Ecuatoriana: 274
Accionpopulistas: 298, 299
ACOPI. *See* Colombian Association of Small Industrialists
Act of Dominican Reconciliation: 169
Acta de la Revolución Argentina: 425
AD. *See* Acción Democrática party
Adams, Richard N.: on Central American local government, 76
Adecos: 211
Adventists: 139
Aeronaves de México: 33
AFL. *See* American Federation of Labor

Africa: 121, 147, 183, 191, 505
Africans: 147, 173
Afro-Europeans: 147, 148, 158
Afuerinos: 343
Agency for International Development: 240
Agrarian Leagues (Paraguay): 381, 390
Agrarian Reform, National Institute of (Cuba): 182
Agrarian Reform Committee (Bolivia): 328
Agrarian Reform Law (Cuba): 191
Agricultural and Livestock Bank (Venezuela): 214
agriculturalists. *See* landowners
agriculture: in colonies, 3; productivity drop in, 5; percentage of workers in, 13; in Nicaragua, 89; in Panama, 119, 141; in Haiti, 146; in Dominican Republic, mechanized, 173; in Cuba, 174; in Venezuela, 201, 206; in Peru, 290, 291, 307, 312; in Bolivia, 316, 327–330; in Chile, 343, 348, 353, 378; in Paraguay, 374, 383, 386, 390; in Argentina, 395, 412; in Uruguay, 442, 445. *See also* reform, agrarian
agronomy: 125
Agrupación Política 14 de Junio (Dominican Republic): 161
Aguirre Cerda, Pedro: 350, 351, 521

545

AID. *See* Agency for International Development

AID. *See* Democratic Institutionalist Alliance

Alajuela, Costa Rica: 92, 108, 110

Alaska: 290

Alberdi, Juan Bautista: 481–483

alcaldes: 126

alcaldes mayores: 3

alcohol: taxes on, 49

alcoholism: 317

Alegría, Ciro: 289, 500

Alemán Valdes, Miguel: 27, 31, 42, 53

Alende, Oscar: 418

Alessandri, Jorge: 355, 362, 363, 364, 366, 368

Alessandri Palma, Arturo: 351, 355, 365

Alfaro, Eloy: 270, 273

Alianza Popular Revolucionaria Americana: 295, 296, 500

Allende, Ignacio: 20

Allende Gossens, Salvador: 357, 362, 363, 364, 371

Alliance for Progress: programs of, 133, 136; attitudes toward, 142; and Ecuador, 286; and Bolivia, 334; and Paraguay, 381, 384, 389; and Brazil, 449; mentioned, 129, 308

Almazán, Juan Andreu: 26

Almond, Gabriel A.: on parochials, 284

alonsistas: 410

Alonso, José: 410, 411

Alsogaray, Julio: 424

alternación: 237

Alto Perú: 313

Altos Hornos de México: 30

Alvarado, Pío Jaramillo: on independence, 6

Alvarez, Adolfo: 425

Alvarez, Luis H.: 28, 44

Alvarez de Arenales: 314

Amadeo, Mario: 426

Amalia: 498 n.29

Amazon: 246, 268, 290, 328, 460

América Latina de Hoy, La: 477

American Federation of Labor: 135

American Revolutionary Popular Alliance. *See* Alianza popular Revolucionaria Americana

Americano Ilustre: 202

Amiama Tío, Luis: 161

amparo: legal cases of, 75

Anaya, Ricardo: 324

ANAPO. *See* National Popular Alliance

Anarcho-Syndicalists: Argentina, 409; Chile, 350, 351

anarchy: 6, 202, 314, 490

Ancha Base: 210

Andes Mountains: in Venezuela, 200; in Peru, 289, 299, 305; in Ecuador, 268; in Bolivia, 327, 328, 374; in Chile, 337, 338; in Argentina, 393, 496

Andrade, Ramiro: 257

Anglicans: 139

Antarctica: 338

anti-Americanism: 40, 97, 122, 130, 132, 140, 163, 189, 265. *See also* United States

anti-Castroism: 97, 107. *See also* Castro, opposition to

anticlericalism: in Mexico, 20, 25, 26, 43; in Central America, 64; in Panama, 139; in Cuba, 183; in Venezuela, 202, 209; in Colombia, 233; in Ecuador, 273; in Argentina, 398; in Uruguay, 440; mentioned, 7, 97

anti-communism: 84, 87, 160, 183

Antioquia, Department of (Colombia): 244, 250

Antofagasta, Bolivia: 316

Antofagasta, Chile: 316

Anzoátegui: 225

AP. *See* Acción Popular

Aparceria: 241

APRA. *See* Alianza Popular Revolucionaria Americana

aprismo: 295, 298, 381

Aprista parties: 100–102

Apristas: 295–299 passim, 304, 309, 311, 382, 413

Apurímac Valley: 307

AR. *See* Acción Revolucionario

Arabs: 10

Aragua (state): 228

Aramburu, Pedro E.: 141, 408, 415, 417

Arbenz Guzmán, Jacobo: 79, 80, 520

Arce y Cespedes, Armando: 322

Architects, Association of: 186

Arco, Juan Galindo de: 134

ARENA. *See* National Renovation Alliance

Arendt, Hannah: 496, 499

Arequipa, Peru, 292, 298, 299

arevalismo: 79

Arévalo, Juan José: 79–80, 508
Arevalo Martinez, Rafael: philosophy of, 488–491; mentioned, 495, 502
Argentina: nationalism in, 12, 414, 425; revolutions in, 16, 421, 481; Roman Catholic Church in, 96, 398, 405, 496, 411–412, 426; literacy in, 109, 441; and Bolivia, 314; livestock in, 328, 393, 394; races in, 393, 394; geography, 393–394; agriculture, 393, 394, 395, 412; natural resources in, 393, 398, 414, 422; transportation in, 393, 422; industry in, 394, 395; population in, 394, 403; urbanization in, 395; landowners, 395, 396 Table 1, 412; industrialization, 395, 413, 414; education, 395, 414, 425; lower classes, 395, 396 Table 1, 397; illiteracy in, 396; middle sectors, 396 Table 1, 397, 407, 415; upper classes, 396 Table 1, 397, 415; liberalism, 397, 413; reforms, 397, 413, 414; conservatism, 397, 407, 413, 416; anticlericalism, 398; and International Monetary Fund, 398, 414; dictatorship in, 398, 432, 481, 496, 498; government structure of, 399–404; Constitutions of, 399, 401, 402, 404, 413, 482, 483; government functions of, 404, 406; labor, 406, 409–411, 415, 416, 426, 518; legalists, 408, 409, 411, 423; *gorilas* in, 408, 409, 423; leftists, 409, 410, 411, 416, 421, 424, 426; General Confederation of Labor in, 410, 411, 415; interest groups in, 412; strikes in, 414; industrialists in, 415; League of the South in, 417; problems facing, 422; foreign debt of, 422; gross national product of, 422; railroads in, 422; inflation in, 422; and Chile, 424; and Dominican Republic, 424; Communique 150 of, 424; foreign policy of, 425; social security, 426; and Brazil, 432; and the CIA, 521; mentioned, 8, 17, 23, 252, 315, 323, 338, 339, 374, 375, 376, 381, 434, 441, 497, 511, 513, 515, 522
—military: power of, 398, 399, 405, 424, 441, 512, 520, 521; position of, 406–409; and Peronists, 423, 424, 425; mentioned, 254, 414, 473

Argentina (continued)
—Peronists: position of, 398, 399, 405, 417; opposition to, 413, 414, 418, 422; discussed, 415–416; acceptance of, 415, 423, 424; mentioned, 408, 410, 414, 417, 422
—political parties: Federalists, 396, 412; Radical Civic Union, 397, 398, 399, 412, 413, 421; Conservatives, 397, 398, 412, 416, 418, 420; Anarcho-Syndicalists, 409; Radicals, 409, 412, 420; Federal Union party, 411; Liberals, 412; Unitarians, 412; Christian Democrats, 412, 417, 420, 421; Intransigents, 413; Unionists, 413; Intransigent Radical Civic Union, 413, 415, 418, 421; Popular Radical Civic Union, 413, 415, 423, 424; Labor party, 415; National Federation of Parties of the Center, 416; Democrats, 416; Popular Conservative Democrats, 416, 421; Progressive Democratic party, 417; Social Christian Union, 417; Union of the Argentine People, 418; strength of, 418–419; Democratic Social party, 419, 420; organization of, 420, 421; Socialist party, 421; Popular Union party, 423
Argentine Communist party: 417
Argentine Meat Producers Corporation: 412
Argentine Socialist party: 416
Arguedas, Alcides: on Bolivian Indians, 318
Arias, Arnulfo: 121, 131, 132, 134
Arias, Harmodio: 132, 133
Arias, Ricardo: 133
Ariel: 483–485, 490, 522
Aristide, Achille: 505
aristocracy: 6–11 passim. *See also* landowners; upper classes
Aristotle: 489
armed forces. *See* military
Armed Forces of National Liberation: 205, 211, 225–226
army. *See* military
ARNE. *See* Acción Revolucionaria Nacional Ecuatoriana
Arosemena, Carlos Julio: 271, 273, 274, 281, 283
Arosemena, Díaz: 132

Arosemena Gomez, Otto: 272
Arrais, Miguel: 449, 468
Artibonite River: 146
Artigas (province): 435
Artime, Manuel: 195
Asia: 121, 191
Asocaña: organization of sugar growers, 249
Asociación de Agricultores de Pamaxán: 71 n.6
Asociación de Caficultores de Oriente: 71 n.6
Asociación de Mayo: 481
Asociación General de Agricultores de Occidente: 71 n.6
Asociación General de Comerciantes Guatematecos: 71 n.6
Asociación General de Industriales de Guatemala: 71 n.6
Asociación General de Salineros de Guatemala: 71 n.6
Asociación Guatemalteca de Agricultores: 71 n.6
Asociación Guatemalteca de Institutiones de Seguros: 71 n.6
Asociación Guatemalteca de Productores de Aceites Esenciales: 71 n.6
Asociación Guatemalteca de Productores de Algodón: 71 n.6
Asociación Nacional Republicana. *See* Colorado party
Asociación Rural: 445
Asociación Venezolana Independiente: 212
Association of Agriculturalists and Cattlemen: 249
Association of Cuban Bankers: 186
Association of Cuban Sugar Cane Planters: 186
Asturias, Miguel Angel: 498 n.32, 501
Asunción, Paraguay: 316, 374, 375, 383, 389
Ataide, Tristão: 457
Ateneo de lo República: 426
Atlantic Ocean: 231, 430
Aucas (Indians): 268
audiencias: 3, 115, 126
Auténticos: 177, 179, 181, 194
Authentic Revolutionary party: 33
authoritarianism: in Mexico, 38; in Central America, 57; in Haiti, 150, 152, 154–155, 156; in Venezuela, 202, 203; in Uruguay, 434; in Ar-

authoritarianism (continued)
gentina, 441; mentioned, 2, 6, 488, 501
Autocratic Republic: Chile, 365
automobiles: 236, 238, 265
Autonomists: 412
Avellaneda, Alfonso Ruiseco: 53
AVI. *See* Asociación Venezolana Independiente
Avila, Federico: on Bolivian Indians, 318
Avila Camacho, Manuel: 26, 36, 42
Ayala, Eusebio: 376
ayllu: 500
Aymará (language): 291
Azuela, Mariano: 499
azules: 408

Báez, Buenaventura: 159
Bahia: Brazil, 457, 458, 464
Baja California: 26, 29, 32, 40, 49
Balaguer, Joaquín: 161, 166, 169
Ballivián, Adolfo: 315, 316
bananas: in Central America, 66; in Costa Rica, 92, 94; in Panama, 124, 137; in Ecuador, 267; in Guatemala, 501; mentioned, 291
Banco Agrícola Mercantil: 71 n.6
Banco Agrícola y Pecuario: 223
Banco Central: 349
Banco de México: 48
Banco Ejidal: 44
Banco Nacional: 192
Banda Oriental (Uruguay): 432
Bandera Roja: 299
banderón, El: 503
bandits: 235, 238, 239, 241, 254
Bantoue-Africaine philosophy: 505, 506
Baoruco Mountains (Dominican Republic): 157
BAP. *See* Agricultural and Livestock Bank
Barager, Joseph: on election of Arturo Illia, 399
Barbarina, Luis Alfonso: 257
Barbosa, Rui: 456, 506
Barquisimeto, Venezuela: 206
Barranca Birmeja, Colombia: 259
Barranquilla, Colombia: 257
Barrerras, Antonio Imbert: 165
barriadas: 430

Barrientos, Ortuno, René: 332, 335, 336

Barros, Ademar de: 460, 462, 466, 468

Barrios, Gonzalo: 204

Barrios, Justo Rufino: 65

Bases y puntos de partida para la organización política de la República Argentina: 483

Batista, Fulgencio: regimes of, 176, 177, 178, 182, 183, 193, 511; coup by, 177, 186; and Castro, 179; exile of, 179; abdication of, 179, 184; and military, 184; loss of U.S. support for, 189; opposition to, 225, 512; mentioned, 182, 511, 514

Batistianos: 179, 186, 189, 194

Batlle, César: 444

Batlle, Lorenzo: 444

Batlle, Luis: 444

Batlle y Ordóñez, José: as implementor of nationalism in Uruguay, 12; administration of, 433–435; system of, 434–435, 436; anticlericalism of, 440; and military, 442; rise of, 485; mentioned, 432, 443, 509

Batllismo: 434, 436

bauxite: 158

Bay of Pigs invasion: 183, 184, 185, 190, 195, 512

Bejarano, Ramón C.: 388

Belaúnde, Fernando: candidacy of, 297; administration of, 300, 303, 304, 307, 311; election of, 303; mentioned, 298

Belice: 503

Bellegarde, Dantes: 506

Bello, Andrés: 508

Beltrán, Pedro: 303

Benavides, Oscar: 296, 498

Benelux countries: 200

Beni River: 327

Bentez Zenteño, Raul: 29

Berzola, María: 324

Betancourt, Rómulo: and Acción Democrática party, 208; administration of, 208, 209, 213, 214, 217, 219, 226; and military, 216; and agrarian reform, 223; and John F. Kennedy, 224; support of, 225; mentioned, 100, 204, 210, 222, 512

Betancourt Doctrine: 225

bismuth: 325

Blanco, Andrés Eloy: 208

Blanco Fombona, Rufino: 498, 502

Blancos: early history, 432; position of, 433, 436; in power, 435; and *Colorados,* 437; mentioned, 439, 441

Blanksten, George: on role of Roman Catholic Church in Argentina, 405

Bloque Revolucionario Universitario Cristiano: 163

Bocas del Toro: 119

Bogotá, Colombia: uprisings in, 178; founding of, 232; construction in, 235; Eighth Inter-American Conference in, 234, 370; bombing in, 241; mentioned, 239 n.14, 244, 249, 251, 253, 492, 495

Bogotazo: 241, 254

Bohan Mission, Bolivia: 325

Boletin, El: 42

Bolisario: 490

Bolívar, Simon: leadership by, 202, 232; on military, 388; hopes of, 481, 494; and Henry Clay, 502; mentioned, 269, 315, 483, 484, 490, 495

Bolívar, Department of (Colombia): 245, 246

Bolivia: as Upper Peru, 313; and Spain, 313, 314; natural resources, 313, 316, 320, 324, 325, 327, 329; and Peru, 314, 317; education in, 314, 319, 330, 331; governmental structure of, 315; constitution of, 315; dictatorship in, 315, 316; and Brazil, 316; and Chile, 316; and Paraguay, 316; and Gran Chaco War, 316, 317; tin of, 316, 319–326 passim, 332, 334; political parties of, 316, 319, 320, 321, 322, 332–334, 336; military power in, 316, 319, 320, 321, 323, 332, 335, 512; mining in, 316, 319, 323, 325, 327; transportation in, 316, 328; industry in, 316, 328; nationalism in, 317; races in, 317, 318, 319, 321, 322, 328, 329, 330; communications in, 317, 318, 321, 322, 335; landowners in, 317, 320, 329; labor in, 319, 320–324 passim, 326, 333, 518; foreign exchange in, 319, 320, 328, 334; taxes, 319, 325; Standard Oil Company in, 319, 327; illiteracy in, 319, 330, 331, 335; sharecroppers in, 320; secret police of, 320; social security, 320; terrorism, 320; leftists in, 320, 321, 322, 324, 328, 334; exiles from, 321, 323; strikes in, 321, 334; students in,

Bolivia (continued)
321, 334; miners in, 322, 323, 324, 325, 330, 331, 333, 334; 1952 uprising in, 323, 328, 333, 335; and United States, 326, 331, 332, 333, 334; inflation in, 326, 332; Gulf Oil Corporation in, 327; South American Gold and Platinum Company in, 327; agricultural zones of, 327; agriculture of, 327–328, 332; exports, 328; urbanization in, 328, 329; reform, 328, 329–330, 334; imports, 328, 332; upper classes, 330; suffrage, 331, 334; middle sectors, 333; and Alliance for Progress, 334; guerrillas in, 336; flag, 368; mentioned, 38, 307, 338, 374, 430, 515
Bolivian Labor Central: 330
Bolo, Father Salomon: 299
Bon Dieu, Le: 149
Bonilla, Frank: 348
Bonilla, Policarpo: 66
Borno, Haiti: 150
Bosch, Juan: administration of, 164, 169; mentioned, 100, 160, 162, 165, 167
Bourbons: 4
Boyaca, Department of (Colombia): 232, 243
Boyer, Jean: 149
bracero: 48
Brasília monument: 476
Brazil: end of ties with Portugal, 5; nationalism in, 12, 451, 463, 470; revolution in, 16; supernaturalism in, 17; population, 17, 394; and Venezuela, 225; military power of, 225, 449, 452–455 passim, 458, 459, 461, 465, 466, 468, 469, 470, 471–472 passim, 507, 512, 520; and Bolivia, 316; natural resources of, 328, 448, 457; and Paraguay, 374, 390; and Perón, 422; and Argentina, 432; geography of, 447–450 passim; and Soviet Union, 448; and Great Britain, 448; communication in, 448, 457, 458, 463, 470, 472, 475; races, 448, 451, 458, 507, 508; and United States, 448, 458, 470, 472; transportation, 448, 475; and Roman Catholic Church, 449–452 passim, 456, 461, 463–464, 468, 469, 471, 507; and Alliance for Progress, 449; Portuguese language used in, 449; left-

Brazil (continued)
ists in, 449, 450, 454, 458, 460, 463, 464, 468, 469; middle sectors in, 449, 451, 452, 454, 458, 463, 464, 466, 468, 470, 471, 473, 474; slums in, 449, 451, 457, 465, 466, 467, 472; industries in, 449, 454, 462; unemployment in, 449, 475; peasant leagues in, 450; sharecroppers, 450; dictatorship in, 450, 454, 460, 463, 465, 474, 475; labor in, 450, 454, 473; lower classes in, 450, 465, 466, 468, 470, 472, 474, 475; literacy in, 451; nationalities in, 451, 452, 464; upper classes of, 451, 465, 474; Constitutions of, 452, 454, 457; slavery in, 452, 456, 506, 507; regionalism in, 454; government structure in, 455; education in, 456, 469; Catholic University of, 457; ultranationalism in 457, 468; landowners in, 459, 462, 465; conservatism in, 461, 464, 467, 471, 472; inflation in, 462, 475; liberals in, 463; radicals in, 463, 467; students in, 464, 472; industrialists in, 465; reforms in, 466, 467, 472, 476, 511; taxes in, 467, 476; Independence Day, 470; mobilization in, 471, 472; illiteracy, 471, 472; Carnival of, 472; crops, 477; political writings in, 506–508; and CIA, 520; mentioned, 4, 23, 252, 340, 375, 376, 430, 443, 445, 503, 511, 515
—political parties: party systems of, 106; Republican party, 452, 453, 459; Conservative party, 452, 465; other parties, 452, 456, 464; discussion of, 459–461; National Renovating Alliance, 459, 461, 468; Brazilian Democratic Movement, 459, 461, 468; Social Progressive party, 460, 461; Social Democratic party, 460, 461, 464; National Democratic Union, 460, 461, 464; Brazilian Labor party, 460, 465
Brazilian Democratic Movement: 459
Brazilian Institute of Democratic Action: 464
Brazilian Labor party: 460, 464
Brazilian Populist movement: 471
British: 8, 175, 339, 375, 480
British Guiana: 224
British Honduras: 28

Brizola, Leonel: 465–468 passim
brotherhoods: 71 n.6
BRUC. *See* Bloque Revolucionario Universitario Cristiano
Buddhism: 152
Buencos, Chile: 450
Buenos Aires, Argentina: 375, 376, 384, 394, 395, 396, 399, 403, 407, 412, 415, 424, 439, 481, 496
Buenos Aires Unitarians: 396
Buga, Colombia: 240
Bundy, McGeorge: 458
Busch, Germán: 319
Bustamante, José: 296
bwanga: 505

Caamano, Dominican Republic: 163
Caballero, Bernardino: 376
caballeros: 245, 247
cabildos: 5
cacao: 92, 124, 158, 201, 202, 270, 327
Cáceres, Andrés: 290
cacique: 71
Cadíz, Spain: 59
Caesarism: 208
Caldera, Rafael: 209, 222
Calderón Guardia, Rafael: as founder of Partido Republicano Nacional, 98, 103, 104; and Ulate, 106; popularity of, 113; mentioned, 95, 97, 99, 106, 109, 111
Calderonistas: 104, 106
Cali, Colombia: 235, 244, 251, 253, 258
California: 17, 65, 127, 290, 338
Callao, Peru: 292, 298
Calle, La: 322
Calles, Plutarco Elias: 25, 36
Calvin, John: 9
Camara, Helder: 458, 464
Cámara Central de Comercio de Chile: 348, 349
Cámaras Unidas de Comercio e Industria: 71 n.6
Cámera de Industriales: 71 n.6
Cámera Mercantil de los Productos del País: 445
campesinos: Panama, 120; Cuba, 174, 188, 192; Venezuela, 205, 206, 230; Bolivia, 330, 331, 333, 335; Colombia, 488
Campo de Mayo: 408
Campos, Roberto: 474

Canada: 340
Canal Zone: influence of in Panama, 116; as liability to Panama, 116, 119; employment in, 119; as asset to Panama, 119, 120; trade in, 120, 124; North Americans of, 121; amount paid for, 127; sovereignty of, 130, 134, 141, 142; as haven for political refugees, 131; salary in, 136; labor in, 136; United States in, 140, 141; mentioned, 135, 512. *See also* Panama; Panama Canal
Cannes Festival: 470
cantegriles: 430
Cape Town, South Africa: 338
capital: in Mexico, 33, 48; in Panama, 120, 134, 135; private, 129, 134; Peru, 307; Chile, 349; Uruguay, 433; Brazil, 462; mentioned, 8, 9, 12, 40, 48, 307, 433, 462
capitalism: Calvin's ethic of, 9; private, 35; of State, 35; in Guatemala, 78; Cuba, 185, 192; Chile, 357; Uruguay, 435
carabineros: 318, 322
Caracas, Venezuela: 200, 206, 221, 226, 230
Caracas Museum: 25
caraqueños: 202, 230
Cárdenas, Lazaro: 25, 27, 30, 36, 40, 42, 47
Carías Andino, Tiburcio: 83
Caribbean: 92, 157, 172, 175, 200, 232, 394
cariocas: 469, 470
Carlotta: 21
Carnival: Brazil, 472
Caro, Miguel Antonio: 233
Caroní River: 223
Carranza, Venustiano: 23, 24
Carrera, Rafael: 64, 65
Cartagena, Colombia: 232, 244
Cartago (province): 92, 93, 108, 110
Casa-grande & senzala: 507
casas brujas: 123
CASC. *See* Confederación Autónoma de Sindicatos Cristianos
caste: Haiti, 149; Dominican Republic, 159
Castello Branco, Humberto: 225, 469, 474
Castilla, Ramon: 293
Castillo Armas, Carlos: 69, 81, 511
Castro, Cipriano: 203

Castro, Fidel: and Panama invasion, 139; invasion of Cuba by, 161, 178, 181, 188; regime of, 170, 172, 179, 183, 184, 186, 187, 188, 189, 191–193, 194, 196, 224; ideology of, 179, 180; as *caudillo,* 180; personality of, 180; as Prime Minister, 182; and 1940 Constitution, 182; and Roman Catholic Church, 183; and military, 184; in United States, 189; and United States, 189, 512; opposition, 194, 195, 271; goals and techniques, 196; and Colombia, 257; and guerrilla, 336, 511; mentioned, 28, 82, 87, 96, 128, 142, 173, 174, 225, 240, 381, 514

Castro, Raúl: 182

Castroites: 93, 298, 299

Catamarco (province): 403

Catavi, Bolivia: 320, 324

Catholics. *See* Roman Catholic Church

Catholic Electoral League: 463

Catholic parties: 68

Catholic University: Brazil, 457

Catholic University Youth organization: Brazil, 464

Catorcistas: 161

cattle: as industry, 9; in El Salvador, 86; in Nicaragua, 88; in Costa Rica, 92; in Panama, 119; in Dominican Republic, 158; in Venezuela, 200; in Colombia, 245; in Paraguay, 374; in Argentina, 394; in Uruguay, 430, 441, 445

Cauca River: 238, 245, 246

caudillismo: 74, 167

caudillo: as prototypal political leader, 5; in Central America, 71; in Honduras, 83; in Nicaragua, 88; in Dominican Republic, 165; in Cuba, 179; in Venezuela, 199, 203, 216; in Bolivia, 315; in Argentina, 396; in Uruguay, 432; mentioned, 6, 8, 72

CCI. *See* Independent Peasant Front

CDR. *See* Committee for Revolutionary Defense

CDT. *See* Confederación Dominicana de Trabajadores

cement: 88, 120, 154

Central America: education in, 57, 61; reform in, 57, 61; politics in, 57, 62, 67–70, 72, 77; governments, 57, 64, 74, 75, 101; social structure in, 59–63, 70; races in, 59, 62, 63; control

Central America (continued) in, 59, 63, 64; commerce in, 59, 73; Roman Catholic Church, 60, 70, 72; labor in, 61, 62, 72; industry in, 61, 66, 72; rural-urban relations in, 62; foreign interests in, 62, 64, 66, 67; factionalism in, 63, 64, 65, 76; anticlericalism in, 64; conservatives in, 64, 65; liberals in, 64, 65, 66; military in, 64, 70; agriculture in, 66, 477; interest groups in, 70–73; political instability in, 70, 90; freedoms in, 74, 77. *See also* Costa Rica; El Salvador; Guatemala; Honduras; Nicaragua

Central American Common Market: 90

Central de Trabajadores del Uruguay: 446

Central Oberra Boliviana: 324, 328

Central Planning Council: Cuba, 182

Central Railroad: Paraguay, 374

Central Unica de Trabajadores de Chile: 351, 352

Central University: Ecuador, 277, 278

centrales: 249, 250

Center for Training in [Civil] Service: Paraguay, 389

CEPCH. *See* Confederación de Empleados Particulares de Chile

Cerro de Pasco, Peru: 298

Cervantes, Jose Trinidad: 43

Cervantes, Luis: 499

CFP. *See* Concentración de Fuerzas Populares

CGE. *See* General Economic Confederation

CGT. *See* Confederación General de Trabajo

Chaco War Veterans Party: 333

chafarotes: 254

Chagres (province): 123

Chaîne de Mateux, Haiti: 146

Chapultepec, Castle of: 21

Charcas, Audiencia of: 313, 315, 316

Chaves, Federico: 377

Chaves, Juan Ramón: on Paraguay's elections, 378; on political parties, 379

chef de section: 154

Chiari, Roberto: 129, 133–134

Chibás, Eduardo: 178, 181, 188

Chibcha Indians: 232

Chihuahua, Mexico: 21, 47

Chihuahua City, Mexico: 45

Child of the Dark: 466
Children of Sanchez, The: 17, 52
Chile: natural resources of, 8, 13, 316, 338, 348, 350, 358, 367, 370, 477; nationalism in, 12, 339, 356; labor in, 14, 337, 345, 346, 347, 348, 350–353, 357, 365, 370; government of, 16, 365–368; Christianity in, 41, 356; literacy rate in, 108, 345, 353, 365; foreign policy of, 293, 339, 356, 358, 424; Christian Democrats of, 258, 264, 299, 344, 347, 348, 352, 382, 417, 440; and Bolivia, 314, 316; lower classes, 337, 340–344 passim, 355, 360; middle sectors, 337, 344, 345, 350, 355, 356, 359, 365, 371, 521; reforms, 337, 344, 347, 355, 356, 357, 365, 369, 370, 371; political parties, 337, 345, 346, 348, 349, 350, 353–360, 362, 365, 370, 371, 521; Indians, 339; and Spain, 339; population, 339–343 passim; Roman Catholic Church, 339, 347, 354; utilities, 340; urbanization, 340, 341, 342; communications, 340, 345, 346, 367; transportation, 340, 367; housing, 340, 370; natural disasters, 341; illiteracy, 341; slums, 341, 364; landowners, 342, 344, 361; income, 343, 344, 370; agriculture, 343, 348, 353, 370; strikes, 344, 350, 370; upper classes, 345, 349, 354, 359, 363, 371, 521; education, 345, 355, 365, 370; inflation, 345, 370; taxation, 345, 370; rightists, 346, 350, 354, 362, 323, 369, 371; military, 347, 350, 367; management groups, 348–350, 352; students, 348, 359, 371; industry, 348, 370; electoral system, 360–365; Constitutions of, 361, 365, 368; mentioned, 8, 11, 14, 23, 113, 253, 515
—leftists: Socialists, 346, 347, 348, 350, 352, 353, 357–359, 362, 364, 365, 370, 371, 521; Communists, 12, 346, 347, 348, 351–354 passim, 357–359, 362, 365, 370, 371, 521; Marxists, 352, 362, 371; others, 358; mentioned, 369
Chile, University of: 341, 342, 348, 371
Chimbote, Peru: 298
Chimbote Steel Mill: 298
China: 132, 189, 190, 384
Chiriquí, Panama: 119

"Chispas": 238
chocolate: 158
cholo: 269, 291
chombos: 121
Christian Democratic parties: in Mexico, 42; in Central America, 68; in Guatemala, 69; in El Salvador, 70, 88; in Panama, 131, 134, 135; in Venezuela, 204, 258, 417; in Colombia, 256, 258, 259, 264; in Peru, 258, 297, 299, 303, 304; in Bolivia, 334; in Paraguay, 378, 379, 383–384, 385, 389; and Organization of American States, 383; in Argentina, 411, 417, 420, 421; Italian, 417; in Uruguay, 439, 440; mentioned, 300, 311
—Chile: support, 347, 354; power, 348, 350; and labor, 353; and reform, 360, 364; mentioned, 258, 264, 299, 344, 355, 356–357, 359, 362, 363, 369, 370, 371, 417, 440
Christianity: 152, 356
Christians: 149, 252
Christophe, Henri: 146, 148
chromite: 173
Chrysler Motor Company: 292
Chuquisaca, Audiencia of Charcas: 314
Church. *See* Roman Catholic Church
Cibao Valley: 157, 158
CID. *See* Democratic Institutionalist Coalition
Cienfuegos, Camilo: 180
Citadel: of Henri Christophe, 146
Ciudad Bernardino de Sahagún, Mexico: 51
Ciudad Guayana, Venezuela: 223
Civil Engineers, Association of: Cuba, 186
Civil party: Peru, 293, 294
civil war: in Costa Rica, 95, 98, 101, 106, 109, 114; in Venezuela, 203; in Colombia, 234; in Paraguay, 377; in Uruguay, 437
Clarin: 346
Clay, Henry: 502
Cleveland, Grover: 224
Clothing Workers Union: 410
Club Guatemala: 71 n.6
CNC. *See* National Confederation of Peasants
coal: 8, 30, 393
COB. *See* Central Obrera Boliviano
Cochabamba, Bolivia: 314, 319, 327, 335

Cochabamba, University of: 314
coffee: in Central America, 66, 477; prices of, 82, 86, 238, 240, 250; in El Salvador, 86; in Costa Rica, 92, 93, 94, 114; in Haiti, 146; in Dominican Republic, 158; in Venezula, 201, 202; in Colombia, 235, 236, 238, 240, 244, 250; in Bolívia, 327; in Brazil, 477
cold war: 172, 190, 197
Colombia: population explosion in, 17, 252; Roman Catholic Church in, 96, 233, 247, 247 n.17, 251–253, 265; and Panama, 126, 127, 233 n.4; uprisings in, 178, 233, 234, 247; Ecuador, 202, 268; geography, 231–232; and Spain, 232; and Viceroyalty of Peru, 232; and Viceroyalty of Nueva Granada, 232; races in, 232; natural resources in, 232, 259; anticlericalism in, 233; slavery in, 233; labor in, 233, 234, 249–250, 257, 260; education, 233, 236, 242–244; passim, 245, 251, 252, 254; leftists in, 233, 248, 250, 253, 256–259 passim, 264; Constitutions of, 233, 251; railroads of, 234; taxes in, 234, 238, 245, 249, 251, 260, 261; reform in, 234, 246, 255; housing, 235; employment, 235; coffee of, 235, 236, 239, 240, 244, 250; dictatorship in, 235–236, 511; bandits in, 235, 238, 241, 254; students, 236, 240, 241, 251, 258, 263; newspapers, 236, 241; *paridad* agreement, 237; unemployment in, 237, 239, 265; government structure in, 237, 259–262; industrialists of, 238; landowners of, 238, 241, 245; automobiles of, 238, 265; guerillas in, 239, 240, 254, 259; inflation in 239, 240, 265; loans in 240–241; exports of, 240, 241; upper classes of, 240, 244–245, 246, 253, 258, 264, 265; military tribunals of, 240, 253–254, 519; and United States, 240, 265; share cropping in, 241, 245; lower classes of, 242, 242 n.14, 262, 264; illiteracy in, 242, 242 n.15; *minifundias* in, 243; middle sectors of, 243, 243 n.16, 247, 253, 258, 264; sugar in, 244, 246, 258; strikes in, 244, 249, 251, 258; livestock, 245, 246; Concordat of 1887, 252; *Bogotazo* in, 254; factionalism in, 256; voting

Colombia (continued)
in, 262, 263, 264; *campesinos* in, 488; mentioned, 8, 18, 116, 478, 486, 492, 503, 515, 518
—political parties: Liberals of, 106, 234, 237, 247–248, 249, 250, 253, 255–256, 262, 263, 264, 437, 494; Conservatives of, 106, 234, 237, 247–248, 249, 253, 255–256, 262, 263, 264, 437, 494; Frente Nacional of, 255, 258, 259, 263, 264; Christian Democrats of, 256, 258, 259, 264; mentioned, 241
Colombian Anarchist Movement: 258
Colombian Association of Small Industrialists: 250, 251
Colombian Embassy: Peru, 296
Colombian Institute of Agrarian Reform: 246
Colombian Student Worker Movement: 258
Colón, Panama: 123
Colorado: 268
Colorado party: Paraguay, 376, 377, 378, 379–381, 383, 384, 385, 386, 388, 389, 392; Argentina, 408; Uruguay, 432, 433, 434, 435, 437, 439, 441, 444; mentioned, 382, 391
Colorado River: 28
Columbia University: 497
Columbus, Christopher: 158
COMACH. *See* Confederación Marítima de Chile
Comercio, El: 298
COMIBOL. *See* Corporación Minera de Bolivia, La
Comisión Interministerial de Cooperacion Popular: 303
Comité de Forces Democratique: 150
Comité por Organización Política y Electoral Independiente: 208, 209, 224, 226, 228, 230
Command Corps: Argentina, 407
Commandos of Workers: Bolivia, 322
Committee for Revolutionary Defense: Cuba, 185
Common market: 129, 370
communications: Haiti, 146, 156; Cuba, 188, 194; Venezuela, 203, 221, 228; Peru, 290, 309, 310; Chile, 340, 345, 346, 367; Paraguay, 374, 380, 389; Brazil, 448, 463, 470, 472; mentioned, 488
Communique 150: 409, 424

Communism: in Mexico, 28, 40, 41, 42; in Central America, 69; in Guatemala, 78, 79, 80; in Honduras, 84; in El Salvador, 86, 87; in Nicaragua, 89; in Costa Rica, 93, 95, 98; and Roman Catholic Church, 97; in Panama, 130; in Haiti, 150; in Dominican Republic, 160, 165, 169; Venezuela, 172, 205, 211, 218, 226; Castro as, 179; and Fidelistas, 180, 181; in Colombia, 256, 258–259, 264; Ecuador, 271, 273, 274; in Peru, 295, 297, 298, 299, 305, 308, 311; Chinese, 299; Bolivia, 321, 324, 328, 333; in Chile, 346–348 passim, 351–354 passim, 357–359, 362, 364, 365, 370, 371, 521; in Paraguay, 377, 379, 384; in Argentina, 409, 410, 411, 424, 426; in Uruguay, 439, 440; in Brazil, 449, 454, 460, 468; in United States, 479; mentioned, 106, 117, 172, 265, 284, 350
—Cuba: control, 175, 179; and labor, 177, 186; attacks on, 182; and armed forces, 185; and Castro, 187; alignment with, 190; acceptance of, 193; influence in, 194; mentioned, 178, 183, 196, 502
Communist Parti Socialiste Popular: 150
Communists' Thirteenth National Convention: 359, 371
Communist Youth organization: 258
communitarianism: 357
compadrazgo: 494
Compañía Nacional de Subsistencias Populares: 48, 50
Compañía Tubos Moore: 249
Comte, Auguste: 8, 21, 484, 486
comunas: 386
Comunidad: 382
CONACO. *See* Corporación Nacional de Comerciantes
CONASUPO. *See* Compañía Nacional de Subsistencias Populares
CONATREL. *See* Confederación Nacional Trabajadores Libre
Concentración de Fuerzas Populares: 274, 275
concentration camps: 321, 391
Concepción, Chile: 338, 342
Concepción, Paraguay: 374
Concepción, University of: 348
Concepción del cosmos: 488

Concha Córdoba, Monsignor Luis: 253, 258
Concordat of 1860: 152
Concordat of 1887: 252
Confederación Autónoma de Sindicatos Cristianos: 162, 163
Confederación de Empleados Particulares de Chile: 352
Confederación de la Producción y del Comercio: 349, 355
Confederación de Trabajadores de América Latina: 89
Confederación de Trabajadores de Chile: 351
Confederación de Trabajadores de Nicaragua: 89
Confederación de Trabajadores de Panamá: 135
Confederación de Trabajadores de Venezuela: 211, 220
Confederación de Trabajadores Peruanos: 300
Confederación Dominicana de Trabajadores: 162
Confederación General del Trabajo: Chile, 351
Confederación Marítima de Chile: 352
Confederación Nacional Trabajadores Libre: 162
Confederation of Colombian Workers: 249
Confederation of Cuban Workers: 186
Confederation of Ecuadorian Workers: 277
Confederation of Greater Colombia: 269
Confederation of Labor: Paraguay, 383
Confessions: 483
Confites, Cayo: 178
Consejo Supremo Electoral: 218
conservatism: economic, 41; in Mexico, 43; in Central America, 65; in Honduras, 83; in Dominican Republic, 164; Burkean, 276; in Peru, 297; in Argentina, 397, 407, 413, 416; in Brazil, 452, 461, 464, 465, 467, 471, 472; mentioned, 93
Conservatives: in Mexico, 21, 25, 26; in Central America, 64; in Nicaragua, 66, 70, 501; in Guatemala, 69, 71 n.6; in Honduras, 85; in Costa Rica, 97, 99; in Colombia, 106, 264; in Dominican Republic, 169; Vene-

Conservatives (continued)
zuela, 172, 200, 202, 209, 229; Cuba,
181; Colombia, 233, 234, 237, 247–
248, 249, 253, 255–256, 262, 263,
437, 494; in Ecuador, 270, 272–273,
276; in Peru, 298, 299; in Bolivia,
316, 319, 333–334; in Chile, 346,
350, 354–355, 356, 357, 359, 363,
365; in Paraguay, 381; in Argentina,
397, 398, 412, 416, 418, 420; in
Uruguay, 433; in Latin America,
520, 521; mentioned, 7, 11, 106, 107,
172, 179, 501
Consorcio Pesquero del Perú: 292
Constant Botelho de Magalhães, Benjamin: 456
constitutionalism: Latin America, 480
Constitutionalist party: Dominican Republic, 163; Peru, 294
Constitution of 1824: Brazil, 452
Constitution of 1830: Uruguay, 432
Constitution of 1832: Colombia, 232
Constitution of 1853: Argentina, 399,
401, 402, 404, 482, 483
Constitution of 1857: Mexico, 20, 24
Constitution of 1860: Peru, 293
Constitution of 1863: Colombia, 233
Constitution of 1869: Ecuador, 270
Constitution of 1879: Guatemala, 73
Constitution of 1880: Peru, 294
Constitution of 1886: Colombia, 233,
251
Constitution of 1891: Brazil, 457
Constitution of 1901: Cuba, 183
Constitution of 1904: Panama, 125
Constitution of 1906: Ecuador, 270
Constitution of 1917: Mexico, 43
Constitution of 1920: Peru, 294
Constitution of 1925: Chile, 361, 365,
368
Constitution of 1929: Ecuador, 282
Constitution of 1933: Peru, 296, 309
Constitution of 1934: Uruguay, 437
Constitution of 1934: Brazil, 454
Constitution of 1940: Panama, 125;
Cuba, 176, 194, 195; Paraguay, 376,
381, 385
Constitution of 1946: Ecuador, 277,
279, 281; Panama, 125, 128; Ecuador, 278, 282
Constitution of 1949: Costa Rica, 112
Constitution of 1956: Guatemala, 75
Constitution of 1961: Venezuela, 212

Constitution of 1963: Dominican Republic, 164, 167
Constitution of 1967: Brazil, 476
constitutions: 2, 5, 57
consumer goods: 192
Continental System: 20
continuismo: in Central America, 74,
83
continuistas: 408
Contra o militarismo: 507
Control Obrero: Bolivia, 326
conventillos: 430
convivencia: 297, 299
Cooperativa de Ganaderos de Guatemala: 71 n.6
Cooperativa de Ganaderos de Occidente: 71 n.6
Copacabana Beach, Brazil: 451
COPEI. *See* Comité por Organizacion
Política and Electoral Independiente
Copeyanos: 210, 211, 227
copper: Cuba, 173; Peru, 291, 292,
294; Bolivia, 316; Chile, 338, 370,
477
Coquimbo, Chile: 338
Cordillera Central Mountains: 157
Cordillera Septentrional Mountains:
157
Córdoba, Department of (Colombia):
236
Córdoba (province): 394, 421
coregimientos: 126
CORFO: 369
Corporación de Guayana: 223
Corporación de Ventas de Salitre y
Yodo: 349
Corporación Minera de Bolivia, La:
324
Corporación Nacional de Comerciantes: 307
Corporación Venezolana de Fomento
223
Cornejo Chávez, Hector: 299
Corrientes, Argentina: 403
Corvalán, Luis: 358
Costa e Silva, Marechal: 463, 474, 476
Costa Rica: governmental organization
of, 63, 95, 98, 99, 107–108, 110,
113; political parties of, 65, 92, 93,
95, 97–110; and Nicaragua, 89, 113;
geography of, 91–92, 114; democracy of, 91, 95, 114; United Fruit
Co. in, 92; cattle, 92; crops in, 92,

Costa Rica (continued)
93, 94, 112; education in, 92, 93, 96, 109; races in, 92, 93, 101; class system in, 92, 99, 100, 102, 107; mass media of, 92, 109; colonization of, 93–94, 114; landowners of, 93, 102; dictators in, 94–95; taxation in, 94, 101; foreign policy of, 95; military in, 95–96, 110, 114; civil war in, 95, 98, 101, 106, 109, 114; leftists in, 95, 98, 107 n.12; Roman Catholic Church in, 96–97, 110; exiles in, 96, 99, 107; professors in, 97, 98, 102; students in, 97, 98, 110; labor in, 98; unemployment in, 98; social security in, 98; rightists in, 99, 100; private enterprise in, 100, 104; social reform, 101; economic development in, 101, 102, 107; anti-Castroism in, 107; pro-United Statesism in, 107; civil liberties in, 108; literacy in, 109, 113; political decision-making in, 110–114; Constitution of, 112; housing, 113; industrialization in, 114; mentioned, 382, 511, 515

Costa Rica, University of 97, 104

cotton: in Nicaragua, 88; in Cuba, 192; in Venezuela, 202; in Peru, 290, 292; mentioned, 294

Council of the Indies: 3

counterrevolution: Guatemala, 81–83

Country Club: Guatemala, 71 n.6

Court of Cassation: Haiti, 153

Creelman, James: 22

Creole (tongue): 147

creoles: 4, 5, 59, 63

Crespo, Joaquín: 203

criollos: 4, 375

CROM. *See* Regional Confederation of Mexican Workers

CSE. *See* Consejo Supremo Electoral

CTAL. *See* Latin American Workers Confederation

CTC. *See* Confederation of Colombian Workers

CTC. *See* Confederation of Cuban Workers

CTCH. *See* Confederación de Trabajadores de Chile

CTE. *See* Confederation of Ecuadorian Workers

CTM. *See* Mexican Confederation of Workers

CTP. *See* Confederación de Trabajadores de Panamá

CTP. *See* Confederación de Trabajadores Peruanos

CTV. *See* Confederación de Trabajadores de Venezuela

cuartelazo: 15

Cuba: Castro's invasion of, 161, 178; and Soviet Union, 171, 172, 177, 189, 190, 192; strategic position of, 171, 173, 190, 197; geography of, 172–173; dictatorship in, 172, 176, 177, 178, 179, 182, 186, 187, 189, 193; modernization, 172, 177; agriculture in, 173, 174, 175, 186, 190, 192, 196, 477; industries, 173, 174, 183, 186, 192; and Spain, 173, 175; slaves in, 173, 175; natural resources of, 173, 175, 185; literacy in, 173, 193; races in, 173, 502–504; economy of, 174, 175, 177, 191; landowners in, 174, 175, 186; labor in, 174, 176, 177, 182, 183, 186, 187, 188, 191; middle sectors of, 175, 176, 177, 183, 186, 187, 188, 193; nationalism of, 175, 177, 189; Roman Catholic Church in, 175, 183, 194; gangsterism in, 176; politics of, 176–181 passim; reforms, 176, 177, 182, 191; students of, 176, 178, 179, 187, 188, 193; Constitutions of, 176, 182, 183, 194, 195; military in, 176, 184; exiles from, 177, 181, 184, 186, 189, 193, 194; lower classes of, 177, 183, 188, 192, 195; upper classes of, 177, 186, 193; guerillas of, 179, 184, 191, 194, 197, 311, 511; totalitarianism, 179, 188, 196; leftists in, 180, 185, 193; government organization of, 182, 185; religion in, 183; social welfare in, 183, 187; education in, 183, 187, 191, 193; capitalism in, 185, 192; communications in, 188, 194; and China, 189, 190; and other countries, 189, 191, 200, 284, 339; domestic policy of, 191–193; consumer goods, 192; moderates in, 193; effect of Revolution on, 172, 181, 196; influence of, 274; image of, 514; mentioned, 18, 28, 225, 364, 384, 446, 502, 503, 511, 512, 515

—Communists: as state of, 171, 189, 193; and labor, 177, 186;

Cuba (continued)
—Communists (continued)
   control by, 179, 185; and Castro,
   179, 187; attacks by, 182; alignment with, 190; influence of, 194;
   mentioned, 178, 183, 502
—United States: interest of, 172,
   174; assistance from, 176, 183; opposition to, 189; influence of, 189;
   policy of, 189, 190, 197; mentioned, 177, 179, 521
Cuban Communist party: 180, 181
Cuban People's party: 178
Cuban Revolution: effects of, 172, 181,
   196, 276; under Communists, 175;
   myths concerning, 178; ideology of,
   180, 190; popularity of, 191, 193,
   225; mentioned, 16, 171, 177, 200,
   431, 502
Cuban Revolutionary Council: 195
Cuenca, Ecuador: 273
Cuernavaca, Mexico: 26
Cul de Sac Plain (Haiti): 146
Cunday, Colombia: 235
Cundinamarca, Department of (Colom-
   bia): 245, 250
Cunha, Euclides da: 457
Cunill, Pedro: on Chile's mushroom
   settlements, 341
Curicó (district): 360, 362, 363
CUT. *See* Central Unica de Trabaja-
   dores de Chile
Cuzco, Department of (Peru): 311
CVF. *See* Corporación Venezolana de
   Fomento
CVP. *See* Venezuelan Petroleum Cor-
   poration
Czechoslovakia: 311

Danzós Palomino, Ramón: 41
Darien jungles: 117
Darió, Ruben: 502
DCG. *See* Christian Democratic party
d'Eca, Raul: on progress of Latin
   America, 2
decentralization: 126
DeGaulle, Charles: 418
delegados: 386
Demetrio: 499
democracy: barriers to establishment
   of, 6; in Mexico, 22; in Central
   America, 57; in Guatemala, 66, 79;
   in Costa Rica, 91, 95; in Panama,

democracy (continued)
   128, 129, 141; in Latin America,
   172; in Cuba, 183; mentioned, 41,
   309, 488
Democratic Alliance: 297
Democratic Christian party: 274
Democratic Front. *See* Frente Demo-
   crático
Democratic Institutionalist Alliance:
   334
Democratic Institutionalist Coalition:
   275
Democratic party: 294
Democratic Revolutionary Front: 194
Democratic Socialist party: 416, 418,
   420
Democrats: United States, 106; Argen-
   tina, 416
Democristianos: 299
Département du Nord (Haiti): 148
despotism: 64, 66, 132, 175, 270
Dessalines, Jean Jacques: 148, 153
Dewey, John: 508
D'Hondt representation: 218, 361, 402
Diario de Costa Rica: 100
Diario, El: 318
Diaro Ilustrado, El: 346
Díaz, Felix: 23
Díaz, Porfirio: 21, 30, 36, 509, 522
Díaz Lanz, Pedro: 180
Díaz Ordaz, Gustavo: 28, 45
Díaz Torres: 44
Dickman, Enrique: 416
dictators: concepts of, 2, 484; in Mex-
   ico, 22, 23, 38; in Guatemala, 66,
   78; in Costa Rica, 94; of Central
   America, 101; in Dominican Repub-
   lic, 160, 164, 166, 168, 170, 497–
   498; in Cuba, 172, 176, 177, 178,
   179, 182, 186, 187, 189, 193; in
   Venezuela, 205, 498; in Colombia,
   235–236, 511; in Peru, 294, 308; in
   Bolivia, 315, 316; in Chile, 351, 358;
   in Paraguay, 375, 390; in Argentina,
   398, 481, 496, 498; in Uruguay, 432,
   434; in Brazil, 450, 454, 460, 463,
   465, 474, 475; in Latin America,
   512, 521; in Haiti, 520; mentioned,
   55, 364, 488
Diez de Medina, Fernando: on Bolivian
   Indians, 318, 330
DIGEPOL: Venezuelan national police,
   214, 217
diputados de partido: 47

disarmament: 95
Dogma Socialista: 481
dollar diplomacy: 174
Dominican Republic: political parties of, 106, 160, 161, 163, 164, 169; and Europe, 157; agriculture in, 157; exports of, 157, 158; economy of, 157, 159; and Haiti, 157, 159, 167; urbanization in, 158; population of, 158; geography of, 158; mining in, 158; Spain in, 158, 159; races of, 158, 159; slums in, 159; dictatorship in, 159, 160, 164, 166, 168, 170; labor in, 159, 162, 163; landowners in, 159, 164, 166; Roman Catholic Church of, 159, 164–165; anti-communism in, 160; exiles from, 160, 161; students in, 160, 163; leftists in, 160, 163, 165, 169, 170; nationalism in, 161, 163; government of, 161, 167, 168; rightists in, 161, 169, 170; military in, 163, 165–166, 169; upper classes in, 164, 165; constitutions of, 164, 167; lower classes of, 164, 169; middle sectors of, 164, 169, 170; OAS in, 169, 170; reforms in, 170; mentioned, 100, 145, 146, 173, 179, 424, 483, 497–498, 512, 515
—United States: occupation of, 18, 96, 159, 161, 163, 164, 165, 170, 512, 520; mentioned, 160, 169, 521
Dominicans: 252
Doña Barbara: 498
Draper, Theodore: on Bay of Pigs invasion, 195; on Castroism, 180
DRF. *See* Democratic Revolutionary Front
Dulles, John Foster: 130
Durán, Julio: 362, 363
Dutch: 451, 480
duties: 271, 281, 386
Dutra, Eurico: 471
Duvalier, François: opposition to, 149, 150; election tactics of, 151; authoritarianism of, 151, 152, 154–155, 520; excommunication of, 153; and army, 154; mentioned, 481, 509
Duverger, Maurice: 102, 102 n.11

earthquakes: 341
Easter Island: 338

Echeverría, Esteban: theories of, 481; on inalienable rights, 482; mentioned, 491, 495
Echandi, Mario: 95, 99, 103, 106, 113
Echandistas: 104, 106
Ecuador: Roman Catholic Church in, 96, 270, 273, 275, 276, 286; and Colombia, 202, 268; as part of Gran Colombia, 232, 232 n.2; crops of, 267, 268; Indians of, 267, 268, 269, 273, 282, 284, 287, 500; exports of, 267, 268, 270; population of, 267, 268, 282, 286; upper classes in, 267, 269, 273, 282; political parties of, 267, 270, 271–279 passim; military of, 267, 271, 275–276, 283, 286; illiteracy in, 267, 284; geography of, 268; races in, 268, 269, 284; transportation, 268, 270; and Peru, 268, 277; as part of Confederation of Greater Colombia, 269; Spanish in, 269; lower class, 269; middle sectors of, 269, 282; urbanization in, 269, 286; education, 270, 273; Constitutions of, 270, 277, 277 n.11, 278, 279, 281, 282; nationalism in, 270, 284; leftists in, 271, 273, 274, 275, 277; reform in, 271, 273, 276, 277; students in, 271, 276–277, 286; taxes in, 271, 280, 285; customs duties in, 271, 281; strikes in, 271, 283; riots in, 271, 284; Conservatives in, 272–273; Liberals in, 272–273; Social Christians, 273; rightists, 273, 275; landowners, 273, 275; labor in, 273, 276–277; government organization of, 278, 279, 279 n.12, 280–282; "functional" senators of, 279, 282, 283; literacy in, 282; and Cuba, 284; and Alliance for Progress, 286; mentioned, 92, 340, 512, 513, 515
Eder, Harold: 240
Eder family: 258
education: in Mexico, 25, 29, 258; in Central America, 57; in Honduras, 85; in Costa Rica, 93, 94, 96; in Panama, 122, 123, 124–125, 126, 129, 134, 140–141; in Haiti, 150; in Cuba, 183, 187, 191, 192; in Venezuela, 201, 203, 204, 206, 207, 219, 224; in Colombia, 233, 236, 242–244 passim, 245, 251, 252, 254; in Ecuador, 270, 273; in Peru, 310; in Bolivia, 319, 330, 331; in Chile, 345,

education (continued)
355, 365; in Paraguay, 375, 380,
383, 384, 389, 390; in Argentina,
395, 414, 425; in Uruguay, 434, 435;
in Brazil, 456, 469; in Latin America, 492, 494; in United States, 494;
mentioned, 8, 11, 17, 61
Eighth Inter-American Conference:
234
Eisenhower, Dwight D.: 116 n.4
ejidatarios: 34
ejidos: 26, 27, 43, 47
El Arado Sugar Plantation and Mill:
249
El Petén (region): 58
El Salvador: government organization
of, 63, 74; liberals in, 65; Guatemalan intervention in, 64, 66; political parties in, 68, 70, 86, 87; Constitutions of, 74, 75, 87; reform in,
85, 86, 87; military in, 85, 86, 87;
classes in, 85, 86, 87, 71; strike in,
86; agriculturalists in, 86; coffee in,
86; Communists in, 86, 87; landowners of, 87; students in, 87. *See also*
Central America
empresa agrícola: 329
Encarnacion, Paraguay: 374
encomienda: 3, 60
England. *See* Great Britain
Enriquillo Plain: 157
Entre la libertad y el miedo: 488
Equiguren, Luis Antonio: 498
era de Trujillo, La: 497
Escalante, Aníbal: 180
Escambray Mountains: 179, 194
Escola Superior de Guerra: 462
Espectador, El: 236
Estigarriba, José Felix: 317, 376, 381
estancias: 430
estancieros: 433, 435
Estime, Dumarsais: 154
Estrada Cabrera, Manuel: 66, 509
Europe: 9, 21, 121, 125, 157, 190, 382,
425, 483
Europeans: 173, 339
exiles: in Costa Rica, 96, 99, 107; from
Haiti, 150, 154, 155; from Domini-
can Republic, 160, 161; from Cuba,
177, 181, 184, 186, 189, 193, 194,
195; from Peru, 308, 500; in Bolivia, 321, 323; from Paraguay, 376,
384, 388, 390; from Brazil, 457;
mentioned, 4

existentialism: 486, 489, 523
exporters: 92
exports: from Panama, 124; from
Haiti, 146; from Dominican Republic, 157; from Cuba, 174; from Colombia, 240, 241; from Ecuador,
267, 268, 270; from Peru, 291; from
Bolivia, 324, 328

factionalism: 63–66 passim, 256, 407–
408
Facundo: 496, 498, 498 n.32
Facundo Quiroga, Juan: 496–497
Falange Nacional: Chile, 356, 363
Falangists: El Salvador, 86
FALN. *See* Armed Forces of National
Liberation
Family Electoral Alliance: 464
FAR. *See* Revolutionary Armed Forces
FAR. *See* Fuerza Armada Revolucio-
naria
Fascism: 233, 320, 382
fascists: 386
Father's Day: 124
favelas: 430, 451, 466
FCV. *See* Federación Campesina de
Venezuela
FD. *See* Frente Democrático
FDT. *See* Federación Dominicana de
Trabajo
FEDEAGRO. *See* Federación Nacional
de Asociaciones de Productos Agro-
pecuarios
FEDECAMARAS. *See* Federación de
Cámaras de Comercio e Industria
FEDETAV. *See* Independent Federa-
tion of Workers of Valle
Febrerismo: 382
Febrerista party. *See* Partido Revolu-
cionario
Febreristas: 377, 378, 379, 381–382
FECH: 348
Federación Campesina de Venezuela:
211
Federación de Cámaras de Comercio e
Industria: 212
Federación de Estudiantes Domínica-
nos: 163
Federación Dominicano de Trabajo:
162
Federación Nacional de Asociaciones
de Productos Agropecuarios: 212
Federación Obrera de Chile: 350, 357

Federación Rural: 445
Federación Sindical de Trabajadores Mineros: 324
Federal District: Mexico, 28, 37, 47; Venezuela, 230
Federalists: 296, 412
Federal Union party: 411
Federal War: 202
Fédération de Travaillers Haitiens: 150
Fédération Haitienne Travaillers: 150
Federation of Cuban Women: 181
Federation of University Students: 277
FENALCO. *See* National Merchants Federation
FEP. *See* Popular Electoral Front
Fe Sangre Victoria: 42
feudalism: 60, 78, 79, 175, 329, 353, 358, 479, 501
FHT. *See* Fédération Haitienne Travaillers
Fiallo, Viriato: 161
Fiat: 51
Fidelismo: 191, 193, 211
Fidelistas: working with Conservatives, 172; in Cuba, 179, 180, 196; and Communists, 180, 181; in Venezuela, 210; mentioned, 190, 212
Fignole, Daniel: 150, 508
Figueres, José: roles of, 89, 95, 99, 101; popularity of, 102, 112, 113; in center wing of party, 105; feud of with Ulate, 106; and Calderón, 106; administration of, 113; mentioned, 96, 103, 108, 109, 113, 382, 508
Figueristas: 106
fincas: 93, 94, 179, 244, 245, 254
fish: 291
fishing: 88, 290, 327
Fitzgibbon, Russell H.: 513
FLIN. *See* National Liberation Front
FLN. *See* Frente de Liberación Nacional
Flores, Juán José: 269
FND. *See* Frente Nacional Democrático
FNPC. *See* National Federation of Parties of the Center
FOCH. *See* Federación Obrera de Chile
Fonseca, Deodoro da: 507
Fonseca, Deogracias: 236
force vitale: 505, 506
Forces Armées Révolutionaires Haitiennes: 150

Ford, Davis and Bacon report: on effects of Bolivian mine nationalization, 326
Ford Motor Company: 292
FOUPSA. *See* Frente Obrero Unido Pro Sindicatos Autónomos
FOUPSA-CESITRADO. *See* Frente Obrero Unido Pro Sindicatos Autónomos-Central Sindical de Trabajadores Dominicanos
Fragua: 163
France: and Latin America, 21, 146, 203, 314, 432; mentioned, 5, 7, 20, 116, 200, 368, 444, 480
Francia, José Gaspar Rodríquez de: 375
Franciscans: 252
Franco, Rafael: 376, 382, 426
Franklin, Albert B.: on Roman Catholic Church in Ecuador, 276
FRAP. *See* Frente de Acción Popular
Frapistas: 359, 360, 364, 371
free masonry: 183
"Free Port of Colón": 120
FRB. *See* Bolivian Revolutionary Front
Frei Montalva, Eduardo: on governmental changes, 16; advisers to, 347; administration of, 353, 369, 370; ideology of, 356–357; election of, 361, 364; mentioned, 363, 521
Freile Posso, Guillermo: 275
French: in Latin America, 118, 127, 148, 339, 464, 483; mentioned, 10, 480
French (language): 147
French Revolution: 496
Frente de Acción Popular: 358, 362, 363, 371
Frente de Liberación Nacional: 299
Frente Democrático: in Peru, 296; in Chile, 349, 362, 363, 365
Frente [de Transformación] Nacional: 248. *See also* Frente Nacional
Frente Electoral del Pueblo. *See* Popular Electoral Front
Frente Nacional: creation of, 237, 248, 264; and military, 253; explanation of, 255–256; opposition to, 257, 258; mentioned, 244, 245, 249, 259, 263, 264
Frente Nacional Democrático: 210, 228
Frente Obrero Unido Pro Sindicatos Autónomos: 162

Frente Obrero Unido Pro Sindicatos Autónomos-Central Sindical de Trabajadores Dominicanos: 162, 163
Frente Universitario Radical Revolucionario: 163
Freyre, Gilberto: 447, 458, 507, 508
Friedman, John: on term "intellectual" in underdeveloped society, 61
Friendship among Peoples, Institute for: 183
Frondizi, Arturo: overthrow of, 404, 408–409, 512; administration of, 406, 410, 413, 414, 415, 417, 421; and Intransigent Radical Civic Union, 413, 414; conflict with Allende, 418; mentioned, 398
fruit: 327, 393, 394, 477
Frutos, Juan Manuel: 377
FSB. *See* Bolivian Socialist Falange
FTH. *See* Fédération Travaillers Haitiens
Fuerza Armada Revolucionaria: 311
Fundamental Law of February 7, 1959: 182
fundos: 342, 343
FURR. *See* Frente Universitario Radical Revolucionario

Gainza, Gabino: 63
Gaitán, Jorge Eliécer: 233, 234, 254
Galápagos Islands: 268, 279
Galíndez, Jesus de: 497
Gallegos, Rómulo: 204, 208, 223, 498
Gálvez, Juan Manuel: 84, 85
gamonal: 71
gangsterism: 176
García-Godoy, Héctor: 169
García Moreno, Gabriel: 270, 273
Garde d'Haiti: 149, 154
Garza, David: on liberation movement in Mexico, 40
Garza García, Nuevo Leon: 53
gauchupines: 20
GDP. *See* gross domestic production
gendarmerie: 154
General Association of University Students: 86
General Confederation of Labor: 409, 410, 411, 415
General Economic Confederation: 412
General Motors: 292
General Strike Committee: 84

General Union of Mexican Workers and Peasants: 34, 40
gens de couleur: 147
geography: of Central America, 58; of Costa Rica, 91–92; of Venezuela, 200–201; of Colombia, 231–232; of Ecuador, 268; of Peru, 289–290; of Chile, 337–339; of Paraguay, 373–375; of Argentina, 393–394; of Uruguay, 429–430; of Brazil, 447–450 passim
Germans: 10, 189, 339, 464
Germany: 490
Gesti culador, El: 500
Gestido, Oscar: 444
Ghioldi, Américo: 417
GFOCH. *See* Gran Federación Obrera de Chile
Gironde: 496
Glade, William P.: on Mexico's economic policy, 47–48
Gobineau, Joseph: 457
gold: in California, 65, 127; in Mexico, 30; in Cuba, 173, 175; from Venezuela, 201, 223; mentioned, 93
Goldwater, Barry: 43
Golfito (area): 92
golpe de estado: 15
Gómez, Juan Vicente: 203, 206, 498
Gómez, Laureano: administration of, 234, 237, 252, 259; descendants of, 256; overthrow, 511; mentioned, 233, 255
Gómez Hurtado, Alvaro: 255
Gómez Morín, Manuel: 43
González, J. Natalicio: 377, 380
González Navarro, José: 211
González Torres, José: 43, 44
González Videla, Gabriel: 349, 351
Good Neighbor Policy: 176
gorilas: 408, 409, 423
Goulart, João: overthrow of, 448, 464, 465, 512; and agricultural workers, 450; regime of, 464, 465, 471, 472, 473; mentioned, 454, 460, 461, 467, 468, 469, 475
Goytía, Victor E.: 133
Granada (area): 65
Gran Chaco: Bolivia, 316; Paraguay, 374, 376, 391
Gran Chaco War: impact of, 317, 319, 381; mentioned, 316, 320, 322, 333, 373, 377
Gran Colombia: 202, 232

Gran Federación Obrera de Chile: 350
Grand Chaco: 394, 403
Granma: 188
Grant, Ulysses S.: 159
Grau San Martín, Ramón: 176, 177, 181, 182, 183, 186
Great Britain: debts to, 21, 203; intervention of in Central America, 65; and Venezuela, 203, 224; and Paraguay, 377; and Brazil, 448; and Uruguay, 432, 433, 434; mentioned, 110, 116, 200, 431, 479, 496
Great War (Uruguay): 437
Green, Thomas Hill: 490
"gringos": 115
grito de dolores: 20
gros nègre: 148, 153
gross domestic production: 374
gross national product: 31, 422, 442
Groups of Honor: 322, 323
Guadalajara, Mexico: 28, 29, 52
Guadalupe Hidalgo, Treaty of: 20
Guairá Rapids: 375
Guajira, the: 232
Guanaban (state): 449, 455, 463, 467, 469
Guancasts (peninsula): 92, 93, 96, 108, 110
Guaraní: 373, 374
Guaraní (language): 375, 391
Guardia, Ernesto de la: 128, 131, 133
Guardia Nacional. *See* National Guard
Guatemala: revolution in, 16, 77–79, 81–83, 90; population distribution in, 58; Indians in, 59, 76, 78, 81, 81 n.14, 82, 501, 517; *mandamiento* system in, 60; Central American domination by, 63, 64; Ladinos of, 64, 81, 81 n.14, 82; political parties in, 65, 68, 69, 83; Roman Catholic Church in, 65, 77, 82; reforms in, 65, 78, 80, 82; dictatorship in, 66, 78; democracy in, 66, 79; leftists in, 69, 78, 79, 82; upper class in, 71, 71 n.6, 77, 79, 82; Constitution of, 73, 75, 83; government of, 74, 79–80, 81, 83; military in, 77, 82; foreign corporations in, 78; labor unions in, 78; feudalism in, 78, 79; middle sector in, 78, 79, 80; students in, 78, 82; revolutionaries in, 79, 80; lower classes in, 80; United States in, 81, 520, 521; landowners in, 82;

Guatemala (continued)
crops in, 501; mentioned, 28, 84, 92, 94, 488, 503, 511, 512, 513, 515
Guatemala City, Guatemala: 63, 82
Guayana Highlands: 200, 201
Guayaquil, Ecuador: 268, 270, 271, 275, 284
guayaquilenos: 268, 285
guerillas: Cuba, 179, 184, 191, 194, 197, 511; Venezuela, 216, 224, 226; Colombia, 239, 240, 254, 259; Peru, 305, 311; Bolivia, 336; Paraguay, 377; Mexico, 499; mentioned, 112, 497
Guerra de Quince Años: 314
Guerrero, Lorenzo: 89
Guerrero, Vicante: 20
Guevara, Ernesto "Che": 182
Guevara Arze, Walter: 332, 333
Guevara Morena, Carlos: 274, 275
Guido, José María: 399, 410, 417
Guillén, Nicolás: 502–504, 509
Guión Roja: 377
Gulf of Gonaives: 146
Gulf of Mexico: 175
Gulf Oil Corporation: 327
Guzmán Blanco, Antonio: 202, 215

hacendado: 175
Haedo, Eduardo Victor: 443
Haiti: geography of, 145, 146; population of, 146–148, 505; land of, 146, 148; and France, 146, 148; communications in, 146, 151, 156; crops of, 146, 154; African culture in, 147; languages of, 147; Afro-Europeans in, 147, 148; nationalism in, 147, 151, 154; Roman Catholic Church in, 147, 152; middle sectors in, 147, 150, 152; Revolution of 1946, 147, 154, 156; illiteracy in, 147, 155, 156; lower classes in, 148, 149, 156; Negroes in, 148, 149, 152, 156; slaves, 148, 505; government of, 149, 151, 153, 155–156; spiritualism, 149, 153; finances, 149, 156; education in, 149, 156; and United States, 149, 156, 520; Communists in, 150; strikes in, 150; urbanization in, 150; students in, 150; labor in, 150; exile groups from, 150, 154, 155; politics of, 150, 156; authoritarianism in, 151, 152, 154–155, 156; Protestants

Haiti (continued)
in, 152; Constitutions of, 152; military of, 153–155; reform in, 156; taxes, 156; and Dominican Republic, 157, 159, 167; literature of, 504, 505, 506; dictatorship in, 520; mentioned, 173, 481, 515
Haiti Sun: 151
Hamburg, Germany: 338
Hamilton, Alexander: 456, 483
Hanke, Lewis: on Carías regime, 83
Hapsburgs: 21
Hare system: 108
Harvard: 458
Havana, Cuba: 176, 179, 187, 190, 225
Havana, University of, 178, 194
Haya de la Torre, Raul: 101, 295, 296, 297, 298, 299, 413, 500
Hay-Bunau-Varilla Treaty: 127
health: Panama, 120, 123, 124, 127; Haiti, 156; Venezuela, 203, 204, 209, 224, 227; Bolivia, 331; Paraguay, 380, 384, 390; Argentina, 426
Hegel, G. W. F.: 486
Hennessey, C. A. M.: on Cuba's politics, 175; on Cuba's mass media, 188
Herard, Charles: 149
Heredia, Costa Rica: 92, 108, 110
Hernández, José: 497
Hernández Martínez, Maximiliano: 66, 85
Herrera, Luis Alberto de: 437, 443
Hertzog, Enrique: 321, 322
Heureaux, "Lilis": 159, 162, 170
Hicks, Frederic: on Paraguay's political parties, 379
Hidalgo, Miguel: 20
highways: in Mexico, 33, 48, 50; in Panama, 119; in Colombia, 234; in Peru, 292, 307; in Bolivia, 328; in Paraguay, 374
Hispaniola: 145, 157
Hobbes, Thomas: 488
Hochschield, Mauricio: 320, 322, 324
Hofernes: 490
Holleran, Mary P.: on military despotism in Central America, 64
hombres de Macias: 19, 499
Honduras: population distribution of, 58; government of, 63, 74; Guatemalan intervention in, 64, 66; Liberals in, 65, 85; United States in, 67; political parties in, 68, 70, 85;

Honduras (continued)
upper class in, 71, 84; Constitution of, 74; suffrage in, 83; labor in, 83, 84–85; conservatism in, 83, 85; Communists in, 84; strike in, 84; middle sector in, 84, 85; reform in, 85; education in, 85; military in, 85; mentioned, 38, 511, 512, 515. *See also* Central America
Honduras Right-Wing: 85
hookworm: 147
houngans: 153
housing: in El Salvador, 86; in Costa Rica, 113; in Panama, 122, 123, 129, 134; in Dominican Republic, 158; in Cuba, 187; in Venezuela, 203, 204, 224, 227, 230; in Colombia, 235; in Peru, 292, 312; in Chile, 340, 370; in Paraguay, 380; in Uruguay, 430
Housing Institute: 389
Hoy: 188
Huacho, Peru: 298
Huasipungo: 478, 500
Huber, Ernst Rudolf: 484
Huerta, Adolfo de la: 25
Huerta, Victoriano: 23, 498
Huila, Department of (Colombia): 245
Humboldt Current: 290

IAN. *See* Agrarian Reform Institute
IBAD. *See* Brazilian Institute of Democratic Action
Ibáñez, Carlos: 351, 363, 368
Ibarrola, Adolfo Christlieb: 53
Ica, Peru: 298
Icaza, Jorge de: 478, 500
ICT. *See* Instituto de Crédito Territorial
ideales de mayo y la tirania, Los: 481
idealism: 12, 483–484
Illia, Arturo: election of, 399; administration of, 410, 422, 424–425; political party of, 423; mentioned, 410
illiteracy: in Panama, 125; in Haiti, 147, 155, 156; in Cuba, 193; in Venezuela, 209, 221, 224; in Colombia, 242, 242 n.15; in Ecuador, 267, 284; in Peru, 301, 307; in Bolivia, 319, 330, 331, 335; in Chile, 341; in Argentina, 396; in Brazil, 471, 472; in Latin America, 516
Imaz, José Luis de: 522

IMF. *See* International Monetary Fund
immigrants: 9, 10, 339, 483
Imparcial, El: 71 n.6
Imperial French Army: 21
importers: 174, 251
imports: in Panama, 124; in Venezuela, 202, 224; in Colombia, 251; in Bolivia, 328, 332; in Uruguay, 443
Incas: 290, 293, 315, 318, 329, 500
INCE. *See* National Institute of Educational Cooperation
income: in Mexico, 49; in Panama, 120, 129; in Cuba, 174; in Venezuela, 201; in Peru, 292; in Chile, 343, 344, 370; in Paraguay, 374
INCORA. *See* Colombian Institute of Agrarian Reform
Independence Day: Bolivia, 315; Brazil, 470
Independent Federation of Workers of Valle: 258
Independent Liberal party: 70
Independent Peasant Front: 40
Indians: in Mexico, 20, 29, 33, 517; in Central America, 59; in Guatemala, 59, 60, 76, 78, 81, 82, 90, 501, 517; in Costa Rica, 92, 93, 101; in Panama, 120, 121, 126; in Dominican Republic, 158; in Cuba, 173; in Venezuela, 201; in Colombia, 232; in Ecuador, 267, 268, 273, 284, 287, 500; in Peru, 291, 299, 307, 308; in Bolivia, 317, 318, 319, 321, 322, 328, 329, 330; in Chile, 339, 375; in Paraguay, 391; in Argentina, 393, 394; in Uruguay, 431, 439; in Brazil, 448, 458, 507, 508; in Latin America, 517; mentioned, 3, 4, 6, 9, 485, 486, 501
industrialists: native, 11; in Costa Rica, 92, 100, 101; in Venezuela, 211; in Colombia, 238; in Argentina, 412, 415; in Brazil, 465; in Latin America, 493
industrialization: in El Salvador, 86; in Costa Rica, 114; in Panama, 118, 120; in Cuba, 174, 183, 186, 192; in Venezuela, 201, 202, 207, 223; in Peru, 290, 307, 308, 311; in Bolivia, 328; in Paraguay, 384; in Argentina, 395, 398, 413, 414; in Brazil, 462; in Latin America, 519; mentioned, 11, 12, 13, 61

Industrialization, Department of: 183
industry: in Mexico, 43, 52; in Panama, 119; in Cuba, 173; in Venezuela, 204; in Peru, 291; in Bolivia, 316; in Chile, 370; in Paraguay, 389; in Argentina, 394, 395; in Uruguay, 434, 443, 445; in Brazil, 449, 454, 462; in Latin America, 494; in United States, 494; mentioned, 5, 9, 11, 26, 35, 74
inflation: in Colombia, 239, 240, 265; in Bolivia, 326, 332; in Chile, 345, 370; in Uruguay, 435, 442; in Argentina, 422; in Brazil, 462, 475; mentioned, 14
inquilinos: 343
Inquisition: 20
INRA. *See* National Institute of Agrarian Reform
Institute for Agrarian Reform: 389
Institute of Social Security: 224
Institutional Act Number Two: 461, 475
Institutional Revolutionary party: 299
Instituto Agrario Nacional: 214, 223
Instituto de Crédito Territorial: 235
Instituto de Estudios Políticos: 381, 383
Inter-American Development Bank: 239, 332
Inter-American Peace Force: 424
interdentes: 386
Interministerial Commission of Popular Co-operation: 303
International Bank for Reconstruction and Development: 210, 239
International Coffee Agreement: 250
International Confederation of Free Trade Unions and Inter-American Regional Organization of Workers: 162
International Conference of Catholic Youth: 209
International Monetary Fund: and Colombia, 239 n.11, 240; in Bolivia, 332; and Argentina, 398, 414; mentioned, 246
International Petroleum Company: 307
Intransigent Radical Civic Union: 413, 414, 415, 418, 421
Intransigents: 398, 413
Ipanda: 490

IPC. *See* International Petroleum Company
Iquique, Chile: 350
Irazú (volcano): 103
Irigoyen, Hipólito: 398
iron: 30, 172, 199, 223, 338, 430, 457
Islam: 152
Island of Chiloé: 338
Israel: 109
Italians: 10, 339, 431, 464
Italy: 203, 233, 386, 394, 409, 417
Iturbide, Augustín de: 20, 63

Jaguaribe, Helio: 458
Jamaica: 92
Jamaicans: 121
James, Daniel: on regime of Jorge Ubico, 78
Japan: 490
Jaramillo, Rubén: 40
Jaramillo Girardo, José: 237
Jefferson, Thomas: 456
Jesuits: Colombia, 250, 252, 253; in Chile, 347; in Paraguay, 373, 374
Jesus, Carolina de: 466
Jews: 139
Jiménez, Juan Isidro: 159
Jiménez de Quezada, Gonzalo: 232
Jivaros: 268
Johnson, John J.: on interests of middle sector, 11; on the middle sectors, 35
Johnson, Kenneth: on political instability, 16; mentioned, 513
Johnson, L. B.: 116
Juan Fernández Islands: 338
Juárez, Benito: 20, 21, 24, 497, 509
juge de paix: 153
Julião, Francisco: 450, 451, 465
Jurado Nacional de Elecciones. *See* National Election Jury
Justo, Brother Ramón: 252
Justo, Juan B.: 416

Kafka, Franz: 490
Kant, Immanuel: 480
Kautsky, John: generalizations of on social divisions in traditional societies, 6–7
Keenleyside Mission: on Bolivian Indian, 317, 328
Kennedy, John F.: 116 n.4, 224, 466

kidnapping: 225, 240, 320
Kling, Merle: on political instability, 16
Kubitschek, Juscelino: 455, 471, 475, 476
Kundt, General: 316

laberinto de la soledad, El: 487, 523
labor: in politics, 10, 69; codes of, 14, 98; in Mexico, 24, 42, 54; in Central America, 61, 62, 72, 77; in Guatemala, 78; in Honduras, 83, 84–85; in Nicaragua, 89; in Panama, 135–136; in Canal Zone, 136; in Haiti, 150; in Dominican Republic, 160, 162–163; in Cuba, 174, 176, 182, 183, 186, 187, 188, 191; in Venezuela, 202, 207, 209, 211–212, 220, 227, 518; in Colombia, 233, 249–250, 257, 260; in Ecuador, 273; in Peru, 298, 299, 300, 307, 309, 310; in Bolivia, 319, 320, 322, 323, 324, 326, 333, 518; in Chile, 337, 347, 349, 350–353, 357, 359, 365, 370; in Paraguay, 383, 384, 385, 389; in Argentina, 406, 409–411, 416, 426, 518; in Uruguay, 433, 434, 443, 444, 445–446; in New Zealand, 435; in Brazil, 453, 473; mentioned, 9, 13, 72, 98, 490
Labor party: Argentina, 415; Brazil, 465
La Brea, Peru: 307
La Brea Pariñas Commission: 307
Lacerda, Carlos: 454, 467, 469, 476
Ladinos: 64, 81, 81 n.14, 82, 90
La Follette, Robert: 434
Lake Enriquillo: 157
Lake Maracaibo: 200
lámpara de Aladino, La: 502
Landázuri, Cardinal: 301
landowners: in Central America, 60, 64, 72; in Guatemala, 82; in El Salvador, 87; in Costa Rica, 92, 93, 100, 102; in Panama, 119, 122, 139, 141; in Haiti, 148; in Dominican Republic, 159, 164, 166; in Cuba, 174, 175, 186; in Venezuela, 204, 206; in Colombia, 238, 241, 245; in Ecuador, 273, 275; in Peru, 295, 300; in Bolivia, 317, 320, 329; in Chile, 342, 344, 361; in Paraguay, 381, 389; in Argentina, 395, 396

landowners (continued)
Table 1, 397, 407, 412; in Brazil, 460, 462, 465; mentioned, 6, 71
La Paz, Bolivia: 314, 319, 320, 322, 327, 333, 334, 335
La Paz, University of: 314
La Plata (viceroyalty): 432
La Rosca: 320, 322
Larraín, Monsignor: 252
Larrazabal Brothers: 216
Larrazabal, Wolfgang: 204, 216, 230
latifundias: wiping out of, 30, 47; in Central America, 60; in Colombia, 245; in Bolivia, 329, 330; in Argentina, 395; in Uruguay, 431, 435; in Brazil, 507; mentioned, 8, 93
latifundistas: 245, 318, 518. *See also* landowners
Latin America: violence in, 477, 478; leftists in, 479; feudalism in, 479; and United States, 479, 483, 501, 503, 512, 520; and Roman Catholic Church, 479, 517; rightists in, 479, 520, 521; liberalism in, 480; constitutionalism in, 480; and France, 483; middle sectors in, 492; education in, 492; industrialization in, 492, 494, 518; industrialists in, 493; taxes in, 493, 517; tyranny in, 495–500; military in, 512; dictatorship in, 512, 521; urbanization in, 516; illiteracy in, 516; Indians in, 517; students in, 518; welfare in, 518; over-population of, 519; reform in, 519
Latin American Free Trade Area: 223, 225
Latin Workers Confederation: 40
Laureanistas: 237
Lauroalzatistas: 256
La Vega Real: 157, 158
Law for the Defense of Democracy: 351
lead: 291
League of Agrarian Communities: 34
League of Nations: 490
League of the South: 417
League of States: 490
Lec. *See* Liga Eleitoral Católica
Lechín Oquendo, Juan: 322, 323, 326, 332, 334
leftists: in Mexico, 26, 39, 41, 54; in Guatemala, 69, 82; in Central America, 72; in Costa Rica, 107 n.12; in

leftists (continued)
Dominican Republic, 161, 163, 169, 170; in Latin America, 172, 479; in Venezuela, 205, 209, 225, 226, 227, 228; in Colombia, 233, 248, 250, 253, 257, 258; in Ecuador, 274, 275, 277; in Peru, 297, 298, 308, 311; in Bolivia, 333, 334; in Chile, 346, 357–359, 364, 369, 370, 371; in Paraguay, 382; in Argentina, 421; in Brazil, 458, 469; mentioned, 195, 509. *See also* Communism; Marxists; Socialists; Stalinists; Trotskyites
Leftist Revolutionary party: 333, 334
Legionaries: 376
Leguía, Augusto B.: 294, 509
Leiva, Jorge: 237, 256
leivismo: 255
lemas: 438, 444
Lémus, José María: 86
Lenin, Nikolai: 493
Leninism: 180, 193
León (area): 65
León, Guanajuato: 41
León, Mexico: 47
Leoni, Raúl: election of, 205, 208; and CTV, 211; administration of, 214, 217, 222, 225, 228, 229, 230; and military, 216; mentioned, 204, 210, 219
Lerdo de Tejada, Sebastian: 20, 21, 24
Lescot, Elie: 154
Levant: 10
ley de hacienda: 49
ley del gusto: 486
ley fuga: 22, 23
Ley Júarez: 20
Ley Lerdo: 20
Liberación Nacional party: as majority-bent party, 102; leadership differences within, 105; strength of, 105 Table 1, 108, 114; activities of, 109; mentioned, 97, 99, 102, 107, 112, 114
Liberal party: in Honduras, 85; in Panama, 135; in Bolivia, 334; in Chile, 354–355, 357, 359, 362, 365; in Paraguay, 376, 377, 378, 380, 381; in Brazil, 452
Liberal Radical party: 378, 379
liberalism: in Mexico, 20; in Argentina, 397, 413; democratic 480–483; mentioned, 491, 495, 501, 509. *See* Liberal party; liberals

Liberals: in Mexico, 21; in Honduras, 60, 68; in Central America, 64, 65, 66; in Nicaragua, 66; in Colombia, 106, 233, 234, 237, 247–248, 249, 250, 253, 255–256, 262, 263, 264, 437, 494; in Panama, 133; in Cuba, 181; in Venezuela, 202; in Ecuador, 270, 272–273, 276; in Peru, 299; in Bolivia, 316; in Chile, 346, 354; in Argentina, 412; in Brazil, 463; mentioned, 7, 179
Liga Federal de Acción Rural: 445
Liga de Defensa Comercial: 445
Liga Eleitoral Católica: 463
Ligas Agrarias: 383
Light and Power union: 411
Lima, Alceu Amoroso: 457
Lima, Peru: 290, 292, 298, 299, 306, 307, 310, 336, 430
Lima, viceroy of: 313
Limantour, José Y.: 21
Limón (area): 92, 107, 110
Linares Briceño, Antonio: 216
Lincoln, Abraham: 497
Lippmann, Walter: 508
Lisboa, João Francisco: 506
literacy: in Costa Rica, 94, 108, 113; in Chile, 108, 345, 353, 365; in Uruguay, 109, 430; in Argentina, 108, 441; in Panama, 124; in Venezuela, 206; in Paraguay, 375, 389; in Brazil, 451
livestock: in Venezuela, 201; in Colombia, 245, 246; in Ecuador, 268; in Peru, 312; in Paraguay, 374, 386; in Argentina, 395; in Uruguay, 429, 431
llaneros: 202
llanos: 200, 201
Lleras Camargo, Alberto: administration of, 234, 237, 246, 252, 257; opposition to, 256; writings of, 492–495; on government intervention, 493; mentioned, 255, 509
Lleras Restrepo, Carlos: administration of, 240–242, 265; opposition to, 256; mentioned, 255, 257, 261
Lobato, Monteiro: 457
localism: 64
Locke, John: 482, 488
Lombardo Toledano, Vicente: 26, 37, 40, 89
Lonardi, Eduardo: 411
London, England: 250

López, Alfonso: 233, 234, 248, 250, 251, 253
López, Francisco: 376
López, Jacinto: 34, 40
López Arellano, Oswaldo: 85
López Contreras, Eleazar: 203
López Mateos, Adolfo: 27, 30, 38, 43, 47
López Michelson, Alfonso: 248, 256, 257
Los de abajo: 24, 499
Lota-Coranel (area): 342
lottery: 50
L'Ouverture, Toussaint: 153
lower class: in Central America, 70; interest groups of, 71, 72; in Guatemala, 80; in Nicaragua, 89; in Costa Rica, 92, 101, 107; in Panama, 122, 125, 135; in Haiti, 149, 156; in Dominican Republic, 164, 165, 169; in Cuba, 177, 184, 188, 192; in Venezuela, 205, 206, 216, 219, 227; in Colombia, 242, 242 n.14, 262, 264; in Ecuador, 269; in Chile, 337, 340–343, 344, 355, 360; in Argentina, 395, 397; in Uruguay, 431, 441, 444; in Brazil, 450, 465, 466, 468, 470, 472, 474
Lozano Díaz, Juan: 85
lumber: 88, 328
Lutherans: 139

MAC. *See* Colombian Anarchist Movement
Machadistas: 179
Machado: 186
Machiavelli: 496
Maciel, Antonio: 457
Madero, Francisco I.: 22, 55, 434, 498
Madrazo, Carlos: 53
Madrid, Spain: 410, 415, 422
Magdalena, Department of, 232
Maggi, Carlos: on Uruguayans, 440
Magloire, Paul: 150, 153, 154, 155
malaria: 147, 224, 317
Maldonado Sández, Braulio: 40, 45
Manchester tradition: 381
mandamiento system: 60
manganese: 173, 430
Manuelita: 258
manzanillos: 238, 238 n.9
Maoists: 311
Mao Tse-Tung: 40, 41

MAP. *See* Military Assistance Program
Maracaibo, Venezuela: 206, 221
Maracay, Venezuela: 200, 206
marble: 430
Marbury vs. Madison: 403
Marcha: 437
Marmol, José: 498
Marshall, John: 403
Martí, Jose: 175, 196, 502
Martín Fierro: 497
Martínez Trueba, Andrés: 437
Martz, John D.: on social change in
   Honduras, 84
Marx, Karl: 493
Marxism: 39, 41, 45, 98, 180, 193,
   250, 295, 359, 382, 487, 509
Marxists: Chile, 352, 357, 360, 362,
   364, 371; Brazil, 449, 463, 464, 468;
   mentioned, 180, 226, 299, 333, 426
masombos: 4
Massif du Nord, Haiti: 146
Masters and the Slaves, The: 507
Mater et Magistra: 165, 250
Matin, Le: 151
Matos, Hubert: 180
Maximillian: 21
Mayas: 517
mazorca: 496
Mazzini, Giuseppe: 481
McKinley, William: 502
MDB. *See* Brazilian Democratic Move-
   ment
MDP. *See* Movimiento Democrático
   Peruano
meat: 9, 14, 124, 433
Medellín, Columbia: 10, 18, 244, 251
Medicine, National Union for Workers
   of: 186
medicine, socialized: 27
medieros: 343
Medina Angarita, Isaías: 203, 228
Medinistas: 228
Melbourne, Australia: 338
Melgar, Colombia: 236
Melgarejo, Mariano: 316
Melindez family: 66
Melo, Antônio: 464
Mendes de Almeida, Carlos: 458
Méndez, Epifanio: 381
Méndez Montenegro, Julio: 83
Mendoza, Alberto: 322
Mendoza Heredia, Guillermo: 42
Mendoza Heredia, Rubén: 42
Mercurio, El: 346

Meriño, Fernando: 164
meseta central: 91, 94, 114
mestizos: in Mexico, 20; in Central
   America, 59; in Panama, 121, 122;
   in Cuba, 173; in Ecuador, 269, 284;
   in Peru, 291; in Bolivia, 318; in
   Chile, 340; in Argentina, 394; men-
   tioned, 3, 6, 501
Metal del Diablo: 323
Metalurgical Workers Union: 410
Methodists: 13
Metropolitan Museum of Art: 470
Mexican Armed Forces: 54
Mexican Communist party: 39
Mexican Confederation of Workers:
   26, 37
Mexican Revolution: 12, 16, 30, 52,
   63, 381
Mexican Revolutionary party: 26, 36–
   37
Mexican Social Security System: 47
Mexican Treasury: 23, 26
Mexico: labor in, 14, 24, 28, 42, 54;
   population explosion in, 17, 28, 48;
   politics in, 19, 20–28, 36–46, 52, 53,
   299, 463; Constitutions of, 20, 24,
   43; education in, 25, 28; Conservatives in, 25, 26, 41, 43, 53; anticlericalism in, 25, 26, 43; and United
   States, 25, 27 n.2, 65, 498; oil in,
   26, 30; leftists in, 26, 39, 40, 41, 42,
   43, 45, 54; foreign investors in, 26,
   48; social welfare in, 27, 28, 38, 50,
   51; reform in, 27, 33, 40, 43, 47;
   mining in, 30; government of, 33,
   37, 41–47 passim, 111; economy of,
   33, 47, 48, 52, 292; society of, 34,
   35; Indians in, 34, 517; dictators in,
   43; industry in, 43, 52; public policy
   of, 47–51; urbanization in, 48;
   taxes in, 48–49; lottery in, 50; students in, 54; racism in, 54; control
   of Central America by, 63; and
   Peru, 303; guerillas in, 499; mentioned, 113, 130, 175, 252, 295,
   301, 344, 390, 391, 434, 483, 485,
   486, 487, 497, 498, 500
Mexico City, Mexico: 17, 21, 37, 41,
   51
Mexico, University of: 53, 54
Miami, Florida: 194
Michoacán Torrés, Jose Gonzales: 43
MID. *See* Movement of Integration
   and Development

middle class. *See* middle sectors
Middle East: 339
middle sectors: interests of, 11, 71, 72; in Mexico, 34, 35; in Central America, 61, 70; in Guatemala, 78, 79, 80; in Honduras, 84, 85; in El Salvador, 86, 87; in Nicaragua, 89; in Costa Rica, 92, 99, 100, 101; in Panama, 122, 125, 140, 143; in Haiti, 147, 152, 156; in Dominican Republic, 164, 169, 170; in Cuba, 174, 175, 176, 177, 183, 186, 187, 188, 193, 194; in Venezuela, 205, 206, 216, 219; in Colombia, 243, 243 n.16, 247, 254, 258, 264; in Ecuador, 269; in Peru, 292, 298; in Bolivia, 333; in Chile, 337, 344, 345, 350, 355, 356, 359, 365, 371, 521; in Argentina, 395, 396 Table 1, 397, 398, 407, 415; in Uruguay, 431, 435, 440, 441, 444; in Brazil, 449, 451, 452, 454, 458, 461, 463, 465, 466, 468, 470, 471, 473, 474, 476; in Latin America, 492; mentioned, 4, 11, 35
military: in Central America, 64, 70, 72; in Guatemala, 77, 82, 83; in Honduras, 85; in El Salvador, 85, 86, 87; in Costa Rica, 95, 110, 114; in Haiti, 153–155; in Dominican Republic, 163, 165–166, 169; in Cuba, 176, 184; in Venezuela, 203, 204, 211, 212, 216, 220; in Colombia, 236; in Argentina, 254, 399, 404, 406–409, 411, 423, 424, 425, 441, 473, 512, 520; in Ecuador, 267, 271, 275–276, 283, 286; in Peru, 293, 294, 295, 297, 300, 301, 302, 303, 308, 309; in Bolivia, 316, 319, 320, 321, 323, 332, 335, 512; in Chile, 347, 350, 367; in Paraguay, 374, 377, 386, 387–388, 391; in Uruguay, 441, 442; in Brazil, 449, 452, 453, 454, 455, 458, 459, 461–463, 465, 466, 468, 469, 470, 472, 473–474, 475, 507, 512, 520; in Latin America, 512; mentioned, 5, 7, 8, 11, 16, 60, 95
Military Assistance Program: 335, 512, 518
MIN. *See* Movement of National Intransigence
Minas Gerais (state): 449, 452, 453, 455, 458, 459, 460, 473

minerals: 118, 173, 201, 232, 324, 335
Minha Formação: 506
minifundia: 263, 265, 395, 518
mining: in Chile, 13, 367; as bulwark of Mexican economy, 30; in Dominican Republic, 158; in Peru, 291, 292; in Bolivia, 319, 323, 325, 327; mentioned, 3, 5
MIR. *See* Movement of Intransigence and Renovation
MIR. *See* Movimiento de Izquierda Revolucionaria
Miranda (state): 230
Miristas: 218, 225, 226
Miró Cardona, José: 195
Misiones (area): 393
missiles: 171, 192
missionaries: 127, 295
Mitre, Bartolomé: 481, 509
MLN. *See* National Liberation Movement
MNR. *See* Movimiento Nacional Revolucionario
mobility: 7, 35, 206, 220, 230, 293, 450
mobilization: 471, 472
moderates: 181, 194
modernization: in Cuba, 172, 177; in Venezuela, 205; in Ecuador, 272; in Peru, 302, 312
MOEC. *See* Colombian Student Worker Movement
Molas López, Felipe: 377
Molina, Gerardo: 258
Monagas, Gregorio: 202
Monagas, José Tadeo: 202
Moncado military barracks: 178, 180
Moneda, La: 366
Mongols: 485
Montagnes Noires: 146
Montaña Cuéllar, Diego: 258
Montenegro, Carlos: on effect of Gran Chaco War, 317
Monterrey, Mexico: 10, 29, 50
Montevideo, Uruguay: 384, 430, 433, 445
montuvio: 269
Moors: 507
MOP. *See* Mouvement Ouvrier Paysan
Morais, José Emirio de: 468
Morales, Augustín: 316
mordida, la: 4
Morelos, José Maria: 20, 40

Morínigo, Higinio: 377, 390
Morones, Luis: 25, 26
Morrow, Dwight: 25
Moscow: 161, 190, 211, 274, 299, 334, 358
Mosquera, Tomás Cipriano de: 233
Mother's Day: 124
Mouvement Ouvrier Paysan: 150
Mouvement Renovation Nationale: 156
Movement of Integration and Development: 418
Movement of Intransigence and Renovation: 414
Movement of National Intransigence: 414
Movement for Revolutionary Recovery: 195
Movement of Syndical Unity and Coordination: 410, 411
Movimiento Democrático Peruano: 297, 298–299, 300
Movimiento de Izquierda Revolucionaria: 205, 226, 299
Movimiento Nacional Revolucionario: 320, 321, 322, 324, 325, 326, 327, 328–330, 331–332, 334, 335
Movimiento Popular Colorado: 380
Movimiento Popular Dominicano: 161
Movimiento Revolucionario Liberal: 248, 255, 256–257, 259, 263
MPC. *See* Popular Christian Movement
MPD. *See* Movimiento Popular Dominicano
MRL. *See* Movimiento Revolucionario Liberal
MRP. *See* Revolutionary Movement of the People
MRR. *See* Movement for Revolutionary Recovery
MSC. *See* Social Christian Movement
MUCS. *See* Movement of Syndical Unity and Coordination
mulâtres: 147, 148, 149, 154
mulatto: 121, 122, 268
mundo es ancho y ajeno, El: 500
Munio, Dana: on Conservative governments in Central America, 64–65
Muñiz, Ramon: 416
mushroom settlements: 341

Mutual El Pueblo: 292
mysticism: 17

Nabuco de Araujo, Joaquim Aurelio Barreto: 506
Nación, La: 346
Nacional Financiera: 33
Napoleon: 20, 452
Napoleon III: 21
Napoleonic Code: 293
Naranjo Villegas, Abel: 252
Nardone, Benito: 443, 445
Nariño, Department of: 243, 246
Nash, Manning: on Guatemalan Indian communities, 76, 81
National Agrarian Institute: 227
National Association of Cuban Sugar Mill Owners: 186
National Association of Industrialists: 244, 248, 249, 251
National Autonomist party: 412
National Bar Association: 186
National Chamber of Commerce: 445
National Chamber of Industries: 445
National Civic Democratic Movement: 273
National Civic Union: 332
National Confederation of Peasants: 37
National Constituent Assembly: 378
National Democratic Union: 460, 461, 464
National Election Jury: 297, 302
National Epic: 376
National Exporting Council: 250
National Federation of Coffee Growers: 250
National Federation of Parties of the Center: 416, 417
National Federation of Public School Teachers: 310
National Federation of Velasquistas: 274
National Financiers: 48
National Front. *See* Frente Nacional
National Guard: of Nicaragua, 88; of Panama, 131, 133, 135, 139, 142, 143
National Institute of Agrarian Reform: 192
National Institute of Educational Cooperation: 214

National Leftist Revolutionary party: 334
National Liberation Army: 240, 241
National Liberation Front. *See* Frente de Liberación Nacional
National Liberation Movement: 40, 41, 53, 54, 69, 83
National Merchants Association. *See* Corporación Nacional de Comerciantes
National Merchants Federation: 244, 248, 249, 251
National Odriist Union. *See* Union Nacional Odriísta
National party. *See* Partido Nacional
National Patriotic Coalition: 133
National Patriotic Front: 271
National Peasants Confederation: 34
National Police: 165
National Popular Alliance: 256, 257–258, 259, 263
National Railroads: 50
National Renovating Alliance: 459, 461, 468
National Revolutionary Committee: 323
National Revolutionary party: 25, 26, 36
National School of Public Administration: 237
National Secretariat of Communications and Public Works: 48, 50
National Secretariat for Social Assistance: 235
National Students Union: 472
National Tax Division: 238
National Union party: 297
National University: in Colombia, 234, 236, 239 n.13, 240, 258; in Paraguay, 375, 381, 383, 386
nationalism: in Central America, 61; in Panama, 120, 130, 131, 141; in Haiti, 147, 151, 154; in Dominican Republic, 161, 163; in Cuba, 175, 177, 180, 189; in Venezuela, 203, 207, 209; in Peru, 293; in Bolivia, 317; in Chile, 339, 356; in Paraguay, 375, 379, 391; in Argentina, 414, 425; in Brazil, 451, 463, 470; mentioned, 11, 12, 117
Nationalist Liberal party: 70, 89
Nationalists: in Honduras, 70; in Cuba, 181; in Argentina, 411, 412
naturaleza: 484, 502

Navas Pardo, Rafael: 236
Nazi party: 484
nazism: 382
Needler, Martin C.: on Velasco Ibarra, 275
Negroes: in Central America, 59; in Costa Rica, 92; in Panama, 121, 122, 126; in Haiti, 147, 148, 152, 156; in Dominican Republic, 158, 159; in Colombia, 232; in Ecuador, 269; in Peru, 291; in Paraguay, 375; in Argentina, 394; in Brazil, 451, 458, 507, 508; in Cuba, 502; mentioned, 4, 154
neo-capitalism: 67, 71
neo-fascism: 54
neo-feudalism: 67, 88
nepotism: 120, 494
Neruda, Pablo: 502
New Hampshire: 157
New Spain: 20
New York, New York: 116, 338
New York Stock Market: 294
New Zealand: 435
newspapers: in Costa Rica, 109; in Panama, 137; in Haiti, 150; in Venezuela, 221; in Colombia, 236; in Peru, 310; in Bolivia, 318, 320, 322, 335; in Chile, 346; in Paraguay, 376, 377, 382, 389; in Uruguay, 437, 441, 446; in Brazil, 457, 458, 463, 470, 472, 475; mentioned, 188
Nicaragua: government of, 63, 65, 70, 74; and Guatemala, 64; and United States, 66, 88, 96, 520; Conservatives in, 66, 501; foreign capital in, 67, 88; political parties in, 68, 70; upper class in, 71; Constitution of, 74, 75; neo-feudalism in, 88; industries in, 88; National Guard of, 88; reforms in, 88; Communists in, 89; labor in, 89; lower class in, 89; middle sectors in, 89; and Costa Rica, 89, 113; exiles in, 194; mentioned, 92, 93, 94, 96, 99, 502, 511, 515, 520. *See also* Central America
Nicaraguan Political party: 70
nickel: 158, 173
Nietzsche: 484, 486
Niteroi, Brazil: 450
nitrates: 14, 316, 338, 350
Nixon, Richard: 511
Noticias de Ultima Hora, Las: 346
Nova Scotia: 157

Nouel, Adolfo: 164
nucleo escolar: 330
Nueva Granada, Viceroyalty of: 127, 232, 232 n.2
Nuestra América: 502
Nuestra revolución industrial: 492
Nuevo Casas Grandes, Mexico: 45
Nuñez, Rafael: 233

OAS. *See* Organization of American States
Oaxaca, Mexico: 31
Obregón, Alvaro: 23, 24, 29, 36, 486
Obrerismo Organizado de Nicaragua: 89
Ocampo, Melchor: 20, 24
October Revolution: 208, 209, 216, 229
ODECA. *See* Central American Common Market
Odria, Manuel: 296, 297, 298, 300, 301
Odriístas: 297, 304, 311
Oduber, Daniel: 101, 103, 104, 114
Office of Agrarian Affairs: 82
Office of Economic Opportunity: 304
Oficina de Control Político: 320
oil. *See* petroleum
Ojeda, Gonzalo de: 323
O Jornal de Timon: 506
ojos de los enterrados, Los: 501
oligarchy: in Panama, 127, 130; in Ecuador, 272, 276; mentioned, 6, 7, 289
Olivares, José Trueba: 42
Onganía, Juan Carlos: 423, 425–426
Ordónez, Luis E.: 236
Organic Law of Municipalities: 306
Organization of American States: 96, 169, 170, 225, 383, 511, 512
Organization of Petroleum Exporting: 223
Oribe, Manuel: 432
Orientals: 173, 291, 318, 441
Oriente: 268, 277
Oriente Province, Cuba: 178, 179, 187
Orinoco River: 200, 201, 223, 246
Orlich, Francisco: 101, 104, 112
Ornes, Horacio: 160
Orozco, Pascual: 22
Ortega y Gasset, José: 484
Ortiz Rubio, Pascual: 25
Ortodoxos: 178, 180, 181, 188, 194
Oruro, Bolivia: 322

Orwell, George: 490
Os sertões: 457
Osorio, Oscar: 69, 96
Ospina Pérez, Mariano: 234, 250, 255
Ostria Gutiérrez, Alberto: 320
Our Lady of Asunción Catholic University: 375
Ovando Candia, Alfredo: 335
Overman: 486
overpopulation, 16, 519
Ozama River: 158

Pacem in Terris: 250
Pacific Ocean: 92, 231, 290, 337
pacto social: 481
PADENA. *See* Partido Democrático Nacional
Padgett, L. Vincent: on role of Revolutionary Institutional party, 39; on downfall pattern of state governors in Mexico, 51
Padilla, Juan Ignacio: 42
Paéz, José Antonio: 202
Palacios, Alfred: 416
Palena dispute: 338
paloma de vuelo popular, La: 503
pampas: 393
PAN. *See* National Autonomist party
PAN. *See* Party of National Action
Pan American highway: 92
Pan, Luis: 417
Panama: politics in, 67, 116, 117, 119, 122, 129–137; and Spain, 115, 126; Socialists in, 116; significance of, 116; economics of, 116–119 passim, 127; and Canal Zone, 116, 117, 119, 120; government of, 116, 120, 125–126, 134, 137–139; labor in, 116, 135–136, 141; 1964 riots in, 116 n.4, 117, 119, 131, 133, 134, 135, 139; students in, 117, 125, 128, 130, 140–142; investments in, 118; geography of, 118; natural resources in, 118, 120, 124, 133; industrialization in, 118, 119, 120; population of, 118, 119, 120, 123; transportation in, 118, 119, 120, 127; tourism in, 118, 124; and French, 118, 127; commerce in, 119; cattle in, 119; land in, 119, 120; agriculture in, 119, 120, 124, 137, 141; landowners in, 119, 122, 135, 141; United Fruit Company in, 119, 136; per capita

Panama (continued)
income in, 120; races in, 120, 121, 122, 126, 132; health in, 120, 123, 129; education in, 120, 123, 124–125, 129, 134, 140–141; lower class in, 120, 125, 135; economic nationalism in, 120, 130, 131, 141; citizenship in, 121; housing in, 122, 123, 129; reform in, 122, 129, 133, 135; illegitimacy in, 123; slums in, 123; urbanization in, 123; employment in, 123, 136; literacy in, 124; imports of, 124; illiteracy in, 125; Constitutions of, 125, 128; middle sectors in, 125, 140, 141, 143; taxes in, 126; and Costa Rica, 126; slaves in, 126; colonial period of, 126–127; and Colombia, 121, 126, 127, 233 n.4; oligarchy in, 127, 130; racism in, 130; National Guard, 131, 139, 142, 143; minimum wages in, 133, 136; social security in, 133, 136; unemployment in, 134, 141; strikes in, 135, 136; communications in, 137; Castro-sponsored invasion of, 139; Roman Catholic Church in, 139; anticlericalism in, 139; upper class in, 139–140; religion in, 139, 141; and Alliance for Progress, 134–136; mentioned, 502, 511, 512
—United States: 1903 treaty with, 103; economic relations with, 119, 120, 124, 134, 135, 142; sentiments toward, 122, 132, 142; influence of, 124, 131; significance to, 126; railroad built by, 127; as political issue, 130; and sovereignty over Canal Zone, 130, 134, 142; mentioned, 116, 117, 118, 126, 128
Panama Canal: 116, 128, 137, 173, 502. *See also* Canal Zone
Panama Canal Company: 119
Panama City, Panama: 123
Panameñista party: 134, 135
Pando, César: 299
Panistas: 43
Panoptico (penitentiary): 320
PAP. *See* Partido Aprista Peruano
papa verde, El: 501
PAR. *See* Partido Acción Renovadora
Paraguay: taxes in, 120, 386; Bolivia and, 316; population of, 317, 373, 374, 375; geography of, 373–375;

Paraguay (continued)
Jesuits in, 373, 374; per capita income in, 374; petroleum in, 374; communications in, 374; transportation in, 374, 375, 380; livestock in, 374, 386; and Brazil, 374, 376, 390; and agriculture, 374, 383, 390; and United States, 374, 380, 389, 390; lack of class distinction in, 375; and Spanish, 375; nationalism in, 375, 379, 391; military of, 375, 377, 386, 387–388, 391; education in, 375, 380, 383, 384, 389, 390; Roman Catholic Church in, 375, 383, 385, 386; literacy in, 375, 389; dictatorship in, 375, 390; Indians of, 375, 391; students in, 376; in Argentina, 376; and Uruguay, 376; Protestants in, 376; political parties of, 376–379, 390; newspapers in, 376, 377, 380, 382, 389; Constitutions of, 376–377, 381, 385; labor in, 376, 383, 384, 385, 389; exiles from, 376, 384, 388, 390; and Great Britain, 377; guerillas in, 377; leftists in, 377, 379, 381, 382, 384, 386; civil war in, 377, 382; reform in, 380, 381, 382, 383, 389; health in, 380, 384, 390; propoganda in, 380, 389; upper classes in, 381; and Alliance for Progress, 381, 384, 389; landowners in, 381, 389; industry in, 384, 389; government structure of, 385–388; and United Nations, 390; concentration camp in, 391; slums of, 391; mentioned, 151
Paraguay River: 317, 374
Paraguayan Leninist Communist party: 384
Paraguayan War: 483
Paraguayan Workers' Confederation: 385
Paraíba (state): 453
Paraná River: 375, 394
Pardo, José: 294
Pardo, Manuel: 293
paredón: 176, 184
paridad: 237
Pariñas, Peru: 307
Paris, France: 481
Paris, Gabriel: 236
Parkinson's Law: 494
Parliamentary Republic: 365

parochials: 284
Parti Unique de l'Action Révolutionaire et Gouvernementale: 150
Partido Acción Renovadora: 70
Partido Aprista Peruano: 297–298, 304
Partido Comunista Dominicana: 161
Partido Comunista Paraguayo: 384
Partido Comunista Peruano: 299
Partido Comunista Venezolano: 211, 225
Partido de Acción Nacional: 41
Partido de Conciliación Nacional: 70
Partido Dominicano: 160
Partido Institucional Democrático: 69, 83
Partido Liberación Nacional: 100–102
Partido Liberal Evolucionisto: 161
Partido Nacional: Chile, 355; Uruguay, 435 n.9
Partido Nacionalista de Mexico: 42, 45
Partido Obrero Revolucionario: 328
Partido Reformista: 161
Partido Republicano Nacional: 98–99, 100
Partido Revolutionario de Unificación Democrática: 69, 86, 87
Partido Revolucionario Dominicano: 160, 162, 163, 169
Partido Revolucionario Febrerista: 376, 381–382
Partido Revolucionario Social: 161
Partido Socialista Popular: 160, 180
Partido Trujillista: 160
Partido Unificación Nacional: 104
Partido Unión Nacional: 99–100
Party of National Action: 26, 28, 43, 45, 47, 52, 53
Patagonia (region): 393
patents: 367
Patiño, Simon: 322, 325
Patria: 376
patrón: 6, 113, 177, 179
Pax Porfiriana: 21, 55, 498
Paysandú, Uruguay: 430
Paz, Octavio: on love, 487; mentioned, 523
Paz Estenssoro, Víctor: and Movimiento Nacionalista Revolucionario, 320; in exile, 321; administration of, 323, 324, 328, 331; election of, 323, 335; overthrow of, 332, 335–336, 512; mentioned, 334, 511
PCA. *See* Argentine Communist party
PCB. *See* Bolivian Communist party

PCC. *See* Cuban Communist party
PCD. *See* Partido Comunista Dominicana
PCN. *See* Partido de Conciliación Nacional
PCT. *See* Traditional Conservative party
PCV. *See* Partido Comunista Venezolano
PDC. *See* Christian Democratic party
PDCP. *See* Popular Conservative Democrats
PDP. *See* Progressive Democrat party
Peace Corps: 304
"Pearl of the Antilles": 173
Pearson's Magazine: 22
Peasant Leagues: 450
Pedro I: 452
Pedro II: 452, 508
Peiping. *See* Peking
Peking: 161, 190, 211, 274, 299, 334, 358, 384
Pekingistas: 359
pelucones: 353
PEMEX. *See* Petróleos Mexicanos
Peña, Lázaro: 180
Peña Hermosa (concentration camp): 390
Peñaranda, Enrique: 320, 322
peninsulares: 4, 59, 63
Pensadores: 318
Peralta Azurdia, Enrique: 83
Pérez Jiménez, Marcos: rule of, 204, 223, 301; fall of, 215; and military, 216; mentioned, 208, 211, 217, 224, 230, 483, 509
Pérez Salinas, P.B.: 211
Pernambuco (state): 449, 450, 458, 465, 506
Perón, Juan Domingo: administration of, 398, 406, 409, 412, 415; overthrow of, 405, 407, 408, 409, 412, 418, 511; in Madrid, 410, 415; excommunication of, 411; attempt of to return, 422; mentioned, 509
Peronism: 398, 409, 411
Peronists: position of, 398, 399, 405, 417; and labor, 409–411, 416; power, 412; opposition to, 413, 414, 418, 422; discussed, 415–416; acceptance of, 415, 423, 424; election victories of, 423; and military, 424, 425
Perry, Ralph Barton: 480

Petróleos Mexicanos: 26, 31, 50
Peru: government of, 16, 302–306, 308, 309; political parties in, 41, 102, 258, 293–300 passim, 303, 309, 310, 500; Viceroyalty of, 232, 232 n.2; and Ecuador, 268, 277; oligarchy in, 289; fishing in, 290, 291; agriculture in, 290, 291, 292, 307, 312, 328; Incas of, 290, 291, 299, 307, 308; transportation in, 290, 292, 307; communications in, 290, 298, 299, 309, 310; population of, 290, 306; races in, 291; languages in, 291; exports of, 291; diversification in, 291, 292, 307; industry in, 291, 292, 307, 308, 311; natural resources of, 291, 292, 307, 328; schools in, 292, 294; middle sectors of, 292, 298; housing in, 292, 312; and Chile, 293; and Spain, 293; nationalism in, 293; political history of, 293–297; Constitutions of, 293, 294, 296, 309; military power in, 293, 294, 295, 297, 299, 301, 302, 303, 308, 309; reforms in, 293, 295, 298, 299, 302, 308, 311; Roman Catholic Church in, 293, 295, 300, 301, 302; depression in, 294; foreign capital in, 294, 307; dictatorship in, 294, 308; Communists in, 295, 297, 298, 299, 305, 308, 311; and Soviet Union, 295, 299; students in, 295, 299, 310; landowners in, 295, 300; social security in, 296; Conservatism in, 297, 298, 299; *convivencia* in, 297, 299; labor in, 298, 299, 300, 307, 309, 310; and Peking, 299; and Liberals, 299; traditionalism in, 300; upper class in, 300; suffrage in, 301; electoral system in, 301–302; illiteracy in, 301, 307; modernization in, 302, 311; and Mexico, 303; Peace Corps of, 304; departments of, 304, 306; Andes of, 305; guerillas in, 305, 311; and United States, 308; strikes in, 308, 310; violence in, 308, 311; exiles from, 308, 500; minimum wages in, 310; education in, 310; livestock in, 312; and Bolivia, 314, 317; mentioned, 15, 92, 93, 97, 100, 175, 337, 338, 413, 443, 498, 508, 515, 518, 521
Peruvian Democratic Movement. *See* Movimiento Democrático Peruano

Peruvian Savings and Loan League: 292
Pétion, Alexandre: 148
petroleum: in Mexico: 26, 30, 33; in Venezuela, 31, 199, 200, 203, 204, 209, 222, 230, 477; in Panama, 120, 124; in Cuba, 173; in United States, 201; in Colombia, 259; in Peru, 291, 307; in Bolivia, 320, 327; in Chile, 338, 370; in Paraguay, 374; in Argentina, 393, 398, 414, 422; in Uruguay, 434; in Brazil, 457
Phalange, La: 150
Pharmacists, National Association of: 186
Piadreahita Arango, Ruben: 236
Picado, Teodoro: 95, 98
PID. *See* Partido Institucional Democrático
Piérola, Nicolás de: 294
Pietri Uslar, Arturo: 222, 508
Pilcomayo River: 316
pipiolos: 354
PIR. *See* Leftist Revolutionary party
Pisco, Peru: 298
Pistarani, Pascual: 425
pistolismo: 176
pitucos: 441
PL. *See* Liberal party
Plan de Iguala: 20
Platt Amendment: 176, 189
Plaza, Leónidas: 273
Plaza Lasso, Galo: 271, 272, 273, 282, 283
PLE. *See* Partido Liberal Evolucionista
PLUNA: airlines, 430
plutocracy: 349
PN. *See* Partido Nacional
PNM. *See* Partido Nationalista de Mexico
PNR. *See* National Revolutionary party
poblaciones callampas: 341
poesía negra: 503
Polar, Mario: 303
police: 166, 182, 347, 380
Ponce Enríquez, Camilo: 271, 273, 275, 279
Pope John XXIII: 165, 299
Pope Pius IX: 293
Pope Pius XII: 411
Popular Action Front. *See* Frente Acción Popular
Popular Action group: 464

Popular Action party. *See* Acción Popular
Popular Alliance: 133
Popular Christian Movement: 332
Popular Conservative Democrats: 416
Popular Electoral Front: 41, 45, 54
Popular Front: 350, 351, 521
Popular Radical Civic Union: 413, 414, 415, 418, 423, 424
Popular Radicals: 423
Popular Socialist party: 39, 40, 45, 47, 52
Popular Union: 415, 423
population: in Latin America, 16–17; of Mexico, 28, 29, 48; in Central America, 57, 58–59; of Panama, 118, 120, 123; in Haiti, 146–148, 505; in Dominican Republic, 158; in Venezuela, 201, 219, 229; in Colombia, 252; in Ecuador, 267, 268, 282, 286; in Peru, 290, 306; in Bolivia, 317; in Paraguay, 317; in Chile, 339–340, 341, 342, 343, 362; in Paraguay, 373, 374, 375; in Brazil, 394; in Argentina, 394, 403; in Uruguay, 430
POR. *See* Revolutionary Workers party
porfiriato: 21, 38
Port au Prince, Haiti: 146, 155, 156
Portales, Diego: 365
Portes Gil, Emilio: 25
Porto Alegre, Brazil: 449
Portobelo, Panama: 127
Portugal: 2, 3, 5, 432
Portuguese: 4, 450, 452, 470, 480, 507
Potash, Robert: on Argentine military, 406
Potosí, Bolivia: 383
"Poujadism": 444
PPS. *See* Popular Socialist party
PR. *See* Partido Reformista
PR. *See* Revolutionary party
PRA. *See* Authentic Revolutionary party
Pradistas: 299
Prado, Francisco: 411
Prado, Manuel: administration of, 293, 300, 303, 307; election of, 296; party of, 299; mentioned, 298
Prat Eschaurren, Jorge: 363
PRD. *See* Partido Revolucionario Dominicano
Presbyterians: 139
press: 1, 74, 316. *See also* newspapers
Prestes, Julio: 452

PRI. *See* Revolutionary Institutional party
Price-Mars, Jean: 505
Prieto, Luis B.: 204, 208
PRIN. *See* National Leftist Revolutionary party
"Principles and Actions of the National Revolutionary Movement": 322
Prío Socarras, Carlos: 177, 181, 182, 183, 186, 511
PRM. *See* Mexican Revolutionary party
Program of Economic Development and Social Well-Being: 86
Program of Economic and Social Development: 125
Progressive Democratic party: 417, 418
Promoción Popular: 370
Prosa política: 502
Protestants: 152, 183, 376
PRSC. *See* Partido Revolucionario Social Cristiano
PRUD. *See* Partido Revolucionario de Unificación Democrática
PSA. *See* Argentine Socialist party
PSD. *See* Democratic Socialist party
PSD. *See* Social Democratic party
PSP. *See* Partido Socialista Popular
PSP. *See* Communist Parti Socialiste Popular
PSP. *See* Social Progressive party
PSR. *See* Revolutionary Socialist party
PSR. *See* Socialist Revolutionary party
PTB. *See* Brazilian Labor party
PTJ. *See* Technical Judicial Police
Puerto Rico: 503
Pueto Limón, Costa Rica: 92
Punta Arenas, Chile: 338
Punta del Este, Uruguay: 370
Puntarenas (province): 92, 108, 110, 112
PURS. *See* Socialist Republican Union party

Quadragesimo Ano: 250
Quadros, Jânio: 455, 458, 465, 466, 468, 471
Quechua (language): 219, 500
quedantistas: 408
Querétaro, Mexico: 21
Querétaro Club: 20
Quindío (region): 238

Quintero, José Humberto: 215
quiteños: 268
Quito, Ecuador: 268, 269, 270, 273, 277, 284

race: 59, 121, 130, 485
racism: 54, 62, 173, 457
RADEPA. *See* Razón de Patria
Radical Civic Union: 312, 321, 397, 398, 399, 409, 413, 414, 420, 467
Radical Liberals: 273, 274
Radical party: 346, 349, 354, 355, 359, 362, 365, 370
radicalism: 180
radicals: in Costa Rica, 97; in Brazil, 463
radio: in Brazil, 463, 470, 472; mentioned, 151, 188, 221, 290, 346, 389
railroads: in Central America, 66, 94; in Panama, 118, 119, 127; in Ecuador, 270; in Uruguay, 430, 433, 434; mentioned, 9, 33, 112, 234, 316, 374, 390, 422
Raimondi, Antonio: 294
Rand, Ayn: 493
Rangel, Rafael: 257
Ray, Manuel: 195
raza cósmica, La: 486
Razón, La: 321
Razón de Patria: 320
Rebel Army: 182, 184, 185
Rebel Pioneers: 181
Rebellion in the Backlands: 457
Recabarren, Luis Emilio: 350, 357
Recife, Brazil: 458
Reds. *See* Colorado party
reform: political, 79, 82; tax, 129, 133, 238, 255, 276, 308; mentioned, 4, 18, 192, 193, 293, 295, 298, 302, 311, 354, 355, 356, 365, 369, 389, 397, 506, 509, 511
—agrarian: in Mexico, 30, 40, 47; in Central America, 61; in Guatemala, 78, 80, 82; in Honduras, 85; in El Salvador, 86; in Panama, 129, 135; in Cuba, 182, 191; in Venezuela, 199, 201, 204, 209, 212, 223; in Colombia, 234, 246, 255; in Ecuador, 271, 273, 276; in Bolivia, 328, 330; in Chile, 344, 357, 360, 370, 371; in Paraguay, 383; in Argentina, 413, 414; in

reform (continued)
—agrarian (continued)
Latin America, 519; mentioned, 156
—economic: in Guatemala, 65; in Honduras, 84; in El Salvador, 88; in Haiti, 156; in Cuba, 176, 177; in Peru, 299; in Chile, 347; in Paraguay, 381, 382; in Uruguay, 436, 466; mentioned, 204
—land: in Mexico, 24; in El Salvador, 85, 86; in Bolivia, 328, 334; in Chile, 370; in Paraguay, 380; in Brazil, 472, 476; mentioned, 467
—social: in Mexico, 27, 33; in Central America, 57, 61; in Guatemala, 82; in El Salvador, 88; in Costa Rica, 101; and Roman Catholic Church, 165; in Dominican Republic, 170; in Cuba, 176, 177; in Venezuela, 204, 227; in Chile, 337; in Paraguay, 381, 382
Reforma: 20, 21
Regaldo, Tomás: 66
regimientos: 126
Regional Confederation of Mexican Workers: 24, 26
regionalism: 104, 113, 200, 454, 499
Remón, José A.: 128, 131, 132–133, 511
repartimiento: 60
Repetto, Nicolás: 416
Republican party: in Bolivia, 316; in Brazil, 452, 453, 459
republicanism: 400
Republicano Nacional party: 95, 97, 102–109 passim
Republicans: 181
Republique d'Haiti et la Republique Dominicaine, La: 505
Rerum Novarum: 250
resources: economic, 2, 16; political, 5, 6, 15; natural, 22, 40, 329, 358, 414, 430, 448, 457; mentioned, 120, 185
Revolt of the Masses, The: 484
Revolución: 186
Revolution of 1810: 481
Revolution of 1946: 147, 154, 156
Revolutionary Armed Forces: 184, 196
Revolutionary Directorate: 377
Revolutionary Institutional party: 26, 34–39 passim, 41, 42, 43, 50–53 passim, 102, 103, 390, 463

Revolutionary Movement of the People: 195
Revolutionary party: 83
Revolutionary Socialist party: 333
Revolutionary Workers party: 334
Revuelta, Wálter: 335
rice: 86, 192, 202, 328, 332
Riggs, Fred W.: on Latin America, 522
rightists: in Mexico, 25, 41, 53; as Roman Catholics, 41; in El Salvador, 87; in Costa Rica, 100; in Dominican Republic, 161, 169, 170; in Venezuela, 216; in Ecuador, 273, 274, 275; in Chile, 346, 354–355, 362, 363, 369, 371; in Latin America, 479
Rio de Janeiro, Brazil: foreign minister conference in, 225; slums of, 451, 465, 466, 467, 472; mentioned, 422, 430, 448, 450, 457, 473
Rio Grande do Norte (state): 451
Rio Grande do Sul (state): 449, 450, 453, 455, 459, 463, 465, 468, 469, 476
Rio Negro: 430
Rio Protocol: 277, 284
Rio Yaque del Norte: 157
riots: in Panama, 116 n.4, 117, 119, 131, 133, 134, 135, 139; in Ecuador, 271, 284; in Chile, 350; mentioned, 112
Rivadavia, Comodoro: 496
River Plate: 375
Rivera, Julio Adalberto: 70, 87
Rivera, Fructuoso: 432
Rivera Concha, Alvaro: 268
Robles, Marco: 116, 129, 131, 134, 139, 140
Roca, Blas: 180
Rocafuerte, Vicente: 270
Rodo, Jose Enrique: theories of, 483, 484; on democratic and spiritual life, 484; mentioned, 12, 488, 490, 491, 495, 501, 502
Rodríguez, Abelardo: 26
Rodríguez, Carlos Rafael: 180
Rodríguez, Valmore: 208, 211
Rojas Pinilla, Gustavo: dictatorship of, 235, 236, 259; *coup d'etat* by, 235, 253; resignation of, 245, 251, 256; appeal of, 248; support of, 256, 257; and National Popular Alliance, 257; mentioned, 237, 244, 254, 407, 511
Roldanillo (region): 246

Rolón, Raimundo: 377
Romain, Jacques: 150
Roman Catholic Church: in Mexico, 20–21, 22, 24; in Central America, 60, 64, 70, 72; in Guatemala, 65, 77, 81; in Argentina, 96, 398, 405, 406, 411–412, 426; in Costa Rica, 96–97, 110; in Colombia, 96, 233, 247, 247 n.17, 251–253; in Ecuador, 96, 270, 273, 275, 276, 286; in Panama, 139; in Haiti, 146, 152; in Dominican Republic, 159, 164–165; in Cuba, 175, 183, 194; in Venezuela, 200, 204, 215, 224; in Peru, 295, 300, 301, 302; in Chile, 339, 347, 354; in Paraguay, 375–376, 383, 385, 386; in Uruguay, 434, 439; in Brazil, 449, 450, 451, 452, 456, 461, 463–464, 468, 469, 471, 507; in Latin America, 479, 517; mentioned, 2, 4, 7, 16, 41, 68, 95, 121, 125, 265, 489
Rome: 209
Roosevelt, Franklin D.: 176
Roosevelt, Theodore: 67, 126
Rosas, Juan Manuel de: 432, 481, 496, 498, 522
Rossi: 105
Rostow, W. W.: 493
Rotary Clubs: 71 n.6
Rousseau, Jean Jacques: 480, 482
royalists: 5
Rubio, César: 500
Ruíz Cortines, Adolfo: 27
Ruiz Novoa, Alberto: 253
Rural Society: 412
rurales: 22, 36
Russia. *See* Soviet Union

Saavedia, Bautista: on Bolivian mining companies, 325
Sáenz Peña, Roque: 397, 434
Saint Dominique (colony): 148
St. John, Sir Spenser: on Haitian government, 151
Salazar, Felipe: 257
Sales, Eugenio: 451, 464
Saltillo, Mexico: 52
Samudio, David: 129, 133, 135
San Andrés (island): 503
San Cristóbal, Venezuela: 200, 306
San Francisco de Macoris, Dominican Republic: 158

San Francisco Xavier, University of: 314
San Francisco, California: 116
San Isidro Air Base: 166
San José, Costa Rica: 92, 97, 106 n.12, 107, 109
San Juan del Norte: 65
San Juan Valley: 157
San Marcos, University of: 294
San Pedro de Macoris, Dominican Republic: 158
Sánchez Cerro, Luis: 294, 296
Sánchez Viamonte, Carlos: 416
"Sangre Negra": 238
Sanjinés, Federico Fortún: 335
Santa Anna, Antonio López de: 20, 483
Santa Cruz y Calahumana, Andrés: 314, 317
Santa Fe (province): 394, 417, 496
Santa Marta, Colombia: 232
Santana, Pedro: 159
Santander, Department of: 241, 259
Santander, Francisco de Paula: 232
Santiago, Chile: 340–342, 344, 355, 361, 364
Santiago de los Caballeros, Dominican Republic: 159
Santo Domingo, Dominican Republic: 158, 168
Santo Domingo de Guzmán: 157
Santos, Brazil: 449
Santos, Eduardo: 234, 248, 508
São Paulo, Brazil: 449, 451, 460, 462, 463
São Paulo (state): 449, 452, 453, 455, 458, 459, 460, 468, 473
Saravia, Aparicio: 432, 434, 442
Sarmiento, Domingo F.: 481, 496, 497, 498
Savings and Housing, Institute of: 183
Scandal of Petroleum and Iron, The: 457
Scandinavia: 109
Schick Guitiérrez, René: 89
Schneider, Ronald M.: on regime of Arévalo, 80
schools: in Costa Rica, 93, 94, 108; in Haiti, 149; in Peru, 292, 294; in Bolivia, 330; mentioned, 11, 16
Schopenhauer, Arthur: 489
SCOP. *See* National Secretariat of Communications and Public Works

Sears, Roebuck and Co.: 225
Second Congress of Private Economic Organizations of Paraguay: 384
Seleme, Antonio: 323
selva: 290
SENDAS. *See* National Secretariat for Social Assistance
señor presidente, El: 498 n.32
Seoane, Edgardo: 303
sertanejos: 457
Servicio Cooperativo Interamericano de Educación: 331
Severo, Angel Cabral: 161
Shakespeare: 506
sharecroppers: 240, 245, 320, 343, 450
sheep: 393, 430, 441
Sierra (Ecuador): 268, 277, 281
Sierra de los Organos: 173
Sierra Maestra: 173, 179, 225
Sierra Neiba: Dominican Republic, 157
Sierra Nevada de Mérida: 200
Siglo, El: 236, 346
Siles, Hernán: 316, 322, 323, 328, 331
Siles Salinas, Luis Adolfo: 333
Siles Zuazo, Hernán: 332, 333
Silva Henriquez, Raúl: 347
silver: 30, 93, 291, 313
Silvert, Kalman: on upper class Chileans, 345
Sinarquistas: 41, 42, 45, 54
Sindicato Patronal de Industriales: 71 n.6
sindicatos: 330
Siquieros, David Alfaro: 41
sisal: 146, 154
slavery: in Central America, 60; in Panama, 126; in Haiti, 148, 505; in Cuba, 173, 175; in Colombia, 233; in Brazil, 452, 456, 506, 507; in United States, 507
slums: in Mexico, 29, 47, 52; in Costa Rica, 93; in Panama, 123; in Dominican Republic, 158; in Venezuela, 219, 227, 230; in Peru, 291; in Chile, 341, 364; in Paraguay, 391; in Brazil, 449, 451, 457, 465, 466, 467, 472; in Ecuador, 500
Smith, E. T.: 189
Social Christian party: 334
Social Christian Union: 417
Social Christians Movement: 273, 274
Social Democratic party: 172, 333, 460, 461, 464

Social Institutes: 475
Social Justice: 415
Social Progressive party: 460
social security: in Central America, 77; in Costa Rica, 98; in Panama, 133, 136; in Venezuela, 224; in Peru, 296; in Bolivia, 320; in Argentina, 426; in Uruguay, 434
Social Security Institute: 50
Social Statics: 486
socialism: in Mexico, 28, 43; in Central America, 69; in Dominican Republic, 160; in Cuba, 185; in Colombia, 233; in Ecuador, 274; in Bolivia, 319; in Chile, 357; in Paraguay, 381; mentioned, 13, 41, 79, 93, 493, 509
Socialist Labor party: 358
Socialist Republican Union party: 334
Socialist Revolutionary party: 274
Socialists: in Panama, 116; in Ecuador, 273; in Chile, 346, 347, 348, 350, 351, 352, 354, 357–359, 362, 365, 371, 521; in Argentina, 409, 416, 421; in Uruguay, 439, 440; in Brazil, 450; mentioned, 106
Sociedad de Fomento Fabril: 348, 349
Sociedad Nacional de Agricultura: 348
Sociedad Nacional de Minerías: 348, 349
Salano Lima, Vicente: 416
Solano López, Francisco: 376, 483
Solari, Juan Antonio: 417
Somoza, Anastasio: 88, 89, 511
Somoza, Luis: 89
son entero, El: 503
Sonora, Mexico: 49
Sorzano, Tejada: on Bolivian mining conditions, 324
South American Gold and Platinum Company: 327
Soviet Union: and United States, 89, 171, 173; Cuba as ally of, 171, 172, 177, 189, 190, 193; and cold war, 190; and Peru, 295; and Chile, 358; and Brazil, 448
Spain: and America, 2, 3; Golden Age of, 4; weakened by Napoleon, 20; Mexican debts to, 21; colonial period of, 59; in Central America, 63; wars of independence against, 94; and Panama, 115, 126; in Dominican Republic, 158, 159; in Cuba, 173, 175; in Venezuela, 202; in Co-

Spain (continued)
lombia, 232; and Ecuador, 269; and Peru, 293; in Bolivia, 313, 314; legal codes of, 314; and Chile, 339; and Paraguay, 375; in Uruguay, 432; mentioned, 233, 394, 409, 425, 426
Spanish: 59, 92, 121, 201, 232, 431, 464, 480
Spanish (language): 291, 345
Spanish-American War: 502
Spencer, Herbert: 484, 486
spiritualism: 149
squatters: 135
Stalinists: 322, 358
Standard Oil of New Jersey: 307, 319, 327, 457
steel: 31, 33, 370
Stokes, William: on power relationship, 16
strikes: in Guatemala, 82; in Honduras, 84–85; in El Salvador, 86; in Panama, 135, 136; in Haiti, 150; in Cuba, 186; in Colombia, 244, 249, 251, 258; in Ecuador, 271, 283; in Peru, 308, 310; in Bolivia, 321, 334; in Chile, 344, 350, 370; in Paraguay, 376; in Argentina, 414
Stroessner, Alfredo: administration of, 377, 381, 384, 387, 391; on military, 388; mentioned, 509
students: in Mexico, 54; in Guatemala, 78, 82; in El Salvador, 87; in Costa Rica, 97, 98, 110; in Panama, 116, 124, 128, 130, 131–132, 140, 141; in Haiti, 150; in Dominican Republic, 160, 163; in Cuba, 176, 178, 179, 187, 188, 193; in Venezuela, 204, 208, 209, 226, 229; in Colombia, 236, 240, 241, 251, 258, 263; in Ecuador, 271, 276–277, 286; in Peru, 295, 299, 310; in Bolivia, 321, 334; in Chile, 348, 359, 371; in Paraguay, 376; in Brazil, 472; in Latin America, 518; mentioned, 72
Suarez, Pino: 23, 498
sublemas: 438, 444, 445
Sucre, Antonio José de: 314
Sucre, Bolivia: 314
SUDENE. *See* Superintendency of the Northeast
Sueldo, Horacio: 417
suffrage: for women, 27, 79, 83, 203, 282, 301, 361; in Haiti, 155; in Dominican Republic, 168; in Vene-

suffrage (continued)
zuela, 203, 204, 213, 218; universal, 203, 204, 213, 218, 262, 334; in Ecuador, 282; in Peru, 301; in Bolivia, 331, 334; in Chile, 361; in Paraguay, 389; in Argentina, 397; in Uruguay, 446
sugar: workers in, 162, 163; in Cuba, 173, 174, 175, 185, 186, 189, 190, 192, 196, 477; in Colombia, 244, 246, 258; in Peru, 292, 328; in Bolivia, 327, 332; mentioned, 86, 88, 124, 146, 157, 190, 202, 290, 393, 477
Sumner, William Graham: 508
Superintendency of the Northeast: 449
Superior War College: 462
supernaturalism: 17
superpatriots: 116
superstition: 252
Supreme Electoral Tribunal: 112
Supreme Tribunal of Elections: 108
surrealism: 486
Swiss: 339

Táchira (state): 203
tachirense: 203
Taft, William Henry: 67
Tamayo, Franz: 318, 319
Tampico, Mexico: 24
Tareja Valley: 327
tariffs: 120, 433, 436, 443, 490, 493
taxes: levying of, 48; exemptions from, 49; income, 88, 129, 138, 156, 234; other types, 94, 129, 249, 251, 280, 319; in Costa Rica, 101; in Panama, 126; in Venezuela, 214; in Colombia, 238, 245, 249, 251, 255, 260, 261; reforms in, 255, 308; in Ecuador, 271, 280, 285; in Peru, 308; in Bolivia, 319, 325; evasion of, 325; in Chile, 345, 370; in Paraguay, 386; in Brazil, 467, 476; in Latin America, 517
Taylor, Philip B.: on Mexico, 38
Technical Judicial Police: 214, 217
Tegucigalpa, Honduras: 84
Tejada, Lydia: on Groups of Honor, 322; on 1952 Bolivian uprising, 323
television: 137, 188, 221, 346, 463, 470, 472
Tercera de la Hora: 346
Terra, Gabriel: 437, 442

terrorism: 112, 205, 216, 217, 225, 320
terrorists: 207, 211, 218, 311
Texas: 92, 290
theocracy: 41, 270
theology: 175
Third Reich: 484
Thousand Days War: 233, 247
Three Flags: 415
tidal waves: 341
Tiempo, El: 236, 241
Tierra del Fuego: 337, 393
Timon: 506
tin: 316, 319, 320, 321, 322, 323–326, 332, 334
Tinoco, Federico: 95
"Tiro Fijo": 238, 238 n.8, 239
tobacco: 158, 186, 192, 327
Tobar Doctrine: 225
Tolima: 235, 236
Tonton Macoute: 155
Toro, José David: 319
Torre, Lisandro de la: 417
Torres Restrepo, Camilo: 239, 239 n.31, 253, 258
totalitarianism: in Latin America, 172; in Cuba, 179, 188, 194, 196; mentioned, 55, 490, 496, 499
tourism: 48, 112, 118, 124, 174, 434
Toyota Company: 51
trachoma: 317
Traditional Conservative party: 70
Tragic Ten Days: 23
transportation: in Panama, 120; in Cuba, 173; in Ecuador, 268; in Peru, 290, 307; in Chile, 340, 367; in Paraguay, 374, 380; in Argentina, 393; in Uruguay, 430; in Brazil, 448, 475
Trejos, José Joaquín: 103, 114
Tribuna, La: 298, 309, 376
Tribunal of Accounts: 386
trienio: 204, 208, 209, 210, 211, 224
Trinidad Mountains: 173
Trotskyites: 322, 324, 328, 358
Trujillo, Peru: 298
Trujillo, Rafael Leonidas: assassination of, 160, 161, 164, 512; suppression by, 163; dictatorship of, 164, 167, 170, 497–498; use of army by, 166; mentioned, 162, 178, 483, 512, 520, 522
Trujillo, Venezuela: 200
tuberculosis: 147, 324
Turbay, Gabriel: 234
turco: 10

tyranny: 495–499
"Tyranny, The": 193

Ubico, Jorge: 66, 78, 82
UCN. *See* Unión Cívica Nacional
UCR. *See* Radical Civil Union
UCRI. *See* Intransigent Radical Civic Union
UCRP. *See* Popular Radical Civic Union
Ucurena, Bolivia: 329
UDELPA. *See* Union of the Argentine People
UDN. *See* National Democratic Union
Ugarte Palayo, Alirio: 210
UGOCM. *See* General Union of Mexican Workers and Peasants
Ulate, Otilio: election of, 98, 99; and Unión Nacional party, 99, 100, 103, 104; relations of with Echandi, 103, 105; and Figueres, 106; and Calderón, 106; candidacy of, 111; as compromiser, 113; mentioned, 95, 109
Ulatistas: 104, 106
Ultima Hora: 321
ultranationalism: 457, 468
Underdogs, The: 499
underemployment: 431
UNE. *See* National Students Union
unemployment: in Mexico, 50; in Costa Rica, 98; in Canal Zone, 119; in Panama, 134, 141; in Venezuela, 227; in Colombia, 237, 239, 265; in Chile, 342; in Uruguay, 435, 442; in Brazil, 449, 475
Unidad: 299
Unificación Nacional: 114
Unión Cívica: 439
Unión Cívica Nacional: 161, 169
Unión Nacional party: 97, 98, 102, 103, 104, 105 Table 1, 106, 108, 109
Unión Nacional Odriísta: 297, 298, 304
Unión Nacional Sinarquista: 41, 45, 46
Union National des Travaillers: 150
Union National Étudiants Haitiens: 151
Union National Ouvriers d'Haiti: 151
Union of Colombian Workers: 249
Union of Communist Youth: 181
Union of the Argentine People: 417

Unión Republicana Democrática: 204, 208, 210, 228, 230
Unión Revolucionaria de Juventudes: 274
uniones de facto: 123
Unionists: 413
unions, labor: in Mexico, 28; in Panama, 135, 141; in Haiti, ·150; in Dominican Republic, 160, 162, 163; in Cuba, 186; in Venezuela, 211, 220, 225; in Colombia, 234, 249–251; in Ecuador, 276–277; in Peru, 298, 299, 300, 310; in Bolivia, 320, 321, 322, 323, 324, 330, 333, 518; in Chile, 345, 346, 347, 348, 350–353, 357, 365, 370; in Paraguay, 383, 385, 389; in Argentina, 409–411, 415, 426, 518; in Uruguay, 433, 434, 445–446; in Brazil, 451, 454, 473; mentioned, 13, 14, 24, 490
Unitarians: 412
unitarism: 481
United Democratic Opposition: 87
United Front for National Liberation: 384
United Fruit Company: 68, 84, 92, 119, 136, 501
United Nations: 147, 326, 390, 505
United Nations Mission: 325
United States: and Latin America, 12, 479, 483, 501, 503, 512, 520; intrusion by, 18; and Mexico, 20, 23, 25, 26, 27 n.2, 39, 48, 65, 498; tourists of, 48; Constitution of, 64, 261, 399, 453; and Central America, 65, 67; and Honduras, 67, 84; and Nicaragua, 67, 88, 520; "dollar diplomacy" of, 67, 174; military assistance programs of, 73, 512, 518; and Soviet Union, 89, 171, 173, 190, 197; in Guatemala, 81, 520, 521; southern Democrats of, 106; feelings toward, 170, 171, 502–504; legislators of, 112, 401, 402; foreign policy of, 116, 339; military of, 23, 67, 96, 122, 140, 149, 156, 165, 478; in Canal Zone, 127, 141; capitalism of, 136; in Haiti, 149, 156, 520; in Dominican Republic, 159, 160, 161, 163, 164, 165, 169, 170, 512, 520, 521; imperialism of, 178; Castro in, 189, 512; petroleum productions in, 201; and Venezuela, 224; and Co-

United States (continued)
lombia, 240, 265; President of, 280; Vice-President of, 281; and Peru, 308; as model of constitutional democracy, 209, 380; collective bargaining in, 310; and Bolivia, 326, 331, 332, 333, 334; urban population of, 340; and Chile, 356; and Paraguay, 374, 380, 389, 390; government of, 400; political parties of, 418; and Brazil, 448, 458, 470, 472; and Communists, 479; education in, 494; industries in, 494; and Puerto Rico, 503; slavery in, 507; and Bay of Pigs, 512; mentioned, 7, 9, 28, 29, 80, 363, 371, 395, 401, 434, 450
—Cuba: intervention in, 172, 174, 176; military assistance to, 183; influence on, 189; nationalization of properties by, 189; policy toward, 189, 190, 197; exiles from, 189, 194, 195; mentioned, 177, 179, 521
—Panama: influence in, 116, 124, 131; significance of, 116, 126; economic ties with, 119, 120, 124, 127, 134, 135, 142; sentiments in 122, 132, 142; 1903 treaty with, 127; and sovereign rights over Canal Zone, 127, 130, 134, 141, 142; mentioned, 115, 117, 118, 125, 233 n.4
United States Embassy in Mexico: 23
United States General Accounting Office: 112
United States Information Service: 241
Unity Nucleus: 414
Universidad Central de Venezuela: 226
Universidad de los Andes: 492, 495
Universidad Libre: 258
Universidad Nacional. *See* National University
Universidad Nacional de Panamá, La: 125
University Confederation: 330
University Council: 330
Un Pueblo en la Cruz: 320
UNO. *See* Unión Nacional Odriísta
UNOH. *See* Union National Ouvriers d'Haiti
UNS. *See* Union Nacional Sinarquista
UNT. *See* Union National des Travaillers

upper classes: in Central America, 60, 66, 70, 71; in Panama, 67, 139–140; in Guatemala, 77, 79, 82; in Honduras, 84; in El Salvador, 85, 86; in Costa Rica, 100, 101; in Haiti, 147; in Dominican Republic, 164, 165, 169, 170; in Cuba, 177, 186, 193; in Venezuela, 205, 206, 219; in Colombia, 240, 244–245, 246, 253, 258, 264, 265; in Ecuador, 267, 269, 273; in Peru, 300; in Bolivia, 330; in Chile, 345, 349, 354, 359, 363, 371, 521; in Paraguay, 381; in Argentina, 396 Table 1, 397, 415; in Uruguay, 431, 440, 444; in Brazil, 451, 465, 474
Upper Peru: 313
urbanization: in Mexico, 29, 48, 51; in Panama, 123; in Haiti, 150; in Dominican Republic, 158; in Venezuela, 205, 206, 207, 227; in Ecuador, 269, 286; in Bolivia, 328; in Chile, 340, 341, 342; in Argentina, 395; in Uruguay, 430, 440, 441; in Latin America, 492, 516, 518–519; mentioned, 9, 11, 13, 16
URD. *See* Unión Republicana Democrática
Uribe, Alvaro: 257
Uribe Uribe, Rafael: 233, 248
URJE. *See* Unión Revolucionaria de Juventudes Ecuatorianas
Urquidi, Victor: on economic concept of Mexico, 52
Urquiza, José Antonio: 42
Urriolagoitia, Maneito: 321, 323
Urrutia, Manuel: 180, 182
ursurpador, El: 498
Urubamba Valley: 307
Uruguay: nationalism in, 12; labor in, 14, 433, 434, 443, 444, 445–446; literacy in, 109, 430; geography of, 429–430; livestock in, 429, 430, 431, 441, 445; population growth in, 430; housing in, 430; transportation in, 430, 433, 434; natural resources in, 430, 434; urbanization in, 430, 440, 441; welfare system in, 431; underemployment in, 431; middle sectors of, 431, 435, 440, 441, 444; races in, 431, 439; upper class of, 431, 440, 444; lower class in, 431, 441, 444; Spanish in, 432; and France,

Uruguay (continued)
432; Portuguese in, 432; and England, 432, 434; *Colorados* of, 432, 434, 435, 439, 444; Constitution of, 432, 437; *Blancos* of, 432, 434, 436, 439, 443; utilities in, 433; exports from, 433; conservatives in, 433; foreign capital in, 433; tariffs in, 433, 436, 443; industry in, 433, 443, 445; wool in, 433, 445; dictatorship in, 434; public corporations in, 434; social security in, 434; education in, 434, 435; Roman Catholic Church in, 434, 439; capitalism in, 435; *Partido Nacional* of, 435 n.9; unemployment in, 435, 442; inflation in, 435, 442; reforms in, 436; plural executive of, 436, 438; civil war in, 437; parties of, 437–440; newspapers in, 437, 441, 446; Christian Democrats in, 439, 440; leftists in, 439, 440; military in, 441, 442; agriculture in, 442, 445; imports of, 443; *sublemas* in, 444, 445; legislative process in, 444; suffrage in, 446; mentioned, 14, 268, 376, 450, 485, 515
Uruguay River: 394, 432
Uruguayan War: 496
Usigli, Rudolfo: 500
Uslar Pietri, Arturo: 210, 212, 228, 230
U.S.S.R. *See* Soviet Union
UTC. *See* Union of Colombian Workers
utopianism: 488–491

Valdivia, Chile: 364
Valencia, Guillermo León: 237, 239, 240, 253, 256, 260, 437
Valencia, Venezuela: 200, 206
Vallarino, Bolívar: 135, 139
Valle, Department of: 239, 240, 249, 256, 257, 258
Valle de Cauca: 232, 245
Vallejo, Joaquín: 239
Valparaíso, Chile: 338, 350, 361, 364, 370
Vanderbilt, Cornelius: 65
Vandor, Augusto: 410, 411
vandoristas: 410, 411
Vanguardia Revolucionario Dominicano: 160

Varela, Benigno: 425
Vargas, Getúlio: in Brazil, 113; administration of, 450, 453, 454, 463, 465, 466, 471; and poor, 451; and political parties, 460; opposition to, 460, 474; support for, 469; suicide of, 511; mentioned, 459, 467, 507
Varona, Manuel Antonio de: 194
Vasconcelos, José: on basic human species, 485; on law of three stages, 486; mentioned, 25, 27 n.2
Vásquez, Horacio: 159, 168
Vatican: 152, 251
Vekemans, Roger: 347
Velasco Ibarra, José María: 267, 271, 272, 273, 274, 282, 285
Velasquistas, National Federation of: 274
vendepatria: 12
Venezuela: government of, 16, 213–216; population explosion of, 17, 201, 219, 229; petroleum production of, 31, 199, 200, 203, 204, 209, 222, 230, 477; Christian democracy of, 41; rightists in, 172, 200, 202, 209, 216, 229, 233; leftists in, 172, 205, 209, 211, 218, 225, 226, 227, 228; economy of, 199, 201, 205, 222–224; natural resources of, 199, 201, 223; reform in, 199, 202, 204, 209, 212, 223, 227; modernization of, 199, 205; geography of, 200–201; livestock, 200, 201; Roman Catholic Church in, 200, 204, 215, 224; middle sectors in, 200, 216, 219; and Cuba, 200, 224; industrialization in, 201, 202, 204, 207, 223; agriculture in, 201, 202, 206; foreign investment in, 201, 203; education in, 201, 203, 204, 206, 207, 219, 224; health in, 201, 203, 204, 209, 224, 227; imports to, 201, 224; races in, 201, 232; Federal War in, 202; Spain in, 202; authoritarianism in, 202, 203; nationalism in, 202, 207, 209; labor in, 202, 207, 209, 211–212, 220, 227, 518; anticlericalism in, 202, 209; Liberals in, 202, 233; communications in, 203, 221, 228; civil war in, 203; foreign debt of, 203; housing in, 203, 204, 224, 230; *trienio,* 204; landholders in, 204, 206; stu-

Venezuela (continued)
dents in, 204, 208, 209, 226, 229; military in, 204, 208, 211, 216, 220; urbanization in, 205, 206, 207, 227; lower class in, 205, 206, 216, 227; upper class in, 205, 206, 219; terrorism in, 205, 207, 211, 216, 217, 218, 225; dictatorship in, 205, 498; literacy in, 206; mobility in, 206, 220, 230; political parties in, 208–211, 220, 221, 227, 228, 230, 258, 382, 417; October Revolution of, 208, 209, 216, 229; illiteracy in, 209, 221, 224; *Fidelismo* in, 210, 211; Constitution of 1961, 212; suffrage in, 213, 218; taxation in, 214; guerillas in, 216, 225; electoral system of, 217, 218; socialization patterns in, 219; slums in, 219, 227, 230; social welfare in, 222, 224; foreign relations of, 222, 224–225; and United States, 224; social security in, 224; and England, 224; and Brazil, 225; and OAS, 225; unemployment in, 227; under Viceroyalty of Nueva Granada, 232 n.2; mentioned, 14, 97, 101, 105, 301, 334, 483, 511, 518

Venezuelan Petroleum Corporation: 214, 222

Venezuelan Revolution: 204

Veracruz, Mexico: 21, 23, 27, 28

Verástegui: 236

Verba, Sidney: on parochials, 284

Verissimo, Erico: 508

Vermont: 157

Viaje e Ipanda: 488–491

Vicos experiment: 500

Viento fuerte: 501

Villa, Francisco: 476

Villa, Pancho: 22, 24

Villa Rica: 235

Villalba, Jóvito: 210, 228

Villarrica, Paraguay: 374

Villarröel, Gualberto: 320, 321, 322, 333

Villeda Morales, Ramón: 70, 85

Vincent, Sténio: 154

Vision: 16, 495

vodun. *See* voodoo

vodun houngan: 149

volcanic eruptions: 341

voodoo: 149, 152, 153

VRD. *See* Vanguardia Revolucionaria Dominicana

wages: minimum, 88, 133, 136, 310, 320, 343; mentioned, 187

Wagley, Charles: on barriers to social change, 17

Walker, William: 65, 96, 502

War of 1879–83: 293

War of the Pacific: 338

War of the Triple Alliance: 373

Wars of Reform: 20

Washington, D.C.: 190

Wessin y Wessin, Elias: 166

West Indians: 132

West Indies: 92, 121

wheat: 328, 394

White Book: 324–325

Whites. *See* Blancos

Wide and Alien is the World: 289

Wilches, Bishop: 252

Wilgus, A. Curtis: on progress of Latin America: 2

Willauer, Whiting: 84

Wilson, Henry Lane: 23, 498

Wilson, Woodrow: 23, 434

wool: 433, 445

World Bank: 332

world market: 119, 174, 177

World War I: 9, 12, 13, 176, 294, 350

World War II: 12, 27, 30, 35, 117, 125, 174, 189, 265, 324, 328, 343, 351, 383, 440

xenophobia: 11, 117, 207, 275, 490

Xingu River: 450

Yacimientos Petrolíferos Fiscales Bolivianos: 320, 327

yaws: 147, 317

Ycaza Tigerino, Julio: on liberal democracy, 501; on influence of United States, 501

Ydígoras Fuentes, Miguel: 82

Yeroví Indaburo, Clemente: 272, 512

Ynsfrán, Edgar L.: on Paraguayan exiles, 390; on Paraguayan political parties, 391

Young Italians: 481

YPFB. *See* Yacimientos Petrolíferos Fiscales Bolivianos

Yucatán: 28
Yugoslavia: 359
Yungas, Bolivia: 319, 327

Zapata, Emiliano: 23, 24, 55, 476
Zaragoza, General: 21

Zayistas: 179
Zea, Leopoldo: 508
Zelaya, José Santos: 66
Zermeño, Manuel: 42
zinc: 291
Zudáñez, Jaime: 314